May, 15–18, 2016
Banff, Alberta, Canada

I0038178

Association for Computing Machinery

Advancing Computing as a Science & Profession

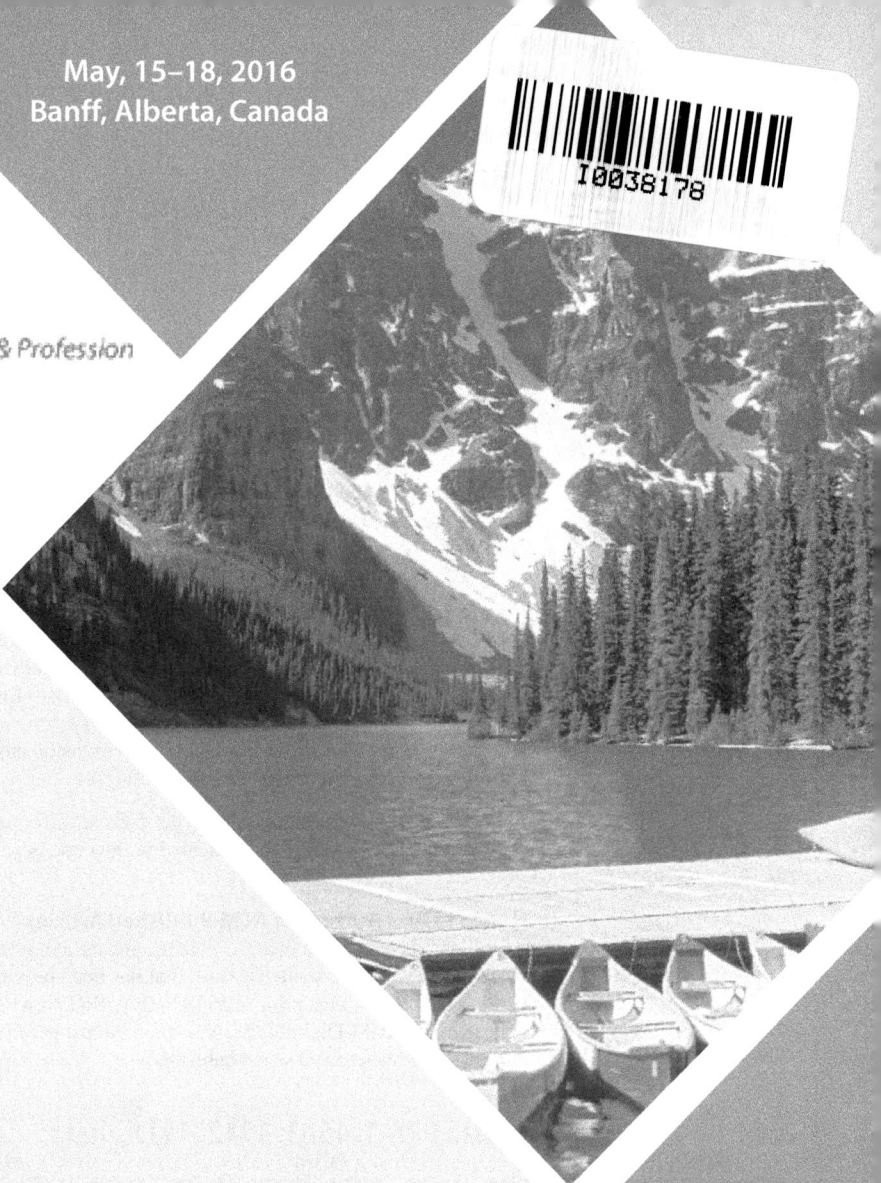

SIGSIM-PADS'16

Proceedings of the 2016 annual ACM Conference on
Principles of Advanced Discrete Simulation

Sponsored by:
ACM SIGSIM

Association for Computing Machinery

Advancing Computing as a Science & Profession

The Association for Computing Machinery
2 Penn Plaza, Suite 701
New York, New York 10121-0701

Copyright © 2016 by the Association for Computing Machinery, Inc. (ACM). Permission to make digital or hard copies of portions of this work for personal or classroom use is granted without fee provided that copies are not made or distributed for profit or commercial advantage and that copies bear this notice and the full citation on the first page. Copyright for components of this work owned by others than ACM must be honored. Abstracting with credit is permitted. To copy otherwise, to republish, to post on servers or to redistribute to lists, requires prior specific permission and/or a fee. Request permission to republish from: permissions@acm.org or Fax +1 (212) 869-0481.

For other copying of articles that carry a code at the bottom of the first or last page, copying is permitted provided that the per-copy fee indicated in the code is paid through www.copyright.com.

Notice to Past Authors of ACM-Published Articles
ACM intends to create a complete electronic archive of all articles and/or other material previously published by ACM. If you have written a work that has been previously published by ACM in any journal or conference proceedings prior to 1978, or any SIG Newsletter at any time, and you do NOT want this work to appear in the ACM Digital Library, please inform permissions@acm.org, stating the title of the work, the author(s), and where and when published.

ISBN: 978-1-4503-3742-7 (Digital)

ISBN: 978-1-4503-4478-4 (Print)

Additional copies may be ordered prepaid from:

ACM Order Department
PO Box 30777
New York, NY 10087-0777, USA

Phone: 1-800-342-6626 (USA and Canada)
+1-212-626-0500 (Global)
Fax: +1-212-944-1318
E-mail: acmhelp@acm.org
Hours of Operation: 8:30 am – 4:30 pm ET

Printed in the USA

Message from the Conference Chairs

Welcome to the annual *ACM Conference on Principles of Advanced Discrete Simulation (SIGSIM-PADS)*, the flagship conference for ACM's Special Interest Group on Simulation and Modeling (SIGSIM). The conference dates back to the annual PADS conference which began in 1985. Originally focusing exclusively on parallel and distributed simulation technologies and applications, the conference has since broadened its scope to encompass all aspects of modeling and simulation, including parallel and distributed execution, focusing on topics at the intersection of modeling and simulation and computer science.

We are pleased to hold this year's conference in Banff, Alberta Canada. Banff provides a wonderful setting for the conference and offers many opportunities for outdoor activities and recreation. We hope you will enjoy the conference, the town of Banff, and the surrounding mountains.

We wish to thank the many individuals who help make this year's conference possible. First, we thank the program committee members and additional external referees who provided timely reviews of the paper submissions, and participated in discussions concerning paper selection. In addition, we recognize the other members of the organizing committee for their contributions to the conference, including Jason Liu (Proceedings Chair), Philip Wilsey (Ph.D. Colloquium Chair), Dong (Kevin) Jin (Publicity Chair), and Holly Rush (Registration Chair and administrative support). Osman Balci did a terrific job with the web site, providing updates as soon as they were submitted. We thank the ACM Special Interest Group on Simulation both for their continued support, and for providing fellowships to students to help enable them to attend the conference. Finally, we wish to express special thanks to our two keynote speakers, Frederica Darema and David Jefferson for sharing their thoughts and insights with conference attendees.

We have an excellent program to offer our attendees this year. New this year is a special interest in data-driven simulation with several sessions dedicated to this emerging topic. All papers submitted to the conference were rigorously reviewed with all papers receiving 3 referee reports. We thank the program committee and additional referees for their diligent efforts to provide timely, critical reviews and feedback to the authors. This process resulted in a total of 20 submissions accepted as full papers and 6 papers accepted as short papers. We expect everyone will appreciate the high-quality papers and presentations in the conference this year.

This year's candidates for the best paper award are listed below. As is customary, the winning paper will be announced at the conference itself. Selected papers from the conference will also be invited to be extended to create a special issue of the *ACM Transactions on Modeling and Computer Simulation (TOMACS)* journal.

> *DSSnet: A Smart Grid Modeling Platform Combining Electrical Power Distribution System Simulation and Software Defined Networking Emulation* by Christopher Hannon, Jiaqi Yan and Dong Jin

> *Modeling a Million-Node Slim Fly Network using Parallel Discrete Event Simulation* by Noah Wolfe, Misbah Mubarak, Christopher D. Carothers, Philip Carns, and Robert Ross

> *Automated Memoization for Parameter Studies Implemented in Impure* Languages by Mirko Stoffers, Daniel Schemmel, Oscar Soria Dustmann and Klaus Wehrle

We congratulate the authors of the paper winning the best paper award for the 2015 conference. Well done!

> *FatTreeSim: Modeling a Large-scale Fat-Tree Network for HPC Systems and Data Centers Using Parallel and Discrete Event Simulation* by Ning Liu, Adnan Haider, Xian-He Sun and Dong Jin.

This year's Ph.D. Colloquium included eight students who prepared brief presentations as well as posters concerning their research. The Ph.D. Colloquium speaker was Dong (Kevin) Jin whose keynote presentation was entitled "Early Career Experiences." We thank Kevin for his presentation as well as the students for their participation.

The meeting this year will include many interesting presentations as well as excellent opportunities for networking. We hope you enjoy the conference!

Richard Fujimoto
ACM SIGSIM-PADS'16 General Chair
Georgia Institute of Technology,
Atlanta GA, USA

Brian Unger
ACM SIGSIM-PADS'16 Co-General
Chair and Local Arrangements Chair
University of Calgary, Alberta Canada

Christopher Carothers
ACM SIGSIM-PADS'16 Program Chair
Rensselaer Polytechnic Institute,
Troy NY, USA

Table of Contents

Session on M&S Areas and Applications 2

Session Chair: Christopher Carothers *(Rensselaer Polytechnic Institute)*

SIGSIM-PADS '16 Program Committee

Anastasia Anagnostous, *Brunell University, UK*

Peter Barnes, *Lawrence Livermore National Laboratory, USA*

Fernando J. Barros, *University of Coimbra, Portugal*

Wentong Cai, *Nanyang Technological University, Singapore*

Laurent Capocchi, *University of Corsica, France*

Paul Fishwick, *University Texas at Dallas, USA*

Philippe Giabbanelli, *University of Cambridge, UK*

Drew Hamiliton, *Mississippi State University, USA*

David Jefferson, *Lawrence Livermore National Laboratory, USA*

Kevin Jin, *Illinois Institute of Technology, USA*

Laxmikant Kale, *University of Illinois at Urbana-Champaign, USA*

Darren Kerbyson, *Pacific Northwest National Laboratory, USA*

Jason Liu, *Florida International University, USA*

Margaret Loper, *Georgia Tech Research Institute, USA*

Madhav Marathe, *Virginia Tech, USA*

Misbah Mubarak, *Argonne National Laboratory, USA*

Navonil Mustafee, *University of Exeter, UK*

David Nicol, *University of Illinois at Urbana-Champaign, USA*

Ernest Page, *MITRE Corporation, USA*

Kalyan Perumalla, *Oak Ridge National Laboratory, USA*

Francesco Quaglia, *Sapienza University of Rome, Italy*

George Riley, *Georgia Institute of Technology, USA*

Hessam Sarjoughian, *Arizona State University, USA*

Young-Jun Son, *University of Arizona, USA*

Steffen Strassburger, *Technical University of Ilmenau, Germany*

Claudia Szabo, *University of Adelaide, Australia*

Simon Taylor, *Brunel University, UK*

Andreas Tolk, *Old Dominion University, USA*

Stephen Turner, *Nanyang Technological University, Singapore*

Adelinde Uhrmacher, *University of Rostock, Germany*

Gabriel Wainer, *Carleton University, Canada*

Philip Wilsey, *University of Cincinnati, USA*

Yiping Yao, *National University of Defense Technology, USA*

Levent Yilmaz, *Auburn University, USA*

SIGSIM-PADS 2016 Sponsor

InfoSymbioticSystems/DDDAS and Large-Scale Dynamic Data and Large-Scale Big Computing for Smart Systems

Frederica Darema
Mathematics, Information, Life Sciences Division
Air Force Office of Scientific Research
Arlington, VA, 22203 USA

ABSTRACT

The presentation will discuss InfoSymbiotics/DDDAS, a paradigm which unifies systems' modeling and instrumentation aspects, and is creating new and revolutionary capabilities for improved understanding, analysis, and optimized, autonomic management and decision support of operational of engineered and natural multi-entity systems, and including human and societal systems. Key underlying concept in DDDAS is the dynamic integration of instrumentation data and executing models of the system in a feedback control loop - that is on-line data are dynamically incorporated into the systems' executing model, to improve the modeling accuracy or to speed-up the simulation, and in reverse the executing model controls the instrumentation to selectively and adaptively target the data collection process, and dynamically manage collective sets of sensors and controllers. DDDAS is timely and in-line with the advent of Large-Scale-Dynamic-Data and Large-Scale-Big-Computing. Large-Scale-Dynamic-Data encompasses the traditional Big Data with next wave of Big Data, and namely dynamic data arising from ubiquitous sensing and control in engineered, natural, and societal systems, through multitudes of heterogeneous sensors and controllers instrumenting these systems, and where the opportunities and challenges at these "large-scales" relate not only to the size of the data but the heterogeneity in data, data collection modalities, data fidelities, and timescales, ranging from real-time data to archival data. DDDAS entails the dynamic integration of the traditional high-end/mid-range parallel and distributed computing with the real-time data-acquisition and control. Thus, in tandem with the important new dimension of dynamic data, DDDAS implies an extended view of Big Computing, which includes a new dimension of computing - the collective computing by networked assemblies of multitudes of sensors and controllers. The DDDAS paradigm, driving and exploiting these notions of Large-Scale Dynamic Data and Large-Scale Big Computing, is shaping research directions and engendering transformative impact in a range of natural and engineered systems application areas. Spanning application areas from the nanoscale to the terra-scale and the extra-terra-scale environments, examples of advances and new capabilities that will be presented include: materials analysis and decision support for structural systems; manufacturing systems; cellular, neural, and biorobotic systems; environmental systems; critical infrastructure systems, such as urban and air transportation, energy powergrids, and smart agriculture. In addition the challenges, opportunities, and advances that have been made in the systems software for these Large-Scale-Big-Computing and Large-Scale-Big-Data environments will also be addressed in the talk.

Permission to make digital or hard copies of part or all of this work for personal or classroom use is granted without fee provided that copies are not made or distributed for profit or commercial advantage and that copies bear this notice and the full citation on the first page. Copyrights for third-party components of this work must be honored. For all other uses, contact the Owner/Author(s). Copyright is held by the owner/author(s).

SIGSIM-PADS, May 15–18, 2016, Banff, Alberta, Canada.
ACM 978-1-4503-3742-7/16/05.
DOI: http://dx.doi.org/10.1145/2901378.2901405

An Adaptive Road Traffic Regulation with Simulation and Internet of Things

Shanthini Rajendran, Suresh Rathnaraj Chelladurai, Alex Aravind[*]

Department of Computer Science
University of Northern British Columbia
Prince George, BC, Canada - V2N 4Z9
(rajendr,chellads,csalex)@unbc.ca

ABSTRACT

Traffic congestion is a growing concern in most cities across the world. It is primarily caused by a sudden increase in the number of vehicles in a relatively small number of roads and intersections, while other roads have the capacity to accommodate more traffic. In such situations, distributing traffic to roads in a balanced way could alleviate congestion. With the help of modern technology such as Internet of Things (IoT) and simulation, road users can be encouraged to choose their route on-the-fly, by providing necessary information such as projected travel time on the next leg. In extreme situations, traffic on some critical roads could be adaptively reduced by even introducing levy. A simple solution like providing road traffic information, benefits and penalties, etc., ahead in each intersection would allow travellers to make cognizant choices and therefore could lead to a better, more efficient traffic distribution.

To implement the proposed system, simulation and IoT must be brought together by a suitable communication middleware system so that they can work in synchrony. Implementing an actual IoT infrastructure and then testing the cause and effects of traffic congestion with the system in-place is a daunting task. Simulation would help us to test and validate the IoT system for functionality, performance, and scalability. In this paper, we propose a novel framework for integrating IoT and simulation using a message-oriented middleware in the context of an adaptive traffic regulation system and then demonstrate the framework with the help of a prototype implementation.

Categories and Subject Descriptors

C.4 [**Computer System Organization**]: Performance of Systems; D.2.8 [**Software Engineering**]: Metrics—*performance measures*

[*]Corresponding author

Permission to make digital or hard copies of all or part of this work for personal or classroom use is granted without fee provided that copies are not made or distributed for profit or commercial advantage and that copies bear this notice and the full citation on the first page. Copyrights for components of this work owned by others than ACM must be honored. Abstracting with credit is permitted. To copy otherwise, or republish, to post on servers or to redistribute to lists, requires prior specific permission and/or a fee. Request permissions from permissions@acm.org.

SIGSIM-PADS '16, May 15-18, 2016, Banff, AB, Canada

© 2016 ACM. ISBN 978-1-4503-3742-7/16/05. . . $15.00

DOI: http://dx.doi.org/10.1145/2901378.2901406

Keywords

Simulation, Road traffic, Internet of things, Dynamic data-driven, Traffic regulation,Traffic congestion

1. INTRODUCTION

Urbanization is an increasing phenomenon worldwide. One of the direct impacts of this phenomenon is the increased traffic in cities. Increased traffic often leads to traffic jams (congestion) when not managed properly, and therefore is a major problem. Traffic congestion has several negative effects such as travel delay, larger number of accidents, increased carbon emission, increased pollution, etc. So, a smart traffic management system is an urgent need across the globe to avoid traffic congestion. In a broader sense, distributing traffic in urban areas contributes significantly to the society's safety and welfare. Fewer congested routes means fewer frustrated drivers and hence a proportionally safer road environment. However, with the increase in the number of vehicles on the road, the problems and challenges on city traffic continue to rise.

1.1 Internet of Things and Road Traffic

Recent times have witnessed IoT explosion ubiquitously. The ability to connect millions of devices to the internet and source data in realtime is a great asset and has been put to thorough use in building traffic solutions that effectively manage congestion. Traditional approaches to IoT solutions follow client-server model, where there is a common point of data aggregation, such as a gateway or a base station. Designing IoT solutions based on a middleware architecture, would allow us to view each sensing device as a service point. All the services can be monitored and accessed from the cloud. We also have access to information from different sensors that may not be part of our system (data sourcing). Interaction of thousands of wireless devices leads to continuous flow of events and massive amounts of data are being generated. The challenge now is "how to deal with this massive flow of online data? "[30]

In the past two decades, many intelligent solutions have been proposed to manage traffic in smart ways. Some of them include placing cameras strategically at intersections for monitoring traffic, sensors and more novel technologies such as Intelligent Transportation Systems (ITS) and Vehicular Ad-hoc Networks (VANETs). Currently, most of the proposed intelligent transport systems are either expensive and therefore cannot be offered to all roads, or not sophisticated enough to be deployed widely. The rise of Internet of Things (IoT) in this decade could allow us to sense, collect, and aggregate information from the most mundane sources possible. Every day, there are new improvements in creating and maintaining compatible communication standards, extending device interfaces to cover as many devices and sensors as possible and much more. Vehicles, roads, intersections provide the capability to house sensors. The development of various communication protocols, multi-hop message transmission protocols allow us to have Vehicle-to-Vehicle and Vehicle-to-Infrastructure communication systems. With the availability of very tiny powerful computers such as Raspberry PI, Intel Edison, the persistent challenge of a "resource-constrained" environment too is lifting off. We are at a crossroad, with the free availability of such different and powerful technologies at our disposal. In this paper, we focus on the amalgamation of IoT, dynamic data processing and analysis, simulation, messaging middleware, and mining repository to build a better, adaptive traffic regulation system.

Since the early 1990's, computer simulation has been used as a vital tool in modeling complex dynamic systems [8, 12]. Traffic systems are quite dynamic and simulation is extensively used to model and study its various aspects and implementation choices. It is easier and more flexible to change parameters and view cause/effect analysis, bottlenecks and various other factors in a simulation system than in the actual system. With the advancement of IoT, simulation can be not only used for modeling and simulation of a system before its implementation but also can be heavily used for prediction of specific aspects of the system during its operation, as illustrated in Figure 1 for a traffic application.

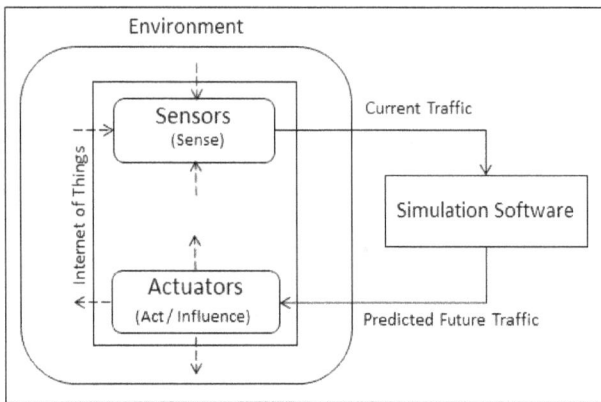

Figure 1: Integration of IoT and Simulation

Here, IoT feeds information of current traffic to the simulator. Then, the simulator can simulate and predict future traffic based on the current state and trend, and that information can then be feed back to influence the traffic. This idea is incorporated into our proposed framework.

In the past, the above mentioned components have been used and well understood mostly in isolation. Bringing them together to solve traffic congestion is what we emphasize in this paper. In such integrated systems, software occupies the major portion of the system including simulation system. Particularly, messaging middleware and mining repository are backbone of the system on which the rest hang. Therefore, messaging middleware and mining repository must be

chosen with care based on the mainstream software development standards and trends. To set the context for our selection of middleware components, let us briefly review the software development trend.

1.2 Software Development Trend

Software engineering is a process dominated by intellectual activities focused on developing software systems with immense complexity and numerous unknowns in computing perspective [25]. For the reusability of code and to reduce complexity, software companies along with research organizations, develop and maintain standards and adopt them as best software engineering practices.

Software engineering has evolved and undergone several stages since 1960. In the beginning, organizations used virtually all custom tools, custom processes, and custom components built in primitive languages. This approach was expensive, not scalable, and hence most projects were never completed [18]. From the experience gained in the previous decade, in 80's and 90's, organizations used more repeatable processes, off-the-shelf tools, and about 70% of their components were built in higher level languages [25]. Even then, they were heavily dominated by custom made tools (70%) and only about 30% of the components were commercial products such as operating systems, database management system, networking, and graphical user interface. With this approach, some of the organizations could achieve success only for small and medium size applications. For the applications of higher complexity, the existing tools would not suffice.

Since the early 2000, almost all organizations including industries started using managed and measured processes and integrated automation environments, and more importantly the trend in usage of various software components took a different turn. That is, about 70% are based on off-the-shelf commercial components and only about 30% of the components need to be custom built [25]. So, the trend in software design and development in industries for quite some time has been towards using mostly off-the-shelf commercial components. Simulation integrated software development practices cannot be an exception. That is, if we expect the design and implementation of our simulation and IoT integrated system framework to be adopted widely, it has to be based mostly on off-the-shelf commercial or open source components.

1.3 Messaging Middleware

Messaging middleware is a software layer or a set of sublayers that connects various heterogeneous domains. The messaging middleware is the glue that holds it all together [20]. Research on middleware systems has been gaining momentum over the years. One of the important advantages of a middleware system is its ability to provide seamless interoperability between various components. This allows the programmer to focus on building standard, adaptable, and effective solutions rather than worrying about the finer details of the underlying layers [30]. A complete list of the advantages and disadvantages of using a message oriented middleware is discussed elsewhere [5].

There are various standards and protocols for building message oriented middleware systems. One of the most popular middleware is the Java Messaging Service. JMS provides a standard API for the Java platform as well as many services for interoperablility within and outside the

Java platform. Integration with other languages such as Ruby, Scala etc is possible but very tricky. Therefore, there was this necessity for a messaging standard that will assure interoperability among different platforms and integration services. AMQP emerged out of this need [13, 15, 2]. At the time of writing this paper, AMQP and its various open source implementations are in practice in some of the most critical systems running in the world, specially in the financial industry.

Advanced Message Queuing Protocol (AMQP) is an important protocol heavily used in recent years. It was developed by John O'Hara of JP Morgan Chase Inc., and is a binary wire transmission protocol. AMQP originated in the financial industry as a solution to the problem of seamlessly connecting different processing platforms together. In order to attain this effortless interoperability, AMQP boasts of a well-defined, structured set of rules or behavior for sending and receiving messages. These rules use a combination of techniques including store and forward, publish and subscribe, peer to peer, request/response, clustering, transaction management and security among many because of which the protocol has become valuable for communication across various operating systems, programming platforms, integration services and hardware devices without compromising on performance [2].

RabbitMQ is an open source implementation of the standard AMQP 0-9-1 and is programmed in Erlang. It provides support for all major operating systems and is also available in languages such as Python, Java, Ruby and .Net. RabbitMQ is very extensible and provides a number of plugins to allow communication with other web protocols such as HTTP, XMPP, SMTP and STOMP [2].

1.4 Mining Repository

Completely automated systems for practical use, though possible theoretically, is a long way to go. For most systems including road traffic, human interaction to offer intelligent decisions based on current and predicted future traffic should be an option for several reasons. Such interaction requires a good analytic support based on the data about past, present, and future. In terms of technology, it needs a scalable mining repository where such data can be deposited and necessary analytics could be derived. An IoT application would greatly benefit by the presence of a mining repository that provides on-going, live support for growing, near-real time data. Such repositories are in practice now.

In a nutshell, we envision that IoT, simulation, mining repository connected by an efficient messaging middleware can play a fundamental role in the advancement of automation integrated future systems.

1.5 Contributions

We first propose a novel framework that integrates simulation and IoT with a message oriented middleware system and mining repository. We then demonstrate the feasibility of the proposed framework by the design and implementation of an adaptive traffic regulation system. Limited simulation experiments were conducted and the results are reported.

The internet of things platform uses sensors to collect data and actuators to influence the system to change its behavior. Discrete event traffic simulation system is used to predict the future traffic behavior based on sensor inputs. Mining repository is used to store sensor data and simulation traces, and

provide analysis support to the users and managers of the system. The messaging middleware is responsible for connecting these components and facilitating message transfer in near real-time. It acts like a "postman" system, distributing the right data at the right time to the right storage system and the right subscriber. The proposed framework is completely reproducible and is built from scratch using open source off-the-shelf components.

The rest of the paper is organized as follows. In Section 2, we explain the proposed framework in detail. Section 3 describes the adaptive road traffic simulator. Simulation experiments and the results obtained are outlined in Section 4 and the paper is concluded in Section 5.

2. PROPOSED FRAMEWORK

In this section, we describe in detail the framework to integrate IoT platform and simulation with a suitable middleware. The proposed framework is shown in Figure 2. It has four main components: (i) The application domain where IoT is deployed; (ii) Simulation system; (iii) Mining repository; and (iv) Messaging middleware.

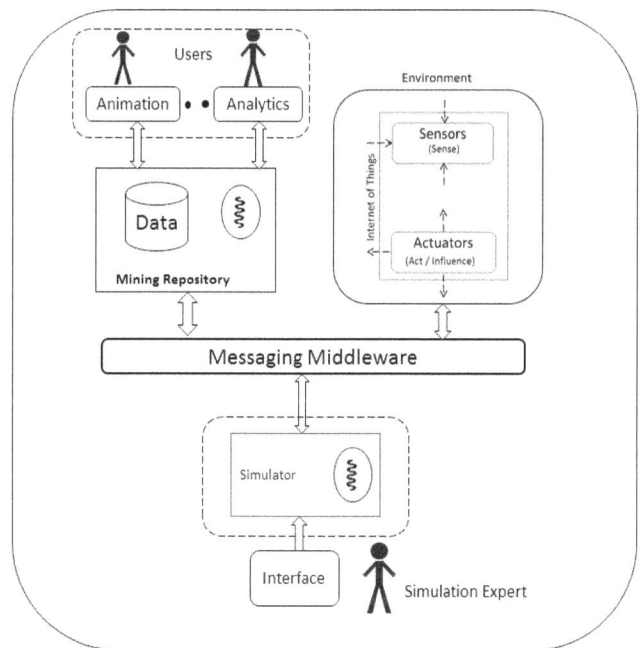

Figure 2: Framework for Smart Regulation System

This framework integrates discrete event simulation and Iot in a simplified way. The application domain where IoT is deployed, may not necessarily be limited to transportation system, rather, this framework can be applied to any practical systems that involve IoT. Next, we will explain the various components of the proposed framework.

2.1 Simulation Component

The simulation component in the framework mainly used to predict the future based on the past and present. It gets it inputs from both IoT (current state) and mining repository (past states). Based on these information, it can simulate and predict the future scenarios, and send that information back to the mining repository. The information stored in the mining repository is then used to derive insights on current state and future states of the system and feed that information back to IoT to influence the current system. Any part of the proposed framework can be modeled and simulated before its actual deployment.

2.2 Internet Of Things

In the proposed system, IoT is primarily used to collect data and influence the system behavior. For our prototype design and implementation, we simulate the presence of an active IoT infrastructure as a part of the traffic simulator.

The IoT infrastructure provided in our simulator, primarily has two components: (i) sensors to collect data; and (ii) actuators to act or influence the system to change. Sensors basically send information such as number of vehicles on the selected road segment. The simulation software, based on the current traffic, in turn predicts future traffic by simulating future scenarios, and sends the relevant information to the actuator component of IoT. The actuator component of IoT then influences the system, and the cycle repeats. The actuator component would be a display board, that will inform the travellers about the present road conditions, time to reach next destination (next intersection, in this case) and the speed limit to be followed.

Simulating an entire IoT system is an effective way to test the design of your system even before developing it. The future is expected to be revolutionized by the integration of IoT and simulation. With simulation, we can test how a target system behaves under different scenarios and road conditions. In summary, to integrate IoT and simulation effectively, we need a middle-ware that is capable of offering message service in near real-time and a scalable mining repository with suitable analytics support. Next, we will discuss about the implementation of such a suitable middleware.

2.3 Messaging Middleware

A messaging middleware helps connecting various heterogeneous devices seamlessly and controls the flow of events extensively by supporting various plugins and interfaces making it very extensible. So, a critical part in realizing the proposed system is using a suitable middleware that could facilitate dynamic data to flow in near real time. Although our framework is generic that any messaging framework can be used, for our prototype implementation we adopt RabbitMQ as our messaging middleware for the following reasons.

1. As it supports a standard messaging protocol AMQP and it is not confined by any proprietary, client specific messaging protocol.

2. All the messages are collected by the RabbitMQ. This type of message storage pattern is very similar to a push-style data flow. All the messages move from where they are produced to where they are consumed in a fluid manner, without having to periodically pull messages at various end points.

Next we briefly explain how RabbitMQ works.

2.3.1 RabbitMQ

RabbitMQ stores messages in queues and acts as a broker between two types of processes, producers and consumers.

There are two core units that form RabbitMQ namely, Queues and Exchanges/Router [26]. In simple terms, every message that is passed through RabbitMQ has to be placed in a queue. The main function of the router is to route the messages from the appropriate producer to the appropriate consumer. Each message consists of a simple header, specifying where it is heading to. The router doesn't read or process the message, it simply delivers the message to the appropriate queues. The consumers on the other hand, can either subscribe to a particular message or keep polling to see if a message is received. The router in RabbitMQ is called as exchanges. Figure 3 shows a simplified architecture of the components involved in the RabbitMQ messaging system [5].

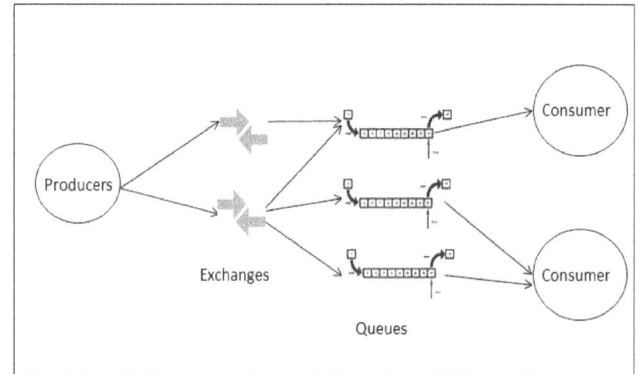

Figure 3: RabbitMQ Architecture

The producers in RabbitMQ generates messages which are then pushed to the exchanges. The exchanges then apply some routing rules on these messages and push each message to the appropriate queues, thus providing a delivery service. The messages can either be directly delivered, or it can be delivered because of an existing subscription system. The routing choices simply depend on the value of the routing key which is available in the header part of the message. This header is constructed by the producer itself. If a particular message is to be sent to more than one queue, then the exchanges take the responsibility of duplicating the message and delivering it to the queues. Consumers always must have a permanent connection with their corresponding exchanges, so that the exchanges may be aware of the exact details of the queues the consumers have subscribed to. In addition to separate queues for consumers, in our prototype system, we also have a common queue that stores all incoming messages to all exchanges in their order of arrival. This common queue is what mining repository is subscribed to. All operations inside RabbitMQ are done in memory and they are transferred to the disk periodically. All the messages in our simulator are time-stamped and their order is maintained consistently throughout the simulation.

2.4 Mining Repository

The most important requirement of a mining repository for the proposed framework is the ability to store and access large data in near real-time and agility for data growth and updates. A near real time search engine with standardized API is its main attraction. Most databases or mining repositories that store large volumes of data, require some sort of sorting, filtering and other such capabilities, to segregate and organise that data so that it can be easy to write queries for searching the data. In this case, offline analysis is the only solution.

Again, any mining repository with above capability can be used in our framework, we adopt Elasticsearch for our prototype implementation. We briefly explain Elasticsearch next.

2.4.1 Elastic Search

Elasticsearch is one of the most popular mining repositories with rich functionalities [19]. We use Elasticsearch in our proposed framework for the following reasons that illustrate its functionality.

1. *Availability and cost:* It is a open source software and that makes it easier to integrate with any application.

2. *Scalability:* When it comes to data storage, we consider scaling from two perspectives. 1) Vertical or scale up - Adding more hardware, powerful servers, 2) Horizontal or scale out - Adding more servers. Elasticsearch is distributed by nature. A running Elastic search server is called a node. Two or more nodes form a cluster. Elasticsearch is heavily supported to run in clusters.

3. *Near real-time Search, Data Analysis, and Visualization:* Elasticsearch stores data in *indexes*. An *index* is analogous to a *database* in a Relational Database Management System (RDBMS). Each document in an Elasticsearch index is a JSON object. All the documents are indexed as soon as they are added to an index, however they are only updated at a pre-defined time interval (1 second). For large scale applications, the Elasticsearch server does not refresh after each update using the default interval because it is costly in terms of disk i/o operations. However, we have the ability to set a custom update interval based on the application.

4. *RESTful API:* Since Elasticsearch is a RESTful server, the most widely used way to communicate with the client is through its REST API. A client normally opens a connection with the Elasticsearch server, posts a JSON Object as a request and receives a JSON object as a response. This is very useful, because there is no restriction on the type of client, the programming languages used. Any client can communicate with the Elasticsearch server with HTTP requests.

5. *Popularity:* It is used by thousands of organizations worldwide including Netflix, Facebook, GitHub, etc.,

In our traffic simulator, we store all the events occurring during the simulation. Each event is associated with a timestamp and is stored on Elasticsearch server in JSON format. By querying the events using the appropriate message, we can get real time results for analysis.

Kibana is the graphical front end for Elasticsearch and provides data visualization and analytic capabilities. Kibana is a browser based interface and provides the capability to search, view and interact directly with the data stored at the Elasticsearch indices. Kibana automatically generates queries for Elasticsearch, the queries are similar to the ones a programmer might write, using the Elasticsearch API. Our kibana dashboard shows us a list of events that are being pushed to the Elasticsearch server at each update.

Kibana allows us to view the events (in our case) logged by the Elasticsearch server, sort and perform search queries on the data presented. Advanced search options such as saving a search, loading a saved search are available and is very handy. Kibana supports visualization tools in the form of various kinds of charts. This allows us to view and compare various scenarios from the live data presented to us and not having to stop and start the simulator again and again. We focus on the business intelligence aspect of Elasticsearch in our simulator, mostly because of ease of use and its plug-in type architecture. There are other scalable search engine solutions that are available like Solr could be used in-place of Elasticsearch.

3. ROAD TRAFFIC SIMULATION

Traffic systems provide a variety of features such as dynamic state change, real time decision making, unexpected congestion etc, that makes it hard to conceive, analyze and test this system. Also, a traffic system consists of many participants with dissimilar interests. Simulation can be a very useful tool to help capture the effect of influencing factors in a real-life traffic system, such as pedestrians, road blockage etc and view the outcomes without disturbing an existing implementation. We briefly review some of the research done in traffic simulation systems. The authors in [12] present an elaborate survey on the state-of-art Intelligent Transportation Systems presently in use across the globe. The authors identify three main research trends on Intelligent Transport Systems (ITS) -

ITS based on Wireless Sensor Networks

An example of an ITS based on WSNs would be Advanced Traveller Information Systems (ATIS) for Indian Cities developed in India in 2014[6]. In this project, over 100 GPS devices and cameras were mounted at intersections. These use wireless communication to transfer information collected on the traffic conditions to the central control center. This information is then converted into data that can be used by travelers, using travel time prediction models and algorithms. The travelers would then be informed about the traffic by the use of strategically placed Variable Message Signs(VMS).

ITS based on Vehicular Sensor Networks

An example of a VSN based traffic control system would be the Mobeyes Project[11]. In this project, all the data sensed by the vehicular nodes are locally processed within the vehicles. The data nodes generate feature-rich data summaries with time and context information. There is no necessity for the road-side infrastructure. Instead of road-side infrastructure, the project has Mobeye data collectors that work more or less like police patrolling agents and collect data from their neighboring vehicular nodes.

Vehicular Ad-hoc Network Simulators

In literature, a road traffic simulator is normally called a VANET simulator. The authors in [3] classify VANET simulation software in three different categories: (a) vehicular mobility generators, (b) network simulators, and (c) VANET simulators. Vehicular mobility generators are useful in creating realistic, accurate patterns of movement of vehicles in various scenarios. *Vehicular mobility generators* fundamentally apply mobility models used in the VANET domain to simulate the movement of vehicles accurately. Output from a vehicular mobility generator will generally be a trace file, containing trip details for each vehicle, spanning across the simulation period. This trace file, can then be used in network simulators such as OMNET++[28], NS3[23] etc for further analysis. *Network simulators* perform in-depth analysis of data packets, packet loss, transmission delays etc. *VANET simulators* allows us to change the behaviour of vehicles based on a given condition within an integrated framework [3]. VANET simulators provide both the ability to generate vehicular mobility as well as network simulation. The VANET simulators specified above, presently, has no support for integration with the Internet of Things[4, 22].

The future is going to be revolutionized by the Internet of Things, specially in the mobility space. Therefore, we see a need for simulators that incorporate necessary support for Internet of Things. In the next section, we describe in detail, our road traffic simulator, that integrates both Internet Of Things and discrete event simulation in this context.

3.1 Simulation System

Traffic simulation models can be classified either as microscopic or macroscopic. In a microscopic model, simulation is centered around an individual vehicle and its performance is evaluated across the entire network. In a macroscopic simulation model, the entire network is modeled and this is used to particularly model large scale systems. In order to retain simplicity, we need a different model that allows us to abstract the required entities and reduce the complexity of the overall system[11]. The various components of a traffic control management system such as vehicle, intersections, road segments, sensors, traffic lights etc are to be modeled independently. Discrete-event simulation supports this type of modeling and provides us with an environment where we can freely integrate the modeled entities. There is a global simulation clock, that controls the entire simulation timerange. Each entity has a list of events associated with it. All events are ordered and executed based on their priority within the event queue. All the events passing through the middle-ware are consistently logged in the mining repository for further data analysis.

The traffic network considered is a simple grid. The nodes in the grid represent intersections and paths connecting the nodes represent the road segments between intersections. The network is connected, meaning there exists a path between two nodes. The IoT part of the system essentially contains a collection of sensors and actuators. In our simulator, there is a sensor-actuator pair at each intersection, in all the directions branching out from that particular intersection. The sensor keeps measuring the number of cars passing the road segment from the chosen intersection to the next intersection, and posting this information continuously to the middle-ware as depicted in Figure 4. The simulator takes the sensor input and uses this input to predict future traffic and the real-time road congestion scenario is passed on to the actuators as messages. The actuator present at each intersection, displays the current congestion statistics, which will then influence the drivers' choice of staying on the same route or taking a different route to their destination. The IoT system can simply send and receive messages from the messaging middleware using AMQP requests.

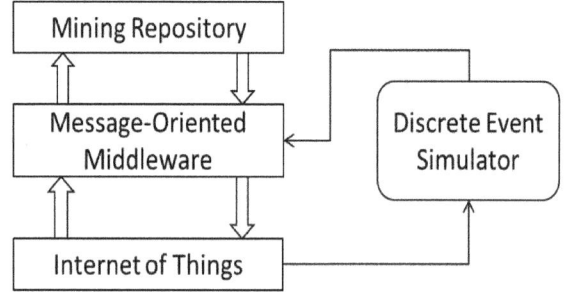

Figure 4: Data Flow within the proposed framework

The simulator can be run on one master computer or on several nodes, with one node acting as the coordinator. It can be implemented in any language, we used JAVA. One key design point of our simulator is that we wanted to make the code as reproducible as possible and that can be achieved only by implementing the simulator using off-the-shelf components. Any traffic simulator which has the capability to send/receive messages following the Advanced Message Queuing Protocol (AMQP) can be used in place. The chosen messaging middle-ware (RabbitMQ) offers us a wide variety of plugins and interfaces for both the IoT environment as well as the mining repository.

We next describe the simulation system components or entities and events of the system.

3.2 System Entities

- Vehicle - represents the model of a vehicle in an actual traffic system. Each vehicle will know its source, destination and will travel from the source to the destination based on the velocity allowed in that road segment. Vehicle has intelligence to take routing decisions based on the available real time sensor information at each intersection.

- Node - represents the model of an intersection in an actual traffic system. A node has four traffic lights, representing a simplified model of a four-way intersection.

- Traffic Lights - represents the model of a traffic signal in an actual traffic system. It controls the flow of vehicles from one intersection to the next.

- Road Segment - represents the model of an actual road connecting two intersections. Each road segment has a maximum capacity that specifies the allowable amount of traffic at a particular time. The speed limit of the road segment varies according to the current load. Current load gives the number of vehicles traversing the road segment at that time. The maximum allowable velocity (V_{max}) is calculated using a *Congestion Formula* given as follows -

$$V_{max} = \text{Max } (10, V_{max}\text{- f(current load)})$$

- Sensor - represents the model of a actual traffic sensor, such as an induction loop or an overhead camera. The sensor reports the number of vehicles passing through the intersection in a real time basis.

3.3 System Events

The simulation basically involves following events.

1. Vehicle Create Event - creates a vehicle with a source, destination and a random velocity in the range (12, 28) m/s. The creation of this event is controlled using a probability distribution.

2. Vehicle Begin Event - denotes the departure of a vehicle from an intersection. Also invokes the Sensor Increment Event.

3. Vehicle Reached Event - denotes the arrival of a vehicle at an intersection. Also invokes the Sensor Decrement Event.

4. Sensor Increment Event - increments the number of vehicles by 1, for that particular road segment attached to the sensor. It also decreases the maximum allowable velocity for that road segment based on the *Congestion Formula*.

5. Sensor Decrement Event - decrements the number of vehicles by 1 when a particular vehicle reaches a node attached to the road segment to which the sensor is connected.

6. Traffic Light Green On Event - enables green light on a particular intersection causing all the vehicles entering the intersection to travel through its associated road segment without stopping at the intersection.

7. Traffic Light Green Off Event - disables green light on a particular intersection and will invoke a Traffic Light Red On Event.

8. Traffic Light Red On Event - enables red light on a particular intersection causing all the vehicles entering the intersection to stop at the intersection and will create a delay before invoking the Vehicle Begin Event.

9. Traffic Light Red Off Event - disables red light on a particular intersection and will invoke a Traffic Light Green On Event.

3.3.1 Simulation Input Parameters

The road network which we have considered as the input for this simulation is stored in a JSON format in the local file system. This JSON file contains the information about the nodes, intersections, road segments and how they are connected to each other. At the beginning of the simulation, the simulator parses through JSON file and converts it to a in-memory graph data-structure. Vehicle Create Event is called for the specified number of vehicles specified in the simulation input parameters and each vehicle gets attributed a random source and a random destination. The shortest path between a given source and destination node is calculated using Dijkstra's shortest path algorithm.

3.3.2 Vehicle Routing

Each vehicle will check the sensor input and chooses it route to the destination accordingly. The vehicle takes into consideration, the maximum allowable speed limit of the K shortest paths to the destination and predicts the time taken for each of the K shortest paths to reach the destination. The vehicle chooses the path which has minimum time to reach the destination and routes to the next node based on this time.

When the current load of a particular road segment increases, the velocity of the cars traveling on that road segment decreases. This decrease is calculated using the formula,

$$\text{New Velocity} = \text{Max (10, Road segment current velocity} - (1.3 * \text{current load))}$$

4. SIMULATION EXPERIMENTS

To demonstrate the functionality of the proposed simulator, we present two experiments to compare the performance of traditional traffic regulation system and adaptive traffic regulation system. The first experiment compares the number of vehicles that reach their destination. The second experiment compares the average time taken by the vehicles to reach the destination.

Experiment 1: Number of vehicles that reach destinations

The simulation parameters used for experiment 1 is given in Table 1.

Parameter	Value
Input Grid Size	50 x 50
Initial Number of Cars	1000
Road Length	[500 to 1600]m
Road Capacity	[50 to 160]
Initial velocity - car	[12 to 28]m/s
Simulation Period	1800 ticks

Table 1: Simulation Parameters for Experiment 1

In this experiment, we show the number of cars that reach the destination with sensor input from the Internet of Things environment in contrast to the scenario wherein the cars are routed without any sensor input. In terms of the number of cars reaching their destination at each simulation clock, we see that the inclusion of sensor data consistently results in increased performance.

The performance gets closer as the cars started decreasing near the end of the simulation.

Experiment 2: Average time to reach destinations

In this experiment, we measure the average time taken by the vehicles in the simulation to reach the destination with and without the presence of the sensor input, while we vary the rate of vehicle generation. The rate of vehicle generation specifies the number of vehicles that will start at the same simulation tick.

The simulation parameters used for experiment 2 is given in Table 2.

In this experiment, we observe that the simulation with sensor input performs fairly well for lower rates of vehicle generation (rate $\leq$ 12). The greater this rate grows, each road segment in the simulation becomes heavily congested. This causes the vehicle to be re-routed to many different paths before reaching the destination. In this scenario, the simulation without sensor input performs comparatively well.

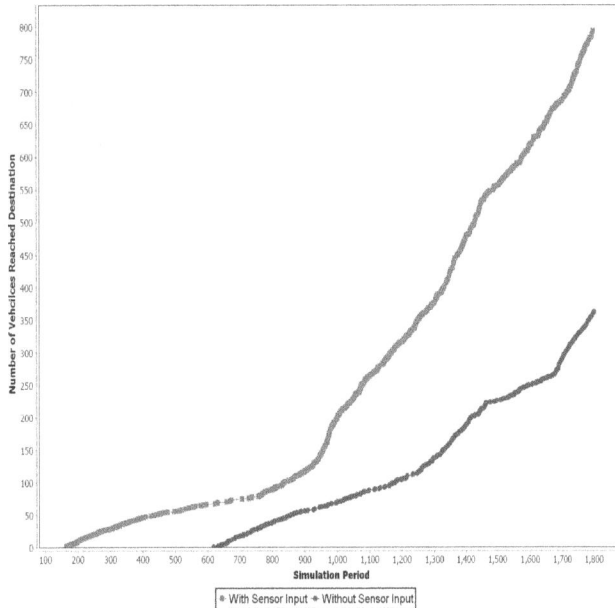

Figure 5: Number of vehicles reached

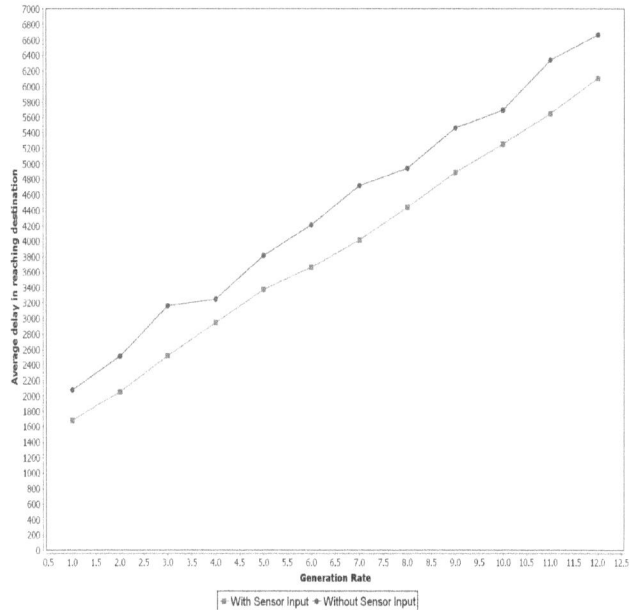

Figure 6: Average Time to Reach Destination

Parameter	Value
Input Grid Size	20 x 20
Initial Number of Cars	1000
Road Length	[500 to 1600]m
Road Capacity	[50 to 160]
Initial velocity - car	[12 to 28]m/s
Simulation Period	1000 ticks

Table 2: Simulation Parameters for Experiment 2

5. CONCLUDING REMARKS

In this paper, we proposed a novel framework integrating simulation, IoT and mining repository using a message-oriented middleware. The efficacy of the framework is demonstrated in the context of simulating traffic congestion. Simulation is used for prediction. IoT again has two components sensors and actuators. Sensors collect data of the current state of the system and feed to the simulation system. Based on the simulation scenarios and data mining, decisions are made to influence the system through actuators. The messaging middleware glue together these components and facilitate effective communication among them. The middleware could easily be hosted as a distributed system making it a very fast and scalable solution. Using Elasticsearch on the data mining for real-time data analysis give the simulator an extra edge at the same time gracefully solving the scalability problem.

We have conducted a limited simulation experiments to demonstrate the proof of concept. Although these experiments give some interesting results, we need to keep in mind that vehicles with human drivers could be different as we have limited knowledge on how each driver will behave based on additional information about the traffic. The proposed system would be more suitable for driver-less vehicular systems. Manual interaction with the system would result in better traffic regulation for vehicles with human drivers. There are several possibilities for further research on

this work including in depth study on road traffic congestion and applying the proposed framework for other applications such as energy system, resource management, etc.

6. REFERENCES

[1] INRIX Report. 2015.
[2] J.O'Hara. Toward a commodity enterprise middleware. *Queue*. 5(4):48-55, 2007.
[3] F.J. Martinez, C.K. Toh, J.C. Cano, C.T. Calafate, and P. Manzoni. A survey and comparative study of simulators for vehicular ad hoc networks (VANETs). *Wireless Communications and Mobile Computing*. 11(7): 813-828, 2011.
[4] M. Piorkowski, M. Raya, A.L. Lugo, P. Papadimitratos, M. Grossglauser, and J.P. Hubaux. TraNS: realistic joint traffic and network simulator for VANETs. *ACM SIGMOBILE mobile computing and communications review*. 12(1): 31-33, 2008.
[5] Nannoni, N. Message-oriented Middleware for Scalable Data Analytics Architectures. 2015.
[6] N. Sivanandam, V. Lelitha Devi, V. Ravi, S. Krishna Kumar. Advanced Traveler Information Systems(ATIS) for Indian Cities. April 2014.
[7] L. Bononi, M. Di Felice, G. D'Angelo, M. Bracuto and L. Donatiello. MOVES: a framework for parallel and distributed simulation of wireless vehicular ad hoc networks. *Computer Networks*. 52(1): 155-179, 2008.
[8] R. M. Fujimoto. Parallel discrete event simulation: Will the field survive? *ORSA J. Computing*. 5(3), 1993.
[9] NS-3 - Discrete Event Network Simulator, accessible at *http://www.nsnam.org*.
[10] E. Baccelli, O. Hahm, M. WÃd'hlisch, M. GuÌĹnes, and T. Schmidt. RIOT: One OS to Rule Them All in the IoT. 2012.
[11] U. Lee, B. Zhou, M. Gerla, E. Magistretti, P.

Bellavista, and A. Corradi. Mobeyes: smart mobs for urban monitoring with a vehicular sensor network. *IEEE Wireless Communications*. 13(5): 52-57, October 2006.

[12] N. Kapileswar and H. Gerhard. A Survey on Urban Traffic Management System Using Wireless Sensor Networks. *Sensors*. 16(2): 1-25, 2016.

[13] M. Albano, L. Ferreira, and A. Alkhawaja. Message Oriented Middleware for smart grids. *Computer Standards & Interfaces*. 38: 133-143, 2014.

[14] A. Dunkels , B. Gronvall, and T. Voigt. Contiki - A Lightweight and Flexible Operating System for Tiny Networked Sensors. *Proceedings of the 29th Annual IEEE International Conference on Local Computer Networks*. 455-462, November 16-18, 2004.

[15] S. Appel, K. Sachs, and A. Buchmann. Towards benchmarking of AMQP. *In Proceedings of the Fourth ACM International Conference on Distributed Event-Based Systems*. 99-100, 2010.

[16] H. Arbabi, and M.C. Weigle. Using DTMon to monitor transient flow traffic. *In Vehicular Networking Conference (VNC), IEEE*. 110-117, 2010.

[17] G. Brambilla, M. Picone, S. Cirani, M. Amoretti, and F. Zanichelli. A simulation platform for large-scale internet of things scenarios in urban environments. *In Proceeding of the of the First International Conference on IoT in Urban Space (Urb-IoT 2014)*. 50-55, 2014.

[18] Brooks Jr, and P. Frederick. "The mythical man-month (anniversary ed.)". (1995).

[19] O. Kononenko, O. Baysal, R. Holmes, and M.W. Godfrey. Mining modern repositories with elasticsearch. *In Proceedings of the 11th Working Conference on Mining Software Repositories*. 328-331, May, 2014.

[20] E. Curry. Message-oriented middleware. *Middleware for communications*. 1-28, 2004.

[21] W.H. Lam. Development of intelligent transport systems in Hong Kong. *In Intelligent Transportation Systems Proceedings*. 1000-1005, 2001.

[22] R. Mangharam, D. Weller, R. Rajkumar, P. Mudalige, and F. Bai. Groovenet: A hybrid simulator for vehicle-to-vehicle networks. *In Third Annual International Conference on Mobile and Ubiquitous Systems: Networking & Services*. 1-8, July 2006.

[23] C. Gustavo. NS-3: Network Simulator 3. UTM Lab Meeting. 20, April 2010.

[24] F. Osterlind, A. Dunkels, J. Eriksson, N. Finne, and T. Voigt. Cross-level sensor network simulation with cooja. *In Local computer networks, proceedings 31st IEEE conference*. 641-648, 2006.

[25] W. Royce, K. Bittner, and M. Perrow. The economics of iterative software development: Steering toward better business results. Pearson Education, 2009.

[26] S. Warren and S. Smallen. Building an Information System for a Distributed Testbed. *Proceedings of the ACM Annual Conference on Extreme Science and Engineering Discovery Environment*. 2014.

[27] ITU Internet Reports 2005: The Internet of Things. 7th edition, 2005.

[28] V. AndrÃąs and R. Hornig. An overview of the OMNeT++ simulation environment. *Proceedings of the 1st international conference on Simulation tools and techniques for communications, networks and systems & workshops*. 2008.

[29] M.A. Chaqfeh and N. Mohamed. Challenges in middleware solutions for the internet of things. *In Collaboration Technologies and Systems (CTS),IEEE*. 21-26, May 2012.

[30] K. Paridel, E. Bainomugisha , Y. Vanrompay, Y. Berbers, and W. De Meuter. Middleware for the internet of things, design goals and challenges. *Electronic Communications of the EASST*. 28, Jun 2010.

Data-Driven Vehicle Trajectory Prediction

Philip Pecher
Georgia Institute of Technology
765 Ferst Drive, NW
Atlanta, GA 30332, USA
philip161@gmail.com

Michael Hunter
Georgia Institute of Technology
Mason Building, 790 Atlantic Drive
Atlanta, GA 30332, USA
michael.hunter@ce.gatech.edu

Richard Fujimoto
Georgia Institute of Technology
266 Ferst Drive
Atlanta, GA 30332, USA
fujimoto@cc.gatech.edu

ABSTRACT

Vehicle trajectory or route prediction is useful in online, data-driven transportation simulation to predict future traffic patterns and congestion, among other uses. The various approaches to route prediction have varying degrees of data required to predict future vehicle trajectories. Three approaches to vehicle trajectory prediction, along with extensions, are examined to assess their accuracy on an urban road network. These include an approach based on the intuition that drivers attempt to reduce their travel time, an approach based on neural networks, and an approach based on Markov models. The T-Drive trajectory data set consisting of GPS trajectories of over ten thousand taxicabs and including 15 million data points in Beijing, China is used for this evaluation. These comparisons illustrate that using trajectory data from other vehicles can substantially improve the accuracy of forward trajectory prediction in the T-Drive data set. These results highlight the benefit of exploiting dynamic data to improve the accuracy of transportation simulation predictions.

CCS Concepts

• **Computing methodologies~Supervised learning**

Keywords

DDDAS; Destination prediction; Path prediction; Route prediction; Trajectory prediction; Markov processes; Pattern recognition; Prediction methods.

1. INTRODUCTION

Route or trajectory prediction algorithms attempt to predict the path that a vehicle will follow in the future assuming its current position is known, but the vehicle's final destination is unknown. These algorithms assume other information is available such as the trajectory taken by the vehicle thus far and/or the routes taken by other vehicles in its vicinity or derived from historical information. As discussed later, several algorithms have been developed to predict future trajectories.

Trajectory and destination prediction finds applications in many areas. For example, in military applications focusing on aerial attack of stationary and unknown ground target [2] and to determine mobility patterns of cell phone users for desirable antenna handoffs for moving vehicles [4].

Permission to make digital or hard copies of all or part of this work for personal or classroom use is granted without fee provided that copies are not made or distributed for profit or commercial advantage and that copies bear this notice and the full citation on the first page. Copyrights for components of this work owned by others than ACM must be honored. Abstracting with credit is permitted. To copy otherwise, or republish, to post on servers or to redistribute to lists, requires prior specific permission and/or a fee. Request permissions from Permissions@acm.org.
SIGSIM-PADS '16, May 15-18, 2016, Banff, AB, Canada
© 2016 ACM. ISBN 978-1-4503-3742-7/16/05…$15.00
DOI: http://dx.doi.org/10.1145/2901378.2901407

It has been suggested that advertising signs can be targeted for nearby locations based on trajectories of approaching travelers [14]. Similarly, mobile apps may suggest restaurants, hotels, or other services based on the driver's expected trajectory [11]. Law enforcement could make use of these models as decision support tools to track the movement of individuals by iteratively sensing the location of a target vehicle, estimating its future location, and redeploying mobile sensors to locations where it is likely to reside in the future [6]. The fuel efficiency of hybrid vehicles can be improved if the system knows the planned route of the driver in advance; automated generation of this information eliminates the need for the driver to explicitly specify this information ([10][5]). This is especially true for routine trips, where the accuracy of personalized trajectory prediction schemes can be particularly good ([13][3][15][19]). Further, the need for such capability is seen in that it has been observed that in practice, in only approximately 1% of all trips does the user specify his/her intended destination ([12]).

Here, we are concerned with the use of trajectory prediction algorithms in the context of dynamic data-driven applications systems (DDDAS) [21]. DDDAS systems involve the use of a control loop that iteratively (1) senses the current state of the system, (2) predicts future system states, and (3) relocates or reconfigures monitoring devices or deploys changes in the operational system to optimize its behavior along one or more dimensions. One use of trajectory prediction is to predict routes to be used by faster-than-real-time microscopic transportation simulation. Such simulations may predict temporal and spatial properties of congestion likely to arise in the future in order to provide travelers with useful information for decision-making, e.g., to determine if an alternate route should be chosen. Today, more drivers are taking advantage of applications that use real-time data to inform them of traffic information such as existing congestion or obstructions (e.g., the mobile app Waze). Accurate simulation results may advise these users of suggested routes and departure times that reduce congestion [14] or reduce travel time globally or individually; we note that these objectives may conflict, and do not necessarily result in identical policies [18].

Similarly, online simulations are often used by transportation engineers to manage the transportation network itself through means such as varying traffic signal timing, ramp metering, or providing travelers with information or recommendations to plan their travel activities. Transportation engineers routinely use microscopic transportation simulation in order to gain insights in traffic, e.g., to determine desirable traffic control policies or logistical considerations of construction projects under a variety of scenarios ([7][20]). Desired output statistics for these models may include the level of congestion and travel times on roads of interest.

Among other factors, the accuracy of these simulation results depends on the validity of the simulation model data that they use.

Specifically, these simulators depend on knowledge of what routes will likely be taken by vehicles in the transportation network. Data-driven transportation simulations require dynamically collected data both to capture the current state of the system as well as to predict future system states. An important question concerns what data and how much data needs to be collected to make reliable predictions. This paper specifically examines the value of utilizing past vehicle trajectory information to provide information for routes likely to be taken by vehicles in the future. Trajectory predictions allow the simulators to use more sophisticated vehicle entity behavior than independent turn probabilities at each intersection.

Sources of dynamic traffic data are numerous. The government uses toll collection transponders, embedded roadway loop detectors [14], automatic license plate recognition, satellite imagery etc., and companies use information collected from drivers who carry smartphones (e.g., Google Maps) and other technologies. Technologies such as Bluetooth and WiFi detectors offer the ability to obtain partial trajectory information of individual vehicles in real-time in an operational transportation network.

Our hypothesis is that dynamic data significantly improves route prediction models. In the evaluation of the prediction models, our aim is to highlight the performance improvement that dynamic data-driven models yield over those that do not utilize such data. The predictive power of dynamic data in urban computing is seen in other areas as well. For example, [24] proposes a cloud-based scheme to predict the travel time of a driver along candidate routes using dynamic data: traffic conditions, time of day, weather, driver behavior, etc. As a result, this system allows GPS navigation systems to find the fastest route for a user, outperforming models that do not utilize this type of dynamic data.

This paper compares methods to predict a driver's future trajectory given the observation of the partial trajectory traversed by the vehicle thus far. For the vehicle whose travel is being predicted we do not assume that we have historical travel information, i.e., common destinations used by that driver in the past. Reliance on such data is problematic due to privacy concerns. This assumption allows the models to be easily applied to different vehicles in a DDDAS application, but will offer lower accuracy than personalized models since the preferred routine destinations of a particular driver are not known. Work by other authors have been used to predict a vehicle's future destination, irrespective of the future route taken to reach it. For example, Krumm's destination prediction model, described later, is based on efficient routes [11]. A modified form of Krumm's model is evaluated in this study.

In this paper, we discuss different methods to predict the trajectory (or route) of a driver on an urban road network and compare their accuracy utilizing the T-Drive trajectory data set. This data set consists of GPS trajectories of over ten thousand taxicabs (15 million data points) in Beijing, China. The performance of the models is measured by how often the next zone (a 1.25 km x 1.25 km square) visited by the vehicle falls within a predicted zone. Our results demonstrate that using route data collected for other drivers substantially improves the accuracy of forward trajectory prediction in the T-Drive data set.

While our primary goal is to show the value of trajectory prediction to drive on-line data-driven simulations, our contributions extend further. First, several proposed trajectory prediction algorithms are compared using a common dataset.

Second, this paper examines the benefit of utilizing dynamic data from other vehicle trajectories in trajectory prediction algorithms. Third, several extensions to previously published prediction algorithms are developed and evaluated.

The next section reviews the destination prediction literature. This is followed by a description of the models examined in this study. The performance of the models using the T-Drive data set is presented, followed by a discussion of future work.

2. RELATED WORK

Early work in destination prediction was developed by Krumm [11]. This work utilizes a Bayesian model that uses the immediate past trajectory taken by a vehicle to predict the vehicle's intended destination. An underlying assumption used in this work is that drivers utilize efficient routes in order to reach their intended destination.

An efficient Markov model for destination and trajectory prediction is presented in [16]. When a prediction is requested, a data structure is traversed that holds the partial trajectory observed for the vehicle thus far. This data structure subsequently provides the empirical distribution of the forward trajectory.

Trajectory prediction using artificial neural networks is described in [14]. The previous five locations visited by the target vehicle are used to estimate the future trajectory by training a feed-forward artificial neural network with two hidden layers consisting of 500 neurons each. These three approaches – Krumm's approach, Markov models, and neural networks are discussed in greater detail later.

In 2008, a Carnage Mellon University group published the PROCAB model (Probabilistic Reasoning from Observed Context-Aware Behavior) [25]. This model uses the current context (e.g., accidents or congestion) and the user's preferences (e.g., fuel efficiency or safety) in order to predict his/her actions, rather than just focus on previous actions for prediction. The model maps actions into a Markov Decision Process (MDP), where intersections are encoded as states and road segments are encoded as transitions. State transitions are associated with a cost, namely the sum-product of road segment features and cost weights obtained from collected training data. The model assumes that drivers attempt to minimize the cost to reach their destination. For destination prediction, it has been reported that PROCAB outperformed Krumm's Predestination algorithm for the first half of the trip. The PROCAB implementation used in [25] takes into account specific road features such as the number of lanes and speed limit. A further challenge in the context of the work discussed here is we assume the destination is unknown; one of the inputs used by [25] for trajectory prediction is the actual destination of the target vehicle.

In [8] the authors suggest using a personalization profile of smartphone users for localized searches. User activities and on-device sensors are queried to build a context profile, including demographical features and previous user activities. The weights of this information along with an environmental profile (weather, temperature, etc.) are trained via an artificial neural network. These profiles are used to rank personalized queries (e.g., local businesses). One could envision utilizing the same model to predict destinations or routes, similar to PROCAB.

In [1] the authors use Krumm's destination prediction model based on efficient routes, but truncate the destination sample space to locations reachable within 30 minutes from the trip's starting location, citing a study [9] that concluded that most driving trips end before that amount of time.

In [19] a hidden Markov model (HMM) is used to estimate a particular driver's destination and route, by using his/her previous trajectories along with driving time. Because personal identification is not specified in the data files of the T-Drive trajectory sample, we apply our Markov model (see Section 3.3) without discrimination towards any particular driver. That is, we train our model using the trajectories of many different drivers, rather than rely on individualized routes.

In [17], historical trajectories are converted into polygons by adding a 10m radius around the observed path. This data is then stored in a database. As soon as a prediction is requested, a polyline is formed through the requesting driver's observed GPS points and the database is checked for any intersecting polygon. If there are multiple results, further filters are applied to obtain the prediction. For example, match of the driver id would rank that particular polygon higher than one from another driver.

Sub-Trajectory Synthesis (SubSyn) [22] addresses the data sparsity problem, as well as privacy concerns, by synthetically generating trajectories from existing routes. These existing routes are decomposed into two-pair nodes and a 1st order Markov Model is used to generate the new trajectories.

Some of the approaches described above are not well suited for use of the T-Drive data set for evaluation. In some cases, necessary information such as source-destination information for trips are not known. Inference of this information from taxi trajectories is not straightforward. Further, the T-Drive sample data is not at a suitable temporal granularity for effective evaluation of some methods; for example, speed data cannot be easily derived.

3. PREDICTION MODELS

The three prediction models compared in this study are described next. These include Krumm's model along with several extensions developed during the course of this study, a model based on artificial neural networks, and a Markov model. Some of these approaches use trajectory information collected from other vehicles. An approach to store this trajectory information, termed Past and Future Trees, is also briefly discussed.

3.1 Krumm's Destination Prediction Algorithm Based on Efficient Routes

Krumm developed a *destination* prediction model based on the intuition that drivers reduce their minimum remaining travel time to their destination as the trip time increases [11], that is, drivers tend to the shortest path to a destination rather than more circuitous routes. Figure 1 illustrates this intuition. According to data collected in the Seattle area. In [11] Seattle was divided into cells measuring 1 km x 1 km. For the study, it was observed that when drivers transitioned between cells they reduced the potential minimum travel time to their destination 62.5% of the time. Krumm utilizes this driver tendency to seek efficient paths to estimate the probability that a given location (i.e. cell) is the driver's destination given the current partial path (i.e. the partial route of the traveler to their current location). That is, suppose a driver has now traversed a partial trajectory P and we wish to determine the estimated probability of the driver's destination being a cell c_i. Each probability $Pr(P|c_i)$ is computed by a product of $\{p, (1 - p)\}$, where $p = 0.625$ and the number of factors is equal to the partial trajectory length (there is a surjective mapping from

the cells of the partial trajectory to $\{p, (1 - p)\}$). A factor of p is selected when the partial trajectory cell brings the vehicle closer to the candidate destination c_i and $(1-p)$ otherwise. All of these candidate $Pr(P|c_i)$'s are then multiplied with the prior probability $Pr(c_i)$, if the cell bias is known, and normalized, so that their sum equals 1 for a valid probability mass of the $Pr(c_i|P)$'s.

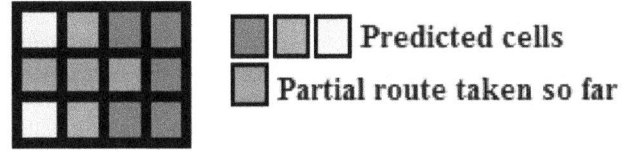

Figure 1: The red cells are assumed to be more likely because they are consistent (in efficiency) with the partial route taken so far (rectilinear distance).

In algorithm format, the prediction algorithm operates as follows:

```
1 For each candidate cell cᵢ
2   p_c = 1
3   For each cell c in partial route P
4     if c is closer to cᵢ than any previous cell in P
5       p_c = p_c * 0.65
6     else
7       p_c = p_c * 0.35
8   P(cᵢ) = p_c
9 Normalize all P(cᵢ) to get a valid probability mass
```

In the above algorithmic description, $Pr(P|c_i)$ is abbreviated as p_c and the cell bias is assumed to be unknown. If the cell bias is known, the probability estimate on Line 8 can be scaled accordingly.

In Section 4.1, we modify this algorithm to use it for *trajectory* prediction, or more precisely, for the *next transition* in the trajectory.

3.2 Artificial Neural Networks

Artificial neural networks (ANN's) map input values to output values and are often used to approximate complex functions (e.g., recognizing handwritten digits). For trajectory prediction, the input layer may encode some number of previously visited locations and the output layer may represent one or more projected future locations. ANN's consist of nodes called neurons (as they are inspired by the brain) and edges that connect them. In a feed-forward ANN (see Figure 2), information flows from the input layer to the output layer, via one or more hidden layers. The nodes in any layer are fully connected to the nodes of their preceding layer. Edges have weights associated with them that determine the strength of the signal sent by the preceding neuron. Typically, the product of the weight and the signal is then received by the neuron to which that the edge points. The signal sent by a neuron is determined by its *activation function*. Sigmoid functions are commonly used in feed-forward ANN's. One of them is the logistic function, $(1+exp(-x))^{-1}$, where x is the total input signal to the receiving neuron. For most values of x, the sigmoid function evaluates to a real number either close to 0 or close to 1. A popular, supervised learning algorithm for training feed-forward ANN's (i.e., determining the edge weights) is the backpropagation algorithm. Usually, the initial weights are randomized after which they are modified to minimize the error via gradient descent.

Since ANN's are often used in prediction to map relevant factors to an estimated output and training data is available, it seems reasonable to assume that we can utilize them for trajectory prediction as well. Just as in the other trajectory prediction models, the partial trajectory of the target vehicle can be used as the input and the output layer can encode a future location of the vehicle. The design of the ANN, including the encoding of the input & output neurons and the architecture of the hidden layers is not trivial. [14] outlines three neuron encoding schemes and opts for the third one in the experiment: (i) A single neuron encodes the location, (ii) each possible location value is associated with a dedicated neuron, and (iii) a neuron encodes a bit in the binary representation. The learning parameters must also be selected carefully, in order to avoid oscillations, high errors, and/or under-training. [14] evaluates the trajectory prediction accuracy of a feed-forward artificial neural network (Figure 2) with sigmoid activation functions on artificially generated data. The input layer consists of the five previously visited locations in the trajectory where each location has multiple input neurons representing the integral location id in binary form. Two hidden layers of 500 neurons are used. Using a training set of 2000, the authors attain a success rate of almost 99% and 64% in their synthetically generated datasets, where the former quantity is tested on a dataset described as an easy data set with very little stochasticity while the latter quantity is tested on a dataset described to contain a considerable amount of random decisions.

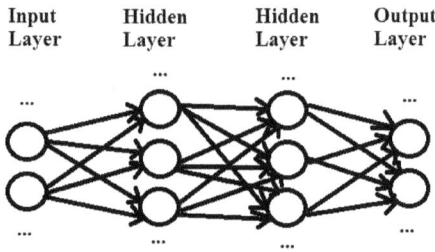

Figure 2: The edges have weights associated with them that set the strength of the value being sent. The circles are neurons that typically send values close to 0 or close to 1.

In order to reduce the training time to an amount comparable to the other tested models, we reduce the hidden layer count to just one and the hidden layer size to just seven neurons. With our fixed learning parameters, ANN's with more hidden layers and/or larger hidden layer sizes performed worse in our profiling tests.

3.3 Markov Models and Trajectory Storage

Pecher et al. [16] proposes a data structure that serves as the fast backbone of an arbitrary-order Markov model. This data structure can be used for a simple trajectory prediction algorithm if it is used to store historical trajectories. If queried order is sufficiently high and/or the data is sufficiently sparse, the future trajectory distribution is obtained from the maximal order for which data is available. A tolerance for minimum sample size can be set by the user. The emphasis on speed makes this implementation especially useful for embedded applications and/or simulation engines where realizations have to be drawn quickly. Historical route data is stored in Past and Future Trees and the data are queried on demand. The Past Tree of a location is queried with the partial trajectory traversed by the target vehicle up to that location. A Future Tree that contains the future trajectory distribution is then returned by the Past Tree. If the user wishes to get an estimate of the location of the target vehicle at some defined time in the future, the model invokes a microscopic traffic

simulation. If storage is more important than access time, a hashtable implementation may be used instead (see Figure 3).

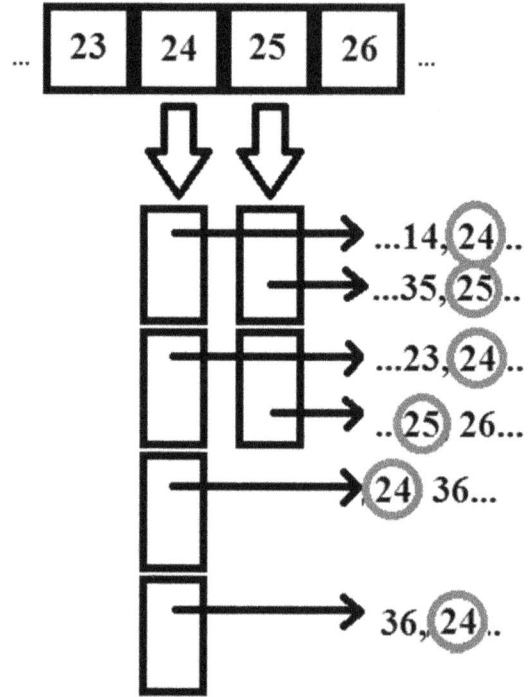

Figure 3: All trajectories that contain the cell 24 are being pointed to by the column 24. Empirical distributions of any Markov order can be obtained quickly by traversing this column.

Suppose the target vehicle is at cell 24, a prediction for the next cell is requested, and the partial trajectory so far is supplied. The 24th column can be accessed in constant time and its elements can be traversed comparing the elements with the partial trajectory observed so far. An empirical distribution can now be constructed by collecting a sufficient number of partial-trajectory matches along this column.

The models discussed thus far – in their current implementation – statically predict the future route with some spatial discretization, but do not specify point estimates for the time needed to reach the points along that route and do not return the projected location at a specific future time. If, rather than the next cell, the projected location of the target vehicle at Δt time units into the future is requested, one can construct a decision tree, T, that enumerates all possible paths in a breath-first fashion. Leaf nodes are tagged with the expected travel time to the intersections represented by those nodes until they exceed Δt. Once all leaf nodes exceed Δt, all locations expected to be reached at Δt time units into the future are tagged with the likelihoods stored in the Past Trees (or with those returned by the models of Section 3.1 and 3.2), and normalized to yield a valid probability mass. For example, if Past Trees are used and all the relevant leaf nodes of T have been enumerated and flagged, the Past Tree column of last observed location of the target vehicle is retrieved (Figure 3), a suitable number of matches of the partial trajectory observed thus far is queried from this column, and used to build an empirical distribution of future locations. Each path from the root node of T to a flagged node can now be used to retrieve the estimated probability from the empirical distribution. All these estimated probabilities are then divided by their sum in order to scale them to a valid probability mass.

3.4 Generating Routes from Probability Maps

The prediction models described above generate probability maps indicating the likelihood the vehicle will reside at particular locations in the future. It is straightforward to use the probability maps to generate future routes. These models can also be used to simulate entity routing in microscopic traffic simulation. For example, if an ANN estimates the next-transition probabilities, one can input a random number into the inverse c.d.f. of the empirical distribution, and generate a next location. This next location, along with the previously visited locations, can be used as an input to the ANN and this process can be repeated. In the same fashion, the probability map returned by Krumm's prediction model based on efficient routes can be used to generate a cell. Lastly, Past Trees can be traversed quickly to construct an empirical distribution function of the next transition and random numbers can be used to obtain a sample of the next decision. In all these cases, a destination should be realized at some point of the simulated trip.

4. EXPERIMENTAL EVALUATION

The data set used for evaluating the accuracy of the models is the T-Drive sample dataset published by Microsoft Research ([24][23]). It consists of 15 million GPS points collected from over 10,000 taxicabs from February 2 to February 8, 2008, in Beijing. The sampling interval between two consecutive GPS coordinates is variable with a mean of 177 seconds (average distance: 623m), but can be as long as 600 seconds. It is important to note that the dataset consists of tour-based data and not origin-destination pairs. In other words, all the origin-destination pairs of sub-trajectories (taxi trips) are hidden in the tours of each taxicab file. The taximeter data of the T-Drive sample data set is not published (as of January, 2016). In our experimental evaluation, we discretize the road network into a two dimensional grid.

From the T-Drive Sample Dataset, we focus on an area that is approximately 100km × 100km: longitude from 116.0 to 117.1 (inclusive) and latitude from 39.6 to 40.5 (inclusive), in decimal degrees. This area was selected by isolating grid cells that have over 100,000 data points at the resolution of 0.1 decimal degrees in both dimensions (approx. 10km × 10km). This region is overlaid with a 96-wide and 80-high cell grid, where each cell maps to a 1.25km × 1.25km area. The relatively coarse grid size was chosen because of the relatively long median sampling interval in the dataset. Finer resolutions would require one to speculate on the path taken by the taxicab between successive reported locations. This is also the reason, in general, why the turn ratio at intersections cannot be determined with certainty in this data sample. To get consistent results, we use the same size for all cells; using variable cell sizes (e.g., determined by the variable sample intervals) could result in an arbitrary grid schema. Taxicab files are only considered if they fall within the above mentioned region. Taxicabs frequently visit certain, popular hubs to drop-off or pick-up passengers. In order to avoid utilizing these "artificial" trips we use a simple heuristic of ignoring the top 5% of the most popular cells, which are more likely to be hub locations, from the results.

We use the first 80% of filtered data points to train the models, and the last 20% of filtered data points to test the models. All interior cells in the grid contain eight neighbors (see Figure 4).

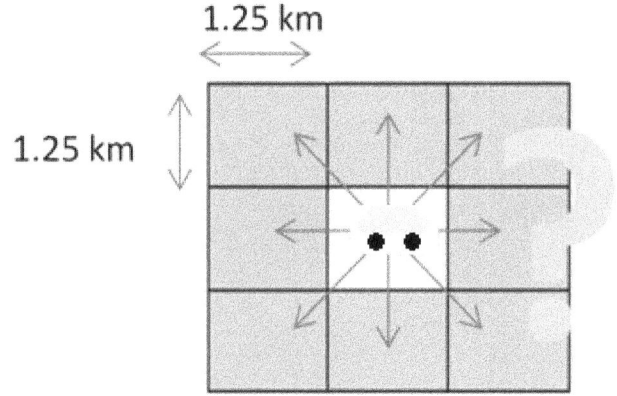

Figure 4: The next zone visited by the taxicab is uncertain, but is restricted to eight possible zones.

We consider the partial trajectory of the taxicab in question in order to predict the next cell visited. To evaluate the accuracy of the models, we assume that we can probe i grid cells, ranging from one to eight, for the presence of the vehicle. For each model, let $A(i)$ denote the measured cumulative probability of capturing the vehicle by greedily selecting the i most probable cells as estimated by the respective model. The objective is to achieve a high probability of detection for small i. In this section, if a model $m2$ is described to be x% *better* or *improved* than model $m1$ (for a specific number of observed grid cells i), x is derived from the distance $A(i)_{m2} - A(i)_{m1}$ - not from a ratio of the two terms.

The test system uses an Intel i7 6700 CPU, 32GB of DDR4-2133 main memory, and a Samsung 840 Evo 1TB solid state disk. Neuroph v2.92 is used for the artificial neural networks in Section 4.3.

4.1 The Efficient Route Model and Extensions

We modify the efficient route algorithm from Section 3.1:

```
1 For each candidate cell cᵢ
2   p_c = 1
3   For each cell c in partial route P
4     If c is closer to cᵢ than the previous cell in P
5       p_c = p_c * 0.75
6     else
7       p_c = p_c * 0.25
8   P(cᵢ) = p_c*Markov(P(P.length-2), P(P.length-1))
9   Normalize all P(cᵢ) to get a valid probability mass
```

We use a less strict condition, on Line 4, to determine whether the vehicle opted for efficient transitions, in order to achieve better accuracy of the prediction of the next transition in the T-Drive sample. In most applications, the sample space of the destination is orders of magnitude greater than the immediate trajectory, so a more discriminatory algorithm is likely to perform better for the prediction of the destination. We also tune the p parameter (Line 5 and 7), denoting the fraction of time a transition is efficient, with respect to the T-Drive sample training set. Lastly, rather than use just the static cell popularity or no adjustment at all, the candidate $Pr(P|c_i)$'s are scaled by the 2nd order Markov estimates on Line 8. *Markov(start, end)* uses the subsequence of P, which starts with cell *start* (inclusive) and ends with cell *end* (inclusive), as arguments, and returns the corresponding Markov probability estimate. The indexing into P is assumed to be zero-based. We will refer to the condition on Line 4 with the term *isCloser* in the subsequent discussion.

For the *modified* Krumm route efficiency model without any historical data for the prior, we noticed very minor changes in the prediction accuracy for low i, as the efficiency likelihood parameter p is varied from 0.55 to 0.95 (using 0.1 increments). Among these, the best results were obtained with p=0.75. In Figure 5, the dark blue plot visualizes the performance, $A(i)$, of this model. This plot, as well as all other plots in Section 4, is derived from evaluating the test set - the last 20% of the data points.

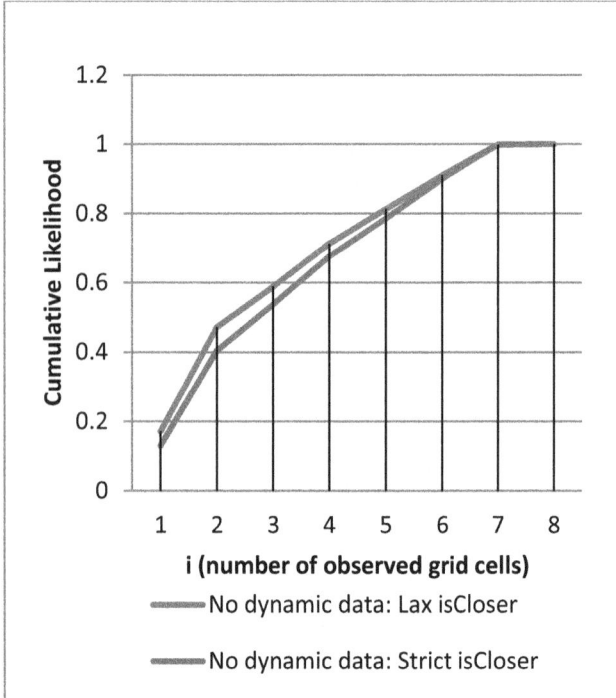

Figure 5: Cumulative likelihood for recapturing the target vehicle at the next cell transition using the path efficiency models (Krumm) with a p=0.75 parameter.

In the Seattle dataset, used in the original study, a value of p equal to 0.65 offered the best results. However, due to the different road network (Seattle vs. Bejing), the different driving population (Microsoft employees vs. cab drivers), slightly different grid size (1.25 km vs. 1.25 km), different objective function (distance to destination vs. next transition) or simply random noise (due to hidden factors) we found that setting p equal to 0.75 performed slightly better in this context. We experimented with dynamically varying the strength of the p parameter for the observed partial trajectory, using higher p parameter values for more current cell transitions than in older transitions. This results in slightly worse performance than a constant p=0.75 for all transitions. Thus, for all subsequent variations of the Krumm route efficiency model, we use p=0.75. We also note that truncating the partial route traversed by the taxicab to two or three cells did not yield any benefits. In other words, using the entire partial trajectory of the taxicab yielded superior results than just considering a limited horizon. Lastly, when deciding if a cell transition is efficient, different distance functions can be used. When we opted for Euclidian distance, rather than rectilinear distance, we obtained slightly worse results. As a result of these two considerations, partial trajectories for the efficient route models will not be truncated and rectilinear distances will be used.

One important algorithm modification that led to the previously mentioned results was the replacement of the efficiency random variable. In the original model, a transition is considered efficient if it brings the vehicle closer to the candidate cell relative to *any* other previously visited cell of the partial trajectory traversed thus far. Instead, we consider a transition efficient if it brings the vehicle closer to the candidate cell relative to the *previously visited* cell only. The original random variable results in slightly worse reacquisition likelihoods as the red-colored plot in Figure 5 illustrates. To be clear, the term *strict isCloser* exclusively refers to the conditional expression in Line 4 of the first algorithm listed in Section 3.1.

The original efficiency standard is stricter, as the comparison is relative to *all* previously visited cells. The sample space of potential destinations is much larger than just the next transition and if the efficiency standard is strict, a large area of potential destinations can be virtually eliminated (with very small assigned probabilities). Our objective is to predict the immediate trajectory, rather than the destination, a likely reason for the better performance of the lax conditional (the conditional on Line 4 of the algorithm listed at the beginning of this section). For all subsequent variations of the Krumm route efficiency model, we only consider a cell transition efficient if it brings the vehicle closer to the candidate cell compared to the previously visited cell only.

4.2 Markov Models

To evaluate the Markov models, we use the Past Tree implementation [16]. We do not set a sample size limit; in other words, we use relevant observations from the entire training set to populate the Past Trees. In our discussion, the term *order-i* refers to using the previous i locations of the target vehicle to make the next prediction. The results of Figure 6 are obtained from the pure order 1, 2, and 3 Markov models:

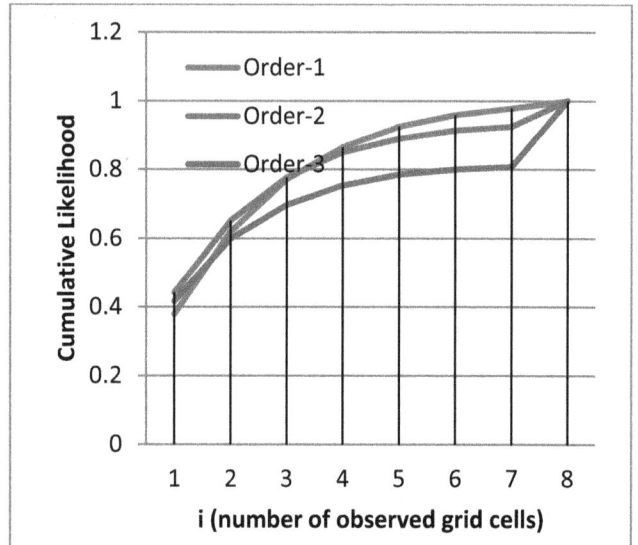

Figure 6: Cumulative likelihood for recapturing the target vehicle at the next cell transition using 1st, 2nd, and 3rd-order Markov models (Past Tree implementation).

Due to over-fitting or data sparsity, the order-3 model performs worse than the order-2 and order-1 model. The order-2 Markov model performs slightly better than the order-1 variant for i=1,2,3 because directional information can be inferred from the previous two destinations. However, there is a slight drop off in this advantage as i increases and the implementation of the order-1 model is easier. Below $i=6$, every Markov model outperforms the models that do not have historical data (the blue and red plots in Figure 5) and the $i=1$ accuracy is over twice as high in the Markov model results. Even though the models without historical data directly infer the immediate future trajectory from the *behavior* (route to current location) *of the target vehicle itself*, the data of *other vehicles* that engaged in the same behavior offers better point estimates on average.

Figure 7 shows the results of Markov models that attempt to use estimates from the next lower orders, after a candidate cell could not be found in the higher order model (due to lack of data). In other words, the estimate is extracted from the highest order model that has the candidate location available. If there is still a miss of the candidate cell in the order-1 model, the static cell popularity is used. There is little benefit of this cascading fallback mechanism at order-1, compared to the plain order-1 model, as the data available at order-1 is quite abundant (i.e., rare fallbacks to static cell popularities). However, the order-2 fallback estimates are on average 1% better from $i=1$ to $i=3$ and 4% better from $i=5$ to $i=7$, compared the plain order-2 model. The order-2 fallback model performs slightly better than the order-3 fallback model.

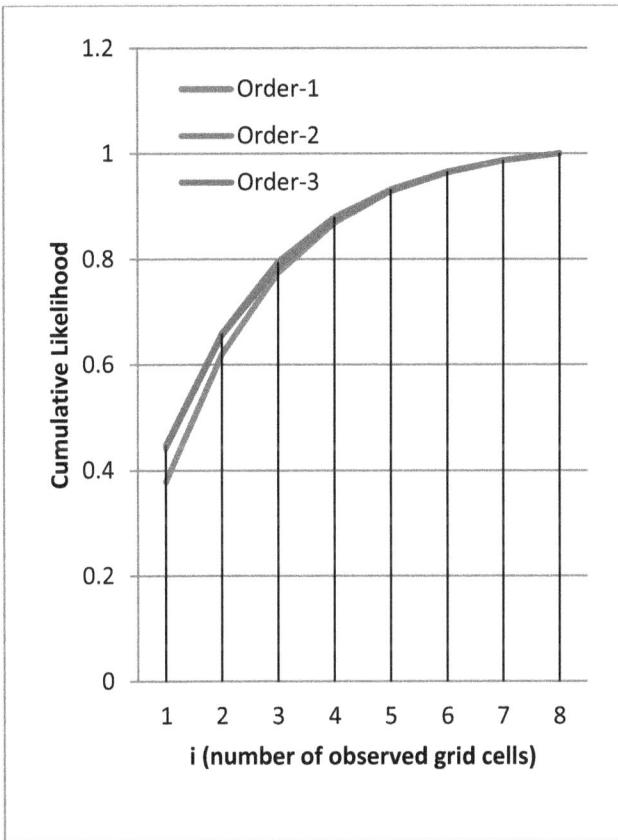

Figure 7: Cumulative likelihood for recapturing the target vehicle at the next cell transition using 1st, 2nd, and 3rd-order Markov models with a cascading fallback mechanism towards lower orders.

If we define the prior (i.e., the cell bias $Pr(c_j)$) in the Krumm route efficiency model as the static cell popularity (how much has each cell been visited by a vehicle in the training dataset), rather than just a uniform constant (in the case where no vehicle density data is available), and then normalize these probabilities for only the eight possible cells, we obtain a significantly improved (relative to the basic route efficiency model) distribution function, as can be seen in the dark blue-colored plot of Figure 8.

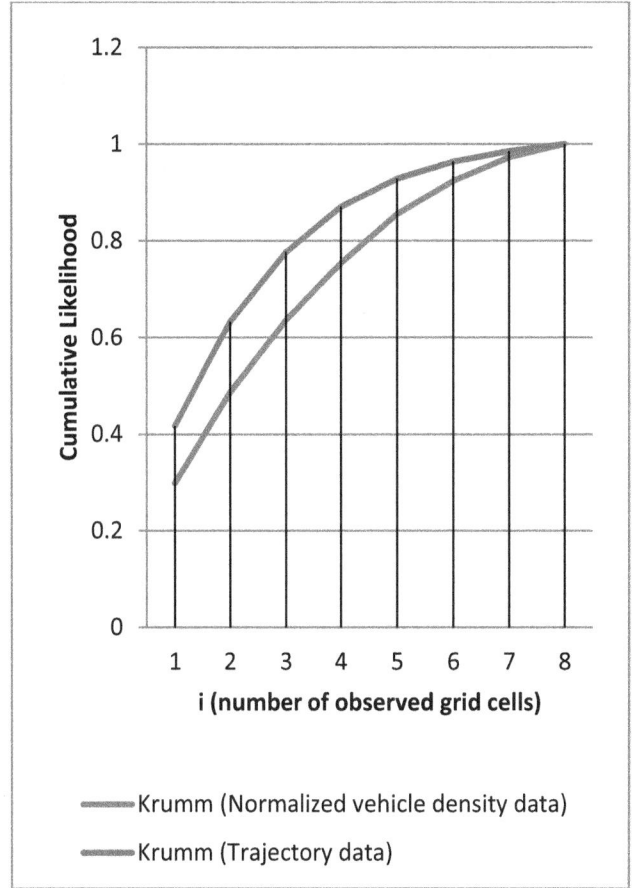

Figure 8: Cumulative likelihood for recapturing the target vehicle at the next cell transition using the modified Krumm models and dynamic data.

When we replace the prior (or the cell bias) in the Krumm route efficiency model with order-2 fallback probability estimates, we obtain reacquisition likelihoods that are improved further (the red-colored plot in Figure 8).

These results illustrate the power of using dynamic data in this particular application. Compared to the original route efficiency model, the probability of correctly predicting the target vehicle's location more than doubles at $i=1$. This advantage is crucial if there are several trials (reacquisition attempts), translating into savings in tracking resources and/or the more likely successful tracking of the target vehicle.

4.3 Feed-Forward Artificial Neural Network

For the feed-forward artificial neural network results, we use a single hidden layer with seven neurons in order to reach a training time comparable to the other models. Our profiling experiments showed that adding significantly more or less than seven neurons to the hidden layer and adding more than one hidden layer worsened the results, fixing the learning parameters described shortly. Omitting the hidden layer completely worsened the results. The activation functions are hyperbolic tangent and the edge weights are learned with the backpropagation algorithm. Because we opt for binary encodings of the input (of the five previously visited nodes, as in the setup in [14]) and our cells are identified with 12 bits, we have 60 (=5×12) input neurons in total. The first six binary values of a binary cell identifier encode the row index, and the last six values encode the column index. The output consists of eight neurons, denoting the prediction of the next cell visited (direction relative to the current cell of the vehicle; see Figure 4), a higher output value being interpreted as a higher likelihood of the next cell visited matching with the cell associated with the given output neuron. Given a step size of 0.2 (based on our results, just slightly better than 0.8), a maximum error of 0.1 (based on our results, as good as 0.01), at most five learning cycles (better than lower values and just as good as most higher values), and including the 5% most popular cells, we obtain the results depicted in Figure 9. The value(s) in parentheses, after the abbreviation ANN, refer to the number of neurons in the hidden layer(s).

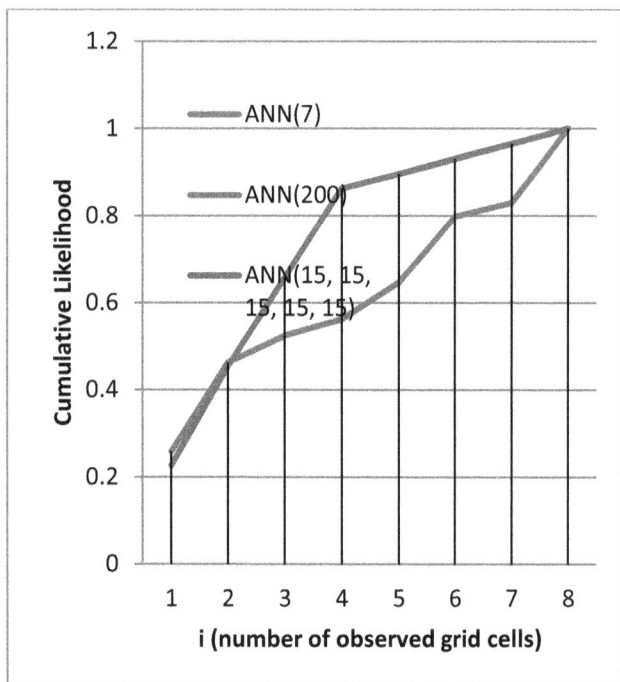

Figure 9: Cumulative likelihood for recapturing the target vehicle at the next cell transition using a feed-forward artificial neural network with one hidden layer, consisting of seven nodes.

The learning parameters are fixed for each ANN model. The performance of ANN(7) and ANN(15,15,15,15,15) is virtually the same. The ANN(7) results are superior to random guessing and the models that are only aware of the partial trajectory traversed by the target vehicle. It took 25.7 sec and 2.3 sec of CPU time to train and test ANN(7), respectively. One possible explanation of the change at $i=4$ is that most of the variation in the output is captured by the most significant bit of the most recent node's row and column index.

5. COMPARISON OF THE MODELS

Figure 10 shows the best performing members of the discussed model families. The blue plot shows the performance of the ANN with one hidden layer of seven neurons

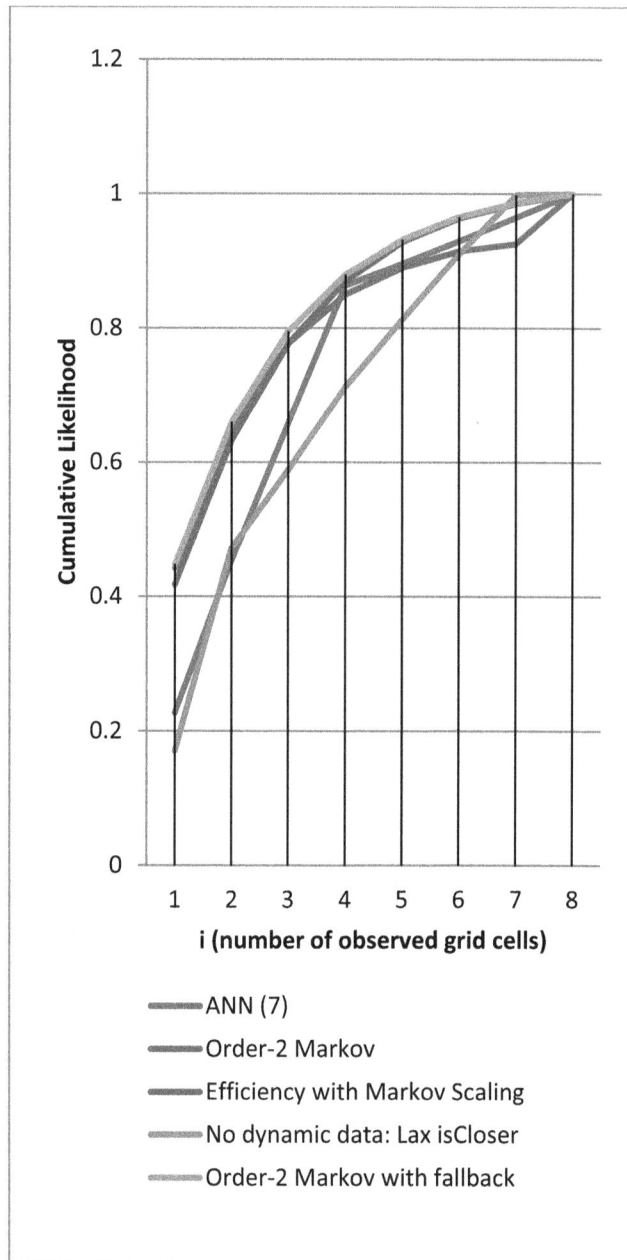

Figure 10: Cumulative likelihood for recapturing the target vehicle at the next cell transition using the best-performing submodels.

The order-2 Markov model with the fallback mechanism outperforms all other models for $i<7$. The preference for efficiency appears to already be implicit in the data. We have also evaluated a tournament predictor (not shown) that uses the estimates from either the hybrid model (efficiency scaled by order-2 fallback estimates) or the order-2 fallback model, depending on how well each model has performed in the current context (the trip progress and specific last two cells visited). For $i<5$, the tournament predictor performs worse than just the order-2 fallback model. While the pure efficiency prediction does not take into account specific features of the Beijing road network or other dynamic factors (cyan), it is – in its modified form (purple) - able to leverage the information that is implicit in the historical order-2 Markov estimates. The modified Krumm model, using the order-2

Markov fallback model in the cell bias term, performs slightly worse than just the pure order-2 Markov model at i=1, perhaps due to the power law nature of popular locations and thus the strong preference of drivers to transition to certain cells. With higher i, however, the skewness of the transition distribution reduces and drivers are likely to still be in transit, when efficiency is still very much relevant. Further investigation is needed to determine appropriate hyper parameters, architectures, and training heuristics to train deep neural networks for trajectory prediction. Our simple ANN architecture is able to outperform the Order-2 Markov model (without fallback) only after i=3, but is dominated by the efficiency-Markov hybrid model across all i.

6. CONCLUSION AND FUTURE WORK

This paper examines different route prediction models on the real-world T-Drive trajectory data sample collected in Beijing, China. All of the models tested can be executed reasonably quickly, even on mobile devices and/or simulation engines. For models making use of large data-sets, queries may be performed in the cloud. Some of the models are provided with the current trajectory of the driver, up to just before the tested zone, while others are provided with a relatively large training set of previously observed trajectories. In all cases where the model is permitted to use historical route data, rather than just the observed partial route, we observe substantial improvement in the forward-trajectory prediction accuracy on the T-Drive trajectory data sample - especially the order-2 Markov models and the Krumm-Markov hybrid model. We would like to emphasize the value of exploiting dynamic data, in accordance with the DDDAS paradigm, for the vehicle tracking problem (see [6]). It becomes especially important to improve the single trial reacquisition probability, when the scheme is repeated for a tracked vehicle. In any case, the economies of scale of the data acquisition costs should be compared to the tracking equipment acquisition and maintenance costs combined with the utility of recapturing the target vehicles. The value of successful trajectory prediction is observed in many commercial and non-commercial applications and is likely to grow as the penetration of smartphones and augmented reality devices increases. The models may also be used to generate accurate trajectories for entities in microscopic traffic simulation.

In the future, we plan to look at more factors and blended models on potentially different conceptual models; for example, roads being modeled rather than zones by randomly selecting among possible subsections in trajectories whose sampling interval may be relatively long. We also plan to investigate the impact in the accuracy of simulation output statistics, when these prediction models are used instead of the traditional inputs. Rather than just predict the forward trajectory statically, we envision predicting the forward trajectory by incorporating time.

7. ACKNOWLEDGMENTS

Funding for this project was provided by NSF Grant 1462503.

8. REFERENCES

[1] Amini, S., Brush, A.J., Krumm, J., Teevan, J., and Karlson, A. 2012. Trajectory-aware mobile search. In Proceedings of the SIGCHI Conference on Human Factors in Computing Systems (CHI '12). ACM, New York, NY, USA, 2561-2564.

[2] Andrew, S. J., Prazenica, R. J., and Jeffcoat, D. E. 2008. Optimal and feedback path planning for cooperative attack. Journal of Guidance, Control, and Dynamics 31, no. 6 (2008): 1708-1715.

[3] Ashbrook, D. and Starner, T. 2003. Using GPS To Learn Significant Locations and Predict Movement Across Multiple Users. Personal and Ubiquitous Computing, 2003. 7(5): p. 275-286.

[4] Cheng, C., Jain, R., and Berg, E.v.d. 2003. Location Prediction Algorithms for Mobile Wireless Systems, in Wireless Internet Handbook: Technologies, Standards, and Applications. 2003, CRC Press: Boca Raton, FL, USA. p. 245-263.

[5] Deguchi, Y., et al. 2004. Hev Charge/Discharge Control System Based on Navigation Information. In: SAE Convergence International Congress & Exposition on Transportation Electronics, Detroit, Michigan USA (2004)

[6] Fujimoto, R., Guin, A., Hunter, M., Park, H., Kannan, R., Kanitkar, G., Milholen, M., Neal, S., and Pecher, P. 2014. A Dynamic Data Driven Application System for Vehicle Tracking. International Conference on Computational Science, Dynamic Data Driven Application Systems Workshop, June 2014.

[7] Fujimoto, R., Hunter, M., Sirichoke, J., Palekar, M., Kim, H-K., and Suh, W. 2007. Ad Hoc Distributed Simulations. In Principles of Advanced and Distributed Simulation.

[8] Gui, F., Adjouadi, M. and Rishe, N. 2009. A contextualized and personalized approach for mobile search. Advanced Information Networking and Applications Workshops, 2009, 966–971

[9] Hu, P.S. and Reuscher, T.R. 2001. Summary of travel trends: 2001 national household transportation survey. Oak Ridge National Laboratory Technical Report ORNL/TM

[10] Johannesson, L., Asbogard, M., and Egardt, B. 2007. Assessing the potential of predictive control for hybrid vehicle powertrains using stochastic dynamic programming. IEEE Transactions on Intelligent Transportation Systems, 8(1):71–83, March 2007.

[11] Krumm, J. 2006. Real time destination prediction based on efficient routes. No. 2006-01-0811. SAE Technical Paper, 2006.

[12] Krumm, J. 2009. Where will they turn: Predicting turn proportions at intersections. Personal and Ubiquitous Computing, 2009

[13] Laasonen, K. 2005. Route prediction from cellular data. In Workshop on Context-Awareness for Proactive Systems (CAPS), Helsinki, Finland, vol. 1617. 2005.

[14] Mikluščák, T., Gregor, M., and Janota, A. 2012. Using Neural Networks for Route and Destination Prediction in Intelligent Transport Systems. In *Telematics in the Transport Environment*, pp. 380-387. Springer Berlin Heidelberg, 2012.

[15] Patterson, D.J., et al. 2004. Opportunity Knocks: A System to Provide Cognitive Assistance with Transportation Services. In UbiComp 2004: Ubiquitous Computing. Nottingham, UK: Springer.

[16] Pecher, P., Hunter, M. and Fujimoto, R. 2014. Past and future trees: structures for predicting vehicle trajectories in real-time. In *Simulation Conference (WSC), 2014 Winter* (pp. 2884-2895). IEEE.

[17] Persad-Maharaj, N. et al. 2008. Real-Time Travel Path Prediction Using GPS-Enabled Mobile Phones. Proc. 15th

World Congress on Intelligent Transportation Systems, ITS America, 2008.

[18] Roughgarden, T., and Tardos, E. 2002. How bad is selfish routing?. Journal of the ACM (JACM) 49, no. 2 (2002): 236-259.

[19] Simmons, R., Browning, B., Zhang, Y., and Sadekar, V. 2006. Learning to predict driver route and destination intent. Proc. Intelligent Transportation Systems Conference, pages 127–132, 2006.

[20] Suh, W., Hunter, M. P., and Fujimoto, R. 2014. Ad hoc distributed simulation for transportation system monitoring and near-term Prediction. Simulation Modeling Practice and Theory 41 (2014): 1-14.

[21] Voronkov, A., and Darema, F. 2004. Dynamic Data Driven Applications Systems: A New Paradigm for Application Simulations and Measurements. In International Conference on Computational Science. 662-669.

[22] Xue, A., Zhang R., Zheng, Y., Xie, X., Huang, J., and Xu, Z. 2013. Destination Prediction by Sub-Trajectory Synthesis

and Privacy Protection Against Such Prediction. IEEE International Conference on Data Engineering (2013).

[23] Yuan, J., Zheng, Y., Zhang, C., Xie, W., Xie, X., Sun, G., and Huang, Y. 2010. T-drive: driving directions based on taxi trajectories. In Proceedings of the 18th SIGSPATIAL International Conference on Advances in Geographic Information Systems, GIS '10, pages 99{108, New York, NY, USA, 2010. ACM.

[24] Yuan, J., Zheng, Y., Xie, X., and Sun, G. 2011. Driving with knowledge from the physical world. In The 17th ACM SIGKDD international conference on Knowledge Discovery and Data mining, KDD '11, New York, NY, USA, 2011. ACM.

[25] Ziebart, B. D., Maas, A. L., Dey, A. K., and Bagnell, J. A. 2008. Navigate like a cabbie: Probabilistic reasoning from observed context-aware behavior. In Proceedings of the 10th international conference on Ubiquitous computing, pp. 322-331. ACM, 2008.

GraphPool: A High Performance Data Management for 3D Simulations

Patrick Lange, Rene Weller, Gabriel Zachmann
University of Bremen, Germany
{lange,weller,zach}@cs.uni-bremen.de

ABSTRACT

We present a new graph-based approach called GraphPool for the generation, management and distribution of simulation states for 3D simulation applications. Currently, relational databases are often used for this task in simulation applications. In contrast, our approach combines novel wait-free nested hash map techniques with traditional graphs which results in a schema-less, in-memory, highly efficient data management. Our GraphPool stores static and dynamic parts of a simulation model, distributes changes caused by the simulation and logs the simulation run. Even more, the GraphPool supports sophisticated query types of traditional relational databases. As a consequence, our GraphPool overcomes the associated drawbacks of relational database technology for sophisticated 3D simulation applications. Our GraphPool has several advantages compared to other state-of-the-art decentralized methods, such as persistence for simulation state over time, object identification, standardized interfaces for software components as well as a consistent world model for the overall simulation system. We tested our approach in a synthetic benchmark scenario but also in real-world use cases. The results show that it outperforms state-of-the-art relational databases by several orders of magnitude.

CCS Concepts

•Theory of computation → Data structures and algorithms for data management;

Keywords

3D Simulation System; Graph Database; Nested Hash Maps; Simulation Database

1. INTRODUCTION

Today, there are numerous 3D simulation applications available including virtual testbeds for space robotics or industrial automation and many more. The goal of such

Permission to make digital or hard copies of all or part of this work for personal or classroom use is granted without fee provided that copies are not made or distributed for profit or commercial advantage and that copies bear this notice and the full citation on the first page. Copyrights for components of this work owned by others than the author(s) must be honored. Abstracting with credit is permitted. To copy otherwise, or republish, to post on servers or to redistribute to lists, requires prior specific permission and/or a fee. Request permissions from permissions@acm.org.

SIGSIM-PADS '16, May 15 - 18, 2016, Banff, AB, Canada

© 2016 Copyright held by the owner/author(s). Publication rights licensed to ACM.
ISBN 978-1-4503-3742-7/16/05. . . $15.00

DOI: http://dx.doi.org/10.1145/2901378.2901379

3D simulations is usually to simulate a given model and to provide the users visual feedback, most often in real-time. Usually, many independent inhomogeneous software components need to communicate and exchange data in order to simulate the model as well as to provide data for the visual feedback [20, 23]. This data exchange is usually done concurrently in highly parallel manner in order to preserve a fast simulation and immersive visual feedback to the user. Therefore, current simulations rely on some kind of data which is concurrently shared between all software components. For instance the 3D geometries of the objects, like the spacecraft and its' individual components in spaceflight simulations, but also their dimensions, their mass, their position and orientation in the world space and other physical properties that are required for the simulation. During the simulation runs, several components need access to that data, e.g. input/output devices, the renderer, a physically-based simulation component, etc. The data is not always pre-defined and fixed, but it may change during the simulation run. For instance, the physically-based simulation module changes the positions and orientations according Newtons laws of motion. Moreover, it is possible that several simulation components, like input devices controlled by the user and the physically-based simulation, want to access and manipulate the same data at the same time.

To summarize, 3D simulations (and simulations in general) require a data management that is easy to handle and guarantees fast access to data for both, reading and writing while maintaining a consistent simulation state even in heavily concurrent access scenarios [17].

Currently, relational databases are often used for this task. They are well-researched, easy-to-use and deliver out-of-the-box functionality for a consistent data management. Unfortunately, they also have some drawbacks when considering 3D simulation applications.

For instance, they do not scale well to massively parallel access due to their inherent serialization of access queries. Moreover, the relational data model requires a strict definition of a schema (consisting of tables with the defined data fields in row-column format) prior to storing any data. This constraints typical simulation engineering tasks such as capturing new simulation data which was previously not considered or introducing simulation behavior changes due to new data formats and content. Finally, simulation application developers usually use object-oriented programming languages to build 3D simulation applications as handling object-oriented data is nowadays most efficient.

In contrast to this, the data needs to be collected from many tables (often hundreds or thousands in today's simulation applications) and combined before it can be provided to the application. Similarly, when writing data, the write access needs to be coordinated, separated and performed on many tables [6]. This results in a fundamental mismatch exists between the way a simulation application would like to see its data and the way it's actually stored in a relational database.

We present a novel approach that overcomes these disadvantages of relational database technology for the use in 3D simulations.

Our approach uses wait-free hash map techniques in graph-based schema-less, in-memory resident manner in order to store object-oriented content. As a result, the time-consuming serialization as well as table-based coordination and separation of relational databases are eliminated. Even more, the wait-free hash map techniques allow high performance access even for massive numbers of concurrent read and write operations. Consequently, our data management incorporates a highly responsive low-latency data access for any number of simulation components accessing it. Finally, our approach implements the same functionality as state-of-the-art relational databases such as aggregate queries as well as caching strategies.

The system can be used to flexibly build simulation applications in various fields of applications, like high fidelity end-to-end spaceflight simulations [19] or self-optimizable virtual testbeds [21].

In summary, our contribution of this paper is a centralized data management approach for high performance 3D simulations that incorporates

- high scalability due to wait-free access for all simulation components to the simulation state
- high performance because it is completely in-memory resident
- high adaptability due to graph-based schema-less data storage of object-oriented content

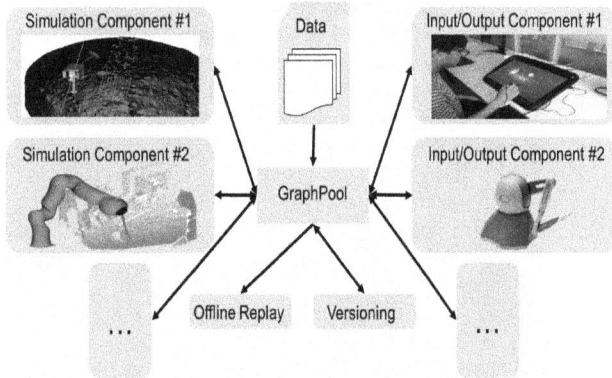

Figure 1: Architecture of a 3D simulation system, using our GraphPool approach: All software components concurrently access the centralized GraphPool which stores the complete simulation data.

Another advantage of our GraphPool is the support of all common kinds of query operations like storing and managing static and dynamic data while enabling sophisticated query types of traditional relational databases. Furthermore, our GraphPool incorporates a versioning mechanism which generates a queryable archive of the complete simulation. As a result, simulation components can be used in an online viewing mode to replay a simulation run step by step, allowing analysis and debriefing. Figure 1 gives an overview of the overall architecture.

2. RELATED WORK

Research in combining database, simulation and rendering methodology has attracted increasing interest in the last decade because databases have been integrated into 3D simulation systems in many different ways. Though many attempts have been made to incorporate database technology into 3D simulation systems, to our knowledge, no one has used in-memory schema-less technology with wait-free access behavior before.

State-of-the-art research in the integration of database technology into 3D simulations use standard full-fledged SQL databases because they are easy-to-use and deliver out-of-the-box functionality for a consistent data management. [17, 13] introduced schema and data synchronization for distributed 3D simulations with a versioning interface. In more basic applications, databases have been used to store additional meta-information (e.g. about scene objects [25, 3]). More sophisticated approaches use the database to store the scene data itself [25], where some do support collaboration [9, 24, 5, 15, 16] while others do not [1, 7]. A flexible support for different data schemata is not widespread among these systems [5, 7, 16]. The simplest realizations allow schema alteration by adding attributes to generic base objects [11]. The more advanced systems support different static [12] or dynamic [7] schemata. However, these data management approaches can only alter their relational table schema based on a new schema delivered by another simulation architecture component (e.g. a simulation server). Consequently, this schema alteration is done manually by hand and is only distributed automatically. In all applications, the table schema alteration is complex and computationally expensive.

To summarize, the above mentioned related studies were focussed on combining traditional relational databases with simulation technology. However, traditional database technology has three main technical limitations:

- the adaptability to object-oriented data due to rigid table-based schema
- the scalability to massive amounts of components accessing the database in real-time manner
- the performance with respect to massively parallel read and write operations due to serialization of access queries

The database research community established in-memory resident databases and the NoSQL ("Not-only" SQL) methodology to compensate for these technical limitations shared by the majority of relational database implementations. NoSQL started out as industry developments in companies such as Amazon, Google, Twitter or Facebook which discovered these serious limitations of relational database technology [10].

In order to overcome these limitations, database architects had sacrificed many of the most central aspects of relational databases, such as joins and fully consistent data, while introducing many complex and fragile pieces into the operations puzzle. They simplified the database schema and introduced various query caching layers. Finally, schema devolved from many interrelated fully expressed tables to something much more like a simple key/value look-up in an attempt to address these new requirements. [6].

Relational and NoSQL data models are very different. The relational model takes data and separates it into many interrelated tables consisting of rows and columns. These tables reference each other through foreign keys that are stored in columns as well. Every piece of data is then stored only once in one table. Consequently, the relational model minimizes the amount of storage space required, which was a key requirement when relational database were created due to expensive hardware [6]. However, space efficiency comes at expense of increased complexity when inserting and looking up data. Developers generally use object-oriented programming languages to build 3D simulation applications as handling object-oriented data is nowadays most efficient. In contrast to this, the data needs to be collected from many tables (often hundreds or thousands in today's simulation applications) and combined before it can be provided to the application. Similarly, when writing data, the write needs to be coordinated, separated and performed on many tables [6]. Consequently, a fundamental mismatch exists between the way a simulation application would like to see its data and the way it's actually stored in a relational database.

Another major difference is that relational technologies have rigid schemas while NoSQL models are schema-less [6]. The relational data model requires a strict definition of a schema (consisting of all tables with the defined data fields in row-column format) prior to storing any data. This requirement makes typical simulation engineering tasks such as capturing new simulation data which was previously not considered or introducing simulation behavior changes due to new data formats and content extremely disruptive and frequently avoided.

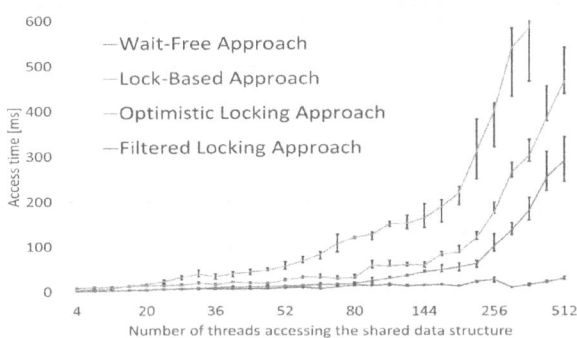

Figure 2: Performance comparison of wait-free and lock-based concurrency control management implementations, which are traditionally used for simulation applications. Adopted from [22].

This is the exact opposite of the desired behavior in the area of simulation and modelling, where developers need to rapidly, and constantly, incorporate new types of data to enrich their simulation models and applications. In comparison, schema-less databases allow the format of the data being inserted or changed at any time, without application disruption [6].

When introducing such a data management we will immediately encounter the well-known problem of concurrent data structures and race conditions which constitutes another challenge of implementing a centralized solution.

In the past, several concurrency control management (CCM) approaches have been proposed to solve this kind of parallel access. In order to avoid problems of traditional lock-based CCMs such as thread starvation or deadlocks, wait-free approaches based on hash maps for realtime interactive systems had been introduced [20, 22, 23]. Wait-free approaches guarantee access to the shared data structure in a finite number of steps for each thread, regardless of other threads accessing the shared data structure by introducing a few atomic operations [18]. This means that these approaches do not need any traditional locking mechanism in order to preserve a consistent data state. Experiments have shown a superior performance of wait-free approaches with respect to traditional locking approaches as Figure 2 illustrates. These wait-free approaches not only support structured data such as arrays or list but also use fast hash key operations in order to find and retrieve the stored data inside the used hash table. Due to their excellent scalability, they are perfectly suited for simulation applications which need to support massive parallel access. Consequently, using wait-free data structures as a data access backbone can highly improve the performance and scalability of a simulation data management.

3. GRAPHPOOL CONCEPT

In this section, we describe the three concepts of our novel GraphPool approach which overcomes the limitations of the presented related work.

First, in order to improve the overall scalability for massive amounts of concurrent simulation components, we introduce a sophisticated wait-free concurrency control management based on hash maps. Second, in order to improve the overall adaptability and performance of the data management, we use object-oriented data formats as data storage backbone. As a result of this, the time consuming separation of data into interrelated tables of relational database technology is eliminated. Third, in order to provide a comparable data management system to common relational databases, we implement relational core and aggregate queries within our approach.

In order to implement these concepts, our approach introduces a central world state (CWS), based on wait-free access using data replication [20, 22]. The CWS is stored in our GraphPool, acting as a centralized data management. This means, the GraphPool is used for storing and managing all parts, dynamic as well as static, of the shared simulation model in a consistent object-oriented data schema. This object-oriented approach correlates to typical 3D construction and environmental data used in 3D simulation applications.

During runtime, every simulation component can replicate any parts of the CWS into its local world state (LWS) while local changes are tracked and written back into the CWS. These read and write processes execute in wait-free behaviour, without synchronisation [20, 22]. As mentioned above, not only are all static parts of a 3D simulation model (e.g. the 3D environment) are stored in the GraphPool, but also all dynamic objects which are changed by the running simulation. These changes are likewise written to the CWS, hence communicating the new state of the simulation model to the CWS. Consequently, the GraphPool drives the simulation itself as it represents the central communication (dataflow and workflow) hub.

Many more advantages arise from using centralized data management system for a simulation system [17]: Different applications (e.g. for authoring) can be employed using its standardized interfaces, an inherent rights management provides means for fine grained access control, consistent data schema, solution to object identification ("id problem"), and (spatial) queries allow very selective loading and changing of the simulation model.

As described in [20, 22], we developed wait-free synchronization methods based on local and global guarding principles with atomic operations allowing simulation components to efficiently access hash maps. Wait-free concurrency approaches guarantee access to the shared data structure in a finite number of steps for each thread, regardless of other threads accessing the shared data structure. Consequently, wait-free approaches deliver high performance access even for massive numbers of concurrent components as evaluations have shown [20, 22].

In order to achieve this wait-free behavior for all data transactions, we identify all kinds of data that need to be shared between different components, e.g. simulation time or the transformations of the objects in the scene. This data is arranged into logically structured data packets. For instance, the 3D geometry of a car but also its' individual components in a car simulation, such as mass, position, velocity or acceleration are logically arranged into one data packet. We store these data packets in a hash map and assign a set of unique key-identifiers (object-key and member-keys) to each of these data packets. The member-key references the complete data packet while member-keys reference a specific data type within the packet. This combination of identifiers and hash map bucket is denoted as GraphNode. All GraphNodes are registered in our GraphPool and memory is reserved for the data. The GraphPool connects all GraphNodes into a graph-based lookup structure and constructs thereby the CWS. If any component wants to access the data, it simply has to look up the key in the GraphPool.

Hash maps outperform other container types (e.g. lists or arrays) due to their constant lookup, insertion and deletion time of $\mathcal{O}(1)$ which makes them perfectly suitable for a high performance data management. Our nested hash map approach enables row and column based queries for the stored data. From a relational database point of view, a GraphNode is a 1-by-n schema-less table in which all columns n can be accessed separately by n member-keys. Figure 3 illustrates this concept with an simple person data example while Figure 4 illustrates the main concept of the GraphPool consisting of GraphNodes.

As all intermediate states of the simulation are made persistent in the GraphPool, a simulation run can easily be captured by our versioning mechanism. This versioning mechanism generates a time-stamped history of all GraphNodes.

These recorded time-stamped GraphNodes represent a queryable archive of the complete simulation. Every simulation component can be used in an off-line viewing mode to replay a simulation run step by step, allowing analysis and debriefing of the complete simulation.

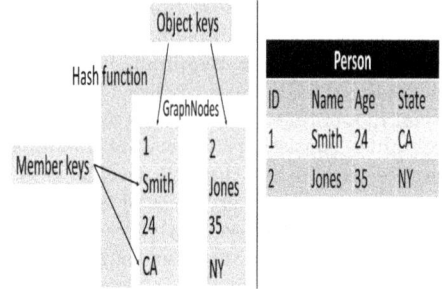

Figure 3: Comparison of GraphPool approach and rigid table schema: In contrast to a rigid table schema (right), GraphNodes store the data in a nested hash map. The data is then available via object- and member-keys (left).

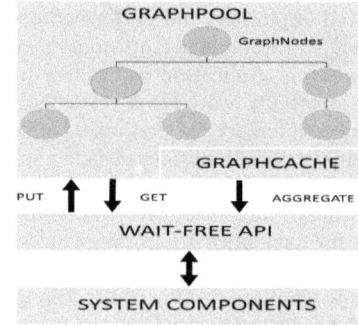

Figure 4: Access workflow of system components using the GraphPool. The stored data is available is via relational core (put, get) and aggregate functions.

3.1 Property Graph Model for Nested Hash Maps

In order to allow for relational core and aggregate functions, we arrange the GraphNodes in a property graph structure. We define this graph structure as $\mathcal{G} = \{\mathcal{N}, \mathcal{R}, \mathcal{K}, \mathcal{P} \mathcal{L}\}$ with $\mathcal{N}$ nodes, $\mathcal{R}$ relationships, $\mathcal{K}$ keys, $\mathcal{P}$ properties and $\mathcal{L}$ labels.

The property graph contains connected GraphNodes which can hold any number of properties within its hash map. GraphNodes can be tagged with labels representing their different roles in the simulation domain. Labels can serve as a contextualization for GraphNode and relationship properties. Furthermore, labels may also denote constraint or metadata information of GraphNodes.

Every relationship provides a directed, named semantically relevant, connection between two GraphNodes. A relationship always has a direction, a start node, an end node and a type.

The relationship type can be arbitrary, for instance a weight, cost, time interval, distance or inheritance/tree structure. GraphNodes can share any number or type of relationships because they are stored efficiently, without sacrificing performance. In order to enable fast traversal of the GraphNodes, the GraphPool can navigate between GraphNodes regardless of relationship direction.

Furthermore, we follow the consistent rule that no broken links shall be present in the graph. Since a relationship always has a start and end GraphNode, a GraphNode can not be deleted without also deleting its associated relationships. Consequently, an existing relationship will never point to a non-existing endpoint. Moreover, the GraphPool provides a versioning mechanism that archives every previous state of the GraphNodes as a time-stamped version. This mechanism provides transparent access to these historic states. A user interface element or any other component of the simulation system can then set a reference time and the versioning interface takes care of reloading the appropriate versions of the object data. Furthermore, there is no global main loop required; each simulation component can access the GraphNodes, i.e. read or write, at any point in time.

Figures 5 and 6 illustrate our property graph structure.

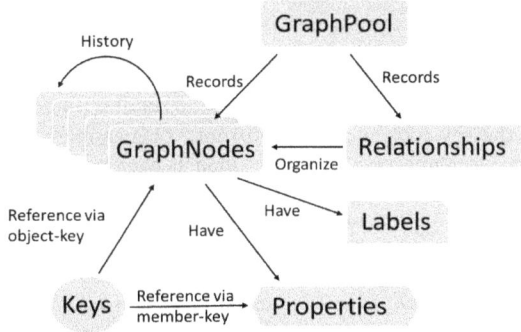

Figure 5: The building blocks of our property graph model: The GraphPool consists of linked GraphNodes which can be accessed via their object- and member-keys.

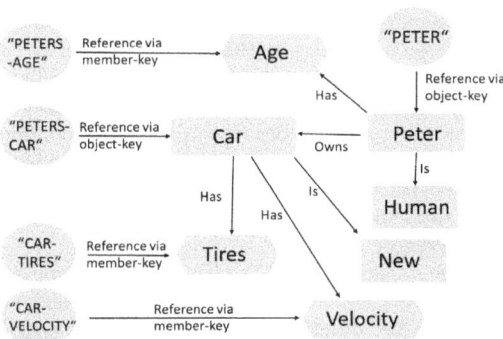

Figure 6: Property graph model example illustrating the use of member- and object-keys, relationships as well as labels.

3.2 Relational Core & Aggregate Queries

In this section, we described how relational core and aggregate queries can be implemented within our property graph structure with caching. The GraphPool has to provide two relational core functionalities:

- Pushing a local world state (LWS) to the central world state (CWS), respectively putting values into the GraphPool
- Retrieving a local world state (LWS) from the central world state (CWS), respectivey getting values from the GraphPool

The CWS is thereby defined by the complete set of GraphNodes which are stored in the GraphPool. As a result, the LWS is a subset of these GraphNodes which a simulation component can access by the GraphPools put and get function.

The put function is used to update a GraphNode via its object-key in the GraphPool. If the object-key is not already stored in the pool, it simply creates a new GraphNode. Otherwise the existing GraphNode will be updated. The value can be retrieved in constant time using our hash function as described below. The get function is used to retrieve an existing GraphNode from the GraphPool.

We presented local [20] and global [22] guarding principles as well as merge strategies [22] for solving this kind of access in wait-free manner. In short, we differentiate between consumer and producer simulation components. Consumer components only read a set of GraphNodes whereas producer components read and write a set of GraphNodes. Therefore, each GraphNode maintains two copies of the data, a producer reference and a consumer reference. These references are used from the corresponding simulation components. This means, that read requests of a GraphNode will return the consumer reference and that write requests of a GraphNode will return the producer reference.

If a consumer wants to read a value, it calls the get function and the GraphPool returns the current consumer copy. This is decided via an access request which every get query has to contain. Moreover, it increments a local atomic marker (see Algorithm 2) of the consumer reference. If the consumer has finished reading, the consumer decrements the local marker again. In addition, it checks whether the local marker is zero and, in case no consumer is reading it anymore, deletes the consumer reference. If the memory can not be directly deleted, the GraphPool will take care of releasing the memory at a later time point as described in [22].

Writing access also begins with a call of the get function in order to retrieve the data which should be manipulated. In this case, the GraphPool returns the producer reference and sets the ownership of the system component. This ownership is an atomic id of the producer reference, which is set and checked in the get and put function. In the get function, the producer reference is marked with the corresponding producer id. When the write operation is conducted, the producer checks whether its id is the current one. If this is not the case, another producer has udpated the producer reference in the meantime (see Algorithm 1). This means that another system component has changed the GraphNode and the changes have to be merged in order to preserve a consistent GraphNode state. The needed merge is then implemented as described in [22]. In short, conflicting producer references are sorted into a producer queue and the GraphPool calls a merge function that processes the merges of those GraphNodes. In order to do so, every GraphNode contains a merge strategy (e.g. first-come first-serve or averaging the values). Algorithms 1 and 2 illustrate the implementation.

In contrast to the above introduced relational core functionalities which use single data, relational aggregate functions use multiple data. Aggregate functions are essential functions of relational databases. These functions collect in their original implementation the values of multiple columns and rows. They use this collection as input on certain criteria which further filter the result. Typically, selective (equal, not, smaller, greater, between) and numerical (average, min, max, sum) operators are most commonly used for aggregate functions.

Algorithm 3 illustrates the general implementation of an aggregate function in our graph structure. First, the corresponding hash is determined. If the result of the aggregate function was computed before, we take the value from the GraphCache. If not, we recalculate the result of the aggregate function. In order to do so, we collect the corresponding data and apply the associated aggregate function onto this data and store the result in the GraphCache.

Algorithm 1 GraphPool::put($\mathcal{K}$ object-key, $\mathcal{V}$ value)

$\mathcal{R}$ retired graph node
if $\mathcal{K} \in$ GraphPool **then**
  $\mathcal{N}$ graph node = GraphPool[$\mathcal{K}$]
  if $\mathcal{V}_{Id} = \mathcal{N}.Producer.Id$ **then**
    $\mathcal{N}.Producer = \mathcal{V}$
    $\mathcal{R} = \mathcal{N}.Consumer$
    $\mathcal{N}.Consumer = \mathcal{V}_{clone}$
  else
    $\mathcal{N}.Producer.Queue(\mathcal{V})$
    $\mathcal{R} = \mathcal{N}.Consumer$
    GraphPool.notify
  end if
else
  GraphPool.insert(pair($\mathcal{K},\mathcal{V}$))
end if
GraphCache.update($\mathcal{K}$)
return $\mathcal{R}$

Algorithm 2 GraphPool::get($\mathcal{K}$ object-key, $\mathcal{A}$ access)

---
if $\mathcal{K} \notin$ GraphPool **then**
  return empty
else
  $\mathcal{N}$ graph node = GraphPool[$\mathcal{K}$]
  if $\mathcal{A}$ is producer **then**
    $\mathcal{N}.Producer.Id = \mathcal{A}.Id$
    return $\mathcal{N}.Producer.Clone$
  else
    $\mathcal{N}.Consumer.MarkerIncrement$
    return $\mathcal{N}.Consumer$
  end if
end if

3.3 Wait-Free Caching

Caching is widely used in database technology to store results of expensive aggregate query results. This enables the database to quickly deliver previously computed results. We also provide a caching strategy based on a tree data structure, called GraphCache.

The GraphCache supports two types of workflows. First, if a GraphNode is updated in the GraphPool from a system

---

Algorithm 3 aggregate($\mathcal{K}$ object-keys, $\mathcal{I}$ member-keys, $\mathcal{A}$ aggregator)

$\mathcal{H} = \text{getHash}(\mathcal{K}, \mathcal{I}, \mathcal{A})$
if $\mathcal{H}_{valid}$ **then**
  return GraphCache.get($\mathcal{H}$)
end if
$\mathcal{C}$ = empty collection
for $\mathcal{K}_i \in \mathcal{K}$ **do**
  $\mathcal{N}$ GraphNode = GraphPool[$\mathcal{K}_i$]
  $\mathcal{C} \mathrel{+}= \mathcal{N}[\mathcal{I}]$
end for
$\mathcal{R} = \mathcal{A}(\mathcal{C})$
GraphCache.set($\mathcal{H},\mathcal{R}$)
return $\mathcal{R}$

---

component by calling the put function, the associated stored data in the GraphCache is marked as outdated. Second, if an aggregate query is used, either a cached result is returned or the associated nodes in the GraphCache are marked as valid and the corresponding data is updated.

For the first case, the GraphPool has to support a GraphCache traversal via object-key in order to find those hash values which (partly) consist of the given GraphNode. For the second case, the GraphPool needs to support a traditional cache traversal via hash value in order to find the corresponding cached query result.

Consequently, our GraphCache is accessible via its two roots: the key-root and the hash-root. This enables fast access because unnecessary tree traversal is avoided (see Figure 7).

Due to the main principle of wait-free access of the underlying concurrency control management [20, 22], we propose a wait-free caching approach in order to maintain overall wait-free access control of the GraphPool. When a wait-free data management system is implemented, every access workflow to the stored data has to be wait-free, in order to guarantee the wait-free behavior of the complete system [22]. Therefore, we initialize the complete GraphCache at simulation startup. This initialization at startup has the advantage that cache entry insertion and deletion does not have to be implemented in wait-free manner, but only the update. This update process can be implemented with an atomic boolean, which is used as an indicator that sores whether a cache entries is outdated or not. The GraphCache initialization involves all possible combinations of object-, member-keys and aggregate query types because the queries conducted by the system components are unknown. This results in a tree structure with $o \cdot m \cdot a$ nodes, where o is the number of object-keys, m is the number of member-keys and a is the number of aggregate types.

In detail, the initialization of the GraphCache involves the creation of two root nodes, the key-root $\mathcal{KR}$ and cache-root $\mathcal{CR}$. These roots are created at first. The GraphCache further consists of three node levels: object-keys, member-keys and aggregate types. In order to generate all hash entries for all possible combinations of object-keys, member-keys and aggregate keys, we iteratively combine them: Object-keys are added to $\mathcal{KR}$ as nodes and all member-keys are added to the object-key nodes. Finally, all aggregate types are added to the member-key nodes (see Algorithm 4). After the initialization, the GraphCache can be directly used for caching operations.

Algorithm 4 initGraphCache($\mathcal{O}$ object-keys, $\mathcal{M}$ member-keys, $\mathcal{A}$ aggregate types)

$\mathcal{KR}$ = key root
$\mathcal{CR}$ = cache root
for $\mathcal{O}_i \in \mathcal{O}$ **do**
  $\mathcal{R}$ = node with $\mathcal{O}_i$
  for $\mathcal{M}_i \in \mathcal{M}$ **do**
    $\mathcal{T}$ = node with $\mathcal{M}_i$
    for $\mathcal{A}_i \in \mathcal{A}$ **do**
      $\mathcal{U}$ = node with $\mathcal{A}_i$
      $\mathcal{T}_{i-childs}$ += $\mathcal{U}$
    end for
    $\mathcal{R}_{i-childs}$ += $\mathcal{T}$
    $\mathcal{CR}_{childs}$ += hash($\mathcal{O}_i, \mathcal{M}_i, \mathcal{A}_i$)
  end for
  $\mathcal{KR}_{childs}$ += $\mathcal{R}$
end for

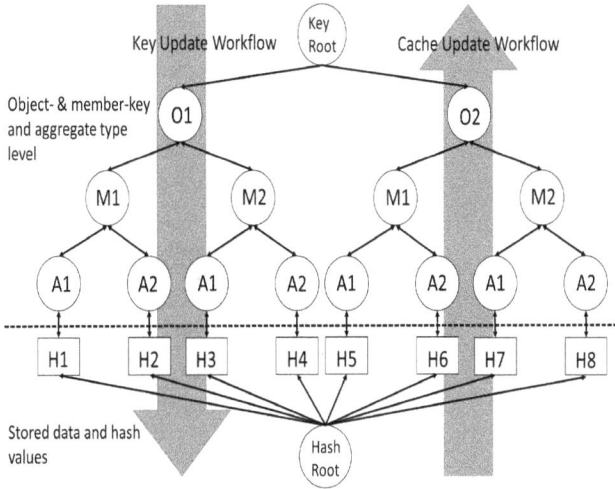

Figure 7: The GraphCache: Updates based on object keys are traversed via the key-root while updates based on hash values are traversed via the hash-root.

Algorithm 5 hash($\mathcal{K}$ object-keys, $\mathcal{M}$ member-key, $\mathcal{A}$ aggregate-type)

$\mathcal{V}$ = empty hash value
$\mathcal{P}$ = prime number
$\mathcal{H}$ = hash function
for $\mathcal{K}_i \in \mathcal{K}$ **do**
  $\mathcal{V} = \mathcal{V} \cdot \mathcal{P} + \mathcal{H}(\mathcal{K}_i);$
end for
$\mathcal{V} = \mathcal{V} \cdot \mathcal{P} + \mathcal{H}(\mathcal{M});$
$\mathcal{V} = \mathcal{V} \cdot \mathcal{P} + \mathcal{H}(\mathcal{A});$
return $\mathcal{V}$

The GraphCache contains a large number of cache entries for sophisticated simulations. We use a uniform distribution of hash values in order to avoid collisions for cache lookup. In order to deliver such a uniform distribution of hash values, even for massive amounts of cache entries, we use a prime-based hash generation in order to generate unique hash values for all concatenations of object- and member-keys with respect to all defined aggregate functions (see Algorithm 5).

Algorithm 6 prune($\mathcal{O}$ object-keys, $\mathcal{M}$ member-keys, $\mathcal{A}$ aggregate-types)

for $\mathcal{N} \in \mathcal{KR}$ **do**
  if $\mathcal{N}_{key} \in \mathcal{O}$ **then**
    remove $\mathcal{N}$ and all children from $\mathcal{KR}$
  else
    for $\mathcal{C} \in \mathcal{N}_{childs}$ **do**
      if $\mathcal{C}_{member} \in \mathcal{M}$ **then**
        remove $\mathcal{C}$ and all children from $\mathcal{N}$
      else
        for $\mathcal{M} \in \mathcal{C}_{childs}$ **do**
          if $\mathcal{M}_{aggregate} \in \mathcal{A}$ **then**
            remove $\mathcal{M}$ and all children from $\mathcal{C}$
          end if
        end for
      end if
    end for
  end if
end for

Howeer, most of these possible key combinations will never be used during runtime. In order to reduce the memory overhead, we propose a pruning strategy that removes unused nodes from the GraphCache. The main idea is to remove those nodes which have not been used by the simulation application after a predefined timespan.

Consequently, the input for the pruning is a set of object-keys $\mathcal{OK} = \{\mathcal{O}_0, ..., \mathcal{O}_k\}$, a set of member-keys $\mathcal{MK} = \{\mathcal{M}_0, ..., \mathcal{M}_l\}$ and aggregate types $\mathcal{AT} = \{\mathcal{A}_0, ..., \mathcal{A}_n\}$ which have not been used as input for any aggregate query. The pruning is conducted in three phases. First, we remove all child nodes and sub-trees of the key-root $\mathcal{KR}$ which contain a $\mathcal{O} \in \mathcal{OK}$. Second, we remove those nodes which contain a $\mathcal{M} \in \mathcal{MK}$ from the remaining nodes. Finally, we remove those nodes which contain a $\mathcal{A} \in \mathcal{AT}$ (see Algorithm 6).

3.4 Relational Database Import & Export

Currently, most 3D simulation system rely on relational databases. In order to keep the implementation overhead small when moving existing systems to our GraphPool, we present an automatic import and export mechanism. The export of GraphPool data to relational databases can be easily realized in two steps: First, the empty tables for the property graph model objects are generated: Nodes, keys, relationships, labels and history. Second, all GraphNodes of the GraphPool are traversed and for every GraphNode, the label, the relationship and the member variables are stored in the aforementioned tables. Additionally, the history of every GraphNode is traversed in order to store the data in the corresponding table. Switching both steps realizes the import of database tables into our GraphPool.

Algorithm 7 illustrates the GraphPool export implementation and Figure 8 shows the resulting rigid table schema:

Algorithm 7 export($\mathcal{G}$ GraphNodes, $\mathcal{N}$ Nodes table, $\mathcal{R}$ Relationships table, $\mathcal{L}$ Labels table, $\mathcal{K}$ Keys table, $\mathcal{H}$ History table)

---

for $\mathcal{G}_i \in \mathcal{G}$ **do**
  Store $\mathcal{G}_i.Label$ in $\mathcal{L}$
  for $\mathcal{R}_i \in \mathcal{G}_i.Relationships$ **do**
    Store $(\mathcal{R}_i.Type, \mathcal{R}_i.From, \mathcal{R}_i.To)$ in $\mathcal{R}$
  end for
  for $\mathcal{H}_i \in \mathcal{G}_i.History$ **do**
    Store $(\mathcal{G}_i.Id, \mathcal{H}_i.Id)$ in $\mathcal{H}$
    Store $(\mathcal{H}_i.Id, \mathcal{H}_i.Object, \mathcal{H}_i.Member)$ in $\mathcal{N}$
  end for
  for $\mathcal{D}_i \in \mathcal{G}_i.Member$ **do**
    Store $\mathcal{D}_i$ in $\mathcal{K}$
  end for
  Store $\mathcal{G}_i.Object$ in $\mathcal{K}$
  Store $(\mathcal{G}_i.Id, \mathcal{G}_i.Object, \mathcal{G}_i.Member)$ in $\mathcal{N}$
end for

KEYS	
KEY	DATA

GRAPHNODE		
ID	MEMBER-KEY	OBJECT-KEYS

LABELS	
ID	Label

RELATIONSHIPS		
TYPE	FROM	TO

HISTORY	
ID	ID

Figure 8: The resulting rigid table schema for importing and exporting the GraphPool.

4. CASE STUDY

Our approach enables the implementation of very different categories of 3D simulation applications. Exemplarily, we present the application to a high fidelity dynamics and spacecraft EDL (entry, descent and landing) end-to-end spaceflight mission simulator [19, 2].

More precisely, we adopted our system to a simplified version of ESAs ARCHEO-E2E system [4] that defines a reference architecture for spacecraft engineering feasibility studies. Instruments of the spacecraft, as well as the environment, including the spacecraft's orbit and attitude, are simulated and defined as simulation components within the software architecture. The sensor input (e.g. camera and range finder measurements) for the instruments is synthesized from the simulated environment. In our implementation, all this synthesized data and the current world state (e.g. spacecraft pose, positions of celestial bodies, sensor configurations, scene nodes) are represented as GraphNodes in our central GraphPool. The instruments and the physically-based simulation read and write the entries periodically. Consequently, this scenario has a large amount of concurrent read- and write operations on our GraphPool. Figure 9 shows the visual output of the simulation in which a spacecraft conducts scientific experiments while orbiting an asteroid.

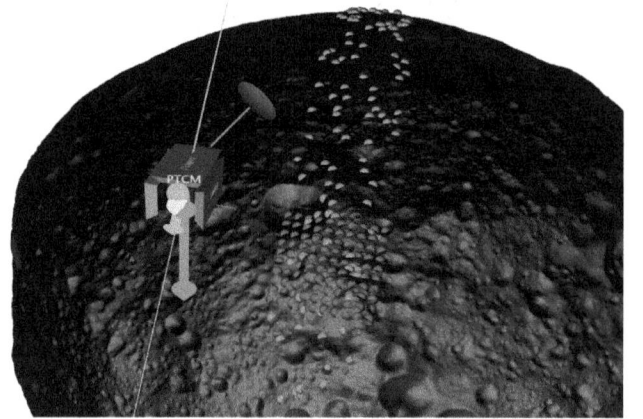

Figure 9: Use case study: A spacecraft is orbiting an asteroid. Rangefinder (red) and landmark (green) measurements are generated for spacecraft self-localization [14, 8] purposes.

5. EVALUATION

We implemented our GraphPool in C++. We performed experiments on a machine with an Intel Core i7 quad core processor with enabled Hyperthreading, operated by Windows 7 64 bit and 8GB of memory.

We applied different experiments to measure the performance as well as the quality of our approach. For the quality measurement, we used the use case scenario described above. However, as the scenario is domain-dependent, it can be hardly used to evaluate the performance of our approach. Hence, we additionally implemented a synthetic benchmark for performance measurements.

The GraphPool contained 1000 GraphNodes for the synthetic benchmark. We performed 10,000 read-, write- and aggregate queries for each test. Each test was additionally repeated 100 times and we averaged the resulting timings. The access to the GraphPool was modelled with an equal read/write distribution of concurrent system components. The transactions to the GraphPool and its competitors varied in size from 1 Byte to 1 Megabyte. We compared the performance of our new approach with three competitors. The first competitor was a lock-based implementation of our GraphPool. The other two competitors were a relational SQLite database and a MySQL database. We compared the performance with the traditional on-disk option as well as in-memory resident versions of the databases. Furthermore, we validated if the results from our GraphPool implementations yield the same results as the database competitors.

Our results show, that, in case of a single component, our wait-free GraphPool outperforms all in-memory and relational databases for every query type in several orders of magnitude. However, the traditional lock-based implementation of the GraphPool is slightly outperformed by in-memory resident relational databases. In this case, the lock acquisition introduces a computational overhead with respect to the wait-free implementation. In addition, standard relational databases can not compete with the in-memory databases and GraphPool implementations (see Figure 10).

This performance gain of our GraphPool increases with an increasing number of components accessing the data management systems. In this case, the wait-free access shows its strengths when several components simultaneously access the GraphPool. Like in the single access case, the in-memory relational database slightly outperforms the lock-based GraphPool implementation. The in-memory and relational databases are again outperformed by the wait-free GraphPool by several orders of magnitude (see Figure 11).

Overall, our evaluation underlines the aforementioned technical limitations of 3D simulation systems which rely on relational databases: The relational databases scale not very well with many concurrent components accessing them. Furthermore, our evaluation shows that the hash map backbone of our GraphPool can effectively solve the problems of the rigid table format of relational databases because no transformations of object-oriented data into tables is necessary. Additionally, the wait-free access of the GraphPool improves the overall performance even for massive concurrent read and write operations. In summary, our approach improves the overall system performance of 3D simulations by several orders of magnitude in all access query cases.

6. CONCLUSION

We presented a novel in-memory resident, schema-less, wait-free GraphPool for high performance 3D simulation applications.

Our GraphPool supports all common kinds of data operations like storing and managing static and dynamic parts while maintaining the support of sophisticated query types of traditional relational databases. Additionally, our GraphPool represents a central communication hub that drives the simulation itself. Every simulation run is implicitly logged by the GraphPools versioning techniques. This allows subsequent replay, analysis and archiving of the complete simulation. During runtime, simulation components can replicate any parts of the central world state into their local world state while local changes are tracked and written back into the central world state. Our approach has already proven its feasibility, real-time performance and flexibility in a high fidelity space robotics application.

The results of our synthetic benchmarks show that our approach is able to outperform state-of-the-art relational database driven simulation applications by several orders of magnitude.

We believe that our approach can be applied to a wide variety of 3D simulations (such as industrial automation, process or manufacturing simulations) where it will improve the performance.

In the future, we would like to extend the GraphCache technique. It would be desirable to remove the initial setup phase of the GraphCache while maintaining its wait-free behavior. Probably, this could be done by using unique prime numbers as identifiers for the components using the GraphCache. These identifiers could be used for unique cache access determination, which would result in "private" GraphCaches for every component accessing the GraphPool.

7. ACKNOWLEDGMENTS

This research is based upon the project KaNaRiA, supported by German Aerospace Center (DLR) with funds of the German Federal Ministry of Economics and Technology (BMWi) under grant 50NA1318.

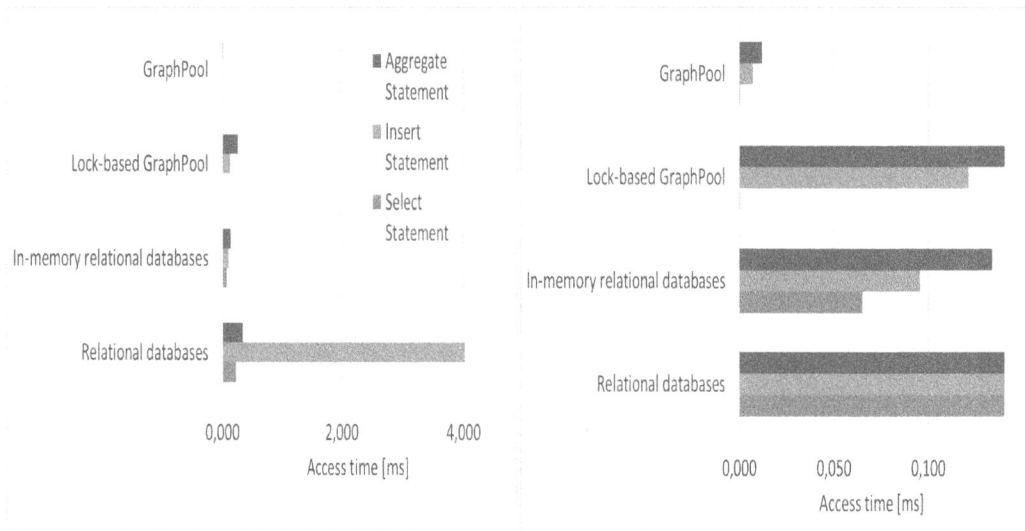

Figure 10: Performance comparison of core & aggregate queries: Overall (left), our GraphPool outperforms all competitors for all query types for single-component access. In detail (right), in-memory resident relational databases outperform the traditional lock-based implementation of the GraphPool.

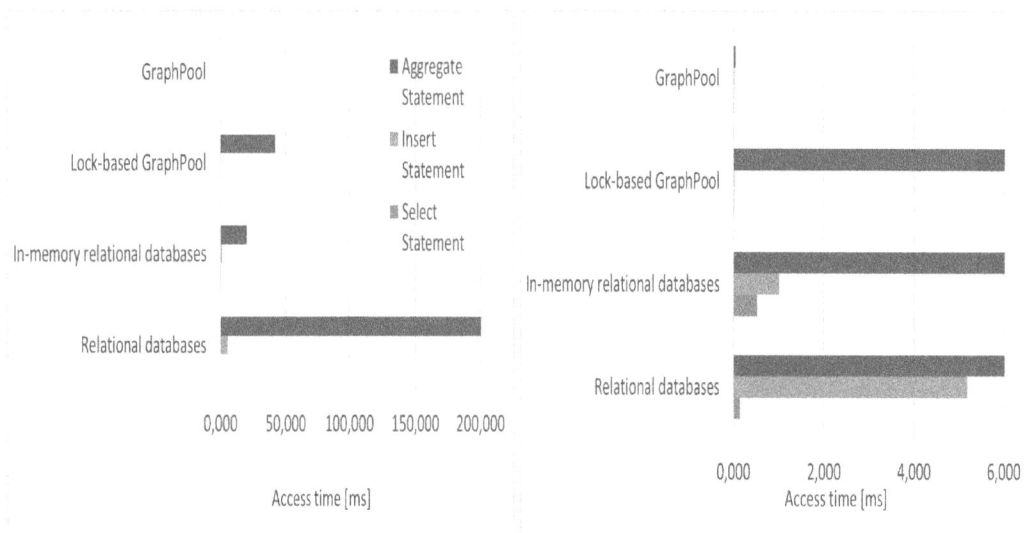

Figure 11: Performance comparison of core & aggregate queries: Overall (left), our GraphPool outperforms all competitors for all query types for multi-component access. In detail (right), in-memory resident relational databases outperform the traditional lock-based implementation of the GraphPool.

8. REFERENCES

[1] A. Vakaloudis, B. Theodoulidis. Spatiotemporal Database Connection to VRML. *Proceedings 9th UL Electronic Imaging & Visual Arts Conference*, 1998.

[2] A. Probst, G. Peytavi, D. Nakath, A. Schattel, C. Rachuy, P. Lange, et al. Kanaria: Identifying the Challenges for Cognitive Autonomous Navigation and Guidance for Missions to Small Planetary Bodies. *International Astronautical Congress (IAC)*, 2015.

[3] B. Damer, S. Gold, D. Rasmussen, et al. Data-Driven Virtual Environment Assembly and Operation. *NASA Ames Research Center: VIB Workshop Report*, 2004.

[4] C. de Negueruela, M. Scagliola, D. Giudici, J. Moreno, J. Vicent, A. Camps, H. Park, P. Flamant, R. Franco. ARCHEO-E2E: A Reference Architecture for Earth Observation end-to-end Mission Performance Simulators. *Simulation and EGSE facilities for Space Programmes*, ESA ESTEC, 2012.

[5] C. Watanabe, Y. Masunaga. VWDB2: A Network Virtual Reality System with a Database Function for a Shared Work Environment. pages 190 – 196, 2002.

[6] Couchbase. Why NoSQL? *Whitepaper*, 2014.

[7] D. Schmalstieg, G. Schall, d. Wagner, I. Barakonyi, G. Reitmayr, J. Newman, F. Ledermann. Managing Complex Augmented Reality Models. *IEEE Computer Graphics and Applications*, 27:48–57, 2007.

[8] D. Nakath, C. Rachuy, J. Clemens, K. Schill. Optimal rotation sequences for active perception. In *Proc. SPIE Multisensor, Multisource Information Fusion: Architectures, Algorithms, and Applications 2016*. SPIE Press, 2016.

[9] E. von Schweber. SQL3D - Escape from VRML Island. *SIGGRAPH VRML Consortium*, 1998.

[10] G. Burd. NoSQL. *Whitepaper*, pages 5–12, 2011.

[11] G. van Mare, R. Germs, F. Jansen. Integrating 3D-GIS and Virtual Reality. Design and Implementation of the Karma VI System. *10th Colloquium of the Spatial Information Research Center*, 1998.

[12] J. Haist, V. Coors. The W3DS-Interface of Cityserver3D. *European Spatial Data Research: Next Generation 3D City Models*, pages 63–67, 2005.

[13] J. Rossmann, M. Schluse, R. Waspe, M. Hoppen. Real-Time Capable Data Management Architecture for Database-Driven 3D Simulation Systems. *Database and Expert Systems Applications*, pages 262 – 269, 2011.

[14] J. Clemens, T. Reineking, T. Kluth. An evidential approach to SLAM, path planning, and active exploration. *International Journal of Approximate Reasoning*, 2016.

[15] K. Kaku, H. Minami, T. Tomii, H. Nasu. Proposal of Virtual Space Browser Enables Retrieval and Action with Semantics which is Shared by Multi Users. *21st International Conference on Data Engineering Workshops (ICDEW)*, pages 1259–1259, 2005.

[16] K. Walczak. Dynamic Database Modeling of 3D Multimedia Content. *Interactive 3D Multimedia Content*, pages 55–102, 2012.

[17] M. Hoppen, M. Schluse, J. Rossmann, B. Weitzig. Database-Driven Distributed 3D Simulation. *Proceedings of the Winter Simulation Conference*, 2012.

[18] M. Herlihy. Wait-free synchronization. *ACM Transactions on Programming Languages and Systems*, pages 206–209, 1991.

[19] P. Lange, A. Probst, A. Srinivas et al. Virtual reality for simulating autonomous deep-space navigation and mining. *24th International Conference on Artificial Reality and Telexistence (ICAT-EGVE 2014)*, 2014.

[20] P. Lange, R. Weller, G. Zachmann. A Framework for Wait-Free Data Exchange in Massively Threaded VR Systems. 2014.

[21] P. Lange, R. Weller, G. Zachmann. Multi Agent System Optimization in Virtual Vehicle Testbeds. *EAI SIMUtools*, 2015.

[22] P. Lange, R. Weller, G. Zachmann. Scalable Concurrency Control for Massively Collaborative Virtual Environments. *ACM Multimedia Systems, Massively Multiuser Virtual Environments (MMVE)*, 2015.

[23] P. Lange, R. Weller, G. Zachmann. Wait-Free Hash Maps in the Entity-Component-System Pattern for Realtime Interactive Systems. *IEEE VR 9th Workshop on Software Engineering and Architectures for Realtime Interactive Systems (SEARIS)*, 2016.

[24] S. Julier, y. Baillot, M. Lanzagorta, D. Brown, L. Rosenblum. BARS: Battlefield Augmented Reality System. *NATO Symposium on Information Processing Techniques for Military Systems*, pages 9 – 11, 2000.

[25] T. Manoharan, H. Taylor, P. Gardiner. A Collaborative Analysis Tool for Visualisation And Interaction With Spatial Data. *Proceedings of the Seveneth International Conference on 3D Web Technology*, pages 75 – 83, 2002.

Knowledge Discovery for Pareto based Multiobjective Optimization in Simulation

Patrick Lange, Rene Weller, Gabriel Zachmann
University of Bremen, Germany
{lange,weller,zach}@cs.uni-bremen.de

ABSTRACT

We present a novel knowledge discovery approach for automatic feasible design space approximation and parameter optimization in arbitrary multiobjective blackbox simulations. Our approach does not need any supervision of simulation experts. Usually simulation experts conduct simulation experiments for a predetermined system specification by manually reducing the complexity and number of simulation runs by varying input parameters through educated assumptions and according to prior defined goals. This leads to a error-prone trial-and-error approach for determining suitable parameters for successful simulations. In contrast, our approach autonomously discovers unknown relationships in model behavior and approximates the feasible design space. Furthermore, we show how Pareto gradient information can be obtained from this design space approximation for state-of-the-art optimization algorithms. Our approach gains its efficiency from a novel spline-based sampling of the parameter space in combination within novel forest-based simulation dataflow analysis. We have applied our new method to several artificial and real-world scenarios and the results show that our approach is able to discover relationships between parameters and simulation goals. Additionally, the computed multiobjective solutions are close to the Pareto front.

CCS Concepts

•Computing methodologies → Model development and analysis;

Keywords

Knowledge Discovery in Simulation; Multiobjective Optimization; Association Rule Mining; Spline Interpolation; Correlation Analysis; Pareto Principle

1. INTRODUCTION

Traditional simulation-based optimization approaches [25, 21] usually require pre-defined objective functions in order to use optimization techniques to find a local or global minimum for the specified simulation. Unfortunately, such objective functions are not available in blackbox simulation problems. In these blackbox simulations, but also in regular simulations, is the analysis of the model behavior and the determination of the valid design space, respectively, usually done manually by simulation experts. This manual analysis is generally performed by identifying a few distinct parameters according to the simulation project scope given as a set of simulation goals. An optimization is not conducted by a simulation itself, but rather through execution of multiple simulation runs. In order to reduce complexity and number of runs, the input parameters of each single run have to be varied cleverly [27]. The simulation expert usually takes an educated guess based on his experience which parameters might be influential on the project scope and therefore time and effort is invested in experimenting with these focus parameters in a fixed system configuration environment. Hence, for each simulation run, the input configuration has to be adjusted if the simulated model performance does not meet scenario or engineering expectations. Currently, this adjustment of input parameters in simulations is either done externally by simulation experts that need to guide the simulation process, or by defining a number of scenarios. These scenarios are pre-defined by simulation experts to cover almost all aspects of the simulation model. The use of expert guidance can lead to quite effective simulation results. However, such experts are rare and expensive. Additionally, its not always feasible to have an expert available for configuring and supervising the simulation. Nevertheless, this approach is widely used [13] but yields many disadvantages as this workflow is based upon subjective judgment of simulation results. These judgments are insufficient for efficiently solving this problem because they can not survey the whole underlying multiobjective problem of the simulation model, especially for blackbox simulations.

[13] refers to this as the "trial-and-error approach" to finding a good solution and recommends that simulation experts should spend more time in analyzing than building the model. Furthermore, pre-defined scenarios may lead to less optimal adaptation [12].

Consequently, it would be beneficial to automatically compute suitable input configurations for a given simulation model without the need of an expert guiding this process [28]. In addition, recent simulation models are dominated by a multiobjective optimization problem (MOP) because many real world problems involve decisions based on multiple and conflicting criteria [17].

Permission to make digital or hard copies of all or part of this work for personal or classroom use is granted without fee provided that copies are not made or distributed for profit or commercial advantage and that copies bear this notice and the full citation on the first page. Copyrights for components of this work owned by others than the author(s) must be honored. Abstracting with credit is permitted. To copy otherwise, or republish, to post on servers or to redistribute to lists, requires prior specific permission and/or a fee. Request permissions from permissions@acm.org.

SIGSIM-PADS '16, May 15 - 18, 2016, Banff, AB, Canada

© 2016 Copyright held by the owner/author(s). Publication rights licensed to ACM. ISBN 978-1-4503-3742-7/16/05. . . $15.00

DOI: http://dx.doi.org/10.1145/2901378.2901380

There is already a number of computational methods for solving MOP [9, 32] available. However, they usually do not consider the generation of vast amounts of simulation model behavior results that can be easily derived from simulation data farming. Although, this data could be used to deliver additional (gradient) information to traditional MOP solving approaches. In the best case, optimization approaches can directly benefit from this information.

In this paper, we present a different approach which is directly based on this observation and the idea of so-called *Knowledge Discovery in Databases (KDD)* [36]. Unlike traditional approaches for solving MOP, KDD in simulations is not limited to a static, pre-determined input dataset for model behavior and optimization. Instead, the simulation can be used as an generator for new data by itself. This enables us to investigate the whole bandwidth or at least the largest part of possible model behavior by conducting cleverly designed simulation data farming in order to discover surprises and potential [11, 35] which can be re-used in the MOP solving process, too. More precisely, we adapt techniques from KDD research to multiobjective Pareto optimization in blackbox simulations with unknown objective functions. Our approach autonomously builds an active model between simulation input and simulation goals which is capable of

- approximating the feasible design space for a Pareto based optimization by uncovering unknown causal relations in large parameter sets between simulation input and model behavior which are assumed to be unknown non-linear objective functions.
- computing Pareto gradient information from this design space approximation which can be used in state-of-the-art multiobjective optimization solvers.

As our approach is completely autonomous, it does not need any supervision from simulation experts. Another advantage of our approach is its performance. It gains its efficiency from a novel spline-based sampling of the parameter space in combination with a novel forest-based simulation dataflow analysis. The only pre-condition is that the simulation output has to be deterministic.

2. RELATED WORK

Research in combining KDD and simulation methodology has attracted increasing interest in the last decade. [24] explored the landscape characterization problem with a support vector machine (SVM) by analyzing the complete input parameter space. The approach assumed a non-goal oriented simulation, in which the simulation model can be reduced to a single function f which updates the simulation state x with parameter set θ via $x_{k+1} = f(x_k, \theta)$. They defined the landscape characterization problem by determining the set of points θ in which a pre-defined simulation state is achieved. This approach can neither be applied to single-objective nor multi-objective based simulations in which the simulation model is governed by a set of (possible) contradictory functions $f_i, ..., f_n$ as the approach does not concern any contradictory goals within the simulation. [4] determined dynamic adaptation strategies for agent-based traffic simulations via supervised learning. They extracted parameter patterns in the from of decision trees in stochastic simulation by simulating the simulation model several times. These generated decision trees are valid for linear relationships between input parameters and model "what if"

studies. The approach is further restricted to a small number of simulation input parameters as the approach involves a runtime which is quadratic in the number of input parameters. Likewise, [26] neglected multiobjective simulation properties. They investigated the application of KDD in simulation of aircraft engine fleet management. They applied a linear regression to all input parameters $x_i, ...x_n$ for one simulation goal state y resulting in a model of the form $y = C + \alpha_1 x_1, ..., \alpha_n x_n$. This model was used to determine the cost drivers in aircraft fleet management. These cost drivers were then classified by a clustering algorithm into low- or high cost classes, describing the main cost drivers for the given fleet management simulation. [27] proposed an approach for uncovering unknown relationships in model behavior. They conducted large scale experiments by replicating pre-defined experiment definitions. The resulting simulation data output was clustered and presented in various plots and charts in order to reveal unknown relationships for the simulation experts and is consequently highly depending on the simulation expert. KDD approaches based on multiobjective (respectively Pareto) simulations (such as [34, 20, 23, 6]) focussed on extracting additional information from pre-determined Pareto sets or analzying these sets within the simulation. Consequently, they can be used to neither approximate the feasibile design space nor to compute a Pareto solution itself.

In summary, all of the above mentioned studies were focused on building passive models between simulation input and goal-related simulation output while minimizing the simulation parameter scope or by focusing on single-objective linear simulation models. These passive models deliver coarse granularity parameter relationship information which can be used to neither approximate the feasible design space nor to compute a Pareto gradient information (e.g. distance or gradient information of the analyzed data with respect to the Pareto front). Moreover, they are highly depending on the simulation expert supervising the KDD process. In addition, they are also not applicable to non-linear simulation models in which the objective functions are not available. Consequently, they can not be used as input for multiobjective optimization algorithms in order to compute suitable configurations.

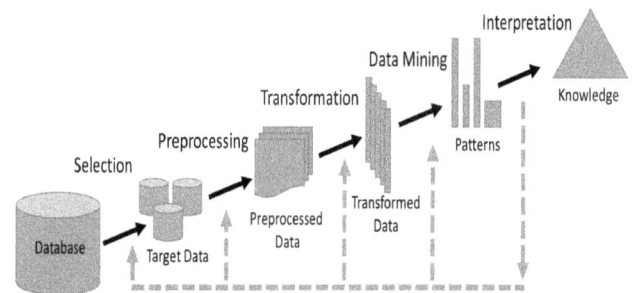

Figure 1: The traditional Knowledge Discovery in Databases (KDD) process: Low level data is extracted and data mining methods generate specific representations. Manual evaluation of these representations leads finally to low level data knowledge. Adapted from [36].

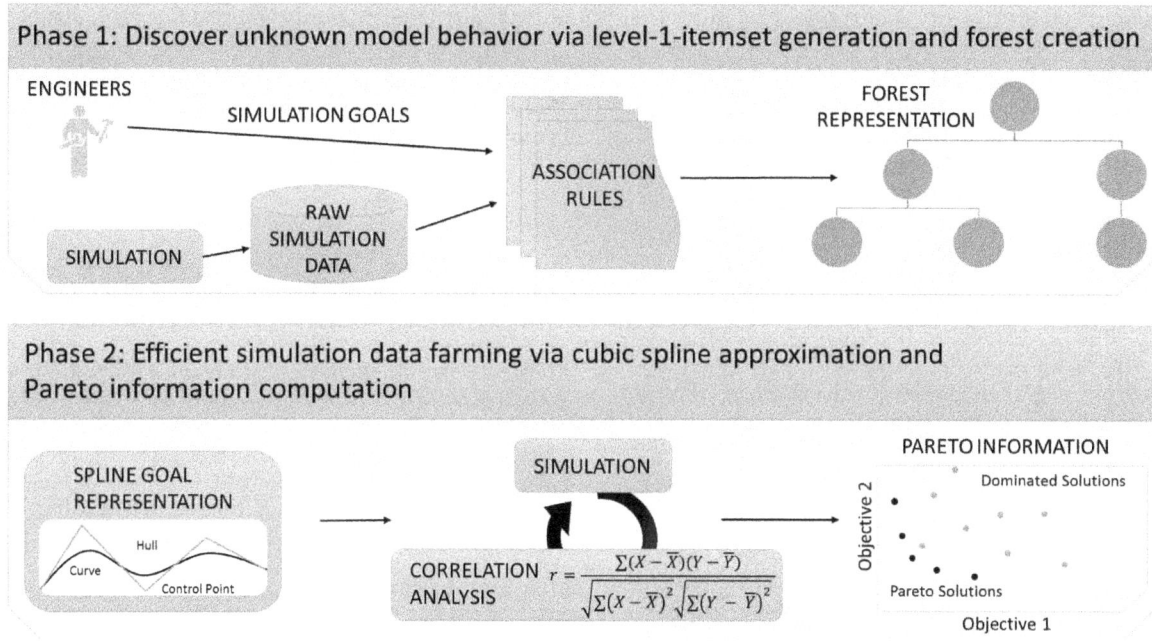

Figure 2: Our autonomous knowledge discovery process: First, all causal relations between input parameters and simulation goals are uncovered. Second, simulation data farming is efficiently conducted in order to approximate the feasible design space as well as to compute Pareto gradient information.

3. OUR KNOWLEDGE DISCOVERY PROCESS

Originally, Knowledge Discovery in Databases (KDD) is defined as making sense of data collections that are too big to manually review each and every single record. Input sources for such kinds of data are complex simulations, graphs, or data warehouses [37]. [36] describe the KDD process as multiple steps to ultimately transform low level data into useful knowledge (see Figure 1). In detail, the KDD process is a highly interactive five-step-process that requires many decisions made by the user. Some of these steps (e.g. target data selection or interpretation of patterns) have to be iteratively repeated by the user for convincing results. Hence, KDD is a semi-automatic process because the user is ultimately responsible for interpretation and evaluation of mining results. This particularly applies for the evaluation of the usefulness of the generated knowledge [36].

Today, simulation models are dominated by a multiobjective optimization problem (MOP) because many real world problems involve decisions based on multiple and conflicting criteria [17]. The optimal decisions have to consider the best trade-off among these criteria. This is actually the goal of multiobjective optimization. Such multiobjective optimization problems can be found in many situations, for example, in product design where several criteria must be simultaneously satisfied [5, 31, 33]. We define MOP according to [17]: Given a subset X of $\mathbb{R}^n$ and p functions $f_j : X \Rightarrow \mathbb{R}$ for $j = 1, 2, ..., p$, MOP is defined as:

$$(MOP) \min_{x \in X} F(x) = (f_1(x), f_2(x), ... f_p(x)) \qquad (1)$$

where $F : X \Rightarrow \mathbb{R}^p$ is the objective function vector. We assume that X is of the form $X = \{x = (x_1, x_2, ..., x_n) \in \mathbb{R}^n : a_i \leq x_i \leq b_i, i = 1, 2, ..., n\}$, where a_i and b_i are the lower

and upper bound of the ith component of variable x, respectively. When the objective functions conflict with each other, no single solution can simultaneously minimize all scalar objective functions $f_j(x), j = 1, ..., p$. Consequently, it is necessary to introduce a new notion of optimality in multiobjective problems. A most commonly used one is that of Pareto optimality or Pareto efficiency, which is an important criterion for evaluating economic and engineering systems. The definition of Pareto optimality can be provided by using Pareto dominance relation [1]:

- Let $x_u, x_v \in X$ be two decision vectors. $F(x_u)$ is said to dominate $F(x_v)$ (denoted $F(x_u) \prec F(x_v)$) if and only if $f_i(x_u) \leq f_i(x_v) \forall i \in \{1, 2, ..., p\}$ and $f_j(x_u) < f_j(x_v) \exists j \in \{1, 2, ..., p\}$
- A point $x* \in X$ is globally Pareto optimal if and only if there is no $x \in X$ such that $F(x) \prec F(x*)$. Then, $F(x*)$ is called globally efficient. The image of the set of globally efficient points is called the Pareto front. In general, computational methods cannot guarantee global Pareto optimality [18], but at best local Pareto optimality that is defined as:
- A point $x* \in X$ is locally Pareto optimal if and only if there exists an open neighborhood of $x*$, $B(X*)$, such that there is no $x \in B(x*) \cap X$ satisfying $F(x) \prec F(x*)$. $F(x*)$ is then called locally efficient. The image of the set of locally efficient points is called the local Pareto front.

The goal of MOP is to identify a subset of the Pareto optimal points ($\mathcal{P}*$) which is able to represent the Pareto front or to compute a single trade-off solution $x \in \mathcal{P}*$. In general, identifying the set of all Pareto optimality points is not a tractable problem and mostly impossible, particularly when the knowledge on the structure of the problem is very minimal or not available [17].

In this work, we present the application of an completely automatic knowledge discovery process to reveal causal relationships between simulation input parameters and pre-defined simulation goals with respect to blackbox simulations with an underlying multiobjective model behavior. The result of our knowledge discovery process is an approximation of the feasible design space as well as Pareto information which can be directly used for solving the multiobjective optimization problem of the model.

Three main challenges arise when applying KDD techniques to these problems:

First, engineers who specify the simulation model as well as simulation experts have limited and hence incomplete knowledge about the simulation model behavior with respect to the complete parameter input space. Consequently, the assumed relations between pre-defined simulation goals and parameter space input are incomplete or wrong. Unfortunately, efficiently computing viable solutions for MOP requires at least a correct approximation of the relationship between the parameter input space and the objective functions. This means, all relations between a simulation input parameter and a pre-defined simulation goal within the simulated model behavior have to be determined. Second, KDD requires extensive simulation data farming in order to yield useful results. This simulation data farming can lead to a computationally very expensive KDD process because this complexity usually grows at least quadratically with the amount of input parameters [4]. Hence, the simulation data farming constraints (selection and sampling of convenient input parameters) have to be minimized. Third, diverse algorithms exist for computing a solution to MOP, such as gradient descent [15, 14], simulated annealing [8, 32] or evolutionary algorithms [9, 10]. The proposed knowledge discovery process should yield Pareto information in such a way that this information can be directly used in such different optimization approaches.

In order to overcome these challenges, our knowledge discovery process differs in many ways from the above described standard KDD process (see Figure 2). Basically, our process is split into two main phases: association rule based dataflow analysis and simulation data farming with relationship analysis. The first phase reveals unknown model behavior and constructs a simulation goal based forest data structure which enables fast simulation data farming. The second phase utilizes this forest in order to analyse the unknown model behavior. This analysis is used to approximate the feasible design space and consequently to compute the needed Pareto information for MOP optimization. In the following, we will detail both phases of our main algorithms.

4. FOREST-BASED ASSOCIATION RULE MINING

Our knowledge discovery process starts with the determination of possible causal relations between simulation input parameters and simulation goals. We define a possible causal relation with an existing dataflow inside the simulation denoted as $f_j\{x_i, ..., x_n\} \mapsto \mathcal{G}_j$ where $\mathcal{G}_j$ is a pre-defined simulation goal which maps the parameters $\{x_i, ..., x_n\}$ with an objective function f_j to a satisfaction value or goal state. Since our approach assumes a blackbox simulation, no mapping between parameters $\{x_0, ..., x_n\}$ and simulation goals $\{\mathcal{G}_0, ..., \mathcal{G}_j\}$ as well as explicit forms of $\{f_o, ..., f_j\}$ is known

in advance. The simplest, and computationally most expensive, approach would be to brute-force analyze all given parameters for every simulation goal in order to reveal unknown model behavior. This would result in a simulation data farming computational complexity of:

$$\mathcal{O}((n^2 - n) \cdot g) \qquad (2)$$

where

g : number of simulation goals
n : number of simulation model input parameters

Sophisticated simulations easily inherit hundreds or thousands of input parameters with large parameter spaces. This would result in computationally very expensive brute-force analysis of the complete knowledge discovery process.

In order to overcome this limitation, we present several ideas to accelerate the computation. We start with a fast Association Rule Mining (ARM) which uncovers the complete dataflow of the simulation by analyzing all dataflow transactions. These transactions can be used to determine the parameter mapping $\{x_i, ..., x_n\}$ as well as for identifying f_j of $f_j\{x_i, ..., x_n\} \mapsto \mathcal{G}_j$.

The main idea is to use the traditional ARM Apriori [30] algorithm with low support and high confidence settings. In order to enable data farming parallelization and pruning of the analyzed workflow, we transform the original list output of the Apriori algorithm into a disjoint union of tree data structures called forest.

Following the original definition by [30], the problem of ARM is defined as: Let $I = i_i, i_2, ..., i_n$ be a set of n binary attributes called *items*. Let $D = t_1, t_2, ..., t_n$ be a set of transactions called the database. Each transaction in D has a unique transaction ID and contains a subset of the items in I. An association rule is an implication expression of the form $X \Rightarrow Y$, where X and Y are disjoint itemsets, i.e., $X \cap Y = 0$. Further, $X, Y \subseteq I$.

To illustrate these concepts, we use a small example from the supermarket domain: $\{butter, bread\} \Rightarrow \{milk\}$ meaning that if butter and bread are bought, customers also buy milk.

The strength of an association rule can be measured in terms of its support and confidence. The support value of X with respect to T is defined as the proportion of transactions in the database which contains the item-set X given as $\sigma(X) =| \{t_i \mid X \subseteq t_i, t_i \in T\} |$. Confidence, on the other hand, measures the reliability of the inference made by a rule. Both are mathematically defined as:

$$Support, s(X \Rightarrow Y) = \frac{\sigma(X \cup Y)}{N} \qquad (3)$$

$$Confidence, c(X \Rightarrow Y) = \frac{\sigma(X \cup Y)}{\sigma(X)} \qquad (4)$$

Apriori [30] is an algorithm for frequent item set mining and association rule learning over transactional databases. It proceeds by identifying the frequent individual items in the database and extending them to larger and larger item sets as long as those item sets appear sufficiently often in the database. The output of the Apriori algorithm is a list of level-k-itemsets: $\{\{X_0, ..., X_k\} \Rightarrow Y\}_{s,c}$.

Algorithm 1 GenerateForestStructure

$\mathcal{O}$ = list of objective references $\{X_0, ..., X_g\}$
$\mathcal{L}$ = list of level-1-itemsets rules: $\{\{X\} \Rightarrow Y\}$ from the Apriori algorithm
$\mathcal{F}$ = forest root node
for $\mathcal{O}_i \in \mathcal{O}$ **do**
    $\mathcal{M}$ = tree root node with $\mathcal{O}_i$
    $\mathcal{M}_{childs}$ = GenerateTreeStructure($\mathcal{M}$, $\mathcal{L}$, $\mathcal{O}_i$)
    $\mathcal{F}_{trees}$ += $\mathcal{M}$
end for

Algorithm 2 GenerateTreeStructure

$\mathcal{R}$: read relations of $\mathcal{O}_i$ as $\bigcup_{X \Rightarrow Y \in \mathcal{L}} := \{X \mid \forall Y = \mathcal{O}_i\}$
for $\mathcal{R}_i \in \mathcal{R}$ **do**
    $\mathcal{C}$ = child node of $\mathcal{M}$ with $\mathcal{R}_i$
    $\mathcal{C}_{childs}$ = GenerateTreeStructure($\mathcal{C}$, $\mathcal{L}$, $\mathcal{R}_i$)
end for
return $\mathcal{M}$

In our scenario, we are only interesting in direct relations represented as consistent association rules. More precisely, we are interested in level-1-itemset rules which have high confidence c and low support s as they describe direct parameter relations [30]. Due to the inherent structure of a simulation dataflow, which is constituted by the simulation workflow, repeating patterns of data access emerge. For instance, a physically-based simulation of Newton's law will always modify the position and velocity of certain simulated objects. This physically-based simulation will update the corresponding objects every time step in the simulation, generating such repeating patterns. These patterns especially appear when different simulation goals are related to the same parameters. This is usually a valid assumption for every multiobjective optimization problem. Consequently, the list-based output of the Apriori algorithm is not suitable for efficiently analyzing the simulation dataflow as it can not represent these repeating patterns. These patterns would lead to additional effort in the simulation data farming process because the repeating relations would need to be analyzed multiple times.

We present a novel idea based on forest data structures in order to overcome these repeating patterns. The main idea is to generate for every simulation goal $\mathcal{G}$ a tree which denotes the level-1-itemset dataflow result of the ARM process for this particular simulation goal. Within these trees, repeating transactions will manifest as duplicated sub-trees which can be effectively pruned. Figure 3 additionally illustrates the first step of our knowledge discovery process, namely the forest generation.

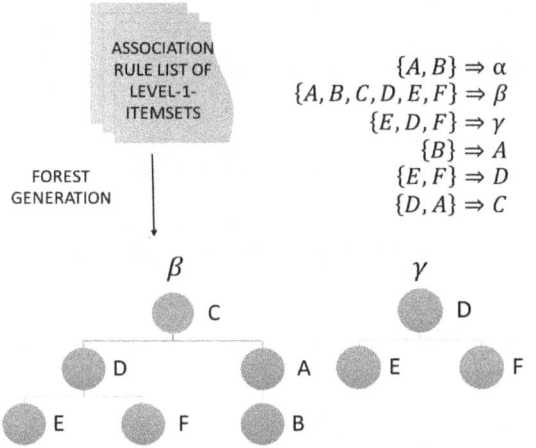

Figure 3: Level-1-itemsets are generated by the Apriori algorithm. The list based output is transformed into a forest structure which facilitates efficient simulation data farming. Repeating data access patterns from the simulation workflow result in prunable (green & orange) sub-trees of our forest.

Our utilization of the simulation transaction data as well as our forest data structure introduction reduces original computational complexity because we focus now in our simulation data farming phase only actual relationships:

$$\mathcal{O}((n^2 - n) \cdot g) \Rightarrow \mathcal{O}(k \cdot g) \qquad (5)$$

where

k : number of simulation goal related input parameters with $k \leq n$

4.1 Cubic Spline based Simulation Data Farming & Sampling

In order to determine causal relations our knowledge discovery process needs to farm simulation data after the dataflow determination of the blackbox simulation. As stated before, a brute-force analysis would lead to computationally very expensive behavior of the complete knowledge discovery process.

In this section, we present the next step of our knowledge discovery process which involves our efficient farming of simulation data for the given parameter and simulation goal relations. As mentioned before, repeating transaction patterns of the simulation workflow will result in duplicated sub-trees in the forest.

As a consequence, we can simply prune a node n that does not have a causal relation to its parent node p. This relation is obviously valid for all trees in the forest. Consequently, all sub-trees of n can be removed of all forest trees. In the following, we present two algorithms to discover these causal relations as well as to minimize the sampling rate of the parameter space without losing objective value information. First, we define a spline approximation of the unknown objective function and second, we describe a recursive correlation analysis in Section 4.2.

Algorithm 3 ForestSampling

```
for 𝒯 ∈ 𝓕 do
    for 𝒩 ∈ 𝒯 do
        𝒮_goal = splineApprox(𝒩, 𝒯_goal)
        𝒮_parent = splineApprox(𝒩, 𝒩_parent)
        𝒞_goal = correlationAnalysis(𝒮_goal)
        𝒞_parent = correlationAnalysis(𝒮_parent)
        if 𝒞_parent < ε or 𝒞_goal < ε then
            Remove all subgraphs of 𝒩 in 𝓕
        end if
    end for
end for
```

Algorithm 4 SplineApproximation

```
𝒟 = x_0, x_{k/2}, x_k
𝒮 = a spline based on 𝒟
ℛ = amount of remaining samples: k − 3
ℰ = list of rejections
while ℛ > 0 and ℰ < ε_rejections do
    𝒳 = evenly distributed x ∈ X
    𝒟 += 𝒳
    𝒴_sim = simulation result of 𝒳
    𝒴_spline = 𝒮(𝒳)
    if | 𝒴_sim - 𝒴_spline | < ε_deviation then
        ℰ += 𝒳
    end if
    𝒮 = rebuild spline based on 𝒟
    ℛ = ℛ - 1
end while
```

We assume that every relationship between a parameter $x = x_0, ..., x_k$ with parameter space k, unknown objective function f and utility value $y = y_0, ..., y_k$ can be formally represented as a continuous function $f_j\{x_i, ..., x_n\} \mapsto \mathcal{G}_j$. It would be possible to perfectly determine the behavior of f with respect to x by brute-force sampling the whole parameter space k. However, in real world applications k can be arbitrary large, therefore a brute-force sampling of the parameter space is infeasible. In order to overcome this challenge, we propose an approach based on cubic splines. A spline is a function that is piecewise defined by low-degree polynomials. Splines are often preferred in interpolation problems over higher-degree polynomial interpolation approaches because spline interpolation avoids the problem of Runge's phenomenon, i.e. oscillations that occur in interpolations between points when using high degree polynomials. Furthermore, even splines based on even polynomials can accurately approximate a given non-linear function.

The general idea of cubic splines is to represent the function by a different cubic function on each interval between data points. For n data points, the spline $S(x)$ is the function

$$S(x) = \begin{cases} C_1(x), x_0 \leq x \leq x_1 \\ C_i(x), x_{i-1} \leq x \leq x_i \\ C_n(x), x_{n-1} \leq x \leq x_n \end{cases} \quad (6)$$

where each C_i is a cubic function. The most general cubic function has the form

$$C_i(x) = a_i + b_i x + c_i x^2 + d_i x^3 \quad (7)$$

The main idea of our simulation data sampling and farming is to minimize the amount of samples n which are used to approximate the original behavior of f. In order to realize that, we iteratively approximate the unknown objective function f with a cubic spline. This spline is iteratively updated with more sampled data until the spline approximates f within a specified error degree. Algorithm 4 and Figure 4 illustrate this concept.

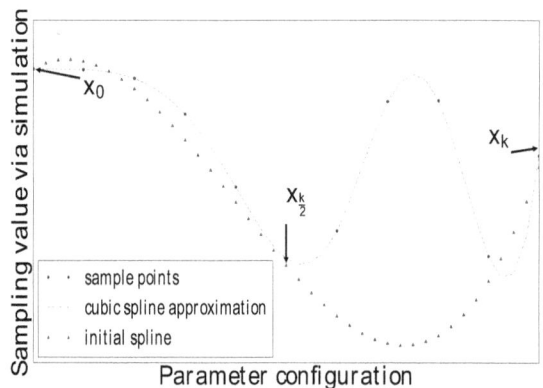

Figure 4: Spline approximation of a unknown objective function f: The spline is initialized with three initial sampled data points. The spline is iteratively updated until it approximates the unknown objective function within a certain error degree.

4.2 Recursive Correlation Analysis

When we have defined the cubic spline which represents the objective function f output $y = \{y_o, ..., y_n\}$ for a given parameter space $x = \{x_o, ..., x_n\}$, the next step is to determine whether or not a causal relation is present between x and y. This correlation analysis is needed as a spline approximation itself does not contain any correlation or causality information and can therefore approximate any given signal. Due to the fundamental property of self-containment of a simulation, confounding variables can be neglect as they would also be part of the workflow which would be uncovered by our ARM approach (see Section 4). Therefore, correlation alone can be used to determine the causal relation between x and y. In order to do so, we approximate the cubic spline representation s of f with segments which prove correlation. If the complete cubic spline s can be represented with such segments, we assume correlation and therefore causality between x and y.

Correlations between variables can be measured with the use of different indices (coefficients), such as the Pearson product correlation coefficient r [19]. It measures the linear correlation between two variables X and Y, giving a value between +1 and -1, where +1 describes total positive correlation, 0 no correlation and -1 total negative correlation.

$$r = \frac{\sum_{i=1}^{n}(x_i - \bar{x})(y_i - \bar{y})}{\sqrt{\sum_{i=1}^{n}(x_i - \bar{x})^2} \cdot \sqrt{\sum_{i=1}^{n}(y_i - \bar{y})^2}} \qquad (8)$$

where

n : number of elements in X resp. Y
x,y : elements of X and Y
$\bar{x},\bar{y}$: sample mean $\bar{x} = \frac{1}{n}\sum_{i=1}^{n} x_i$ (analogously for $\bar{y}$)

However, non-linear objective functions (e.g. polynomials with degree ≥ 2) can not be correctly modelled with r. We therefore propose to recursively compute the Pearson coefficient. If the signal can not be described with r, we recursively split the signal in the middle and analyze the remaining signals. The causal relation is proven when the complete signal can be described with $\{r_k\}$, where k is the number of coefficients. Algorithm 5 and Figure 5 illustrates this concept:

Algorithm 5 RecursiveCorrelationAnalysis($\mathcal{S}$ spline)

$\mathcal{C}$ empty correlation segments
r_{xy} = pearson coefficient of $\mathcal{S}$[0,n]
if $|r_{xy}| >= r_{threshold}$ **then**
    $\mathcal{C}$ += $\mathcal{S}$[0,n]
else
    $\mathcal{C}$ += recursiveCorrelationAnalysis($\mathcal{S}[0,\frac{n}{2}]$)
    $\mathcal{C}$ += recursiveCorrelationAnalysis($\mathcal{S}[\frac{n}{2}$,n]$)
end if
return $\mathcal{C}$

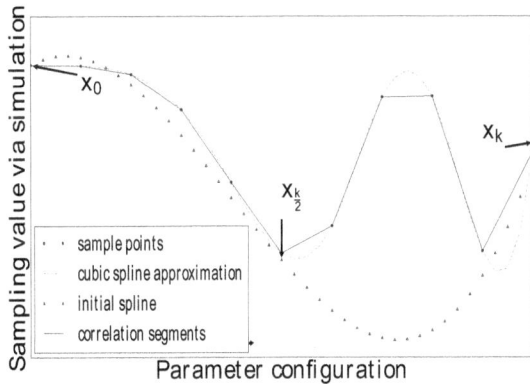

Figure 5: Result of the correlation analysis: Segments which prove linear correlation computed for the Spline representation of the objective function.

4.3 Determination of Pareto Information

After the determination of all causal relations between parameters $\{x_0, ..., x_p\}$ and simulation goals $\{g_0, ..., g_k\}$ (resp. objective functions $\{f_0, ..., f_k\}$) we can approximate the feasible design space for every parameter x_i. This feasible design space approximation can be used to efficiently compute suitable Pareto information for optimization algorithms.

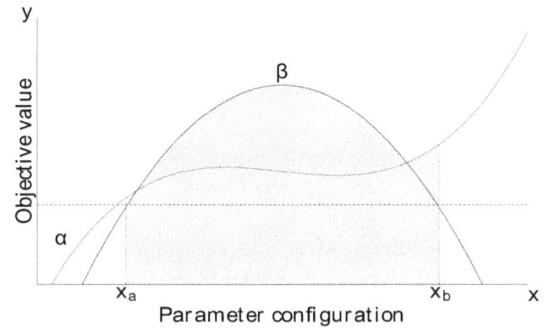

Figure 6: Approximation of feasible design space for a obtained parameter and simulation goal (α, β) relationship and given minimum objective value (dotted line): $x_a, ..., x_b$ determines the feasible parameter configurations.

The feasible design space constitutes a sub-set $\{\{x_i, ..., x_j\}, ..., \{x_n, ..., x_m\}\} \subseteq \{x_o, ..., x_k\}$ with $0 \leq i, i < j, n < m, j < n, m \leq k$. Figure 6 illustrates this concept for a parameter which is related to two simulation goals α, β.

Depending on the extracted design space, different outcomes are possible: singleobjective as well as multiobjective optimization problems. Singleobjective optimization problems can be directly solved by regular optimization algorithms. Multiobjective structures require Pareto information to solve conflicting objective functions. In the last case, we can further utilize our feasible design space approximation to generate Pareto gradient information.

An additional challenge appears if the same parameter contributes to different objective values at different time steps in the simulation (e.g. a fuel state/configuration in a car simulation which changes over time). Because of configurations like this, we prefer to define a spline of the objective function for each simulation time step individually. This results in a list of splines: $\{S(\{x_k\})_{t_0}, ..., S(\{x_k\})_{t_n}\} = \{\{y_k\}_{t_0}, ..., \{y_k\}_{t_n}\}$ for n time steps with:

$$S(\{x_k\})_{t_i} = \{y_k\}_{t_i} \qquad (9)$$

where

t_i : simulation time
$\{x_k\}$: parameter space
$\{y_k\}$: objective values of the corresponding objective
        function

In the easiest case, every input parameter $x_i \in x_k$ would result in every time step in the same objective value y_i, hence $y_{i_{t_0}} = y_{i_{t_1}} = ... = y_{i_{t_n}}$. In this case, only one spline is needed to describe the relationship. In the other case, we define the deviations of x_i over the simulation time as

$$\alpha_t(x_i) = \{y_0, ..., y_m\} \qquad (10)$$

where

$\{y_0, ..., y_m\}$: objective values for all simulation steps m

Additionally, we introduce a weighting function for this case in order to achieve smooth gradient transitions for the simulation behavior over the simulation time. We define this weighting as a Gaussian alignment of $\{y_o, ..., y_m\}$.

$$\omega_{x_i t} = \frac{e^{-k^2} \alpha_t(x_i) + ... + e^{-g^2} \alpha_{t_m}(x_i)}{m} \qquad (11)$$

where

$k > m, k = 1, m$: number of simulation time steps
g : the Gaussian weight

In order to generate the required Pareto information, we transform this parameter space and objective space of the corresponding relations into a new representation which we call Pareto space.

The transformation into the Pareto space is implemented with $\omega_{x_i t}$:

$$\omega_{pareto}(x_i) = \frac{\sum \Theta_i (|\frac{o}{n} - \frac{o}{\sum_{j<n}^{j=0} f_j(x_i)} \cdot \omega_{x_i t}(x_i)|)}{k} \qquad (12)$$

where

$1 \leq o \leq 100$: weighting factor
k : the number of non-empty utility functions
n : the number of related simulation goals
Θ : the Pareto weighting factor

We construct the Pareto space ω_{pareto} for all given Pareto goal weightings $\Theta_0, ..., \Theta_n$. Figures 7 and 8 additionally illustrate the definitions:

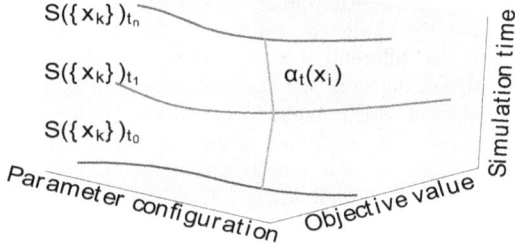

Figure 7: Graphs and deviation of a causal relationship between a parameter and a simulation goal.

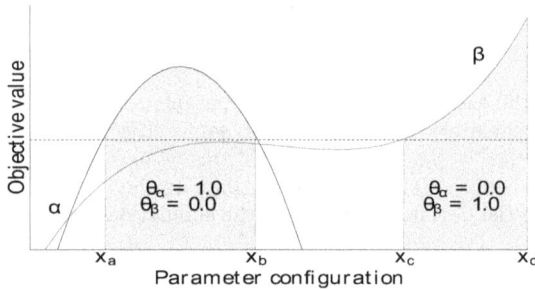

Figure 8: The Pareto gradient is determined by the amount of related simulation goals as well as Pareto weight Θ. The gradient information is computed for every sampling data point and constitutes our Pareto space. For every weighting Θ, a different Pareto space ($\{x_a, ...x_b\}$ and $\{x_c, ...x_d\}$) is constructed.

5. USE CASE STUDIES

We present two diverse use case studies from the fields of engineering and biology to illustrate the broad range of applications of our presented approach. First, we use Kepler's orbital mechanics which are used in space flight to describe celestial body and spacecraft movement. Second, we use the non-linear differential Lotka-Volterra equations [3] which are frequently used to describe the dynamics of biological systems in which to species interact, one as a predator and the other as prey. In both use case scenarios, the model behavior is unknown to our knowledge discovery process. Known to our approach are only the available input parameters as well as simulation goal measurements.

5.1 Spaceflight Orbit Optimization

5.1.1 Scenario

Usually spaceflight navigation solutions, especially autonomous interplanetary cruise flight, use optical measurements of reference bodies (e.g. Sun, Earth, Mars, Jupiter) to compute their position [2]. On-board optical systems take pictures of these reference bodies with respect to stars with known celestial locations. These images are used to compute the angular position of a spacecraft with respect to the reference bodies. These measurements are essential as spacecraft self-localization is needed throughout the complete mission [2]. Consequently, spacecraft trajectory calculation to target destinations has to consider possible reference bodies as well as optical system placing on the spacecraft for a given mission scenario.

The main idea of this use case is to compute a orbit for a interplanetary cruise flight to a target body in such a way that optical measurements to two reference bodies are guaranteed in order to ensure that spacecraft self-localization is possible.

5.1.2 Methodology

In celestial mechanics, Kepler's orbital elements can be used to uniquely identify a specific orbit in space. A Keplerian orbit is an idealized, mathematical approximation of an orbit for a particular time span. Each Kepler orbit is defined with six elements (see Figure 9), namely eccentricity e, inclination i, semimajor axis a, longitude of ascending node Ω, argument of periapsis ω and mean anomaly at epoch M.

Solving Keplers Equation $M(t) = E(t) - esin(E)$ for the eccentric anomaly $E(t)$ which defines the cartesian position of the specified orbit object can then be done with an appropriate method numerically, e.g. via Newton-Raphson iteration until $|E_n - E_{n-1}| \leq k$, where k defines the allowed deviation for the orbit (see Equation 13).

$$E_n = E_{n-1} - \frac{E_{n-1} - e \cdot sin(E_{n-1}) - M}{1 - e \cdot cos(E_{n-1}} \qquad (13)$$

$\vec{r}$ is then defining the object position in cartesian coordinates with respect to the eccentric anomaly and support vectors $\vec{P}, \vec{Q}$:

$$\vec{r} = a \cdot (\vec{P} \cdot (cos(E) - e) + \sqrt{1 - e^2} \cdot \vec{Q} \cdot sin(E)) \qquad (14)$$

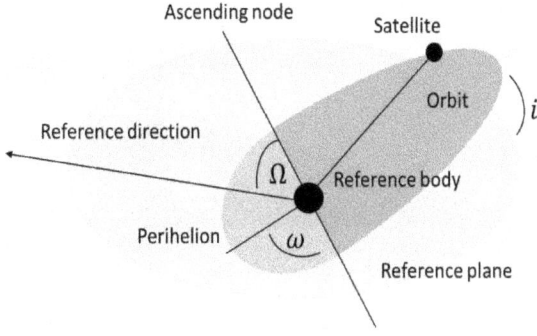

Figure 9: Illustration of the Keplerian orbital elements.

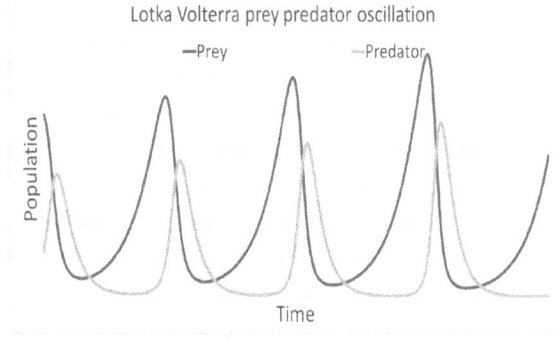

Figure 10: Illustration of the Lotka-Volterra equations: Periodic oscillation between preys and predators occur.

The two target bodies as well as the spacecraft are represented by their Kepler orbits around the Sun $k_1 = \{e, a, i, \omega, \Omega, M\}$, $k_2 = \{e, a, i, \omega, \Omega, M\}$, $k_{sc} = \{e, a, i, \omega, \Omega, M\}$. The required field of view of the sensor measurements are represented by

$$\cos \alpha = \frac{(\vec{r_{target}} - \vec{r_{sc}}) \cdot \vec{p}}{|(\vec{r_{target}} - \vec{r_{sc}})| \cdot |\vec{p}|} \leq t \quad (15)$$

where

$\vec{p}$: the aligned payload vector
t : the allowed angle of the payload field of view
$\vec{r_{sc}}$: the spacecraft position
$\vec{r_{target}}$: the target position

5.2 Lotka-Volterra Optimization

5.2.1 Scenario

The prey-predator system is a widely used simulation model of biological systems in which two species interact with each other. It consists of a dynamical non-linear system modeled by two differential equations, known as the Lotka-Volterra equations [3]. The equations model the evolution of two populations evolving in a common environment: preys and predators. Predators need to consume preys to survive, and preys spontaneously reproduce.

Due to the non-linear behavior of the Lotka-Volterra equations and further constraints (e.g. environmental conditions as the seasons which affect birth and death rate of the species) which can be added to the model, determining suitable input for observed real world ecosystem data is a challenging problem [22]. Therefore, the main idea of this use case is to determine a suitable input parameter set for the Lotka-Volterra equations in order to achieve a steady state between preys and predators for a given time span.

5.2.2 Methodology

The Lotka-Volterra model involves four parameters:

α : preys reproduction rate
β : preys death rate due to predators
δ : predators death rate in absence of preys
γ : predators reproduction rate according to consumed preys

The population evolution is given by these two differential equations:

$$\frac{dx(t)}{dt} = x(t)(\alpha - \beta y(t)) \quad (16)$$

$$\frac{dy(t)}{dt} = -y(t)(\delta - \gamma x(t)) \quad (17)$$

where $x(t)$ is the prey population at time t and $y(t)$ is the predator population at time t. Figure 10 further illustrates the behavior of the model.

6. EVALUATION

We implemented our knowledge discovery process and optimization approach in C++. We performed our experiments on a machine with Intel Core i7 quad-core processor with Hyperthreading enabled and 8GB of memory.

We applied different experiments to measure the performance as well as the quality of our approach. For the quality measurement, we used the use case scenarios described above. Both use case simulations were used to evaluate whether the computed Pareto gradient information are suitable for converging towards the Pareto front.

However, both scenarios are relatively small and can be hardly used to evaluate the performance of our approach. Hence, we additionally implemented a synthetic benchmark for performance measurements. We included three standard optimization algorithms: gradient descent, simulated annealing and evolutionary algorithms. The synthetic benchmark is based on blackbox simulations. We generated random objective functions for arbitrary simulation input parameters with mixed polynomials up to degree ten. These objective functions are further linked arbitrary times together with various simulation input parameters in order to generate multiobjective constraints.

Such multiobjective optimization problems do not have a single, accepted measure for solution quality [16], in contrast to single objective optimizations that have single global optimum, it is more complicated to measure the quality of any solution produced by a optimization algorithm.

We use the GD (Generational Distance) measurement [7] that provides an estimation of the distance of the current solution to the Pareto front. In other words, $GD = 0$ indicates that all solutions are placed on the Pareto front. We first compute the minimum Euclidean distance $\delta_i, i = 1, 2, ..., n_p$ of each solution where n_p is the number of solutions found.

The Generational Distance is then defined as:

$$GD = \frac{\sqrt{\sum_{i=1}^{n_p} \delta_i^2}}{n_p} \qquad (18)$$

Figure 11 shows the mean average computation time for the implemented Association Rule Mining approach in our synthetic benchmark. Our approach generates level-1-itemsets for more than 10.000 simulation input parameters in less than a second (see Figure 11). Moreover, our approach is able to generate our forest data structure of up to 100 simulation goals for these 10,000 parameters in less than 100 milliseconds (see Figure 12). Consequently, our approach is able to analyze large scale simulations very effectively. Figure 13 shows the average sampling rate of our cubic spline based interpolation needed for successfully approximating an unknown objective function with parameter space $k = 100$. The sampling rate depends on the polynomial degree of the unknown objective function. We compared our spline based approach with an approach which randomly samples the parameter space. The results show that our approach needs less samples for determining the objective function.

All three optimization algorithms we tested directly benefit from our Pareto information. Here, we compared how close the algorithms optimize towards the Pareto front when using our provided Pareto gradient information or not. When using the provided Pareto gradient information from our approach, the algorithms find solutions closer to the Pareto front by up to 38% for gradient descent, 44% for simulated annealing and 81% for a evolutionary approach (see Figure 14).

Surprisingly, evolutionary algorithms benefit most from our Pareto information. We believe, that with an increasing number of conflicting goals, even our Pareto space inherits many local minima, which adversely affect gradient descent and simulated annealing.

We used our use case scenarios to measure the quality of our approach. In the prey predator system, our approach was successfully able to compute a suitable input parameter set in order to achieve a steady simulation state. Figure 15 shows initial and the optimized model behavior. In our space flight scenario, our approach obtained an optimized flight orbit of the spacecraft with respect to the needed sensor measurements (see Figure 16). In both use case studies, our approach computed suitable solutions based on our Pareto space and it achieved the desired simulation goal state.

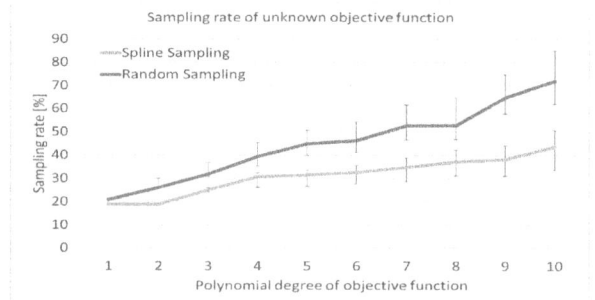

Figure 12: Our forest generation algorithm is able to generate the corresponding tree structures for more than 100 goals in less than 100 milliseconds.

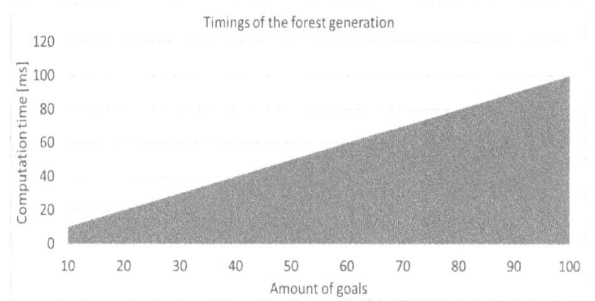

Figure 13: Our cubic spline algorithm is able to efficiently approximate unknown objective functions with less than half of the available parameter space even for high degree polynomials.

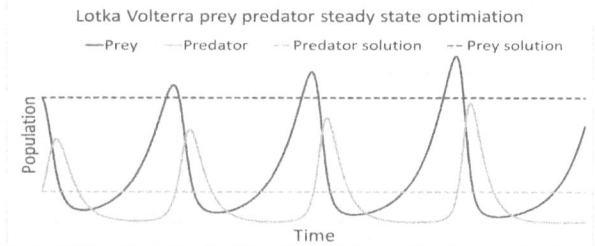

Figure 15: Evaluation of the Lotka-Volterra use case study: Our approach is able to compute Pareto information in order to achieve a steady state in the population.

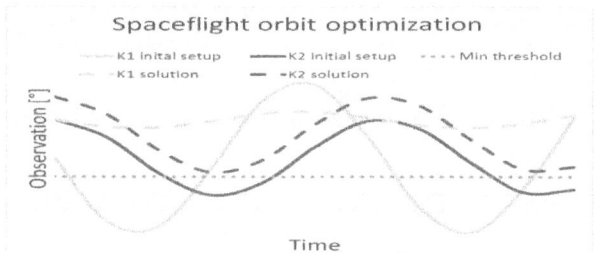

Figure 16: Evaluation of the spacecraft flight use case study: Our approach is able to compute Pareto information in order to achieve the desired orbit for suitable observation possibilities.

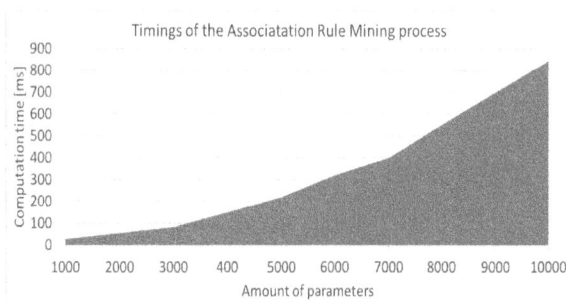

Figure 11: Our customized Association Rule Mining approach is able to analyze several thousands of parameters for generating level-1-itemsets in less than a second.

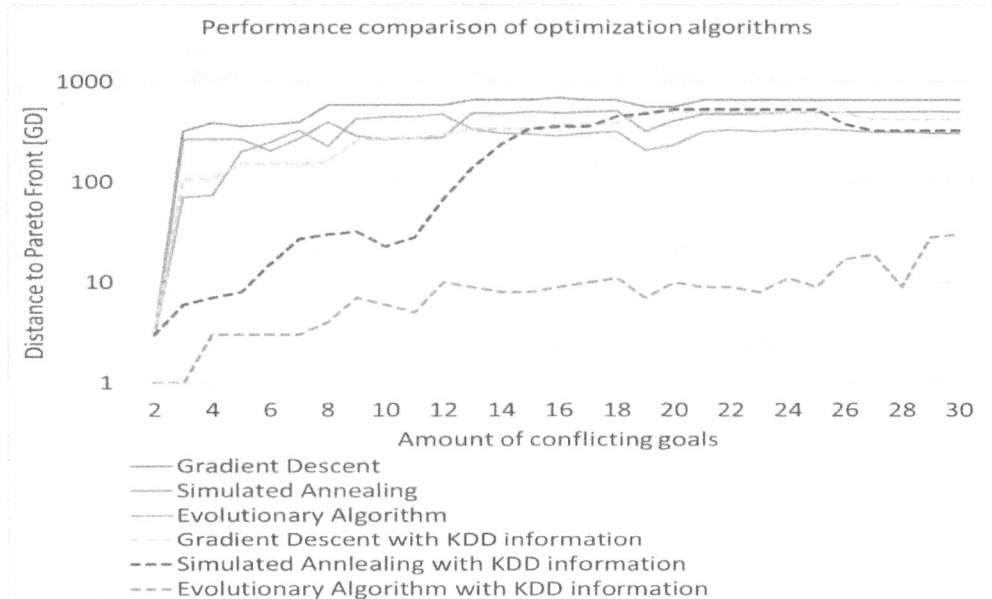

Figure 14: Our Pareto information directly benefit gradient descent, simulated annealing and evolutionary approaches and deliver results closer to the Pareto front.

7. CONCLUSION

We presented a novel knowledge discovery process for active model building of multiobjective optimization within deterministic blackbox simulations.

Our process automatically builds an active model between simulation input and simulation goals which is capable of

- approximating the feasible design space for a Pareto based optimization by uncovering unknown causal relations in large parameter sets between simulation input and model behavior which are assumed to be unknown non-linear objective functions.
- computing Pareto gradient information from this design space approximation which can be used in state-of-the-art multiobjective optimization solvers.

Our knowledge discovery process is completely autonomous and does not need any supervision from a simulation expert.

The results from our case studies and synthetic benchmarks show that our approach is able to analyze large scale simulations with tens of thousands of parameters in less than a second while providing suitable Pareto information for state-of-the-art multiobjective optimization algorithms. Due to its generality, our approach is applicable to a wide variety of simulation domains such as engineering design problems, including layout, design, and process optimization.

In the future, we would like to extend our approach to support intelligent, heuristic-based simulation data farming and sampling. In detail, our approach could sample directly in the direction of the Pareto front in order to improve the simulation data farming process. In order to realize this, a sampling heuristic is needed which should be in a direct feedback-loop with our proposed Pareto gradient optimization. Furthermore, an evaluation of our approach with standard optimization via simulation problems as provided by [29] is planned. Finally, it would also be beneficial if our approach could support stochastic simulations.

This would incorporate that our spline-based sampling technique needs to adapt to randomness in the sampling of objective values.

8. ACKNOWLEDGMENTS

This research is based upon the project KaNaRiA, supported by German Aerospace Center (DLR) with funds of the German Federal Ministry of Economics and Technology (BMWi) under grant 50NA1318.

9. REFERENCES

[1] Ajith Abraham, Lakhmi C. Jain, Robert Goldberg. Evolutionary Multiobjective Optimization: Theoretical Advances and Applications. *Springer Verlag*, 2005.

[2] Alena Probst, Graciela Peytavi, David Nakath, Anne Schattel, Carsten Rachuy, Patrick Lange, et al. Kanaria: Identifying the Challenges for Cognitive Autonomous Navigation and Guidance for Missions to Small Planetary Bodies. *International Astronautical Congress (IAC)*, 2015.

[3] Alfred J. Lotka. Elements of Physical Biology. *Williams and Wilkins*, 1925.

[4] Andreas Lattner, Joerg Dallmeyer, Ingo Timm. Learning Dynamic Adaptation Strategies in Agent-Based Traffic Simulation Experiments. *Ninth German Conference on Multi-Agent System Technologies (MATES)*, pages 77–88, 2011.

[5] Benjamin Wilson, David Cappelleri, Timothy W. Simpson, Mary Frecker. Efficient Pareto frontier exploration using surrogate approximations. *Optimization and Engineering*, pages 31–50, 2001.

[6] Catarina Dudas, Amos H. C. Ng, Henrik Bostroem. Post-Analysis of Multi-Objective Optimization Solutions Using Decision Trees. *Intelligent Data Analysis*, 19:259–278, 2015.

[7] David A. van Veldhuizen, Gary B. Lamont. Evolutionary Computation and Convergence to a Pareto Front. *Late Breaking Papers at the Genetic Programming Conference*, 1998.

[8] Dongkyung Nam, Cheol Hoon Park. Multiobjective Simulated Annealing: A Comparative Study to Evolutionary Algorithms. *International Journal of Fuzzy Systems*, 2, 2000.

[9] Eckart Zitzler, Lothar Thiele. Multiobjective Evolutionary Algorithms: A Comparative Case Study and the Strength Pareto Approach. *IEEE Transactions on Evolutionary Computation*, 3:257–271, 1999.

[10] Eckhart Zitzler. Evolutionary Algorithms for Multiobjective Optimization: Methods and Applications. 1999.

[11] Gary E. Horne, Theodore E. Meyer. Data Farming: Discovering Surprise. *Winter Simulation Conference*, pages 1082–1087, 2005.

[12] J. Westra, F. Dignum, V. Dignum. Guiding User Adaptation in Serious Games. *Agents for Games and Simulations II*, pages 117–131, 2011.

[13] Jack P.C. Kleijnen, Susan M.Sanchez, Thomas M. Cioppa. A User's Guide to the Brave New World of Designing Simulation Experiments. *INFORMS Journal on Computing (Summer 2005)*, 17:263–289, 2005.

[14] Jean-Antoine Desideri. Multi-Gradient Descent Algorithm (MGDA) for Multiobjective Optimization. *Comptes Rendus Mathematique*, 350:313–318, 2012.

[15] Joerg Fliege, B. Fux. Svaiter. Steepest Descent Methods for Multicriteria Optimization. *Mathematical Methods of Operations Research*, 3:479–494, 2000.

[16] John D. Siirola, Steinar Hauan, Arthur W. Westerberg. Computing Pareto Front Using Distributed Agents. *Computers and Chemical Engineering*, 29:113–126, 2004.

[17] Jong-Hyun Ryu, Sujin Kim, Hong Wan. Pareto Front Approximation With Adaptive Weighted Sum Method in Multiobjective Simulation Optimization. *Winter Simulation Conference*, pages 623–633, 2009.

[18] Jorge Nocedal, Stephen J. Wright. Numerical Optimization. *Springer Verlag*, 1999.

[19] Karl Pearson. Mathematical Contributions to the Theory of Evolution. *Philosophical Transactions of the Royal Society*, 187:253–318, 1896.

[20] Kazuyuki Sugimura, Shigeru Obayashi, Shinkyu Jeong. Multi-Objective Design Exploration of a Centrifugal Impeller Accompanied With a Vaned Diffuser. *ASME/JSME Joint Fluids Engineering Conference*, 2007.

[21] L. Jeff Hong, Barry L. Nelson. A Brief Introduction to Optimization via Simulation. *Winter Simulation Conference*, 2009.

[22] C. B. L. Pons. A Multi-Agent System for Autonomous Control of Game Parameters. *IEEE International Conference on Systems, Man and Cybernetics (SMC)*, 2013.

[23] Martin Liebscher, Katharina Witowski, Tushar Goel. Decision Making in Multi-Objective Optimization for Industrial Applications - Data Mining and Visualization of Pareto Data. *8th World Congress on Structural and Multidisciplinary Optimization*, 2009.

[24] M.C. Burl, D. DeCoste, B.L. Enke, D. Mazzoni, W.J. Merline, L. Scharenbroich. Automated Knowledge Discovery from Simulators. *Sixth SIAM International International Conference on Data Mining*, pages 82–93, 2006.

[25] Michael C. Fu. Optimization via Simulation: A Review. *Annals of Operations Research*, 53:199–248, 1994.

[26] Michael Painter, Madhav Erraguntla, Gary Hogg, Brian Beachkofski. Using Simulation, Data Mining, And Knowledge Discovery Techniques For Optimized Aircraft Enginee Fleet Management. *Proceedings of the Winter Simulation Conference*, pages 1253–1260, 2006.

[27] Niclas Feldkamp, Soeren Bergmann, Steffen Strassburger. Knowledge Discovery in Manufacturing Simulations. *ACM SIGSIM PADS*, pages 3–12, 2015.

[28] Patrick Lange, Rene Weller, Gabriel Zachmann. Multi Agent System Optimization in Virtual Vehicle Testbeds. *EAI SIMUtools*, 2015.

[29] R. Pasupathy. SimOpt: A Library of Simulation Optimization Problems. *Winter Simulation Conference*, pages 4075–4085, 2011.

[30] Rakesh Agrawal, Tomasz Imielinski, Arun Swami. Mining Association Rules between Sets of Items in Large Databases. *ACM SIGMOD Conference*, 1993.

[31] Ravindra V. Tappeta, John E. Renaud. An Interactive Multiobjective Optimization Design Strategy for Decision Based Multidisciplinary Design. *40th AIAA/ASME/ASCE/AHS/ASC Structures, Structural Dynamics, and Materials Conference and Exhibit*, pages 78–87, 1999.

[32] Sanghamitra Bandyopadhyay, Sriparna Saha, Ujjwal Maulik, Kalyanmoy Deb. A Simulated Annealing-Based Multiobjective Optimization Algorithm: AMOSA. *IEEE Transactions on Evolutionary Computation*, 12:269–283, 2008.

[33] Songqing Shan, Gary G. Wang. An Efficient Pareto Set Identification Approach for Multiobjective Pptimization on Black-box Functions. *Journal of Mechanical Design 127*, 5:866–874, 2004.

[34] Sunith Bandaru, Kevin Deb. Automated discovery of vital knowledge from Pareto-optimal solutions: First results from engineering design. *IEEE Congress on Evolutionary Computation (CEC)*, pages 1–8, 2010.

[35] Susan M. Sanchez. Simulation Experiments: Better Data, Not Just Big Data. *Winter Simulation Conference*, pages 805–816, 2014.

[36] Usama Fayyad, Gregory Piatetsky-Shapiro, Padhraic Smyth. From Data Mining to Knowledge Discovery in Databases. *AI Magazine (Fall 1996)*, 17:37–54, 1996.

[37] William J. Frawley, Gregory Piatetsky-Shapiro, Christopher J. Matheus. Knowledge Discovery in Databases: An Overview. *Springer Verlag*, 1992.

Coupling Simulation with Machine Learning:
A Hybrid Approach for Elderly Discharge Planning

[Applied to Hip Fracture Care in Ireland]

Mahmoud Elbattah
National University of Ireland Galway
m.elbattah1@nuigalway.ie

Owen Molloy
National University of Ireland Galway
owen.molloy@nuigalway.ie

ABSTRACT

Healthcare systems are increasingly challenged by the phenomenal growth of population ageing. Healthcare executives are, and will be, in an inevitable need of evidence-based artifacts for decision making. The paper addresses issues in the context of discharge planning for elderly patients with application to hip fracture care in Ireland. A hybrid approach is embraced that integrates simulation modeling with machine learning in an attempt to improve the validity of the simulation model outputs. In terms of simulation modeling, a discrete event simulation model is used to model the elderly patient's journey through the care scheme of hip fracture. In tandem with the simulation model, predictive models are used to guide the simulation model. Specifically, the predictive models are used to make predictions on the inpatient length of stay and discharge destination of simulation-generated patients. On a population basis, the simulation model provides demand predictions for healthcare resources related to discharge destinations, with a focus on long-stay care such as nursing homes. Our results suggest that there may be a need to reconsider the geographic distribution of nursing homes within particular areas in Ireland in order to keep abreast of the foreseen shift in demographics. Furthermore, the incorporation of machine learning within simulation modeling is claimed to improve the predictive power of the simulation model.

Keywords

Discrete Event Simulation; Machine Learning; Elderly Healthcare; Discharge Planning; Hip Fracture Care.

1. INTRODUCTION

The world has been witnessing a remarkable increase in the growth of population ageing [29-31]. Moreover, the acceleration of ageing will likely increase over the coming decades [32]. In Europe, the proportion of people aged 65 years or over has already exceeded that younger than 15 years in 2008, and that proportion is expected to double by 2060 [33]. More significantly, the proportion of very old people aged 80 years or over is expected to triple between 2008 and 2060 [34].

Permission to make digital or hard copies of all or part of this work for personal or classroom use is granted without fee provided that copies are not made or distributed for profit or commercial advantage and that copies bear this notice and the full citation on the first page. Copyrights for components of this work owned by others than ACM must be honored. Abstracting with credit is permitted. To copy otherwise, or republish, to post on servers or to redistribute to lists, requires prior specific permission and/or a fee. Request permissions from Permissions@acm.org.
SIGSIM-PADS '16, May 15-18, 2016, Banff, AB, Canada
© 2016 ACM. ISBN 978-1-4503-3742-7/16/05...$15.00
DOI: http://dx.doi.org/10.1145/2901378.2901381

Likewise in Ireland, the numbers and proportion of elderly people are increasing rapidly. As reported [35] by Ireland's Health Service Executive (HSE), the increase in the number of people over 65 is approaching 20,000 per year. As a result to that demographic transformation, a considerable rise in the demand for healthcare services is in prospect. For instance, the prevalence of chronic diseases is anticipated to increase by 20% by 2020. Figure 1 plots the trend of ageing in Europe and Ireland from 2004 to 2013.

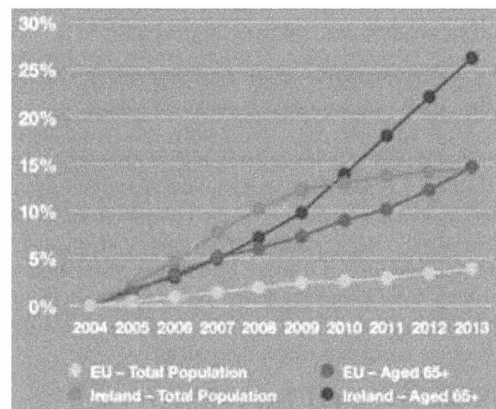

Figure 1. The ageing population trend in the EU and Ireland from 2004 to 2013 [35].

Given this challenge, there is an imperative need for insightful planning in order to cope with the growing elderly-driven demand for healthcare. Healthcare executives are faced by dilemmas for making appropriate decisions in response to the changing profile of population.

In this context, the focus of the study centralised around the care scheme of hip fracture. In particular, we were concerned with discharge planning for elderly patients who undergo hip fracture care. Hip fracture care was purposefully considered for two arguments. First, hip fracture care can represent an adequate exemplar of elderly healthcare. Plentiful studies [37-39] identified hip fractures as exponentially increasing with age, despite the existence of variability of rates from country to another. In Ireland, around 3,000 people sustain hip fractures annually [40], which will unavoidably increase owing to the ageing population. Second, the care delivery of hip fractures has a considerable importance, whereas the HSE identified hip fractures as one of the most serious injuries resulting in lengthy hospital admissions and high costs [44].

In relation to the elderly care of hip fracture, the paper aimed at endorsing two complementary categories of questions including: i) Population-level questions, and ii) Individual patient-level questions. Table 1 poses the questions in detail.

Table 1. Questions of interest.

Category of Questions	Question
Population-Level	Q1) What is the expected proportion of elderly patients discharged to home, or long-stay care?
	Q2) How adequate is the geographic distribution of long-stay care facilities with respect to the demographic profile of elderly people in Ireland?
Individual Patient-Level	Q3) Given an elderly patient's characteristics, how to predict the length of stay in acute facilities?
	Q4) Given an elderly patient's characteristics, how to predict the discharge destination?

In light of the aimed questions, a combined approach was embraced that integrated simulation modeling with machine learning techniques. At the population scale, a simulation model was developed to provide a projected perspective of elderly discharged patients. At the individual patient scale, machine learning models were used to make predictions on the inpatient length of stay (LOS), and discharge destination.

Broadly, we attempted to make contributions in two aspects. First, the study presented the potential usage of machine learning for reducing the uncertainty of non-deterministic behaviour underlying simulation models. We argue that the incorporation of simulation modeling and machine learning can yield an improvement in the predictive power of simulation models. Second, useful insights were gained in relation to the expected demand for hip fracture care due to population ageing. The insights were provided based on a well-rounded picture corresponding to the demographic profiles, structure, and capacity of the healthcare system in Ireland.

2. APPROACH OVERVIEW

The adopted approach mainly consisted of two integrated parts. On one hand, a discrete event simulation model served as the core component. The model assumptions were primarily set using a dataset stemmed from the Irish Hip Fracture Database (IHFD) [6], and other data sources described at Section 4.1 in detail.

On the other hand, two machine learning models were developed in order to predict the LOS and discharge destination for every elderly patient generated by the simulation model. The prediction models were developed and tested using Microsoft Azure Machine Learning [7], described at Section 3 in detail. The predictions were obtained from the models via web services enabled by the Microsoft Azure platform. Figure 2 sketches an overview of the approach.

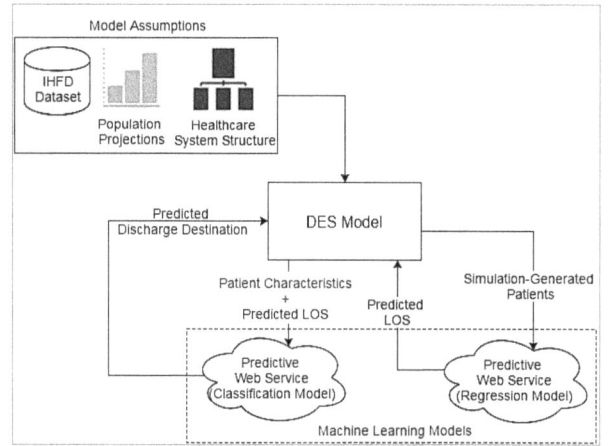

Figure 2. Overview of the approach.

3. MACHINE LEARNING MODELS

This section delineates the developed machine learning models, and their performance evaluation. As mentioned before, two models were used to predict the inpatient LOS and discharge destination. Specifically, a regression model was trained for predicting the LOS, and another multi-class classification model for predicting the discharge destination.

3.1 The Role of Machine Learning

"Even though the assumptions of a model may not literally be exact and complete representation of reality, if they are realistic enough for the purpose of our analysis, we may be able to draw conclusions which can be shown to apply to the world." [1].

The "realism" of simulation modeling has been a central issue. According to [2-5], all models, including simulation models, are invalid with respect to complete reality. However, a simulation model does not need to be a complete representation in order to be useful, as above-stated by [1]. However, a simulation model should attempt to represent a level of reality, which can be acceptable in accordance with the questions of interest.

In this respect, we embraced machine learning in an attempt to realise a higher level of model reality. Given historical patient records, machine learning models were trained to make predictions on important outcomes related to patient discharge. In conjunction with the simulation experiments, the predictive models were utilised to carefully predict the inpatient LOS and discharge destination for each elderly patient generated by the simulation model.

3.2 Source of Training Data

The study used a dataset extracted from the Irish Hip Fracture Database (IHFD) [6] for training both of the regression and classification models. The IHFD repository is the national clinical audit developed to capture care standards and outcomes for patients with hip fractures in Ireland. The IHFD records contain ample information about the patient's journey from admission to discharge. Particularly, a typical patient record included 38 data fields such as gender, age, type of fracture, date of admission, time to surgery and LOS. The dataset consisted of 2,024 patient records for the year 2013.

3.3 Data Anomalies

A data anomaly was defined as an observation that appears to be inconsistent with the remainder of the dataset [15], or more generally as any data that is unsuitable for the intended use [16]. This section describes data anomalies exposed within the IHFD dataset, and the procedures conducted to deal with them.

3.3.1 Outlier Removal

In order to prevent the odd influence of outliers, we considered only the samples whose LOS were no longer than 40 days. The excluded outliers represented approximately 8% of the overall dataset. Figure 3 plots a histogram of the LOS used to identify the outliers.

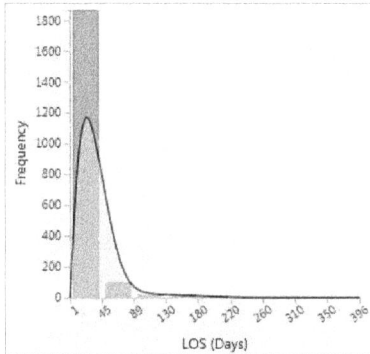

Figure 3. Histogram and probability density of the LOS variable. The outliers can be observed when the LOS becomes longer than 40 days.

3.3.2 Dealing with Data Imbalances

The training data was originally obtained in a form of an imbalanced dataset, which was accounted for having an adverse impact on prediction quality [12]. The problem of imbalanced data was acknowledged as one of the profound challenges in machine learning research [13]. In our case, imbalanced training samples were outstanding for inpatient LOS longer than 20 days, and discharge destinations where a patient was transferred to acute hospital after surgery. In addition, training samples for male patients, and particular age groups were obviously underrepresented. Figure 4 shows the imbalanced histograms of the LOS and discharge destination.

In order to cope with the imbalance constraint, over-sampling technique [14] was adopted. The underrepresented samples were resampled at random until they approximately contained as many examples as the other well-represented samples.

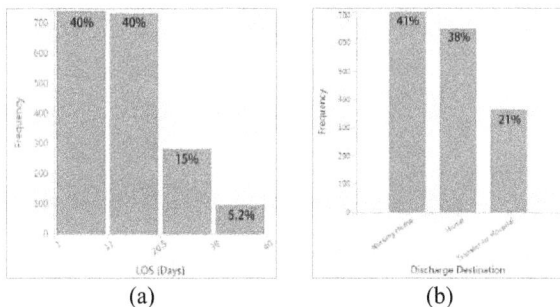

| (a) | (b) |

Figure 4. The imbalanced training samples, where figures (a) and (b) plot histograms of inpatient LOS and discharge destination respectively.

3.4 Prediction of LOS: A Regression Model

The inpatient LOS has a pivotal importance within healthcare schemes. On one hand, the LOS was suggested by numerous studies [8-10] as a significant outcome measure for potential quality improvement. On the other hand, study [11] demonstrated that there is an evident relationship between the LOS and discharge destination. Moreover, the LOS was recognised as the main component of the overall cost of hip fracture care [17]. Therefore, discharge planning is significantly contingent on the predictability of inpatient LOS. A regression forest [45] model was developed for that purpose.

3.5 Prediction of Discharge Destination: A Multi-Class Classifier

Predicting discharge destination has a strategic importance in order to estimate the overall needed capacity of nursing homes for example. The discharge destinations include home, nursing home, or transfer-to-hospital where acute post-surgery care is needed. The intuition was that a discharge destination can be predicted based on patient's characteristics and the LOS, which was predicted separately by the regression model. A random forest [45] model was developed for predicting the discharge destination.

3.6 Feature Selection

Initially, the dataset contained 38 features, however they were not all relevant. Intuitively irrelevant feature were simply excluded. In addition, the most influential features were decided based on the technique of permutation feature importance [18]. Table 2 presents the set of features used by the predictors, and their associated importance scores.

Table 2. Selected features in descending order with respect to importance score.

Predictor Model	Selected Features	
	Feature	Importance Score $\approx$
LOS Regression Model	Source Hospital	0.71
	Patient Age	0.50
	ICD Diagnosis	0.46
	Patient Residence Area	0.40
	Fracture Type	0.39
	Patient Sex	0.29
	Fragility History	0.22
Discharge Destination Classifier	Source Hospital	0.44
	Patient Age	0.35
	LOS	0.21
	Patient Residence Area	0.20
	Patient Sex	0.13

3.7 Predictors Evaluation

The predictive models were tested using a subset from the dataset described in Section 3.2. The randomly sampled test data represented approximately 40% of the overall dataset. The prediction error of each model was estimated by applying 10-fold cross-validation. Table 3 presents evaluation metrics of the LOS regression model, while Figure 5 shows the confusion matrix of the discharge destination classifier.

Table 3. Average 10-fold cross-validation accuracy of the LOS predictor.

Relative Absolute Error	Relative Squared Error	Coefficient of Determination
≈0.26	≈0.17	≈0.83

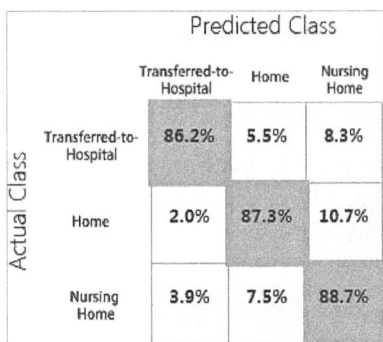

Figure 5. Average 10-fold cross-validation accuracies of discharge destination classifier.

4. SIMULATION MODELING

4.1 Sources of Data

The collection of high-quality information and data on the system of interest is a key determinant of the validity and credibility of a simulation model [19]. As alluded to earlier in Section 3.2, the study utilised a high-quality schema-based dataset derived from the IHFD database. Full descriptions of the dataset fields were available in the form of a data dictionary [43]. Mainly, the assumptions, limitations and parameters of the simulation model were constructed based on admission and discharge records from that dataset.

In addition, projections of population were essentially needed to address the population-level questions of interest. On one hand, the study used population projections prepared by the Central Statistics Office (CSO) [20]. The population information contained comprehensive information about the population in specific geographic areas in terms of age and sex. However, the simulation model focused only on population aged 60 years and over, in line with the study scope. Figure 6 plots the elderly population projections for the years ranging from 2016 to 2026.

On the other hand, we acquired further demographic statistics from the HSE Health Intelligence. The demographic statistics included information about the regions that currently structure the Irish healthcare system into 9 geographic regions called "Community Health Organizations", commonly abbreviated as CHO. Although, the statistics included only the year 2014, they were useful for setting necessary assumptions regarding the CHOs, which are described in the next section. Figure 7 [23] shows the geographic boundaries of the 9 CHOs. Figure 8 plots the reported elderly populations in 2014 with respect to every CHO. Further information on the bed capacities of nursing homes was obtained using reports from the Health Information and Quality Authority (HIQA) [36].

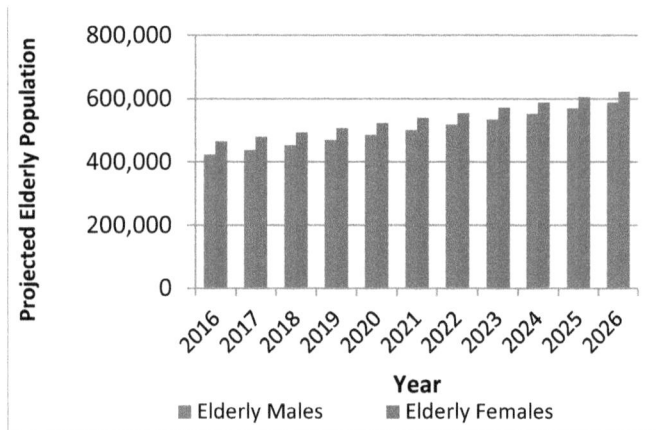

Figure 6. Projected populations aged 60 and over from year 2016 to 2026. The left-sided column represents elderly males, while the right-side one represents elderly females.

Figure 7. The geographic boundaries of the Community Health Organisations (CHOs).

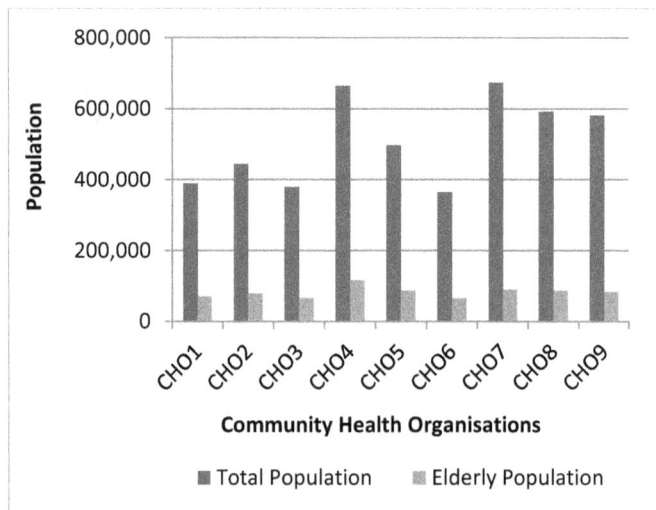

Figure 8. The population profiles of the 9 CHOs in 2014. The right-sided column represents the total population, while the left-sided column represents the elderly population aged 60 and over.

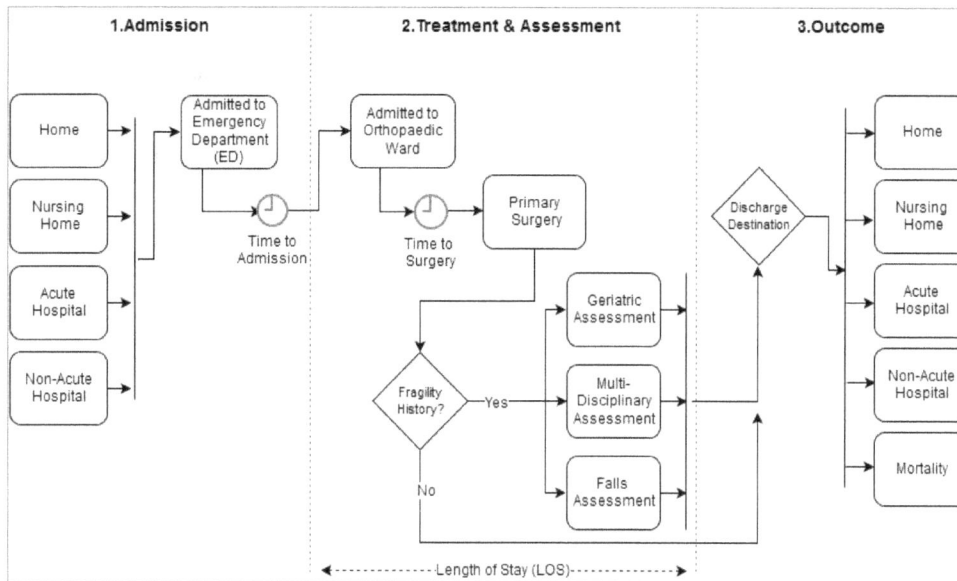

Figure 9. The elderly patient journey over the scheme of hip fracture care.

4.2 Conceptual Model

4.2.1 Elderly Patient Journey

Simulation modelling is both art and science with conceptual modelling lying more at the artistic end [21]. In this sense, the conceptualization of the elderly patient journey was an important step towards understanding and implementing the simulation model.

Figure 9 sketches the journey of an elderly patient in a process fashion from admission to discharge. The journey is divided into three stages as follows: i) Admission, ii) Treatment and Assessment, and iii) Outcome. The journey begins from an admission source, where it can be one of the following: i) Home, ii) Nursing Home, iii) Acute Hospital, and iv) Non-acute hospital. Initially, the patient is usually received at the Emergency Department (ED). After admission to an orthopaedic ward, the primary surgery should be performed within 48 hours, asserted as a measure of care quality [22]. After surgery, the patient can possibly undergo various assessments based on the history of falls and fragility of each patient. Eventually, the discharge destination is decided as follows: i) Home ii) Nursing Home, or iii) Non/acute hospital.

4.2.2 Model Assumptions and Simplifications

A set of assumptions and simplifications were decided while maintaining the simulation model as a reasonably approximate representation of the actual system. Table 4 presents what simplifying assumptions were made and why.

Table 4. Model assumptions and simplifications.

Assumption / Simplification	Reason / Purpose
The rate of hip fracture in the total population aged 60 and over was set as 407 for females and 140 for males per 100,000.	The rate was defined by [24].
Elderly patients were assumed as those aged 60 and over, although usually considered as aged 65 and older [25].	To conform to the pre-set hip fracture rate, which included those aged 60 and over.
The model did not consider the scenario of patient transfer from an acute hospital to another during treatment course.	To simplify the patient's journey, where treatment course was bounded within a single acute hospital.
The model used the same age distribution for both male and female elderly patients.	For the purpose of simplification, since both distributions were slightly different.
The model assumed a discrete uniform distribution for patient's fragility history, whether positive or negative fragility.	It was not appropriate to use the original distribution of the fragility history variable, since the field values were missing for more than 34% of the records.
The elderly population for each CHO was computed by applying a (fixed) percentage of the nation-wide projected population on a yearly basis from 2016 to 2026. For example, the elderly population of CHO1 was computed as 9.5% of the total elderly projected population in 2016, whereas 9.5% was the actual percentage in 2014.	Due to lack of population information with respect to the 9 CHOs. The study obtained the population profiles of the CHOs for the year 2014 only.

51

4.3 Simulation Model Development

4.3.1 Simulation Approach

Discrete Event simulation (DES) was decided as the simulation modeling approach. The DES approach was robustly preferred for the following reasons:

- It facilitated structuring the model into entities, which naturally represented the real system's components.

- The entity-based modeling enabled to consider demographic aspects on the individual patient level. For instance, the properties of elderly patients were determined differently according to the CHOs.

- It could produce a realistic sequence of events corresponding to those underlying the elderly patient journey.

4.3.2 Model Implementation

Based on the conceptual model and the empirical data, a discrete event simulation model was developed. The simulation model was implemented using the DESMO-J framework [26], a discrete event simulation library developed in Java.

The main entity of the simulation model represented the elderly patient. On the population level, the projected elderly patients were generated with regard to the CHOs' population profiles. On the patient level, each patient was assigned a set of attributes that characterised age, sex, area of residence, fracture type, fragility history and diagnosis type. Further, every CHO was structured as a set of acute hospitals and nursing homes, which were specified with accurate bed capacity using information from the HIQA organisation [36].

The arrival rate of elderly patients was constructed as before-mentioned in Section 4.2.2. Further statistical assumptions were included using probability distributions derived from the IHFD dataset.

In tandem with the simulation model, the already-trained machine learning models were utilised to guide the simulation model to predict the LOS and discharge destination of simulation-generated elderly patients.

4.4 Model Verification and Validation

4.4.1 Model Verification

In order to examine the logic and suitability of the model, it was verified qualitatively and quantitatively. Throughout the simulation model's development, a set of verification tests [28] were conducted as follows:

- Structure-Verification Test: The model structure was checked compared to the actual system. Specifically, it was verified that the model structure mirrored reality in terms of the underlying CHOs, and associated elderly populations.

- Extreme Conditions Test: The equations of the simulation model were tested in extreme conditions. For example, flows of patients were set at extreme conditions (e.g., there is no elderly population aged 60 or over).

- Parameter-Verification Test: The model parameters and their numerical values were inspected to correspond conceptually and numerically to reality. Specifically, probability distributions of patient attributes output from the model were compared against those derived from the real system, such as age, sex and fracture types for example.

4.4.2 Model Validation

According to [27], the most definitive test of simulation model validity is comparing outputs of the simulation model to those of the actual system. Similarly, we used the variables of discharge destination and LOS as a measure of the approximation between the simulation model and the actual system.

On one hand, Figure 10 provides a histogram-based comparison between the actual system and the simulation model regarding the discharge destination. The comparison showed that the distributions of the actual and simulated data were relatively close. However, the comparison revealed that the model slightly underestimated and over-estimated the proportion of patients discharged to nursing homes, and acute hospital respectively.

On the other hand, Figure 11 compares the actual system's average LOS to that of the simulation model with respect to the 9 CHOs separately. The figure clearly shows that the simulated CHOs' average LOS matched the actual system very well, without any significant over- or under-estimations. Overall, validation and verification tests proved that the simulation model can be suitable for answering questions from the perspective of the study's intended objectives.

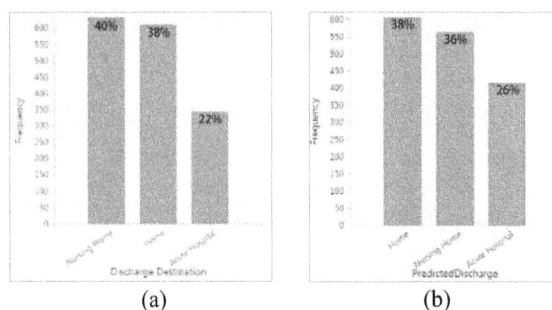

(a)   (b)

Figure 10. Histograms of the discharge destination for the actual system and simulation model, where (a) and (b) represent the actual system and simulation model respectively.

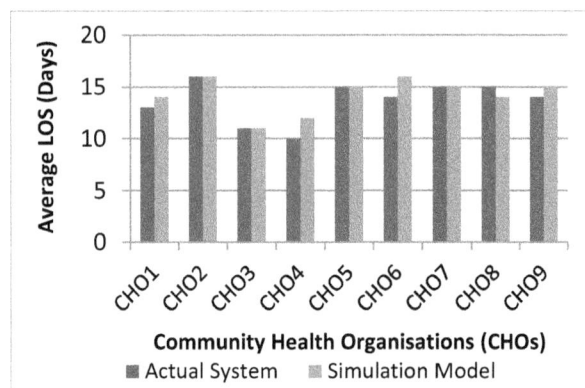

Figure 11. CHO-based comparison between the actual system and simulation model in terms of average LOS.

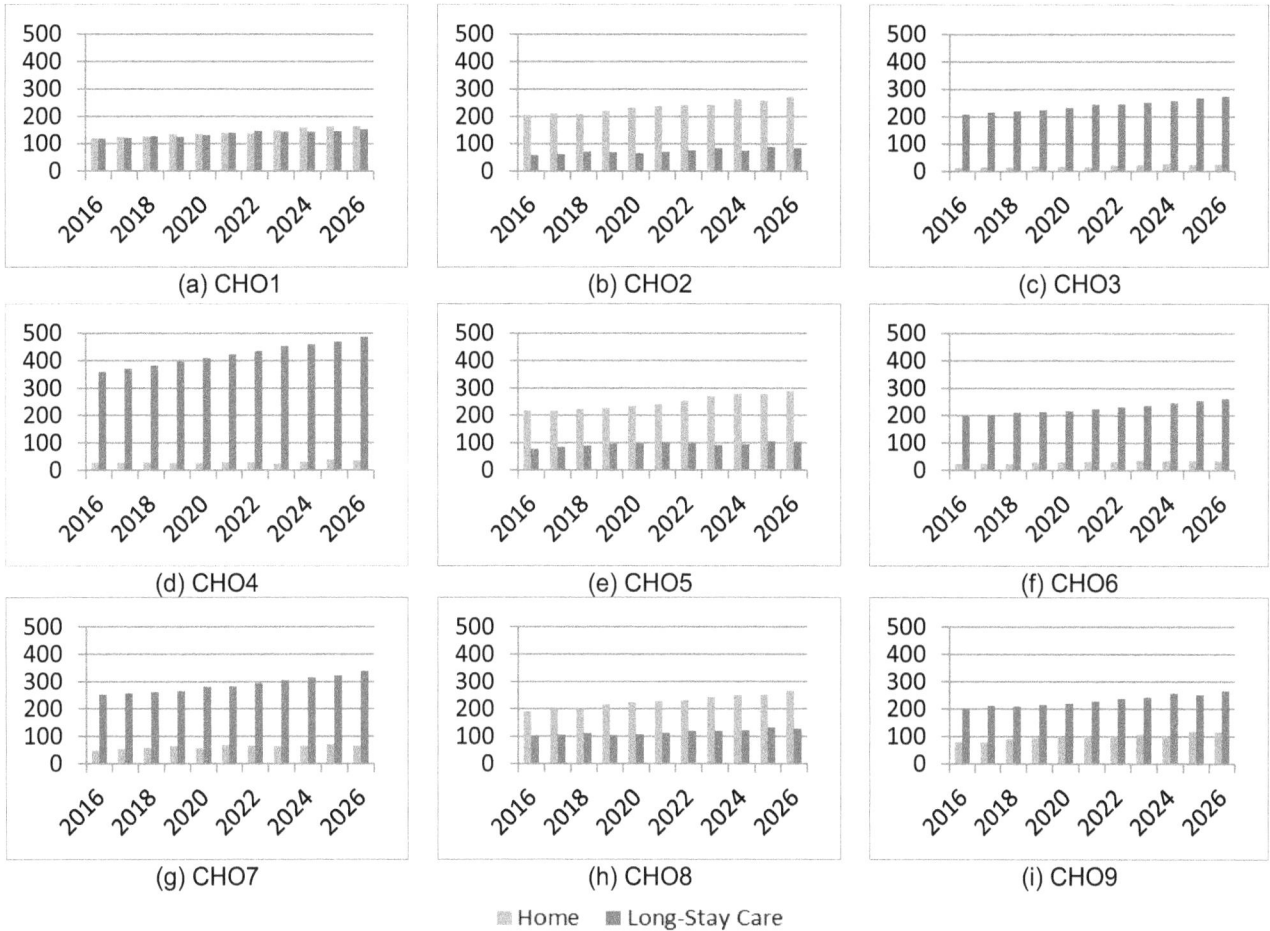

Figure 14. Predicted demand for discharge destinations with respect to the 9 CHOs individually from 2016 to 2026.

5. RESULTS & DISCUSSION

The outputs of the simulation model were interpreted in terms of the following: i) The total number of elderly patients discharged per year, and ii) The expected demand for long-stay care as a discharge destination. Figure 12 jointly plots the projections of elderly male and female patients from 2016 to 2026. As expected, the discharged female patients constantly surpassed the male ones due to the pre-set disparate rates of arrival.

Figure 13 shows the projected elderly patients with regard to the discharge destinations. The model expected that patients discharged to long-stay care can significantly be dominant over home-discharged patients. Furthermore, the demand for long-stay care was expected to keep growing over the simulated period. This expectation agreed with the official HSE report [44] that acknowledged that less than one-third of hip-fracture patients go directly home after their hospital treatment.

Figure 14 refines the understanding of the model results with respect to every CHO individually. Given the 9 sub-plots in Figure 14, it could be concluded that most CHOs can likely have significantly higher demands for long-stay care as a discharge destination. Specifically, CHO4 and CHO7 had the highest expected demand for long-stay care, which conformed with that CHO4 and CHO7 comprised the highest elderly population nation-wide (Section 4.1). On the contrary, CHO2, CHO5 and CHO8 were expected to experience higher levels of home-discharged patients, and fewer demands for long-stay care.

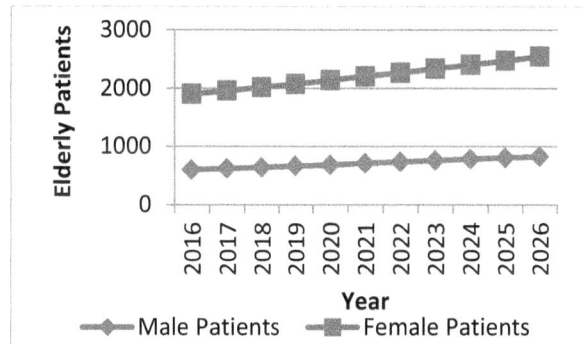

Figure 12. Projections of elderly discharged patients.

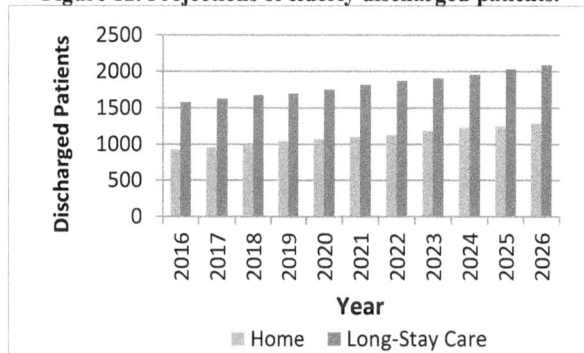

Figure 13. Projected elderly patients with respect to discharge destinations from 2016 to 2026.

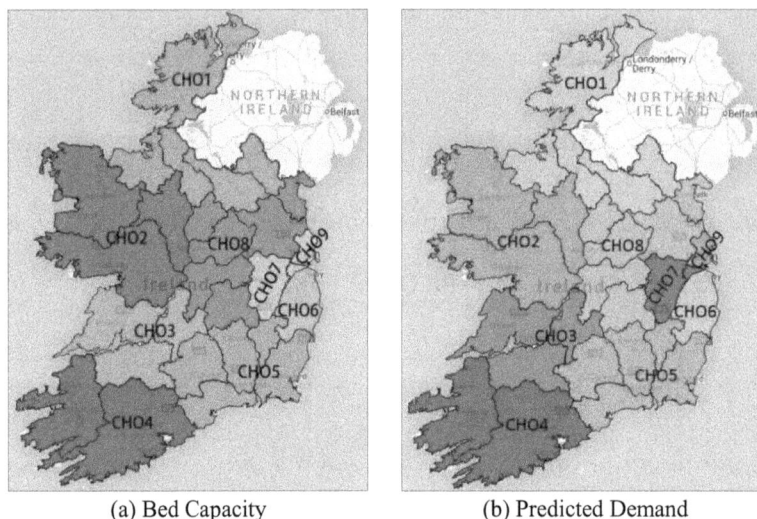

(a) Bed Capacity   (b) Predicted Demand

Figure 15. Heatmap: Bed capacity of nursing homes against predicted demand for long-stay care. Figure (a) visualises the current bed capacity of the 9 CHOs with reference to nursing homes as an example of long-stay care. Bed capacity of a given CHO is visually indicated by red (high) and green (low) in Figure (a). Figure (b) visualises the expected demand for long-stay care in every CHO. Predicted demand of a given CHO is visually indicated by red (high) and green (low) in the Figure (a). The relatively mismatched colours in Figures (a) and (b) might infer a discrepancy of the geographic distribution of nursing homes.

Further observations could be drawn in relation to the capacities of long-stay care facilities in the CHOs. Nursing homes were used as a concrete example of long-stay care resources due to the availability of quality information on their capacities nationwide (Section 4.1). However, other facilities of long-stay care may exist such as rehabilitation institutions. Comparing bed capacities of nursing homes against predicted demands, it turned out that a relative capacity-demand discrepancy might exist within some CHOs. For instance, the CHO2, CHO5 and CHO8 were predicted to experience the lowest levels of demands, though they were reported to have significantly higher bed capacities. Furthermore, the CHO4, CHO7 and CHO3 might probably be in need of higher bed capacities in the future, whereas they were predicted to have the top levels of demands for long-stay care. Figure 15 visualises a heat map of the 9 CHOs with regard to the current bed capacity and expected demand produced by the simulation model. Similarly, Figure 16 comparatively plots the bed capacity and the accumulative demand for long-stay care within every CHO.

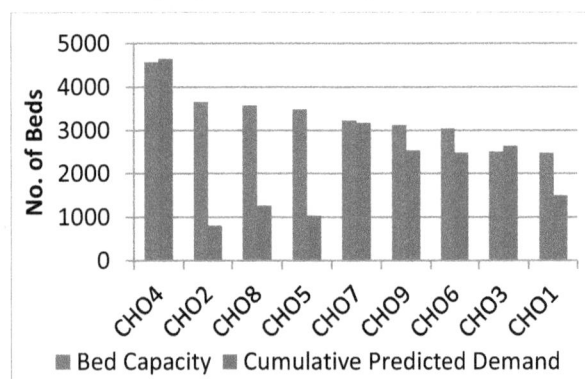

Figure 16. Capacity-demand analysis with respect to long-stay care in every CHO. The bed capacities of nursing homes are used as an example of long-stay care facilities.

6. RELATED WORK

The literature was reviewed in the context of studies that endorsed elderly care planning, particularly in Ireland. Study [41] used modeling and simulation to address elderly care pathways within the Irish healthcare sector. The developed model was used to assess financial and performance issues related to the flow of elderly patients. While the study [42] used a System Dynamics methodology in order to map the dynamic flow of elderly patients in the Irish healthcare system. The model was claimed to be useful for inspecting the outcomes of proposed policies to overcome the delayed discharge for elderly patients.

However, the literature obviously lacked similar studies with a specific focus on hip fracture care in Ireland, to the best knowledge of the authors. In addition, the literature generally laid little emphasis on endeavours that incorporated simulation–based methods and machine learning.

7. STUDY LIMITATIONS

We acknowledge the limitations of the study as follows:

- Only public acute hospitals were considered, from which the IHFD records were obtained.

- The records of the IHFD dataset did not evenly represent the 9 CHOs.

- The real data obtained by the study covered only a single year, which was 2013.

- The rate of hip fractures was assumed as a constant over the simulated interval, however it might increase or decrease in reality.

8. CONCLUSIONS

The significance and complexity of discharge planning have increased owing to the mounting challenge of population ageing. The study presented an approach that integrated simulation modeling with machine learning techniques. The incorporation of machine learning is claimed to reduce the uncertainty underlying the simulation model, in turn improving its validity and credibility for decision making.

A discrete event simulation model was developed, which modelled the elderly patient's journey from admission to discharge. Furthermore, the model endeavoured to blueprint the geographic structure of the Irish healthcare system by accurately mimicking the Community Health Organisations (CHOs). In conjunction with simulation experiments, the trained predictors guided the simulation model by making predictions on the inpatient length of stay and discharge destination.

The model outputs realised a population-based perspective of the demand for hip fracture care, regarding elderly patients in particular. The projections of elderly discharged patients were compared to the present bed capacities of nursing homes, as an ideal example of long-stay care. The results revealed that the current geographic distribution of nursing homes may not match with the projected demographic profile of elderly patients within particular regions (CHOs) in the future. Generally, the study can carry useful insights for understanding the anticipated demand for elderly care with reference to the geographic structure of the healthcare system in Ireland.

References

[1] Cohen, K.J. and Cyert, R.M., 1965. Simulation of organizational behavior. Handbook of Organizations, Rand McNally.

[2] Ashby, W.R., 1970. Analysis of the system to be modeled. The process of model building in the behavioral sciences, pp.94-114.

[3] Stanislaw, H., 1986. Tests of computer simulation validity: what do they measure?. Simulation & Games.

[4] Gershenson, C., 2001. Complex philosophy. arXiv preprint nlin/0109001.

[5] Abu-Taieh, E.M. ed., 2009. Handbook of Research on Discrete Event Simulation Environments: Technologies and Applications: Technologies and Applications. IGI Global.

[6] https://www.noca.ie/irish-hip-fracture-database, accessed on 26/12/2015.

[7] Barga, R., Fontama, V. and Tok, W.H., 2015. Predictive Analytics with Microsoft Azure Machine Learning.

[8] O'Keefe, G.E., Jurkovich, G.J. and Maier, R.V., 1999. Defining excess resource utilization and identifying associated factors for trauma victims. Journal of Trauma and Acute Care Surgery, 46(3), pp.473-478.

[9] Englert, J., Davis, K.M. and Koch, K.E., 2001. Using clinical practice analysis to improve care. Joint Commission Journal on Quality and Patient Safety, 27(6), pp.291-301.

[10] Guru, V., Anderson, G.M., Fremes, S.E., O'Connor, G.T., Grover, F.L., Tu, J.V. and Consensus, C.C.S.Q.I., 2005. The identification and development of Canadian coronary artery bypass graft surgery quality indicators. The Journal of thoracic and cardiovascular surgery, 130(5), pp.1257-e1.

[11] Brasel, K.J., Lim, H.J., Nirula, R. and Weigelt, J.A., 2007. Length of stay: an appropriate quality measure?. Archives of Surgery, 142(5), pp.461-466.

[12] Japkowicz, N. and Stephen, S., 2002. The class imbalance problem: A systematic study. Intelligent data analysis, 6(5), pp.429-449.

[13] Yang, Q. and Wu, X., 2006. 10 challenging problems in data mining research. International Journal of Information Technology & Decision Making, 5(04), pp.597-604.

[14] Japkowicz, N., 2000, July. Learning from imbalanced data sets: a comparison of various strategies. In AAAI workshop on learning from imbalanced data sets (Vol. 68, pp. 10-15).

[15] Hodge, V.J. and Austin, J., 2004. A survey of outlier detection methodologies. Artificial Intelligence Review, 22(2), pp.85-126.

[16] Sarsfield, S., 2009. The data governance imperative. IT Governance Publishing.

[17] Johansen, A., Wakeman, R., Boulton, C., Plant, F., Roberts, J. and Williams, A., 2013. National Hip Fracture Database: National Report 2013. Clinical Effectiveness and Evaluation Unit at the Royal College of Physicians.

[18] Altmann, A., Toloşi, L., Sander, O. and Lengauer, T., 2010. Permutation importance: a corrected feature importance measure. Bioinformatics, 26(10), pp.1340-1347.

[19] Law, A.M. and Kelton, W.D., 1991. Simulation modeling and analysis, 1991. New York: McGrae-Hill Inc.

[20] http://www.cso.ie/en/statistics/population/

[21] Shannon, R.E., 1975. Systems simulation: the art and science (Vol. 1). Englewood Cliffs, NJ: Prentice-Hall.

[22] British Orthopaedic Association and British Geriatric Society, The Care of Patients with Fragility Fracture ("Blue Book"), BritishOrthopaedic Association and BritishGeriatric Society, London,UK, 2007.

[23] http://www.hse.ie/eng/services/publications/corporate/CHO_Chapter_1.pdf

[24] Dodds, M.K., Codd, M.B., Looney, A. and Mulhall, K.J., 2009. Incidence of hip fracture in the Republic of Ireland and future projections: a population-based study. Osteoporosis international, 20(12), pp.2105-2110.

[25] Rosenberg, M. and Everitt, J., 2001. Planning for aging populations: inside or outside the walls. Progress in Planning, 56(3), pp.119-168.

[26] Lechler, T. and Page, B., 1999, October. DESMO-J: An object oriented discrete simulation framework in Java. In Proceedings of the 11th European Simulation Symposium (pp. 46-50).

[27] Law, A.M., 2009, December. How to build valid and credible simulation models. In Simulation Conference (WSC), Proceedings of the 2009 Winter (pp. 24-33). IEEE.

[28] Martis, M.S., 2006. Validation of simulation based models: a theoretical outlook. The Electronic Journal of Business Research Methods, 4(1), pp.39-46.

[29] Lloyd-Sherlock, P., 2000. Population ageing in developed and developing regions: implications for health policy. Social science & medicine, 51(6), pp.887-895.

[30] United Nations. World Population Ageing 2007 (United Nations, New York, 2007).

[31] Christensen, K., Doblhammer, G., Rau, R. and Vaupel, J.W., 2009. Ageing populations: the challenges ahead. The Lancet, 374(9696), pp.1196-1208.

[32] Lutz, W., Sanderson, W. and Scherbov, S., 2008. The coming acceleration of global population ageing. Nature, 451(7179), pp.716-719.

[33] Rechel, B., Grundy, E., Robine, J.M., Cylus, J., Mackenbach, J.P., Knai, C. and McKee, M., 2013. Ageing in the European union. The Lancet, 381(9874), pp.1312-1322.

[34] European Commission. 2009 Ageing report: economic and budgetary projections for the EU-27 Member States (2008–2060).Luxembourg: Office for Official Publications of the European Communities, 2009.

[35] Health Service Executive. Annual Report and Financial Statements 2014, 2014.

[36] https://www.hiqa.ie/social-care/find-a-centre/nursing-homes

[37] Cooper, C., Campion, G. and Melton Iii, L.J., 1992. Hip fractures in the elderly: a world-wide projection. Osteoporosis international, 2(6), pp.285-289.

[38] Melton, L.J., 1996. Epidemiology of hip fractures: implications of the exponential increase with age. Bone, 18(3), pp.S121-S125.

[39] Gullberg, B., Johnell, O. and Kanis, J.A., 1997. World-wide projections for hip fracture. Osteoporosis international, 7(5), pp.407-413.

[40] Ellanti, P., Cushen, B., Galbraith, A., Brent, L., Hurson, C. and Ahern, E., 2014. Improving Hip Fracture Care in Ireland: A Preliminary Report of the Irish Hip Fracture Database. Journal of osteoporosis, 2014.

[41] Ragab, M., Abo-Hamad, W. and Arisha, A., 2012. Capacity Planning for Elderly Care in Ireland Using Simulation Modeling.

[42] Rashwan, W., Ragab, M., Abo-Hamad, W. and Arisha, A., 2013, December. Evaluating policy interventions for delayed discharge: a system dynamics approach. In Proceedings of the 2013 Winter Simulation Conference: Simulation: Making Decisions in a Complex World (pp. 2463-2474). IEEE Press.

[43] http://www.hpo.ie/hipe/hipe_data_dictionary/HIPE_Data_Dictionary_2015_V7.0.pdf

[44] http://www.hse.ie/eng/services/publications/olderpeople/Executive_Summary_-_Strategy_to_Prevent_Falls_and_Fractures_in_Ireland%E2%80%99s_Ageing_Population.pdf

[45] Breiman, L., 2001. Random forests. Machine learning, 45(1), pp.5-32.

Granular Time Warp Objects

Nazzareno Marziale, Francesco Nobilia, Alessandro Pellegrini and Francesco Quaglia
nazzareno.marziale@gmail.com, f.nobilia@gmail.com, pellegrini@dis.uniroma1.it, quaglia@dis.uniroma1.it
DIAG – Sapienza, University of Rome

ABSTRACT

A recent trend has shown the relevance of PDES paradigms where simulation objects are no longer seen as fully disjoint entities only interacting via events' scheduling. Particularly, mutual cross-state access (as a form of state sharing) can represent an approach enabling the simplification of the programmer's job. In this article, we present a multi-core oriented Time Warp platform supporting so called *granular objects*, where cross-state access is transparently enabled jointly with the dynamic clustering (granulation) of objects into groups depending on the volume of mutual state accesses along phases of the model execution. Each group represents an island where activities are sequentially dispatched in timestamp order. Concurrency is still preserved by enabling the optimistic execution of the different islands. Granulated objects do not pay synchronization costs due to mutual causal inconsistencies. Also, the underlying Time Warp platform does not pay memory management (e.g. memory access tracing) overheads to determine that mutual accesses are taking place within a group. Overall, the platform transparently (and dynamically) determines a well-suited granulation of the overall model state, and a corresponding level of concurrency, depending on the actual state access pattern by the simulation code. As far as we know, this is the first study where the problem of clustering Time Warp simulation objects is addressed for the case of in-place cross-object state accesses by the application code, and where dynamic granulation of multiple objects in a larger one is supported in a fully transparent manner. We integrated our proposal in the open source ROOT-Sim platform.

Categories and Subject Descriptors

I.6.8 [**Simulation and Modeling**]: Types of Simulation—
Discrete Event, Parallel

Keywords

PDES; Multi-thread; Linux; Kernel Support; Synchronization

Permission to make digital or hard copies of all or part of this work for personal or classroom use is granted without fee provided that copies are not made or distributed for profit or commercial advantage and that copies bear this notice and the full citation on the first page. Copyrights for components of this work owned by others than ACM must be honored. Abstracting with credit is permitted. To copy otherwise, or republish, to post on servers or to redistribute to lists, requires prior specific permission and/or a fee. Request permissions from permissions@acm.org.

SIGSIM-PADS '16, May 15-18, 2016, Banff, AB, Canada

© 2016 ACM. ISBN 978-1-4503-3742-7/16/05. . . $15.00

DOI: http://dx.doi.org/10.1145/2901378.2901390

1. INTRODUCTION

Historically, Parallel Discrete Event Simulation (PDES) [9] has been based on a programming paradigm where (i) the overall simulation model state is partitioned into disjoint sub-states, each one associated with a so called simulation object (or Logical Process—LP), (ii) the memory access operations by the event-handling routine are confined within the state of the LP targeted by the event, and (iii) interactions across the LPs solely occur by the exchange of messages carrying *timestamped* simulation events.

Although this paradigm fully fits loosely-coupled parallel architectures, where LPs are executed concurrently on distributed memory systems, the sliding towards multi/many-core off-the-shelf technology has renewed challenges and opportunities in the design of shared memory oriented PDES environments (see, e.g., [6, 23, 24]).

This aspect also involves the development of innovative programming paradigms, and their associated runtime support, where the application software is no longer limited to perform per-event state access/update operations in data separation across the LPs. Rather, state-wide in-place access by event-handlers, exploiting shared memory in the underlying multi-core machine, is nowadays considered as a powerful means for improving programmability of complex models and further increasing model execution speedup [16]. Just to provide a few examples, it can avoid the coding of complex cross-LP event patterns in case some data embedded within the state of a given LP need to be known while processing an event occurring at some other LP. Also, for (very) large models, where such data awareness would involve large amounts of LPs, the possibility to directly access the target data in-place while coding the event-handlers for whatever LP would also lead to avoiding large message-exchange overhead.

Following this research trend, in this article we present the design of a multi-core oriented Time Warp PDES environment supporting so called Granular LPs (GLPs). Our proposal is based on enabling in-place access to the state of whatever LP by the event-handlers, particularly by inheriting the basic mechanisms already offered by the support presented in [16]. However, differently from such proposal, we also enable the dynamic grouping of multiple LPs, thus forming islands that are managed by the runtime PDES environment as if the modeler had specified them to represent a same (larger) object within the whole simulation model.

Overall, while we support the same PDES programming model as in [16], the granulation process leads to some major differences in the runtime behavior of the underlying Time Warp system. On the one hand, a GLP does not pay any rollback-related synchronization cost due to mutual causal inconsistencies of its member LPs, given that all of them are always scheduled sequentially and according to timestamp ordering of the events they receive as input. On the other hand, once a GLP has been dynamically formed, runtime tracing/identification of memory operations by event-handlers, which indiscriminately access the states of its members, does not need to be carried out, thus avoiding the associated costs. This occurs because GLP members do never execute concurrently, thus any event-handler accessing the overall GLP state always observes a consistent (although speculatively-generated) snapshot. Contrarily, the absence of granulation in [16] led this proposal to rely on simulation-lifetime cross-state access tracing (via an ad-hoc Linux memory management support). This is exploited to apply an explicit LPs' synchronization protocol enabling consistent snapshot access when multiple LPs' states are touched by in-place memory operations by some event-handler.

In our proposal, concurrency and the potential for exploiting model parallelism are still preserved by keeping the different GLPs—or individual LPs not involved in the dynamic granulation process—executing according to optimistic synchronization. Also, a GLP is dynamically formed only in case the runtime support determines that a group of LPs exhibits (along a specific model execution phase) significant cross-state dependencies, caused by repeated in-place accesses to their states while processing individual events. This might be the case of, e.g., an agent-based simulation model where some LP represents an individual, and other LPs represent a portion of the environment, and at a certain point multiple individuals start interacting repeatedly with the same portion of the environment—a scenario just coded via in-place access to the state of multiple LPs by some event-handler. If this is no longer the case, the GLP is un-grouped so as to slide along classical concurrent speculative execution of its members. The dynamic granulation process is driven by a self-adapting policy, which is used to determine how long a GLP should exist, given that it is expected to provide some revenue in terms of synchronization efficiency. Our policy is based on a mixture of space-efficient probabilistic data structures and machine learning.

As hinted, our proposal is specifically designed to reduce both direct (e.g., due to speculation) and indirect (e.g., due to memory access tracing) synchronization costs, as compared to the original cross-state synchronization approach in [16]. Further, it targets the reduction of the overhead when LPs are tied/untied to a given GLP. To this end, a GLP has multiple input/output queues, one for each LP belonging to it. This poses algorithmic challenges, and requires, as it will be shown, to redesign as well traditional operations characterizing the execution of a Time Warp-based simulation, such as the *schedule*, the *rollback*, and the *coasting forward* phase (in case of checkpoint-based rollback).

The remainder of this article is structured as follows. An overview of the cross-state synchronization approach is given in Section 2, so as to summarize the results from [16] which are exploited in the current proposal. In Section 3 we discuss the innovative architectural organization of a Time Warp system supporting the granulation process, and the algorithms it uses. An assessment of validity and effectiveness of our proposal is presented in Section 4. In Section 5 we discuss related work.

2. CROSS-STATE SYNCHRONIZATION RECAP

The proposal in [16] allows the event-handler of DES models developed in C technology to access (and alter) the state of multiple LPs while processing any individual event. Therefore it provides and enhanced support for model development, which does not only rely on cross-LP scheduling of events in order to code the dependencies across the different model's portions. Rather, in-place read/write operations are enabled targeting any (dynamic) memory location that represents a valid buffer included in the state of whichever concurrent LP. This type of operation is referred in [16] to as *cross-state access*.

Cross-state accesses must be supported in such a way to ensure that the state snapshot observed by the event-handler is consistent, although generated by a speculative execution. Hence, the LPs whose states are actually accessed while processing an individual event all need to figure as aligned (in logical time) to the timestamp of the event. This is achieved by encapsulating the cross-state access within an atomic action that is, in its turn, based on an ad-hoc synchronization protocol triggered on demand, if and only if a cross-state access materializes. Such a materialization is detected in [16] by relying on an advanced Linux oriented virtual memory management architecture able to track at runtime the access to the state of whichever LP.

The architecture delivers memory buffers (in reply to `malloc` requests by the application code) via a non-anonymous scheme, where the buffers destined to serve memory requests by an LP are guaranteed to fall within a memory *stock* formed by a 1GB-wide segment of contiguous virtual addresses just reserved for hosting the state of that LP. Hence, with stock-based allocation, the virtual memory pages destined to host memory buffers included in the state of an LP correspond to contiguous pages whose virtual-to-physical memory translation is associated with a single entry of the second-level x86-64 page table, which is called PDP—Page Directory Pointer.

A special device file (whose driver is loaded into the Linux kernel via an external module) is used to communicate via the `SET_VM_RANGE ioctl` command, implemented within the module, what is the range of virtual addresses associated with a given simulation object. Before CPU-dispatching an event at some LP, the worker thread in charge of the execution communicates to the kernel module what is the LP which will be activated via another `ioctl` command called `SCHEDULE_ON_PGD`. This command activates a kernel-level logic implemented in the module which installs a *sibling page table* on the `CR3` (page-table pointer) register of the CPU-core running the worker thread. The per-thread sibling page table is constructed so that initially the thread has access only to the pages destined to keep the dispatched LP state—trying to access any other LP state while processing the event generates a fault.

The fault is efficiently intercepted by the kernel module, which gives control back to the worker thread (thus, outside of the execution context of the LP, thanks to ULT support). In this way, the execution of the current event—hence of the associated LP—is interrupted, and it could be eventually restarted without worrying about any housekeeping operation which took place in the meanwhile[1]. In

---

[1]We recall that the LPs' execution contexts—including their stacks—are separated in this system.

addition to blocking the execution of the LP, the worker thread sends a *rendez-vous start* control message towards the LP whose state is the target of the intercepted memory access (cross-state) operation. Such control messages carry system-events that are silently (with respect to LPs' activities) exchanged by worker threads. System-events do not cause the actual dispatching of the target LPs for state updates, although they are incorporated into the LPs' event lists as place-marks. Independently of whether the rendez-vous start event is located in the past or future of the target LP logical time, this LP will eventually re-align its logical time to the rendez-vous timestamp either via a rollback operation, if the rendez-vous start event was a straggler, or by executing events until the rendez-vous is reached.

When an LP reaches a rendez-vous start event in logical time, it is temporarily blocked, and the Time Warp platform sends back to the LP originating the cross-state access a rendez-vous ack control message, which puts this LP back to the *ready* state. In this way, the event that was temporarily blocked due to cross-state access interception could be restarted from the machine instruction which caused the fault. Nevertheless, this time, when the `SCHEDULE_ON_PGD` command is executed before reactivating the LP, the kernel module will be instructed to open the access to the memory stocks of both the LPs involved in the cross-state access, thus allowing in-place memory access by the event-handler to both their states. This scenario could be repeated more than once per each event, thus synchronizing multiple LPs and opening the access to all their states. When the execution of an event that caused a cross-state synchronization is completed, the worker thread sends to all the LPs that were involved in the synchronization a *rendez-vous unblock* control message, which brings all them back into the ready state, for normal processing.

By the above description, the materialization of a cross-state access leads to a non-persistent relation between two or more LPs. In fact, given that cross-state synchronization is operated on a per-event basis, after the finalization of the event that led to cross-state accesses, the involved LPs start again executing alone along their own simulation trajectories. However, in general contexts, a cross-state access by the application code could be the evidence that two (or more) LPs are actually starting to execute in a synergistic way, in terms of overall simulation model execution trajectory. In this scenario, the cross-state synchronization protocol as introduced in [16] might require the exchange of a large number of control messages—which in turn might produce a large amount of rollbacks as well. Our innovative LPs' granulation process aims at avoiding adverse runtime synchronization dynamics associated with such a synergic execution of the LPs, while still supporting the flexible programming model offering the possibility to perform in-place accesses to whatever state information by the event-handler.

3. GRANULAR LOGICAL PROCESSES

3.1 The Grouping Algorithm

Our support for instantiating and managing GLPs inherits the memory management architecture presented in [16]. However, the materialization of cross-state accesses by the application software, beyond being used for synchronizing the involved LPs, is also used to determine a relation across them, which will drive the formation (or fading) of GLPs.

As hinted, we consider the fact that two LPs are involved in a cross-state synchronization as a possible materialization of a synergistic execution phase. To keep track of this, we rely on a matrix $LpDependencies$, the size of which is $numLPs \times numLPs$. Every time that a cross-state access involving LP_i and LP_j is detected at runtime according to the technique described in Section 2, we increment the value of the two matrix elements $LpDependencies[i,j]$ and $LpDependencies[j,i]$. $LpDependencies$ represents therefore a matrix of cross-state dependency counters, where every element (i,j) tells how many cross-state dependencies involving LP_i and LP_j have been detected along some execution phase[2].

The $LpDependencies$ matrix can be mapped to an incidence matrix of a directed multigraph $G = (V, E)$ where the set of vertices V keeps the identifiers of all the LPs currently running in the system, and the set of edges E is defined as $E = \{\{i,j\} : i, j \in V \wedge LpDependencies[i,j] > 0\}$. Nevertheless, before converting it to an actual incidence matrix, we apply some filtering aimed at reducing the possibility of capturing spurious cross-state relations (depending on the events' logic). This is because the GLP concept targets the runtime optimization achievable in scenarios where actual synergistic execution due to cross-state accesses is statistically significant. Hence, cross-state relations which are detected only seldom should not be taken into account for driving the dynamic formation of GLPs. Overall, we use a threshold τ_{dep} to filter out all the spurious cross-state dependencies, thus building a so called *cross-state dependency multigraph* $G = \{\{i,j\} : i, j \in V \wedge LpDependencies[i,j] \geq \tau_{dep}\}$ and deriving its incidence matrix which we refer to as IMG. If no edge exists in G between two LPs, say LP_i and LP_j, then we set the value of the IMG element (i,j) to the special value $\perp$. These data structures are exploited to determine the formation of GLPs according to the following scheme.

Periodically (say after n cycles of GVT computation) IMG is accessed to determine what is the highest value of cross-state access counts for each LP_k thus determining the index:

$$MaxDep_k = \max_{i \in [0, numLPs-1], i \neq k} \{IMG[k,i]\}$$

where the element $\perp$ is assumed to be the lowest value in the domain where the maximum is searched. These indices are used to build a so called $LpGranulation$ vector, which is a vector of tuples each one structured as $\langle MaxDep_k, group \rangle$ $\forall k \in [0, numLPs - 1]$. Initially, the value $group$ for all the elements of the vector is set to the special value $\perp$. This configuration tells that LP_k, associated with the k-th row of the $LpGranulation$ vector, has its highest dependency counter set to $MaxDep_k$ and belongs to the special group $\perp$, meaning that LP_k still belongs to no group.

This construction transforms the multigraph G into another oriented multigraph $\bar{G}$ such that the set $\bar{V} \equiv V$, but if $\{i,j\} \in \bar{V}$, then $\{i,k\} \notin \bar{V}$ $\forall k \neq j$. This means that every node $i \in \bar{V}$ has at most one edge connecting it to another node $j \in \bar{V}$, with $i \neq j$, and by construction $j = MaxDep_i$.

---

[2]This matrix is a logical construction, while the actual counters have been embedded in our implementation within LP control blocks, which keep recoverable information. Consequently, updates if the matrix entries associated with rolled back computation are discarded.

A graph visiting algorithm on $\bar{G}$ is then used to determine the formation of GLPs as groups of LPs[3]. We iterate over all indices $k \in [0, numLPs - 1]$, and for each value k we execute the recursive function REGROUP($LpGranulation$, k, $\bot$) shown in Algorithm 1. The goal of this recursive function is to determine whether the selected LP already belongs to a group. In the negative case, if the passed value for the group ID is not $\bot$, then the target LP is aggregated into the passed group (line 6), otherwise a new group is created, which is associated with the ID of the passed LP (line 8). In the positive case, no action is taken for the current LP, and the group the LP belongs to is returned (line 3). Both cases (namely, lines 6 and 8), are associated with *tentative groups*, which could be later confirmed or discarded. If the LP was associated with a tentative group, a recursive call is issued to REGROUP() (line 11), selecting as the target LP the *MaxDep* one of the current LP, and passing the ID of the group which the current LP belongs to. The group ID of the current LP is then updated with the return value of this call, which is done so as to backwards propagate the creation of new groups or the agglomeration to existing ones (line 13). Line 11 can either confirm a tentative group for a given LP, or supersede it with a different one.

Algorithm 1 GLP Construction

```
1:  procedure REGROUP(LpGranulation GLP, int LPid, int group)
2:      if GLP[LPid].group ≠⊥ then
3:          return GLP[LPid].group
4:      end if
5:      if group ≠⊥ then
6:          GLP[LPid].group ← group
7:      else
8:          GLP[LPid].group ← LPid
9:      end if
10:     if GLP[LPid].MaxDep ≠⊥ then
11:         GLP[LPid].group = REGROUP(GLP, GLP[LPid].MaxDep,
    GLP[LPid].group)
12:     end if
13:     return GLP[LPid].group
14: end procedure
```

We show in Figure 1 an example execution of Algorithm 1 for a scenario with 8 LPs. In the example, LP_0 exhibits a large number of cross-state dependencies involving LP_3, LP_1 shows no cross-state dependency, LP_2 is dependent on LP_6, LP_3 has no dependencies, LP_4 depends on LP_1, LP_5 depends on LP_6, LP_6 depends on LP_4.

Algorithm 1 is first invoked on LP_0, which belongs to no group (i.e., the *group* field of row 0 of *LpGranulation* is set to $\bot$), and therefore a new group with ID set to 0 is created (line 8). Then, since $MaxDep_0 = 3$, line 11 is executed as REGROUP($LpGranulation$, 3, 0). Therefore, for LP_3, the group is set to 0 (line 5), and the value 0 is returned again at line 13, confirming the tentative group. Thus, LP_0 and LP_3 now both belong to group 0, say to a same GLP. The execution then selects LP_1 which does not belong to any group: a new group with ID set to 1 is created. Then, LP_2 is selected, which is the most interesting execution case of this example. First, this LP is set to tentative group 2 (line 8), and then the graph visiting selects LP_6. Since LP_6 belongs to no group, the new tentative group with ID 6 is created, and the visiting goes to LP_4, leading to the creation of a new tentative group with ID 4. When the visit reaches LP_1, line 3 is executed, as LP_1 already belongs to group

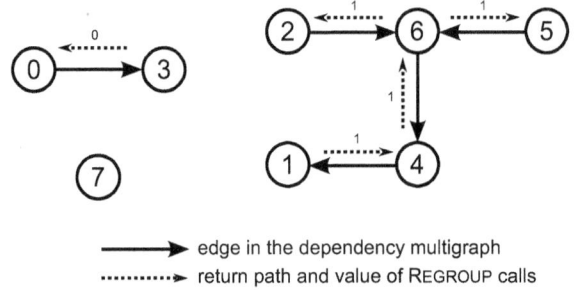

Figure 1: REGROUP **execution with 8 LPs.**

1. Therefore, all tentative groups for LPs 4, 6, and 2 are backwards superseded by group 1 (as per lines 11 and 13). The actual execution for LPs 3 to 7 can be trivially deduced from the already analyzed execution steps. It is interesting to note that LP_7 belongs to a group formed by a single LP.

Once the graph visiting algorithm is completed, every LP belongs to a group. We note that in the scenario where no dependencies at all were detected (namely, all the elements in *LpDependencies* are found to be set to a value smaller than the threshold value τ_{dep}), Algorithm 1 creates $numLPs$ groups, each one keeping a single LP. In this case, our GLP scheme boils down to a traditional Time Warp execution, although augmented with cross-state synchronization support according to [16].

Given that groups are defined after an observation period where the materialization of cross-state dependencies has been tracked, a scenario where such cross-state dependencies, although playing a role in the construction of the G graph, were spanned over no longer actual execution phases could arise. In other words, the locality of the dependencies might vary over time according to a non-uniform distribution leading to the identification of synergistic executions no longer in place at a given point in time.

In order to capture this scenario, we have coupled the *LpDependencies* matrix with a matrix keeping timestamps values, called *TimeDependencies*[4], which records at the element (i, j) the latest wall-clock time at which the corresponding counter in *LpDependencies* was incremented. Thus, we resort to an additional threshold called $\tau_{freshness}$ which is used when building the incidence matrix for the dependency multigraph G. In particular, if a given counter element (i, j) is higher than τ_{dep}, then an edge (i, j) is added to E if, and only if, $CurrentTime - TimeDependencies[i, j] < \tau_{freshness}$. In this way, stale interactions are filtered out.

By the algorithm structure, we guarantee that if a GLP is formed, then it contains sets of LPs whose cross-state dependencies have been (recently) observed to be more intense than the ones observed for LPs that belong to different groups.

Clearly, GLPs as defined by the presented algorithm are abstractions, and need to be finally managed by the runtime system according to specific rules which we discuss in the next section. The discussion and the proposed GLPs' management approach will also cope with scenarios of underparallelism, where less GLPs than worked threads would be generated (as a corner case) by blindly running the presented

---

[3]From now on we will use the terms GLP and group, or GLP ID and group ID, interchangeably.

[4]This second matrix is still managed so as to make its entries recoverable in rollback phases.

grouping algorithm without taking into account the available level of parallelism in the underlying PDES platform.

3.2 Management of GLPs

After the graph visiting algorithm is completed, we consider the groups as *determined*, but not yet active—we say that the groups are not *revealed* yet. Revealing a group requires some more actions to be taken since the execution of the LPs is asynchronous, just like prescribed by the Time Warp algorithm. Hence we need to put the LPs forming a determined GLP on phase. This task is carried out according to the following scheme.

Once a GLP, say $\mathcal{G}$, is determined, the input queues of all the LPs belonging to it are examined. We recall that every LP is associated with a last (speculatively) processed event[5], referred to as bound event, which is the last correctly executed event in the speculative portion of the simulation trajectory of that LP. For each $LP_k \in \mathcal{G}$, the event e_k, associated with timestamp T_{e_k} which is the event next to LP_k's bound is selected[6]. From this pool of events, we determine the *group revelation bound* as the event $\hat{e}$ such that $T_{\hat{e}} = \max_{k \in \mathcal{G}}\{e_k\}$. Once this event—which is the next event farthest in the simulation time future—is executed at the corresponding LP, we consider the group as *revealed*.

Nevertheless, once a GLP is determined, some preliminary steps are immediately taken by the worker threads in order to CPU-schedule the events occurring at the GLP members. In other words, every operation carried out by worker threads somehow considers groups of LPs, rather than individual LPs. This is achieved by letting each worker thread receive a temporary binding of a set of LP groups, depending on the total workload of the LPs in the groups, according to the load-sharing scheme proposed in [22], which we inherit in our Time Warp implementation supporting GLPs.

Assuming, as commonly done in literature, that the CPU-scheduling operation by the worker thread works according to the Smallest-Timestamp-First (STF) policy, all the LPs in any GLP are guaranteed to execute their events in a timestamp ordered fashion (since they are all bound to a single worker thread). We can therefore augment the notion of a group $\mathcal{G}$ by introducing the *group bound*, which is the last processed event by any LP_k belonging to $\mathcal{G}$. The group bound advances whenever any LP executes an event, and goes back whenever a straggler event is received and a rollback operation is required involving elements in $\mathcal{G}$. When a group is determined (but not yet revealed) we set the group bound to the oldest LP bound in the group. When an event is executed at a certain LP of a group, both the LP bound and the group bound advance to the next event.

As mentioned before, a group is revealed whenever $\hat{e}$ is executed. With the notion of group bound, this means that a group is revealed when the group bound corresponds to $\hat{e}$. At this point the members of the group do no more execute as individual entities, rather as a single entity, say the GLP they form. Referring to the cross-state access model described in Section 2, from a technical point of view this means that upon the schedule operation of any LP in the GLP, the `SCHEDULE_ON_PGD` command receives as input the IDs of all the LPs belonging to the corresponding group,

---

[5]This might correspond to the INIT event of the simulation in case no model specific event was ever scheduled for that LP.

[6]If LP_k has no event next to the bound, we consider its bound.

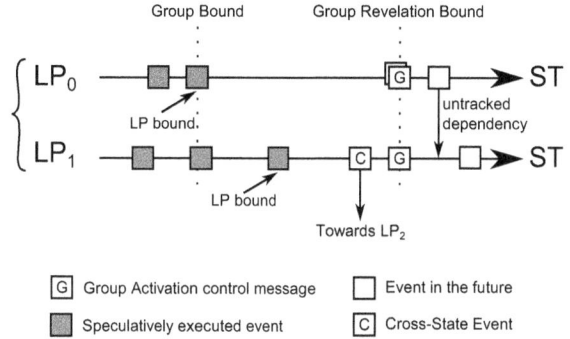

Figure 2: Revelation of a group: need for synchronization.

so that the states of all of them can be accessed without the need for tracing memory accesses and synchronizing the execution (given that the snapshot associated with the union of these states has a logical time compliant with the timestamp of the CPU-scheduled event destined to some GLP member—although the snapshot is generated speculatively). In case of contemporary events within a GLP, any tie-breaking function (see, e.g., [13]) could be applied at GLP level.

A particular case might arise, related to the revelation of a group. Consider the scenario depicted in Figure 2. A group is composed of two LPs, namely LP_0 and LP_1, whose next events are at times $T_0 > T_1$. Therefore, $\hat{e}$ is selected as the next event of LP_0 at time T_0. Since the group is determined but not revealed yet, the STF-based scheduler selects LP_1 for execution. The next event generates a cross-state dependency, which is still tracked (we recall that, until a group is not revealed, the forward execution phase is similar to the traditional Time Warp with cross-state synchronization). This cross-state dependency is materialized towards some LP which is outside the group, say LP_2, and there is no limit in the amount of wall-clock time to wait for LP_2 to send a rendez-vous ack control message. In the meanwhile the speculative execution continues, and LP_0 is selected for event processing (we recall that the LP blocked for synchronization is temporarily skipped by the STF-based scheduling policy, as described in [16]). LP_0 executes $\hat{e}$, thus the group is revealed and the execution starts according to the GLP logic: any LP has access to all the states of the LPs belonging to the group. LP_1 is still blocked waiting for the rendez-vous ack control message. While processing its next event, LP_0 generates an untracked dependency, namely it accesses LP_1's state with no detection by the cross-state access tracking system. While this is the goal of the GLP abstraction, this execution is incorrect since LP_1 has not completed the execution of its event (it's blocked waiting for a rendez-vous ack control message), and therefore the memory access by LP_0 does not see a consistent state.

To overcome this issue, we augment the logic associated with the determination of the group revelation bound. In particular, after having selected $\hat{e}$, a *group-activation control message* is sent towards all the LPs in the group. Additionally, each group is associated with a *group state*, part of the *group control block*[7]. This group state is associated with a

---

[7]The *group control block* is a per-group data structure which keeps all the control information related to it—we will fill

61

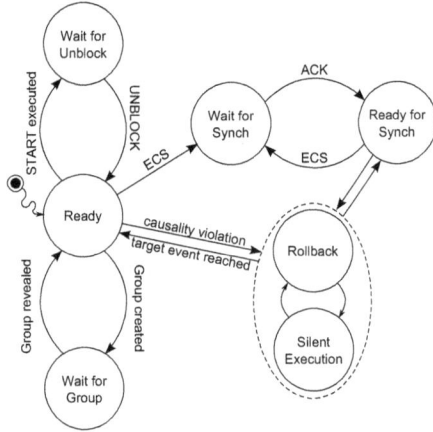

Figure 3: State machine for groups.

state machine which, as we will see later, determines the execution cycle of a group. Once a group is determined, it starts in the *wait-for-group* state. We note as well that the corner case where all LPs in a determined group have no event next to the bound leads to selectling as the group-revelation bound the timestamp associated with the bound event farthest in the simulation time. This wait-for-group state is associated with an *activation-bound counter*, again placed in the group control block and initially set to the number of LPs in the group. Whenever some LP belonging to the group reaches the group-activation control message, the simulation kernel moves it to the block state (so that no other event is processed by it until the group is revealed), and the activation-bound counter is decreased. Thus, if this counter reaches zero, it means that all the LPs in the GLP are synchronized to the revelation bound. At this point, the worker thread sets the group and all its LPs as ready. From now on, the scheduler will rely on the group state to drive the activities of the group, hence of the GLP. In particular, whenever a cross-state dependency is materialized towards some LP belonging to a different group, the whole GLP goes into the wait-for-synch state. Similarly, all the other states characterizing the original cross-state synchronization protocol in [16] are mapped to the GLP state. The state machine for a group is shown in Figure 3.

The overall logic to compute and install groups is reported in Algorithm 2. For the sake of performance, it is devised mostly as a non-blocking algorithm [11], except for a final synchronization point where all the worker threads hit a barrier. The idea behind this algorithm is that while one thread (which we refer to as the *master thread*, as the check at line 6 indicates) computes the new groups, it is pointless for the other worker threads to wait for this task to complete. Rather they can keep on processing simulation events. To let other worker threads continue processing, we rely on counters which described the *group determination era*, namely a global shared counter (*group_era*) and a set of thread-private counters (*my_group_era*). When the master thread starts computing the new GLPs, the new group control blocks (which keep as well pointers to LP-related information) are computed on a global data structure. When the GLPs are all determined, via repeated calls to REGROUP(), this data structure with the relevant fields during the forthcoming discussion.

the global *group_era* counter is incremented (line 10). At every main simulation loop cycle, all the other worker threads compare the value of *group_era* with their private value of *my_group_era* (line 16), and only if it is incremented they start installing the groups (line 20, for other worker threads). In this way, even though the GLPs' determination procedure takes a bit of time, the speculative execution can continue at other worker threads. Installing groups requires all the worker threads to make a private copy of the shared group control blocks on thread-private storage, and rebinding the LPs belonging to their groups on them. This algorithm requires an additional modification, related to the determination of $\hat{e}$. In fact, this should be done by the worker threads only after that the GLPs have been bound to them (lines 14 and 22). The thread barrier at the end of the algorithm is required so as to ensure that when the new GLPs are determined, no worker thread restarts executing events before all the worker threads have a coherent view on what LPs they are in charge of CPU-scheduling.

Algorithm 2 GLP Management Algorithm

```
 1: new_LP_groups[]
 2: LP_groups[] (thread-private)
 3: group_era
 4: my_group_era (thread-private)
 5: procedure GROUPCOMPUTE( )
 6:     if MASTERTHREAD( ) then
 7:         for i ∈ [0, numLPs − 1] do
 8:             REGROUP(LpGranulation, i, ⊥)
 9:         end for
10:         group_era ← group_era + 1
11:         SANITIZEGROUPS( )
12:         INSTALLGROUP( )
13:         THREADBARRIER( )
14:         Compute Group Revelation Bounds for all bound groups
15:     else
16:         if my_group_era == group_era then
17:             return
18:         end if
19:         my_group_era ← group_era
20:         INSTALLGROUP( )
21:         THREADBARRIER( )
22:         Compute Group Revelation Bounds for all bound groups
23:     end if
24: end procedure
```

An additional operation is required for avoiding under-parallelism in the model execution. In particular, it could be the case that due to the detected cross-state dependencies the number of determined GLPs according to the algorithm devised in Section 3.1 is smaller that the total number of available worker threads. To avoid under-parallelism scenarios, the master thread executes the SANITIZEGROUPS() routine (line 11), which takes care of this. In particular, if the number of GLPs $\mathcal{NG}$ is smaller than the available number of worker threads C, additional $C - \mathcal{NG}$ groups are instantiated. To determine which LPs should fall into these new groups, the *LpDependencies* matrix is scanned, so as to determine what are the LPs with the smallest number of interactions, and they are taken out of their determined groups according to a greedy approach.

An alternative approach to cope with discrepancies between C and $\mathcal{NG}$ would be the one of dynamically shrinking the amount of available worker threads. This would not be a means to avoid under-parallelism with respect to the amount of worker threads (e.g. the amount of CPU-cores potentially available within the hardware platform), rather for driving the level of parallelism (hence the actual synchronization dynamics) exclusively on the basis of cross-state dependen-

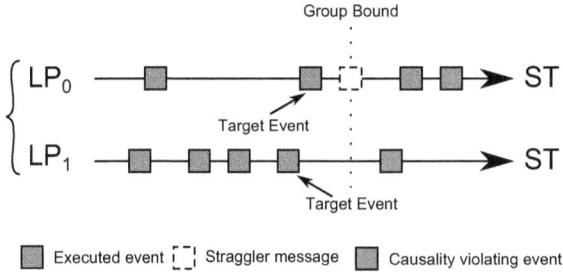

Figure 4: Group rollback.

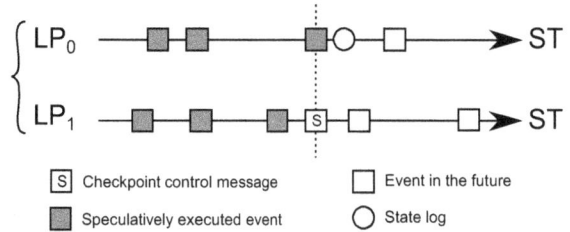

Figure 6: Group checkpoint control messages.

3.3 Managing Rollbacks

Concerning the reception of straggler messages, the execution of the rollback operation must take into account GLPs, rather than single LPs. In fact, a straggler must rollback the entire GLP, as shown in Figure 4. In particular, in the depicted example, LP_0 receives a straggler message keeping event e at timestamp T_e, which is smaller than the bound of both LP_0 and LP_1. We note that rolling back as well LP_1 in this case is not an option. In fact, nothing prevents the received straggler to manifest a cross-state dependency when executed in forward mode. Nevertheless, since both LPs belong to the same group, LP_0 has direct access to LP_1's simulation state. Therefore, if LP_1 is not rolled back as well, LP_0 would see an inconsistent snapshot, related to a simulation time in the future.

Whenever a straggler message e_{str} is received, associated with timestamp T_{str}, the GLP's state is set to the *rollback* state, meaning that a causality violation was detected. At this point, all the LPs that are members of the GLP must rollback to a previous consistent simulation state. The first task is therefore to identify such a consistent state. If we consider a GLP $\mathcal{G}$ composed of $|\mathcal{G}|$ LPs, we select from each $LP_i, i \in [0, |\mathcal{G} - 1|]$ the *target event* $\bar{e}_i$ associated with a timestamp $T_{\bar{e}_i} < T_{str}$. A *group-consistent* simulation state for $\mathcal{G}$ is the state $\bar{S}_{\mathcal{G}} = \bigcup_{i=0}^{|\mathcal{G}|-1} S_i$ such that each S_i keeps the effects of the execution of all the events in the i-th input queue up to the execution of $\bar{e}_i$, included.

The goal of the rollback operation is thus to realign the LP bound of every $LP_i, i \in [0, |\mathcal{G} - 1|]$ to $\bar{e}_i$. In case the simulation engine bases its rollback operation upon checkpoint/restore primitives, it would appear sufficient to select at each LP_i the simulation state checkpoint S_i^t such that $t < T_{str}$, and then execute the coasting forward phase. Unfortunately, this simple solution could be easily proven wrong in a twofold way. Consider, in fact, the example shown in Figure 5, where GLP $\mathcal{G}$ is already revealed. The first anomaly is related to the way the coasting forward phase is usually carried out. In fact, according to [12], the traditional coasting forward phase leads the LP to silently reprocess events until the simulation state is realigned to the desired point. Referring to Figure 5, this means that LP_0 is selected, its checkpoint is restored, and events e_1, e_2, and e_3 are reprocessed. Then, LP_1 is selected, its state is restored as well, and events e_4, e_5, and e_6 are silently replayed. The problem is related to the fact that e_5 generates a cross-state dependency towards LP_0. Since the group is already revealed, dependency detection is disabled across the two involved LPs, and LP_1

directly accesses LP_0's state. Nevertheless, since LP_0 has already reprocessed e_3, LP_1 observes an inconsistent snapshot, in a way which goes undetected. The second anomaly is similar in spirit, but is actually related to the replay of e_1 at LP_0. In fact, e_1 generates a cross-state dependency towards LP_1, but: i) LP_1 has not yet restored its previous checkpoint, and ii) even if the checkpoint were already restored, it would be associated with a simulation state farther in simulation time.

To solve these inconsistencies, two changes to the traditional Time Warp operations should be actuated. First, a *group-log* operation should be supported in case of checkpoint-based rollback of GLPs, which is depicted in Figure 6. In particular, the checkpointing period χ should be evaluated at the GLP level, so that any data structure required to keep track of how many events have been processed since the last log should be kept in the group control block. Once the checkpointing system detects that a state checkpoint should be taken, a copy of the LP's state at which the last event was executed is immediately taken. Additionally, a *checkpoint control message* is sent towards all the other LPs in the group. Once the other LPs in the group are scheduled, this control message is found in the input queue, and the simulation kernel immediately takes a checkpoint state. The control message can be immediately discarded, as checkpoints are ephemeral and do not survive a rollback operation to a lower logical time—therefore a checkpoint control message should be never replayed during a coasting forward phase. In this way, whenever a checkpoint is selected during a rollback operation, it is guaranteed that any other LP in a given GLP has a checkpoint associated with the same simulation time instant, thus preventing the above second anomaly to occur[8]. This is a necessary condition in case of a rollback, and must be ensured as well in the case the group has just been determined. To this end, the execution of a group-activation control message involves as well taking a state snapshot.

As for the first anomaly, it arises from the fact that a GLP must be considered as a unique object, although associated with multiple input queues (the input queues of its member LPs). Therefore, the anomaly can be tackled by replaying events according to their timestamp order in a GLP coasting

---

[8]Clearly, the actual checkpoint operation can be optimized using common literature techniques such as incremental checkpointing ones [18, 19, 25], which might fit larger grain LPs, just like GLPs. In our implementation, and in the presented experimental study, we rely on a baseline periodic non-incremental checkpointing scheme. A deeper study of the interactions between the GLP concept and optimized checkpoint/restore schemes, or even reverse computing schemes for state recoverability (see, e.g., [5, 7]), is planned as future work.

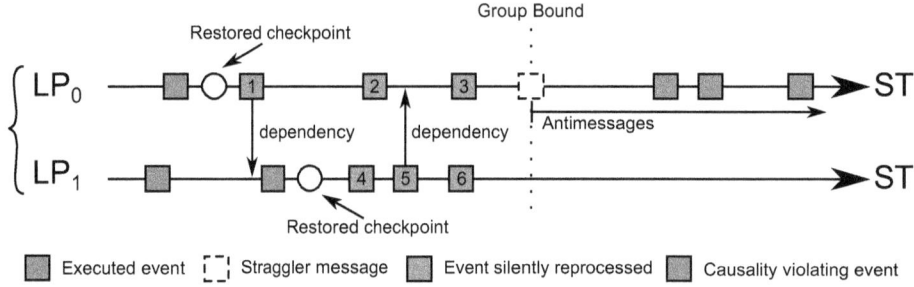

Figure 5: Inconsistent execution of traditional rollback/coasting forward phase with active groups.

forward pahse, independently of the LP queue in which they are found. To this end, the traditional STF scheduler can be used during the GLP silent execution phase. This means that the actual silent reprocessing of the events is carried out by the same scheduling operation that is used in forward execution mode, although this time operating at GLP level. To prevent that duplicate messages are sent by LPs, the whole group is moved to the *silent execution* state. In this way, whenever some LP generates a new event destined to any LP in the system, this event is simply discarded—it was already sent before. To determine when the group should leave the silent execution state and enter again the ready state, it is sufficient to check when the group bound is reached. At that point, all the events involved in the GLP coasting forward figure as already reprocessed. An example of this type of execution is depicted in Figure 7, where events e_1, e_2, e_3, e_4, and e_5 are processed in the correct order by the STF scheduler. Event e_3 is involved in a cross-state dependency, but it anyhow observes a consistent GLP snapshot.

In case a rollback operation falls before a GLP is revealed—which is detected by checking if the timestamp of a straggler message falls before the group revelation bound—the group is brought back to the wait-for-group state, so that cross-state dependencies are again runtime tracked according to the original proposal in [16].

3.4 Lifetime of GLPs

So far we have discussed our GLP proposal in terms of group determination, activation, and speculative execution. A question which should be still answered is related to the lifetime of a group: how long should a GLP exist in a given simulation run? While detecting when a synergistic execution starts could be easy, thanks to the runtime tracking of cross-state dependencies when LPs are not granulated, determining when such a phase ends is a non-trivial achievement, given the fact that when a group is revealed, cross-state dependencies are no longer traced (in fact, memory access to any state of the LPs belonging to the group is directly allowed by the runtime system to the worker thread that is in charge of managing the GLP). To this end, when a group is created, a simulation-time interval $\delta_{\mathcal{G}}$ is determined. This interval is computed as the average simulation-time increment that the model reaches in a given GVT phase. $\delta_{\mathcal{G}}$ is therefore a parameter which depends on the simulation model and its current execution phase, which captures the "speed" at which the parallel simulation is being carried out. As a first estimation, we set a GLP lifetime to $L_{\mathcal{G}} = k_{\mathcal{G}} \cdot \delta_{\mathcal{G}}$, where $k_{\mathcal{G}}$ is a per-GLP value which is initially set to 3.

Therefore, whenever a group is detected, we immediately schedule a *group-untie control message* to all the LPs in the GLP at simulation time $T_u = GVT + L_{\mathcal{G}}$, where GVT is the GVT value which was reduced when the group was detected. This event is associated with an additional counter in the group control block, which is initially set to the number of LPs in the GLP. Whenever such an event is executed by a LP (still at platform level, with no real dispatching of the application code), the counter is decremented, and when it reaches zero the group is considered as *untied*. LPs belonging to an *untied* group could be mapped to different worker threads when a LP rebinding phase is executed, and they again rely on the traditional Time Warp protocol, augmented with cross-state access tracking as in the original proposal in [16]. The group-untie control message should be kept in the input queue, as its effects are not transient: a rollback operation targeting a simulation-time instant which falls before the group-untie moment must re-activate the group, and therefore these control messages might be replayed.

This first estimation of $L_{\mathcal{G}}$ clearly needs to be improved at runtime. In fact, a synergistic execution phase which led to tying a number of LPs in a GLP could be either shorter or longer. To this end, whenever a group is determined, we generate a sort of *group fingerprint*, which is able to capture the size and the LPs which are belonging to the GLP. This fingerprint is based on a Bloom filter [2] using 3 hash functions, which is a space-efficient probabilistic data structure, telling whether an element is a member of a set. When a group is determined at turn i, we compute the Bloom filter B_i. At the next step, when groups are determined again, for each group we compute the Bloom filter B_{i+1}. Note that, by Algorithm 1, if the dependencies do not change significantly, the same LPs are tied into the same GLP. Therefore, we can compute the approximation of the intersection of the two Bloom filters according to the result in [20] as:

$$-\frac{m \ln\left[1 - \frac{X_i}{m}\right]}{k} - \frac{m \ln\left[1 - \frac{X_{i+1}}{m}\right]}{k} + \frac{m \ln\left[1 - \frac{X_i | X_{i+1}}{m}\right]}{k} \tag{1}$$

where m is the size of the filters, k is the number of hash functions (3 in our case), X_i is the number of bits set in the i-th filter. $X_i | X_{i+1}$ denotes the bitwise OR between the two filters. Counting the number of bits set in a given word (a problem also know as the *population count*) could be a costly operation. There are nevertheless specific hardware supports for this (e.g., the `popcnt` instruction on modern x86 processors) or extremely optimized software routines for this [14].

64

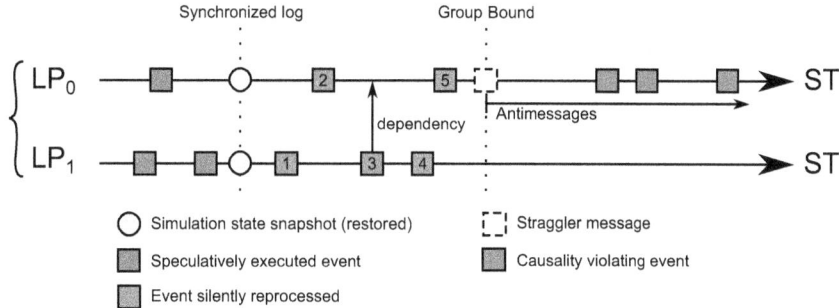

Figure 7: Group-rollback operation.

This number is an estimation of how much two instances of a GLP associated with a given ID are different[9]. We set the threshold τ_{dif}, which is used to apply a hill climbing algorithm to self-tune the value $k_\mathcal{G}$ of the group in the following way:

$$k'_\mathcal{G} = \begin{cases} k_\mathcal{G} \cdot (1 + \alpha) & \text{if } dif_\mathcal{G} \geq \tau_{dif} \\ k_\mathcal{G} \cdot (1 - \alpha) & \text{otherwise} \end{cases} \quad (2)$$

where $\alpha \in [0, 1]$ is a tuning parameter which tells how fast the value $k_\mathcal{G}$ should be adapted, and $dif_\mathcal{G}$ is the outcome by Equation (1). On the basis of Equation (2), GLPs last longer in case they don't change very much, while they are untied more frequently in case the synergistic phases are short.

4. EXPERIMENTAL STUDY

We have implemented the support for GLPs within the ROOT-Sim [21] package[10], an open source Time Warp-based general purpose simulation platform hosting simulation models developed using the C programming language. This platform already offers the baseline support for cross-state synchronization as presented in [16].

In this section we provide experimental data achieved by testing our proposal running the implementation of a multi-robot exploration and mapping simulation model, as developed in [15] according to the results in [8]. In this model, a group of robots is set out into an unknown space, with the goal of fully exploring it, while acquiring data from sensors (e.g., cameras, lasers, ...) which are used to map the environment. The robots are equipped with enough processing power to elaborate the sensors data online (thus, the map is constructed during the exploration), so as to allow them to rely on the acquired knowledge to drive the exploration in a more efficient way. Specifically, whenever a robot has to make a decision about which direction should be taken to carry on the exploration, it is done by relying on the notion of *exploration frontier*. By keeping a representation of the explored world, the robot is able to detect which is the closest unexplored area which it can reach, computes the fastest way to reach it and continues the exploration.

The robots explore independently of each other until one coincidentally detects another robot. Whenever two robots enter a proximity region, they perform three different actions: i) they use their sensors to estimate their mutual physical position—recall that they are just in *proximity*; ii)

they verify the goodness of their position hypothesis by creating a rendez-vous point (not to be confused with rendevous control messages in the underlying Time Warp platform supporting granulation) in the explored part of the region, and trying to meet again there; iii) if the hypothesis is verified, they exchange the data acquired during the exploration, thus reducing the exploration time and allowing for a more accurate decision of the actions to be taken. Additionally, in case step ii) succeeds (i.e., the robots actually meet in the rendez-vous point), it means that the estimation of their respective position is correct. Therefore, they can form a *cluster*, i.e. they can start exploring the environment in a collaborative way. This collaborative exploration can take place in two different ways. On the one hand, they jointly define (by relying on *cost* and *utility* functions, as defined in [8]) their next exploration targets, so that they can minimize the time required for a complete environment exploration. On the other hand, they might decide to make a *guess* about the position of other robots (the total number of which is known) which are not part of the cluster yet. In the latter case, one of the robots (the one for which the utility/cost ratio is convenient) targets the hypothesized position. If a robot is found there, the aforementioned steps are carried out, so as to increase the knowledge of the environment.

Discovering the presence of a nearby robot is a crucial step while coding this simulation model. In fact, in case of reliance on classical PDES programming schemes not based on cross-state access, either the robots must communicate to each other their current position (thus exponentially increasing the number of exchanged messages, say cross-scheduled events, which in turn can limit the performance of the simulation), or they have to notify it to specific simulation objects (i.e., the regions), again increasing the number of messages exchanged. Additionally, to estimate the respective position of the robots, many simulation events could be required. In this specific case, these events should be marked with the same timestamp, thus requiring efficient (but non-negligible in cost) tie-breaking approaches, like the one in [13]. Third, exchanging map information could entail a data transfer non-negligible in size, posing a huge burden on the communication subsystem.

This model is therefore a good test-case for exploiting the innovative programming paradigm based on cross-state access, and to test the advantages from granulating LPs according to the new mechanisms we have presented (just supporting this programming model). In our implementation (as said aligned with the one in [15]), we rely on two different types of LPs, namely active ones (implementing the robots) and passive ones (implementing regions of the ex-

---

[9]Recall that the ID of a GLP corresponds to the ID of some LP belonging to the GLP.

[10]The full source code of our implementation is available at https://github.com/HPDCS/ROOT-Sim.

ploration environment). More specifically, the environment is represented as a square region, divided into hexagonal cells. This choice allows us to define a meaningful mobility model for the robots, and at the same time allows us to define proximity regions which are used by the robots to detect the presence of other ones in the nearby. Also, in our model, periodic events occurring into any cell are envisaged as the basis for modeling the evolution (inside the cell) of any phenomenon characterizing the dynamic change in the state of the explored region.

At simulation startup, each passive simulation object creates random obstacles (which prevent the robots from reaching any neighbour cell), mimicking a rescue scenario, where an open space is modified by an accident and the robots are used to explore it for rescue activities. At the same time, each passive LP instantiates in its private simulation state (by relying on a traditional `malloc` call) a *presence vector*. Each entry of the vector is associated with a specific robot. Whenever a robot enters a given cell, it explicitly informs the LP taking care of the cell's state by exchanging an event, piggy-backing a pointer to a buffer in the robot's simulation state which keeps the representation of the explored map. When the cell processes this event, it stores the pointer in the presence vector, which is then scanned to synchronize the information in the map. In particular, all the robots' states are in-place accessed, so as to copy the information from one state to the other. This operation clearly triggers cross-state synchronization and may lead to granulate LPs temporarily residing in a given area, together with the LP modeling the specific portion of the environment where they reside.

To test the GLP proposal we have compared the execution time for this simulation model when run with the granulation support, and without granulation thus running with the baseline cross-state synchronization protocol (labeled as CS). We have also run the same identical model on top of a serial engine based on a classical calendar-queue scheduler. Finally, for completeness of the analysis, we have run a version of the same model coded by only relying on the traditional paradigm where cross-state access is not employed/supported, thus basing the interactions among the different parts/entities in the model exclusively on the cross-scheduling of events across the different LPs. For all the tests we run a model with 1000 LPs, the 10% of which represent robots, and the remaining 90% represent sub-regions of the overall bi-dimensional region to be explored.

The hardware architecture used for running the experiments is a 64-bit NUMA machine, namely an HP ProLiant server, equipped with four 2GHz AMD Opteron 6128 processors and 64 GB of RAM. Each processor has 8 cores (for a total of 32 cores) that share a 12MB L3 cache (6 MB per each 4-cores set), and each core has a 512KB private L2 cache. For the parallel runs we configured the simulation platform to use 32 worker threads.

The total execution time for the simulations are reported in Figure 8 for the different settings of the underlying simulation engine (where each reported sample is averaged over 10 runs). For GLP-based runs, we have also considered the variation of the threshold parameter τ_{dep}, which we recall can be used to filter out cross-state dependencies that are less valuable (say, their volume is lower than others) while building the GLPs. Also, in GLP-based runs, the granulation process is actuated after the first GVT computation

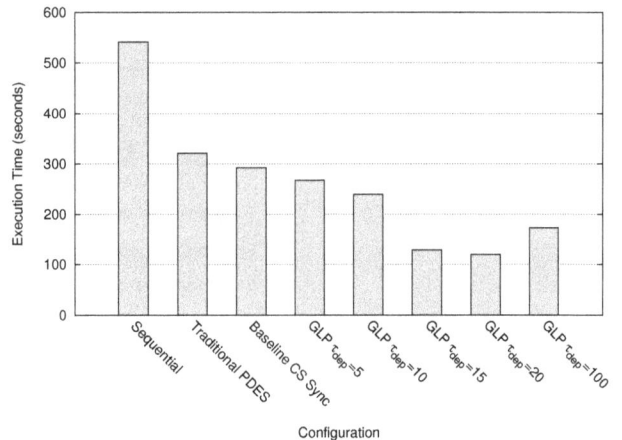

Figure 8: Total execution time.

round that is subsequent to the fading (due to lifetime expiration) of previously formed groups[11].

By the results we observe that all the platform configurations offering support for in-place cross-state access outperform the traditional PDES scenario, not admitting cross-state accesses. Nevertheless, the baseline CS synchronization scheme offers a limited gain, while the integration of the new granulation support leads to noticeable performance improvements. These improvements are better for larger values of the parameter τ_{dep}, indicating that a more accurate selection of actually valuable cross-state dependencies can drive significantly better granulation decisions, leading to more efficient synchronization dynamics, which lead the execution time to be almost 3 times lower compared to both the traditional PDES case and the baseline CS synchronization scheme. An additional observation concerns the step reduction of the execution time with GLPs when increasing τ_{dep} from 10 to 15. From the collected statistics we noted that this phenomenon is due to the fact that up to the value $\tau_{dep} = 10$, scenarios were generated where granulation involved multiple LPs representing distinct sub-regions, which does not favor concurrency since the model let each robot LP to move around, with the constraint of residing at any time in a single region. Hence, at any time instant, some event can only lead to cross-state access involving a region and its hosted robots. Different sub-regions, and their currently hosted robots, should be therefore allowed to execute concurrently to favor parallelism, by placing them in different GLPs. Nevertheless, our solution allows to be sufficiently resilient to this scenario. In fact, the first value of τ_{dep} where some thrashing phenomenon is observed (which in turn affects the overall performance) is observed only for a much higher value, namely $\tau_{dep} = 100$.

5. RELATED WORK

The LP granulation scheme we have presented can be seen as a means to bias synchronization dynamics in order to let a Time Warp system improve its performance in contexts where different portions of the simulation model exhibit more strict interdependencies (along different phases of the simulation run). The consequence would be an improve-

---

[11]In all the parallel runs the GVT period has been set to 1 second.

ment of fruitful usage of computing resources while carrying out speculative processing of DES models. This is the objective of classical load balanging/sharing approaches proposed in literature (see, e.g., [4, 10, 22]). However, these proposal are bound to scenarios where the interactions across the model portions are explicit and only occur via the classical event cross-scheduling approach (in-place state-wide access to the model state is not supported/considered).

More generally, to the best of our knowledge, there are not many proposals focusing on enabling non-explicit inter-dependencies between different LPs for the case of optimistic PDES. The work in [17] tackles the issue of transparently supporting the access to a shared state portion of the model by whichever event on multi-core Time Warp platforms, which is anyhow confined to global variables. This work presents state management/recoverability operations that allow concurrent event-handlers, CPU-scheduled to run events at multiple LPs, to observe a consistent global snapshot of such shared portion even in the case they do not notify their operations via explicit event exchange. Beyond a few technical differences—such as the reliance on application software instrumentation in [17] vs the employment of kernel-supported memory management facilities in order to runtime detect the materialization of an in-place access to some state portion in our proposal—the proposal in [17] does not entail mechanisms for dynamically determining the level of correlation of the memory (read/write) operations involving the overall model state. Rather, our granulation mechanism targets the dynamic discovery of such correlation so as to dynamically create islands of the model state where in-place access by the application code is enabled in a synchronization efficient manner.

In [6] the authors present the concept of Extended LP (Ex-LP). An Ex-LP is a collection of LPs that explicitly expose towards other (Ex-)LPs a certain amount of attributes, which can be implicitly accessed/modified. The access to exposed attributes is synchronized by relying on the Software Transactional Memory (STM) paradigm. In this sense, memory accesses to the shared portion of the state (the exposed attributes) is as well speculative, and could be subject to undo (via transaction aborts). This proposal anyhow requires pre-declaration of the state portions that can be subject to in-place concurrent access (since these must be accessed via STM demarcated code blocks) and there is no concept of dynamic clustering of different state portions in order to apply cluster oriented synchronization mechanism aimed at improving the runtime efficiency. Contrarily, in our proposal we do not require any pre-specification of what state portions will be accessed in-place by a same event-handler execution instance, and we support the dynamic clustering scheme with associated runtime change of the synchronization dynamics. Overall, we improve both flexibility of model coding (via the support for state-wide in-place access) and the potential for higher fruitful usage of resources.

The notion of *Kernel Process* (KP) is presented in [3]. A KP is a sort of PDES kernel-level thread instance that handles a collection of LPs by managing a single event-list of their events. The core objective is to optimize operations such as the fossil collection (memory recovery), which can pay-off even if false rollbacks can occur due to updates of the unique (merged) event list caused by stragglers or anti-messages (leading to rollback LPs in a KP that could still be considered as causally consistent). In our proposal the clus-

tering of the LPs on a same thread is enabled dynamically (although with no explicit fusion of the event lists of the clustered LPs, rather by adopting a multi-list management approach), depending on the cross-state dependencies that are materialized at runtime and on the choice by the underlying granulation mechanisms. Further, our Time Warp environment supports a different programming model where in-place access to whatever state location is enabled. We feel that the event-list management features/optimizations at the core of KPs could be somehow integrated with our granulation support to further improve the performance of the runtime system.

The proposal in [1], still targeting multi-core architectures as we do, proposes a technique called Dynamic Local Time Window Estimates (DLTWE), in which each processor communicates time estimates of its next inter-processor event to its neighbors, which use the estimates as bounds for advancement. The proposal specifically targets spatial simulations, in which different (close) sub-volumes could be interested by a rollback operation. A selective rollback function is described, which allows to reduce the effects of rollbacks at LPs managing "close" entities. Contrarily, we do not impose any topology or predetermined relation across the LPs, which is an implicit outcome thanks to the different supported programming model (based on in-place state access everywhere). Moreover, we limit the effect of a rollback too for applications exploiting such a programming model by explicitly avoiding causal inconsistencies across LPs that are dynamically granulated together.

6. CONCLUSIONS

In this article we have introduced the concept of granular Time Warp simulation objects, and the design of a runtime PDES platform enabling the granulation process. This leads to dynamically clustering the baseline Time Warp objects, thus forming larger entities that advance in logical time as individual larger-grain objects, whose elements do never give rise to causality errors towards each other. This is achieved by jointly supporting a programming model where the simulation code can be written in such a way to access in-place the state of whichever object (either granular or not) while processing each individual event, an approach that stands as a valuable alternative to traditional PDES only based on event exchanges for coding interactions across the objects. Such cross-state accesses are what drive the formation of granulated objects, which are aimed at clustering the baseline objects that along specific execution phases shown larger volumes of cross-state dependencies. Also, this mechanism leads to runtime configurations where the level of parallelism is dynamically determined on the basis of the level of coupling of the objects, as determined by cross-state dependencies materialization. We tested our proposal against traditional Time Warp and a variant with cross-state support but no granulation, for the case of a multi-robot exploration simulation model run on a 32-core machine. By the study we report a 3x improvement in the model execution speed thanks to our proposal.

7. REFERENCES

[1] P. Bauer, J. Lindén, S. Engblom, and B. Jonsson. Efficient Inter-Process Synchronization for Parallel Discrete Event Simulation on Multicores. In *Proceedings of the 3rd ACM SIGSIM Conference on*

Principles of Advanced Discrete Simulation, SIGSIM-PADS, pages 183–194. ACM Press, 2015.

[2] B. H. Bloom. Space/Time Trade-offs in Hash Coding with Allowable Errors. *Communications of the ACM*, 13(7):422–426, 1970.

[3] C. D. Carothers, D. W. Bauer, and S. Pearce. ROSS: A High-performance, Low-memory, Modular Time Warp System. *Journal of Parallel and Distributed Computing*, 62(11):1648–1669, 2002.

[4] C. D. Carothers and R. M. Fujimoto. Efficient Execution of Time Warp Programs on Heterogeneous, NOW Platforms. *IEEE Transactions on Parallel and Distributed Systems*, 11(3):299–317, 2000.

[5] C. D. Carothers, K. S. Perumalla, and R. M. Fujimoto. Efficient Optimistic Parallel Simulations Using Reverse Computation. *ACM Transactions on Modeling and Computer Simulation*, 9(3):224–253, 1999.

[6] L.-l. Chen, Y.-s. Lu, Y.-P. Yao, S.-l. Peng, and L.-d. Wu. A Well-Balanced Time Warp System on Multi-Core Environments. In *Proceedings of the 25th Workshop on Principles of Advanced and Distributed Simulation*, PADS, pages 1–9. IEEE Computer Society, 2011.

[7] D. Cingolani, A. Pellegrini, and F. Quaglia. Transparently Mixing Undo Logs and Software Reversibility for State Recovery in Optimistic PDES. In *Proceedings of the 2015 ACM SIGSIM Conference on Principles of Advanced Discrete Simulation*, SIGSIM-PADS, pages 211–222. ACM Press, 2015.

[8] D. Fox, J. Ko, K. Konolige, B. Limketkai, D. Schulz, and B. Stewart. Distributed Multirobot Exploration and Mapping. *Proceedings of the IEEE*, 94(7):1325–1339, 2006.

[9] R. M. Fujimoto. Performance of Time Warp Under Synthetic Workloads. In *Proceedings of the Multiconference on Distributed Simulation*, pages 23–28. Society for Computer Simulation, 1990.

[10] D. W. Glazer and C. Tropper. On Process Migration and Load Balancing in Time Warp. *IEEE Transactions on Parallel and Distributed Systems*, 4(3):318–327, 1993.

[11] M. P. Herlihy. Wait-free Synchronization. *ACM Transactions on Programming Languages and Systems*, 13(1):124–149, 1991.

[12] D. R. Jefferson. Virtual Time. *ACM Transactions on Programming Languages and System*, 7(3):404–425, 1985.

[13] H. Mehl. A Deterministic Tie-breaking Scheme for Sequential and Distributed Simulation. In *Proceedings of the 6th Workshop on Parallel and Distributed Simulation*, PADS. ACM Press, 1992.

[14] R. E. Odeh and D. E. Knuth. *The Art of Computer Programming. Volume 1: Fundamental Algorithms.*, volume 64. Addison-Wesley Professional, mar 1969.

[15] A. Pellegrini and F. Quaglia. Programmability and Performance of Parallel ECS-based Simulation of Multi-Agent Exploration Models. In *Proceedings of the 2nd Workshop on Parallel and Distributed Agent-Based Simulations*, PADABS, pages 395–406. LNCS, Springer-Verlag, 2014.

[16] A. Pellegrini and F. Quaglia. Transparent Multi-core Speculative Parallelization of DES Models with Event and Cross-state Dependencies. In *Proceedings of the 2nd ACM SIGSIM Conference on Principles of Advanced Discrete Simulation*, SIGSIM-PADS, pages 105–116. ACM Press, 2014.

[17] A. Pellegrini, R. Vitali, S. Peluso, and F. Quaglia. Transparent and Efficient Shared-State Management for Optimistic Simulations on Multi-core Machines. In *Proceedings of the 20th International Symposium on Modeling, Analysis and Simulation of Computer and Telecommunication Systems*, MASCOTS, pages 134–141. IEEE Computer Society, 2012.

[18] A. Pellegrini, R. Vitali, F. Quaglia, A. Pellegrini, and F. Quaglia. Autonomic State Management for Optimistic Simulation Platforms. *IEEE Transactions on Parallel and Distributed Systems*, 26(6):1560–1569, 2015.

[19] R. Rönngren, M. Liljenstam, R. Ayani, and J. Montagnat. Transparent Incremental State Saving in Time Warp Parallel Discrete Event Simulation. In *Proceedings of the 10th Workshop on Parallel and Distributed Simulation*, PADS, pages 70–77. IEEE Computer Society, 1996.

[20] S. J. Swamidass and P. Baldi. Mathematical Correction for Fingerprint Similarity Measures to Improve Chemical Retrieval. *Journal of Chemical Information and Modeling*, 47(3):952–964, 2007.

[21] The High Performance and Dependable Computing Systems Research Group (HPDCS). ROOT-Sim: The ROme OpTimistic Simulator. https://github.com/HPDCS/ROOT-Sim, 2012.

[22] R. Vitali, A. Pellegrini, and F. Quaglia. Load Sharing for Optimistic Parallel Simulations on Multi-core Machines. *ACM SIGMETRICS Performance Evaluation Review*, 40(3):2, 2012.

[23] R. Vitali, A. Pellegrini, and F. Quaglia. Towards Symmetric Multi-threaded Optimistic Simulation Kernels. In *Proceedings of the 26th Workshop on Principles of Advanced and Distributed Simulation*, PADS, pages 211–220. IEEE Computer Society, 2012.

[24] J. Wang, D. Jagtap, N. B. Abu-Ghazaleh, and D. Ponomarev. Parallel Discrete Event Simulation for Multi-core Systems: Analysis and Optimization. *IEEE Transactions on Parallel and Distributed Systems*, 25(6):1574–1584, 2014.

[25] D. West and K. Panesar. Automatic Incremental State Saving. In *Proceedings of the 10th Workshop on Parallel and Distributed Simulation*, PADS, pages 78–85. IEEE Computer Society, 1996.

Online Data Extraction for Large-Scale Agent-Based Simulations

Daniel Zehe, Vaisagh Viswanathan
TUM CREATE
1 CREATE Way
138602 Singapore
+6566014015
{daniel.zehe,vaisagh.viswanathan}@tum-create.edu.sg

Wentong Cai
Nanyang Technological University
639798 Singapore
+657904600
aswtcai@ntu.edu.sg

Alois Knoll
Technische Universität München (TUM)
85748 Munich Germany
+498928918104
knoll@in.tum.de

ABSTRACT

Cloud-based simulation systems reduce the upfront hardware costs of running high-performance experiments and increases the ease with which simulation experiments can be repeated. The data being generated by simulations can be large. Commonly used data storage systems such as relational databases can handle large amounts of data, but the analysis is a challenging problem. Moreover, handling this amount of data in cloud services can be both expensive (bandwidth and storage costs) and time-consuming. However, a lot of the data that is generated by agent-based simulations does not contribute directly to the purpose of the experiment being conducted. We propose an extension to cloud-based simulation systems that rather than storing raw simulation output data, uses stream data processing to generate the result dataset while the simulation is running. This can then be used to store only the data required for later use, this saving both time and money.

CCS Concepts

•Computing methodologies → Modeling and simulation; Data assimilation; *Agent / discrete models; Simulation environments; Simulation tools;*

Keywords

Online Data Extraction, Time-variant Relational Algebra, Cloud-based Simulation, Agent-based Simulation

Permission to make digital or hard copies of all or part of this work for personal or classroom use is granted without fee provided that copies are not made or distributed for profit or commercial advantage and that copies bear this notice and the full citation on the first page. Copyrights for components of this work owned by others than the author(s) must be honored. Abstracting with credit is permitted. To copy otherwise, or republish, to post on servers or to redistribute to lists, requires prior specific permission and/or a fee. Request permissions from permissions@acm.org.

SIGSIM-PADS '16, May 15 - 18, 2016, Banff, AB, Canada

© 2016 Copyright held by the owner/author(s). Publication rights licensed to ACM.
ISBN 978-1-4503-3742-7/16/05. . . $15.00

DOI: http://dx.doi.org/10.1145/2901378.2901384

1. INTRODUCTION

The computational resources required for modern urban system simulations [18, 4] are increasing; this has also resulted in more high resolution output data being generated. Moreover, availability of much cheaper storage options[1] has resulted in data being generated at unprecedented velocities, volumes and varieties [19, 8]. Depending on the run time of a single simulation, the design decision is often taken to record as much as possible in order to reduce the number of simulation runs.

However, despite the price reduction in persistent storage, analyzing large amounts of data can still be problematic. Large data sets have to be loaded into the memory of one or multiple machines in order to do the necessary post-processing of the data. If the main memory of the system is exhausted, a distributed or stream-processing workflow has to be used. This adds an additional overhead for the user. There is a need for more efficient methods for handling the large datasets that are generated, especially with the increasing availability of cloud computing resources and cloud-based simulation services [21]. As stated in [13], "transferring data-sets to a centralized machine is thus expensive (due, for example, to network communication and other I/O related costs)".

A possible solution to this problem is to do the data analysis while the simulation is running and store only the processed data set necessary for the given experiment, i.e. the *result data set*. Such a solution would be most useful for large workflows where, traditionally, huge amounts of data have to be transfered between two consecutive steps. A possible approach to this would be to leverage on the *IEEE 1516* High Level Architecture (HLA) [6] which is popular in the simulation community. A data processing federate could be created which collects the data from the running simulations, and processes and writes it to persistent storage as required. However, the limited data transfer rate and the large overhead of publishing all information either reduces the simulation performance significantly or necessitates a larger simulation "cool-down" phase during which all data is analyzed and transmitted to a single data analysis federate.

---

[1]http://www.mkomo.com/cost-per-gigabyte-update

Most simulation experiment post-processing workflows start with obtaining data sets from databases, but since the size of these data sets is increasing steadily an online data extraction methodology as presented in this paper can be useful. We describe formally the components and advantages of an online data extraction methodology for agent-based simulation (specifically cloud-based simulations), in which data processing at simulation time is used to minimized the use of slower persistent storage. Using a relational algebra context of modelling the data output of a simulation does not break the post-processing workflow of many experiments. Agent-based simulations are have been taken as an example, since a set of agents of the same (or similar) type can be interpreted as a table or relation.

Using a relational algebra to model the data output of a simulation is beneficial since it does not interfere with the established post-processing workflot of many experiments. Agent-based simulations are a good example to use a relational representation of the output data, since a agents can be grouped together and be seen as a relation with tuples of state-variables.

As part of the literature review, we explore the current research in big data and stream processing as well as data description languages. Subsequently, we introduce the structure and overall working of a data-analysis component for a cloud-based simulation system. This is followed by a formal relation-algebra-based description of the data output, but unlike traditionally relational algebra, can be used to describe time-variant data. Finally, we use two traffic simulation examples to demonstrate the working and advantages of the proposed system.

2. RELATED WORK

2.1 Relational Data Description

Relational data models are widely used in the database domain where they are used to describe data by using tables from which data can be accessed and operations be executed on. The data entries are called *tuples* and share the same structure (i.e. fields) within a single database table. The advantages of the relational data description language and relational algebra are that they enable the analysis and optimization of complex and large amounts of data by using formal mathematical methods. Despite the limited number of operations, complex manipulations can be created on structured data. Relational databases were first introduced by Codd [5] and later refined by Darwen and Date [7]. In this paper, we leverage on the well-developed work in relational algebra, with a temporal component extension in order to deal with time-variant data sources that characterize simulations.

2.2 Big-Data and Stream Processing

Ranja [13] commented on the fact that the data that is being generated on the internet has been and will keep increasing rapidly over the next couple of years. This is similar to the data being generated by simulations. Individual simulations produce a lot more data than the average node on the internet. Cloud-based simulation services [22] can result in multiple concurrent simulations in the cloud at unprecedented rates which will increase the data output significantly. Ranja [13] postulates that relational databases will be unable to cope with the massive data anymore. In contrast, state-of-the-art data mining algorithms work on main memory. However, main memory is much more expensive and invariably inadequate to store the amount of data generated.

Another point to be considered is the network and I/O costs involved in the transfer of data between the storage location and the analytics computer [13]. Ranja proposes an ecosystem for data processing that involves a high velocity *data ingestion layer* that communicates with the actual *data analytics layer*, which then pushes the resulting data sets to a *data storage layer*. This kind of data analytics frameworks have different advantages and drawbacks. While the Apache Hadoop [17] distributed stream processing toolchain is more suited for historic/existing data analysis, Spark [20] and Storm streaming processing are better suited for online data-streams with highly variable (in terms of amount and type) data.

For general big data processing, different tools already exist. Tools like Apache Mahout[2] and GraphLab[3] have a large number of implemented data analysis algorithms available for use. These offer an easy-to-use off-the-shelf experience for researchers. On the other hand, building a system with such tools for simulation data analysis, that might be outside the realm of standard big data processing, presents its own set of challenges. A distributed system that relies on message passing and queuing for a general purpose application programming interface (API) is more applicable for simulations. Apache Kafka[4] for distribution of incoming data streams is an example of such a system. This usually works in conjunction with Hadoop, Storm[5] or Spark[6] to distributed high-velocity data processing payloads. Such data needs to be stored in a NoSQL database structure like MongoDB [3] or Casandra [11]; in these systems large amounts of data are stored in easily accessible structures.

Babcock et al. [2] give an overview of data streaming models and current issues in data stream processing systems. They acknowledge that there are different groups of data streaming models that handle data differently and differs from conventionally stored data in (1) availability (online vs. offline), (2) order of data elements, (3) undefined or unbound size of the stream and (4) the unavailability of historical data, since after processing the input data is discarded.

2.3 Data Extraction Techniques for Simulations

For many simulations the data export focuses on writing to a comma-separated, XML-based or application-specific binary data format. This might be acceptable for small amounts of data coming from small-scale simulations or rarely updated variables, where the final amount of raw data is rather small. For large-scale simulations, saving raw data might be desirable but infeasible due to I/O constraints. Many simulation tools, output only aggregated values or rely on visualization to transport information in the form of recordings (animation or video) or images. Prominent examples are material simulations, where the forces on a digital workpiece is shown as an overlaid heat map [10, 16].

---

[2]http://mahout.apache.org
[3]http://graphlab.org
[4]http://kafka.apache.org
[5]http://storm.apache.org/
[6]http://spark.apache.org

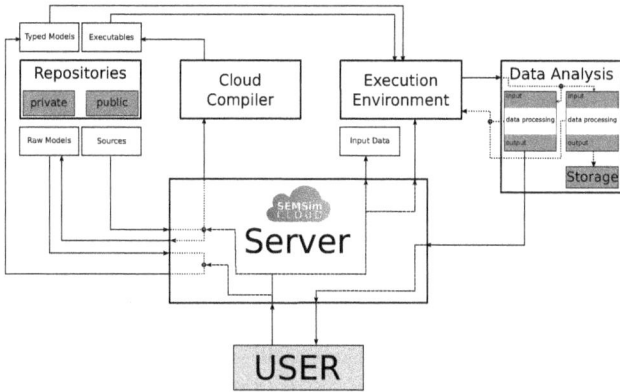

Figure 1: Cloud-based Simulation Reference Architecture. The user interacts with the system through RESTful APIs and the entire system runs on public or private cloud instances.

Schützel et al. [14] describe a stream-based reference architecture for a data management system that interacts with all the components of a simulation workflow. The described approach starts from the experiment setup, the actual execution of the simulation up to adding a "processing graph" and a storage engine. Data management has a mediating role between all steps of a simulation and passes data between the different steps of an experiment. This mediator role is also active for different simulations within one experiment run.

In a different publication, Schützel et al. [15] have presented that the extraction of simulation data is dependent on the structural dimension of the simulation entities as well as the sequential dimension that describes the order in which the data is being generated. They describe the *ML-Rules Data Extraction Language* and also the *SystemXtract Language*. The latter one uses sequential logs to reconstruct the structural and sequential information of the simulation state and passes it to the analysis application.

3. ONLINE DATA PROCESSING SYSTEM

We have previously presented SEMSim Cloud Service, a simulation cloud service for agent-based simulations with a special focus on traffic simulations [22]. In this paper we use the SEMSim Cloud Service as the reference model for giving context and for describing the proposed model. However, the methods developed are not SEMSim specific in any way. In the next section, we give a brief overview of the Cloud Service [22].

3.1 SEMSim Cloud Service

The cloud service consists of 6 main components as shown in Figure 1, of which the *Data Analysis* component is the focus of this paper.

1. The **user-interface** is represented through *representational state transfer* (REST) APIs. Through the use of APIs and non-fixed front-end, the user can tailor a use-case specific front-end for the simulation experiment.

2. These API calls are then translated by the **cloud service server** component which executes cloud service

actions like allocation and deallocation of cloud resources as well as starting, monitoring and stopping of simulation experiments.

3. A **repository** for models (algorithms with parameters), types (parameter configurations for models), source code (for implemented models and simulation engine) and executables (compiled source code) is the main component of the cloud service. It can offer private repositories to privileged users or publicly available repositories to all user. This allows different domain experts to develop, validate and test models before being used by a non-domain expert.

4. The **cloud compiler** takes the source code from the repository and compiles it into an executable that can be used by the execution environment.

5. An **execution environment** is the heart of the cloud-based simulation service. It executes an executable from the repository together with parameterized models and input data to form a simulation run.

6. **Data Analysis** is an integral part of any simulation experiment and is connected to the execution environment to use the data being generated by a simulation run to deduce results by analyzing it directly. Data storage or forwarding the data stream to a visualization can range from megabytes to terabytes for a single simulation run, depending on the simulation experiment.

The complete system relies on public cloud resources allocated from cloud service providers (e.g., Google Compute Engine[7], Amazon AWS[8], Microsoft Azure[9]). These resources, mostly virtual machines but also virtual networks and virtual storage, are allocated according to the specifications of the experiment and deallocated after the experiment has finished. The data generated is stored in the cloud as well. In order to guarantee the security of the input data into the simulation, all data is encrypted until they are used in the simulation itself. Generated output data can also be encrypted, if required. The focus in this paper is on the data analysis part which is described in more detail next.

3.2 System Design

In the proposed system, the simulation instance's output data is first formally defined in a relational algebra as presented in Section 4.1. This enables us to leverage on the effectiveness and power of relational algebra in our simulation data manipulation. Once the simulation is running, a high performance simulation can output data in several ways. The naive and standard approach is to output all state variables of all agents whenever they change. However, by doing so, the bandwidth required would be very high (as illustrated in Section 5.1). A better strategy would be that external programs can subscribe to updates of variables as required for the analysis. This means that subscribers either get an update of the variable whenever it changes, at certain intervals or, if sufficient for the analysis, just once to initialize. This is a contrast to receiving always all data,

---

[7]https://cloud.google.com/compute/
[8]https://aws.amazon.com
[9]https://azure.microsoft.com/

whenever a state changes in the simulation. A constraint is that the update interval, in which state changes can be received, should not be smaller than the time between two events that change an attribute in the simulation (e.g., if the simulation event occurs every 1s then an update frequency of 500ms is not allowed).

This data-stream is then received by stream processing scripts. As the data is received in batches (e.g., every 1 second), and in temporal order[10], an event-based processing framework, that instantiates a new thread/process is very favorable. This also allows for scaling the processing to multiple nodes, due to its limited dependency.

Once the data has been processed by the scripts (which may even be a chain of different processing steps), this final result data set is either stored in persistent storage, or sent to a visualization client.

In order to extend a simulation engine in the cloud with a stream processing engine, the simulation engine needs to provide an API that exposes the state of the simulation to an external data sink. This API should present the data in such a way, that once requested, each change in the agent's state will be transmitted to the requester. This process continues for as long as the simulation is running, or until the request is specifically terminated by the requester. Additionally, the data sink should have some form of caching to reduce the amount of data being transferred at every change. The actual processing can be done using existing stream processing tools like Hadoop or Spark, as introduced in Section 2, which either distributes the data to be processed to one or multiple worker nodes.

3.3 Implementation

The data request scripts, that define what data is streamed from the simulation is, for ease of use, in an SQL-like language called *SimuSQL*, to ensure compatible with offline analysis of the data. An exemplary query on the output data-model of a traffic simulation requests data of electric vehicles (EV) that have the time variant property *State-of-Charge* (SOC) at an update rate of 1 second.

```
SELECT * from EV WHERE SOC>0.3 AT 1 SECOND
```

The extension `AT 1 SECOND` is added to specify how often an update of the data should be provided by the simulation. When omitting this parameter, a new data item is sent whenever available. The related concepts are described in more detail in Section 4. The data analysis middleware should take care of static/non-changing content and inject this accordingly, to ensure that the simulation can omit that data if unchanged – transparent caching.

The most important part of the cloud service, in the context of the proposed data analysis system, is an interface which the data analysis middleware provides, that the processing framework can access and request data from . This interface needs to be separate from the simulation itself, but should use locality in the data center to ensure fast data transfer. The middleware accepts requests in the above defined *SimuSQL* and returns data when available. It also takes care of the transparent caching of the data. The connection to the simulation has to be via open socket connections that support fast data transfers.

---

[10]note that the transport protocol can change the receive order

As can be seen in Figure 2 the data-processing starts with calling the SELECT statement towards the data analysis middleware component (step ❶). Note, that the user initiating this data-processing work flow can be different from the user that designed or started the simulation experiment. The select statement is the trigger to instantiate a connection between the simulation and the data analysis middleware. For this specific call, the first callback will be towards the initialization function of the data analysis middleware (step ❷). This is different from any other succeeding callback, because the simulation will transmit the entire current state. This includes, unlike to all other callbacks, the static data as well. All following callbacks will only include the time-variant data, as well as the key to identify the tuple unambiguously (step ❸). Should a new agent be added to the simulation and should it satisfy the conditions stated in the initial request, it's data will be fully included. The data analysis middleware has to ensure that the static data from the initial data set is merged with the time-variant data stream. After the data has been prepared, the entire data set is presented to the stream processing toolchain. At the end of processing, data can be stored as a result data set or streamed out to a different data-sink. Since there is no historical data injected into the stream of data, the processing component needs to take care of passing values from one step to the next. The data will be sent from the simulation to the data analysis middleware and passed to the processing component until a cancel request is sent (step ❹).

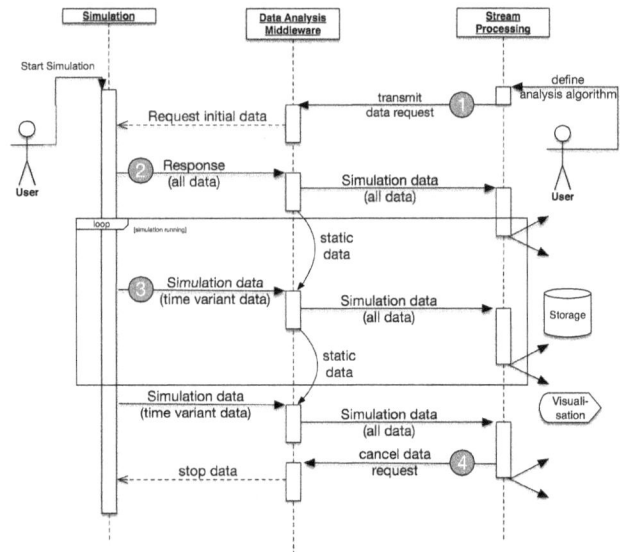

Figure 2: Sequence diagram depicting the workflow of the data analysis including the data processing. The Data Analysis middleware combines the time-variant data and the static data and passes it on to the analysis processing. Finally the result is send to storage or visualization.

The data transmitted from the simulation is not a constant stream of data. Depending on the execution speed of the simulation itself, the output will change once the state of an agent changes or a new agent is added to the simulation. For example, the position of all vehicles in a traffic simulation, will be updated rather frequently (in the range of a few seconds), while the occupancy of a car park will be updated more infrequently (in the range of a few minutes)[11]. The data analysis middleware needs to know when all data is in the same logical time step in order to pass this block of data to the processing component. In order to handle this, *landmarks*, a concept proposed by Gama et al. [9], can be introduced into the stream by the simulation. These are meta information on which the receiver, in our case the data analysis middleware, can deduce the end of a data concurrent stream of information.

Figure 3 shows how the landmarks are inserted into the data stream of serialized data objects from the simulation. Each rectangle represents information from a specific agent. The *Entity Types* are different classes in the object-oriented framework in a simulation. The order in which entities of different types are put on the stream can vary (see A and B in Figure 3), as long as there are no 2 entity updates of the same type between 2 landmarks. It can also happen that for different entity types the amount of data varies. Also, not all entities need to be updated between two landmarks (compare B and C in Figure 3). The data-analysis middleware needs to keep track of this. It is done to ensure the reduction of bandwidth usage, by avoiding unnecessary transfers of information.

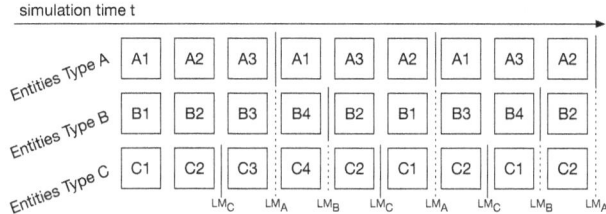

Figure 3: The Simulation inserts landmarks into the stream of updates of state changes for each entity type. The data analysis middleware detects the landmarks and discards all old information from the changed entities and replaces it with the newly received. Should an agent's state not change, the previous value is kept by the data analysis middleware.

To ensure data consistency between the simulation data model and the output data model, the landmarks play an important role. The entities that have not been updated since the last landmark, their old values are still to be considered valid. Between different entity types the time stamp of the landmarks for each type is compared by the middleware component and a consistent set of data is presented to the processing component.

4. FORMAL SIMULATION DATA REPRESENTATION

The data in an agent-based simulation can be described in multiple ways. In this paper we propose that this data be in relational algebra. This provides the advantage that constructs from a *structured query language* (SQL) can be used to retrieve data from the simulation or to store the data in a data sink (for a relational database with the same

structure). In agent-based simulation, each set of agents of the same type can be perceived as tuples in a relation of a database. Therefore, the approach representing the output data-model in the form of relations is favorable, since many (post-processing) algorithms and work-flows already work on database structured data as input. Should there be a very heterogeneous agent-population, where agents can not be grouped together into relations, each agent will then form its own relation with only one time-variant tuple.

Since some of the data will change over the course of the simulation, a temporal component needs to be added to the relational schema. Mahmood et al. [12] have given an overview of how to encode temporal information into a relational data model with a focus on database use-cases. This approach is not restricted to databases and can be applied to generic relational data. This temporal relational data model can be adapted to be used in describing output data from an agent-based simulation. The difference here is that there is no (or only limited) data of the past available. Future states can be seen as starting or ending points of data output. The data analysis middleware will only receive data from the simulation when the requested time is reached. This means, in practical use, a request on a future state of an agent in the system can trigger an event to start outputting the data at that event and not sooner.

4.1 General Simulation Data Representation

The general definition of relational data models, is to characterize the well-defined structure of databases, called a database schema. One could describe the state variables of the agents in an agent-based simulation as a schema with time-varying data. The formal description of an n-ary tuple of states is usually done by writing the name of the tuple (class name) followed by a comma separated list of the state variable names in parentheses [5]. Primary keys describe a field or a set of fields which characterizes the tuple unambiguously. This primary key is indicated by underlining the respective variable names. For the temporal dependency as described in [12], an extra field is added to the relation to describe its temporal activation (when the value is valid). It is also possible to add a field for each variable of the relation, but this increases the number of variables in a relation significantly, since for each variable field an extra field for activation is required.

Since we do not have to worry about the actual time when a state variable is active, we only need to indicate that a field might change its value over the course of the simulation adding an extra field for each of the state-variable is unnecessary. We are proposing the indication of time-variance by adding that the variable is a function of time (e.g. *variablename(t)*).

$$A(\underline{f_1, f_2, ..., f_k}, f_{k+1}, f_{k+2}, ..., f_{k+n}, f_{k+n+1}(t), ..., f_{k+n+m}(t))$$

shows agent A with $n \in \mathbb{N}_{>0}$ static state variable names, $m \in \mathbb{N}_{>0}$ time-variant state variable names and $k \in \mathbb{N}_{>0}$ state variable names that unambiguously describe one $(m + n + k)$-ary tuple.

Time-variant Relational Algebra

Since traditional relational algebra has no concept of time-variant fields or tuples, the individual simple functions like projection (Π), selection (σ), Cartesian product ($\times$) and nat-

---

[11]Note that all time information is simulation time, not real-time

ural join (⋈) have to be translated to equivalent time-variant operations. In all following operations the n-ary tuple for a given relation has to be determined, such as that the tuples that are included in the result set before doing the algebraic function are the most recent tuples for a given primary key in respect to the time τ given. This is also expressed in Equation 1.

$$TS(id_i) : \text{all Timestamps for a given } id_i$$
$$ID(ts_i) : \text{all IDs for a given } ts_i$$
$$\alpha : \Pi_{a_1,...,a_n}, \sigma_{a\theta v}, \bowtie, \times, ...$$
$$Dom(\alpha(R(\tau))) : \text{Domain of operation from } \alpha$$
$$\text{on relation R at time } \tau$$
$$Dom(\alpha(R(\tau))) = \big[\forall A(id_1, t_1) : [t_1 \in TS(id_1), t_1 \leq \tau$$
$$\wedge \nexists t_2 \in TS(id_1), t_1 < t_2 \leq \tau]$$
$$\wedge [\nexists A(id_2, t_2) : t_2 \in TS(id_2), t_1 < t_2 \leq \tau$$
$$\wedge id_1 = id_2]\big] \tag{1}$$

Table 1 shows two exemplary relations that are used to demonstrate the time-variant operations in this section. The column TS is the time-stamp of the respective values.

Table 1: Example Relations

Relation1				Relation2		
ID	**V1**	**V2**	**TS**	**ID**	**V3**	**TS**
1	A	C	0	1	E	0
2	B	H	0	2	F	0
1	J	C	1	1	G	1
3	C	D	2	2	L	1
2	I	C	2			

Time-variant Projection

A projection $\Pi_{a_1,...,a_n}(R)$ returns a set of data items that contain the components $a_1, ..., a_n$ of relation R and disregards all other fields in the set of tuples. The time-variant projection includes indication for what time τ this operation should be applied. $\Pi_{a_1,...,a_n}(R(\tau))$ returns all n-ary tuples from the time-variant set R that satisfy the result of Equation 1. The projection in Table 2 outputs the variable V1 and the ID at time $\tau = 1$ from Relation1.

Table 2: $\Pi_{ID,V1}(Relation1(1))$

ID	V1
1	J
2	B

Time-variant Selection

A selection $\sigma_{a\theta v}(R)$ returns a set of data items from the set of n-ary tuples R that satisfies the restriction expressed by attribute a, the binary operation $\theta \in \{<, \leq, =, \neq, \geq, >\}$ and the constant value v. The time-variant version of a selection needs to include the indication for what time τ this operation should be applied. $\sigma_{a\theta v}(R(\tau))$ returns all tuples that satisfy the restriction, but are also part of the result set generated by Equation 1. The selection in Table 3 outputs the variables of Relation1 with the condition that variable V2 is equal to D.

Table 3: $\sigma_{V2=D}(Relation1(2))$

ID	V1	V2
3	C	D

Time-variant Natural join

A natural join $R \bowtie S$ returns a set of data item from the sets of tuples R and S that have at least one matching attribute $\exists a_r \in R \wedge \exists a_s \in S; a_r = a_s$ in a resulting tuple. The time-variant version of this natural join includes indications for what times τ_S and τ_R this join should be applied. $R(\tau_1) \bowtie S(\tau_2)$ return all tuples as the standard join would, but under the constraint that the relations R and S are first reduced to the result generated by Equation 1. The natural join in Table 4 joins Relation1 and Relation2 at $\tau_1 = 1$ and $\tau_2 = 2$.

Table 4: $Relation1(1) \bowtie Relation2(2)$

ID	V1	V2	V3
1	J	C	G
2	B	H	L

Time-variant Cartesian product

The Cartesian product of $R \times S$ returns a set of data items from tuples R and S in which there is no matching attribute name $\nexists a_r \in R \wedge \nexists a_s \in S; a_r = a_s$. The time-variant version of the Cartesian product needs to include in what times τ_1 and τ_2 the tuples need to be included in the operation. $R(\tau_1) \times S(\tau_2)$ returns all standard Cartesian product tuples that are part of the result set that satisfy the Equation 1 for τ_1 and τ_2. The Cartesian product in Table 5 joins Relations1 and Relation2 at $\tau_1 = 1$ and $\tau_2 = 0$.

Table 5: $Relation1(1) \times Relation2(0)$

ID	V1	V2	V3
1	J	C	F
2	B	H	F
1	J	C	E
2	B	H	E

This extension to the standard relational algebra can be used when the data in a database contains additional information about the time of activation of a respective tuple.

5. CASE STUDY

As case studies for strengthening the need to reduce the amount of data stored in persistent storage, we are first evaluating the speed in which data needs to written to a storage medium and what current technologies support how many agents and simulation speeds. Secondly, we are giving an example on how the above described workflow can be used for an actual cloud based traffic simulation experiment.

5.1 Data Amount Model

In the following section we compare the amount of data that is being generated by a simulation and try to fit it to a suitable data processing framework. For this we consider the writing speed of conventional storage mediums like HDD or SSD as well as network-based distributed data processing solutions. First, we develop a model to estimate the amount of data that is being generated by a simulation.

For this we assume an agent-based simulation with $n_A \in \mathbb{N}_{>0}$ number of agents, the update frequency of the agents t_s (in seconds), the run time of the simulation T (in seconds) as well as the function $g(\tau)$, the percentage of agents being updated at given time. Additionally, the run time performance as a *real time factor RTF* (how much faster than real-time) needs to be considered as well as the number of state variables $s \in \mathbb{N}_{>0}$ each agent can have. An exemplary function $g(\tau)$ can be seen in Figure 4.

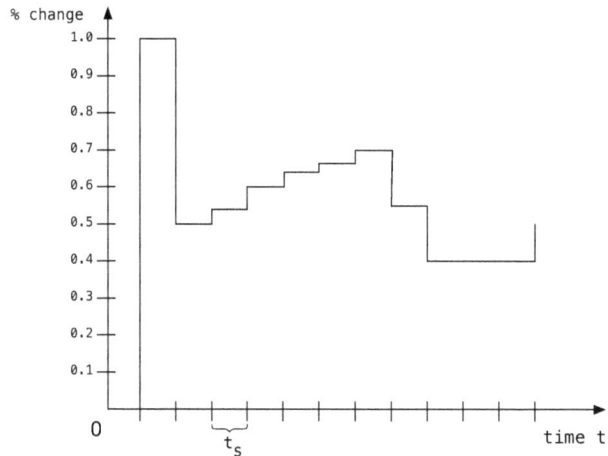

Figure 4: Time-variant percentage of agents changing in the simulation. t_s describes the time between subsequent simulation steps.

The final mathematical model to determine how many values will have to be saved or transmitted is:

$$TotalValues = \sum_{t=t_0}^{T} g(t) * n_A * s \tag{2}$$

All variables are double values on a 64 bit system, the memory footprint is different from the space required when outputting into CSV format. The precision $p \in \mathbb{N}_{>0}$ needs to be regarded as well, since this will influence the number of bytes that need to be written to disk. If the precision is 10 digits, a string representation of the number with ASCII coding would need 11 bytes, due to the decimal point. This is 3 bytes more than in the computer's main memory.

$$CSVsize = TotalValues * (p+1) \tag{3}$$

In order to evaluate if a certain storage medium can be used, the specification of common hardware write speeds need to be collected. For this we are considering conventional hard drives with a writing speed of 80 - 160 MB/s as well as solid state disk with a writing speed of 400 - 1000 MB/s. Additionally, state-of-the-art network transfer speeds for local networks need to be considered, since the data analysis is not be done on the same machine as the simulation is being executed. Current data center interconnections technologies are Ethernet, Infiniband or fiber optical connections. They range from $10-40GB/s$, $56GB/s$ to $>100GB/s$ respectively. The output bandwidth in bytes per second is defined

Table 6: Agent count vs. writing speed

	5000	8000	80000	800000
	103.76 MB/s	166.02MB/s	1.66GB/s	16.6GB/s
HDD	✓	-	-	-
SSD	✓	✓	-	-
10G Ethernet	✓	✓	✓	-
56G Infiniband	✓	✓	✓	✓
100G Fibre	✓	✓	✓	✓

as

$$OutputSpeed = \frac{CSVSize}{\frac{T}{t_s}} * RTF \tag{4}$$

Conventional way of processing simulation output data also requires to read data into main memory. There are also limits on main memory of a single system. A distributed processing workflow has to be used in such cases. This allows to distribute workload to multiple worker nodes and use a single aggregation node to combine the results. this works very well, when the data has little or no dependencies. The developed model can help to design the right data analysis workflow for the agent-based simulation that is to be run.

Data amount example

In a simple example where we vary the number of agents in a 24-hour simulation with each agent having 25 state variables that change throughout the simulation. The time step is 1 second and the RTF is 100. Over the course of the simulation with each time step 50% of the agents change and their state has to be outputted. Assuming a precision of 16 digits.

This would result in $87.55GB$ of total data and 1.04 MB per simulated second of simulation time when considering 5000 agents. Multiplying it with the RTF of 100, it results in $103.76MB/s$ that have to be written to storage. This would be possible with all the listed storage options in Table 6. The introduction of more agents into a simulation will have the effect that the simulation data can not be written out anymore and the systems capability is exhausted.

In the presented system, the large data would only be transfered from the simulation to a distributed processing workflow.

This mean the large amount of data generated by a simulation is streamed to the processing systems using high throughput network communications. Since the processing system might be distributed, even a lower capability virtual machine can handle the incoming connections. This allows for shorter turnaround times, between the end of a simulation, since a hard-disk-based approach would need to wait until all data is written before reading it from the storage medium. Once the simulation output data bandwidth exceed the capability of the medium, the I/O presents a bottleneck to the simulation experiment.

5.2 Traffic Simulation Cloud Service

The SEMSim simulation engine [1, 18] is used in the SEMSim traffic simulation cloud service. The *Scalable Electromobility Simulator* (SEMSim Traffic) is an agent-based traffic simulation engine. It is part of the SEMSim platform, which also includes a power system simulation [4]. This allows researchers to study the holistic effects of electromobility on an entire city/region through simulation.

Within the SEMSim traffic simulation each agent is represented as driver-vehicle-units (DVU) which consists of driver behavior and vehicle component models. Depending on the specific agent the actual models can vary.

The simulation uses a hybrid time-stepped and event-based execution model. Specific events like agent movement have predefined intervals, whereas other events, like the decision making of the driver or the update of the air-conditioning, are scheduled at different intervals. This gives the flexibility to vary the update of certain models more frequently than others.

An exemplary simulation experiment [4] with electric vehicle agents in a city-scale network and the objective is to determine the locations and State-of-Charge (SoC) of all electric vehicles that have an SoC of less than 0.3.

5.2.1 Traffic Simulation Data

In a nanoscopic agent-based traffic simulations like SEMSim Traffic, the agents are the vehicles and their driver. The behavior of the driver directly influences the state of the vehicle. For example, the decision by the driver model to increase the velocity directly influences the acceleration, fuel consumption and, ultimately, the velocity of the vehicle itself. Since the vehicle is not the only entity in a traffic simulation, the output data representation also needs to consider other entities:

- *Roads*: Consist of links and lanes [18], used for routing and movement.

- *Car Parks*: Hold a certain number of vehicles.

- *Traffic Lights*: Regulate the traffic at intersections and control the flow of vehicles.

- *Other Infrastructure Components*: Bus Stops, Crosswalks, Tram/MRT stations

An agent-based traffic simulation is usually modeled in an object-oriented framework, all the entities can have inheritance to child-models with larger amounts of data (see Figure 5). A vehicle only contains the very basic attributes like speed, location and geometric dimensions, while more specific vehicle implementations (e.g., electric, fuel-cell, ICE) can have more specific model attributes that influence the speed or location. The same applies for driver behavior. The output data relations for this example, containing only a subset of all entities in the simulation, would be:

```
Vehicle(vehicleID,geometry,
    velocity(t),location(t))
EV(vehicleID,batterySize,currentCapacity(t))
ICE(vehicleID,MotorPower,tankSize,
    tankfilled(t))
Road(ID,name,startpoint,endpoint)
Link(ID,startpoint,endpoint)
Lane(ID,startpoint,endpoint,leftlane,rightlane)
CarPark(ID,location,totalSlots, freeSlots(t))
Trip(ID,vehicleID,FromLocation,ToLocation)
```

This relation scheme needs to be known to the user that is developing the processing scripts, because these are the relations a *SimuSQL* query can return results for.

5.2.2 Time-variant Relational Data Model

The data required from the simulation is the vehicle location as well as the information of the SoC. A time-variant relation algebra expression would look like the following when

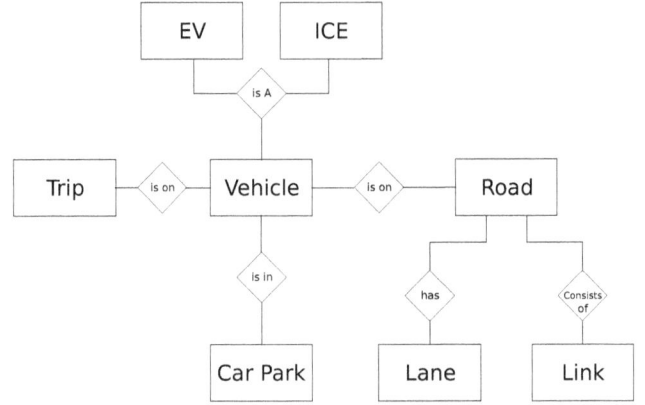

Figure 5: ER output data Model for a agent-based traffic simulation

considering that t is the current time t_{now}:

$$\text{LowSOCAgents}(t_{now}) = \text{Vehicle}(t_{now}) \bowtie$$
$$\sigma_{currentCapacity/batterySize<0.3}(EV(t_{now})) \quad (5)$$

$$\Pi_{vehicleID,location,batterySize,currentCapacity}$$
$$(\text{LowSoCAgents}(t_{now})) \quad (6)$$

This projection will return the vehicle ID, the location of the vehicle, the current capacity of the battery as well as the total battery size. Due to the selection in equation 5, the natural join only includes those agents that have an SoC of less than 0.3. The SoC is defined as the current capacity of the battery over the maximal battery size. The equation 6 applies a projection on the result tuples of equation 5. This is the formal description and operations that can be used to optimize queries using time-variant relational algebra. The following section expresses the same query as an *SimuSQL* statement which is queried from the processing script to the data analysis middleware.

5.2.3 Stream Output for Traffic Simulations

After we have introduced the data that a traffic simulation is generating, and the formal time-variant relation algebra optimization that has been performed, the translation into a *SimuSQL* query and the workflow at the data analysis middleware will be shown now.

A *SimuSQL* query to obtain the location and the SoC of all vehicles in the simulation that have less than 0.3 would be:

```
SELECT vehicleID,Location,currentCapacity/
    batterySize as SOC from EV natural
    join Vehicle WHERE currentCapacity/
    batterySize < 0.3;
```

This will return a time-variant tuple of all vehicles containing the location as well as batterySize as a fixed value whenever a vehicle has an SoC (currentCapacity/BatterySize) of less than 0.3. Since there is no update interval (e.g. **AT 1 SECOND**) specified, the data is streamed whenever changed in the simulation.

This query will be forwarded to the data analysis middleware where it is translated into a statement requesting information from the vehicle object as well as the inherited properties from the EV object in the simulation. The first request will transmit the entire state of the simulation regarding the vehicles and the EVs to the data analysis middleware. The transparent caching structure in the data analysis middleware will then cache the time-invariant variables, like the `batterySize` in this case and pass the entire data stream to the processing engine. Here the processing of spatial information of vehicles is performed and the result of clustering "low SoC agents" is transmitted to the database and/or pushed to a visualization engine, which eventually displays this information. In parallel to the processing, the simulation continues running and data continues being sent to the data analysis middelware. With any subsequent stream of data after the initial one (containing the `batterySize`), only the primary key, in this case the `vehicleID`, together with the time-variant information (e.g. currentCapacity) is forwarded. In the above example, data analysis middleware takes care of inputting the `batterySize` from the transparent cache and forwards it to the processing engine. To the processing engine, the simulation looks like a normal SQL database; however, in the background the simulation is changing the data constantly, while the cloud service is trying to minimize the data transmitted between the simulation and the data analysis middleware and the processing engine.

6. CONCLUSIONS

In this paper we have presented an approach to reduce the data generated by simulation experiments and to couple the data analysis to the simulation execution. This is especially useful for cloud based simulation experiments, where the costs of running simulation experiments is low, but long term storage and transfer of large amounts of data can be really expensive. The proposed system uses stream processing of data during its generation and a relational data model of the possible output data generated by a simulation experiment. This enables experiment designers to formally model the simulation output data with a time-variant relational data model.

We propose a formalism that indicates time variance on a simple relational model, where all operations have to regard the time at which the data was created. Since this method introduces another layer of middleware into the simulation work-flow, the middle-ware component presents a possible bottleneck to the system. This needs to be evaluated in experimental studies, but since the middle-ware discards any historical data, the execution, even of complex queries, is expected to be fast.

Possible use-cases of this model is an online data visualization application that can show results, and possible interactions with the simulation while it is still running. (Semi-)Manual exploration of different simulation and model configurations could be much more engaging and fruitful. This can be used for visualization of the data but also for decision support systems that deliver results while the simulation is still running.

7. ACKNOWLEDGMENTS

This work was financially supported by the Singapore National Research Foundation under its Campus for Research Excellence And Technological Enterprise (CREATE) programme.

8. REFERENCES

[1] H. Aydt, Y. Xu, M. Lees, and A. Knoll. A multi-threaded execution model for the agent-based semsim traffic simulation. In G. Tan, G. Yeo, S. Turner, and Y. Teo, editors, *AsiaSim 2013*, volume 402 of *Communications in Computer and Information Science*, pages 1–12. Springer Berlin Heidelberg, nov 2013.

[2] B. Babcock, S. Babu, M. Datar, R. Motwani, and J. Widom. Models and issues in data stream systems. In *Proceedings of the Twenty-first ACM SIGMOD-SIGACT-SIGART Symposium on Principles of Database Systems*, PODS '02, pages 1–16, New York, NY, USA, 2002. ACM.

[3] K. Banker. *MongoDB in Action*. Manning Publications Co., Greenwich, CT, USA, jan 2012.

[4] D. Ciechanowicz, D. Pelzer, and A. Knoll. Simulation-based approach for investigating the impact of electric vehicles on power grids. In *Proceedings of IEEE PES Asia-Pacific Power and Energy Engineering Conference 2015*, Nov 2015.

[5] E. F. Codd. A relational model of data for large shared data banks. *Communications of the ACM*, 13(6):377–387, jun 1970.

[6] J. Dahmann and K. Morse. High level architecture for simulation: an update. In *Distributed Interactive Simulation and Real-Time Applications, 1998. Proceedings. 2nd International Workshop on*, pages 32–40, Jul 1998.

[7] H. Darwen and C. J. Date. The third manifesto. *SIGMOD Rec.*, 24(1):39–49, mar 1995.

[8] W. Fan and A. Bifet. Mining big data: current status, and forecast to the future. *ACM sIGKDD Explorations Newsletter*, 14(2):1–5, dec 2012.

[9] J. Gama and P. Rodrigues. Data stream processing. In J. Gama and M. Gaber, editors, *Learning from Data Streams*, pages 25–39. Springer Berlin Heidelberg, sep 2007.

[10] P. Kurowski. *Engineering Analysis with SolidWorks Simulation 2012*. SDC Publications, apr 2012.

[11] A. Lakshman and P. Malik. Cassandra: a decentralized structured storage system. *ACM SIGOPS Operating Systems Review*, 44(2):35–40, apr 2010.

[12] N. Mahmood, S. M. A. Burney, and K. Ahsan. A logical temporal relational data model. *CoRR*, abs/1002.1143, jan 2010.

[13] R. Ranjan. Streaming big data processing in datacenter clouds. *IEEE Cloud Computing*, 1(1):78–83, may 2014.

[14] J. Schützel, H. Meyer, and A. M. Uhrmacher. A stream-based architecture for the management and on-line analysis of unbounded amounts of simulation data. In *Proceedings of the 2Nd ACM SIGSIM Conference on Principles of Advanced Discrete Simulation*, SIGSIM PADS '14, pages 83–94, New York, NY, USA, may 2014. ACM.

[15] J. Schützel and A. M. Uhrmacher. Targeted extration of simulation data. In *Distributed Simulation and Real Time Applications (DS-RT), 2015 IEEE/ACM 19th International Symposium on*, Oct 2015.

[16] S. Tickoo. *Autodesk Simulation Mechanical 2015 for Designers*. CADCIM Technologies, sep 2014.

[17] V. K. Vavilapalli, A. C. Murthy, C. Douglas, S. Agarwal, M. Konar, R. Evans, T. Graves, J. Lowe, H. Shah, S. Seth, B. Saha, C. Curino, O. O'Malley, S. Radia, B. Reed, and E. Baldeschwieler. Apache hadoop yarn: Yet another resource negotiator. In *Proceedings of the 4th Annual Symposium on Cloud Computing*, SOCC '13, pages 5:1–5:16, New York, NY, USA, oct 2013. ACM.

[18] V. Viswanathan, D. Zehe, J. Ivanchev, D. Pelzer, A. Knoll, and H. Aydt. Simulation-assisted exploration of charging infrastructure requirements for electric vehicles in urban environments. *Journal of Computational Science*, 12:1–10, jan 2016.

[19] X. Wu, X. Zhu, G.-Q. Wu, and W. Ding. Data mining with big data. *Knowledge and Data Engineering, IEEE Transactions on*, 26(1):97–107, Jan 2014.

[20] M. Zaharia, T. Das, H. Li, S. Shenker, and I. Stoica. Discretized streams: an efficient and fault-tolerant model for stream processing on large clusters. In *Proceedings of the 4th USENIX conference on Hot Topics in Cloud Ccomputing*, pages 10–10. USENIX Association, jun 2012.

[21] D. Zehe, W. Cai, A. Knoll, and H. Aydt. Tutorial on a modeling and simulation cloud service. In *Proceedings of the 2015 Winter Simulation Conference*, dec 2015.

[22] D. Zehe, A. Knoll, W. Cai, and H. Aydt. Semsim cloud service: Large-scale urban systems simulation in the cloud. *Simulation Modelling Practice and Theory*, 58, Part 2:157 – 171, nov 2015. Special issue on Cloud Simulation.

A Simulator for Distributed Cache Management in Friend-to-Friend Networks

Keynan Pratt
University of Calgary
Calgary, AB Canada
kjpratt@cpsc.ucalgary.ca

Carey Williamson
University of Calgary
Calgary, AB Canada
carey@cpsc.ucalgary.ca

ABSTRACT

Multimedia streaming services such as YouTube and Netflix consume a staggering amount of Internet bandwidth [1]. Furthermore, traditional mechanisms such as proxy caches, content distribution networks, and redundant traffic elimination are rendered ineffective by copyright concerns, regulatory issues, and the growing prevalence of end-to-end encryption. One possible solution is a peer-to-peer caching system with social relationships at the core of its topology construction. A social topology carries an implicit level of trust, and induces a relatively high degree of correlation between users that can be exploited by the system as a whole. For example, two users with shared interests are more likely to have relevant videos in cache for each other. This short paper discusses the design of a simulator for such a system to provide insight into the performance of different cache management policies.

CCS Concepts

•**Networks** → *Network simulations;* Network performance modeling; •**Computing methodologies** → *Simulation tools;* Massively parallel algorithms;

Keywords

Friend-to-Friend, F2F, P2P, Distributed Caching, Parallel-DES, Simulation, Haskell

1. INTRODUCTION

Friend-to-Friend (F2F) systems are a sub-class of *Peer-to-Peer (P2P)* systems. The primary distinction is that F2F systems operate with a constrained topology based on social relationships. In F2F systems, a user node may only peer with nodes for which the user knows the operator. This constraint allows the system to assume that the other nodes are trustworthy.

A notable example of an F2F system is *Freenet* [5]. Freenet is a well-known anonymity system that uses heuristic-based

Permission to make digital or hard copies of all or part of this work for personal or classroom use is granted without fee provided that copies are not made or distributed for profit or commercial advantage and that copies bear this notice and the full citation on the first page. Copyrights for components of this work owned by others than ACM must be honored. Abstracting with credit is permitted. To copy otherwise, or republish, to post on servers or to redistribute to lists, requires prior specific permission and/or a fee. Request permissions from permissions@acm.org.

SIGSIM-PADS '16, May 15-18, 2016, Banff, AB, Canada

© 2016 ACM. ISBN 978-1-4503-3742-7/16/05. . . $15.00

DOI: http://dx.doi.org/10.1145/2901378.2901398

routing to achieve expected log-squared routing distance without any node having knowledge of the network beyond its immediate connections [5]. Additionally, the system may assume connected nodes have more properties in common than would randomly chosen nodes. Examples of such commonalities include geo-location, shared interests, education level, and socio-economic background.

This short paper describes work in progress towards a simulator for Netflix content delivery in F2F networks. One motivation for this simulator is the growing volume of media streaming traffic on campus networks. For example, recent work at the University of Calgary studied five months of campus Internet traffic [10]. Of the 2 PB of data analyzed, more than 500 TB of traffic was identified as Netflix video. Detailed analysis showed that a 12 TB cache at the campus edge could save approximately 250 TB of Internet traffic. However, even if Netflix could be persuaded to position edge nodes on every university campus, this would not solve the general case, leaving other services such as Hulu, Amazon Prime, and YouTube to install their own edge nodes. Additionally, university edge caching is made ineffective by the growing use of end-to-end encryption. This necessitates an end system solution that can operate on the encrypted data.

This work-in-progress paper outlines the construction of a simulation engine that, based on limited empirical measurements, can guide the construction and optimization of a distributed caching system. The remaining sections of this paper discuss the design of the simulator, as well as its key components for topology generation, workload generation, and cache management.

2. DESIGN RATIONALE

The Haskell language was chosen for the simulator. Haskell is a pure functional language known for its mathematical rigor. In particular, the strict type system (and the requirement that all side-effect causing code be made explicit) prevent many common programming errors that could undermine the results of simulation. Additionally, the simulator's architecture is built on Cloud Haskell[1], a message-passing library based on Erlang's OTP framework that can achieve high reliability and linear process scaling [2].

In the design of the simulator, two key properties must be maintained: the simulation must be agnostic about the data source; and the simulation must scale well with respect to the size of the social graph, and the number of content requests.

---

[1]https://haskell-distributed.github.io/

In the long term, we wish to examine the efficiency of various cache management strategies and synchronization policies for F2F networks. In the initial prototype, synthetically generated data will be produced with a range of parameters to identify the properties under which each policy performs well. Thus, the simulation uses the following interface:

```
simulate :: (Cache c, Generator ContentEvent g)
        => Graph
        -> Map Vertex g
        -> Map Vertex c
        -> Process SimResults
```

where *Graph* and *Map* are standard Haskell containers, and *Process* refers to the Cloud Haskell *distributed.process*. *Process* monad.

The network topologies are assumed to be static. While social topologies are dynamic, it's assumed that changes of any one node are slight enough to have little or no impact on system behavior.

The core simulator engine operates as follows. Once simulation has begun, the graph $G(V, E)$ is partitioned using an approximation algorithm. The result is k sets containing approximately $|V|/k$ vertices each, where k is the number of processes over which the computational load is to be distributed. Each process p_i has ownership of one set M_i of *master nodes*. Process p_i constructs the set $S_i = \{v \mid u \in M_i, v \notin M_i, (u, v) \in E \lor (v, u) \in E\}$. For all $v \in S_i$, a slave replica of the master cache is created. Whenever the master cache is modified, the new entry and the simulation time at which it was inserted are transmitted to every process that possesses a slave replica. If, at time t, the process p_i attempts to read from a slave cache where the master replica is owned by p_j, it first applies any updates it has received from p_j prior to time t. If the last update received from p_j occurred at or after time t, the read of the slave replica succeeds. If the read of the slave replica fails, then the process p_i announces an update with no content occurred at time $t - 1$; it then pauses simulation. p_i continues receiving updates and resumes simulation when a read of the slave replica succeeds.

The simulator design ensures deadlock-free operation. To understand this, assume process p_i is blocked waiting for an up-to-date slave replica for a node managed by p_j at time t. Then, if p_j is blocked it must be the case that p_j is blocked waiting for an event that happens prior to $t - 1$, so p_j can't be blocked waiting for an event from p_i. It is easy to see how this property generalizes to many processes. Thus, deadlock is not possible in the discrete-event simulator.

3. TOPOLOGY GENERATION

The simulator currently supports several social network topology models. Of primary interest are graphs that are small-world and scale-free, as observed in real-world social networks. We consider Watts-Strogatz (WS), Barabási-Albert, and the Stochastic Block Model. For comparison, we also include the Erdős-Rényi model of random graphs.

For each of these models, the graphs generated are analyzed to understand the properties that influence the simulation results. We focus on the graph diameter, radius, average path length, clustering coefficient, and degree distribution. Brief descriptions of these metrics and properties are given below.

3.1 Graph Properties

3.1.1 Eccentricity

The eccentricity of a vertex v, denoted $\varepsilon(v)$, is the length of the shortest path $P(v, u)$ to the vertex u that is farthest away from it (i.e., there exists no vertex w such that $P(v, w) > P(v, u)$).

3.1.2 Radius & Diameter

The radius of a graph is given by $\min_{v \in V} [\varepsilon(v)]$ and the diameter is given by $\max_{v \in V} [\varepsilon(v)]$

3.1.3 Clustering Coefficient

There exist two common methods for measuring the clustering coefficient of a graph, specifically:

$$C^{\Delta} = \frac{3 * number\ of\ triangles}{number\ of\ connected\ triplets\ of\ vertices}$$

and the Watts-Strogatz clustering coefficient [12]:

$$C^{WS} = \frac{\sum_i (c_i^{ws})}{|V|} \qquad c_i^{WS} = \frac{2e_i}{k_i(k_i - 1)}$$

where, for vertex v_i, e_i is the number of connected neighbors and k_i is the degree of the vertex.

3.2 Graph Models

All simulated graph models accept the input parameter $n = |V|$. We constrain the parameter d_{avg}, the average degree of a vertex, to be within one order of magnitude of that observed in online social networks. According to PEW research [7], the average Facebook user has 338 friends. Thus d_{avg} is constrained to the range $[10, 4000]$. The same PEW study estimated the median number of friends at 200, with 39% of users having less than 100 friends and 15% having more than 500. This gives us a rough approximation of the slope of the degree distribution to be emulated when constructing scale-free graphs.

3.2.1 Erdős-Rényi Graphs

In an Erdős-Rényi graph, the existence of every edge is sampled according to a Bernoulli distribution with probability p [8]. Values of p are chosen such that $p = \frac{|E|}{n}$ and $p > \frac{log(n)}{n}$. The latter constraint ensures that with high probability (w.h.p.), the graph is connected [9].

3.2.2 Watts-Strogatz Graphs

The Watts-Strogatz model [13] is designed to produce graphs with a notably higher *clustering coefficient* than in Erdős-Rényi graphs. The model takes two additional parameters: k where $2|k$ and $n \gg k \gg \log n \gg 1$; and $\beta \in [0, 1]$. The graph is initially constructed as a ring lattice with neighborhood size k. Therefore the graph will contain $\frac{nk}{2}$ edges. Every edge is moved according to probability β. If $\beta = 0$, the lattice structure is preserved. As β approaches unity, the graph resembles an Erdős-Rényi graph where $p = \frac{nk}{2n^2}$. Additionally, as β goes to 1, the average path length rapidly approaches $\frac{\log n}{\log k}$, and the clustering coefficient degrades to $\frac{k}{n}$. The small-world properties of these graphs are most prominent for intermediate values of β, before the clustering coefficient drops, and the average path length shrinks. One limitation of this model is the unrealistic degree distribution. The WS degree distribution tends

(a) Erdős-Rényi Graph   (b) Watts-Strogatz Graph   (c) Barabási-Albert   (d) q-Clique Tree

Figure 1: Graph examples for $n \approx 30$ and $d_{avg} \approx 4$

Table 1: Small ($n \approx 30$, $d_{avg} \approx 4$, $\beta = 0.28$)

Model	Diameter	Avg Path Length	C^{WS}
Erdős-Rényi Graphs	6	2.559	0.134
Watts-Strogatz	5	2.578	0.133
Barabási-Albert	4	2.308	0.238
q-Clique Tree	3	1.80	0.810

Table 3: Large ($n = 10,000$, $d_{avg} = 20$, $\beta = 0.28$)

Model	Diameter	Avg Path Length	C^{WS}
Erdős-Rényi Graphs	5	3.401	0.002
Watts Strogatz	5	3.744	0.269
Barabási-Albert	5	3.065	0.011
q-Clique Tree	5	3.064	0.875

Table 2: Medium ($n = 1000$, $d_{avg} = 10$, $\beta = 0.28$)

Model	Diameter	Avg Path Length	C^{WS}
Erdős-Rényi Graphs	6	3.307	0.009
Watts Strogatz	6	3.660	0.263
Barabási-Albert	5	2.989	0.036
q-Clique Tree	5	2.787	0.874

towards a Poisson, while observed social networks have a power-law distribution.

3.2.3 Barabási-Albert Graphs

The Barabási-Albert model [3] produces scale-free graphs. From an initial graph containing n_0 vertices, the remaining $n - n_0$ vertices are added. For each additional vertex, m edges are created. Each edge connects the vertex to an existing vertex v_i with probability $p_i = \frac{d_i}{2E}$ where d_i is the current degree of v_i. The resulting graph has degree distribution roughly $P(d) \sim d^{-3}$. Scale-free graphs are ultra-small-world with average path length $\frac{\log n}{\log \log n}$. However, as n grows, the clustering coefficient tends towards $n^{-0.75}$, much lower than observed in social networks.

3.2.4 Recursive Clique Trees

Recursive Clique Trees, as discussed by [6], are deterministically generated hierarchical graphs that exhibit both the small-world and scale-free properties. The graph is constructed according to two parameters q and t, where q is the clique size, and t is the recursive depth. The graph grows exponentially with parameter t, while q controls both the clustering coefficient and the degree distribution.

Examples of the four graph models are shown in Figure 1, with their graph metrics given in Table 1.

4. WORKLOAD GENERATION

Workload generation is focused on content requests that reflect general viewing habits. As a control, one class of generator samples *independently* from the empirical Zipf-like distribution identified by [10]. However, it is reasonable to consider correlation between the viewing habits of friends in a social network, as well as for content events to depend on previous events observed by the same node. The correlations arise from common interests, social recommendation, word-

of-mouth, and social engagement. Dependence is most pronounced in terms of viewing habits. After watching episode 6, a user is very likely to watch episode 7, and extremely unlikely to watch episode 28.

In order to include these dependencies in our simulation, samples are taken from a composition of multiple distributions, each of which is unique to a particular node. Each node starts with the same distribution as the control. As events are processed the distribution is updated to reflect the correlation and dependence outlined above. The primary technique used is the Least-Recently-Used (LRU) stack model commonly used for modeling temporal locality in caching simulations.

A practice among some viewers is to "binge watch" specific TV series. Thus, there will be a strong tendency to watch only a small number of series at a time, consuming one to completion before moving on. Additionally, in order to accurately reflect the real world, new content will become available mid-simulation. The arrival of new content may interrupt the current series being viewed.

5. CACHING ARCHITECTURE

The design of an effective caching architecture is the main motivation for our simulator. It is desirable to avoid a cross-network query if the query would fail. Therefore, each node maintains a Bloom filter [4] of each neighbor's cache. Tuning the size of the Bloom filter relative to the cache size will be an important optimization question during simulation.

Prior to their deployment of end-to-end encryption, Netflix was known to buffer video via multiple HTTP request-response operations. In a production system, each individual HTTP request must be representable as a cache query. Additionally, each request would specify a time offset into the video. The flexibility offered by this API must be mirrored in a production cache. Therefore, each video occupies a single entry in the cache, though the entry may be incomplete or even contain holes. In order to minimize message-passing overhead in simulation, each movie or TV episode is treated as a single cache entry, storing only the integer identifying the video requested.

Common cache management policies such as FIFO, LRU, and LFU will be considered. However, traditional caching policies are applied in a single user environment; the distributed environment creates opportunities for unique cache semantics. Consider the perception of a single node. It does this node no good for all of its neighbors to store the most popular piece of content. As soon as the closest neighbor has the content in cache, the node ceases to gain benefit from other neighbors caching the same content. In some sense, cache space is wasted if they do so. The neighbor, when pulling a piece of content, may choose not to cache it.

Recall that the social topology is small-world and therefore has a high clustering coefficient. In other words, your friends are frequently friends with each other. Assume that a node can discover or approximate the distance of each neighbor to the closest source (i.e., Netflix server), and to any mutually connected neighbors. Let the in-network availability of a piece of content γ be defined as the percentage of neighbors who have a mutual neighbor who has the content and is closer to them than to the source. Then, the node may choose to store the content with probability $p = f(\gamma)$. Two functions of interest are:

$$f(\gamma) = 1 - \gamma \quad \text{and} \quad f(\gamma) = 1 - S(12\gamma - 6)$$

where $S(x)$ is the sigmoid function. An alternative measure of availability would be for each node to provide each neighbor with a second Bloom filter suggesting the pieces of content to which it has nearby access. This measure would produce lower message overhead and greater accuracy at the expense of leaking information to nodes without a direct connection.

6. CURRENT CHALLENGES

6.1 Random Number Generation

One unexpected technical challenge was random number generation. Implementations of common pseudo-random number generators (PRNG), such as the Mersenne twist, are available in Haskell. However, these implementations may be incomplete, or have drawbacks such as the inability to safely split the period across multiple parallel streams. We have implemented the xorshift-128-plus algorithm to serve as the underlying U(0,1) PRNG. While no PRNG is known to pass all of the standard TestU01 [11] statistical tests, xor0shift passes many more of these tests than does the Mersenne twist, which is believed to be the most popular PRNG in use today. Additionally, the xorshift-128-plus is fast, requires minimal state, and has a period many orders of magnitude larger than required in most simulations.

6.2 Parallel Performance

Our simulator is designed to exploit the inherently distributed nature of the problem. Each simulated node depends only on having current knowledge of its neighbors. Simulation run-time is expected to scale linearly with the number of vertices in the social graph for a fixed value of d_{avg}. To see why this is true, consider the extreme case $n = k$, where all edges cross partition boundaries. Then for a given content event, the node must process d incoming messages, perform the update reading from d slave replicas, and broadcast d outgoing messages. Each process will need to remain in near lockstep, so the entire simulation will progress at the rate of the slowest node (with highest degree). Synchronization overhead in a partition is bounded by the number of partition-crossing edges, while event processing time is bounded by the degree of the node.

The key to simulation performance will be good partitioning of the vertices.

An optimal partitioning minimizes the number of edges between processes and the number of slave replicas that need to be maintained. The upper bound on the number of crossing edges for a 2-cut is $\frac{nd}{2}$. As the slope of the distribution increases, efficient partitioning is expected to become more likely.

Inefficient partitioning results in higher memory usage and higher communication overhead when cache updates are broadcast. Provided $n \gg d_{avg}$, performance should scale well if k is increased proportionally. As either k or d approach n, message overhead will become large.

7. FUTURE DIRECTIONS

The path to a working simulation is clear in most respects. It is still necessary to identify a good partitioning algorithm for each graph model. The implementation is expected to be complete in time to present preliminary results in May.

8. REFERENCES

[1] V. Adhikari, Y. Guo, F. Hao, V. Hilt, Z. Zhang, M. Varvello, and M. Steiner. Measurement study of netflix, hulu, and a tale of three cdns. *IEEE/ACM Transactions on Networking*, 23(6):1984–1997, Dec 2015.

[2] J. Armstrong. Erlang. *Communications of the ACM*, 53(9):68, 2010.

[3] A. Barabási and R. Albert. Statistical mechanics of complex networks. *Reviews of Modern Physics*, 74(January):48–94, 2002.

[4] B. Bloom. Space/time trade-offs in hash coding with allowable errors. *Communications of the ACM*, 13(7):422–426, 1970.

[5] I. Clarke, O. Sandberg, B. Wiley, and T. Hong. Freenet: A distributed anonymous information storage and retrieval system. *Designing Privacy Enhancing Technologies.*, pages 46–66, 2001.

[6] F. Comellas, G. Fertin, and A. Raspaud. Recursive graphs with small-world scale-free properties. *Physical Review E - Statistical, Nonlinear, and Soft Matter Physics*, 69(3 2):2–5, 2004.

[7] M. Duggan and A. Smith. Social media update 2013. *Pew Internet and American Life Project*, 2013.

[8] P. Erdös and A. Rényi. On random graphs. *Publicationes Mathematicae*, 6:290–297, 1959.

[9] P. Erdos and A. Renyi. The evolution of random graphs. *Publ. Math. Inst. Hungar. Acad. Sci*, 5(1):17, 1961.

[10] M. Laterman. NetFlix and Twitch Traffic Characterization. Master's thesis, University of Calgary, 2015.

[11] P. L'Ecuyer and R. Simard. TestU01: A c Library for empirical testing of random number generators. *ACM Transactions on Mathematical Software*, 33(4), 2007.

[12] Q. Telesford, K. Joyce, S. Hayasaka, J. Burdette, and P. Laurienti. The Ubiquity of Small-World Networks. *Brain Connectivity*, 1(5):367–375, Dec. 2011.

[13] D. Watts and S. Strogatz. Collective dynamics of 'small-world' networks. *Nature*, 393(6684):440–2, 1998.

Agent-based Simulation Modeling of Low Fertility Trap Hypothesis

Jeongsik Kim*, Kasin Ransikarbum*, Namhun Kim*, Euihyun Paik+

*Department of Human and Systems Engineering,
Ulsan National Institute of Science and Technology
UNIST-gil 50, Ulsan, South Korea
{jskim0, kasinr, nhkim}@unist.ac.kr
+Electronics and Telecommunications Research Institute
Gajeong-ro 218, Daejeon, South Korea
ehpaik@unist.ac.kr

ABSTRACT

Advances in information technology enable researchers to utilize big data in analyzing social behaviors in scientific ways. While an interest to evaluate economically effective policies is increasing worldwide, testing hypothesized policies with a real society is highly risky. To overcome this difficulty, we present an agent-based social simulation model based on the low fertility trap hypotheses, which includes human network, social heterogeneity, demographic condition, and economic activity. We aim to 1) analyze the interaction between economic state transitions and demographic events in terms of ageing, low fertility, and economic instability and 2) use the social simulation model to support political decision making based on real case study data from South Korea. An initial designed experiment shows that ageing and low fertility are mutually related to individual economic capability. Low fertility is also found to be a consequence of creating an economic buffer against consumption and well-being of people in a society, especially with a high number of elderly. This current study is the first phase of the hybrid simulation model integrating the statistical-based micro simulation and system dynamics simulation approaches in our on-going work to create the hybrid demographic simulation model using South Korean case study to better understand social phenomena and to provide economic solutions during crises.

Keywords

Agent-based Simulation; Economic Life Cycle; Social Simulation; Demographic Simulation; Low Fertility Trap

1. INTRODUCTION

With an advance development in computer science and information technology, computational simulations have played an important role in studying human behaviors for the last few decades [1]. The key advantage of computational simulation is its ability to test and verify when experimenting with a real system is not feasible [2]. In addition, as an experiment with a complex

Permission to make digital or hard copies of all or part of this work for personal or classroom use is granted without fee provided that copies are not made or distributed for profit or commercial advantage and that copies bear this notice and the full citation on the first page. Copyrights for components of this work owned by others than ACM must be honored. Abstracting with credit is permitted. To copy otherwise, or republish, to post on servers or to redistribute to lists, requires prior specific permission and/or a fee. Request permissions from Permissions@acm.org.

SIGSIM-PADS '16, May 15-18, 2016, Banff, AB, Canada
© 2016 ACM. ISBN 978-1-4503-3742-7/16/05...$15.00
DOI: http://dx.doi.org/10.1145/2901378.2901399

system involving society, demography, and economy requires high risk and cost of experimentation; using a simulation approach is a key tool, which can deal with such complex system.

Recent simulation approaches to a human society have been developed to integrate diverse sectors of a society to capture social dynamics with multi-level observations (e.g., [3-7]). These models are broadly categorized into either statistical-based approach (e.g. microsimulation model (MSM)) or rule-based approach (e.g. agent-based model (ABM) and system dynamics model (SDM)). Although MSM can take advantage of empirical data in the form of transition probability to simulate a future society, there are limitations in predicting with uncertain knowledge, dealing with insufficient data, and increasing of model complexity [8]. On the other hand, while SDM and ABM can enable the analysis of emergent behaviors with the capability of adapting prescriptive rules, it has the fundamental drawbacks of discrepancy with the real data and the high cost of finding reasonable rules [5-7]. While SDM is used as a top-down approach, ABM is considered as a bottom-up simulation with agent interactions [2]. These modeling methodologies have been proposed to capture various aspects of social dynamics. ABM in particular is developed to discover interactions and relationships between different individual agents and stocks in emergent phenomena of a society [9-11]. Moreover, a hybrid simulation approach integrating ABM with multiple simulation methods has recently gained attention as a new solution for complex system in manufacturing applications. However, the hybrid approach in the social-demographic study is at the infant level [12, 13].

In the current research, we develop an agent-based simulation module of a hybrid model for a demographic-economic study and conduct a designed experiment to test the impact of social and demographic elements on economic policies. The outline of this paper is as follows. We discuss the proposed agent-based simulation modeling framework based on the low fertility trap hypothesis in Section 2. Then, Sections 3 and 4 present an experimental design and initial results, respectively. Finally, we conclude our research and provide future directions in Section 5.

2. MODELING LOW FERTILITY TRAP
2.1 Agent-based Simulation Approach

The agent-based simulation model proposed in the current study implements social phenomena of ageing and low fertility. An ageing society is often cited as one of the biggest problems in many developed countries [14]. It is also expected to cause an economic burden for the next generation and this burden in turn causes the lower fertility ending up with a financial crisis for the whole society [14-16]. To capture interactions of these phenomena, we design an agent with a set of discrete states of demographic events based on the Economic Life Cycle (ELC). We then use this model as a preliminary test bed for political welfare services.

Obtaining proper social-demographic data related to human network has been challenging in certain countries, including South Korea which is the original system of the developed model in the current research. South Korean statistical records show that the ageing ratio is predicted to be at the world top level [14]. However, available demographic and economic data in South Korea cover a relatively short period and are very dynamic [17]. Unstable and insufficient data can prohibit the development and the validation of statistical approach in the social and demographic simulation models. This issue is critical for the statistical-based simulation models, which are developed using accumulated empirical data with social indices. Thus, the rule-based approach is used in the current study to reduce the dependency on long-term empirical data.

2.2 Low Fertility Trap Hypotheses

Lutz *et al.* [13] suggest that when the fertility decreases below a certain level, it will be difficult to recover from the low fertility. They call this phenomenon the low fertility trap and discuss its root from three mechanisms in terms of demography, sociology, and economy. Low Fertility Trap Hypotheses (LFTHs) are these mechanisms for serving low fertility and its downward spiral. The hypotheses are listed below.

> *LFTH-1: Fewer births today means fewer potential mothers in the future*
> *LFTH-2: Lower actual fertility in previous cohorts will decrease ideal family size for the younger cohorts*
> *LFTH-3: If fertility is decided by the combination of economic aspirations and expected income, ageing population induced by low fertility will cause higher aspiration and lower expected income and the fertility will decrease*

Our previous study (Kim *et al.* [18]) presents an agent-based model implementing demographic mechanism (*LFTH-1*) and a decrease of fertility by ageing population. The modeling framework is summarized in Figure 1. It shows that an increase in the ageing ratio of the population increases the mean age of fertility and decreases the fertility rate. This is due to that the elderly agents depend their economic status on the younger agents, who are at the age for fertility. To be precise, if every person needs money to spend each year to continue to live on, living longer implies that more money are needed and can be an issue due to insufficient financial earnings. It then follows that an insufficient economic status of an elderly person may cause the person to depend on the younger agent. Thus, the latter may decide to postpone his or her savings for fertility in order to support the elderly's insufficient economic status under the longer ageing condition. In other words, the decision for postponing or giving up a chance for fertility is used as a temporary countermeasure to deal with insufficient economic status and to live in a better economic situation as a whole.

In this research, we extend the previous model based on the *LFTH-3* to capture demographic and economic dynamics in ageing population by low fertility. The decision for fertility according to current economic capability and economic aspiration from parents is further discussed in section 2.3, which will be tested with welfare services next. We note that the *LFTH-2* is in the list in our on-going future research.

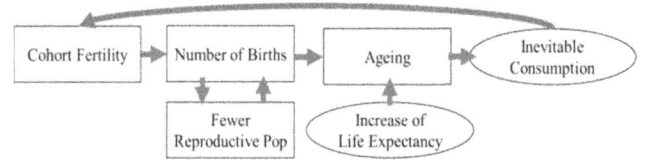

Figure 1. Relationship between low fertility and ageing population [18]

2.3 Demographic-Economic Model

The demographic-economic model presented in this section is developed using AnyLogic 7.1 software. Agents stay in a virtual society and each agent may have connections with other agents in its kinship. The inputs of the model are the combinations between the distribution of life expectancy and policies for economic support. Observations of the model include number of fertility, mean age of fertility, and individual financial status.

The agent in the simulation model represents a human who lives over his or her lifetime. He or she may form a family and have a child, work to receive income, spend money, and eventually die at some ages. Each agent experiences a simplified cycle of economic activity including 'education', 'labor', and 'retirement' during his or her life and each transition occurs once at a specified age. In our model, we use coins to represent monetary activities to investigate an economic status of each agent. Initially, we assume that these agents will spend constant coins during each step for individual activities and can earn coins only during the labor stage. A simple example of the above demographic-economic relationship is illustrated in Figure 2.

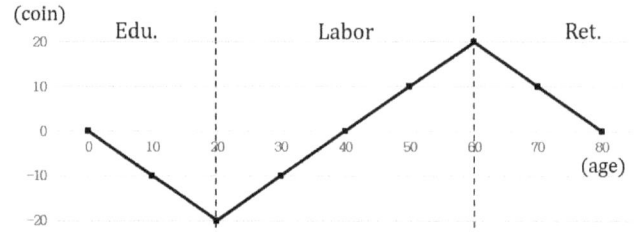

Figure 2. The example of demographic-economic relationship of an agent's lifetime ('education' period = 0-20 steps, 'labor' period = 20-60 steps, and life expectancy = 80 steps)

An agent will require cost of living based on Equation (1), which accounts for the propagation of economic aspiration from parent agent to the child agent. Then, when each agent is at the labor stage, the tax will be required based on Equation (2). Next, an agent will consider reproducing a new agent when reaching a certain age range. The agent will judge if he/she has enough economic capability for reproduction according to Equation (3) by considering several factors including cost of living, tax payment, welfare benefits, etc. The reproduced agent starts with zero years old and will die (leave the system) at the age given by the distribution of death by age in each scenario. Then, the new agent becomes connected with the parent agent in kinship. This connection allows the monetary dependence between the parent and child agents when an agent has no saved coin to spend. It follows that every newborn agent has no any coins at the beginning and will depend on his or her parent agent until certain ages (i.e., 'labor' state).

$$Cost\ of\ living\ (C) = (1 - 0.5 \cdot k_d) \cdot I + k_d \cdot C_p \qquad (1)$$

$$Tax\ (T) = I \cdot TS \qquad (2)$$

$$Fertility = P + (I - T) \cdot RT_R - C \cdot RT_D - (C - S_{Ch}) \cdot TP_E \qquad (3)$$

, where k_d = Coefficients for propagation of economic aspiration, C_p= Cost of living of the parent agent, I = Income, TS = Tax size, P = Current property, RT_R = Residual time to retirement, RT_D = Residual time to death, S_{Ch} = Subsidy for childcare from system, and TP_E = Time for Education period

On one hand, a retired agent without any coins will secure cost of living from his or her connected agents. The economic status of the retired agent with no coins will be negative when there are no connected agents or when the supports are not possible from these connected agents. On the other hand, an agent at the edge of life expectancy may propagate his or her residuary coins or debt to his or her offspring.

The initial conditions of the simulation model are as follows. At the first 30 steps, 100 agents are generated for each step. As they are zero years old and are the first generation, each agent will have coins to pay for his or her own educational fee. We note that this initial condition will be relaxed later using the warmup analysis when the statistical outputs are collected. During each step (i.e., each year), every agent computationally processes seven events in sequence, which include getting old, being dead, deciding fertility, earning income, consuming a coin, exchanging or transferring a coin, and reporting its own status to the simulation control (Figure 3).

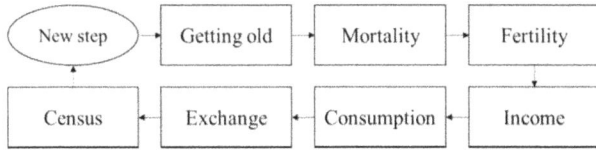

Figure 3. Individual event-order during a step

3. DESIGNED EXPERIMENT
The simulation experiments are conducted with different scenarios to understand the impact of ageing phenomenon (i.e., ageing society) to the combined demographic-economic indices based on essential demographic events and ELC. All the experimental scenarios are conducted on a personal computer (PC) with an Intel (R) Core (TM) with its processor i7-3770 @ 3.40 GHz. The system type is 64-bit OS on Windows 7 and the maximum available memory is set as 4GB.

To verify ageing phenomena with *LFTH*-3 and test political policies, different scenarios are generated based on economic growth (EG), ageing parameter (AP), initial life expectancy (ILE), political support type (PT), and tax size (TS) as summarized in Table 1. In particular, the EG and AP factors both consist of two levels (0.00 or 0.15), the ILE factor consists of three levels (75, 80, or 85), the PT factor consists of three levels (None, Childcare, or Pension), and the TS consists of two levels (10% or 20%). Thus, it follows that the total scenarios required for the simulation analysis are $2 \cdot 2 \cdot 3 \cdot (3 \cdot 2 - 1) = 60$ scenarios. We next discuss the experimental factors below.

In all scenarios, an agent will be removed from the system when his or her age (i.e., simulation steps) is equal to the sum of initially assigned life (i.e., mean age of ILE) and the additional life based on AP factor. The additional life represents wellbeing of an agent to live longer. In particular, the AP can be set to either 0 for no additional life or 0.15 for higher ageing from additional life. We note that the AP factor of 0.15 is the empirical increasing scale of mean age at death of those people aged over 60 from 1990 to 2010 in South Korea [14].

Table 1. Summary of scenarios (Note: there is no TS option when PT = 'None')

Ageing Parameter	Initial Life Expectancy	Economic Growth	Political Type	Tax Size
0.00	75	0.00	None	10%
0.15	80	0.15	Childcare	20%
	85		Pension	

The initial life expectancy of every agent is randomly assigned by a specified mean age and age distribution. In all scenarios, the mean of initial ILE for an agent is assumed to be 75, 80, or 85 steps. This mean value indicates the starting economic status of an agent in a virtual society to decide how residuary coins will be handled when he or she is dead. The distribution of the ILE is assumed to be triangular on 11 consecutive integers centered at a specific mean (e.g. 70-80, 75-85, or 80-90).

The EG implies an increase of individual income. It can be set to either 0 for constant income or 0.15 for higher income by 15%. The EG factor of 0.15 is used to investigate a balance between economic capability and consumption because fertility rate decreases with higher ageing phenomena without any changes in yearly income.

In addition, agents will pay taxes and some of them may get supported by a selective welfare service. That is, a system (e.g., government) can choose not to support any coins with no tax (i.e., None) or exchange coins by one of the two methods: Childcare (Ch) or Pension (Pe). The Ch service supports some coins for parent agents to encourage them to have a baby. That is, an agent, who decides to have a baby, will receive certain amount of coins from the system. The Pe service is used to support some coins for a retired agent, who has no coins or has to depend on his or her connected agents. A retired agent without any coins will also secure some coins from the stored tax. The size of support will depend on the TS of either 10% or 20%. All stored tax will be equally distributed to support zero-coin objects every year.

4. RESULTS AND DISCUSSION
To verify the model and analyze the *LFTH-3* outlined above, we generate 30 replications for each scenario resulting in 30*60 = 1800 simulation trials. After obtaining all the outputs from all trials, the results are analyzed in terms of demographic events, economic level, and the combined effect of both in this section. In each trial run, the model is run for totally 260 simulation steps with a step of one year. Then, the first 60 steps are excluded from a statistical interpretation accounting for the initial effect or the warmup period. That is, the statistical output for each trial run is based on the 200-step run to ensure that long-term effect is incorporated.

Initially, the economic-demographic relationship is verified. When we vary between AP=0.00 and AP=0.15, but keep other parameters fixed with EG=0.00 and PT='None', it is clear that excessive consumption itself worsens the ageing ratio over time (i.e., higher ageing ratio). The ageing ratio also tends to be stable when μ=75. This is due to that these agents have enough coins to spend during their lifespan, but is not the case in other conditions. The ageing ratio in this case is calculated based on the proportion of the agents with age higher than 60 years old. Observations shows that ageing cause an imbalance between economic capability and consumption and this imbalance results in the postponement of fertility and economic stability as explained in the section 2.2. In other words, ageing and low fertility are mutually related to individual economic capability. Low fertility can be seen as a consequence of creating an economic buffer against consumption and well-being of people in a society especially with a high number of elderly.

We note that the current study in this paper shows the verification study of the model with regard to the economic-demographic relationship, while the other scenarios pertaining to political changes are being studied. We are also analyzing South Korea data to validate our proposed model.

5. CONCLUSION

The scope of previous studies in demography has been restricted by the risks and costs of experimenting with a real society. As the key advantage of computational simulation is its ability to test and verify when experimenting with a real system is not feasible, we developed an agent based simulation model based on a simplified economic life cycle (ELC) in this paper. A designed experiment is then conducted based on demographic, economic, and political scenarios. Our initial results show that the ageing phenomenon significantly affects the low fertility and economic states when economic capability is a key factor for living and reproduction. Continuing from the current work, we are studying how other scenarios related to political policy and tax status impact the agents living in the system.

Additionally, to reflect the South Korean economic and demographic situation, the current model will be further extended and integrated with the system dynamics and microsimulation approaches as an integrated hybrid model. The authors are also collecting the empirical data of South Korean society to validate the developed simulation model. That is, the demographic and financial distribution of population will be used as the basis to define the initial population and coefficients related to ELC structure, demographic information, and economic relationship between agents.

6. ACKNOWLEDGMENTS

The authors would like to thank South Korean Electronics and Telecommunications Research Institute to support this project (10047117, Development of Distributed / Parallel Multi-Dimensional Demographic Micro Simulation Technologies for Population Dynamics and Socio-Economic Experimentation).

7. REFERENCES

[1] Billari, F.C., Ongaro, F., and Prskawetz, A. 2003. Introduction: Agent-based Computational Demography. In *Agent-based computational demography: Using simulation to improve our understanding of demographic behavior*, F.C. Billari, and A. Prskawetz, Ed. Physica-Verlag HD, Heidelberg, 1-17. DOI=10.1007/978-3-7908-2715-6_1

[2] Borshchev, A. and Filippov, A. 2004. From system dynamics and Discrete Event to Practical Agent-based Modeling: Reasons, Techniques, Tools. In *Proceedings of the 22nd international conference of the system dynamics society*, Oxford, England, July 25-29.

[3] Cassells, R., Harding, A., and Kelly, S. 2006. Problems and Prospects for Dynamic Microsimulation: A Review and Lessons for APPSIM. NATSEM, University of Canberra.

[4] Spielauer, M. 2013. The LifePaths Microsimulation Model : An Overview. Ottawa: Statistics Canada.

[5] Morand, E., Toulemon, L., Pennec, S., Baggio, R., and Billari, F. 2010. Demographic Modelling: the State of the Art. Paris, INED. FP7-244557 Project Sustain City 39.

[6] Spielauer, M. 2011. What is Social Science Microsimulation? *Social Science Computer Review*. 29, 1, 9-20.

[7] Li, J. and O'Donoghue, C. 2013. A Survey of Dynamic Microsimulation Models: Uses, Model Structure and Methodology. *International Journal of Microsimulation* 6, 2, 3-55.

[8] Silverman, E., Bijak, J., Noble, J. 2011. Feeding the Beast: can Computational Demographic Model? In *Proceedings of the Eleventh European Conference on the Synthesis and Simulation of Living Systems*. MIT Press, 747-754

[9] Noble, J., Silverman, E., Bijak, J., Rossiter, S., Evandrou, M., Bullock, S., Vlachantoni, A., and Falkingham, J. 2012. Linked Lives: the Utility of an Agent-based Approach to Modeling Partnership and Household Formation in the Context of Social Care. In *Proceedings of the Winter Simulation Conference*. 1-12. Winter Simulation Conference.

[10] Wu, B.M., Birkin, M.H. 2012. Agent-based Extensions to a Spatial Microsimulation Model of Demographic Change. *Agent-based models of geographical systems* (Jan. 2012), 347-360.

[11] Balbo, N., Billari, F., and Melinda, M. 2013. Fertility in Advanced Societies: A review of Research. *European Journal of Population* 29, 1-38.

[12] Brailsford, S. C., Silverman, E., Rossiter, S., Bijak, J., Shaw, R. J., Viana, J., and Vlachantoni, A. 2011. Complex Systems Modeling for Supply and Demand in Health and Social Care. In *Proceedings of the Winter Simulation Conference*. 1125-1136. Winter Simulation Conference.

[13] Swinerd, C. and McNaught, K. R. 2012. Design Classes for Hybrid Simulations Involving Agent-based and System Dynamics Models. *Simulation Modelling Practice and Theory* 25, 118-133.

[14] National Center for Korean statistics, [Online] URL: http://kostat.go.kr/. Accessed: Nov. 05, 2015

[15] Brar, K. S., Sajjad, M., and Ahn, C. W. 2015. Policy Evaluation by Analysing Population Emergent Behaviour with a Microsimulation and Multi Agent Based Model. In *International Symposium on Agents, Multi-agent Systems and Robotics*. 83-86. IEEE.

[16] Lutz, W., Skirbekk, V., and Testa, M. R. 2006. The Low-fertility Trap Hypothesis: Forces that may Lead to Further Postponement and Fewer Births in Europe. *Vienna yearbook of population research*, 167-192.

[17] Park, Y., Kim, H., Choi, B. and Kim, K. 2009. A Study on Applying Microsimulation to the Korean Population Structure. *Journal of the Korean Data Analysis Society* 11, 2, 881-893.

[18] Kim, J., and Kim, N. 2015. Preliminary Research on an Agent-Based Simulation of Economic Life Cycle in Demography. In Proceedings of Asia Simulation (Jeju, Korea, Nov. 4-6, 2015). Springer-Verlag.

The Future of Parallel Discrete Event Simulation

David Jefferson
Lawrence Livermore National Laboratory

ABSTRACT

Parallel discrete event simulation (PDES) has been a subject of research since the late 1970s. By now we know a lot about the general outlines of the subject. However, there is still an immense amount of research and development to do. In this talk I will summarize what I believe PDES has contributed to computer science and other fields so far, what the current status is, where I think we are still deficient as a field, and where I think our R&D priorities should be in the future.

Keywords

parallel discrete event simulation; extreme scale; synchronization; modeling

Permission to make digital or hard copies of part or all of this work for personal or classroom use is granted without fee provided that copies are not made or distributed for profit or commercial advantage and that copies bear this notice and the full citation on the first page. Copyrights for third-party components of this work must be honored. For all other uses, contact the Owner/Author(s). Copyright is held by the owner/author(s).

SIGSIM-PADS, May 15–18, 2016, Banff, Alberta, Canada.
ACM 978-1-4503-3742-7/16/05.
DOI: http://dx.doi.org/10.1145/2901378.2901404

A Role-dependent Data-driven Approach for High Density Crowd Behavior Modeling

Mingbi Zhao
School of Computer
Engineering
Nanyang Technological
University
Singapore 639798
zhao0149@ntu.edu.sg

Jinghui Zhong
School of Computer
Engineering
Nanyang Technological
University
Singapore 639798
jinghuizhong@ntu.edu.sg

Wentong Cai
School of Computer
Engineering
Nanyang Technological
University
Singapore 639798
aswtcai@ntu.edu.sg

ABSTRACT

In this paper, we propose a role-dependent data-driven modeling approach to simulate pedestrians' motion in high density scenes. It is commonly observed that pedestrians behave quite differently when walking in dense crowd. Some people explore routes towards their destinations. Meanwhile, some people deliberately follow others, leading to lane formation. Based on these observations, two roles are included in the proposed model: leader and follower. The motion behaviors of leader and follower are modeled separately. Leaders' behaviors are learned from real crowd motion data using state-action pairs while followers' behaviors are calculated based on specific targets that are obtained dynamically during the simulation. The proposed role-dependent data-driven model is trained on crowd video data in one dataset and is then applied to two other different datasets to test its generality and effectiveness. The simulation results demonstrate that the proposed role-dependent data-driven model is capable of simulating crowd behaviors in crowded scenes realistically and reproducing collective crowd behaviors such as lane formation.

CCS Concepts

•Computing methodologies → Modeling and simulation; *Artificial intelligence;* Computer graphics;

Keywords

Crowd simulation; data-driven models; leader-follower behavior

1. INTRODUCTION

Public places where a lot of people gathering together (e.g., shopping malls and train stations) appear more and more common in modern days, especially in big cities. In these high density crowd scenes, the behaviors of pedestrians are quite different from those in low density ones, because pedestrians are more difficult to move freely due to the lack of available space. High crowd density may

Permission to make digital or hard copies of all or part of this work for personal or classroom use is granted without fee provided that copies are not made or distributed for profit or commercial advantage and that copies bear this notice and the full citation on the first page. Copyrights for components of this work owned by others than ACM must be honored. Abstracting with credit is permitted. To copy otherwise, or republish, to post on servers or to redistribute to lists, requires prior specific permission and/or a fee. Request permissions from permissions@acm.org.

SIGSIM-PADS '16, May 15-18, 2016, Banff, AB, Canada
© 2016 ACM. ISBN 978-1-4503-3742-7/16/05. . . $15.00
DOI: http://dx.doi.org/10.1145/2901378.2901382

result in serious safety issues. A number of tragedies have already happened in many high density public places in the past few years [1, 2]. Therefore, understanding and simulating crowd behaviors in high density scenes is of great usefulness for the public safety. It can provide effective tools to evaluate evacuation strategies and building structures, and to train the skills of rescue team.

In crowded scenarios, pedestrians automatically form collective motion patterns such as walking in lanes, moving faster along the edge of crowd, forming stop-and-go wave and so on. These self-organized macroscopic behaviors help to improve overall walking efficiency and avoid traffic congestions. Several models have been developed over the last few years to simulate crowd dynamics in high density scenes. Most of them are defined based on the current knowledge as well as the hypothesis and assumptions observed from pedestrians motion. The typical examples include modeling the social interactions among pedestrians as forces [14, 15] and determining future velocities based on bio-mechanical energy spent [12]. By defining proper formulas based on the modelers' domain knowledge, this kind of methods are able to reproduce some of the collective crowd dynamics such as lane formation. However, developing this class of crowd models requires tremendous domain knowledge and manual effort, which can be quite time consuming. Besides, calibrating the initially designed model is also a trial task.

Recently, data-driven crowd modeling approaches have been proposed to automate modeling process. These approaches are inspired by human decision-making process where pedestrians are likely to make their decisions based on past experience when encountering a new situation [18]. The key idea is to learn knowledge such as state-action pairs from real pedestrians and then utilize the learned knowledge to drive pedestrians' behaviors, so that the simulated behaviors can match the observed real pedestrians' behaviors [8, 22, 24]. However, the existing data-driven models mainly aim at generating realistic motion behaviors in low density scenarios, many of which cannot be directly applied to high density scenarios, because pedestrians behave quite differently in high density scenarios from those in low density cases.

To overcome the above issues, this paper proposes a role-dependent data-driven crowd modeling approach to generate realistic crowd dynamics in high density scenes so that the simulated behaviors can match the real world crowd data. The key idea is to model pedestrians' behaviors separately according to their roles. According to Wolff [39], people usually have two choices when walking in a high density situation. The first is to move behind pedestrians in front. Another option is to "intrude into the oncoming pedestrians". Therefore, two roles are included in the proposed model: follower and leader. After sensing environment features, followers decide to follow pedestrians in front that have the same destinations of their own; whereas leaders attempt to explore their paths through other pedestrians. The role of each pedestrian is updated at every time step based on the sensed environment features. State-action pairs which are specifically designed for high density scenarios are generated from leaders' behaviors in real crowd data to drive leaders' motion in simulation. To test the effectiveness and generality of the proposed model, two narrow corridor scenes with different crowd densities are applied and the proposed model is compared with two other models qualitatively and quantitatively in terms of reproducing crowd behaviors in real crowd data.

2. RELATED WORK

2.1 Leader-Follower Concept in Crowd Modeling

The leader follower concept is widely used in simulating crowd dynamics. In [30, 31], different roles (trained leader, untrained leader etc.) are applied to simulate pedestrians evacuating a building with many rooms. The roles are manually assigned to pedestrians in order to study the effect of different personnel composition on crowd evacuation process. Leaders are simulated by the same crowd models as other pedestrians except that they are more familiar with the building's internal structure. In the proposed model, agents automatically determine their roles periodically during simulations. Leader-follower concept is also used in simulating the behaviors of pedestrians walking in a small group [19, 21, 34, 36, 37]. These models pay more attentions on investigating the influence of small groups on the overall crowd dynamics. Typically the group size is fixed and the roles are assigned beforehand and are unchanged during simulations. Other researchers focus on modeling realistic following behaviors. Rio et al. [33] proposes a speed control model to visually adjust the follower's speed when he/she follows a leader on a straight path. Danchner and Warren [9] model how a follower aligns his walking direction (i.e., heading) according to the direction of a leader and they validate their model against human motion data. Realistic following behaviors are investigated, modeled and calibrated in [23] based on real kinematics data collected during experiments. The existing works mainly focus on modeling following behaviors between pairs of pedestrians; whereas the model proposed in this paper is applied to high density scenarios.

2.2 High Density Crowd Behavior Modeling

Crowd dynamics of high density scenes is modeled mainly from two distinct points of view. Firstly, macroscopic models consider the crowd as a whole and predict pedestrians' motion based on formulas derived from fluid dynamics [10, 16, 40]. On the other hand, microscopic models treat each pedestrian as an independent entity with the ability to sense, think, and act. The microscopic models are flexible to simulate varying crowd behaviors by assigning different parameter settings to different agents. The microscopic modeling approaches have become more and more popular nowadays owe to its simple implementation, high flexibility and effectiveness. Furthermore, by controlling the behaviors of single agents, macroscopic crowd behaviors can be generated. One of the classic microscopic models is social force model [15] and its variants [7, 29]. In these models, social interactions between pedestrians are defined by repulsive and attractive forces which determine the movement of pedestrians. Cellular automaton models [5, 6, 25, 41] are also very popular in simulating crowd dynamics in crowded scenarios. The CA models simplify the motion prediction process by reducing the search space into discrete choices. The simulation space is divided into equal-sized cells. Cells that located around a pedestrian are the candidate moving locations of that pedestrian. Various cell selection rules are defined in different models to drive the pedestrian into one of these candidate cells. In [13], a least-energy-based model is proposed based on the assumption that pedestrians update their motion in order to minimize the total energy spent. Two simple heuristic rules are proposed in [26] based on domain knowledge to predict crowd motion. Inspired by cognitive science result, Ondřej [27] proposes a synthetic vision-based approach to control pedestrian's locomotion from information obtained from visual stimuli. The major difference between these work and the work reported in this paper is that these models are manually designed based on assumptions and prior knowledge, while the proposed model learns the required knowledge from existing data.

2.3 Data-driven Modeling

Data-driven models learn the required knowledge from real crowd motion data to drive agents' behaviors so that the simulated behaviors can match those observed from the data. The data sources are mostly videos filmed from bird's-eye view and data collected from human tracking devices. Based on these collected crowd data, three common approaches are established so far. First, crowd data is used to calibrate the parameter settings of the crowd models [17, 28, 32, 35, 45]. The common parameter estimation methods include evolutionary algorithm, maximum likelihood estimation, and simplex algorithm. Calibrating parameters using real data can make the predicted crowd trajectories similar to that observed in crowd videos to some degree and thus improving the realism of crowd models. Second, some data-driven modeling techniques drive virtual pedestrians by directly searching for similar situations in real crowd data and then copying correspondent actions [8, 22, 24, 43]. The state-action pairs are constructed from crowd data to describe the regularity of pedestrian's motion, where a state describes the surrounding environment of the subject pedestrian and an action stores the corresponding movement (e.g., velocity) of the subject pedestrian. Other researchers attempt to learn hidden crowd statistics from crowd data. In [46], each pedestrian is modeled as a linear dynamic system with hidden dynamic states. The trajectories of real pedestrians are then used to learn the model parameters. In [44], velocity fields of pedestrians sharing the same starting region and exit region are learned from crowd data using K-means clustering. Other crowd statistics such as frequency of entering the scene and goal selection probability are also learned from crowd videos. These models are mainly focused on low density scenarios and thus may not be effective in high density cases.

3. ROLE-DEPENDENT DATA-DRIVEN MODELING APPROACH

3.1 System Architecture

In this paper, we aim at simulating realistic pedestrians dynamics in high density scenarios and reproducing self-organized collective behaviors observed in real pedestrians. Figure 1 illustrates the overall work-flow of the proposed model. Crowd statistics such as preferred speeds, starting and destination points and timings of entering the simulation area are obtained from real crowd videos to initialize the crowd model. The preferred speeds will be used in the simulation when agents decide to move directly towards their destination points. The simulated pedestrians are assigned with two roles (i.e., leader or follower) at every time step according to their surrounding situations. Driven by their role-dependent motion strategies, pedestrians with different roles move differently. The

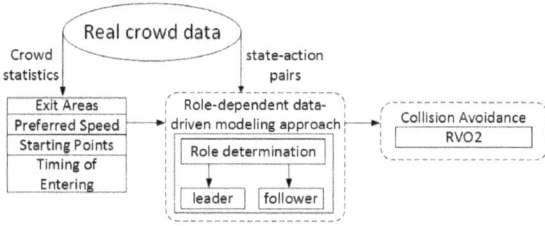

Figure 1: System architecture of the proposed role-dependent data-driven approach.

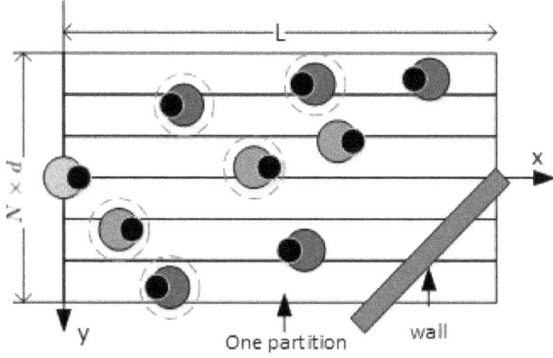

Figure 2: Role determination.

role determination process is also applied to crowd videos before the simulation, where leaders are identified from crowd videos and their motion behaviors are extracted using state-action pairs. The output of our role-dependent model is set as the preferred velocity of a collision avoidance model (RVO2 [38] is used in this paper).

In the remaining of this section, we will first define how to determine the role of each pedestrian, followed by the behavior models of each role, including state-action pairs generation for leaders and following point calculation for followers.

3.2 Role Determination

In the proposed model, pedestrians' behaviors are dependent on their roles which are updated at every time step. The role of a pedestrian is determined by the surrounding environment. It is assumed that each pedestrian has a sensing area, from which he can sense the existence of other pedestrians. The positions and velocities of the observed pedestrians in the sensing area are known by the subject pedestrian. Based on this information, each pedestrian makes a decision to determine where to go at the next time step.

Pedestrians usually put more attention on objects directly in front [20] and thus the sensing area is defined as a rectangle and aligns with the direction of the desired velocity of the subject pedestrian as shown in Figure 2. The desired velocity of the subject pedestrian points to his final destination. The sensing area has $N \times d$ width and L length and is divided into N partitions along the direction of the desired velocity, where N and L are constant parameters. Each pedestrian is modeled as a circle with diameter d, which is set to 0.4 m to approximate the average shoulder width [3].

Other pedestrians located in the sensing area of the subject pedestrian (shown as light blue circle located at the origin of the coordinate system in Figure 2) are referred to as the subject pedestrian's neighbors (shown as red and blue circles in Figure 2). If there is no neighbor observed, the subject pedestrian will walk straightly to his destination in his preferred speed. The positions and velocities of

the neighbors can be sensed by the subject pedestrian, along with other situational information such as static obstacles and the final destination. Neighbors are classified into two groups according to the relative relationship between their velocities and the velocity of the subject pedestrian. Suppose the velocities of the subject pedestrian and a neighbor are $\mathbf{v_s}$ and $\mathbf{v_n}$ respectively. If $\mathbf{v_s} \cdot \mathbf{v_n} > 0$, the neighbor is considered as walking in the same direction (blue circles) as the subject pedestrian. Otherwise, the neighbor is considered as walking in the opposite direction (red circles) as the subject pedestrian.

In each partition, the neighbor who is the closest to the subject pedestrian is defined as an influential neighbor (circles with dashed line). There are at most N influential neighbors for each subject pedestrian. The subject pedestrian's movement is largely influenced by these influential neighbors especially in high density scenarios [11]. Other neighbors blocked by the influential neighbors are filtered out in order to capture only the essential information of the subject pedestrian's current situation.

Pedestrians tend to follow others who have the same walking direction and destination in high density scenes where space is limited. Based on such observation, a pedestrian is identified as a follower according to the following definition.

Definition 1. Follower: A subject pedestrian is identified as a follower at current time step if among all influential neighbors, there exists at least one that meets the following requirements:

1. The influential neighbor is walking in the same direction as the subject pedestrian.

2. The destination of the influential neighbor is the same as the subject pedestrian.

3. The current speed of the influential neighbor is larger than the average walking speed in the scenario.

Setting a requirement on the speed of the influential neighbor prevents pedestrians walking to the congested area. The final destinations of all pedestrians are clustered into different groups. Each group of destinations form an exit region (ER). Pedestrians whose destinations are in the same exit region are considered having the same destination. The influential neighbors that meet the above requirements are identified as potential targets and will be used to determine the preferred velocity of a follower.

Definition 2. Leader: A subject pedestrian is identified as a leader if he/she is not a follower.

A leader has to explore by himself based on the surrounding situation. After role identification, the pedestrians will make the decision according to two separate models which are discussed in the following sections.

3.3 Leader's Behavior Modeling

For leaders, we adopt a data-driven method to model their comprehensive moving behaviors. The surrounding situation of the subject pedestrian (leader) at each time step is represented by a state $\mathbf{S} \in \mathbb{R}^{N+1}$:

$$\mathbf{S} = (\hat{d_1}, ..., \hat{d_i}, ..., \hat{d_N}, ID_{ER}), \quad \hat{d_i} = d_i/L \qquad (1)$$

where d_i is the Euclidean distance to the influential neighbors or static obstacles in partition i. If there is no neighbor or static obstacle sensed in the partition, d_i is set to L. ID_{ER} indicates which exit region the subject pedestrian's final destination belongs to.

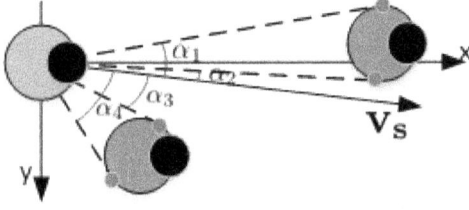

Figure 3: Follower's action determination. v_s indicates the current velocity of the subject pedestrian.

The action of the subject pedestrian $\mathbf{A} \in \mathbb{R}^2$ is a two dimensional vector indicating the preferred velocity of the subject pedestrian which is the average velocity of the subject pedestrian from current time t to $t + \Delta t$ time (Δt is set to 0.5 seconds in this paper).

State-action pairs extracted from videos are stored in a k-d tree using state $\mathbf{S}$ as index which serves as a working memory of leaders. Whenever a leader needs to decide where to move with the observed state $\mathbf{S}_o$, a query is made to search the k-d tree to find a similar situation based on the past experiences. In real-world scenarios, pedestrians usually make different decisions under similar situations [22]. Therefore, we combine k candidate actions to compute the final action. Specifically, one query of the k-d tree using $\mathbf{S}_o$ will return k nearest actions as candidates $\{\mathbf{A}_1, \ldots, \mathbf{A}_i, \ldots, \mathbf{A}_k\}$. The output action $\mathbf{A}$ is the weighted sum of these k nearest actions

$$\mathbf{A} = \sum_{i=1}^{k} w_i \cdot \mathbf{A}_i \qquad (2)$$

where weight w_i of each candidate action $\mathbf{A}_i$ is in proportion to the similarity Sim_i between the observed state $\mathbf{S}_o$ and the corresponding state $\mathbf{S}_i$ of action $\mathbf{A}_i$

$$w_i = \frac{Sim_i}{\sum_{j=1}^{k} Sim_j} \qquad (3)$$

$$Sim_i = exp(-B \cdot D_i) \qquad (4)$$

D_i is the Euclidean distance between the observed state $\mathbf{S}_o$ and the corresponding state $\mathbf{S}_i$ of action $\mathbf{A}_i$. B is a scaling constant that map from Euclidean distance to similarity between 0 and 1.

3.4 Follower's Behavior Modeling

If a pedestrian is determined to follow other pedestrians, there must be at least one potential target. As stated in role determination, they are influential neighbors who are walking in the same direction and have the same exit region with the follower and whose current speeds are large enough. Figure 3 shows a subject pedestrians with two potential targets.

Wolff [39] notes that people prefer walking behind the shoulder of the pedestrian in front, rather than directly behind the pedestrian. It allows them to keep monitoring the situations ahead. Therefore, two tangent lines are generated pointing from the center of the subject pedestrian to the circle that represents one potential target. The directions of these two tangent lines are approximately the directions of the shoulder of the potential target. Therefore, for each potential target, this generates two target points for the subject pedestrian to follow (red small circles on pedestrians in Figure 3). Moreover, people tend to maintain their own pace and thus they wish not to significantly change their current velocities [39]. The angle differences between the subject pedestrian's current heading

Table 1: Datasets description

name	b_{cor}[m]	b_l[m]	b_r[m]	N_l	N_r	$\bar{\rho}$[m^{-2}]
DML1	3.00	0.80	1.20	116	103	1.1675
DML2	3.60	1.60	1.60	140	166	1.6996
DML3	3.00	0.50	0.70	72	63	0.5411

and the directions of two tangent lines are calculated and referred to as changing angles (e.g., $\alpha_1, \alpha_2, \alpha_3$, and α_4 in Figure 3). From n potential targets, $2n$ changing angles need to be calculated. The tangent line direction with the smallest changing angle (α_2 in Figure 3) is selected as the preferred direction of the subject pedestrian and the preferred speed of the subject pedestrian is assigned as the average speed of all potential targets.

4. EXPERIMENTAL RESULT

In this section, we present the simulation results of the proposed model. The proposed model is first learned from trajectories of a real trajectory dataset. Then the learned model is applied to simulate the crowd dynamics in two other scenarios with different densities.

4.1 Datasets

In order to test the effectiveness of the proposed method, three real trajectory datasets DML1, DML2, and DML3 are used for training and testing, which are obtained from well-controlled pedestrians experiments [42]. In the experiments, participants walked through a narrow corridor from two entrances located at two ends of the corridor (Figure 4b). Two synchronized stereo cameras mounted on the rack of the ceiling recorded the pedestrians' movement from bird's-eye view. The pedestrians' trajectories were annotated from videos every 0.0625 second. Figure 4a shows one frame of the video. Scenario parameters such as the width of the corridor b_{cor} and two gates, b_l and b_r were changed in each dataset so that the crowd density and the flow ratio of the opposing stream are different. Table 1 lists the values of these parameters together with the average crowd density of three real pedestrian datasets. The fundamental diagram of three datasets are also shown in Figure 4d. It is clear that the speed-density relationships of three datasets have distinct distributions. DML1 from which leaders' state-action pairs are extracted has medium average crowd density among the three datasets. The learned model is directly applied to DML2, which has higher density than DML1, as well as DML3 which has lower density than DML1. The method to calculate the crowd speed and density will be discussed in Section 4.3.

4.2 Simulation Settings

Crowd statistics such as preferred speeds, starting and destination points and timings of entering the simulation area of agents are initialized using the trajectories of the respective dataset. We consider the first point and the last point of a trajectory from a dataset as the starting position and destination of the corresponding agent respectively. The preferred speed is set as the pedestrian's average speed within the first second of entering the scenario instead of the whole trajectory based on the observation that pedestrians are forced to slow down due to heavy interactions soon after entering the scenario. Exit regions (ERs) are identified by clustering the final destinations of all pedestrians. All the trajectories in DML1 are illustrated in Figure 4c together with four exit regions identified in this scenario.

When RVO2 is used alone, unrealistic motion will happen since the final destinations of pedestrians are mostly behind the corridor

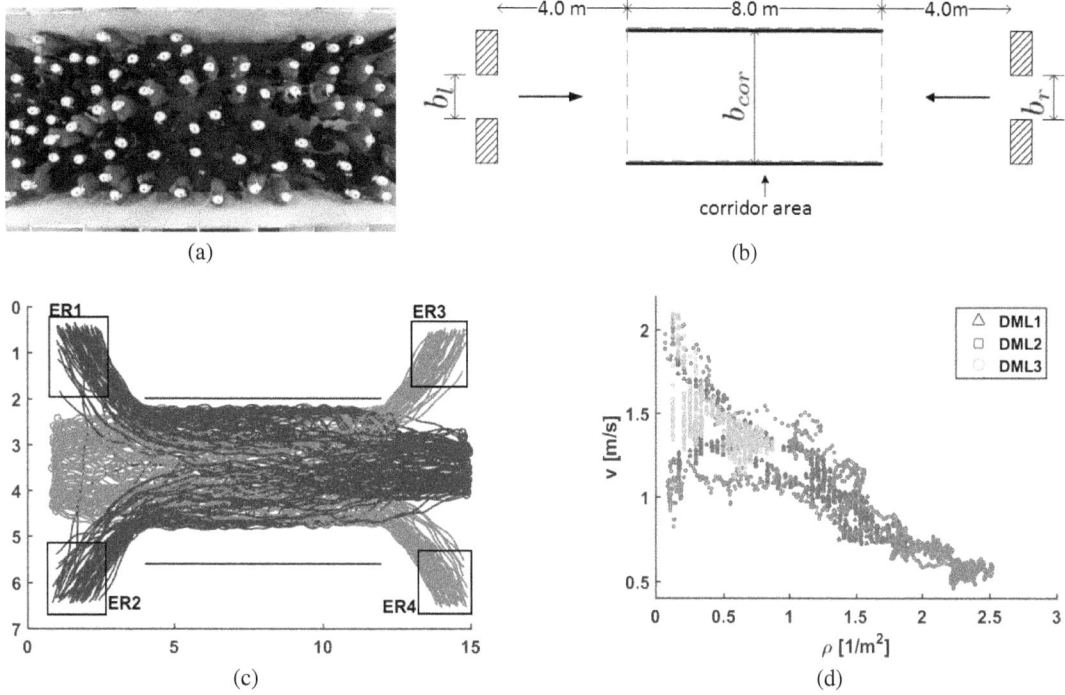

Figure 4: Datasets used in evaluating models. (a) A snapshot of the experiments where participants walk in a narrow corridor. (b) Details of the narrow corridor scenario. (c) Trajectories of pedestrians in `DML1` and four identified exit regions. (d) Fundamental diagram of three datasets used in this paper.

walls. If no path planning method is applied, agents simulated by RVO2 alone will walk directly to the corridor walls. On the other hand, the proposed model, although also uses RVO2 as collision avoidance method, is able to generate realistic pedestrian motion without path planning. We develop a simple yet effective way-point generation approach to guide the motion of the RVO2-simulated agents. Way-points are generated from trajectories in each datasets respectively. Pedestrians with different ERs are likely to have different plans to avoid static obstacles and thus way-points are generated for each ER separately. The key idea is that the places where most people pass through are potential way-points for pedestrians to avoid static obstacles. Therefore, we generate the trajectory density map from all the real trajectories belong to the same ER and identify high density points as candidate way-points. The trajectory density map is generated according to the approach suggested in [44]. The whole experiment area shown in Figure 4b is evenly divided into n cells and each cell is represented by its center point. For each representative point $\mathbf{p}_i$, its local density is calculated by

$$\rho_{\mathbf{p}_i} = \frac{1}{\pi R^2} \sum_{k=1}^{m} exp(-\frac{d(\mathbf{p}_i, \mathbf{p}_k)^2}{R^2}) \qquad (5)$$

where $d(\mathbf{p}_i, \mathbf{p}_k)$ returns the Euclidean distance from the kth point in trajectories to $\mathbf{p}_i$, m is the number of points in all trajectories and R is a constant parameter. Among all representative points, top M points with highest density are selected as the candidate way-points which are then clustered using Gaussian Mixture Model [4]. After clustering, each clustered way-point group is represented by a two dimensional Gaussian distribution parameterized by its mean and covariance matrix. For each pedestrian, his/her next way-point is determined by drawing a sample from the Gaussian distribution of

the next way-point group that has not been reached. A way-point group is considered as "reached" if the way-point sampled from this group is located behind the pedestrian. The trajectory density map and way-points distributions of one exit region of `DML1` are illustrated in Figure 5. The way-points are generated using the trajectories of the respective dataset.

4.3 Model Evaluation

Average crowd speed and density are commonly used to describe the aggregated crowd dynamics in high density scenarios [42]. To evaluate the performance of the proposed model, we compare the simulation results with real crowd data in the following aspects: the relationship between density and speed collected at every time step (i.e., fundamental diagram), density over time and speed over time. The method to measure pedestrian speed and density are based on Voronoi partition as suggested in [42]. At any time step the pedestrians' positions in the scenario can be interpreted as a set of points. A Voronoi diagram is generated upon these points and the corridor area is then decomposed into C Voronoi cells as shown in Figure 6. Each Voronoi cell P_i is represented by its center point (x, y). The density ρ_{xy} and speed v_{xy} of point (x, y) are then computed by:

$$\rho_{xy} = \frac{1}{a_i} \quad \text{and} \quad v_{xy} = v_i(t) \qquad (6)$$

where a_i is the area of Voronoi cell P_i and $v_i(t)$ is the speed of pedestrian in cell P_i. The average density $\bar{\rho}_t$ and speed $\bar{v}_t$ of pedestrians in the corridor area at time step t are then calculated as follows:

$$\bar{\rho}_t = \frac{\sum_1^C \rho_{xy}}{C} \qquad (7)$$

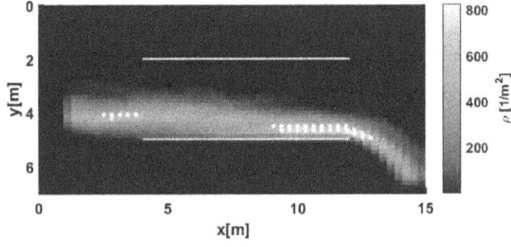

(a)

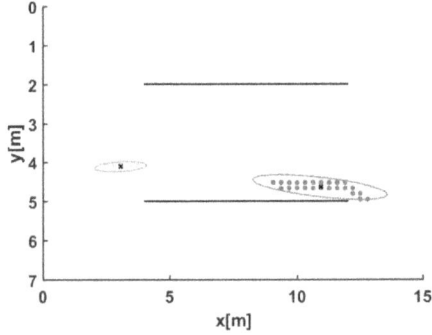

(b)

Figure 5: Way-points generation. (a) Trajectory density map and candidate way-points. (b) Candidate way-points are clustered and modeled by two Gaussian Mixtures, indicated by mean values (cross symbols) and 95% confidence interval error eclipses.

$$\bar{v}_t = \frac{\sum_1^C v_{xy}}{C} \qquad (8)$$

To facilitate description, the proposed model is denoted as Role Dependent RVO2 (RD-RVO2) model. In this evaluation, we compare RVO2 model [38], RVO2 model with way-points (W-RVO2) and our model (RD-RVO2) with real pedestrians data respectively. Each simulation model is run 10 times independently with different random seeds and the average of $\bar{\rho}_t$ and $\bar{v}_t$ from each run are calculated for evaluation.

Figure 7 illustrates the snapshots of the simulations generated by the three models and crowd data in DML2 and DML3, captured at time step 200, 600, and 800 respectively.[1] Red circles represent pedestrians walking from the left to right and blue circles represent pedestrians walking from the right to left. It can be observed that compared to other models, trajectories generated by agents simulated using RD-RVO2 are more similar to those observed in real data. Congestion does not occur in RD-RVO2 throughout simulations in both scenarios, similar to those in the video. Agents simulated using RVO2 go directly to their final destinations in both scenarios. As a result, pedestrians quickly get congested in the middle of the corridor, blocking the way of other pedestrians coming from both directions. However, with the proper guidance of way-points, W-RVO2 is capable of generating congestion-free crowd behaviors in DML3 as well as in the early stage of the simulation in DML2, but it still leads to congestions afterwards in DML2 because of the higher density.

For DML2, the fundamental diagram shown in Figure 8a demonstrates that the density-speed relationship of the crowd simulated

---

[1]The simulation videos can be downloaded from https://drive.google.com/open?id=0Bznmk8A9qnaedDc1TVdxNi02NGs

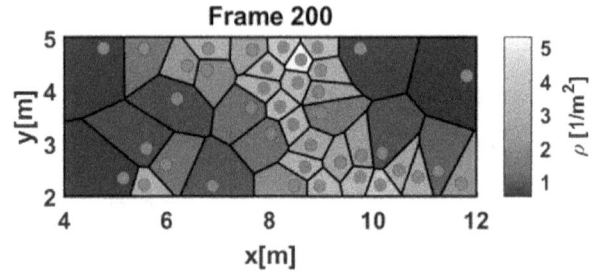

Figure 6: Voronoi partition of the corridor area at one time step. Circles in red represent pedestrians and the density of each Voronoi cell is indicated by its color according to the colorbar on the right.

Table 2: Average travel time steps of pedestrians in the video and agents in simulations.

	Video	RVO2	W-RVO2	RD-RVO2
DML2	319.42	901.73	867.74	380.38
DML3	168.82	344.92	213.84	177.45

by RD-RVO2 well matches that of real pedestrians in the video, while crowd driven by RVO2 and W-RVO2 has higher density with lower speed than real pedestrians in most of the time steps. The results of RVO2 and W-RVO2 indicate that congestions have happened during the simulations. From Figure 8b, the crowd density collected at every time step using crowd video data shows that the crowd density in the corridor area first increases when pedestrians start moving and then stay nearly stable thereafter until the end of the experiment. Among three compared models, RD-RVO2 are most similar to that of real pedestrians. The density of corridor area in RVO2 quickly become much higher than that of real crowd. The density of W-RVO2 first has the same trend as that of real pedestrians in the beginning but then increases to the same value of that in RVO2. Consequently, it takes much longer time for RVO2 and W-RVO2 to finish simulations. Likewise, the crowd speed of real pedestrians gradually decreases as pedestrians keep coming in the corridor area. The crowd speed of agents simulated by RD-RVO2 shows a similar trend while the average speed of simulated agents in RVO2 and W-RVO2 reduces to smaller values (Figure 8c). In simulations, agents will move back if they are blocked by other agents, which rarely happens in crowd videos. An agent is considered as moving back if the angle between his current velocity and the velocity that pointing to his final destination is larger than 90°. Therefore, we keep track the number of agents who are forced to walk back together with their duration of moving back. Specifically, each data point in Figure 8d represents the number of moving back agents whose duration of moving back exceeds the correspondent value in X-axis. From Figure 8d, it can be observed that agents simulated by RVO2 and W-RVO2 move back more frequently for much longer time than that in crowd video data.

For DML3 which has lower crowd density, the fundamental diagram (Figure 9a) indicates that agents simulated by RVO2 still have higher crowd density and lower crowd speed compared to real pedestrians in the video. On contrast, both W-RVO2 and RD-RVO2 are able to generate similar crowd density and speed statistics to that in the video (Figures 9b and 9c). However, Figure 9d reveals that there are more agents moving back in W-RVO2 than that in RD-RVO2. This indicates that RD-RVO2 still offers better performance among three models in simulating crowd motion for DML3.

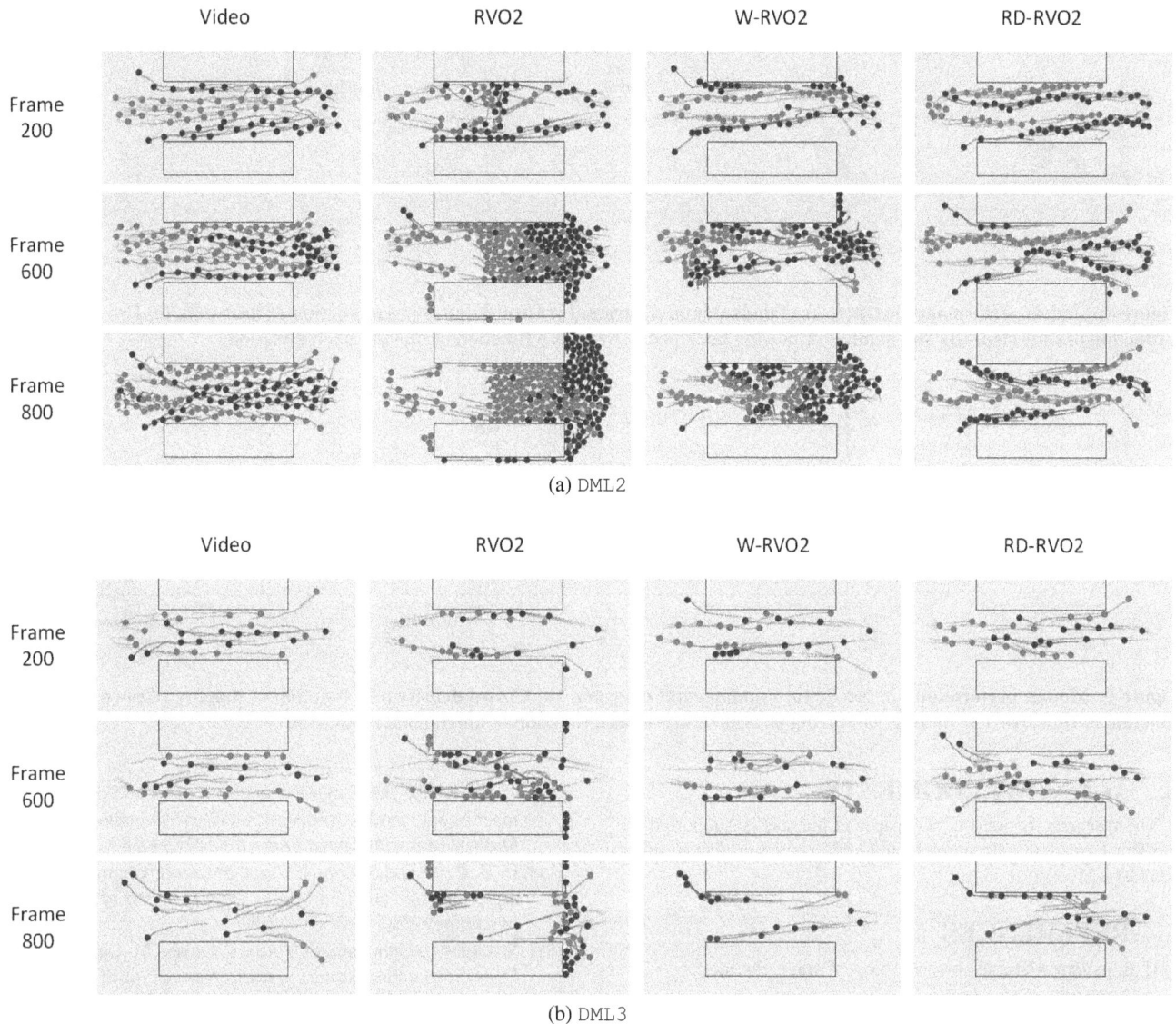

Figure 7: Snapshots of the simulations captured at time step 200, 600 and 800.

From single pedestrian/agent's perspective, the average travel time steps of pedestrians in the video and simulated agents shown in Table 2 demonstrate that the average travel time step of agents simulated using RD-RVO2 is similar to that of pedestrians in the video. Agents simulated using RVO2 take much longer time to reach their destinations due to heavy congestions. Implementing way-point algorithm on top of RVO2 reduces the average travel time steps of agents, indicating that the proposed way-point approach is able to relief the level of congestion during simulation.

5. CONCLUSIONS AND FUTURE WORK

In this paper, we have proposed a role-dependent data-driven model to simulate realistic crowd dynamics in high density scenes. In the proposed model, pedestrians have two distinctive roles, namely, leader and follower. At each time step, a pedestrian can only have one role. Pedestrians first determine their roles and then act accordingly. The leaders' behaviors are learned from real crowd data, while the followers' behaviors are calculated based on the potential targets. To test the effectiveness of the proposed method, the model is first built on a real crowd video data. Then the learned model is applied to two different scenarios. The simulation results have demonstrated that the proposed model is able to simulate pedestrian behaviors in high density crowd more realistically than RVO2 in terms of statistics such as crowd density, crowd speed and average travel time step. Visual observation also reveals high similarity between agents' movement during the simulation using the proposed model and pedestrians' movement seen in the videos. Furthermore, the proposed model can be directly applied to different scenarios without training on the new scenario.

In the current role-dependent model, the role of pedestrians has two types (i.e., leader or follower). Considering more role types in the model may further improve the effectiveness of the current model. Besides, in role determination, neighbors are considered as either walking in the same direction or in the opposite direction as the subject pedestrian. Using more neighbors types may lead to more accurate role determination.

95

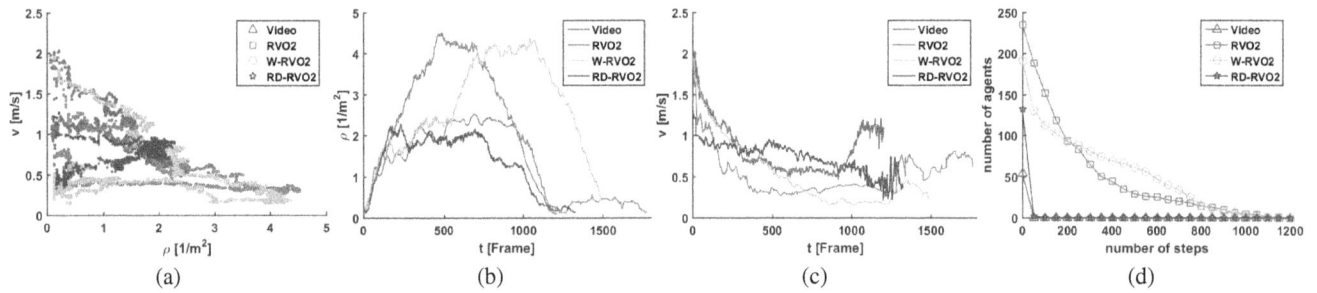

Figure 8: Models performance in `DML2`. (a) Fundamental diagram. (b) Crowd density as a function of time step. (c) Crowd speed as a function of time step. (d) The number of moving back pedestrians as a function of moving back duration.

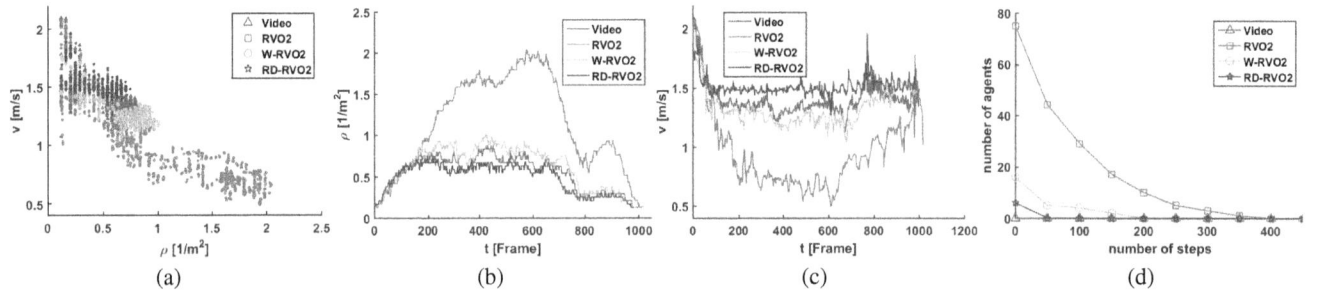

Figure 9: Models performance in `DML3`. (a) Fundamental diagram. (b) Crowd density as a function of time. (c) Crowd speed as a function of time. (d) The number of moving back pedestrians as a function of moving back duration.

6. ACKNOWLEDGMENTS

The research reported in this paper is financially supported by the Tier 1 Academic Research Fund (AcRF) under project Number RG23/14.

7. REFERENCES

[1] https://en.wikipedia.org/wiki/Love_Parade_disaster. Accessed: 2015-12-25.

[2] https://en.wikipedia.org/wiki/Phnom_Penh_stampede. Accessed: 2015-12-25.

[3] Note on human sizes. http://www.roymech.co.uk/Useful_Tables/Human/Human_sizes.html. Accessed: 2015-12-25.

[4] C. M. Bishop. *Pattern recognition and machine learning.* springer, 2006.

[5] V. Blue and J. Adler. Cellular automata microsimulation of bidirectional pedestrian flows. *Transportation Research Record: Journal of the Transportation Research Board*, (1678):135–141, 1999.

[6] V. J. Blue and J. L. Adler. Cellular automata microsimulation for modeling bi-directional pedestrian walkways. *Transportation Research Part B: Methodological*, 35(3):293–312, 2001.

[7] M. Braun. Communication and social cognition. *Cross-cultural survey methods*, 325:57, 2003.

[8] P. Charalambous and Y. Chrysanthou. The pag crowd: A graph based approach for efficient data-driven crowd simulation. In *Computer Graphics Forum*, volume 33, pages 95–108. Wiley Online Library, 2014.

[9] G. C. Dachner and W. H. Warren. Behavioral dynamics of heading alignment in pedestrian following. *Transportation Research Procedia*, 2:69–76, 2014.

[10] C. Dogbé. On the numerical solutions of second order macroscopic models of pedestrian flows. *Computers & Mathematics with Applications*, 56(7):1884–1898, 2008.

[11] H. E. Egeth and S. Yantis. Visual attention: Control, representation, and time course. *Annual review of psychology*, 48(1):269–297, 1997.

[12] S. J. Guy, J. Chhugani, S. Curtis, P. Dubey, M. Lin, and D. Manocha. Pledestrians: a least-effort approach to crowd simulation. In *Proceedings of the 2010 ACM SIGGRAPH/Eurographics symposium on computer animation*, pages 119–128. Eurographics Association, 2010.

[13] S. J. Guy, S. Curtis, M. C. Lin, and D. Manocha. Least-effort trajectories lead to emergent crowd behaviors. *Physical review E*, 85(1):016110, 2012.

[14] D. Helbing, I. Farkas, and T. Vicsek. Simulating dynamical features of escape panic. *Nature*, 407(6803):487–490, 2000.

[15] D. Helbing and P. Molnar. Social force model for pedestrian dynamics. *Physical review E*, 51(5):4282, 1995.

[16] Y. Q. Jiang, P. Zhang, S. Wong, and R. X. Liu. A higher-order macroscopic model for pedestrian flows. *Physica A: Statistical Mechanics and its Applications*, 389(21):4623–4635, 2010.

[17] A. Johansson, D. Helbing, and P. K. Shukla. Specification of the social force pedestrian model by evolutionary adjustment to video tracking data. *Advances in complex systems*, 10(supp02):271–288, 2007.

[18] E. Á. Juliusson, N. Karlsson, and T. Gärling. Weighing the past and the future in decision making. *European Journal of Cognitive Psychology*, 17(4):561–575, 2005.

[19] I. Karamouzas and M. Overmars. Simulating the local behaviour of small pedestrian groups. In *Proceedings of the*

17th acm symposium on virtual reality software and technology, pages 183–190. ACM, 2010.

[20] K. Kitazawa and T. Fujiyama. Pedestrian vision and collision avoidance behavior: Investigation of the information process space of pedestrians using an eye tracker. In *Pedestrian and evacuation dynamics 2008*, pages 95–108. Springer, 2010.

[21] G. Köster, M. Seitz, F. Treml, D. Hartmann, and W. Klein. On modelling the influence of group formations in a crowd. *Contemporary Social Science*, 6(3):397–414, 2011.

[22] K. H. Lee, M. G. Choi, Q. Hong, and J. Lee. Group behavior from video: a data-driven approach to crowd simulation. In *Proceedings of the 2007 ACM SIGGRAPH/Eurographics symposium on Computer animation*, pages 109–118. Eurographics Association, 2007.

[23] S. Lemercier, A. Jelic, R. Kulpa, J. Hua, J. Fehrenbach, P. Degond, C. Appert-Rolland, S. Donikian, and J. Pettré. Realistic following behaviors for crowd simulation. In *Computer Graphics Forum*, volume 31, pages 489–498. Wiley Online Library, 2012.

[24] A. Lerner, Y. Chrysanthou, and D. Lischinski. Crowds by example. In *Computer Graphics Forum*, volume 26, pages 655–664. Wiley Online Library, 2007.

[25] T. J. Lightfoot and G. Milne. Modelling emergent crowd behaviour. In *The Australian Conference on Artificial Life (ACAL)*, pages 159–169, 2003.

[26] M. Moussaïd, D. Helbing, and G. Theraulaz. How simple rules determine pedestrian behavior and crowd disasters. *Proceedings of the National Academy of Sciences*, 108(17):6884–6888, 2011.

[27] J. Ondřej, J. Pettré, A.-H. Olivier, and S. Donikian. A synthetic-vision based steering approach for crowd simulation. In *ACM Transactions on Graphics (TOG)*, volume 29, pages 123:1–123:9. ACM, 2010.

[28] S. Paris, J. Pettré, and S. Donikian. Pedestrian reactive navigation for crowd simulation: a predictive approach. In *Computer Graphics Forum*, volume 26, pages 665–674. Wiley Online Library, 2007.

[29] N. Pelechano, J. M. Allbeck, and N. I. Badler. Controlling individual agents in high-density crowd simulation. In *Proceedings of the 2007 ACM SIGGRAPH/Eurographics symposium on Computer animation*, pages 99–108. Eurographics Association, 2007.

[30] N. Pelechano and N. I. Badler. Improving the realism of agent movement for high density crowd simulation. *University of Pennsylvania, Center for Human Modeling and Simulation*, 2006.

[31] N. Pelechano, K. O'Brien, B. Silverman, and N. Badler. Crowd simulation incorporating agent psychological models, roles and communication. Technical report, DTIC Document, 2005.

[32] J. Pettré, J. Ondřej, A.-H. Olivier, A. Cretual, and S. Donikian. Experiment-based modeling, simulation and validation of interactions between virtual walkers. In *Proceedings of the 2009 ACM SIGGRAPH/Eurographics Symposium on Computer Animation*, pages 189–198. ACM, 2009.

[33] K. W. Rio, C. K. Rhea, and W. H. Warren. Follow the leader: Visual control of speed in pedestrian following. *Journal of vision*, 14(2):4, 2014.

[34] S. Sarmady, F. Haron, and A. Z. H. Talib. Modeling groups of pedestrians in least effort crowd movements using cellular automata. In *Third Asia International Conference on Modeling & Simulation*, pages 520–525. IEEE, 2009.

[35] P. Scovanner and M. F. Tappen. Learning pedestrian dynamics from the real world. In *2009 IEEE 12th International Conference on Computer Vision*, pages 381–388. IEEE, 2009.

[36] M. Seitz, G. Köster, and A. Pfaffinger. Pedestrian group behavior in a cellular automaton. In *Pedestrian and Evacuation Dynamics 2012*, pages 807–814. Springer, 2014.

[37] H. Singh, R. Arter, L. Dodd, P. Langston, E. Lester, and J. Drury. Modelling subgroup behaviour in crowd dynamics dem simulation. *Applied Mathematical Modelling*, 33(12):4408–4423, 2009.

[38] J. Van den Berg, M. Lin, and D. Manocha. Reciprocal velocity obstacles for real-time multi-agent navigation. In *IEEE International Conference on Robotics and Automation*, pages 1928–1935. IEEE, 2008.

[39] M. Wolff. Notes on the behaviour of pedestrians. *People in places: The sociology of the familiar*, pages 35–48, 1973.

[40] S. Wong, W. Leung, S. Chan, W. H. Lam, N. H. Yung, C. Liu, and P. Zhang. Bidirectional pedestrian stream model with oblique intersecting angle. *Journal of transportation Engineering*, 136(3):234–242, 2010.

[41] K. Yamamoto, S. Kokubo, and K. Nishinari. Simulation for pedestrian dynamics by real-coded cellular automata (rca). *Physica A: Statistical Mechanics and its Applications*, 379(2):654–660, 2007.

[42] J. Zhang. *Pedestrian fundamental diagrams: Comparative analysis of experiments in different geometries*. PhD thesis, Forschungszentrum Jülich, 2012.

[43] M. Zhao, S. J. Turner, and W. Cai. A data-driven crowd simulation model based on clustering and classification. In *Proceedings of the 2013 IEEE/ACM 17th International Symposium on Distributed Simulation and Real Time Applications*, pages 125–134. IEEE Computer Society, 2013.

[44] J. Zhong, W. Cai, L. Luo, and H. Yin. Learning behavior patterns from video: A data-driven framework for agent-based crowd modeling. In *Proceedings of the 2015 International Conference on Autonomous Agents and Multiagent Systems*, pages 801–809. International Foundation for Autonomous Agents and Multiagent Systems, 2015.

[45] J. Zhong, N. Hu, W. Cai, M. Lees, and L. Luo. Density-based evolutionary framework for crowd model calibration. *Journal of Computational Science*, 6:11–22, 2015.

[46] B. Zhou, X. Wang, and X. Tang. Understanding collective crowd behaviors: Learning a mixture model of dynamic pedestrian-agents. In *IEEE Conference on Computer Vision and Pattern Recognition (CVPR)*, pages 2871–2878. IEEE, 2012.

Towards PDES in a Message-Driven Paradigm: A Preliminary Case Study Using Charm++

Eric Mikida, Nikhil Jain,
Laxmikant Kale
University of Illinois at
Urbana-Champaign
{mikida2,nikhil,kale}@illinois.edu

Elsa Gonsiorowski,
Christopher D. Carothers
Rensselaer Polytechnic
Institute
{gonsie,chrisc}@rpi.edu

Peter D. Barnes, Jr.,
David Jefferson
Lawrence Livermore
National Laboratory
{barnes26,jefferson6}@llnl.gov

ABSTRACT

Discrete event simulations (DES) are central to exploration of "what-if" scenarios in many domains including networks, storage devices, and chip design. Accurate simulation of dynamically varying behavior of large components in these domains requires the DES engines to be scalable and adaptive in order to complete simulations in a reasonable time. This paper takes a step towards development of such a simulation engine by redesigning ROSS, a parallel DES engine in MPI, in CHARM++, a parallel programming framework based on the concept of message-driven migratable objects managed by an adaptive runtime system. In this paper, we first show that the programming model of CHARM++ is highly suitable for implementing a PDES engine such as ROSS. Next, the design and implementation of the CHARM++ version of ROSS is described and its benefits are discussed. Finally, we demonstrate the performance benefits of the CHARM++ version of ROSS over its MPI counterpart on IBM's Blue Gene/Q supercomputers. We obtain up to 40% higher event rate for the PHOLD benchmark on two million processes, and improve the strong-scaling of the dragonfly network model to $524,288$ processes with up to $5\times$ speed up at lower process counts.

1. INTRODUCTION

Discrete event simulations (DES) are a key component of predictive analysis tools. For example, network designers often deploy DES to study strengths and weaknesses of different network topologies. Similarly, the chip design process makes heavy use of DES to find the optimal layout of the circuit on a new chip. As the complexity of such analyses increases over time, either due to the larger number of components being studied or due to higher accuracy requirement, the capability of DES engines also needs to increase proportionately. Parallel discrete event simulation (PDES) holds promise for fulfilling these expectations by taking advantage of parallel computing. Many scientific domains, e.g. cosmol-

ACM acknowledges that this contribution was authored or co-authored by an employee, or contractor of the national government. As such, the Government retains a nonexclusive, royalty-free right to publish or reproduce this article, or to allow others to do so, for Government purposes only. Permission to make digital or hard copies for personal or classroom use is granted. Copies must bear this notice and the full citation on the first page. Copyrights for components of this work owned by others than ACM must be honored. To copy otherwise, distribute, republish, or post, requires prior specific permission and/or a fee. Request permissions from permissions@acm.org.

SIGSIM-PADS '16, May 15-18, 2016, Banff, AB, Canada

© 2016 ACM. ISBN 978-1-4503-3742-7/16/05. . . $15.00

DOI: http://dx.doi.org/10.1145/2901378.2901393

ogy [22], biophysics [27], computational chemistry [14], etc., have already exploited parallel computing to great effect. Thus, it is natural that PDES should be explored to match the growing requirements posed by domains of interest.

Development of scalable PDES engines and models is a difficult task with many important differences from common High Performance Computing (HPC) applications, which are predominantly from the science and engineering domain. First, while the interaction pattern of common HPC applications can be determined apriori, the communication pattern in most PDES models is difficult to predict. The communication in PDES models is also more likely to be one-sided, i.e. the source entity may create work or data for a destination without the destination expecting it. Second, typical PDES models are asynchronous and do not have a predetermined time step; simulated entities are allowed to proceed through the simulation at a pace dictated by the availability of work. In contrast, many common HPC applications perform iterative operations with similar work repeated across iterations. Third, unlike common HPC applications, the amount of computation per communication byte is typically low for PDES models.

Due to the unique features of PDES described above, MPI [2], the de-facto standard for parallel programming, may not be the best fit for developing PDES engines and models. This is because MPI is suitable for bulk-synchronous models of parallel programming based on two-sided and collective communication. Support for one-sided indeterministic communication, as required by PDES, is limited in MPI [15]. Moreover, long running complex models may require load balancing and checkpointing infrastructure, both of which are programmer's responsibility in MPI. Despite these limitations, Rensselaer's Optimistic Simulation System (ROSS) [6], a PDES engine implemented using MPI, has been shown to be highly scalable for homogeneous models with low communication volume [5].

For models with heavy communication and high complexity, the capabilities and performance of the MPI version of ROSS exhibit limitations. To overcome these limitations, a new version of ROSS is being designed and implemented on top of CHARM++ [4], a parallel programming paradigm which is a better fit for performing PDES. Powered by an intelligent adaptive runtime system, CHARM++ is an alternative method for developing parallel programs based on object-oriented programming in contrast to MPI's processor based programming. Several large scale scientific applications, including NAMD [27], ChaNGa [22], EpiSimdemics [31] and OpenAtom [16], have been developed in

CHARM++. Additionally, the Parallel Object-oriented Simulation Environment (POSE) [30] is a PDES engine implemented as a DSL on top of CHARM++ which explores various scheduling and load balancing techniques but is ultimately limited by poor sequential performance. In this paper, we describe our experience and results related to the CHARM++ version of ROSS. The main contributions of this work are:

- **Suitability of Charm++** for implementing a PDES engine in general, and ROSS in particular, is demonstrated.

- **A Charm++ version of ROSS** is presented along with a detailed description of its design and implementation.

- **Features and benefits** of the CHARM++ version of ROSS are presented.

- **Superior performance** of the CHARM++ version of ROSS over its MPI counterpart is shown on two models running on IBM's Blue Gene/Q supercomputers:

    1. 40% higher event rate is obtained for the PHOLD benchmark on two million processes.

    2. Strong-scaling of the dragonfly network model for simulating different communication patterns is improved to $524,288$ processes with up to $5\times$ speed up at lower process count.

2. BACKGROUND

CHARM++ [4] and ROSS [5] are central to the work presented in this paper. This section first provides an overview of PDES, followed by details of its concrete implementation in ROSS. Finally we introduce CHARM++ and discuss why it is a good fit for PDES.

2.1 PDES

A DES system consists of *Logical Processes* (LPs) and events. LPs represent the entities within the simulation and encapsulate the majority of simulation state. Changes within DES are driven by execution of events that are communicated from one LP to another at specific points in virtual time. In order to obtain a correct simulation, the events must be executed in timestamp order, i.e. causality violations should not happen wherein an event with higher timestamp is executed before an event with a lower timestamp.

For a sequential DES, the simulation progresses in a very straight forward manner: the pending event with the lowest timestamp is processed by its receiving LP. As each successive event is processed, simulation time moves forward. After an event is successfully processed, its memory can be reclaimed by the simulation system.

In PDES, special care must be taken to ensure the correct ordering of events. The LP objects are distributed across concurrent processes with events traversing across the network. Therefore, parallel simulators must handle inter-node communication as well as maintain global synchronization to avoid causality violations. There are two main schools of thought on how to avoiding causality violations in PDES: conservative and optimistic [13, 17, 26]. In a conservative synchronization algorithm, events can only be executed if there is a guarantee that it will not result in a causality violation. In optimistic algorithms, events are executed speculatively and if a causality violation does eventually occur, the simulation engine must recover from it.

In this paper our focus is on the optimistic Time Warp algorithm proposed by Jefferson et al. [17]. In Time Warp, when a causality violation is detected, states of the relevant LPs are reverted to a point in time before the causality violation occurred. This process is referred to as rollback. Once an LP has rolled back to a previous point in virtual time, it is allowed to resume forward execution. In order to correctly rollback an LP, the simulation engine needs to store history information about that LP, which causes an increase in the memory footprint of the program. To mitigate this, the simulation engine periodically synchronizes and computes the Global Virtual Time (GVT). The GVT is a point in virtual time which every LP has safely progressed to, and therefore memory used to store the history before the GVT can safely be reclaimed by the simulator.

2.2 ROSS

ROSS is a framework for performing parallel discrete event simulations. It has demonstrated highly scalable, massively parallel event processing capability for both conservative and optimistic synchronization approaches [5, 6, 8, 20, 25]. For optimistic execution, ROSS mitigates Time Warp state-saving overheads via *reverse computation* [9]. In this approach, rollback is realized by performing the inverse of the individual operations that were executed in the event's forward execution. This reduces the need to explicitly store prior LP state, leading to efficient memory utilization.

Most recently, ROSS optimistic event processing has demonstrated super-linear performance for the PHOLD benchmark using nearly 2 million Blue Gene/Q cores on the 120 rack Sequoia supercomputer system located at LLNL [5]. Barnes et al. obtained 97x speedup at 120 racks from a base configuration of 2 racks for a PHOLD model configured with over 250 million LPs. The peak event rate was in excess of 500 billion events-per-second. PHOLD configurations similar to the one used in Barnes et al. [5] have been used in the results section of this paper.

Using ROSS's massively parallel simulation capability, many HPC system models have been developed as part of a DOE co-design project for future exascale systems. These include models for the torus and dragonfly networks and the DOE CODES storage simulation framework. The torus model has been shown to simulate 1 billion torus nodes at 12.3 billion events per second on an IBM Blue Gene/P system [19]. The dragonfly model has been scaled to simulate 50 million nodes, with a peak event rate of 1.33 billion events/second using 64K processes on a Blue Gene/Q system [25]. We use a similar dragonfly model in the results section of this paper as was used by Mubarak et al. in [25].

2.3 CHARM++

CHARM++ is a parallel programming framework which consists of an adaptive runtime system that manages migratable objects communicating asynchronously with each other. Like MPI, it is available on all major HPC platforms and takes advantage of native messaging routines when possible for better performance. Applications developed for CHARM++ are written primarily in C++ with a small amount of boiler-plate code to inform the runtime system of the main application entities (C++ objects).

Unlike MPI, CHARM++ is more than just a messaging layer for applications. It contains a powerful runtime system that aims to remove some of the burden of parallel program-

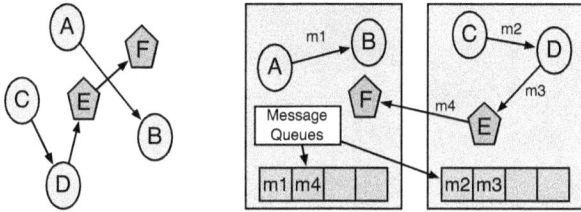

Figure 1: A depiction of communicating chares from the programmers view (left) and the runtime system's view after the chares have been mapped to the processes (right). Arrows represent messages sent between chares.

ming from the application developer by taking care of tasks such as location management, adaptive overlap of computation and communication, and object migration. Broadly speaking, the primary attributes of CHARM++ that we hope to leverage in PDES are: object-level decomposition, asynchrony, message-driven execution, and migratability.

In CHARM++, the application domain is decomposed into work and data units, implemented as C++ objects called chares, that perform the computation required by the application. Thus, the programmers are free to write their applications in work units natural to the problem being solved, instead of being forced to design the application in terms of cores or processes. An application may also have many different kinds of chares for different types of tasks. Note that the user is free to choose the number of chares and is not bound by the number of cores or processes. Figure 1 (left) shows a collection of 6 chares of two different types labeled A, B, C, D, E, and F. Arrows represent communication between chares. This freedom of decomposition is highly suitable for implementing PDES engines and models since they typically have simulated entities of different types whose work and count is determined by the model being simulated.

The runtime system is responsible for mapping the chares defined by an application to cores and processes on which they are executed. The chares interact with each other asynchronously in a one-sided manner: the senders send messages to the destinations and continue with their work without waiting for a synchronous response. This mode of communication is a direct match to the type of communication exhibited by a typical PDES. Figure 1 (right) shows a potential mapping of the 6 chares to specific hardware resources. The runtime system keeps track of the location of each chare and handles sending messages across the network when communicating chares are mapped to different hardware resources.

In CHARM++, chares are message-driven entities, i.e., a chare is scheduled and executed only when it has a message to process from itself or from other chares. Being message-driven makes chares an ideal candidate for representing the entities modeled in a PDES. This is because LPs in a PDES are also typically driven by events that are sent to them. In Figure 1 (right), we see that each process maintains a queue of all messages directed to it's local chares. The runtime system removes messages from these queues, and executes appropriate method on each message's destination chare.

Finally, the chares in CHARM++ are migratable, i.e., the runtime system can move the chares from one process to an-

other. Moreover, since chares are the only entities visible to the application and the notion of processes is hidden from the application, the migration of chares can be done automatically by the runtime system. This allows the runtime system to enable features such as dynamic load balancing, checkpoint/restart, and fault tolerance with very little effort by the application developer. Complex PDES models can take advantage of these features, thus providing a solution to problems posed by long running dynamic models.

3. DESIGN OF THE CHARM++ VERSION OF ROSS

In order to demonstrate the benefits an asynchronous message-driven paradigm can have for PDES, we have created a version of ROSS built on top of CHARM++. Our focus is on improving the parallel performance and taking advantage of features provided by CHARM++ (Section 2.3), while keeping the PDES logic and ROSS API as intact as possible. The design and implementation of the CHARM++ version of ROSS can be divided into five segments, each of which are described in this section: parallel decomposition, scheduler, communication infrastructure, global virtual time (GVT) calculation, and user API.

3.1 Parallel Decomposition

As described in Section 2.1, a typical PDES consists of LPs that represent and simulate entities defined by the model. Whenever an event is available for an LP, the LP is executed. This execution may result in generation of more events for the given LP or other LPs. In the MPI version of ROSS, three main data structures are used to implement this process as shown in Figure 2 (left): Processing Element (PE), Kernel Processes (KP), and Logical Process (LP).

There is a single PE per MPI rank with three main responsibilities. First, the PE manages event memory of its MPI rank with a queue of preallocated events. Second, the PE maintains a heap of pending events sent to LPs on its MPI rank. Third, the PE contains data used when coordinating the GVT computation across all MPI ranks.

KPs are used primarily to aggregate history storage of multiple LPs into a single object to optimize fossil collection. This history consists of events that have been executed by an LP. Fossil collection refers to freeing up the memory occupied by the events that occurred before the current GVT.

LPs are the key component in actually defining the behavior of a specific model. They contain model-specific state and event handlers as defined by the model writer, in addition to storing some meta-data used by ROSS such as their globally unique ID. The pending events received for LPs are stored with the PEs while the events that have been executed by the LPs are stored with the KPs.

The organization of ROSS in MPI, as described above, is mainly driven by the process-based model typical of MPI programs. On each MPI process, there is a single flow of control managing the interaction between a single PE and a collection of KPs and LPs as shown in Figure 2 (left). None of these application entities are recognized by MPI, and hence are managed as passive sequential objects that rely on the MPI process for scheduling and communication.

Decomposition with Charm++: As shown in Figure 2 (right), the CHARM++ version of ROSS consists of three key entities: LPs, LP Chares, and PE Managers. The role

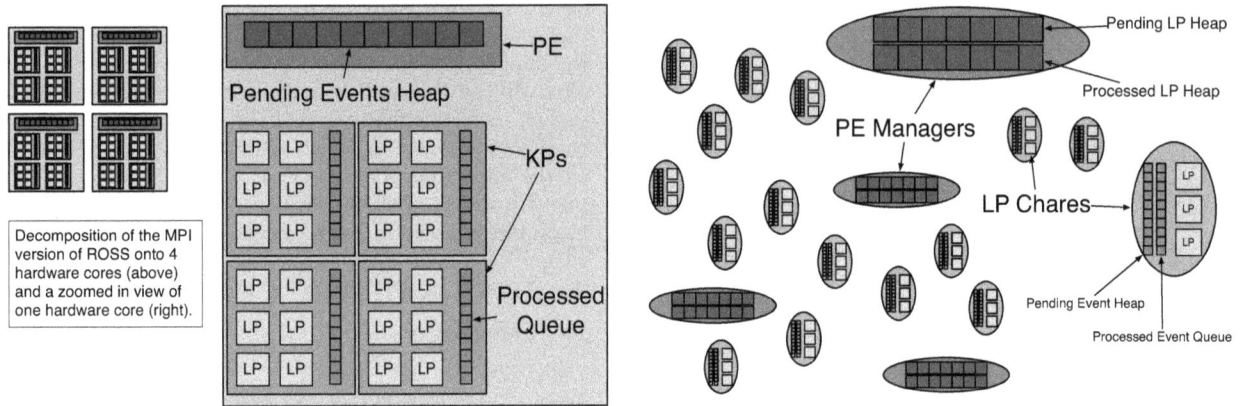

Figure 2: User view of ROSS decomposition in MPI (left) and CHARM++ (right). Boxes are regular C structs, and ovals are chares (known to the CHARM++ runtime system). In the MPI version, the users view requires explicit knowledge of the mapping of entities to hardware, where in the CHARM++ version the runtime system manages this mapping.

and implementation of LPs is same as the MPI version of ROSS in order to preserve the user-level API of ROSS.

LP Chares now encapsulate everything an LP needs to execute. They contain the LPs themselves, which as before hold model-specific state and event handlers, in addition to storing both the pending and past events of its LPs. The charm runtime system is aware of LP Chares and allows communication of events directly between LP Chares. Upon receiving an event, an LP Chare handles any causality violations or event cancellations by performing the necessary rollbacks, and enqueues the new event into its pending queue. This removes the need for event storage at the PE and KP level. The mapping of LPs to LP Chares is left to the user so that a model-appropriate scheme can be used, but the mapping of LP Chares to hardware resources is handled by the runtime system. This also allows the runtime system to migrate LPs as needed which enables features such as checkpointing and dynamic load balancing.

PE Managers are implemented as special chares in CHARM++ which guarantee a single PE Manager chare per process. Similar to PEs in the MPI version, PE Managers still manage event memory and coordinate the computation of GVT; however, they no longer store pending events. Instead, PE Managers maintain a pending LP heap and a processed LP heap, both of which store pointers to LP Chares. The pending heap is sorted based on the timestamp of the next pending event of each LP Chare, and the processed heap is sorted based on the timestamp of the oldest processed event of each LP Chare. The ROSS scheduler is now integrated into the PE Managers and utilizes these LP Chare queues to coordinate event execution and fossil collection among chares co-located with a given PE Manager. By integrating the ROSS scheduler into the PE Manager, the CHARM++ runtime system is now aware of the ROSS scheduler. The changes to the ROSS scheduler are described in more detail in the next section.

Expected cost of basic operations: In the MPI version, the expected cost to add, remove, or execute an event is $\log N$ when N is the number of events in the PE's pending heap. In the CHARM++ version, all event heaps are stored in the LP Chares and only store events for its own LPs, so the cost of any operation on these heaps is approximately

$\log \frac{N}{C}$ where C is the number of chares on the processor/core. In some cases, the addition or removal of an event requires updating the PE Manager-level heaps which incurs an additional $\log C$ operation. Thus, the expected cost to add, remove, or execute an event in the CHARM++ version is at most $\log \frac{N}{C} + \log C = \log N$.

3.2 Scheduling

In the MPI version of ROSS, the scheduler is simply a function called from `main` after the initialization is completed. There are three types of schedulers supported in the MPI version: sequential, conservative, and optimistic. Figure 3a provides a code snippet that shows the simplified implementation of the optimistic scheduler, which is almost always the preferred option for ROSS. The scheduler is primarily an infinite loop that polls the network for driving the communication, performs rollbacks if they are needed, executes events on LPs in batches of size *batch_size*, and performs GVT computation if needed. In the conservative mode, the rollback step is skipped, while in the sequential mode only event execution happens.

As discussed in the previous section, the schedulers in the CHARM++ version of ROSS have been promoted from regular C functions to methods on PE Manager chares. The runtime system schedules all chares, include PE Managers, based on availability of messages for them to process, so the schedulers are implemented as messages to PE Managers. Again, we will focus our detailed discussion on the optimistic scheduler. As shown in Figure 3b, the CHARM++ version of the scheduler has two main tasks: event execution and GVT computation. Unlike the MPI version, the scheduler no longer does network polling (which is now handled by the runtime system), and no longer deals with event queuing or rollbacks (which are now handled by the LP Chares).

When a simulation begins, all PE Managers receive a message that triggers execution of execute_events method. During normal execution, this involves delegating control to LP Chares for event execution by using the pending LP heap, and then sending a message, say M, that should trigger execution of execute_events on the PE Manager. The message M is added to the runtime system's queue, and when the execution of execute_events is complete, control returns to

```
//main control loop in PE
void scheduler () {
  while(1) {
    poll_network (); //drive communication
    //rollback if cancellation event
    //rollback if event(s) with old timestamp
    for (i=0; i<batch_size; i++) {
      //execute events directly on LPs
    }
    if (ready_for_gvt) {
      do_gvt ();
      //perform fossil collection on KPs
    }
  }
}
```

(a) MPI Version : PE drives the execution.

```
void PEManager::execute_events() {
  for (i=0; i<batch_size; i++) {
    /* delegate control to LP Chares
       for event execution */
  }
  if (ready_for_gvt)
    start_gvt ();
  else
    // self-send an execute_events() message
}
void PEManager::gvt_done() {
  /* delegate control to LP Chares
     for fossil collection */
  // self-send an execute_events() message
}
```

(b) CHARM++ Version: PE Manager is one of the chares scheduled when work is available for it.

Figure 3: Simplified versions of the role of PE in optimistic mode.

the runtime system. At this point, the runtime system may perform other tasks such as polling the network or execute methods on other chares based on its queue. Eventually when the message M reaches the top of the runtime system's queue, execute_events is executed again on the PE.

During the execution of execute_events, if it is time to compute the GVT, start_gvt() is called instead of sending the message that triggers execution of execute_events. This starts the asynchronous computation of the GVT, which is described in more detail in Section 3.4. When the GVT computation is complete, a message to trigger execution of gvt_done is sent to PE Managers, which results in delegation of control to the LP Chares to do fossil collection. Finally, a message to trigger execution of execute_events is sent to resume forward progress.

3.3 Communication Infrastructure

ROSS requires communication across processes to deliver events generated by LPs on one process for LPs on different processes. In the MPI version of ROSS, the delivery of events is performed using point-to-point communication routines in MPI. Since MPI's point-to-point communication is two-sided, this requires both the sender and the receiver to make MPI calls. The complexity and inefficiency in this process stems from the fact that the events are generated based on the model instance being simulated, and thus the communication pattern is not know apriori. Whenever an LP, say srcLP, generates an event for another LP, say destLP, the process which hosts destLP is computed using simple static algebraic calculations and the sender process issue a non-blocking MPI_Isend to it. Since the communication pattern is not known ahead of time, all MPI processes post non-blocking receives that can match to any incoming message (using MPI_ANY_TAG and MPI_ANY_SOURCE). Periodically, the scheduler performs network polling to test if new messages have arrive for LPs on the current process. Both these actions, posting of receives that match to any receive and periodic polling, lead to high overheads.

In the CHARM++ version of ROSS, both LPs and the events they generate are encapsulated in LP Chares which the runtime system knows about. Hence, when an LP Chare issues an event for the another LP Chare, the runtime takes

the ownership of the event and delivers it to the destination LP Chare without the involvement of PE Manager. This also means that each LP Chare can detect its own causality violations as soon as it receives events, and take the appropriate course of action immediately. The runtime also performs the lookup of the process that actually owns each LP Chare automatically and does not require any additional support from ROSS. This automation is extremely useful for cases where LPs are load balanced across processes, and their owner processes cannot be computed using simple algebraic calculation. Moreover, since CHARM++'s programming model is one-sided and message driven, there is no need to post receives in advance.

3.4 GVT Computation

Computation of the GVT requires finding the minimum active timestamp in the simulation. Hence, while computing the GVT, all of the events and anti-events (events that cancel an older event) which have not been executed yet have to be taken into consideration. This implies that any event that has been sent by a process must be received at its destination before the GVT is computed. Without such a guarantee, we are at the risk of not accounting for events that are in transit. Alternatively, a sender process can account for the events it sends out in the GVT computation. However, this scheme leads to additional overhead of explicit acknowledgment for every event received by the destination processes to the sender processes, and hence is inferior in terms of performance to the former scheme.

In the MPI version of ROSS, to guarantee that all events are accounted for the ROSS engine maintains two counters: events sent, and event received. When the GVT is to be computed, all execution of events stops and ROSS makes a series of MPI_Allreduce calls interspersed with polling of the network to guarantee communication progress. Once the global sum of the two counters match, all events are accounted for, and the global minimum timestamp of these events becomes the new GVT. Then ROSS resets the counters, performs fossil collection, and resumes event execution.

In the CHARM++ version of ROSS, we have simplified the computation of the GVT by replacing the above mentioned mechanism with a call to CHARM++'s efficient asynchronous quiescence detection (QD) library [1, 28]. The QD library automatically keeps track of all communication in a CHARM++ application, and invokes an application specified *callback* function when the global sum of initiated sends matches the global sum of the receives. The efficiency of the QD library is due to overlap of the library's execution with application progress obtained by performing asynchronous non-blocking communication in the background. Once it is time to compute the GVT, event execution is stopped while ROSS waits for QD to complete. During QD the runtime continues polling the network and delivering messages to chares as normal. Once quiescence is reached, the GVT is computed via a global reduction, and the PE Manager does fossil collection and restarts event execution. Because of the flexibility in QD and the asynchrony of the runtime system there are further opportunities to reduce the synchronization cost of GVT computation discussed in Section 4.4.1.

3.5 User API and Porting Models

One of the major goals when writing the CHARM++ version of ROSS was preserving the existing user API. By making minimal changes to the user API, we hope to make the porting process for models written for the MPI version of ROSS simple and minimalistic. To port a model from the MPI version to the CHARM++ version of ROSS, the majority of changes are performed in the startup code where the model is initialized. Once the simulation of the model begins, the logical behavior of the CHARM++ version is exactly same as the MPI version, and hence there is often no change needed in the LP event handlers or reverse event handlers.

Among the startup changes, the primary change is related to LP mapping. In the MPI version, there are two mapping functions. One of them is used during startup to create LPs on the calling PE, and decide their local storage offset, KP it belongs to, and type of LP it is. The second mapping function is used during execution to determine the PE on which an LP with a given ID exists.

In the CHARM++ version, since LPs are no longer bound to PEs, four mapping functions have to be defined to provide equivalent functionality w.r.t. LP Chares. The first two are used during startup. One is a function that takes an LP Chare index and an offset, and returns the global LP ID that resides on that chare at that offset. The second is a function that takes a global LP ID and returns the type of that LP. The remaining two functions are used for LP lookup during execution. One takes an LP ID and returns the LP Chare on which that LP resides and another takes an LP ID and returns the local storage offset of that LP. These two functions are the inverse of the first function that initially determined placement of LPs.

In addition to the above mapping changes, the models usually require minor changes to their main functions. These changes usually entail setting which maps to use, and setting some other CHARM++ specific variables such as the number of LP Chares a simulation is going to use. Concrete examples of the changes required to port the models are further presented in the results section, where the PHOLD and Dragonfly models are discussed in detail (Section 5).

4. BENEFITS OF THE CHARM++ VERSION OF ROSS

In this section, we describe the benefits of the CHARM++ version of ROSS. These include inherent benefits that the use of CHARM++'s programming model provides in the current version, as well as new features enabled by the runtime system that are being implemented and will be explored in detail in a future publication.

4.1 Better Expression of Simulation Components

One of the most important advantages of using CHARM++ for implementing ROSS is that the programming model of CHARM++ is a natural fit for implementing PDES. In the CHARM++'s programming model, as described in Section 2.3, an application implementation is composed of many chares executing concurrently, driven by asynchronous message communication. When a message is received for a chare, the runtime executes the appropriate method on the chare to handle the message. This model is analogous to PDES where several LPs are created to represent simulation entities and event handlers are executed on the LPs when events are available for them. Thus LPs and events map naturally to chares and messages. Moreover, similar to PDES models, which can have different types of LPs and events to simulate different types of entities and work, there can be many types of messages and chares in CHARM++ to trigger and perform different types of computation. As a result, use of CHARM++ provides a natural design and easy implementation of ROSS, which is in part evidenced by the smaller code base discussed in the next section.

4.2 Code Size and Complexity

Since the CHARM++ runtime system relieves ROSS from managing inter-process communication, network polling, and scheduling computation and communication, the size and complexity of the ROSS code base has been reduced significantly. The communication module of the ROSS code base, which contains a large amount of MPI code for conducting data exchange efficiently, has been removed. This has resulted in a much smaller code base. In fact, the SLOC count (significant lines of code count) has been reduced to nearly half its original value, from $7,277$ in the MPI version to $3,991$ in the CHARM++ version. This is despite the fact that the CHARM++ version of ROSS also includes additional code required for enabling migration of LPs, a feature that is not present in the MPI version. Moreover, since the CHARM++ runtime system manages scheduling of different types of work units (LPs, PEs, communication, etc.), the code base has been simplified since explicit scheduling of these work units need not be done by ROSS.

4.3 Ease and Freedom of Mapping

CHARM++ programmers are encouraged to design their applications in terms of chares and the interactions between them, instead of programming in terms of processes and cores. This relieves the programmers from the burden of mapping their computation tasks to processes and cores, and thus allows them to divide work into units natural to the computation. In ROSS, and in PDES in general, this means that a model writer can focus solely on the behavior of the LPs and map them to chares based on their interactions. As a result, the model writer does not have to worry about clustering the LPs to match the number of processes and cores they may be running on now or in the future. Instead, they can choose the number of chares that is most suitable to their model, and let the runtime assign these chares to processes based on their computation load and communication pattern. A concrete example of this is shown in Section 5.2.4 for the dragonfly network model.

4.4 Features Enabled by CHARM++

In addition to the benefits described above, use of CHARM++ enables many new features that are difficult or infeasible to add to the MPI version of ROSS. Many of these features are currently under development, so their performance implications will be described in a future work.

4.4.1 Asynchronous GVT

As mentioned in Section 3.4, the computation of GVT using ROSS's current scheme has been simplified by the CHARM++ QD library. Moving forward, the flexibility provided by the adaptive and asynchronous nature of the runtime system presents opportunities to further restructure the GVT computation. Since computation and communication in CHARM++ are asynchronous and non-blocking, GVT computation can be adaptively overlapped with event execution. An obvious optimization is to overlap the global reduction performed to compute the GVT post quiescence detection with event execution. A more complex scheme, similar to the one described by Mattern [21], will enable continuous computation of the GVT in the background, without the need for globally synchronizing all processes and intermittently blocking event execution for detecting quiescence.

4.4.2 Migratability

One of the most important benefits of the object oriented programming model of CHARM++ is the ability to migrate chares. The use of LP Chares to host data belonging to LPs enables migration of LPs during execution of a simulation. In terms of implementation, this has been achieved in the CHARM++ version of ROSS by defining a simple serializing-deserializing function for LP Chares using CHARM++'s PUP framework [4]. Migratability of LPs leads to two new features in ROSS: automatic checkpoint-restart and load balancing. When directed by ROSS to checkpoint, the CHARM++ runtime system migrates LPs to disk and the simulation can be restarted as part of a new job.
Load Balancing: In complex, long-running models, load imbalance and excess communication can hinder performance and scalability. Dynamic load balancing algorithms can help address this problem [10, 12] but may add complexity to both the PDES engine, or to specific models. The CHARM++ runtime system eases this burden by making migratability a central tenet of its design. Migratability of LPs enables the CHARM++ runtime system to periodically redistribute LPs in order to balance load among processes and reduce communication overhead. In the current implementation, the CHARM++ version of ROSS is able to utilize basic load balancing strategies provided by the runtime system. Currently, we are working on developing PDES-specific load balancing strategies so that better performance can be obtained for complex models by utilizing extra information provided by the PDES engine and model.

4.4.3 TRAM

One common characteristic of many PDES simulations is communication of a high volume of fine-grained messages in the form of events. These numerous fine-grained messages

can easily saturate the networks, and thus increase the simulation time. To optimize for such scenarios, CHARM++ provides the Topological Routing and Aggregation Module that automatically aggregates smaller messages into larger ones [29]. In the past, Acun et al. [4] have already demonstrated the benefits of using TRAM for PDES simulations using a simple PDES mini-application. Based on those results, we plan to utilize TRAM to further improve the performance of ROSS.

5. PERFORMANCE EVALUATION

Scalable performance is a major strength of ROSS that has lead to its widespread use in conducting large scale simulations [23,24]. One of the primary reasons for the unprecedented event rate obtained by ROSS is its MPI-based communication engine that has been fine-tuned over a decade by the developers of ROSS. Hence, despite the benefits of the CHARM++ version of ROSS described in the previous section, it is critical that it also provides performance comparable to the MPI version of ROSS. In this section, we study the performance of the two versions of ROSS using its most commonly evaluated models - PHOLD and Dragonfly [7,23]. For these comparisons, we have used the latest version of ROSS as of December, 2015 [3].

5.1 PHOLD

PHOLD is one of the most commonly used models to evaluate the scalability of a PDES engine under varying communication load. It consists of a large number of LPs all of which perform similar work. At the beginning of a PHOLD simulation, a fixed number of events are scheduled on every LP. When an LP executes an event at time T_s, it creates a new event to be executed at time $T_s + T_o$. The offset, T_o, equals the sum of a fixed lookahead, T_l and a random delay chosen using an exponential distribution. The new event is sent either to a randomly selected LP with probability p, or to the current LP with probability $1 - p$. T_l, p, and the mean of the exponential distribution are all model input parameters. The only work done by an LP when processing an event is the generation of a few numbers from a random distribution, which results in PHOLD being extremely fine-grained and communication intensive if p is large.

5.1.1 Porting Process

Minimal changes are required to execute the version of PHOLD distributed with ROSS on top of the CHARM++ version of ROSS. First, a few global variables used in PHOLD, e.g. the number of LPs, should be removed since they are provided by the CHARM++ version of ROSS. As such, storing the model specific versions of these variables is redundant. Second, a new simple mapping function that returns the type of LP based on it global ID is required. Since PHOLD only has one type of LP, this mapper is a trivial two-line function that always returns the same LP type.

5.1.2 Experimental Set up

All the experiments have been performed on Vesta and Mira, IBM Blue Gene/Q systems at Argonne National Laboratory. The node count is varied from 512 to 32, 768, where 64 processes are launched on each node to make use of all the hardware threads. On BG/Q, due to disjoint partitioning of jobs and minimal system noise, event rate does not change significantly across multiple trials.

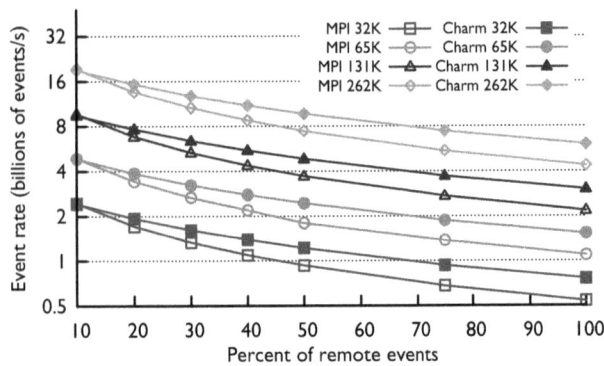

Figure 4: Simulating PHOLD on up to two million processes: for all process counts, CHARM++ version of ROSS provides up to 40% higher event rate in comparison to the MPI version of ROSS.

In these weak-scaling experiments, the number of LPs is fixed at 40 LPs per process (or MPI rank), each of which receives 16 events at startup. The lookahead (T_l) and the simulation end time are set to 0.1 and 8,192, respectively. The percentage of remote events, ($100 * p$), is varied from 10% to 100% to compare the two versions of ROSS under different communication loads.

5.1.3 Performance Results

Figure 4 compares the performance of PHOLD executed using the MPI and CHARM++ versions of ROSS on a wide range of process counts. For both the versions, we observe that the event rate drops significantly as the percentage of remote events increase. This is expected because at a low remote percentage, most of the events are self-events, i.e. they are targeted at the LP which generates them. Hence, the number of messages communicated across the network is low. As the percentage of remote events increases, a higher volume of events are communicated to LPs located on other processes. Thus, the message send requires network communication and the amount of time spent in communication increases, which limits the observed event rate.

At low remote percentages (10 − 20%), both versions of PHOLD achieve a similar event rate irrespective of the process count being used. However, as the percentage of remote events increase, the CHARM++ version of ROSS consistently achieves a higher event rate in comparison to the MPI version of ROSS. At 100% remote events, the CHARM++ version outperforms the MPI version by 40%. This shows that when communication is dominant, the runtime controlled message-driven programming paradigm of CHARM++ is able to better utilize the given resources. At 50% remote events, which is a more realistic scenario based on the dragonfly results from the next section, the CHARM++ version improves the event rate by approximately 28%. Figure 4 shows that these improvements in the event rate are observed on all process counts, ranging from $32K$ processes (512 nodes) to two million processes ($32K$ nodes).

5.1.4 Performance Analysis

To identify the reasons for the performance differences presented in the previous section, we used several performance analysis tools to trace the utilization of processes. For the CHARM++ version of ROSS, we use Projections, a tracing tool built for CHARM++ applications [18]. MPI-

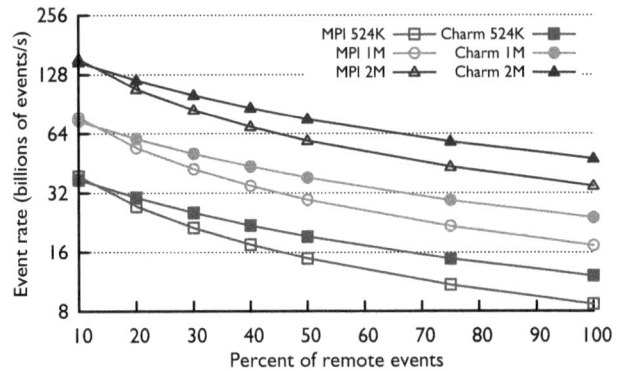

Trace library [11] is used to monitor the execution of the MPI version of ROSS. As a representative of other scenarios, we present the analysis for execution of PHOLD on 32,768 processes with 50% remote events.

Figure 5a shows that for the MPI version of ROSS, as much as $45 − 50\%$ of the time is spent on communication, while the rest is spent on computation. In this profile, communication is time spent in MPI calls, which include *MPI_Isend*, *MPI_Allreduce*, and *MPI_Iprobe*. A more detailed look at the tracing data collected by MPI-Trace shows that half of the communication time is spent in the *MPI_Allreduce* calls used when computing the GVT, while the remaining half is spent in sending, polling for, and receiving the point-to-point messages. A major fraction of the latter half is spent in polling the network for unexpected messages from unknown sources.

In contrast to the MPI version of ROSS, Figure 5b shows that the CHARM++ version of ROSS spends approximately 75% of its time performing computation, while only the remaining 25% is spent in communication. In this profile, communication encompasses sending and receiving of events, global synchronization for the GVT, and any other overheads incurred by the runtime system while performing communication tasks. Since Projections traces are integrated with the CHARM++ runtime system, Figure 5b provides a more detailed breakdown of time spent doing computation. Approximately 12% of the time is spent doing fossil collection, while 55% of time is spent in the main scheduling loop executing events. The remaining 8% is spent managing events, which entails checking for causality violations and performing necessary rollbacks, as well as pushing received events onto the pending events heap of the receiving LP.

The CHARM++ version of ROSS is able to reduce the time spent in communication due to three reasons. First, CHARM++ is a message-driven paradigm, so ROSS does not need to actively poll the network for incoming events. This saves a significant fraction of time since CHARM++ performs such polling in an efficient manner using lower level constructs. Second, the GVT is computed using a highly optimized quiescence detection mechanism in CHARM++, which is based on use of asynchronous operations. Third, since the runtime system schedules execution in CHARM++, it is able to overlap communication and computation automatically. Figure 6 shows the number of messages received over time during event execution between two consecutive GVT com-

106

(a) Usage profile of MPI ROSS

(b) Usage profile of CHARM++ ROSS

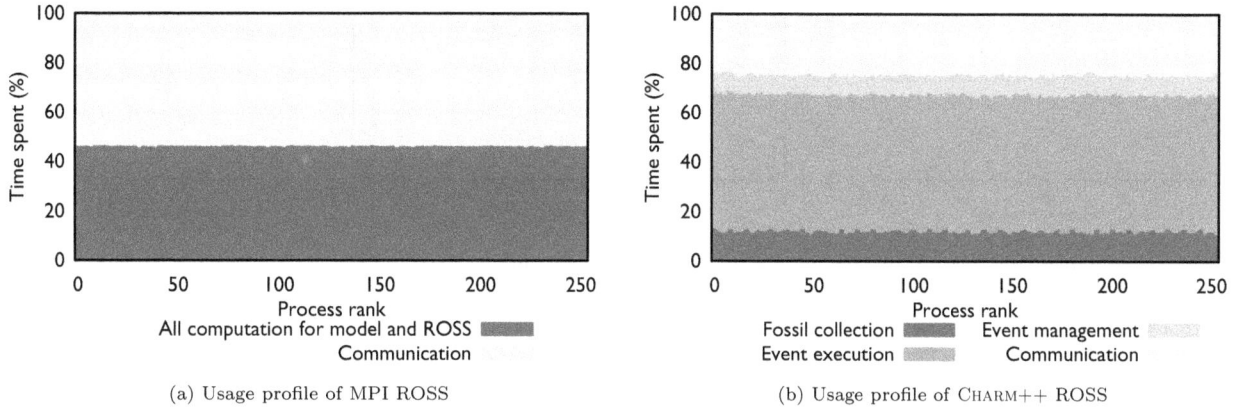

Figure 5: PHOLD model at 50% remote events: CHARM++ version of ROSS spends $20 - 25\%$ time in communication, but MPI version of ROSS communicates for $45 - 50\%$ of execution time.

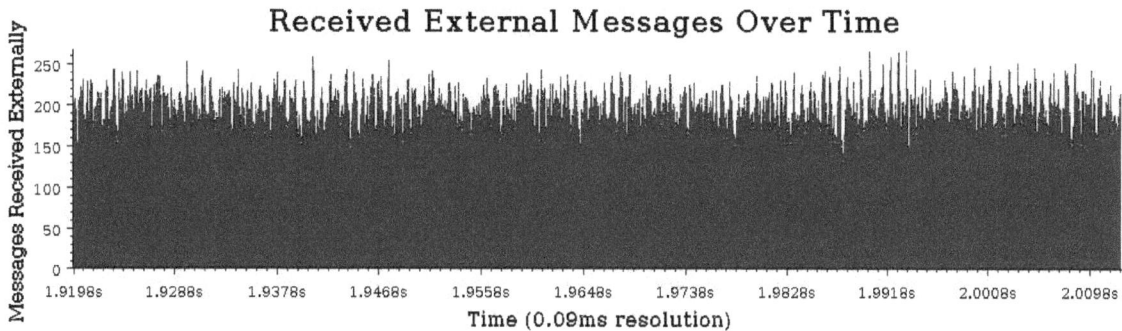

Figure 6: CHARM++ version of ROSS: communication is spread uniformly over the period of event execution between GVT computation.

putations in the CHARM++ version of ROSS. It shows that throughout execution, messages are actively being handled by the CHARM++ runtime system. The runtime system frequently schedules the communication engine, which ensures fast overlapping communication progress.

5.2 Dragonfly

The dragonfly model used in this section, which is similar to the one described in [23], allows us to study the performance of the two ROSS versions on a real application model. The LPs in the model are of three types: routers, terminals, and MPI processes. Three different built in communication patterns are used to drive the simulation from the MPI processes: 1) Uniform random - MPI ranks send messages to randomly selected partners, 2) Transpose - every MPI rank communicates with the MPI rank situated diagonally opposite to it if the ranks are arranged in a 2D grid, and 3) Nearest Nbr - all MPI ranks connected to a given router send messages to other MPI ranks connected to the same router only. As is apparent from their descriptions, these patterns results in completely different types of communication for the simulation engine.

5.2.1 Porting Process

Although, the dragonfly model is a much more complex model than PHOLD, the porting process is still very similar

to the one we described for PHOLD and involves minimal coding changes. The main difference is the use of a model specified mapping of LPs to LP Chares, instead of the default block mapping used by PHOLD. This necessitated a few key changes in the code. First, a few global variables used for mapping in the MPI version of ROSS are tied to the MPI processes, e.g. the variable that stores the number of LPs per MPI process. These variables have been either removed, or changed to be contained in the LP Chares. Second, the mapper that maps LPs to MPI processes is changed to map LPs to LP Chares instead. This change is mainly an API change, as the mapping logic itself remains the same. Third, a new mapper that returns the LP types based on their ID has been added.

5.2.2 Experimental Set up

Experiments for the dragonfly model have been done on Mira and Vulcan, a IBM Blue Gene/Q system at Lawrence Livermore National Laboratory. Allocations of sizes 512 nodes to 8,192 nodes have been used, with 64 processes being executed on every node. As mentioned above, due to the nature of BG/Q allocations, performance statistics had minimal variability between trials. Two different configurations of the dragonfly network are simulated on these supercomputers for the three traffic patterns described above.

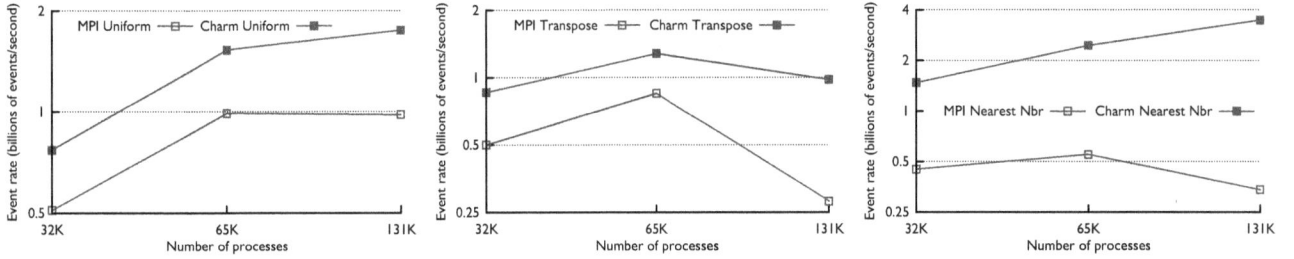

Figure 7: Performance comparison for a dragonfly with $256K$ routers and $10M$ terminals: when strong scaling is done, the CHARM++ version of ROSS outperforms the MPI version.

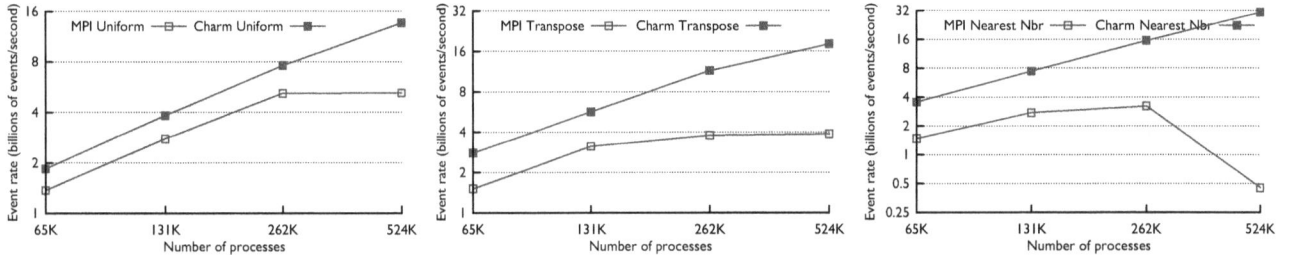

Figure 8: Strong scaling of a dragonfly with $2M$ routers and $160M$ terminals: for all traffic patterns, the CHARM++ version of ROSS scales to $524K$ processes and provides up to $4\times$ speed up over the MPI version.

The first configuration of the dragonfly uses 80 routers per group, with 40 terminals and 40 global connection per router. This results in a system with $256,080$ routers and $10,243,200$ terminals being simulated, with one MPI process per terminal. The second larger configuration consists of 160 routers per group, with 80 terminals and 80 global connections per router. This system contains $2,048,160$ routers and $163,852,800$ terminals in total.

5.2.3 Performance Results

The $256K$ router configuration of dragonfly is simulated on $32K$ to $131K$ processes. Figure 7 shows the observed event rate for these strong scaling experiments using all three traffic patterns. It can seen that for each traffic pattern, the CHARM++ version of ROSS outperforms its MPI counterpart. For two of the traffic patterns, Uniform random and Nearest Nbr, the CHARM++ version provides performance gains up to $131K$ processes. In contrast, the MPI version sees a dip in performance after $65K$ processes. It is worth noting that at $131K$ processes, we are simulating the dragonfly at its extreme limits since there are only one to two routers per process. Though the number of terminals is much higher, a large fraction of communication is directed towards the routers in a dragonfly simulation, which makes it the primary simulation bottleneck.

For the larger $2M$ router configuration, Figure 8 shows distinct patterns in the performance of both versions. At every data point, the CHARM++ version achieves significantly higher event rate than the MPI version. At $524K$ processes, an event rate advantage of $4\times$ is observed for the Transpose pattern. For the Uniform random pattern, $2\times$ improvement in the event rate is observed. The most extreme case is the Nearest Nbr pattern where we see the CHARM++ version achieving more than $2\times$ the event rate of the MPI version at $65K$ processes. This advantage increases to $5\times$ at $262K$

	MPI	Charm
Uniform	51.40%	33.99%
Transpose	34.80%	5.97%
Nearest Nbr	43.11%	0.26%

Table 1: Dragonfly remote event percentage.

processes, and skyrockets to $60\times$ at $524K$ processes, mainly because of the drop in the performance of the MPI version.

5.2.4 Performance Analysis

To analyze the performance for the dragonfly model, we look at two key factors: remote event percentage and efficiency. In these experiments, both these factors are impacted by how LP mapping is performed in the dragonfly model. The mapping in both versions of the dragonfly model is a modified linear mapping that maps each LP type separately. Each execution unit (MPI process in the MPI version, or LP Chare in the CHARM++ version) is assigned approximately the same number of router LPs, terminal LPs, and MPI LPs. To do so, LPs are assigned IDs to preserve locality. If there are x terminals per router, then the x terminals connected to the first router are given the first x IDs, followed by the terminals connected to the second router, and so on. A similar method is taken for assigning the IDs to MPI LPs.

In an ideal scenario, when the number of routers LPs (and hence the number of terminal and MPI LPs) is a multiple of the number of processes, the above mentioned ID assignment guarantees that terminals and MPI ranks that connect to a router are mapped to the same process/execution unit. However, when the number of routers is not a multiple of the number of processes, an even distribution of terminal and MPI LPs to all processes leads to them being on processes different from their router. This results in bad performance for the MPI version of ROSS.

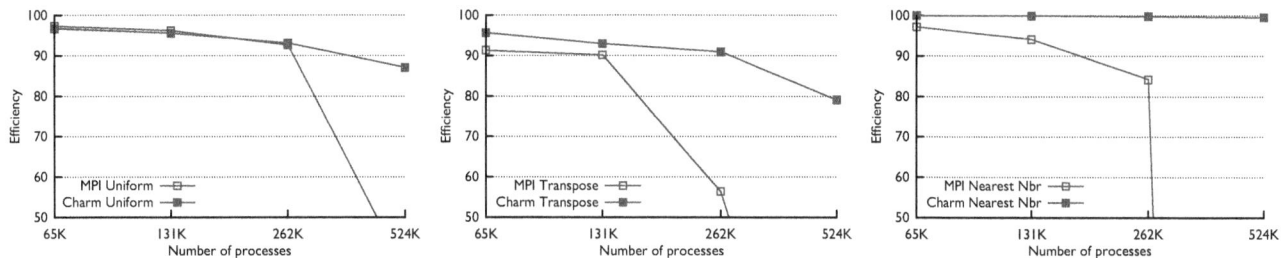

Figure 9: Efficiency comparison: as the process count increases, the efficiency of the CHARM++ version of ROSS decreases at a much slower rate in comparison to the MPI version.

In the CHARM++ version of ROSS this issue is easy to handle. Since the number of LP Chares can be chosen at runtime, we can always ensure that terminal LPs and MPI LPs are co-located with their routers on a single LP chare. This advantage of the CHARM++ version of ROSS follows from the fact that CHARM++ frees the programmer from having to worry about the specifics of the hardware the application is executed on. Instead, the work units of a CHARM++ application are the chares, and we have the flexibility to set the number of chares to yield the best performance. In this particular experiment, the best performance was achieved when there was exactly one router (and it's associated terminals and MPI processes) per chare.

Table 1 provides empirical evidence for the issue described above by presenting the average remote communication for each of the traffic patterns simulated in the dragonfly model. Here, remote communication is the percentage of committed events that had to be sent remotely. It does not include anti-events, or remote events that were rolled back. It is easy to see that the CHARM++ version requires less remote communication for every pattern, since many of the events are sent among LPs within the same chare. This is especially evident in the Nearest Nbr pattern where the CHARM++ version has less than 1% remote events in contrast to 43% remote events for the MPI version.

The mapping and its impact on remote events also directly affects the efficiency of each model. Figure 9 shows the efficiency for the different traffic patterns simulated in the dragonfly model. Here, efficiency is calculated as $1 - \frac{R}{N}$ where R is the number of events rolled back, and N is the total number of events executed. We see that the effect is particularly pronounced for the Nearest Nbr traffic pattern. In the CHARM++ version, nearly all events are sent locally, so there is very little chance for causality errors to occur. Because of this the CHARM++ version maintains 99% efficiency at all process counts, whereas the MPI version drops significantly in efficiency as the process count increases, eventually reaching an efficiency of -705% at $524K$ processes.

6. CONCLUSION

In this paper we have shown the suitability of CHARM++, a parallel adaptive runtime system, for designing and implementing PDES engines and models. The re-targeting of ROSS from MPI has simplified and reduced the ROSS code base, while simultaneously enabling new features such as asynchronous GVT computation and dynamic load balancing. Furthermore, the CHARM++ version of ROSS provides significantly better performance in comparison to its MPI counterpart. In the paper, we showed that as the commu-

nication volume increases in the PHOLD benchmark, the gap in the performance of CHARM++ and MPI version also increases. For the dragonfly model, irrespective of the communication pattern being simulated, the CHARM++ version not only provides higher event rate, it also scales to higher core counts. Moreover, due to the features discussed in this paper (checkpointing and load balancing), the CHARM++ version of ROSS is also better suited for simulating dynamic and complex models with long run times.

7. ACKNOWLEDGMENTS

This work was performed under the auspices of the U.S. Department of Energy by Lawrence Livermore National Laboratory (LDRD project 14-ERD-062 under Contract DE-AC52-07NA27344). This work used resources of the Argonne Leadership Computing Facility at Argonne National Laboratory, which is supported by the Office of Science of the U.S. Department of Energy under contract DE-AC02-06CH11357 (project allocations: PEACEndStation, PARTS, CharmRTS). This work also used resources from the Blue Waters sustained-petascale computing project, which is supported by the National Science Foundation (award number OCI 07-25070) and the state of Illinois.

8. REFERENCES

[1] The charm++ parallel programming system manual. http://charm.cs.illinois.edu/manuals/html/charm++/manual.html, visited 2016-3-20.

[2] MPI: A Message Passing Interface Standard. In *MPI Forum*. http://www.mpi-forum.org/, visited 2016-03-20.

[3] Ross source code on github. https://github.com/carothersc/ROSS, visited 2016-03-20.

[4] B. Acun, A. Gupta, N. Jain, A. Langer, H. Menon, E. Mikida, X. Ni, M. Robson, Y. Sun, E. Totoni, L. Wesolowski, and L. Kale. Parallel Programming with Migratable Objects: Charm++ in Practice. SC, 2014.

[5] P. D. Barnes, Jr., C. D. Carothers, D. R. Jefferson, and J. M. LaPre. Warp speed: executing time warp on 1,966,080 cores. In *Proceedings of the 2013 ACM SIGSIM conference on Principles of advanced discrete simulation*, SIGSIM-PADS '13, pages 327–336, New York, NY, USA, 2013. ACM.

[6] D. W. Bauer Jr., C. D. Carothers, and A. Holder. Scalable time warp on blue gene supercomputers. In *Proceedings of the 2009 ACM/IEEE/SCS 23rd*

Workshop on Principles of Advanced and Distributed Simulation, pages 35–44, Washington, DC, USA, 2009. IEEE Computer Society.

[7] C. D. Carothers, D. Bauer, and S. Pearce. ROSS: A high-performance, low-memory, modular Time Warp system. *Journal of Parallel and Distributed Computing*, 62(11):1648–1669, 2002.

[8] C. D. Carothers and K. S. Perumalla. On deciding between conservative and optimistic approaches on massively parallel platforms. In *Winter Simulation Conference'10*, pages 678–687, 2010.

[9] C. D. Carothers, K. S. Perumalla, and R. M. Fujimoto. Efficient optimistic parallel simulations using reverse computation. *ACM Trans. Model. Comput. Simul.*, 9(3):224–253, July 1999.

[10] M. Choe and C. Tropper. On learning algorithms and balancing loads in time warp. In *Workshop on Parallel and Distributed Simulation*, pages 101–108, 1999.

[11] I.-H. Chung, R. E. Walkup, H.-F. Wen, and H. Yu. MPI tools and performance studies—MPI performance analysis tools on Blue Gene/L. In *SC '06: Proceedings of the 2006 ACM/IEEE conference on Supercomputing*, page 123, New York, NY, USA, 2006. ACM Press.

[12] E. Deelman and B. K. Szymanski. Dynamic load balancing in parallel discrete event simulation for spatially explicit problems. In *Workshop on Parallel and Distributed Simulation*, pages 46–53, 1998.

[13] R. Fujimoto. Parallel Discrete Event Simulation. *Comm. of the ACM*, 33(10):30–53, 1990.

[14] F. Gygi, E. W. Draeger, M. Schulz, B. R. de Supinski, J. A. Gunnels, V. Austel, J. C. Sexton, F. Franchetti, S. Kral, C. W. Ueberhuber, and J. Lorenz. Large-scale electronic structure calculations of high-z metals on the bluegene/l platform. In *Proceedings of the 2006 ACM/IEEE Conference on Supercomputing*, SC '06, New York, NY, USA, 2006. ACM.

[15] N. Jain, A. Bhatele, J.-S. Yeom, M. F. Adams, F. Miniati, C. Mei, and L. V. Kale. Charm++ & MPI: Combining the best of both worlds. In *Proceedings of the IEEE International Parallel & Distributed Processing Symposium (to appear)*, IPDPS '15. IEEE Computer Society, May 2015. LLNL-CONF-663041.

[16] N. Jain, E. Bohm, E. Mikida, S. Mandal, M. Kim, P. Jindal, Q. Li, S. Ismail-Beigi, G. Martyna, and L. Kale. Openatom: Scalable ab-initio molecular dynamics with diverse capabilities. In *International Supercomputing Conference*, ISC HPC '16 (to appear), 2016.

[17] D. Jefferson and H. Sowizral. Fast Concurrent Simulation Using the Time Warp Mechanism. In *Proceedings of the Conference on Distributed Simulation*, pages 63–69, July 1985.

[18] L. V. Kale, G. Zheng, C. W. Lee, and S. Kumar. Scaling applications to massively parallel machines using projections performance analysis tool. In *Future Generation Computer Systems Special Issue on: Large-Scale System Performance Modeling and Analysis*, volume 22, pages 347–358, February 2006.

[19] N. Liu, C. Carothers, J. Cope, P. Carns, R. Ross, A. Crume, and C. Maltzahn. Modeling a leadership-scale storage system. In *Proceedings of the 9th international conference on Parallel Processing and Applied Mathematics - Volume Part I*, PPAM'11, pages 10–19, Berlin, Heidelberg, 2012. Springer-Verlag.

[20] N. Liu, J. Cope, P. Carns, C. Carothers, R. Ross, G. Grider, A. Crume, and C. Maltzahn. On the role of burst buffers in leadership-class storage systems. In *Proceedings of the 2012 IEEE Conference on Massive Data Storage*, Pacific Grove, CA, Apr. 2012.

[21] F. Mattern. Efficient algorithms for distributed snapshots and global virtual time approximation. *Journal of Parallel and Distributed Computing*, 18:423–434, 1993.

[22] H. Menon, L. Wesolowski, G. Zheng, P. Jetley, L. Kale, T. Quinn, and F. Governato. Adaptive techniques for clustered n-body cosmological simulations. *Computational Astrophysics and Cosmology*, 2(1):1–16, 2015.

[23] R. B. R. Misbah Mubarak, Christopher D. Carothers and P. Carns. Modeling a million-node dragonfly network using massively parallel discrete-event simulation. *SCC, SC Companion*, 2012.

[24] R. B. R. Misbah Mubarak, Christopher D. Carothers and P. Carns. A case study in using massively parallel simulation for extreme-scale torus network codesign. In *Proceedings of the 2nd ACM SIGSIM PADS*, pages 27–38. ACM, 2014.

[25] M. Mubarak, C. D. Carothers, R. Ross, and P. Carns. Modeling a million-node dragonfly network using massively parallel discrete-event simulation. In *High Performance Computing, Networking, Storage and Analysis (SCC), 2012 SC Companion,*, pages 366–376. IEEE, 2012.

[26] D. M. Nicol. The cost of conservative synchronization in parallel discrete event simulations. *J. ACM*.

[27] J. Phillips, G. Zheng, and L. V. Kalé. Namd: Biomolecular simulation on thousands of processors. In *Workshop: Scaling to New Heights*, Pittsburgh, PA, May 2002.

[28] A. B. Sinha, L. V. Kale, and B. Ramkumar. A dynamic and adaptive quiescence detection algorithm. Technical Report 93-11, Parallel Programming Laboratory, Department of Computer Science , University of Illinois, Urbana-Champaign, 1993.

[29] L. Wesolowski, R. Venkataraman, A. Gupta, J.-S. Yeom, K. Bisset, Y. Sun, P. Jetley, T. R. Quinn, and L. V. Kale. TRAM: Optimizing Fine-grained Communication with Topological Routing and Aggregation of Messages. In *Proceedings of the International Conference on Parallel Processing*, ICPP '14, Minneapolis, MN, September 2014.

[30] T. L. Wilmarth. *POSE: Scalable General-purpose Parallel Discrete Event Simulation*. PhD thesis, Department of Computer Science, University of Illinois at Urbana-Champaign, 2005.

[31] J.-S. Yeom, A. Bhatele, K. R. Bisset, E. Bohm, A. Gupta, L. V. Kale, M. Marathe, D. S. Nikolopoulos, M. Schulz, and L. Wesolowski. Overcoming the scalability challenges of epidemic simulations on blue waters. In *Proceedings of the IEEE International Parallel & Distributed Processing Symposium*, IPDPS '14. IEEE Computer Society, May 2014.

Automatic Generation of Reversible C++ Code and Its Performance in a Scalable Kinetic Monte-Carlo Application

Markus Schordan   Tomas Oppelstrup   David Jefferson   Peter D. Barnes, Jr.
Daniel Quinlan
Lawrence Livermore National Laboratory
{schordan1,oppelstrup2,jefferson6,barnes26,dquinlan}@llnl.gov

ABSTRACT

The fully automatic generation of code that establishes the reversibility of arbitrary C/C++ code has been a target of research and engineering for more than a decade as reverse computation has become a central notion in large scale parallel discrete event simulation (PDES). The simulation models that are implemented for PDES are of increasing complexity and size and require various language features to support abstraction, encapsulation, and composition when building a simulation model. In this paper we focus on parallel simulation models that are written in C++ and present an approach and an evaluation for a fully automatically generated reversible code for a kinetic Monte-Carlo application implemented in C++. Although a significant runtime overhead is introduced with our technique, the assurance that the reverse code is generated automatically and correctly, is an enormous win that allows simulation model developers to write forward event code using the entire C++ language, and have that code automatically transformed into reversible code to enable parallel execution with the Rensselaer's Optimistic Simulation System (ROSS).

1. INTRODUCTION

Reversible computation is a key concept in parallel discrete event simulation [2, 10]. It is essential in order to achieve high performance for large scale models. In fact, the most highly parallel and fastest discrete event simulation benchmarks ever executed have depended on it [1]. In this paper we will briefly describe reversible computation and its use for optimistic parallel discrete event simulation, and then describe how we produce efficient reversible code from ordinary (non-reversible) code written in standard C++.

1.1 Discrete Event Simulation

Discrete event simulation (DES) is a simulation paradigm suitable for systems whose states are modeled as changing *discontinuously* and *irregularly* at discrete moments of simulation time.

State changes occur at simulation times that are calculated dynamically rather than determined statically as in time-stepped simulations. Most irregular systems whose behavior is not describable by continuous equations and do not happen to be suitable for simple time-stepped models are candidates for DES. Even some systems that are described by continuous equations can benefit from being discretized in an event-driven form.

1.2 Parallel Discrete Event Simulation

Efficient *parallel* discrete event simulation (PDES) is much more complex than the sequential version. The general approach is to divide the simulation and its state into semi-independent parallel units called LPs (logical processes) that generally execute concurrently and communicate asynchronously. Each simulated event (state change) is executed within one LP and affects only that LP's state. Any event may schedule other events for future simulation times. Events scheduled for other LPs must be transmitted to them as event messages with a timestamp indicating the simulation time when the event should be executed. Arriving event messages get enqueued in the event queues of the receiving LPs in increasing time stamp order.

What makes PDES so complex is the synchronization problem. Every LP must execute all of its event messages in strictly non-decreasing timestamp order despite the fact that it does not know in what order events may arrive or what timestamps they may carry. At any hypothetical global snapshot of the parallel simulation taken at a single instant of wall clock time some LPs will be ahead in simulation time and some will be behind., and which LPs are ahead or behind may change during execution. As a result, there is a danger of a *causality violation* when an LP that is behind in simulation time, e.g. at t_1, sends an event message with a (future) timestamp $t_2 > t_1$ that arrives at a receiver that has already simulated to time $t_3 > t_2$. In that case the receiver has already simulated past the simulation time when it *should* have executed the event at t_2, but it would be incorrect to execute events out of order. This is the essence of the PDES synchronization problem.

There are two broad approaches to resolving the PDES synchronization issue, called *conservative* and *optimistic* [4]. Conservative synchronization uses conventional process blocking primitives along with extra knowledge about the simulation model (called *lookahead* information) to prevent the execution from ever getting into a situation in which an event message arrives at an LP with a timestamp in its past. Optimistic synchronization, by contrast, does not try to prevent the simulation from getting into a *causalityviolation*,

ACM acknowledges that this contribution was authored or co-authored by an employee, or contractor of the national government. As such, the Government retains a nonexclusive, royalty-free right to publish or reproduce this article, or to allow others to do so, for Government purposes only. Permission to make digital or hard copies for personal or classroom use is granted. Copies must bear this notice and the full citation on the first page. Copyrights for components of this work owned by others than ACM must be honored. To copy otherwise, distribute, republish, or post, requires prior specific permission and/or a fee. Request permissions from permissions@acm.org.

SIGSIM-PADS '16, May 15-18, 2016, Banff, AB, Canada

© 2016 ACM. ISBN 978-1-4503-3742-7/16/05. . . $15.00

DOI: http://dx.doi.org/10.1145/2901378.2901394

i.e. a situation in which an event arrives at an LP in its past, i.e. with a timestamp $t_2 < t_3$. Whenever that occurs, the simulator rolls back the LP from t_3 to the state it was in at time t_2, cancels all event messages the LP sent after t_2, executes the arriving event, and then re-executes forward from time t_2 to t_3 and beyond. All event executions are therefore *speculative* or *provisional*, and are subject to rollback if the simulation gets into local causality trouble. Most of the time that does not happen and the simulation proceeds forward in parallel. For more detail see [10, 6].

1.3 Motivation for Generation of Reversible Code

In this paper we assume the parallel simulation model is written in C++. Each event is the execution of some event method $E()$ that makes changes to the state variables of the simulation. If that event has to be rolled back to deal with a causality violation, then the simulator needs a way to exactly reverse all of the side effects of $E()$ to return the simulation to the exact state it was in before $E()$ was executed.

However, a C++ method $E()$ will generally destroy information during its forward execution. It will usually overwrite or update some state variables, destroy control information (e.g. by *forgetting* which branch it took at a conditional), and may also delete data structures on the heap. It is not possible in general to write an $E'()$ that can restore information that was actually destroyed by $E()$. But we can frame the problem differently and achieve our purpose.

Instead, for an event method E() written in C++ (with return type void), we generate a derived method, $E^+()$ that is identical to $E()$ except that it is instrumented to save in a side data structure a trace of all of the information that $E()$ would destroy. The simulator uses that saved trace information to undo the side effects of $E^+()$, and it also destroys the side data structure that $E^+()$ created.

If $E()$ does any memory deallocation, we do not actually do the deallocation in $E^+()$ since it cannot be reversed. Instead we defer the actual deallocation of an object (but not the call to its destructor) to be done at *commit time* when we can be sure that $E^+()$ will never need to be reversed. Once the entire simulation has progressed (on all nodes) beyond a certain simulation time t, it is guaranteed that no event at a simulation time $< t$ will ever need to be reversed. At this point the commit function is called for all events at simulation times earlier than t. I/O and certain other issues are also handled at commit time, but they are beyond the scope of this paper.

Our approach is also described in general by K. S. Perumalla in [10] (p.132) as incremental check pointing "Among the checkpointing schemes, incremental checkpointing is in general the most efficient scheme, but is also one of the more challenging ones to implement." - also pointing out that incremental checkpointing can severely interfere with cache behavior and introduce a significant performance penalty in particular in cases when entire data structures are modified. In [13] a method is presented to implement incremental state saving in simulation kernels based on C++. In contrast to our approach, this method is not completely transparent. In particular, the user has to explicitly declare state variables as State<> or RefState<> objects and might have to explicitly make some casts which were not previously needed.

Our work significantly goes beyond the scope of our work in [15] which excluded C++ templates, as we can fully au-

tomate the generation of reversible code for arbitrary C++ code. We demonstrate this by applying it to a complete model in a scalable kinetic Monte-Carlo C++ application. In [15] a small toy model is used and separate benchmarks to demonstrate aspects of memory allocation and deallocation. We present one model code that combines all C++ features, in particular also including templates which are explicitly excluded in [15]. We also generate reversible assignment operators which are required to be provided by the user in [15]. The results presented in this paper are based version 2.0.12 of the Backstroke tool that can generate reversible forward code for the given simulation model code without any intervention or requirements on the user. It also generates a much less convoluted reversible code in comparison to the original code as presented in [15]. To the best of our knowledge, this is the very first paper that presents the transformation of a full C++ simulation model involving all essential features of the C++98 standard.

In Section 2 we present our approach to generating reversible C++ code and how we generate code to address full C++98 and describe the differences to C++11 and obstacles in utilizing the full C++STL. In Section 3 we describe the kinetic Monte-Carlo simulation model and in Section 4 an evaluation of the optimistic parallel execution on an Intel cluster with the ROSS simulator. All reversible code used to implement the reverse function as required with the ROSS simulator is generated automatically and no user intervention is necessary. In Section 5 we present the related work. In Section 6 we conclude on the observed performance and what future potential we see for further performance improvements.

2. GENERATION OF REVERSIBLE CODE

Our approach is a variant of incremental check pointing and the forward-reverse-commit paradigm as described in [10] (Chapter 7.3). This paradigm allows us to address situations in which a program fragment can be executed optimistically "ahead of time", but is found to be incorrect ("too optimistic"), and requires re-execution from a previous state of execution.

This situation occurs in parallel discrete event simulation with optimistic synchronization. We need to reverse events if they turn out to be not on the correct execution path (e.g. because an event that was transmitted on the network arrives with a timestamp that is older than the one that has already been simulated). After the event has been reversed we can then re-execute the event, but also taking into account the events that had occurred with an older time stamp.

Our approach requires that we transform only the forward event function. The forward code is transformed such that it records additional information in a data structure that is used by the reverse and commit methods. No code is generated for the reverse and commit method. They share the same implementation for all variants of transformed forward event codes. We have implemented our approach in a tool called *Backstroke* as source-to-source transformation based on the compiler infrastructure ROSE [12].

In the following sections we describe the code transformation operations, recorded data at runtime, and how the recorded data is used by the reverse and commit methods in the following sections.

2.1 Code Transformations for Intercepting Memory Modifying Operations

For our approach it is sufficient to intercept all memory modifying operations. Measured in bits, we store more information than necessary, but we do not need to store control flow information, because we only restore the sequence of memory locations that have been modified through assignments in one execution of the event method. When the execution of the event method is reversed, we restore the memory locations in reverse order of their modification. For this purpose of restoration, it is irrelevant which execution path was executed by the event method. One can also consider this to be an execution trace of all addresses and their old values before they are overwritten by an assignment. By restoring all those memory locations to their previous value, we can restore the program state before execution of the event function.

This approach allows us to address the effects of memory modifications for all of C++. With C++ come a number of language constructs in addition to the language constructs in C that make the generation of reverse code that can be *executed* in reverse very difficult. This applies in particular to C++ exceptions which are used in many modern C++ codes.

We consider three kinds of memory modifying operations: assignment operators, memory allocation, and memory deallocation. C++ offers 15 different assignment operators, which can modify the memory for all built-in types, two operators for memory allocation (single object and arrays) and two operators for memory deallocation (single object and arrays).

In the following section we define the transformations for all the C++ operators that must be transformed in the forward method.

2.2 Forward Code Generation for Assignment Operators

C++ offers 15 memory modifying operators, eleven variants of assignment and four variants of increment/decrement operators:

1. Assignment: E_1 **=** E_2

2. Assignment with additional operation: E_1 *op* E_2 where $op \in \{$ **+=, -=, *=, /=, %=, &=, |=, ^=, <<=, >>=** $\}$

3. pre/post increment/decrement operators: *op E*, *E op* where $op \in \{$ **++, --** $\}$

For each of the 15 operators we apply a transformation that enables us to record the old value stored at the address that is modified by an assignment and the address itself. The code transformation of assignments is only applied to operations on built-in types. For our approach it is important to be aware of the fact that memory can only be modified through built-in types. In C++ the assignment of user-defined types is defined by a default assignment operator (see Section 2.6). If the default assignment operator is user-defined we transform this implementation in the same way as all other forward code. If the default assignment operator is not user-defined, we generate a reversible default assignment operator. This way, the assignment of user-defined types is addressed as well.

For assignment operators we define the transformation α which intercepts all 15 forms of C++ assignments. The code that is introduced by this transformation is applied to all 15 kinds of assignment operators as a unified operation (including pre- and post-increment/decrement operators). The transformation α is introduced as follows for the different kinds of assignment:

1. E_1 **=** $E_2 \implies \alpha(E_1)$ **=** E_2

2. E_1 *op* $E_2 \implies \alpha(E_1)$ *op* E_2

3. *op* $E \implies op\ \alpha(E)$, E *op* $\implies \alpha(E)$ *op*

For example, let `p` be a pointer to an object and `x` be a data member of this object. Then an assignment of `y` to this member variable can be written as `p->x=y`. The transformation α instruments the left-hand-side of the assignment. The right-hand-side of the assignment remains unmodified as we only require the address of the left hand side of an assignment to access the old value (i.e. the value before assignment). Hence, we perform the transformation α(`p->x`)`=y`. The transformation α introduces a call to a function in the Backstroke library that takes as argument a reference parameter and returns the very same reference. This allows us to keep this transformation local to all expressions and we never need to transform any control flow or normalize code. An example of a transformed code involving assignments is described in Section 2.5.

2.3 Addressing Dynamic Memory Allocation

To address memory allocation we introduce transformation β, and for deallocation we introduce transformation γ. This concept is essentially the same as described in [10] (Chapter 13), but extended for C++ constructors and destructors, and in particular for C++ array allocation and deallocation. The correctness proof provided in [10] also applies for our approach. The only difference is that we split the execution of the destructor from the actual deallocation. In contrast, constructor calls are not separated from the actual allocation. We only need to store the address of the allocated object. Note that all constructors and copy constructors are transformed as well. Strictly, constructors only need to be transformed if the C++ placement **new** operator is used *and* it reuses old data (by not initializing all elements of an object). We discuss aspects of these transformations in detail in Section 2.6.

Let T be a built-in type or a user defined type (class, struct, or union) and E be an expression. Then for every occurrence of the operators **new** and **delete** in a program, we introduce the following transformations

1. **new** T**()** $\implies \beta_1($T$)$.

2. **new** T**()[**E**]** $\implies \beta_2(T,E)$.

3. **delete** $E \implies \gamma_1(E)$.

4. **delete[]** $E \implies \gamma_2(E)$.

For array allocation the expression E specifies the size of the array. For the C++ **delete** operator (e.g. **delete** x, where x denotes the address of an object) we generate code that invokes the destructor of the respective type, store the address of the object to be deallocated, and defer the actual memory deallocation to commit time (i.e. the memory of the object is deallocated when the commit function in the Backstroke library is invoked by the simulator). More details on these transformations can be found in [15]. An example of a generated code involving memory allocation and deallocation is described in Section 2.5. Deallocation of arrays is improved over the method in [15], as described in the next section.

2.4 Semantics of the Transformation Operators for Memory Allocation and Deallocation

Array deallocation has the additional complication that we also need to know (i) the size of the array (which is not explicitly provided in the source code), (ii) apply the destructor for each array element in reverse of the order constructors were called in the forward code, and finally (iii) to deallocate the memory allocated for the array and the memory location storing the size.

Our current implementation is different from the array handling in [15] as we do not rely on the compiler-specific method for storing the array size. We completely replace the array allocation and deallocation by our own allocation scheme. Our allocation scheme mimics the aforementioned allocation scheme by adding a word for storing the size of the array. The pointer returned by our allocation function refers to the actual memory (behind the size field). This mimics the same behavior as the code that is usually generated by C++ compilers, where the size of an array is stored in addition to the array elements. This enables us to ensure that the call to the destructor and the actual memory deallocation can be separated and it is also compiler independent.

2.5 Example: Original and Transformed Model Code Fragment

In Figure 1 we show side by side the original code and the Backstroke transformed code. It is a code fragment from our KMC model where a hash table is implemented for a map abstraction. In our model we use the C++STL interface of various data types (e.g. map, vector, deque, pair and iterators) and use a clean C++ implementation of the relevant C++STL functionality. The GNU C++STL implementation poses some additional engineering obstacles as described in Section 2.13.

The example fragment contains assignments, memory allocation, and memory deallocation. It also shows that the instrumentation on some local variables can be detected and those assignments to those variables are not instrumented. In detail, the variable `used` is a state variable of the hash table that is incremented when a new element is inserted. The left-hand side is instrumented by the α transformation introducing the `rts->avpushT(used)`. The variable `rts` is a global variable that maintains a pointer to a runtime state storage which maintains the states for reverse and commit. The variable `used` is passed by reference (as a C++ reference parameter). The function `avpushT` returns this very same reference allowing to assign the value from the right-hand side. For the **new** operator the transformation β is applied. It introduces the function call `registerAllocationForRollbackT` which only records the pointer value of the allocated memory. Variables p and `last` are local variables, therefore assignments to these variables do not need to be in-

strumented. To the expression `operator p` the transformation γ is applied that introduces the function call `registerDeallocationForCommitT`. This Backstroke library function records the pointer of the object memory to be deallocated and defers the deallocation until commit time. It also invokes the destructor of the respective class of p explicitly without deallocating memory. If a reverse operation is performed then the memory is restored and no memory deallocation is performed.

2.6 C++ Default Assignment Operators of User-Defined Types

C++ allows one to implement a user-defined assignment operator for any user-defined type. A user-defined assignment operator function is invoked whenever an assignment operator is used for this user-defined type. This way alternative semantics for assignment can be implemented. We utilize this C++ feature by generating reversible default assignment operators, if the operator is not provided by the user. In this case the compiler generates a default assignment operator, but since we require a reversible assignment operator we generate an alternative implementation. A provided user-defined assignment operator replaces the default implementation. If the user provided an assignment operator we transform the existing one (like any other function).

In addition C++ also provides copy constructors which allow one to initialize a new object from the values of an existing object. We can also generate reversible copy constructors, but it is not necessary as copy constructors are only applied to uninitialized memory (which does not need to be recorded for reversal). Note that in C++ initialization is not assignment. This distinction is important for reversibility as it suffices to provide reversible assignment operators, but it is not necessary to provide also reversible copy constructors.

Backstroke offers also to generate reversible copy constructors when needed for placement **new**. In C++ it is possible to reuse memory in combination with the C++ placement **new** operator. This requires to also transform member initializer lists to record the value for each initialized data member.

2.7 C++ Code Generation

The generated code contains calls to Backstroke library functions that have been introduced. All code is generated in the C++ namespace Backstroke. It is never necessary to normalize code or transform the control flow in a program. All transformations are local to expressions. The Runtime Library is linked with the transformed forward code. The execution of the forward code computes all data necessary to restore any previous state in the computation of the forward function. All data is maintained in data structures of the Backstroke Library.

2.8 RTSS Operations

The Backstroke library uses a Run Time State Storage (RTSS) to manage the data necessary to restore states to support reversibility. Since our approach follows the Forward-Reverse-Commit paradigm, the essential data structure used internally in the RTSS is a double ended queue. The forward code pushes data on one end of the queue, and the reverse code pops data from the very same end of the queue. The commit function, in contrast, pops

```
template <typename T,typename K> inline
T * Hash<T,K>::Insert(const K &key) {
    int idx = (int) (hash_value<K>(key) % (unsigned int) size);
    used = used + 1;
    table[idx] = new Link(key,table[idx]);


    return &table[idx]->data;
}
template <typename T,typename K> inline
void Hash<T,K>::Remove(const K &key) {
    int idx = (int) (hash_value<K>(key) % (unsigned int) size);
    Link *p = table[idx],*last = 0;
    while(p != 0 && !(p->key == key)) {
        last = p;
        p = p->next;
    }
    if(p != 0) {
        used = used - 1;
        if(last == 0)
            table[idx] = p->next;
        else
            last->next = p->next;
        delete p;
    }
}
```

```
template <typename T,typename K> inline
T * Hash<T,K>::Insert(const K &key) {
    int idx = (int) (hash_value<K>(key) % (unsigned int) size);
    (rts->avpushT(used)) = used + 1;
    (rts->avpushT(table[idx])) = (rts->
        registerAllocationForRollbackT(new Link(key,table[idx
        ])));
    return &table[idx]->data;
}
template <typename T,typename K> inline
void Hash<T,K>::Remove(const K &key) {
    int idx = (int) (hash_value<K>(key) % (unsigned int) size);
    Link *p = table[idx],*last = 0;
    while(p != 0 && !(p->key == key)) {
        last = p;
        p = p->next;
    }
    if(p != 0) {
        (rts->avpushT(used)) = used - 1;
        if(last == 0)
            (rts->avpushT(table[idx])) = p->next;
        else
            (rts->avpushT(last->next)) = p->next;
        (rts->registerDeallocationForCommitT(p));
    }
}
```

Figure 1: Example code fragment from the original code and the Backstroke transformed code showing a templated implementation of the hash function used in a map implementation.

data from the other end, performing the commit operation in the same order as the forward function. Note that we maintain a data queue for each event invocation, and thus, after restoring an event its data queue is guaranteed to be empty after reversal or commit. Note that maintaining this order is important in cases where data for the same memory location is restored multiple times (because multiple writes to the same memory location were recorded). Note that in the reverse method we deallocate memory that has been allocated, but may also restore data in this very same memory. Hence, the order of data restoration and undoing of memory allocation (i.e. deallocation) must be maintained in the reverse function. The commit function only disposes data stored by the forward function and performs the deferred memory deallocation (as a result of the **delete** operator). Since deallocated memory blocks cannot overlap, and no data is restored in the commit function, the order is irrelevant - however, it is conceptually clean to perform it in the same order as the forward function, as memory deallocation is a deferred operation. We do not consider input/output operations in this paper, but the order is also significant when completing deferred output in the commit function. Therefore, we consider a double ended queue as the appropriate abstraction for maintaining data for the forward-reverse-commit approach. Handling of input and output (currently only performed in the initialization of model data and after the end of the simulation) is the subject of future work.

In summary, the essential operations in the RTSS for supporting Backstroke generated reversible forward functions in combination with the reverse and commit functions which are provided by the RTSS, are shown in Table 1.

2.9 Transformation Statistics for the KMC Model

In Table 2 we show the transformation statistics for the KMC simulation model that we evaluate in this paper. We show the results for the non-optimized and optimized ver-

Variant	T1	T2	T3	T4	T5	T6	Total
Non-optimized	136	4	1	4	1	18	166
Optimized	84	4	1	4	1	18	114

Table 2: Overview of the number of applied transformations on the KMC Model code for the non-optimized and the optimized version.

sion. In the optimized version we detect variables that are guaranteed not to be state variables. In C++ terminology these are auto variables, or local variables that have a scope that begins and ends within the event execution. For those we do not need to record any address-value pair, nor do we need to check whether it is allocated on the stack or heap. We can therefore eliminate the instrumentation for the assignment. The columns T1-T6 show the number of instrumentations by language construct as follows

T1 : Assignment operator expression statements (e.g. x=y;)

T2 : Object memory allocation with operator **new**

T3 : Array memory allocation with operator **new[]**

T4 : Object memory deallocation with operator **delete**

T5 : Array memory deallocation with operator **delete[]**

T6 : Default assignment operators that are not implemented by the user and for which a reversible version is generated.

In the last column we show the total number of transformations. The total number of classes is 21, and in 18 classes (see column T6) a reversible default assignment operator is generated. In 3 classes the model writer provided assignment operators which are transformed like any other function to become reversible.

Original	Forward	Reverse	Commit
new	register obj allocation	deallocate obj	dispose obj allocation
delete	register obj deallocation	dispose obj deallocation	deallocate obj
l=r	store (addr(l),val(l))	restore (addr(l),val(r))	dispose (addr(l),val(r))

Table 1: Summary of operations performed by the Run Time State Storage in the Backstroke Library.

2.10 C++ Templates

Any non-trivial C++ code involves templates. Since our transformation is performed source-to-source we need to take templates into account. For each type used in a template the compiler generates a separate instance of the template with the parameter replaced by the actual type. We transform the original template definition without considering instantiations. Let us discuss this in detail for the assignment operator and why this is guaranteed to be correct in combination with the specific semantics implemented in the Backstroke library.

An assignment that occurs in the template function can be either instantiated for (a) a built-in type, or (b) for a user-defined type. For a built-in type (e.g. int) the left hand side of the assignment must be passed to a Backstroke library function to record its address-value pair to support reversibility. For a user-defined type we do not need to record the address-value pair for the left hand side variable because any actual memory-modifying assignments will occur in the underlying reversible assignment operator for that type. However, since we transform the original template (and not the instantiated code) the code transformation is the same for both cases. Here C++11 predicates (part of C++ since C++98 TR1), which determine at compile time whether a type is a build-in type or a user-defined type, come to rescue.

The implementation in the Backstroke library uses these predicates such that the C++ compiler can determine at compile-time whether the provided type to the library function avpushT is a built-in type or a user-defined type. For the user-defined type the function performs a no-op (i.e. fall-through branch). There is no impact on performance as the function has an empty path for this case. If the compiler can also eliminate the function call itself there is no overhead at all for user-defined types for the avpushT on the left-hand-side of the assignment at all. For built-in types the address-value pair is stored. Note that the transformed assignment operator contains an avpushT for each data member of the user-defined type. This is a form of template meta programming that enables us to keep the required source-to-source transformations simple. The combined transformation time and compilation time for the entire model code is less than 3 seconds. Note that operators for built-in types cannot be overloaded in C++. That is why we need to perform a source-to-source transformation (otherwise it would suffice to implement reversible assignment operators for built-in types).

Memory allocation and deallocation operators are independent of the assignment operator semantics. They are only involved when the result of a **new** operation (i.e. a pointer to allocated object memory) is assigned to a variable. Assignment of values and memory allocation and deallocation is treated orthogonally by the separate transformations α, β, and γ.

2.11 Stack vs Heap - The Necessary Check

The Backstroke Runtime Library must ensure that data stored on the runtime stack of the event is not restored in the reverse function because once the event function has been executed, all elements on the event function's runtime stack are popped from the stack by the C++ runtime system. Therefore a compiler/system dependent test is performed for each address-value pair that are about to be stored in the Run Time State Storage (RTSS). If the pointer refers to a stack address, then the pointer is not stored in the RTSS. This is necessary, because otherwise we would restore memory (in the reverse function) that is no longer allocated on the runtime stack after the event function has been executed (in the forward-function). On the other hand, if it is a heap pointer, then the pointer is stored in the RTSS and the reverse and commit functions use this information to perform the proper operations to restore the memory state.

Hence, no information about stack allocated memory is ever stored in the RTSS, only *modified* heap allocated memory is duplicated in the RTSS.

The Backstroke Runtime Library is initialized at the beginning of the simulation. For our model this also involves initializing the simulation with data read from configuration files. Hence, the code performing Input/Output (similar for generating the results of the simulation) is not part of the event function and therefore not reversed.

The Backstroke Library stores the current start address and end address of the thread's stack (currently we use POSIX pthread library function calls to determine the stack's start address and the length of the stack).

2.12 C++98 vs C++11

In this paper we have considered all C++98 language constructs. To support C++11 we have to consider new C++11 language features which are not in C++98, primarily C++11 move constructors and move assignment operators. These allow one to express data movement between variables with the advantage that aliasing can be avoided and the compiler can decide not to copy data if it can remain at the same memory location (i.e. C++11 move semantics allow one to avoid copying of data). Reversible move constructors and move assignment operators are different from the default assignment operators we generated for C++98. Further work is required to support reversible C++11 move semantics. In C++98 unions can only contain POD (plain old data) types (i.e. types with no user-defined constructors). POD types can also be **struct**s that contain only POD types. Because of this restriction, assignment operators cannot be added to types that are used inside unions in C++98. In C++11 this restriction is relaxed and all types can be used inside unions. Therefore, for C++11 we can also generate assignment operators for non-POD types that are used inside unions. Our current implementation for C++98 unions is the same as for structs, and hence copies the same data in a union multiple times. This will be further optimized in future releases of Backstroke.

2.13 C++STL

Our work does not cover all the details required for handling GNU header files yet, which contain C++ language extensions, built-ins, and explicit calls into the C++ standard library. The functions in the C++ standard library that replace parts of implementations of the C++ Standard Template Library must be reversed as well (e.g. several functions of the red-black tree that is used for implementing maps in the C++STL are implemented in the C++ standard library). To fully automate this entire build process with Backstroke requires further engineering work.

An alternative could be the use of a clean STL implementation (e.g. the old SGI C++ STL), but only up-to-date versions of GNU, Intel, and Clang/LLVM support the C++11 standard, which is our target to provide to model developers. For our HPC super computers of interest LLVM is not an option, as no backend exists yet. However, LLVM uses the GCC STL and poses similar engineering challenges to reversibility. It does not require any different code transformations or support in the Backstroke library, but tedious engineering work to address all the additional functions that are implemented in the C++ standard library, for which we also require reversible code. However, we already have completed this work for the C++ `std::list` and `std::map` abstractions. Further work is required to address built-in functions and C++ standard library calls for the remaining STL classes.

3. C++ KMC MODEL

In order to verify robustness and correctness of Backstroke, we have chosen to apply it to a grain evolution simulation using a real world parallel kinetic Monte-Carlo code written for crystal kinetics. The code is named SPOCK (Scalable Parallel Optimistic Crystal Kinetics) and is built on the ROSS discrete event simulator by C. Carothers et al., which uses the Time Warp algorithm to achieve a scalable and robust parallelization. The following sections introduce the ROSS simulator, the kinetic Monte-Carlo method, and the grain evolution application.

3.1 ROSS Simulator

ROSS is a general purpose discrete event simulator developed at RPI by C. Carothers et. al. [5]. Within ROSS, a simulation consists of a set of logical processes (LP's) that communicate with each other through time-stamped event messages. A discrete event process formulated in this way is called a ROSS model. To implement a new model in ROSS one needs to write an initialization function that sets off the initial state of each LP, and an event function which is responsible for processing a received event message for a given LP. The event function also has the opportunity to send further event messages.

After initialization the simulation logically progresses by processing any event messages in simulation time order using the provided event functions for the LP's.

ROSS has been developed over more than 10 years, and is mature software. It has the capability of running simulations in parallel using either conservative or optimistic synchronization. The Time Warp mechanism is the versatile and scalable option in ROSS for running simulations in parallel.

Time Warp is an optimistic approach, where each processor employs speculative execution to process any event messages it is aware of. Causality conflicts, such as when a previously unknown message which should already have been processed is received, are handled through local roll back. During roll back the effects of messages that were processed in error are undone.

In order to use Time Warp in a ROSS model, a reverse event function must be provided. The reverse function is responsible for undoing the state changes that the forward event function incurred for the same message.

The power of Backstroke in this context is that it can automatically generate the appropriate reverse event function for a given forward event function. For complicated discrete event models, this greatly increases productivity since less code needs to be written by hand. In addition, it is much less error prone and reduces the code maintenance burden, compared to hand written reverse code. It can not be stressed enough that even a very minute bug in the reverse code, so that it only almost reverses the effect of the forward event code, is disastrous for Time Warp simulations. Small state differences can make the code address out of bounds, cause exceptions, and result in infinite loops.

3.2 Model: A Parallel Kinetic Monte-Carlo Application

We have applied Backstroke to the event processing code of SPOCK (Scalable Parallel Optimistic Crystal Kinetics), a parallel kinetic Monte-Carlo application for simulation of growth and morphology evolution of crystals.

We will here give an overview of the kinetic Monte-Carlo method, and of crystal evolution simulations. After that we will describe the application of Backstroke to SPOCK and give some performance metrics.

In the kinetic Monte-Carlo method, a physical system is modeled as a set of interacting objects, and their evolution is described by a sequence of discrete events that affect the set of objects.

In our crystal grain simulation, we model a piece of solid as a grid of unit elements. Each unit element represents a microscopic piece of material, big enough to be able to exhibit a well defined crystal orientation, but much smaller than typical grain sizes. These unit elements are commonly called spins, since the nature of grain evolution resembles evolution of magnetic domains, commonly studied by the Ising model in which unit element has a binary state: spin up or down. A spin that has at least one neighbor of a different orientation than itself is defined a boundary spin, and the set of these spins comprise the grain boundaries. It is the evolution and morphology of these boundaries that is of interest in grain evolution simulations.

An event in the grain evolution model is a change in crystal orientation of a spin. The time of the change, and the next orientation of a given spin are given by stochastic variables whose distributions depend on the orientation of the neighboring spins. Typically, it is favorable for a spin to choose a new orientation that maximizes the number of neighbors with that same orientation.

A high level description of a grain evolution algorithm is as follows:

1. Initialize the orientations of all spins.

2. For each spin, sample an event from the corresponding

time and orientation distributions. This event is inserted in the event queue, and serves as a putative event for this spin.

3. Execute the earliest event in the event queue, and advance the simulation time to that of this event.

4. For all spins whose time and orientation distributions changed due to the executed event, retract their current putative events, and sample new ones. Sample a new event also for the spin whose event was just executed. Insert these events in the event queue.

5. If the earliest event in the event queue is past the end time of the simulation, stop. Otherwise, go to 3.

Some notes about this algorithm: For short ranged interactions, in 2D each spin typically has 4 or 8 neighbors, while in 3D this number is often 6 or 26. For longer range interactions the number of neighbors can be much greater. Typically, at each executed event, as many events as the number of neighbors are retracted, and new events are sampled. This means that the vast majority of scheduled events are retracted. This is in contrast to most event driven simulations where retractions are rare. The algorithm description above allows plenty of room for optimization in these grain simulations: often, new orientations are restricted to those present in the neighbors. Therefore, spins in the bulk of a grain, i.e. one which as the same spin as all its neighbors, can not change, and thus no events need to be generated or kept for these spins, which can be the vast majority of spins in the simulating. This saves both memory and computational resources.

4. EVALUATION

As a case for our evaluation of Backstroke, we have chosen to use the 2D Potts grain growth model, where the spins are vertices in regular Cartesian grid on a 2D torus, and each spin interacts with its 8 nearest neighbors. The possible orientations, or spin values, are represented by integers, and a spin can only change orientation to that of one of its neighbors.

The event code was not written with Backstroke in mind, and is a relatively complex C++ code making full use of e.g. templates and overloaded operators. The forward event code size is around 1800 lines including the implementation of all used data types.

To run our grain evolution tests, we choose two system sizes: A smaller system with 128×128 spins divided into a grid of 16×16 LP's, which we run for 100 simulation time units, or a total of 821872 events, and a bigger system with 768×768 spins in 96×96 LP's. We run the big system for 8 time units, or a total of 16174893 events.

The tests were run on an Intel cluster with 16 cores per node, using up to 256 cores. We evaluated the correctness of our simulations by recording for each simulation the final number of committed events as well as intermediate information about the number of orientation changes at well defined simulation times. There is complete agreement of these numbers between all simulations, parallel and sequential, and hand written and automatically generated reverse code. In our runs we used GNU g++ 4.9.3 with the optimization flags "-O3 --finline-limit=1000000". It is

crucial to allow a high amount of inlining to get good performance, as it enables high-level and low-level optimizations on the code instrumentations and the inlined Backstroke library functions.

We include performance data both for simulations using hand written (HW) forward and reverse code, and using reversible code generated by Backstroke (BS) from the hand written forward code. We include measurements of two versions of the Backstroke generated code: One plain version which transforms all assignments and copy constructors, and one optimized version which excludes transformation of assignment to local variables and excludes automatically generated copy constructors.

In summary we find that the BS generated reversible code is 3.4 to 5.9 times slower than the hand written forward and reverse code, with the optimized BS code version being up to 8% faster than the non-optimized version. The performance details can be found in Fig. 2 where the y-axis units are committed events per second. In Fig. 3 we compare the speed (in units of committed events per second) of the hand written code to the Backstroke generated code. The slowdown factor is defined as the speed of the hand written code divided by the Backstroke generated code. We see that the slowdown factor increases significantly as we reach the scaling limit for the small model. In order to gain an understanding of that, we show in Fig. 4 the fraction of total gross executed events that are rolled back. This figure shows that the additional slowdown of the Backstroke generated code in the strong scaling limit is likely due to additional roll backs incurred when running this code.

5. RELATED WORK

Jefferson started the subject of rollback-based synchronization in 1984 [6]. The paper discusses rollback implemented by restoring a snapshot of an old state. In 1999 Carothers et. al published the first paper to suggests using reverse computation instead of snapshot restoration as the mechanism for rollback [2]. It is written in terms of very simple and conventional programming constructs (C-like rather than C++ -like) and instrumenting the forward code to store near minimal trace information to allow reversing of side effects when needed. That paper considers discrete event simulation as one of several applications of virtual time, but in fact it was then and is now the primary application. Although the term "virtual time" is used, you can safely read it as "simulation time".

Barnes et. al demonstrated in 2013 [1], how important reverse computation can be in a practical application area. The fastest and most parallel discrete event simulation benchmark ever executed was done at Lawrence Livermore National Laboratory on one of the world's largest supercomputers using reverse computation as its rollback method for synchronization. The reverse code was hand-generated, and methodologically we know that this is unsustainable, highlighting the need for a way of automatically generating reverse code from forward code, and this is what we address with the work presented in this paper - to have a tool available, Backstroke2, for generating reverse code that can be applied to full C++.

Kalyan Perumalla and Alfred Park discuss the use of Reverse Computation for scalable fault tolerant computations [11]. The paper is limited in a number of ways, but they make a fundamental point, which is that Reverse Compu-

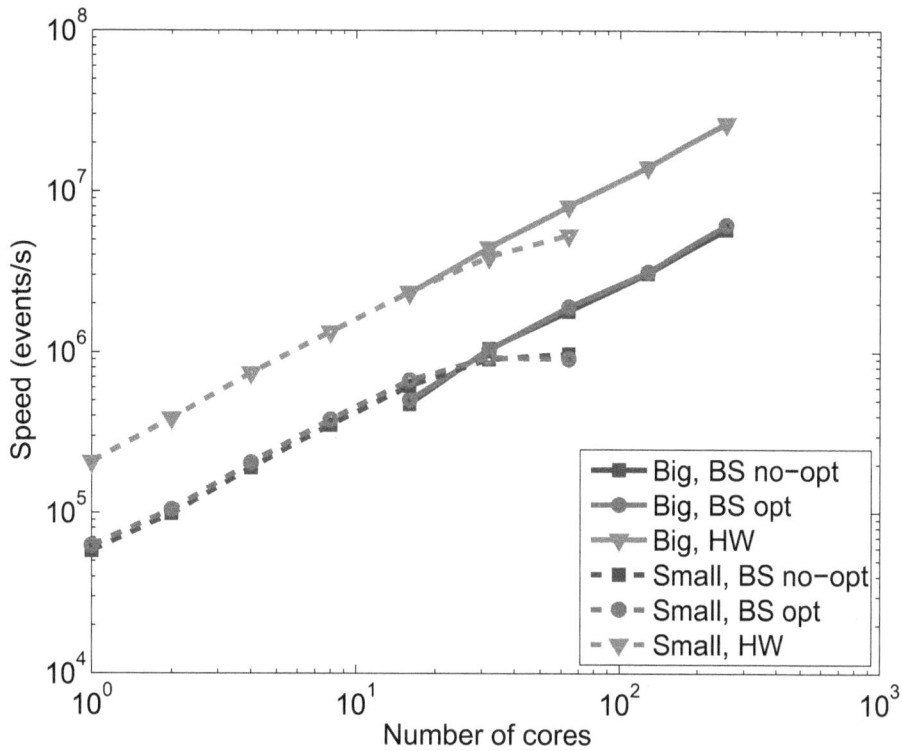

Figure 2: The performance of Potts model of different sizes using various versions of Backstroke instrumented code, as well as hand written reverse code. The big system consists of 768×768 spins, divided into a grid of $96 \times 96 = 9216$ LP's. The small system is 128×128 spins, divided into a grid of $16 \times 16 = 256$ LP's. The simulations are run for 1000 time units.

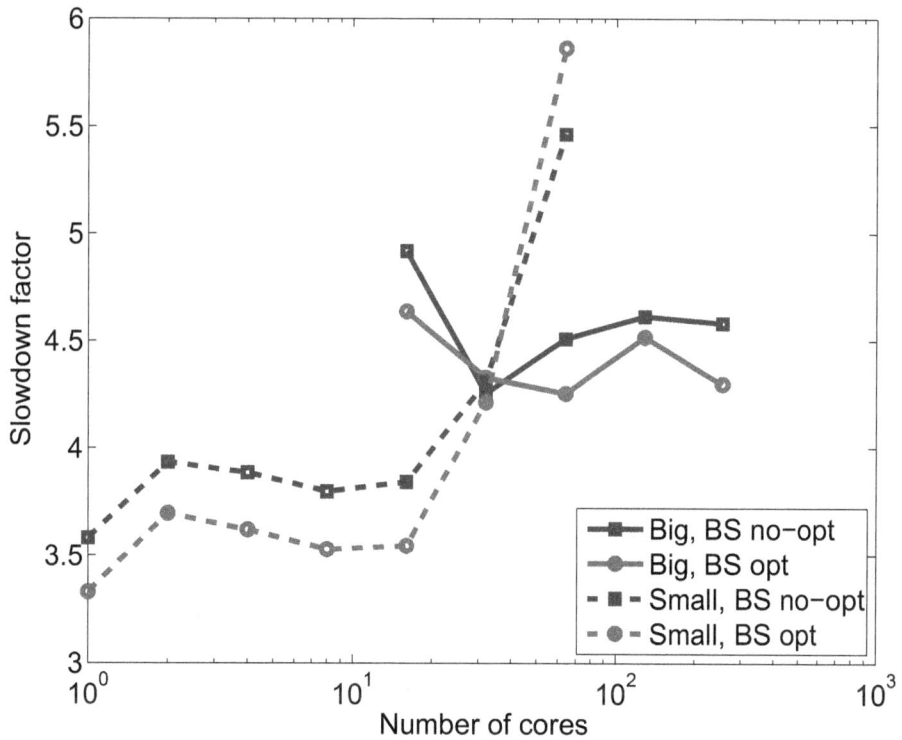

Figure 3: The slowdown factor of using the Backstroke instrumented code compared to hand written reverse code.

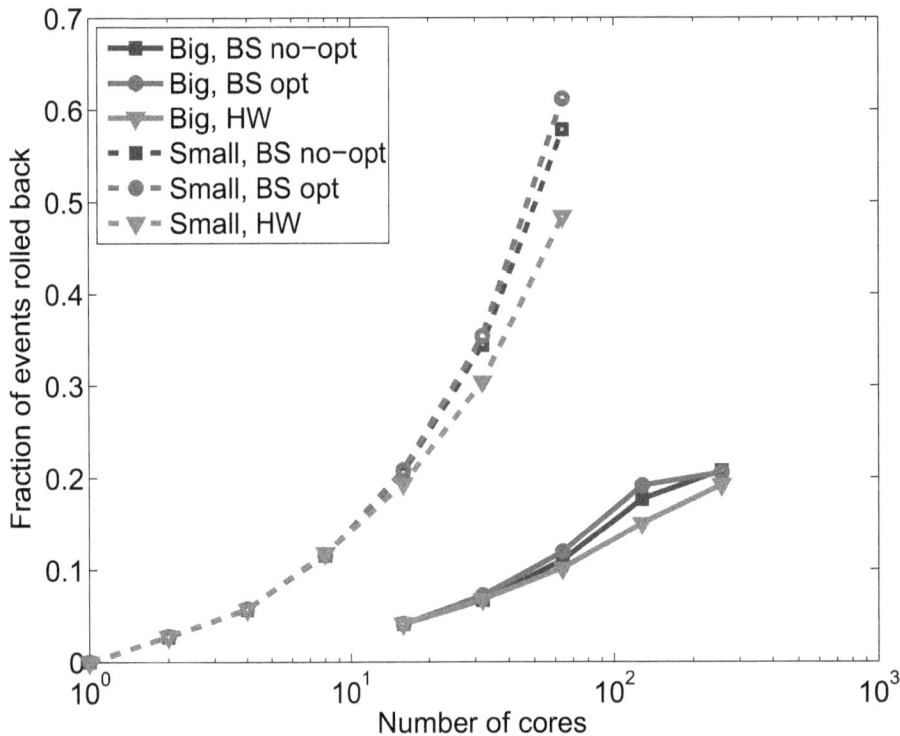

Figure 4: The fraction of events rolled back from the total number of events executed.

tation can be used to recover from faults by mechanisms that are much faster than check pointing mechanisms. The approach presented in this paper uses incremental check-pointing, which reduces the amount of memory that needs to be stored for establishing a checkpoint by only storing the changes to a state, instead of storing the values of all variables (and memory) defining the state of a program.

In [7] Justin LaPre et. al discuss an approach called Low Overhead Runtime Assisted Instruction Negation, LO-RAIN. LORAIN is able to account for, and in many cases reverse, the computation without resorting to state-saving techniques. Similar to our presented work, it also uses Rensselaer's Optimistic Simulation System (ROSS), but couples it with the LLVM compiler to generate the reverse code. The reverse code generation is limited as it cannot handle more sophisticated C++ language features such as virtual functions and exceptions, but since it operates on the LLVM IR, it is independent of the source level language, but it limited to LLVM supported backends. Loops also require user-provided information, which in contrast, our approach does not.

The approach in [16] is similar to [7] as it takes control flow into account and generates code for computing additional information required to reconstruct the execution path that had been take in the forward code, but operates at the source code level. It has similar limitations w.r.t. to C++ language constructs with complicated control flow, in particular virtual method calls and exceptions, which are not addressed.

The scope of our work in this paper clearly goes beyond the work in [15], as we also address C++ templates and the generation of reversible C++ assignment operators, allowing a fully automatic generation of reversible forward code for arbitrary C++ code. The model presented in this paper is

a full model (about 1800 lines in length including the implementation of all used data structures), whereas in [15] only a small model of about 30 lines was used that only performed assignments, but does not perform memory allocation and deallocation. Dynamic data structures are demonstrated in separate benchmarks in [15]. In our model all language constructs are used in the same code.

Our approach presented in this paper is different to [2, 16, 7] as we do not need to take any control flow information into account and address full C++. It is sufficient to consider only a small subset of the C++ language, and by regenerating all other constructs unmodified in the forward code. However, the drawback of our approach is that it is likely to generate a high overhead in the forward code. Therefore, our approach should only be considered as a base level for establishing reversibility of arbitrary irreversible (i.e. information destroying) C++ code that can benefit from the above mentioned approaches for reverse code generation. Approaches to reverse code generation that allow reverse execution usually induce smaller overhead in the forward code as our approach if information is destroyed, or no overhead at all for reversible programs (which do not destroy information).

In [9] an autonomic system is presented that can utilize both an incremental and a full checkpointing mode. At run time both code variants are available and the system switches between the two variants, trying to select the more efficient checkpointing version. With our approach we optimize the incremental checkpointing by reducing the number of instrumentations at compile time by determining with static analysis which memory locations are part of the event object's state and only need to be instrumented. In [3] an instrumentation technique is applied to relocatable object files. Specifically, it operates on the Executable and Linkable

Format (ELF). It uses the tool Hijacker [8] to instrument the binary code to generate a cache of disassembly information. This allows to avoid disassembly of instructions at run time. At run time the reverse instructions are built on-the-fly also using pre-compiled tables of instructions. This approach is similar to our approach as it also pays an instrumentation overhead. The information that it extracts from instructions, the target address and the size of a memory write, is similar to our address-value pairs. With our source-level approach the available type information is sufficient to determine the value size. Since we add the code instrumentations at the source level, our approach has a higher potential for optimization, as a compiler's multiple optimization stages are more likely to minimize the impact of code instrumentations than instrumentations that are added to an already optimized binary. Recently progress has been made also in utilizing hardware transactional memory for further optimizing single node performance [14].

6. CONCLUSION

We have demonstrated an approach to reverse computation that can be applied to full C++ and demonstrated it for a model that makes use of full C++, including templates, operator overloading, memory allocation, placement **new** operator, and user-defined complex data structures. We transform irreversible C++ programs that destroy information into instrumented reversible C++ programs. The instrumentation ensures that all potentially destroyed information is preserved by the transformed forward code such that the provided reverse function can restore a previous program state and the commit function can perform the deferred memory deallocation.

In contrast to other approaches for generating reverse code, we do not need to explicitly take any control flow information into account, but instead store address-value pairs of modified memory locations and record information about all dynamic memory allocation and deallocation. In addition, we generate reversible (copy) constructors and assignment operators. The reversible assignment operators are crucial for supporting user-defined types that are composed of other user-defined types and built-in types. When the forward function is executed it is guaranteed that only heap allocated memory is stored in the Run Time State Storage (RTSS). With a run time check we ensure that stack allocated memory is never stored in the RTSS as the event function's stack frame is only valid while the event function is executing.

To the best of our knowledge, this is the very first publication where a full scale C++ model is automatically transformed such that it can be executed in parallel optimistically on a super computer. Our scaling study still shows a significant performance penalty compared to the manually written reverse code. For the big model we observe a performance penalty between 3.4 and 5.9 for the automatically optimized version. Further, the optimization of the RTSS and improved static analysis to reduce the number of program instrumentations have a great potential to reduce this performance penalty. In this paper we focus on correctness and will address improvements in performance in future work. It is also important to point out that we did not eliminate all the additional data (and its corresponding code) that is necessary to allow for the manual reverse code. The elimination of this code will also improve the performance,

as it is actually superfluous in the automatically reversed model. However, this model was originally developed without Backstroke, and additional work is necessary to remove all this code now.

If a user starts with a new model and uses Backstroke, it is sufficient to write uninstrumented irreversible C++ code (i.e. conservative code). There are no limitations in what features of C++ can be used. Backstroke can be used to automatically transform the model's code and run the code on a parallel computer using the ROSS simulator. This offers a significantly lower entry level for model writers to use parallel discrete event simulation. The performance can be also addressed at the language level by implementing functions as pure functions (in C++ as const functions that do not modify state) as Backstroke does not need to instrument such functions.

In future work we also plan to incorporate approaches that address reversible languages into Backstroke. One example is the Janus language which has been extended to provide a C backend. Such Janus generated reversible C code is suitable to be combined with Backstroke generated code and offers to avoid the Backstroke induced overhead for reversible code fragments. How to efficiently combine both approaches is subject to future research, but it is clear that leveraging other tools that can generate reverse code must be integrated in our approach to reduce the overhead of Backstroke generated code. This optimization opportunity may also motivate users who implement complex PDES models to write parts of their models in reversible subsets of C++ (with possibly some extensions) to achieve better performance. These reversible subsets can then be transformed into a reversible language (e.g. Janus) to leverage an existing C language backend, and combine the generated C code with the Backstroke generated C++ code. Similar, a reversible C compiler can also be utilized in such a work flow.

Thus, possibly in the long run, some kind of hybrid approach, by combining complex C++ code, reversible languages, and reverse code generators, will enable improved productivity in the implementation of PDES models, but also achieve good performance by combining all these approaches in one work flow.

7. ACKNOWLEDGMENTS

This work was performed under the auspices of the U.S. Department of Energy by Lawrence Livermore National Laboratory under Contract DE-AC52-07NA27344, via LDRD project 14-ERD-062. IM release number LLNL-CONF-681318.

8. REFERENCES

[1] P. D. Barnes, Jr., C. D. Carothers, D. R. Jefferson, and J. M. LaPre. Warp speed: Executing time warp on 1,966,080 cores. In *Proceedings of the 2013 ACM SIGSIM Conference on Principles of Advanced Discrete Simulation*, SIGSIM-PADS '13, pages 327–336, New York, NY, USA, 2013. ACM.

[2] C. D. Carothers, K. S. Perumalla, and R. M. Fujimoto. Efficient optimistic parallel simulations using reverse computation. *ACM Trans. Model. Comput. Simul.*, 9(3):224–253, July 1999.

[3] D. Cingolani, A. Pellegrini, and F. Quaglia. Transparently mixing undo logs and software

reversibility for state recovery in optimistic pdes. In *Proceedings of the 3rd ACM SIGSIM Conference on Principles of Advanced Discrete Simulation*, SIGSIM PADS '15, pages 211–222, New York, NY, USA, 2015. ACM.

[4] R. M. Fujimoto. *Parallel and Distribution Simulation Systems*. John Wiley & Sons, Inc., New York, NY, USA, 1st edition, 1999.

[5] A. O. Holder and C. D. Carothers. Analysis of time warp on a 32,768 processor ibm blue gene/l supercomputer. In *Proceedings of the European Modeling and Simulation Symposium (EMSS)*, 2008.

[6] D. R. Jefferson. Virtual time. *ACM Trans. Program. Lang. Syst.*, 7(3):404–425, July 1985.

[7] J. M. LaPre, E. J. Gonsiorowski, and C. D. Carothers. Lorain: A step closer to the pdes 'holy grail'. In *Proceedings of the 2Nd ACM SIGSIM/PADS Conference on Principles of Advanced Discrete Simulation*, SIGSIM-PADS '14, pages 3–14, New York, NY, USA, 2014. ACM.

[8] A. Pellegrini. Hijacker: Efficient static software instrumentation with applications in high performance computing: Poster paper. In *High Performance Computing and Simulation (HPCS), 2013 International Conference on*, pages 650–655, July 2013.

[9] A. Pellegrini, R. Vitali, and F. Quaglia. Autonomic state management for optimistic simulation platforms. *IEEE Transactions on Parallel and Distributed Systems*, 26(6):1560–1569, June 2015.

[10] K. S. Perumalla. *Introduction to Reversible Computing*. CRC Press Book, 2013.

[11] K. S. Perumalla and A. J. Park. Reverse computation for rollback-based fault tolerance in large parallel systems. *Cluster Computing*, 17(2):303–313, June 2014.

[12] D. Quinlan, C. Liao, R. Matzke, M. Schordan, T. Panas, R. Vuduc, and Q. Yi. ROSE Web Page. http://www.rosecompiler.org, 2014.

[13] R. Rönngren, M. Liljenstam, R. Ayani, and J. Montagnat. Transparent incremental state saving in time warp parallel discrete event simulation. In *Proceedings of the Tenth Workshop on Parallel and Distributed Simulation*, PADS '96, pages 70–77, Washington, DC, USA, 1996. IEEE Computer Society.

[14] E. Santini, M. Ianni, A. Pellegrini, and F. Quaglia. Hardware-transactional-memory based speculative parallel discrete event simulation of very fine grain models. In *2015 IEEE 22nd International Conference on High Performance Computing (HiPC)*, pages 145–154, Dec 2015.

[15] M. Schordan, D. Jefferson, P. Barnes, T. Oppelstrup, and D. Quinlan. Reverse code generation for parallel discrete event simulation. In J. Krivine and J.-B. Stefani, editors, *Reversible Computation*, volume 9138 of *Lecture Notes in Computer Science*, pages 95–110. Springer International Publishing, 2015.

[16] G. Vulov, C. Hou, R. Vuduc, R. Fujimoto, D. Quinlan, and D. Jefferson. The backstroke framework for source level reverse computation applied to parallel discrete event simulation. In *Proceedings of the Winter Simulation Conference*, WSC '11, pages 2965–2979. Winter Simulation Conference, 2011.

Development and Experimentation of PDES-based Analytic Simulation

Yi-Ping Yao, Dong Meng, Qing-Jun Qu, Jin Li, Zhi-Wen Jiang
College of Information System and Management
National University of Defense Technology
Changsha, Hunan, 410072, China
ypyao@nudt.edu.cn, donemen@yeah.net, qjqu2012@163.com, dlijin@163.com, zhiwenj@163.com

ABSTRACT

Parallel-discrete-event-simulation-based analytic simulation (PAS) is an effective approach to study complex issues and analyze complex systems. But the complexity and high demand for credibility of PAS make its development and experimentation quite different from traditional information systems. Firstly, this article briefly introduces analytic simulation concept and the difference with training simulation. And then five computational characteristics which cause the huge computation demand are summarized: multi-sample, multi-entity, as fast as possible, synchronization for constraint of causality and complex model calculation. According to these characteristics, a "Sample, Entity, Model" three-level-Parallelization solution (SEMP) is introduced for PAS. The solution can be used to fully exploit the parallelization of PAS and utilize the computing resources in different levels, which is able to meet the growing computation demand of PAS. Finally, in order to improve the development efficiency and credibility of PAS application, based on the accumulation of several years' R&D, we conclude a summary of development and experimentation flow of PAS, and propose four additional VV&A principles to improve credibility, which can be used to guide the development and experimentation of PDES-based analytic simulation.

Keywords

PDES-based Analytic Simulation; three-level-parallelization; development and experimentation flow; VV&A

1. INTRODUCTION

As a third way to understand the world after experiment and theory, analytic simulation is used more and more widely in various fields, such as national economy, national defense military, natural science, social sciences and so on. Analytic simulation plays a very important role in evaluating systems' effectiveness, understanding complex issues, discovering problems existing in the solution, figuring out the optimized solution, enlightening new idea and assisting users to make decisions.

2. Analytic simulation and its characteristics

Analytic simulation is an effective approach to study and analyze complex system, such as choosing a reasonable airline traffic time schedule [3], searching for an optimal solution for a possible crisis and so on. The common goal of this kind of activity is to obtain a large number of simulation results by exploring the undetermined factors of research object. Then, an appropriate statistical method is used to analyze the results to discover and understand the important relationship between the variables hidden in the complex phenomenon, and find out the rules they follow, thereby obtain satisfied solution of the problem.

2.1 The difference between analytic simulation and training simulation

Due to the different application purpose, the model, computing and platform requirements of different types of simulation are different. To sum up, the major difference between analytic simulation and training simulation are listed as follows (see Table 1 [4]).

2.2 The computational characteristics of analytic simulation

In addition to the above mentioned differences with training simulation, analytic simulation also has the following characteristics:

(1) Multi-sample

Analytic simulation is popular for analyzing what-if scenarios in complex processes, such as traffic and epidemic simulation, and these scenarios often belong to the parameters in a large sample space. Moreover, owing to the existence of probability model in the simulation application, each sample often needs to be executed a large number of times to reach the desired probability distribution. So once an analytic simulation has been created, it always needs repeatedly execution, even tens of thousands of times, to study complex problems or systems.

(2) Multi-entity

Analytic simulation usually contains a large number of entities, and these autonomous entities cooperate with each other through interactions to achieve a pre-defined objective.

(3) As fast as possible

The execution time of the analytic simulation usually needs much less than the time of actual activities. "As fast as possible" execution can greatly speed up the simulation procedure, thus we can test samples as much as possible in a relatively short time.

(4) Complex model calculation

Some computational models may only involve simple mathematical calculation, while others can model the complicated behaviors of complex system over time [1]. With the problem to be studied become more and more refined, the inner structure of simulation models become very complicated and the models become increasingly compute-intensive [5]. As a consequence, the computational complexity of the simulation models increase dramatically. Especially when there are multiple inputs need to be

Permission to make digital or hard copies of all or part of this work for personal or classroom use is granted without fee provided that copies are not made or distributed for profit or commercial advantage and that copies bear this notice and the full citation on the first page. Copyrights for components of this work owned by others than ACM must be honored. Abstracting with credit is permitted. To copy otherwise, or republish, to post on servers or to redistribute to lists, requires prior specific permission and/or a fee. Request permissions from Permissions@acm.org.

SIGSIM-PADS'16, May 15-18, 2016, Banff, AB, Canada
© 2016 ACM. ISBN 978-1-4503-3742-7/16/05...$15.00
DOI: http://dx.doi.org/10.1145/2901378.2901385

calculated at the same time, the corresponding model will be invoked separately in a serial manner.

(5) Synchronization for constraint of causality

Analytic simulation is usually a non-tightly coupled collaborative application in which there involves not only huge work of computation, communication and storage, but huge interactions between entities as well. In order to ensure the correctness of the causality of interaction events, a lot of synchronizations are needed between simulation entities.

With the increasing development of the research on simulation applications, the scale of simulation application and the complexity of the models continue to grow, which cause the "rising tide lifts all boats" for the demand of computing resources in analytic simulation. Especially, these above mentioned computational characteristics of analytic simulation propose a very high expectation for computing power. However, Due to the limits of integrated circuit techniques, bus latency, cooling and other physical factors, the performance of single processor has approached to its limit. The gradually failure of Moore's law means that "free lunch is over" [6] for the performance improvement of software based on hardware. The traditional method to obtain a higher computing power by raising CPU frequency is no longer feasible. For a long period of time, parallelization has become the only way to meet the computation demand of analytic simulation. Therefore, parallel processing has become our inevitable choice to improve the executive efficiency of analytic simulation.

2.3 "Sample, Entity, Model" three-level-Parallelization solution and its main challenges

In order to fully exploit the potential parallelism of analytic simulation and make the best utility of given hardware resources, we propose a "Sample, Entity, Model" three-level-Parallelization solution (SEMP) according to the computational characteristics of analytic simulation. The SEMP solution supports parallel executing of simulation at three levels: Multi-replication, Multi-entity and Model Calculation.

Multi-replication Parallelization: In order to explore the uncertainties of the research object and obtain satisfied solution of the problem, analytic simulation often needs to be executed repeatedly with different samples, and these executions are independent between each other. Therefore, in order to improve the efficiency and satisfy the computation demand that arise from the Multi-sample characteristic, different samples should be executed at different computing nodes in parallel manner. The main problems need to be solved include: remote dispatching and scheduling of samples; load balancing of computing nodes; collecting and saving of simulation results automatically.

Multi-entity Parallelization: Multi-replication Parallelization could improve the efficiency of analytic simulation at the Simulation Application layer. But the characteristics of "Multi-entity", "As fast as possible" require the implementation of parallelization among simulation entities to avoid too long running time of a single replication. The development of high performance computing and network technology enable Parallel Discrete Event Simulation (PDES) becomes an important way to solve the above problem. And the main challenges include: synchronization, communication, and high efficiency, transparency, visualization for application development.

Model Calculation Parallelization: With the increasing of model complexity, the computational complexity increases exponentially. And the complex model calculation with a single thread may become one of the main bottlenecks of system execution. Using multi-thread to calculate complex model can improve the efficiency of the system. Some special hardware, such as Multi-core CPU, GPU, FPGA, MIC, is very well suited for accelerating some core algorithms of analytic simulation. For the execution of specific application, these hardware resources are even several times faster than general-purpose processor. The main problems of Model Calculation Parallelization that need to be solved include: multithreading of model calculation; cooperation, communication and load balance between CPU and accelerators; access interference, lock mechanism, communication bottleneck, and interaction mode, etc.

SEMP solution support parallel execution of analytic simulation at three levels to fit the five computational characteristics. It could meet the growing computation demand of analytic simulation by fully exploiting the parallelism.

3. Application of PDES-based analytic simulation

In recent years, owning to the computational characteristics, PAS proposes an increasing demand for computing capacity. To improve system efficiency and meet the real-time requirement of simulation experiments, we propose a method of system development and experimentation, which employs High-Performance-Computer-based Parallel Discrete Event Simulation (HPC-based PDES) technology, according to the event-driven characteristic of PAS.

PAS usually belongs to system simulation, and its development and experimentation is a kind of complicated system engineering. Therefore, a standardized development and experimentation flow is very important for the success of PAS application.

Table 1. Analytic vs. Training

	Analytic Simulation	Training Simulation
Communication	Usually point-to-point, Reliable	Broadcast/multicast, Best Effort
Geographical distribution	Multiprocessor	LAN/WAN
Repeatablity	Yes	Often not essential
Time advance	Unpaced (Event Driven)	Paced with wall-clock time
Time Management & Synchronization requirements	Time stamp order, Synchronization protocol	Receive order, Relaxed
Simulation purpose	Simulation result	Operating/Exercise flow
Simulation model	May be non-interactive	Interactive (Man-in-loop)
Performance requirement	As fast as possible, Speedup	Real-time, Realism
Issues	Efficient execution, Ease of use	Scalable execution (Scalability)
Typical applications	Design, Analysis, Demonstration, Evaluation	Training, Exercise

3.1 Development flow of PDES-based analytic simulation

PAS always includes a large number of entities, and each entity may contain a number of computational models which are developed by different domain experts. Moreover PAS often needs to keep updated to ensure its credibility, and it is necessary to continuously upgrade computational models, improve simulation entities and their interaction relationship and even add new entities and new models. Therefore the development mode of general information system is not suitable for PAS application.

After many years of practice and exploration, we proposed a hierarchical development method (see Figure 1) for PAS system. Firstly, model developer (e.g. domain experts) could develop computational models in accordance with the ReUsable simulation Model development Specification (RUM specification) [7], and provide the method of invoking model and the way of processing its execution results. Application developers could use these models and related information to construct simulation entity (simulation object), and then build simulation applications according to the organization and interaction relationship among these entities. Finally users could execute simulation system to implement simulation experiment according to the multi-sample parameters file, collect and save related execution results.

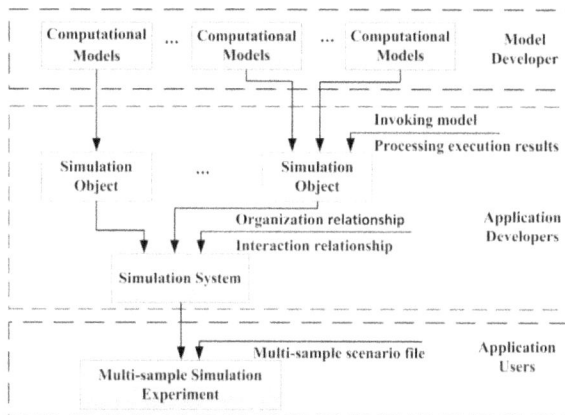

Figure 1. The hierarchical development method for PDES-based analytic simulation system

We proposed a development flow of PAS based on the characteristics of analytic simulation and the above hierarchical development method as follows.

(1) Clarifying evaluation requirement and defining development object

"What to be evaluated" is an important problem to building PAS system, and is also the essential goal of system construction.

(2) Establishing the evaluation index system

Index system gives a detailed and specific representation to evaluation object, which determines the output of system, thus it also determines system composition and development requirement.

(3) Determining functional and performance requirements of modeling object and computational model, and designing and verify conceptual model

Determining functional and performance requirements of modeling object and computational model needs to take the evaluation

requirement into account and adopt proper scale, and it is not encouraged to develop and employ over-detailed models. Conceptual model should correspond with functional requirements of model, and describes the content and behavior of the corresponding entities of the system being simulated. it is particularly important to invite experts to validate conceptual model in prior to the actual development of models.

(4) Clarifying modeling plan and assigning modeling tasks

In order to facilitate the upgrading and replacement of model, modeling of simulation object should adopt technology of parameterization and componentization modeling. To support the reusability of model, the development of model needs to follow RUM specification, which guarantees its openness and extendibility by supporting portability, redevelopment and reutilization of model.

(5) Determining the interface of model initialization, input and output and interaction relationship between models

(6) Developing experiment platform, validating and integrating model

During the model developing, it is necessary to carry on the design and development of integrated software for model integration of PAS system. At the same time some subsystems development is also requested to support the execution of whole project, such as: scenario generation subsystem, resources management subsystem, display subsystem, etc. Before model integration, model developer should test and validate model and submit testing report and validation report which is approved by domain experts.

(7) Integration test, model verification and running test

System will enter joint test phase when model integration and development of each subsystem are finished. Analysis and evaluation of the test results obtained from joint test can be used to validate and evaluate model.

3.2 Experimentation flow of PDES-based analytic simulation

The experimentation flow of typical PAS is shown in Figure 2. Firstly, user utilizes scenario generation subsystem to set simulation scenarios according to experimental purpose; and then experimental planning subsystem generates multi-sample scenario files through the planning of the specified parameters in simulation scenarios; multi-replication scheduling and management tool dispatches multi-sample scenario files and simulation program to different high performance computing nodes and executes them in parallel; execution data and results, which could be used to 2D/3D display and experimental analysis, can be written to database according to the predetermined rules.

4. Improvement of the credibility of PDES-based analytic simulation

PAS is mainly concerned with execution results, and all results are obtained through model calculation, so the credibility of model is very critical. In order to realize model Verification, Validation and Accreditation (VV&A), the VV&A Recommended Practices Guide issued by U S. Defense Modeling and Simulation Office has summarized 12 general applicable principles [2]. This article suggests that the VV&A of PAS should also follow the following principles in addition to the above principles.

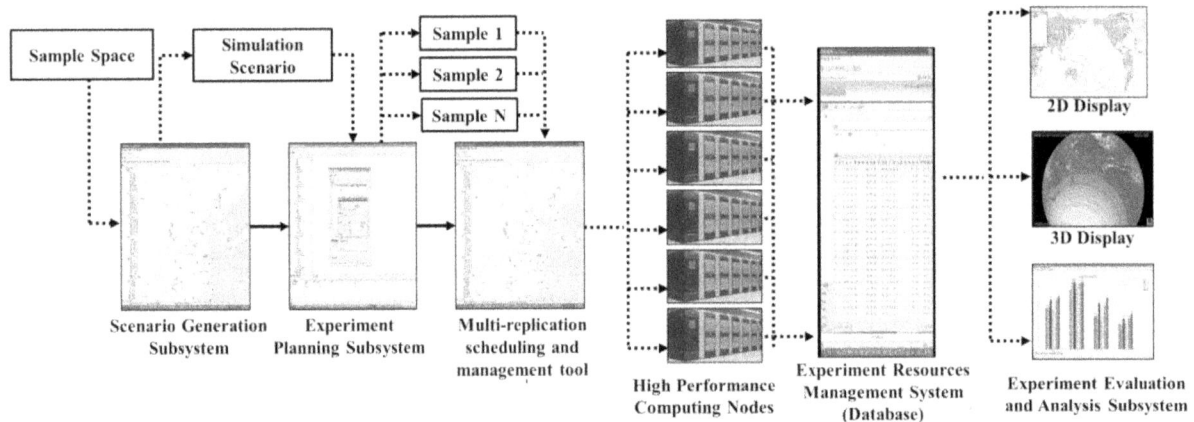

Figure 2. The experimentation flow of typical PDES-based analytic simulation system

Principles 1: Pay more attention to conceptual model

Conceptual model should describe the functional and performance index of real system being simulated. Modeling, model testing and model validation can be implemented correctly only if the real features and behaviors were correctly captured.

Principle 2: Long-term development

The improvement of the credibility of PAS requires long-term accumulation and maintenance. Building PAS system is not a once-for-all project. Because real system, specific issues and human knowledge are always in continuous development, PAS system often needs to be revised and upgraded. So overall, the thoughts of building general information system are not perfectly suitable for the construction of PAS.

Principle 3: User-driven improvement

On the one hand, it is necessary to validate model by user: to verify whether the function and performance realized in model are consistent with the real system (or the description of conceptual model). On the other hand, the system must be used frequently after it has been developed: system or model could be revised, improved and optimized according to constantly using, which is necessary for the development of simulation system.

Principle 4: Verification of conceptual model and review of model validation report

Although building PAS system is a continuous process, strengthen system evaluation is still needed before delivery. Firstly, as the foundation and basis of model VV&A, conceptual model verification is a crucial step in system evaluation. Due to the professional attribute of conceptual model, the verification must be responsible by the corresponding domain experts. Secondly, model validation should be performed by comparing model output to the description of conceptual model. The review of model validation report should be led by user, and model developer and technical experts should also participate in the review.

5. CONCLUSIONS

PDES-based analytic simulation has been becoming an important method to study complex problems, and it will be more and more widely used. Firstly this article presents the concept and characteristics of PAS, the differences between PAS and training simulation and correlative optimization techniques of PAS. And then we conclude a development and experimentation flow of PAS

to guide the development and experimentation. Of note, evaluation index system should be set firstly prior to the actual development of PAS, for it describes the goal of simulation and determines the output of system; Model development specification should be unified because the reusability and the replaceability of model is very important for model reuse and system upgrade; Model credibility is the critical problem for determining the success of PAS system.

6. ACKNOWLEDGMENTS

The research was supported by National Natural Science Foundation of China (no. 61170048) and Research Project of State Key Laboratory of High Performance Computing of National University of Defense Technology (no.201303-05).

7. REFERENCES

[1] Chen, D., Theodoropoulos, G.K., Turner, S.J., Cai, W., Minson, R., and Zhang, Y., 2008. Large scale agent-based simulation on the grid. *Future Generation Computer Systems 24*, 7 (7//), 658-671. DOI=http://http://dx.doi.org/10.1016/j.future.2008.01.004.

[2] Defense U S. Modeling and Simulation Office (DMSO). Verification, Validation and Accreditation (VV&A) Recommended Practices Guide [RP/OL]. http://vva.dmso.mil, Build 2 5, 2004.

[3] Fujimoto, R. M., 1999. Parallel and distributed simulation. In *Proceedings of the 31st conference on Winter simulation: Simulation---a bridge to the future-Volume 1* ACM, 122-131.

[4] Fujimoto, R.M., 1999. Parallel and Distributed Simulation Systems. John Wiley & Sons, Inc., New York, NY, USA, 1999.

[5] LI, B.H., 2004. Some focusing points in development of modern modeling and simulation technology. In *Proceedings of the Third Asian simulation* conference *on Systems Modeling and Simulation: theory and applications* Springer-Verlag, 12-22.

[6] Sutter H, 2005. The Free Launch Is Over: A Fundamental Turn Towards Concurrency in Software [J]. *Dr. Dobb's Journal*, 2005, 30(3): 16-22.

[7] Zhu, F., Yao, Y., Chen, H., and Yao, F., 2014. Reusable component model development approach for parallel and distributed simulation. *The Scientific World Journal 2014*. DOI= http://dx.doi.org/http://dx.doi.org/10.1155/2014/696904

SPOCK: Exact Parallel Kinetic Monte-Carlo on 1.5 Million Tasks

Tomas Oppelstrup
Lawrence Livermore Nat. Lab.
oppelstrup2@llnl.gov

David R. Jefferson
Lawrence Livermore Nat. Lab.
jefferson6@llnl.gov

Vasily V. Bulatov
Lawrence Livermore Nat. Lab.
bulatov1@llnl.gov

Luis A. Zepeda-Ruiz
Lawrence Livermore Nat. Lab.
zepedaruiz1@llnl.gov

ABSTRACT

We have created a scalable implementation of the kinetic Monte-Carlo method, SPOCK (Scalable Parallel Optimistic Crystal Kinetics). Unlike most reported parallel implementations relying on approximation to achieve parallelism, our parallelization is exact and accomplished using the Time Warp paradigm. We demonstrate that our implementation exhibits near perfect scaling for two different and important classes of systems. It runs efficiently on Vulcan, a 24 thousand node BlueGene/Q machine, using all ~400 thousand cores and ~1.6 million MPI tasks. Further, we have run production simulations using the full Vulcan machine and requiring nearly all available system memory. In this paper we demonstrate these results, and discuss some important implementation details. The kinetic Monte-Carlo method is ubiquitous within the natural sciences, and important classes of problems have so far been limited to sequential simulation. For many scientific simulations, an exact parallel implementation of the kinetic Monte-Carlo method has the potential of being game changing.

1. INTRODUCTION

The kinetic Monte-Carlo (KMC) method is a commonly used simulation tool within the natural sciences, and in physics in particular. For example it has been used to study as widely different topics as radiation damage in reactor physics, disease spread in epidemiology, population dynamics in biology, and option pricing in finance. The aim of this paper is to demonstrate scalable and approximation-free parallel KMC. We will do this by showing the scalable performance and capability of our parallel KMC code SPOCK (Scalable Parallel Optimistic Crystal Kinetics) for two different types of physics applications. The organization of this Paper is as follows. First we introduce the KMC method and two different physics applications, then we describe our implementation and parallelization. After that we show the

ACM acknowledges that this contribution was authored or co-authored by an employee, or contractor of the national government. As such, the Government retains a nonexclusive, royalty-free right to publish or reproduce this article, or to allow others to do so, for Government purposes only. Permission to make digital or hard copies for personal or classroom use is granted. Copies must bear this notice and the full citation on the first page. Copyrights for components of this work owned by others than ACM must be honored. To copy otherwise, distribute, republish, or post, requires prior specific permission and/or a fee. Request permissions from permissions@acm.org.

SIGSIM-PADS '16, May 15-18, 2016, Banff, AB, Canada

© 2016 ACM. ISBN 978-1-4503-3742-7/16/05. . . $15.00

DOI: http://dx.doi.org/10.1145/2901378.2901403

performance of our implementation, and conclude with a summary of our results and their significance.

2. THE KMC METHOD

In the kinetic Monte-Carlo (KMC) method, the state of a system is represented as a collection of interacting objects. Their evolution is then modeled by a sequence of events that affect the objects at given time moments. The simulation is typically stochastic, in that the events and their time of occurrence are sampled from known probability distributions.

Logically, the KMC method is inherently sequential in that each event may effect the distribution of future events, and no look-ahead information is in general available. The KMC method has been parallelized before (e.g. [1, 2]) but to our knowledge only by relying on approximations to obtain high scalability. These approximations can result in serious artifacts in the simulation results, and for certain applications an exact parallelization is crucial.

We proceed to describe the nature of KMC simulation in more detail. At any given moment in simulation time (e.g. the initial configuration), we know the event time and event kind distributions for each object. However, unless the event time distributions are particularly simple, we do not have a reasonable representation of the distribution which tells us which event happens first. We can only determine this by sampling: for each object, sample the time and nature of the next event to affect it, then pick the event with the earliest time of these sampled events.

A simplistic KMC simulation algorithm would be to perform this sampling, execute the earliest event, and repeat. For a collection of N objects, the cost is then $O(N)$ samples per executed event, which becomes prohibitively expensive for systems of many objects.

In many systems of physical nature, objects have a finite interaction range, and in what follows we confine ourselves to these kinds of systems. The key point to get an efficient algorithm in this case is to realize that when an event has been sampled for each object, and the earliest one is executed, most sampled events can be retained and reused in the next round of finding the earliest event. Only those events within the interaction range of the object whose event was executed need be discarded and resampled. For the types of distributions commonly used in KMC simulations, this can be proven rigorously, although we will omit the proof here.

Using this result, we can use a priority queue for all sampled events. Now, instead of discarding all sampled events, after each execution of an event, the simulation clock is updated to the time of this event. Then the other scheduled events within interaction range of the just executed event are retracted and removed from the priority queue. For each object that had an event discarded or executed, a new event is sampled and inserted into the priority queue. This makes it possible to process an event in $O(\log N)$ time, where the logarithm comes from the time it takes to update the priority queue, and the constant factor is proportional to the number of events retracted for each event execution.

We are left with an event driven algorithm. Perhaps unlike many event driven algorithms it has the following feature: events are frequently retracted from the event queue. In the applications we will consider below, each object interacts with on the order of a dozen other objects, which means that over 90% of all sampled events get retracted.

In terms of parallelization, our algorithm fits closely the conventional discrete event simulation model, in which logical processes (LP's) act (change state) upon received events, and communicate with each other by sending event messages to themselves or other LP's. The contract of the discrete event simulator is to execute the events in increasing order of simulation time. We can thus use current methods in parallel discrete event simulation to obtain a parallel implementation. Before describing our parallel KMC implementation, we introduce the two physics applications we will use:

Lattice gas dynamics. In a lattice gas, each particle lives on a lattice site, and can move to adjacent sites according to rules and probability distributions that depend on the occupancy of the neighboring sites. By deriving these distributions from Boltzmann factors of an appropriately chosen energy function, this kind of model can for example produce realistic simulations of the kinetics of atoms on a crystal surface, and the growth of a crystal thin films from atom deposition.

Crystal grain evolution. In crystalline materials, the size distribution and the evolution of domains of different crystal orientation, grains, affect greatly the strength and durability of the material. Understanding grain boundary evolution and topology is important in designing advanced materials.

In a simple model of grain evolution, each lattice site, or "spin" in this context, is assigned a value which represents a local crystal orientation. Spins which differ in orientation from one of their neighbors can then flip orientation (spin value) to one of the neighboring orientations. Again, the probability distribution for when to flip and to which value, is a function of the neighborhood. Over time, the average size of the grains grow, and fewer and fewer spins live on the boundaries between grains. Spins in the bulk are inactive, until the boundary moves close enough to affect their interaction neighborhood. Thus a peculiar feature of grain evolution simulations is that they become cheaper the further they progress, since fewer and less of the spins are active.

3. PARALLEL IMPLEMENTATION

The Time Warp paradigm [6] is a robust and scalable approach for parallel discrete event simulation. It is a so called optimistic method, and relies on speculative execution. In this context this means that each processor optimistically executes the events it is aware of. If an event is received

after it should already should have been processed, the receiver must roll back to a time before that processing time, execute the straggler event, and then resume normal operation. When it can be proven that an event will never be rolled back, it can be committed, and the memory associated with it recycled (fossil collected). This time horizon before which no event will be rolled back is called the global virtual time.

We have chosen to build our parallel KMC implementation SPOCK on the publicly available ROSS discrete event simulator [4, 5], which can use Time Warp for parallel execution. ROSS has been developed for over ten years and has shown to scale to the 2 million cores [3]. ROSS employs reverse computation, in that the user supplies not only code for forward execution of events, but also code for reversing the effect of the forward execution. This reverse code is used for rollback. The benefit of this approach is that the user can minimize the amount of extra storage space needed for rollback, which enables more memory to be used for state storage and allows bigger simulations.

Even though ROSS is a quite mature code, the current version lacks some functionality that is important for running large scale KMC simulations. We have made the following modifications to ROSS in order to better support our KMC simulations:

Event retraction. This feature is necessary for our KMC implementation. It can in principle be implemented entirely in user code without modifying the ROSS library. However, adding support for retractions inside ROSS allows more efficient memory management. In particular, assume that an event e causes the retraction of an already scheduled event e'. If e is committed, we know that e' will never have any effect, and thus it can be recycled to the memory pool, even though the global virtual time may not have reached the time at which e' should be executed. We implement for each event a retraction flag, which is unset on event creation. If an event is retracted, the flag is set. Whenever an event with the retraction flag set is executed, the event function returns without modifying any state variables. For each event e that is executed we maintain also a list of the events that were retracted during this execution. This retraction list is used during rollback to un-retract any retractions caused by e. The same list is also used when e is committed, to recycle the memory of all events in the list, which are now known not to cause any effect.

Long timestamps. In ROSS, the timestamp consists only of a floating point number. ROSS does not currently offer any tie breaking mechanism for events with the same timestamp, and our implementation needs to guarantee a deterministic order of event execution. For this reason, we have added support for long timestamps which besides a floating point number to represent simulation time also include a configurable number of lower order bits that can be used to ensure that there are no event ties.

In SPOCK, the interacting objects are particles that live on lattice sites. They have besides position and identity also a spin value represented by an integer. This is used in grain evolution simulations. The logical processes (LP's) form a grid covering the lattice, and each LP owns the lattice points and any occupying particles within its grid cell. It also gets information about neighboring lattice sites from the neighboring LP's, so that it can maintain a coherent ghost boundary. For each particle there is typically an event in the event queue of the corresponding LP. When an event is executed which affects the boundary, this is communicated to the neighboring LP's. As in the algorithm described above, when an event is executed, future events of neighboring lattice sites are retracted, and new events are scheduled. With this implementation we can support both lattice gas models and grain evolution models, as well as combinations of the two, such as growth of poly-crystals through deposition of atoms. In this case particles can diffuse (move) on the crystal surface, but may still have a defined orientation that affects its interaction with the neighboring particles.

4. PERFORMANCE RESULTS

We use the two physical models introduced in section 2 to demonstrate the performance and scalability of our implementation. We show scalability with the lattice gas model, and use the crystal grain evolution model to demonstrate the capability to run large scale science simulations using our code.

4.1 Scaling: Lattice gas model

In the lattice model, the particles live on a simple cubic lattice in 3D, where each particle interacts with the lattice sites up to two nearest neighbor distances in the max-norm (L_∞-norm). We allow at most one particle per lattice site, and assign a zero energy penalty to jump to an empty site within the interaction distance; this mimics interaction through hard core repulsion only. We initialize the lattice so that 20% of the lattice sites (chosen at random from a uniform distribution) are filled. On average, each particle interacts with 24.8 other particles. The left panel of Fig. 1 shows the scaling of this model on up to 24576 nodes on Vulcan. At the largest scale, the simulation ran on close to 400 thousand cores and used nearly 1.6 million MPI ranks (393216 cores and 1572864 ranks to be precise). We see that for large enough models, we obtain near perfect scaling to the full size of the machine. To illustrate the strong scaling behavior in more detail, the right panel shows the fraction of events rolled back as a function of the number of cores used. We see that this starts to increase sharply as we reach the scaling limit. Increased number of rollbacks is one of the signature features of Time Warp simulations nearing the end of scaling. In order to increase the efficiency and push the scaling limits further, dynamic load balance and automatic tuning of Time Warp parameters such as throttling and global virtual time calculations can be employed. These capabilities are not yet present in ROSS, but are expected to become available in future versions.

4.2 Large scale grain evolution model

Our second application consists of a 2D Potts Monte-Carlo grain evolution model. The spin lattice was a 2D square lattice, with 8 interacting neighbors for each spin (all nearest neighbors in the L_∞ norm). The size of the grid was 454646×454646, and thus contained just over 206 billion spins (lattice sites). This was close to the maximum that would fit in the memory on Vulcan, which houses just over 400 terabytes of RAM. This simulation was run first on 24k nodes (the full machine). After the initial grains had coarsened enough, and a large fraction of the spins were in the

bulk and thus inactive, the simulation was continued on 8k nodes. As far as the authors are aware, this is the largest kinetic Monte-Carlo Potts grain growth simulation ever performed by over two orders of magnitude. This current simulation performed at around $3 \cdot 10^9$ events per second on 24k nodes, and around $1 \cdot 10^9$ events per second on 8k nodes. Over the course of the simulation, a total of around 135 trillion events were executed, resulting in around 89 trillion spin flips. The rollback fraction in these simulations varied between 5% and 17%, depending on coarsening stage and number of cores used. We note that the early memory recycling we implemented cuts the memory use for this application nearly in half, and thus allows us to double the simulation size. Furthermore, events scheduled very far into the future are very likely to be retracted. Without the early recycling, they would sit in memory for a long time. Thus the early retraction scheme also allows us to run longer sustained simulations than would otherwise be permitted.

The simulation described here is part of an on-going science campaign to gain better understanding of grain boundary evolution and topology. Further simulation results and physical insights gained will be compiled in a future publication.

5. CONCLUSIONS

We have implemented a highly scalable massively parallel kinetic Monte-Carlo code, that can handle simulation of lattice gases and grain evolution. Our parallelization strategy employs the Time Warp mechanism and is exact in that it reproduces the corresponding sequential execution. This is in contrast to most reported Monte-Carlo parallelizations, which rely on approximations to obtain any significant parallelism and which may thus exhibit serious artifacts in many important applications.

We have shown that our implementation can run efficiently on up to 400 thousand processors and 1.6 million MPI tasks. Further, it can handle hundreds of billions of particles or spins, making it capable of running the largest exact kinetic Monte-Carlo simulations reported so far.

Besides the particular applications we have implemented and demonstrated, it is likely that many other (perhaps most) kinetic Monte-Carlo models can be successfully parallelized in an exact fashion. The consequence is that the scale limits for these types of simulations can be pushed from what fits in memory on a single node, to what fits in memory on the largest super-computer available, and will further continue to grow with the availability of larger machines.

6. ACKNOWLEDGMENTS

This work was performed under the auspices of the U.S. Department of Energy by Lawrence Livermore National Laboratory under Contract DE-AC52-07NA27344, via LDRD project 14-ERD-094. The IM document release number is LLNL-CONF-681474.

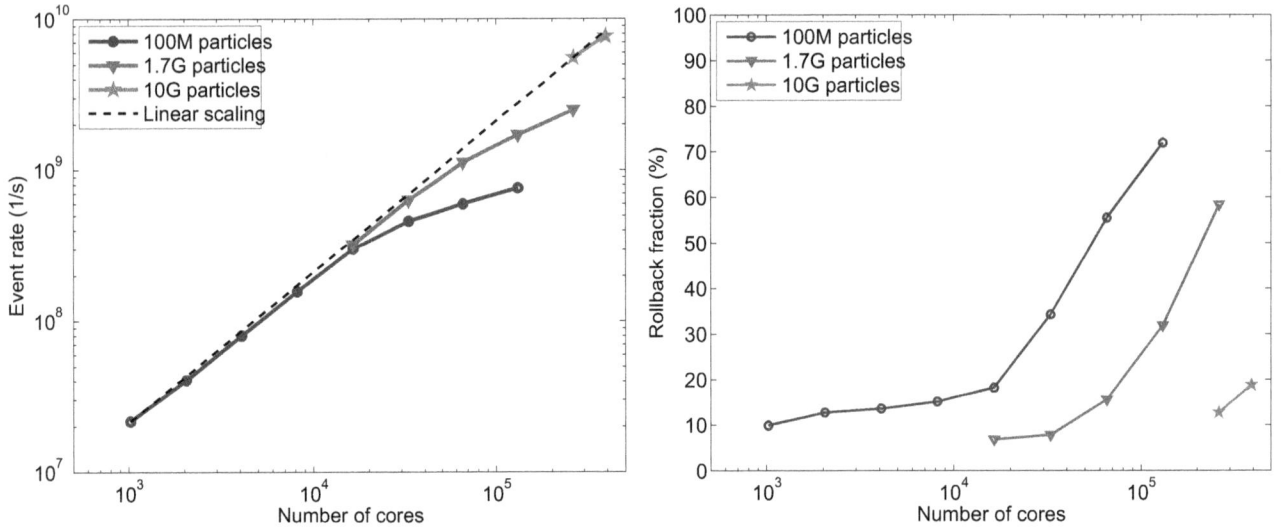

Figure 1: *Left:* Scaling of the SPOCK parallel kinetic Monte-Carlo code on Vulcan, a **24576 node BlueGene/Q** machine. Interaction is through hard core repulsion, and each particle may jump two an empty site up to to nearest neighbors distances away measured in the L_∞-norm. *Right:* Fraction of events rolled back out of the total number of events executed.

7. REFERENCES

[1] S. Plimpton, C. Battaile, M. Chandross, L. Holm, A. Thompson, V. Tikare, G. Wagner, E. Webb, X. Zhou, C. Garcia Cardona, and A. Slepoy. Crossing the Mesoscale No-Man's Land via Parallel Kinetic Monte Carlo. Sandia report SAND2009-6226, October 2009 URL: http://spparks.sandia.gov/

[2] E. Martinez, P. R. Monasterio, and J. Marian. Billion-atom synchronous parallel kinetic Monte Carlo simulations of critical 3D Ising systems. *J. Comp. Phys.*, 230:1359–1369, 2011

[3] P. D. Barnes, Jr., C. D. Carothers, D. R. Jefferson, and J. M. LaPre. Warp speed: Executing time warp on 1,966,080 cores. In *Proceedings of the 2013 ACM SIGSIM Conference on Principles of Advanced Discrete Simulation*, SIGSIM-PADS '13, pages 327–336, New York, NY, USA, 2013. ACM.

[4] C. D. Carothers, K. S. Perumalla, and R. M. Fujimoto. Efficient optimistic parallel simulations using reverse computation. *ACM Trans. Model. Comput. Simul.*, 9(3):224–253, July 1999.

[5] https://github.com/carothersc/ROSS

[6] D. R. Jefferson. Virtual time. *ACM Trans. Program. Lang. Syst.*, 7(3):404–425, July 1985.

DSSnet: A Smart Grid Modeling Platform Combining Electrical Power Distribution System Simulation and Software Defined Networking Emulation

Christopher Hannon
Illinois Institute of Technology
10 West 31st Street
Chicago, Illinois, 60616
channon@hawk.iit.edu

Jiaqi Yan
Illinois Institute of Technology
10 West 31st Street
Chicago, Illinois, 60616
jyan31@hawk.iit.edu

Dong Jin
Illinois Institute of Technology
10 West 31st Street
Chicago, Illinois, 60616
dong.jin@iit.edu

ABSTRACT

The successful operations of modern power grids are highly dependent on a reliable and efficient underlying communication network. Researchers and utilities have started to explore the opportunities and challenges of applying the emerging software-defined networking (SDN) technology to enhance efficiency and resilience of the Smart Grid. This trend calls for a simulation-based platform that provides sufficient flexibility and controllability for evaluating network application designs, and facilitating the transitions from in-house research ideas to real productions. In this paper, we present DSSnet, a hybrid testing platform that combines a power distribution system simulator with an SDN emulator to support high fidelity analysis of communication network applications and their impacts on the power systems. Our contributions lay in the design of a virtual time system with the tight controllability on the execution of the emulation system, i.e., pausing and resuming any specified container processes in the perception of their own virtual clocks, with little overhead scaling to 500 emulated hosts with an average of 70 ms overhead; and also lay in the efficient synchronization of the two sub-systems based on the virtual time. We evaluate the system performance of DSSnet, and also demonstrate the usability through a case study by evaluating a load shifting algorithm.

Keywords

Electrical Power System Simulation; Network Emulation; Software-Defined Networking; Smart Grid; Microgrid

1. INTRODUCTION

Today's utilities increasingly adopt modern communication network technologies to realize their Smart Grid initiatives. For example, the growing development of "smart microgrid", a core component of the future integrated smart gird, is highly dependent on the successful operation of the underlying communication networks. A microgrid focuses on the power distribution system that can operate independently or in conjunction with the traditional main power grid. The microgrid approach focuses on creating a plan for local energy delivery that meets the exact needs of the constituents being served, and introduces huge economic and environmental benefits to our society. For example, the IIT campus microgrid [3] has achieved a 6.58% reduction in annual CO2 emission (saving 3,457,818 kg), and a unit price of 7 cents per kilowatt-hour, while the average price in the U.S. is 10.43 cents per kilowatt-hour in 2015 [2].

To build a resilient and secure networking environment for microgrids and other smart grid applications, we and other researchers envision a software-defined networking (SDN) enabled network infrastructure for the critical power control systems [11,15,17,22,25]. Figure 1 depicts our design of the next-generation IIT campus microgrid. SDN offers the global network visibility, which would enable detailed virtualization and facilitates network and traffic management. With direct and centralized network control integrated with the existing grid control application, we now allow more intelligent utility applications to blossom, such as system-wide configuration verification and context-aware detection systems.

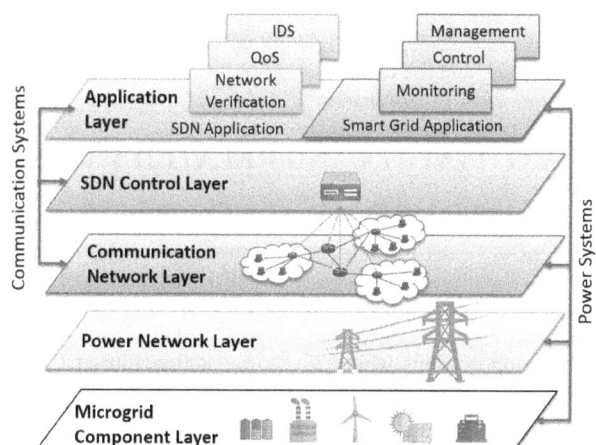

Figure 1: A Multi-Layered SDN-enabled Microgrid Design

However, incorporation of new technologies in such critical control systems is very challenging, because of strong real-time requirements, continuous system availability and many

Permission to make digital or hard copies of all or part of this work for personal or classroom use is granted without fee provided that copies are not made or distributed for profit or commercial advantage and that copies bear this notice and the full citation on the first page. Copyrights for components of this work owned by others than ACM must be honored. Abstracting with credit is permitted. To copy otherwise, or republish, to post on servers or to redistribute to lists, requires prior specific permission and/or a fee. Request permissions from permissions@acm.org.

SIGSIM-PADS '16, May 15–18, 2016, Banff, AB, Canada.
© 2016 ACM. ISBN 978-1-4503-3742-7/16/05. . . $15.00
DOI: http://dx.doi.org/10.1145/2901378.2901383

resource-constrained legacy devices. Therefore, a testing platform targeting such cyber-physical systems is strongly needed for the research community to evaluate the new network technologies and their impact on the power grid systems, before the real deployment. In this paper we present **D**istribution **S**ystem **S**olver **Net**work (DSSnet), a hybrid simulation-emulation testbed incorporating an electrical power distribution system simulator and an SDN-based communication network emulator, with the following features. First, DSSnet enables the modeling of a modern power distribution system and simulates the Intelligent Electrical Devices (IEDs) that make it up. Second, DSSnet enables high fidelity analysis by allowing real networking applications to run in the network emulator and interact with the power simulator. Third, DDSnet provides flexible and direct network programmability by supporting real SDN switch and controller software, an inherent advantage by adopting Mininet [19].

A key challenge is synchronizing the execution of the power simulator and the container-based emulator. This is because all the processes in the emulator execute real programs and use the system clock to advance experiments, while the simulator executes models to advance experiments with respect to its simulation virtual clock. To address this issue, we refine a prior virtual time system [26] and develop a new capability to enable pausing and unpausing the emulation container processes by modifying the Linux kernel. Our underlying design shows how the challenge of synchronizing time and events between the two systems is possible using virtual time, while ensuring high fidelity. We perform extensive evaluation of the system, including system overhead and experiment fidelity in terms of network flow throughput and latency. In addition, we demonstrate the usability of DSSnet with a case study on analyzing the effectiveness of a load shifting algorithm and evaluating the power system impact under a denial-of-service attack.

In the remainder of the paper, Section 2 presents the related work and shows the differences of DSSnet with those existing tools. Section 3 describes the system design and how it addresses the synchronization challenges across two systems. Section 4 presents the component-level implementation. Section 5 evaluates the system performance. Section 6 demonstrate a load shifting application that illustrates the features and benefits of DSSnet. Finally, Section 7 concludes the paper with future works.

2. MOTIVATION AND RELATED WORK

2.1 Combining Power with Communication

The power grid is composed of power generation, transmission, distribution and loads. Traditionally, power is generated in mass quantities from hydro, coal, nuclear, and gas sources. The power is then transmitted at high voltages to distribution systems where the power is distributed to residential and commercial consumers. As the power grid is moving towards a smarter grid, the efficient energy management is increasingly dependent on the underlying communication network supporting reliable information transfer among the various entities in the grid.

With distributed power generation—such as solar and wind energy—and more storage technology, there is a need for understanding the state of the power network in real time. A challenge with the integration of such generation, is the uncertainty and intermittency of the availability of power generation. In order to combat this challenge, there needs to be an infrastructure that allows for the monitoring and control of the system state. To do this effectively, requires a reliable and resilient communication network.

Researchers have developed systems to co-simulate the power and network components of the smart grid [9, 10, 12, 14, 16, 20, 23]. [21] surveys the existing technologies and motivations for co-simulation.

In [23], a system is proposed using OpenDSS to allow for sending real-time signals to hardware integrating with simulation. Real time simulators are used for hardware-in-the-loop simulations, allowing for simulation-emulation closer to the real system [12]. This gives high fidelity, but requires power equipment and often specific simulator hardware. Using a network emulator we make the system closer to that of real hardware deployment, but without the cost or complexity associated with real hardware.

In [20], the authors create a co-simulation between PSLF and ns-2. They use a global event driven mechanism for sending synchronization messages between the two simulators. In simulation, events are sorted by time stamps, typically in a priority queue. To enforce temporal order of events, we take inspiration from the global event queue, and adapt this strategy to integrate the network emulation with the distributed power simulation in DSSnet.

EPOCHS [16] uses commercial power simulators to co-simulate network and power systems through the use of agents. This platform uses agents to effectively co-simulate power and communication elements. The authors define agents as having the properties of autonomy and interaction. That they exhibit properties of mobility, intelligence, adaptivity and communication. In DSSnet, our models run real processes in the network emulation. This allows for us to make use of agents to as entities that exist in both systems.

FNCS [10] is a federated approach for co-simulation of power and electrical simulators by combining multiple power simulators, both distribution and transmission and use ns-3 as a communication simulator. In [9], the same authors improve the synchronization between systems that we take inspiration from in our implementation in Section 4. The difference is that DSSnet is focused on network emulation which has different synchronization challenges due to the inherent difference between the execution mechanisms in simulation and emulation.

There are two main features that set our design apart from the existing tools. The first is that we are using a network emulator rather than a simulator. The emulator allows for higher fidelity by executing real networking programs. The second is that our network emulator supports SDN-based networks.

2.2 Software Defined Networking in Utility

Software defined networking (SDN) is an emerging network technology that separates the data plane from the control plane. The benefit of this is the enhanced ability to have a global view over the network and be able to program network switches to provide functions that were previously too laborious and impossible to do. SDN allows for complex network functions to be created by adjusting network paths and flows in real time — reactively and proactively. This technology can help solve security issues and increase performance in many networks such as data centers, and even in energy infrastructure. However SDN is not widely used yet and does not solve all problems out of the box.

In [17], SDN is proposed to allow for scalable deployment of utility applications. The authors show how SDN can provide network functions to simplify publisher-subscriber roles in intelligent electrical devices (IED) including in phasor measurement unit networks.

In [11], the authors propose a system that combines an SDN emulator with an off-the-shelf high voltage solver. The difference between the system they propose and ours is that we are focused on combining open source tools and that our simulator is for low voltage distribution networks.

In [15], SDN is utilized to increase the performance of SCADA networks. In our testbed we have also modeled SCADA network elements, which can be used to explore how cyber attacks can impact the power grid using different communication models.

In [25] the authors analyze utility communication networks for situational awareness including during blackouts. Through the use of a hybrid power and communication system, situational awareness can be enhanced to increase the resilience of the grid.

Additionally, there has been work to bring existing power grid network protocols such as GOOSE and IEC 61850 into SDN networks [22]. Our testbed can be used to emulate IEC 61850 based communication with the advantage of analyzing the effects in the power simulator.

To summarize, our system is built on top of a network emulator rather than the existing works of network simulation for high fidelity analysis in the context of smart grid, and the emulator we use supports SDN-enabled software switches and protocols.

3. SYSTEM DESIGN

DSSnet integrates a distribution power system simulator, OpenDSS [6], with a network emulator, Mininet [19], using virtual time. The system has the following features:

- Power Flow Studies
- SDN-based Communication Network Modeling
- Smart Grid Control Applications
- Virtual-Time-Enabled Network Emulation

DSSnet is composed of five main components: the communication network emulator, the electrical power simulator, a network coordinator for interfacing with the network and the virtual time system, a power coordinator for interfacing and controlling the simulator, and a virtual time system which manages time and ensures synchronization in DSSnet. Figure 2 depicts the architecture of DSSnet.

3.1 System Design Architecture

3.1.1 Network Emulator

The network emulator in DSSnet contains software switches that emulate the function of real SDN switches. In DSSnet, the hosts represent IEDs in a power network, and each host has its own virtual network ports. Hosts in the emulation have their own namespaces [19] and can run real processes to model IEDs. Any element in the power network that has a communication requirement can be modeled in the emulation, including SCADA elements such as sensors and phasor

measurement units (PMU), and even relays and generators. Load management devices are presented in both systems, such as smart loads and smart meters.

Another benefit to having each model run its own process(es) is that not all network processes need to be present in the simulator. In the network, some hosts interact with the simulator indirectly through other models, such as data collection and storage systems, state estimation applications, voltage and frequency adjustment controllers.

There are drawbacks to using emulation. With each host running its own processes and having their own virtual network adapter, the system becomes more complex, making debugging a challenge. Most importantly, emulation cannot scale to sizes as large as thousands and hundreds of thousands oh hosts like simulation can due to virtualizing hosts which requires many resources. Our future work includes the development of distributed emulation to achieve better scalability, with reference to a prior work on the distributed OpenVZ-based network emulator [28].

3.1.2 Power Simulator

DSSnet models define the power network through elements such as lines, transformers, relays, meters (sensors), loads, capacitors, and generators. Each IEDs behavior in the power simulator can be modeled in the network emulator. However, not all power elements need to be represented in the network emulation, since some elements may exist only in the power network. The power simulator begins by initiating all of the power elements and creating an element matrix representing how the elements affect each other over time. The purpose of the power simulation is to simulate the behavior of utility distribution systems. Functions of the power simulator include power flow snapshot, harmonic study, fault studies, load modeling, and solving dynamic time step power flow [13].

In simulation, the amount of execution time required to solve for the state at a given simulation time step depends on the nature of the request. Typically, small time steps at the level of microseconds may be required for protection studies, while larger time steps at the level of milliseconds may be required for power flow studies while load and generation studies may be at large scales such as seconds, and minutes.

3.1.3 Network Coordinator

The network coordinator starts the network emulation, and creates data structures to maintain a centralized view of the network. The network topology and the IED models are loaded through the coordinator to configure network properties. The role of the network coordinator is also to interface with the communication network emulator for synchronization between the communication and power systems. The coordinator listens for synchronization event requests from the hosts through the event queues. When the coordinator receives a synchronization request, it interfaces with the power coordinator and with the virtual time system to control DSSnet's virtual clock.

3.1.4 Power Coordinator

The power coordinator interfaces with the power simulator. The first task of the module is to initiate the power simulator by setting up the circuit options and initially solving the circuit in a snapshot at time 0. The power coordinator provides an API to modify and the extract values in

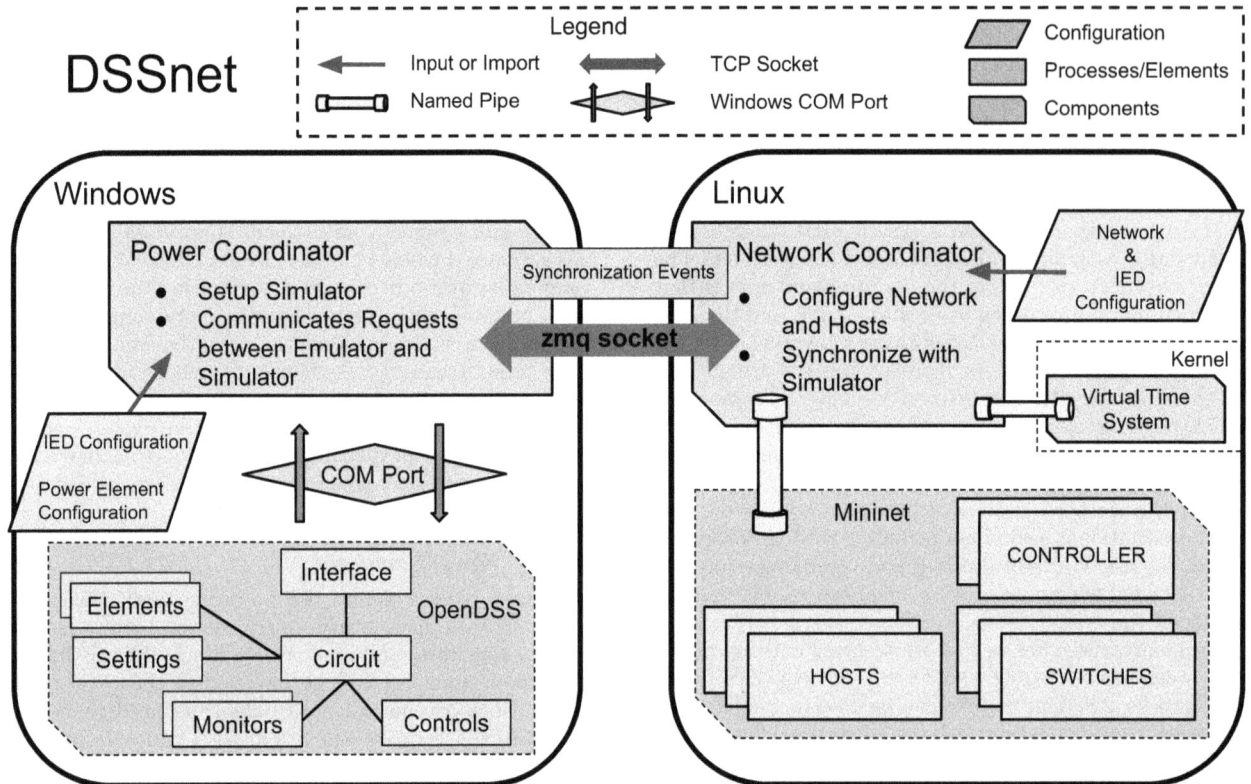

Figure 2: DSSnet system architecture diagram. Note that the power simulator runs on a Windows machine and the network emulator runs on a Linux machine.

the simulator. The simulator is able to accept synchronization events from the network coordinator through the API and return a response accordingly. A role of the module is to advance the simulation's clock to the time stamp of the current event request and to solve the power flow at that time. Additionally, some elements of the power grid may be modeled in the power coordinator as a function of time, such as loads and generation. These elements are not necessarily represented in the communication network, but can still operate on DSSnet's virtual clock.

3.1.5 Virtual Time System

Unlike simulation, the emulation clock elapses with the real wall clock. Therefore, pausing the emulation requires more than just stopping the execution of the emulated entities, but also pausing their clocks. Virtual time can be used to achieve this goal [18, 26]. We choose to extend the work of [27], in which Mininet is patched with virtual time support. However, their motivation is different from ours.

In general, virtual time has at least two categories of application. The first one is to slow down emulation so that it appears to emulated entities that they have sufficient *virtual* resources. Slowing down execution also alleviates the problems caused by resource multiplexing. The work in [27] and [26] fall into this category. Another usage of virtual time is for emulation-simulation synchronization. In DSSnet, we assign every container a private clock, instead of using the global time provided by the Linux OS. The containers now have the flexibility to slow down, speed up or stop its own clock when synchronizing with the simulator.

However, the emulator needs to manage the consistency across all containers. This is achieved by a centralized timekeeper in [18], and by a two-layer consistency mechanism in [26]. A more flexible virtual time system implemented by [26] avoids this problem as emulation takes charge of this responsibility. In practice, the emulator configuration guarantees that all containers are running with one shared virtual clock; Similarly, the container leverages the Linux process hierarchy to guarantee that all the applications inside the container are using the same virtual clock. The two-layer consistency approach is well-suited to this work for pausing and resuming because:

1. All hosts should be paused or resumed when we stop or restart the emulation.

2. All processes inside a container should be paused or resumed when we stop or restart the emulation.

The first task is done by the network coordinator. The second task is implemented based on the fact that processes inside a container belong to the same process group.

3.2 Synchronization

A key challenge in DSSnet is the synchronization between connecting the emulated communication network and the simulated power system. The root cause is that two different clock systems are used to advance experiments. Ordinary virtual-machine-based network emulators use the system clock, and a simulator often uses its own virtual clock. This difference would lead to causality errors as shown in the following example.

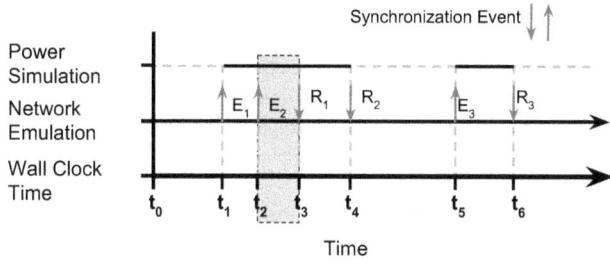

Figure 3: The execution of DSSnet is shown with respect to the wall clock. The network emulation runs concurrently with the power simulation, and is not paused which allows for synchronization errors to occur, when requests arrive before the responses are sent, e.g., R_1 occurs after E_2. The shaded box highlights the location of the error.

In Figure 3, there are three cross-system events (E_i), each with a response (R_i). E_1 occurs before E_2, however, E_2 may require information from R_1. Since the response occurs after the second event, the global causality is violated, and thus reduces experiment fidelity. An example of E_1 is a request to retrieve power flow values while E_2 sets the value of a discharging battery based on the value returned previously. Since the reply R_1 occurs after E_2 this can introduce an error. Furthermore, such errors can be accumulated if the simulation keeps out of synchronization with the emulation.

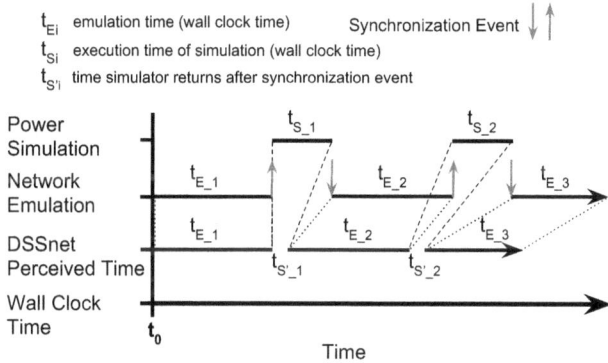

Figure 4: The execution of DSSnet is shown with respect to its own perceived time, i.e., the sum of the emulation execution time (can be dilated or not dilated) and the virtual time elapsed in simulation. The network emulation is paused to allow for the simulation to catch up to the emulation—this also ensures synchronization errors in the early example do not occur.

To address this issue, we develop a virtual time system in Mininet with the new capability to pause the emulator without advancing the emulation virtual clock, while the simulator is running. We adopt this idea, since the experiment advancement in DSSnet by design is driven by the emulation. Before the coordinators permit the simulator to advance over a time interval [a,b), we first ensure that all processes in the emulator have advanced their own clocks to at least time b, to ensure that all input traffic that arrives at the simulator with timestamps in [a,b) are obtained first.

Figure 4 shows the execution of the DSSnet. The total execution time (equation 1) is the total time the emulation is running plus the sum of the time spent executing the simulation. DSSnet's clock (equation 2) is equal to the total time of the emulation plus the sum of the returned simulation virtual times. In this illustrative scenario, we do not include factors like synchronization overhead, parallel execution based on simulation and (possibly) emulation lookahead, and time dilation effect in emulation virtual time, for simplicity.

$$Time_{wall\_clock} = \sum t_{E\_i} + \sum t_{S\_i} \quad (1)$$

$$Time_{DSSnet} = \sum t_{E\_i} + \sum t_{S'\_i} \quad (2)$$

$$ret = \frac{t_{S'\_i}}{t_{S\_i}} \quad (3)$$

where ret's value range is

- $(1,\infty)$ if the power simulation takes longer time to execute than the real time; Thus, emulation virtual time is essential for synchronizing the two systems
- $(0,1]$ if the power simulation takes less or equal time to execute than the real time, i.e., with real-time simulation capability
- 0 if the power simulation time is not considered by the emulation; for instance, recomputing voltage and current change along power lines at nearly light speed.

Synchronization events occur when either system influences the other. One optimization is to divide the global queue into two queues, because synchronization events can be created in two ways: Non-Blocking Events and Blocking Events. For each type of event, we design a queue sorted by time stamps to organize the requests. The non-blocking event queue contains premeditated synchronization events and events that do not require a response to the communication network. For example, the non-blocking event queue can be used to pass messages to the simulation to sample the power flows with meters at periodic intervals. Other examples are power events such as line faults that occur at a specific time.The IEDs are able to influence the power simulation by sending a synchronization event message using the blocking queue. Examples of these classes of synchronization events are that PMUs requesting values from the power simulation and controllable loads changing power values or turning on or off.

By using the non-blocking event queue, we can speed up the overall execution time. In other words, we do not need to pause the emulation for non-blocking events (E_1 and E_3 in Figure 5). However, if a blocking synchronization event (E_2 in Figure 5) occurs before the response R_1, then the emulation is paused at t_2, i.e., the time stamp of E_2. The emulation is resumed at t_4, when response R_2 is returned. In this work, we demonstrate the advantage of having a non-blocking queue with sample events. How to classify the events is not a focus for this paper. In addition, the container-based emulation system introduces opportunities for offering real application specific lookaheads to improve the parallelism performance, which we will explore as our future work.

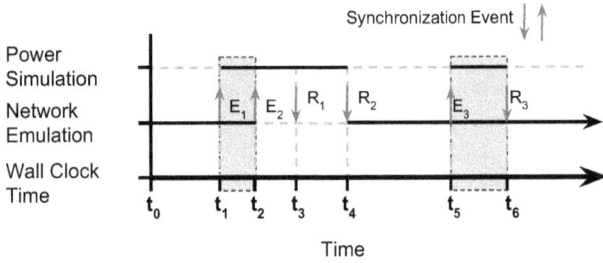

Figure 5: E_1, and E_3 are non-blocking synchronization events and E_2 is a blocking synchronization event from an IED. The network emulation is not paused unless an event in the blocking queue occurs, i.e., the one that requires a response to the communication network. The shaded box represents the portion of the experiment that is running in parallel.

4. IMPLEMENTATION

DSSnet combines Mininet, an SDN emulator, and OpenDSS, an electrical power distribution system solver simulator. This section presents implementation details with our algorithmic contributions.

4.1 Network Coordinator

The network coordinator is implemented as a python program running on the Linux machine. The network coordinator is responsible for (1) initializing the experiment with inputs like network topology and IED configuration, and (2) interfacing with the processes running on Mininet, the virtual time system, and the power coordinator, using named pipes. The network coordinator listens on a named pipe for synchronization calls, and also opens a connection to the power coordinator using ZeroMQ library [7] for python. It sends synchronization event requests and handles the reply from the power simulator.

4.2 Power Coordinator

The power coordinator is implemented as a python program running on the Windows machine. It directly controls OpenDSS through the provided COM port. Because the IED agents may exist in both the power and network systems, the power coordinator maintains a mapping between OpenDSS elements and Mininet hosts for the associated IEDs. The power coordinator listens on a TCP/IP port for a request from the network coordinator. After receiving the request, the message is parsed and handled according to user defined functions. The user has the ability to interface with the provided APIs, such as set_time and solve, but also can implement direct commands or query custom values from OpenDSS, such as PMU value requests, and setting load values. Part of the request specifies if a reply is required to the network coordinator and if so, the power coordinator sends a reply based on the user-defined handler.

4.3 Virtual Time System for Network Emulation

We extended a prior work on virtual-time-enabled Mininet [27], and implement the emulation pausing and resuming capability. To do that, we develop two routines *freeze* and *unfreeze* in the Linux kernel.

4.3.1 Freeze/Unfreeze Interface

The virtual file system provides an interface between the kernel and the user space. Since virtual time is a per-process property, it is more efficient to create a /proc file entry for the associated processes rather than adding system calls. The virtual time interface consists of two extra file entries under /proc/$pid.

- /proc/$pid/dilation A process $pid can enable and disable virtual time, as well as change a new time dilation factor (TDF). To support fractional dilation values, a TDF of x is stored in this entry as $1000x$, since floating point numbers are rarely supported in the Linux kernel.

- /proc/$pid/freeze We can freeze and unfreeze a process $pid according to the written boolean value. A value 1 freezes the entire process group and a value 0 resumes all the processes in this group.

We make a distinction between regular processes and virtual-time enabled processes. In other words, the /proc/$pid/freeze entry is only valid only if /proc/$pid/dilation already has a non-zero value. The emulator can enable a container with virtual time by writing 1000 to the dilation proc file entry. This will turn on the freeze/unfreeze capability without unnecessarily modifying the clock speed. In this work, we use a process calling system call unshare() with flag CLONE_NEWTIME to enable virtual time. This design is motivated and tailored to be compatible with Mininet's programming interface.

We also develop a user space utility program freeze_all_proc. This program can freeze and unfreeze multiple hosts in parallel. In particular, it spawns one pthread for every network host to write its freeze entry in the Proc system. Since the network coordinator always pauses or resumes all hosts, this optimization significantly reduces the running overhead in large-scale network settings.

4.3.2 Freeze/Unfreeze Implementation

To track virtual time using the OS software clock, we add several new fields into the process descriptor task_struct.

- dilation represents the time dilation factor of a time-dilated process. We also use dilation as a flag to indicate whether a process virtual-time-enabled or not.

- physical_start_ns represents the starting time that a process detaches from the system clock and begins to use the virtual time, in nanoseconds.

- physical_past_ns represents the amount of elapsed physical time since the last time inquiry, in nanoseconds.

- freeze_start_ns represents the starting time that a process or a process group is frozen. It is always zero for a non-frozen process.

- freeze_past_ns represents the cumulative time, in nanoseconds, that a running process or a process group remains in the frozen state.

Algorithm 1 shows the procedure to enable, disable and update virtual time. The for-loop (line 33) cascades the update TDF operation to all child processes. The algorithm

Algorithm 1 Set Time Dilation Factor

```
 1: function INIT_VIRTUAL_TIME(tsk, tdf)
 2:     if tdf > 0 then
 3:         __getnstimeofday(ts)
 4:         now ←timespec_to_ns(ts)
 5:         tsk.virtual_start_ns ← now
 6:         tsk.physical_start_ns ← now
 7:         tsk.dilation ← tdf
 8:     end if
 9: end function
10:
11: function CLEANUP_VIRTUAL_TIME(tsk)
12:     tsk.dilation ← 0
13:     tsk.physical_start_ns ← 0
14:     tsk.physical_past_ns ← 0
15:     tsk.freeze_start_ns ← 0
16:     tsk.freeze_past_ns ← 0
17: end function
18:
19: function SET_DILATION(tsk, new_tdf)
20:     old_tdf ← tsk.dilation
21:     vsn ← tsk.virtual_start_ns
22:     if new_tdf = old_tdf then
23:         return 0
24:     else if old_tdf = 0 then
25:         INIT_VIRTUAL_TIME(tsk, new_tdf)
26:     else if new_tdf = 0 then
27:         CLEANUP_VIRTUAL_TIME(tsk)
28:     else if new_tdf > 0 then
29:         OLD_DILATION_TIMEKEEPING(tsk, new_tdf)
30:     else
31:         return -EINVAL
32:     end if
33:     for all child of tsk do
34:         SET_DILATION(child)
35:     end for
36: end function
```

Algorithm 2 Freeze and Unfreeze Process

```
 1: function FREEZE(tsk)
 2:     kill_pgrp(task_pgrp(tsk), SIGSTOP, 1)
 3:     __getnstimeofday(&ts)   /* timespec ts */
 4:     now ← timespec_to_ns(ts)
 5:     tsk.freeze_start_ns ← now
 6: end function
 7:
 8: function POPULATE_FROZEN_TIME(tsk)
 9:     for all child of tsk do
10:         child.freeze_past_nsec ← tsk.freeze_past_nsec
11:         POPULATE_FROZEN_TIME(child)
12:     end for
13: end function
14:
15: function UNFREEZE(tsk)
16:     __getnstimeofday(&ts)   /* timespec ts */
17:     now ← timespec_to_ns(ts)
18:     tsk.freeze_past_ns+ = now − tsk.freeze_start_ns
19:     tsk.freeze_start_ns ← 0
20:     POPULATE_FROZEN_TIME(tsk)
21:     kill_pgrp(task_pgrp(tsk), SIGCONT, 1)
22: end function
```

to freeze/unfreeze processes is shown in Algorithm 2, and is implemented in the Linux kernel. After stopping a group of processes, we record the current time for calculating the process frozen duration once we unfreeze the process. Note that sending SIGCONT to all processes is behind the time keeping function. The reason is that if we resume the process group first, an unfrozen process may be scheduled to run, and possibly query time before we complete populating the freeze_past_ns within the entire container.

5. SYSTEM EVALUATION

5.1 Virtual Time System Overhead in Network Emulation

As described in Section 3, the synchronization between the power simulator and the network emulator requires us to freeze and unfreeze all emulated hosts. These operations bring overhead to synchronization. The overhead is not tolerable when the scale of the networking system grows to hundreds of emulated hosts on a single physical machine, which is quite common in practice [19]. Note that the overhead to freeze/unfreeze processes does not affect the emulation temporal fidelity, which is evaluated in the next section.

We measured the overhead of our pthread-based implementation by repetitively freezing and unfreezing emulated hosts. We varied the number of hosts as 10, 50, 100, 250, 500 in Mininet. For each setting, we repeated the freezing and unfreezing operations for 1000 times, and computed the overhead as the duration from the moment the coordinator issues a freezing/unfreezing operation to the moment that **all** hosts are actually frozen/unfrozen. We added the overhead of freezing operation and the overhead of the associated unfreezing operation, and plotted the CDF of the emulation overhead in Figure 6.

We observe that more than 90% of the operations take less than 100 milliseconds in the 500-host case. For all other cases, more than 80% of the operations consume less than 50 milliseconds. We also observe the average overhead time grows linearly as the number of hosts increases in Figure 7. The error bars indicate the standard deviations of the overhead time, which are caused by the uncertainty of delivering and handling the pending SIGSTOP and SIGCONT signals.

5.2 Accuracy Evaluation

End-to-end throughput and latency are two important network flow characteristics. In this section, we use these two metrics to evaluate the communication network fidelity. We created two emulated hosts connected via an Open vSwitch in Mininet. The links are set to 800 Mbps bandwidth and 10 μs latency. iperf [4] was used to measure the throughput, and ping [5] was used to measure the round-trip-time (RTT) between the two hosts.

5.2.1 End-to-end Flow Throughput

We used iperf to transfer data over a TCP connection for 30 seconds for throughput testing. In the first run, we advanced the experiments without freezing the hosts. In the second run, we froze the emulation for 1 second, and repeated the operation every 1 second for 64 times during the data transmission. We coupled the two experimental results and reported the average throughputs between the

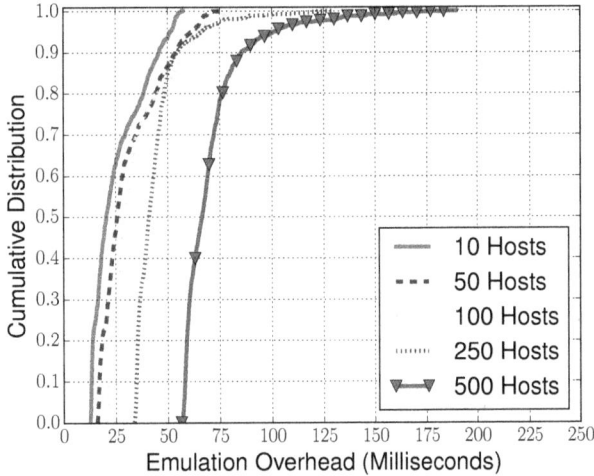

Figure 6: CDFs of Network Emulation Overhead Caused by Freezing/Unfreezing Operations

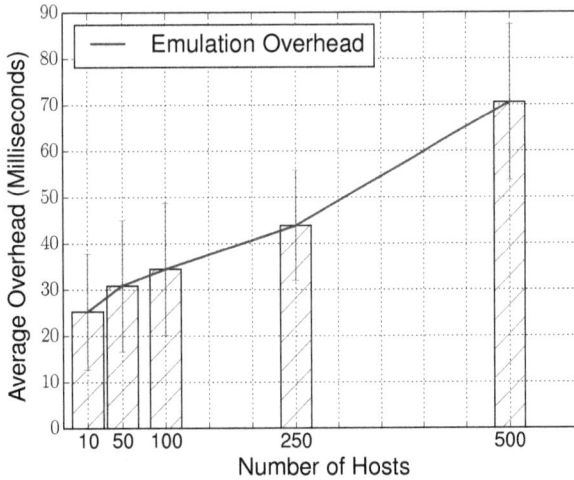

Figure 7: Average Network Emulation Overhead

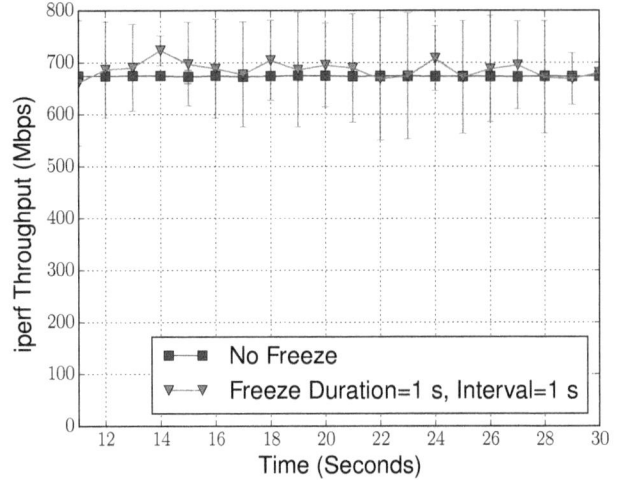

Figure 8: TCP Flow Throughput Comparison, 800 Mbps Bandwidth and 10 μs Link Latency

5.2.2 End-to-end Flow Latency

To evaluate the end-to-end flow latency, we issued 1000 `ping`s with and without freezing the emulator. We skipped the first ping in the results to exclude the effect of ARP and the switch rule installation from the SDN controller. Figure 9 plots the CDF of the round trip time (RTT) for both sets of `ping` experiment. We observed the two lines are well matched in the case of 10 μs link delay, and pausing the emulator does not affect the distribution of RTT. About 80% ping packets are received around 0.2 ms.

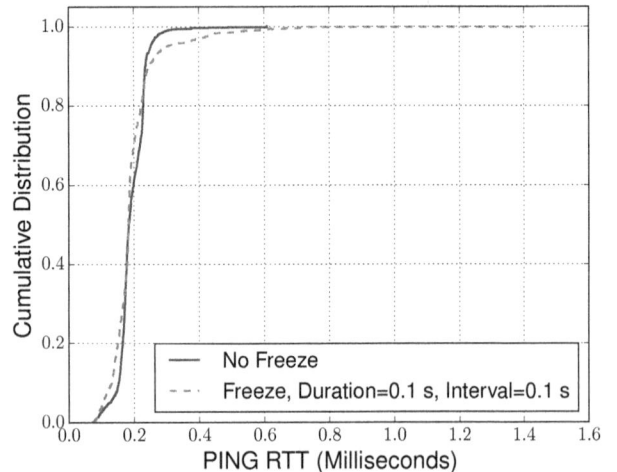

Figure 9: Ping Round-Trip-Time Comparison, 800 Mbps Bandwidth and 10 μs Link Latency

11th second and the 30th second in Figure 8. The error bars represent the 99% confidence interval of the throughputs.

We observed that the average throughputs of the "interrupted" emulation matches well with the baseline results. However, pausing emulation introduces around 11% – 18% deviation. Several sources lead to this deviation. First, while we explicitly generate `SIGSTOP` and `SIGCONT` signals to the containers, those signals are only in the pending state. The actual deliveries depend on the OS scheduler, and the deliveries usually occur when exiting from the interrupt handling. Second, the actual freezing duration depends on the accuracy of the sleep system call. Sleeping for one second has a derivation about 5.027 milliseconds on the testing machine, Dell XPS 8700 with Intel Core i7-4790 3.60 GHZ processor.

When we increased the link latency to 1 millisecond, the observed RTTs in the freezing emulation case were around 1 ms slower than the non-freezing case. One solution is to reprogram the `hrtimer`, but if the target kernel only supports low resolution timers, we need to search in the complicated time-wheel structure, otherwise we can search in a red-black tree. Another approach is to explore the emulation looka-head to increase the synchronization window size, and thus reduce the synchronization frequency between the two systems. We will leave those enhancements as our future work.

6. CASE STUDY: LOAD SHIFTING

DSSnet is designed to be used for smart grid applications that affect both the power grid and the communication network. We now present a case study of analyzing the load shifting problem using DSSnet.

6.1 Load Shifting Problem

We consider a class of loads called "shiftable loads". Shiftable loads are power consuming elements including Hybrid Power Electric Vehicles (HPEV)s, appliances such as dishwashers, pool pumps, Heating and Air Conditioning (HVAC), water heaters, refrigerators, etc. Some of them are preemptive, such as car, pool, HVAC, and others are non-preemptive, such as washing machine, dryer. The demand pattern can be represented with a peak during the day, near 4 pm and an absolute minimum near 4 am [1]. This load shifting problem is surveyed in [24], and a mix integer linear programming algorithm proposed in [8] where the authors considered more constraints on non-preemptive loads. For simplicity we only look at preemptive ones and ignore possible local minima and maxima costs over time. In this case study, we use a novel greedy polynomial time approximate algorithm proposed as follows.

6.1.1 Problem Formulation

Given the following definitions

N_L : number of loads

N_{TS} : number of time slots

L_i : i^{th} load

TS_j : j^{th} time slot

S_i : start time of ith load

F_i : finish time of ith load

c_i : rated power (cost) of ith load

h_i : number of time slots required

P_{ij} : power consumed by i^{th} load at time slot j

V_j : maximum power at j^{th} time slot

Q_i : scheduled or full time steps eligible for i^{th} load

f_j : forecasted price at j^{th} time slot

The problem is to minimize the total cost of power

$$Cost_{total} = \sum_{j=1}^{N_{TS}} \sum_{i=1}^{N_L} P_{ij} * f_j \qquad (4)$$

The following constraints must be satisfied for load requirements.

- Consumption Constraint declares that loads only consume power and do not produce power:

$$\forall (i,j) : P_{ij} \geq 0 \qquad (5)$$

Algorithm 3 Greedy Load Shifting Scheduler
1: Let **L** be the set of all loads
2: Let **TS** be the set of all time slots
3: **function** SCHEDULE(L_i)
4:     **for** $TS_j \in$ **TS** **do**   /* $\mathcal{O}(N_{TS})$ */
5:         **if** $TS_j.sched[L_i.id]$ is **TRUE then**
6:             **Continue**
7:         **else if** $L_i.power > TS_j.volume$ **then**
8:             **Continue**
9:         **else if** $TS_j.time \in [S_i, F_i)$ **then**
10:             $TS_j.sched[L_i.id] \leftarrow$ **TRUE**
11:             $TS_j.volume = TS_j.volume - L_i.power$
12:             **Break**
13:         **end if**
14:     **end for**
15:     RECALCULATE_SCHEDULABILITIES(**L**, **TS**)
16:     BUILD_HEAP(**L**)   /* $\mathcal{O}(N_L)$ */
17: **end function**

- Temporal Power Constraint declares that every load must consume its full power between its start and end time:

$$\begin{cases} \forall i : \sum_{S_i}^{F_i} P_{ij} = h_i * c_i \\[2mm] \forall i : \sum_{j=1}^{S_i} P_{ij} = 0 \\[2mm] \forall i : \sum_{j=F_i}^{TS_{N_{TS}}} P_{ij} = 0 \end{cases} \qquad (6)$$

- Volume Constraint declares that the maximum amount of power available at each time slot cannot be exceeded:

$$\forall j : V_j \geq \sum_{i=1}^{N_L} P_{ij} \qquad (7)$$

6.1.2 Scheduling Algorithm

In order to schedule the loads, we define the schedualability factor p in equation 8:

$$p_i = \frac{h_i}{F_i - S_i - Q_i} \qquad (8)$$

It is the ratio of the number of time periods are required for a load over the number of time slots are available for that load. We maintain all load items in a heap based on this value, and sort time slots by price. We select the load at the top of the heap (the hardest load to schedule), and check if we can add it to the first time slot. Algorithm 3 shows the steps within each iteration. After successful scheduling, we update all load elements schedulability p. The 'slots available' property of the load is decremented by 1, if the new volume of the time slot is smaller than the rated power of the load, and if Q_i has increased. Next we recreate the heap. If any load has a p value less than 1 then the algorithm fails. However, for sufficiently large number of time slots and volumes, this is unlikely. Algorithm 3 will be iterated maximally $N_{TS} * N_L$ times, because each element only has less than N_{TS} time slots. For-loop search takes maximum $O(N_{TS})$ time. Rebuilding the heap after each successful schedule is $O(N_L)$. The total running time of our algorithm is thus $O((N_{TS} + N_L) * N_{TS} N_L)$.

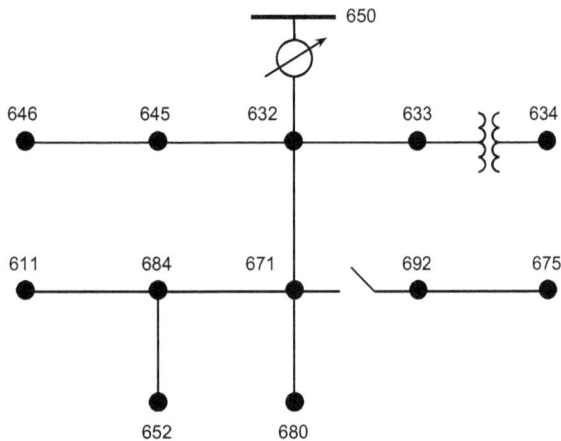

Figure 10: 13-Bus Distribution System

6.2 Experiment Setup

The data to be used for this algorithm consists of loads, prices, and time slots. The load data was modeled from the average daily charge for Electric Vehicles(EVs), and the start time and end time were modeled from the distribution of when people return to their homes in the evening. Other loads were considered that have a shorter duration and varying start time to model appliances. In total, 130 load categories were created, each representing 10 loads. The price used is from real ComEd historic hourly data [1]. The price points between the hours were calculated linearly.

We started our day at the forecasted maximum demand and ran for 6 hours. The time slots were each 5-minute long and spanned a total of 6 hours, generating 72 time slots. The load and time slot data generated represent a time period from 6 pm to 12 am, where people are returning home and plugging in their cars and using appliances. The start times and end times for each load falls within this window.

In this experiment, base loads were arranged according to the specifications of the IEEE 13 bus reference circuit. Shiftable loads replaced the loads connected to buses 611, 652, 680, and 675 in Figure 10. The base load is a linear decreasing value, power equals to $5313 - \frac{3}{20} * t$ with a small amount of noise ($\pm$20kW) added and where t means time in seconds since 6:00 pm. At bus 650, we measured the power entering the distribution system.

Figure 10 depicts the simulated power network. The communication network has one SDN switch at each bus, connected along the power lines. All the links in the communication network are 10 Mb/s links. The coordinator starts Mininet, the load models, and the power application scheduler on the hosts.

The load shifting algorithm runs as a real-time scheduler residing as a power application host in DSSnet. The scheduler is connected to the switch at the substation, which communicates in real time with the loads—hosts in DSSnet—through TCP/IP communication. The performance is evaluated by measuring the state variables within the power simulator. The impact on the power grid are determined by monitoring the power flow into the distribution network at bus 650.

In this setup, the power application scheduler acts as the server and the loads act as clients. The server will send load updates *on* or *off* and the loads will then send the updated value as a synchronization event. During a synchronization event, the power coordinator updates the load variable in the simulator, advances the simulators clock to the time of the emulation and solves the power flow problem. The simulator also samples a monitor at the infinite bus 650 and exports the data in a log file. Because there is no return value injected from the power simulator back to the emulator, these events are sent as non-blocking resulting in a faster overall run time. Both the loads and scheduler are modeled as real processes. To the best of our knowledge, DSSnet is the only smart grid testbed that allows for this kind of interaction between processes.

The importance of using DSSnet to evaluate the smart grid application is to see the effect on the power grid when the communication network experiences changes. What sets DSSnet apart from related works is that in DSSnet, real attack mechanisms can be used rather than just simulating the effects. In this case study, we consider a denial of service attack (DoS). We present a DoS attack at t=7:30, in which the power application server goes offline. The DoS attack can be accomplished by flooding the server with TCP requests and denying any other hosts the ability to connect. Because the load models require communication from the load scheduling server, if the communication is down, they revert back to the default schedule. In this experiment, all communication is blocked from the loads to the scheduler after 90 minutes to emulate a DoS attack.

6.3 Experimental Results

Figure 11 shows the three cases of the load shifting algorithm: the distribution network total power consumption during the experiment window, with and without the load scheduling algorithm, and the load shifting algorithm under the DoS attack.

In this scenario, the utility has a different objective than the consumers. From the utilities point of view, the objective is to flatten the load curve by reducing the peak load. This can be accomplished by providing an artificial market to the consumer. The consumer on the other hand, desires to minimize the cost. In this market, price is forecasted to plan the load shifting. The price listed is the consumer price paid for power. The utilities desired total power is shown in Figure 11.

In each case, the total amount of power in the time window 6:00 pm –12:00 am is the same. The cost of power is calculated using the amount of power used in the 5-minute time slot windows. The hourly quantities are summarized in Figure 11. With the load scheduling algorithm, the total consumer cost of power in the distribution network is $666.01, while without the algorithm the total cost is $713.66. When the load shifting algorithm experiences a DoS attack, the total cost is $688.57. Even when the communication network is under attack, the overall cost has been lowered, due to partial load shifting.

Only when the load scheduling algorithm is used, does the utility see its objective met. When the DoS attack occurs, the total power from 7:30 – 9:00 pm exceeds the utility's goal. This prompts motivation to research mitigation techniques using SDN.

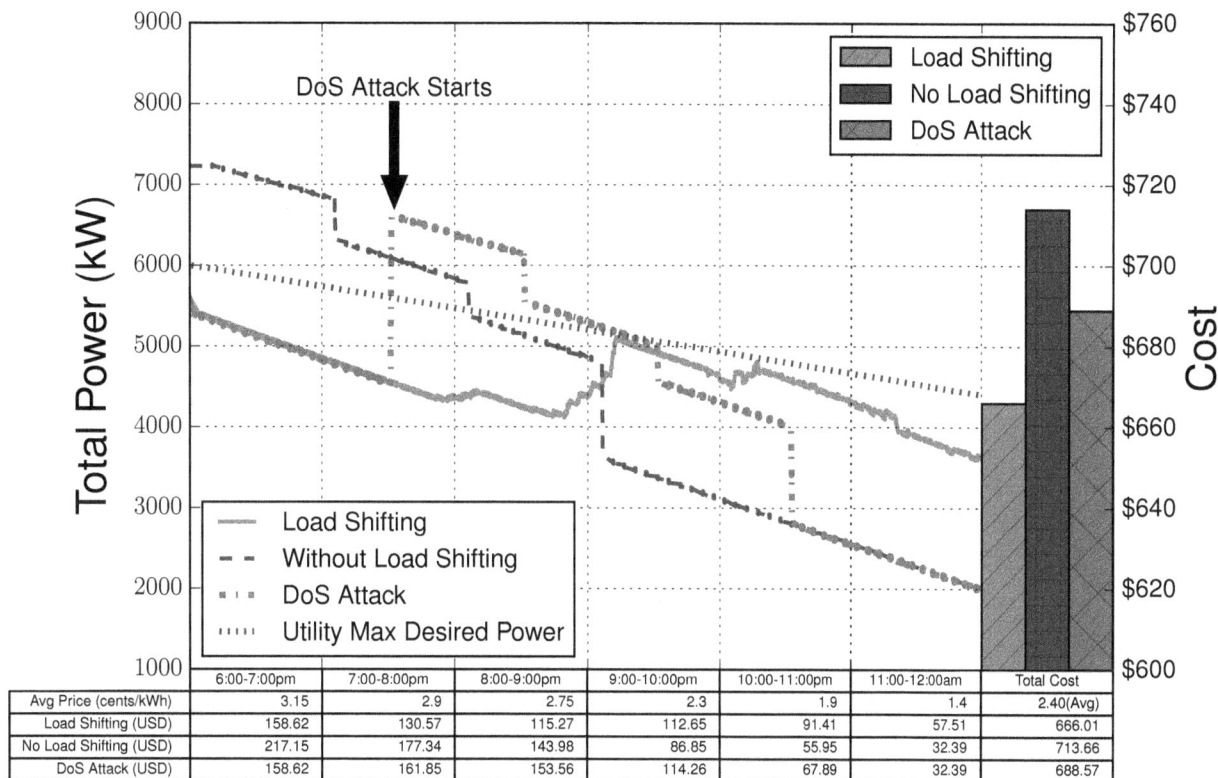

Figure 11: Normal Power Consumption, Power Consumption with Load Shifting Algorithm, Power Consumption with DoS attack, Desired Utility Price. With the load shifting algorithm the power consumption is below the utilities desired limit.

	6:00-7:00pm	7:00-8:00pm	8:00-9:00pm	9:00-10:00pm	10:00-11:00pm	11:00-12:00am	Total Cost
Avg Price (cents/kWh)	3.15	2.9	2.75	2.3	1.9	1.4	2.40(Avg)
Load Shifting (USD)	158.62	130.57	115.27	112.65	91.41	57.51	666.01
No Load Shifting (USD)	217.15	177.34	143.98	86.85	55.95	32.39	713.66
DoS Attack (USD)	158.62	161.85	153.56	114.26	67.89	32.39	688.57

7. CONCLUSION AND FUTURE WORK

We present DSSnet, a testing platform that combines an electrical power system simulator and an SDN-based network emulator. DDSnet can be used to model and simulate power flows, communication networks, and smart grid control application, and to evaluate the effect of network applications on the smart grid. Our future work includes exploring means to extract emulation lookahead to improve the performance of this hybrid system, as well as developing the distributed version of the testbed for large-scale experiments. We also plan to investigate several novel SDN applications for microgrid security and resilience, such as network-wide configuration verification, and context-aware intrusion detection.

8. ACKNOWLEDGMENTS

This paper is partly sponsored by the Maryland Procurement Office under Contract No. H98230-14-C-0141, and the Air Force Office of Scientific Research (AFOSR) under grant FA9550-15-1-0190. Any opinions, findings and conclusions or recommendations expressed in this material are those of the author(s) and do not necessarily reflect the views of the Maryland Procurement Office and AFOSR.

9. REFERENCES

[1] Comed. https://hourlypricing.comed.com/live-prices/?date=20151106. [Last accessed December 2015].

[2] Electric power monthly. https://www.eia.gov/electricity/monthly/epm_table_grapher.cfm?t=epmt_5_3. [Last accessed January 2016].

[3] IIT campus microgrid project. http://www.iitmicrogrid.net/microgrid.aspx. [Last accessed December 2015.

[4] iperf3. http://software.es.net/iperf. [Last accessed December 2014].

[5] iputils. http://www.skbuff.net/iputils/. [Last accessed November 2015].

[6] Opendss program, sourceforge.net. http://sourceforge.net/projects/electricdss. [Last accessed January 2016].

[7] Zeromq. http://zeromq.org/. [Last accessed January 2016].

[8] A. Agnetis, G. De Pascale, P. Detti, and A. Vicino. Load scheduling for household energy consumption optimization. IEEE Transactions on Smart Grid, 4(4):2364–2373, 2013.

[9] S. Ciraci, J. Daily, K. Agarwal, J. Fuller, L. Marinovici, and A. Fisher. Synchronization algorithms for co-simulation of power grid and communication networks. In Modelling, Analysis Simulation of Computer and Telecommunication Systems (MASCOTS), 2014 IEEE 22nd International Symposium on, pages 355–364, Sept 2014.

[10] S. Ciraci, J. Daily, J. Fuller, A. Fisher, L. Marinovici, and K. Agarwal. Fncs: A framework for power system and communication networks co-simulation. In Proceedings of the Symposium on Theory of Modeling & Simulation - DEVS Integrative, DEVS '14, pages

36:1–36:8, San Diego, CA, USA, 2014. Society for Computer Simulation International.

[11] X. Dong, H. Lin, R. Tan, R. K. Iyer, and Z. Kalbarczyk. Software-defined networking for smart grid resilience: Opportunities and challenges. In *Proceedings of the 1st ACM Workshop on Cyber-Physical System Security*, CPSS '15, pages 61–68, New York, NY, USA, 2015. ACM.

[12] C. Dufour and J. Belanger. On the use of real-time simulation technology in smart grid research and development. *Industry Applications, IEEE Transactions on*, 50(6):3963–3970, Nov 2014.

[13] R. C. Dugan. Reference guide, the open distribution system simulator, 2013.

[14] T. Godfrey, S. Mullen, R. Dugan, C. Rodine, D. Griffith, and N. Golmie. Modeling smart grid applications with co-simulation. In *Smart Grid Communications (SmartGridComm), 2010 First IEEE International Conference on*, pages 291–296, Oct 2010.

[15] A. Goodney, S. Kumar, A. Ravi, and Y. Cho. Efficient pmu networking with software defined networks. In *Smart Grid Communications (SmartGridComm), 2013 IEEE International Conference on*, pages 378–383, Oct 2013.

[16] K. Hopkinson, X. Wang, R. Giovanini, J. Thorp, K. Birman, and D. Coury. Epochs: a platform for agent-based electric power and communication simulation built from commercial off-the-shelf components. *Power Systems, IEEE Transactions on*, 21(2):548–558, May 2006.

[17] Y.-J. Kim, K. He, M. Thottan, and J. Deshpande. Virtualized and self-configurable utility communications enabled by software-defined networks. In *Smart Grid Communications (SmartGridComm), 2014 IEEE International Conference on*, pages 416–421, Nov 2014.

[18] J. Lamps, D. M. Nicol, and M. Caesar. Timekeeper: A lightweight virtual time system for linux. In *Proceedings of the 2Nd ACM SIGSIM Conference on Principles of Advanced Discrete Simulation*, SIGSIM PADS '14, pages 179–186, New York, NY, USA, 2014. ACM.

[19] B. Lantz, B. Heller, and N. McKeown. A Network in a Laptop: Rapid Prototyping for Software-defined Networks. In *Proceedings of the 9th ACM SIGCOMM Workshop on Hot Topics in Networks*, Hotnets-IX, pages 19:1–19:6, New York, NY, USA, 2010. ACM.

[20] H. Lin, S. Veda, S. Shukla, L. Mili, and J. Thorp. Geco: Global event-driven co-simulation framework for interconnected power system and communication network. *Smart Grid, IEEE Transactions on*, 3(3):1444–1456, Sept 2012.

[21] K. Mets, J. Ojea, and C. Develder. Combining power and communication network simulation for cost-effective smart grid analysis. *Communications Surveys Tutorials, IEEE*, 16(3):1771–1796, Third 2014.

[22] E. Molina, E. Jacob, J. Matias, N. Moreira, and A. Astarloa. Using software defined networking to manage and control iec 61850-based systems. *Comput. Electr. Eng.*, 43(C):142–154, Apr. 2015.

[23] D. Montenegro, M. Hernandez, and G. Ramos. Real time opendss framework for distribution systems simulation and analysis. In *Transmission and Distribution: Latin America Conference and Exposition (T D-LA), 2012 Sixth IEEE/PES*, pages 1–5, Sept 2012.

[24] H.-C. Sun and Y.-C. Huang. Optimization of Power Scheduling for Energy Management in Smart Homes. *Procedia Engineering*, 38:1822–1827, 2012.

[25] A. Sydney, D. S. Ochs, C. Scoglio, D. Gruenbacher, and R. Miller. Using geni for experimental evaluation of software defined networking in smart grids. *Computer Networks*, 63:5–16, 2014.

[26] J. Yan and D. Jin. A virtual time system for linux-container-based emulation of software-defined networks. In *Proceedings of the 3rd ACM SIGSIM Conference on Principles of Advanced Discrete Simulation*, SIGSIM PADS '15, pages 235–246, New York, NY, USA, 2015. ACM.

[27] J. Yan and D. Jin. Vt-mininet: Virtual-time-enabled mininet for scalable and accurate software-define network emulation. In *Proceedings of the 1st ACM SIGCOMM Symposium on Software Defined Networking Research*, SOSR '15, pages 27:1–27:7, New York, NY, USA, 2015. ACM.

[28] Y. Zheng, D. Jin, and D. M. Nicol. Impacts of application lookahead on distributed network emulation. In *Proc. of the 2013 Winter Simulation Conference (WSC)*, pages 2996–3007, 2013.

Efficient Monte Carlo Evaluation of SDN Resiliency

David M. Nicol
Department of Electrical and Computer
Engineering
University of Illinois at Urbana-Champaign
dmnicol@illinois.edu

Rakesh Kumar
Department of Electrical and Computer
Engineering
University of Illinois at Urbana-Champaign
kumar19@illinois.edu

Software defined networking (SDN) is an emerging technology for controlling flows through networks. Used in the context of industrial control systems, an objective is to design configurations that have built-in protection for hardware failures in the sense that the configuration has "baked-in" back-up routes. The objective is to leave the configuration static as long as possible, minimizing the need to have the controller push in new routing and filtering rules We have designed and implemented a tool that enables us to determine the complete connectivity map from an analysis of all switch configurations in the network. We can use this tool to explore the impact of a link failure, in particular to determine whether the failure induces loss of the ability to deliver a flow even after the built-in back-up routes are used. A measure of the original configuration's resilience to link failure is the mean number of link failures required to induce the first such loss of service. The computational cost of each link failure and subsequent analysis is large, so there is much to be gained by reducing the overall cost of obtaining a statistically valid estimate of resiliency. This paper shows that when analysis of a network state can identify all as-yet-unfailed links any one of whose failure would induce loss of a flow, then we can use the technique of importance sampling to estimate the mean number of links required to fail before some flow is lost, and analyze the potential for reducing the variance of the sample statistic. We provide both theoretical and empirical evidence for significant variance reduction.

Keywords

Software Defined Networking, Reliability, Fast Fail-over, Monte Carlo, Importance Sampling

1. INTRODUCTION

The computer/communication networks in industrial control systems (ICS) are unlike those in enterprise networks. An ICS often has real-time requirements, it always has safety requirements, and in the case of networks used in electrical

Permission to make digital or hard copies of all or part of this work for personal or classroom use is granted without fee provided that copies are not made or distributed for profit or commercial advantage and that copies bear this notice and the full citation on the first page. Copyrights for components of this work owned by others than ACM must be honored. Abstracting with credit is permitted. To copy otherwise, or republish, to post on servers or to redistribute to lists, requires prior specific permission and/or a fee. Request permissions from permissions@acm.org.

SIGSIM-PADS '16, May 15-18, 2016, Banff, AB, Canada

© 2016 ACM. ISBN 978-1-4503-3742-7/16/05. . . $15.00

DOI: http://dx.doi.org/10.1145/2901378.2901401

utilities subject to NERC-CIP regulations, has requirements related to provable limited access to so-called "critical assets". Software defined networking [11] (SDN) is an emerging technology with great promise for aiding the design of ICS networks. A controller with a global view of the network is responsible for creating and installing routing and filtering rules into the network's collection of dumb switches. A standard called OpenFlow exists for expression of the rules and the interaction between controller and switches. Motivated by problems in networks for data centers, SDN's common application is for switches to dynamically communicate routing needs to the controller (e.g., first appearance of a flow) and in response the controller creates and installs rules in multiple switches to address that need, but also achieve system-wide properties such as load-balance.

SDN can be used differently in ICS, there is is value keeping switch configurations static. ICS network engineers like to know *exactly* what their networks are doing, and for the purposes of NERC-CIP audits, explaining a static set of switch rules to an auditor is possible, while trying to analyze an SDN controller program which dynamically *generates* switch rules seems a bridge too far for all involved. Instead, one can engineer all of the configuration rules for all of the network switches in such a way that the flows through the network have pre-defined properties (which we will sometimes call "policies"). The rules are installed when the network comes up, and to the greatest degree possible the switch configurations are left unaltered for as long as possible.

There is a challenge though, in that if the physical infrastructure fails (e.g., a link, or a switch), then some intervention by the controller might be needed to restore full functionality. Fortunately there is a mechanism in the OpenFlow specification that supports so-called "fast fail-over" in which a switch at the point of egress consults a prioritized table of links and pushes the frame through the live link with highest priority. Thus when a link drops, the switch can re-route according to this table without consulting the controller. Of course, careful construction of flow rules is needed to ensure that that local action still leads to ultimate delivery of the frame to its intended destination.

It is relatively straightforward to craft SDN rules which ensure that the failure of any *single* link can be tolerated, in the sense that every flow that formerly crossed that link is still delivered after following the fast fail-over link which covers for the failure. Beyond that, there are unresolved algorithmic issues in crafting configurations that ensure toleration of any 2 (or more) link failures. Still, we don't really anticipate that the network tolerates only one link failure; while subsequent failure of the 1st link's fail-over back-up might indeed cause one or more flows to no longer be routed, there are many links that are logically and physically separated from the first link whose failure could be tolerated just as if they'd been the first failed link. We are led then to a question whose answer this paper supports: how resilient is the network configuration to link failures, where a measure of resilience is the number of link failures may occur before some flow that is supported by the original configuration is no longer supported, what we call a *loss of service*. A moment's reflection though shows that this question needs refinement. One measure might be the absolute minimum number of link failures that can be tolerated, another might be the average number of randomly chosen failures that can be tolerated. We opine that the second version gives a better overall sense of network resilience to normal "wear and tear" failures, while the first might be better to access resilience to attacks by a directed adversary. Note that inducing loss of service through a sequence of link failures in no way implies that the flow cannot be delivered by some other configuration. The point is that when loss of service occurs, new configurations are required of the controller, and in the ICS context we wish to interact with the controller as little as possible.

This paper considers a potential optimization that arises when using Monte Carlo sampling to evaluate a given configuration by estimating the mean number of link failures to loss of service. The standard technique would be to randomly sample sequences of link failures until loss of service occurs, and note the number of link failures involved. Statistical analysis of the sample mean and sample variance yields a confidence interval around the estimate. The technique we develop here does something different called *importance sampling*, which has the effect of tending to make the confidence interval around the mean smaller, for the same number of trials. From a statistical point of view this means that importance sampling is more efficient; for a stated statistical accuracy importance sampling tends to require fewer trials to achieve that accuracy than does ordinary sampling. The challenge when designing importance sampling strategies is to do so in a way that the sample variance is *provably* smaller than ordinary sampling. This is often a challenge, and our presentation of a importance sampling strategy for this problem with analysis of the variance reduction it provides is the key contribution of this paper. We also provide preliminary experimental evidence that importance sampling can reduce the number of samples needed to achieve a given statistical accuracy by an order of magnitude.

2. BACKGROUND

A network orchestrates packet delivery among all network devices by using packet headers. Its configuration drives the two functional components of the networking software: control and data planes. The control plane decides what packet forwarding and header transformations need to occur at network devices, while the data plane performs the actual actions on packets. In the traditional networking architecture, control and data planes coexist on individual network devices, thus requiring manual instrumentation of configuration at individual, heterogeneous devices to implement policy in a variety of configuration semantics. However, the SDN architecture simplifies access to the network config-

uration by logically centralizing the control-plane state in a device called the controller. This centralized state then drives the network devices that perform homogeneous forwarding plane functions [2]. The forwarding plane functions and the interface between controller and networking device are standardized. The OpenFlow specification [3] is one such standard. It provides an abstract model of a network switch. The OpenFlow switch model specifies the operations it performs and its interface with the controller. The packet-forwarding and modification behavior of a switch is driven entirely by the rules installed on it by the controller as part of the network configuration.

The OpenFlow rules support a fast fail-over feature. This is implemented by allowing the rules to choose an output port for a specified set of packets as a function of liveness of links. Hence, it is possible that the configuration may effectively utilize the topological redundancy by specifying rules that reroute traffic if links fail, without the intervention of the controller. However, in order to guarantee that the network configuration provides whatever degree of resilience to link failure is required, it needs to be validated. Such validation requires careful modeling of the network and the results of link failure events. Hence, for a network comprising of OpenFlow switches, a model that predicts the entire network's behavior needs to be constructed. This model needs to take into account the network state and construct data structures that allow for such validation tractably as a function of network's topology and configuration.

In order to model behavior of a network on per-packet basis, Jin et. al. [6] and Lantz et. al. [12] proposed approaches based on discrete-event simulation and container based emulation respectively. These approaches can predict the behavior of a network, given a configuration and offered traffic, but do not consider issues of the resiliency offered by a configuration.

Peyman et. al [9][8] and Khurshid et. al.[10] developed abstractions for representing sets of packets that are processed similarly by individual switches and thus making solution solvable in near real-time for small campus-sized networks. However, neither of these approaches support modeling of rules that support the fast fail-over feature. Thus, we have focused on exhaustive policy validation in an SDN using aggregated sets of packets when fast fail-over rules are used.

The tool we have developed, **Flow Validator** , is able to validate many properties of an SDN configuration. One of these is the ability of the configuration to tolerate failures of network links. This paper addresses how Monte Carlo simulation used to guide evolution of **Flow Validator** evaluations can estimate resiliency to link failure, measured as the mean number of links that must be failed before *some* flow that was supported by the pre-failure configuration is no longer supported. Modification of **Flow Validator** data structures is expensive with each link failure, and so it is worth-while to explore ways of reducing the number of link failure computations needed to derive a useable estimate.

Flow Validator data structures expose much information about all flows through the network. We can analyze those data structures to identify which links, if failed next, will induce loss of service. While the update of data structures to *implement* a link failure is expensive, identification of this set of vulnerable links is comparatively much much faster. The main result of this paper is that this information can be used in an importance sampling scheme for resiliency estimation and provably reduce the variance of the sample statistic.

3. SOFTWARE DEFINED NETWORKS

3.1 The Network Model

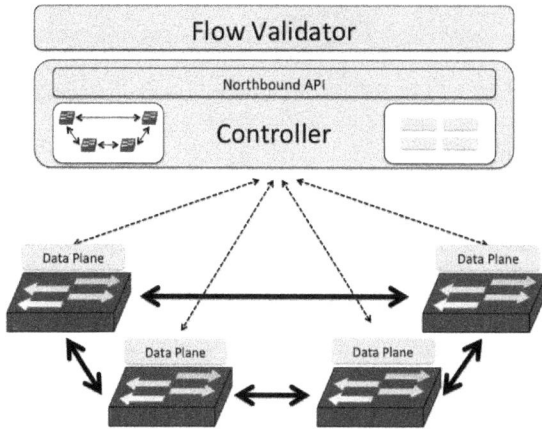

Figure 1: An SDN with a four switch topology connected in a ring.

In an SDN, as Figure 1 depicts, each switch is connected to the controller through a management port. The controller uses this port to gather information about link status and to place forwarding rules on each switch. The information from individual switches is used to construct the state of the entire SDN. The controller makes this state available through a "northbound" API to be used by the applications.

This logically-centralized state comprises a latest snapshot of SDN's topology as well as the data-plane configuration of each switch. Thus, our offline validation application (called Flow Validator) uses this API to access the snapshot of SDN state. The state is used to construct a model to predict the behavior of the SDN on all traffic. If the state of the SDN changes due to a modification of forwarding rules at a switch or a link failure/restoration event, a fresh snapshot of the the state is obtained and any changes are accommodated in the predictive model, incrementally.

3.2 The Switch

In order to predict the behavior of the entire SDN, we need to build a model for individual switches. We use the OpenFlow 1.3 [3] specification to construct one such model for switches, which provides a fast-failover feature.

An SDN switch contains a table processing pipeline and a collection of physical ports. Packets arrive at one of the ports, and are processed by the pipeline comprised of one or more flow tables. Each flow table contains multiple rules. Each flow rule is an atomic unit of decision-making regarding packets going through the pipeline. The decisions take the form of *actions*. During the processing of a single packet, these actions can modify the packet, forward it out of the switch via one or more of switch ports, or drop it. Below we provide more details regarding the OpenFlow specification that are relevant to our model of the switch.

3.2.1 Flow Rule

The set of actions that a switch applies to a packet is governed entirely by flow rules. Each flow rule has two parts:

- Match: A set of packet header field values that the given rule would apply to. Some packet header fields are characterized by single values (e.g. VLAN ID: 1, or TCP Destination Port: 80), while others can take a range of values (e.g. Destination IP Addresses: 10.0.0.0/8). If a packet header field is not specified then it is considered to be a wildcard for the purposes of match operation.

- Instructions: A description of the control operations performed by the flow rule to a matched packet. A switch can apply a variety of actions on the packet. These actions include:

  - Header Modification Actions: These include actions that modify existing protocol headers by adding or removing part of the headers.
  - Output Actions: These include actions that specify the ports on which the packet will be sent out. This can either be a set of ports, or a first live port in a sequence of ports.

3.2.2 Flow Table Pipeline

A switch processes the arriving packets through a pipeline of one or more flow tables. Each flow table is a collection of flow rules sorted by the priority in which they are matched against an arriving packet. A packet matches at most one flow rule in a flow table that has the highest priority.

When a packet arrives at the switch, it is associated with an empty action set and matched against rules in the first table. The action set can be manipulated by instructions in the matching flow rules in each table. Furthermore, the instructions associated with the matching flow rules can select the next table that will process the packet. Before the packet is sent to the next table, the matching flow rule can apply an action to it. If at any table, a matching flow rule for the packet is not found, then the switch stops processing the packet and actions in the associated action set are applied to it. If the action set is empty, then the packet is simply dropped.

The last table applied to a transiting packet chooses the egress port through which the packet is pushed. The table selected for the packet has a list of ports in priority order. The first port in the list whose associated link is live is chosen. Hence, it is possible that the configuration may effectively utilize the topological redundancy by specifying rules that reroute traffic if links fail, without the intervention of the controller. However, in order to guarantee that the network configuration conforms to a given policy in the face of link failures, it needs to be validated. Such validation requires careful modeling of the network and the results of link failure events. Hence, for a network comprising of OpenFlow switches, a model that predicts the entire network's behavior needs to be constructed. This model needs to take into account the network state and construct data structures that allow for such validation tractably as a function of network's topology and configuration.

3.3 Header Space Abstraction

As evident from the operations of a switch previously, in order model to its behavior and reason about properties of an SDN, it is crucial to model sets of packets. To that end, Peyman et. al. proposed a geometric abstraction for representing packet traffic called Header Space [9]. A typical packet contains more than one protocol header, each serving individual control-plane functions. However, the header space abstraction removes individual protocol semantics and represents packets as a point in the $\{0, 1\}^L$ space, where L is the total bit length of the packet headers.

Similarly, sets of traffic are represented as hyper-rectangles in this space. These sets are expressed using wildcards for individual bit positions in an L bit header space expression. The utility of the header space abstraction is in its ability to compactly define sets of traffic by using wildcards for individual bit positions in the header. Such definition of traffic then allows set-theoretic operations such as intersection, union, complementation on it.

3.4 Switch Transfer Function

Peyman et. al. proposed representing a switch as a Transfer Function [9]. The transfer function is an abstract model for operations performed by a switch on the input traffic presented at on one of its ports. The switch *tranfers* a subset of traffic to one or more of its output ports. Beyond describing the subset of traffic that arrives at the output port for a corresponding input port traffic, the transfer function also captures any modifications that the subset of input traffic undergoes by the switch as specified by the OpenFlow specification [3].

3.5 Flow Validator Data Structures

The data structures we use and the analysis we employ in **Flow Validator** for validating flows are well beyond the scope of the present paper. However our purposes here we point out that these data structures describe *every possible flow* through the SDN, and so expose the information we need to characterize each link as one whose next failure will induce loss of service, or not. The basic idea is as follows. Some switches connect to hosts, or to networks that are not part of the SDN fabric, others connect only to other switches. Thus there is a set $\mathcal{H}$ of switch ports connected to links that provide SDN ingress and egress. For every given port $p \in \mathcal{H}$ we present a header space that has wildcards in every dimension. **Flow Validator** pushes the abstraction through the rules and tables in the switch. This will fragment the initial abstraction: only some subspace will find rules that admit that subspace, different header modifications and output actions will be applied, different subspaces may be directed to other egress ports. Following application of the header space abstraction to one switch, we have generated a number of header space abstractions on egress links; each such abstraction is presented to the switch at the other end of the link and the process continues, until we discover the complete description of all flows that enter the SDN at the initial ingress port and are delivered to any egress port. Intuitively, we have computed all flows the SDN will route; we have identified for every link the set of flows that (for the given state of the network) cross that link. With supplementary analysis that is outside of the scope of this paper we can analyze these data structures and for every link determine whether if that link were to fail, every flow using that link

reaches its destination somehow after using the back-up link. An ability to make this differentiation relatively efficiently is a crucial aspect of our approach.

Following selection of a link to fail, when the chosen link is in the set of links whose failures do not induce loss of service, **Flow Validator** needs to compute the impact that that failure has on all the routes impacted by the failure. This step is computationally expensive; not only are routes and their backups recomputed, other data structures that support compliance of the post-failure SDN with other user-defined policies are also recomputed. This expense helps motivate our work in reducing the amount of simulation workload needed to estimate resiliency as we have defined it.

4. MONTE CARLO EVALUATION

A body of sophisticated work exists on using Monte Carlo to estimate network reliability, e.g. see [1] and its references. The model we have for SDN's is in some ways simpler than such work (e.g., to the extent that we are concerned with link failure probabilities, ours are equal and other work considers various more complex relationships), and in some ways harder (e.g., the connectivity of interest to us is that provided by software configuration, and is dynamic, whereas the more typical model of network connectivity is purely topological.)

The idea behind fast fail-over paths is to provide a means by which link failures can be tolerated without calling the controller. A measure of the link failure resiliency then is the mean of the random variable N_F, defined as the number of link failures that can occur until the controller is called to find new routes.

We can express $E[N_F]$ precisely, but first need to identify some notation. Let $\mathcal{L}$ be the set of all switch links with cardinality $N = |\mathcal{L}|$, let $2^{\mathcal{L}}$ denote the power-set (set of all subsets) of $\mathcal{L}$, and for a given $S \in 2^{\mathcal{L}}$ let $Seq(S)$ be the set of all sequences constructed from permutations of S. For example, if $S = \{l_1, l_2, l_3\}$ then $(l_2, l_1, l_3) \in Seq(S)$ and $(l_3, l_2, l_1) \in Seq(S)$, along with four other unique sequences. For a given sequence $\mathbf{L} = (l_1, l_2, \ldots, l_k)$ we will refer to subsequences $\mathbf{L}_0 = ()$, $\mathbf{L}_1 = (l_1), \ldots, \mathbf{L}_j = (l_1, l_2, \ldots, l_j)$, and so on.

For any $S \in 2^{\mathcal{L}}$ and $\mathbf{L} \in Seq(S)$, we define an indicator function $\phi(\mathbf{L})$ to have value 1 if failing links in the order specified by $\mathbf{L}$ induces loss of service (else 0), and define indicator function $\gamma(\mathbf{L})$ to be 1 if $\phi(\mathbf{L}) = 1$ but $\phi(\mathbf{L}_j) = 0$ for all $j = 1, 2, \ldots, len(\mathbf{L}) - 1$ where $len(\mathbf{L})$ is the number of elements of $\mathbf{L}$. In other words, $\mathbf{L}$ is minimal in the sense that as links are failed in the sequence specified by $\mathbf{L}$, the first loss of service is induced by the failure of the last link. We define

$$\mathcal{S} = \{\mathbf{L} \mid \gamma(\mathbf{L}) = 1\}$$

to reference these sequences of interest.

Given a permutation $\mathbf{L}_N$ of all links in $\mathcal{L}$, there is exactly one j for which $\gamma(\mathbf{L}_j) = 1$, and we denote this index by $d(\mathbf{L}_N) = j$. We can express $E[N_F]$ as the expectation over all permutations $\mathbf{L}_N$, each permutation having equal probability $1/N!$:

$$E[N_F] = \sum_{\mathbf{L}_N} d(\mathbf{L}_N)/N!.$$

We partition the permutations into equivalence classes, where $\mathbf{L}_N^{(1)}$ and $\mathbf{L}_N^{(2)}$ are in the same class if and only if $d(\mathbf{L}_N^{(1)}) =$

$d(\mathbf{L}_N^{(2)}) = k$ for some k, and the two permutations are identical in the first k links. That *stopping prefix* uniquely identifies the class. Given $d(\mathbf{L}_N^{(1)}) = k$ we know that the first $k-1$ links did not cause loss of service, while the kth selection did. Some care is needed in expressing the probability of choosing the common prefix. For every sequence $\mathbf{L}_i$ with i links and $\gamma(\mathbf{L}_i) = 0$, let $F(\mathbf{L}_i)$ denote the set of links not in $\mathbf{L}_i$ such that extending $\mathbf{L}_i$ with a member of $F(\mathbf{L}_i)$ induces loss of service. The notation captures the dependence of that set on the first i links chosen; different sequences expose different sets of vulnerable links. Also let $\bar{F}(\mathbf{L}_i)$ denote all links not in $\mathbf{L}_i$ and not in $F(\mathbf{L}_i)$. Now if we choose a sequence of k links with the property that the last link induces loss of service but none of the previous links do, we can express the probability that a uniformly sampled N-length sequence is a member of the equivalence class defined by that prefix. This is obtained by multiplying the probability p_{pre} of sampling the specific prefix times the probability p_{post} of sampling some specific sequence of $N - k$ links that are not in the prefix, times the number of such postfixes. To set up a later comparison with a different distribution, we express each term of the product p_{pre} as the probability of sampling from the set of links that do not induce loss of service times the (uniform) probability of sampling a specific link from that set. We likewise express p_{post} as the probability of sampling from the set of links that do induce loss of service times the probability of sampling a specific link from that set. Thus we express

$$p_{norm}(\mathbf{L}_k) = \Pr\{\text{sample sequence } \mathbf{L}_k\}$$

$$= p_{pre} \cdot p_{post} \cdot \prod_{i=0}^{N-k-1} \frac{1}{N-k-i} \cdot (N-k)!$$

$$= \Big(\prod_{i=0}^{k-2} \frac{|\bar{F}(\mathbf{L}_i)|}{N-i} \cdot p_l(\mathbf{L}_i)\Big) \cdot \Big(\frac{|F(\mathbf{L}_{k-1})|}{N-k+1} \cdot p_f(\mathbf{L}_{k-1})\Big)$$

$$= \prod_{i=0}^{k-1} \frac{1}{(N-i)} \tag{1}$$

where for notational convenience and future use we define

$$p_f(\mathbf{L}_i) = 1/|F(\mathbf{L}_i)|$$

and

$$p_l(\mathbf{L}_i) = 1/|\bar{F}(\mathbf{L}_i)|$$

e.g., the uniform probability of sampling a particular member of of $F(\mathbf{L}_i)$ (alt., $\bar{F}(\mathbf{L}_i)$) at the $(i+1)^{st}$ step.

The point of this rigor is to show that $p_{norm}(\mathbf{L}_k)$ accumulates the probability under uniform sampling of all full length sequences that match in the prefix up to the kth selected link, which first induces loss of service. Therefore if we sample links until we select one that induces loss of service, it is a valid sample of N_F, with a probability given by $p_{norm}(\mathbf{L}_{d(\mathbf{L})})$. For a given k, the probability that $N_F = k$ is given by the sum over all k-length members of $\mathcal{S}$, call this subset $\mathcal{S}_k$, so that

$$E[N_F] = \sum_{k=1}^{N} \sum_{\mathbf{L}_k \in \mathcal{S}_k} k \cdot p_{norm}(\mathbf{L}_k)$$

$$= \sum_{\mathbf{L} \in S} len(\mathbf{L}) \cdot p_{norm}(\mathbf{L}). \tag{2}$$

Equation 2 shows us that Monte Carlo simulation can be used to estimate $E[N_F]$ as follows. An experiment is a sequence of steps where with each step an un-chosen link is randomly selected, and the existing sequence is extended by this selection. On selecting the jth such link, analysis determines whether the failure of that link induces loss of service, and if so the experiment stops. Effectively the simulation determines whether, given the sequence construction after $j-1$ steps, the chosen link is sampled from $F(\mathbf{L}_{j-1})$ (uniformly) or from $\hat{F}(\mathbf{L}_{j-1})$, also uniformly. In the former case value j is the sample of N_F that is recorded, and then another experiment may be run, independent of any other; in the latter case the experiment continues until the stopping condition is encountered. After m experiments the sample mean of the recorded values is our point estimate of N_F, and a confidence interval can be constructed around it in the usual way. For a given N-length sequence $\mathbf{L}_N$ the step where the experiment stops is deterministic, $d(\mathbf{L}_N)$, and so conditioned on this we know that for $i = 1, 2, \ldots, d(\mathbf{L}) - 1$, the sample must draw uniformly at random from $\bar{F}(\mathbf{L}_{i-1})$, and the last sample must draw uniformly from $F(\mathbf{L}_{d(\mathbf{L})-1})$. This is reflected in equation 2.

A class of techniques exist for reducing the overall cost of estimating resiliency called *variance reduction*. In these one conducts the experiments in a way that reduces the variance of the estimator.

4.1 Variance of Estimators

Basic statistical theory teaches that the sample mean we construct from repeated un-biased experiments is a random variable and has a mean that is the same as the mean of the random variable of interest (here, N_F). The confidence we have in a particular sample mean is expressed formally as a confidence interval. The smaller the width of the confidence interval, the greater the confidence we have; the smaller the variance of the probability distribution associated with the sample, the smaller the width of the confidence interval tends to be for the same number of samples.

Classically, when m independent repetitions are performed with m measurements $x_1, x_2, \ldots, x_m$, the sample mean $\hat{\mu} = (1/m) \sum_{i=1}^{m} x_i$ is computed, with confidence interval

$$\hat{\mu} \pm t^* \cdot \frac{s}{\sqrt{m-1}}$$

where $s^2 = \big(\sum_{i=1}^{m}(x_i - \hat{\mu})^2\big)/(m-1)$ is an unbiased estimator of the sampling distribution variance, and t^* is a critical value related to the certainty desired. The smaller $\sqrt{s^2/(m-1)}$, the tighter the interval around $\hat{\mu}$. One commonly seeks to achieve a confidence interval width that is 10% or less of the sample mean. The expression above reveals the limited impact of reducing the confidence interval width by increasing the number of samples: to make the confidence interval smaller by half requires that the number of samples be a factor of four larger.

The variance of N_F is given by

$$var(N_F) = \sum_{\mathbf{L} \in \mathcal{S}} (len(\mathbf{L}) - E[N_F])^2 \cdot p_{norm}(\mathbf{L})$$

$$= \sum_{\mathbf{L} \in \mathcal{S}} \big(len(\mathbf{L})^2 \cdot p_{norm}(\mathbf{L})\big) - E[N_F]^2 \tag{3}$$

where the expectation is taken with respect to the uniform sampling distribution.

The objective of *variance reduction* techniques is to craft a sampling distribution such that the mean value of the sample mean random variable is that of the random variable of interest (again, here N_F), and that the *variance* of the sample distribution (estimated by s^2) is smaller than that of ordinary random sampling, so that the confidence interval tends to be smaller for the same number of experiments. This paper develops ideas from importance sampling to accomplish this.

5. IMPORTANCE SAMPLING

Importance sampling is a different way to reduce the width of the confidence interval, by reducing the sampling variance s^2. One application of the technique is to increase the precision of the confidence interval for a given number of samples, another application is to achieve a desired precision using fewer samples. The problem motivating our work falls in the latter category. It is computationally expensive to execute an experiment, and so we seek means by which we can reduce the number of experiments needed for a desired accuracy.

Importance sampling has a long history, with reference as early as the 1950s by Kahn and Marshall [7]. Description of various techniques in general stochastic systems is reviewed by Glynn and Iglehart [4], its application to rare event simulation detailed by Heidelberger [5], and to communication systems by Smith, Shafi, and Gao [13]. Use of a variety of variance reduction techniques (including importance sampling) is covered by Cancela et. al [1]. Against the backdrop of extensive literature on importance sampling, our work is unique in its application to SDN, and in exploitation of separating links into the class of those that will induce loss of service when next failed, and the class of those that don't.

The basis for importance sampling is very simple. If $\mathbf{L}$ is a random sequence with discrete components having probability mass function $f(\mathbf{y}) = \Pr\{\mathbf{L} = \mathbf{y}\}$, and g is any other probability mass function on the same space with the property that $g(\mathbf{y}) > 0$ whenever $f(\mathbf{y}) > 0$, then if β is a scalar valued function of $\mathbf{L}$ we can write the expected value of $\beta(\mathbf{L})$ as

$$E_f[\beta(\mathbf{L})] = \sum_{\mathbf{y}} \beta(\mathbf{y}) \cdot f(\mathbf{y})$$

$$= \sum_{\mathbf{y}} \beta(\mathbf{y}) \cdot \frac{f(\mathbf{y})}{g(\mathbf{y})} g(\mathbf{y})$$

$$= E_g[\beta(\mathbf{L}) \cdot R(\mathbf{L})] \qquad (4)$$

where E_f denotes the expectation with respect to probability function f, E_g denotes the expectation with respect to probability function g, and the *likelihood ratio function* is $R(\mathbf{y}) = f(\mathbf{y})/g(\mathbf{y})$. This equivalence tells us that an unbiased estimator of $E_g[\beta(\mathbf{L}) \cdot R(\mathbf{L})]$ is also an unbiased estimator of $E_f[\beta(\mathbf{L})]$.

Applying these notions to our problem, the random vectors $\mathbf{L}$ are members of $\mathcal{S}$, i.e., sequences of link failures where the last link failed induces loss of service. $f(\mathbf{L}) = p_{norm}(\mathbf{L})$ is the probability of choosing that sequence of links. To apply importance sampling, at each step when we select a link, the probability distribution need not be uniform, and can depend on previously selected links. We denote the sequence of the first j links by $\mathbf{L}_j$ (with the boundary case of $\mathbf{L}_0 = ()$). Now if $\mathbf{L}_j$ does not cause loss of service and λ is any link not in $\mathbf{L}_j$, we must allow for the possibility that the

biased sampling chooses λ, because the unbiased sampling can. We denote the probability under our sampling scheme of choosing λ to extend $\mathbf{L}_j$ by $p_{samp}(\lambda \mid \mathbf{L}_j)$. Therefore the probability of sampling sequence $\mathbf{L} = (l_1, l_2, \ldots, l_k) \in \mathcal{S}$ under importance sampling is

$$p_{skew}(\mathbf{L}) = p_{samp}(l_1) \prod_{i=2}^{k} p_{samp}(l_i \mid \mathbf{L}_{i-1}).$$

Once a link is chosen that induces loss of service the sampling stops, and we can think of $p_{skew}(\mathbf{L})$ as the probability of choosing some member of the equivalence class defined by prefix $\mathbf{L}$. With this interpretation we see that the skewed sampling is referring to the same underlying sample space as the uniform sampling does, and is just an alternative assignment of probabilities to all full permutations of links.

When a sampled link induces loss of service we need to compute the likelihood ratio $R(\mathbf{L}) = p_{norm}(\mathbf{L})/p_{skew}(\mathbf{L})$, and use $len(\mathbf{L}) \cdot R(\mathbf{L})$ as the value of the experiment.

While the intention of importance sampling is to reduce the variance in the sample mean, it is possible to actually *increase* the variance. Denoting the random sample under importance sampling by $\hat{\mu}$, the variance of $\hat{\mu}$ is given by

$$var(\hat{\mu}) = \sum_{\mathbf{L} \in \mathcal{S}} (len(\mathbf{L}) \cdot R(\mathbf{L}) - E[N_F])^2 \cdot p_{skew}(\mathbf{L})$$

$$= \sum_{\mathbf{L} \in \mathcal{S}} (len(\mathbf{L}) \cdot \frac{p_{norm}(\mathbf{L})}{p_{skew}(\mathbf{L})})^2 \cdot p_{skew}(\mathbf{L}) - E[N_F]^2$$

$$= \sum_{\mathbf{L} \in \mathcal{S}} (len(\mathbf{L})^2 \cdot R(\mathbf{L}) \cdot p_{norm}(\mathbf{L})) - E[N_F]^2. \quad (5)$$

The objective is to define a skewed sampling strategy such that $var(\hat{\mu}) < var(\mu)$. Subtracting the expression in equation 5 from the variance of N_F (equation 3) we see that variance is reduced when the right-hand-side of the equation below is positive:

$$var(\mu) - var(\hat{\mu}) = \sum_{\mathbf{L} \in \mathcal{S}} len(\mathbf{L})^2 (1 - R(\mathbf{L})) \cdot p_{norm}(\mathbf{L}) \quad (6)$$

$$= \sum_{\mathbf{L} \in \mathcal{S}} len(\mathbf{L})^2 (1 - \frac{p_{norm}(\mathbf{L})}{p_{skew}(\mathbf{L})}) \cdot p_{norm}(\mathbf{L})$$

This expression gives a clue to a skewed sampling approach that reduces variance. Suppose that $p_{skew}(\mathbf{L})$ could be constructed to be proportional to $len(\mathbf{L}) \cdot p_{norm}(\mathbf{L})$. Applying this to the expression above we obtain

$$var(\mu) - var(\hat{\mu}) =$$

$$= \sum_{\mathbf{L} \in \mathcal{S}} len(\mathbf{L})^2 (1 - \frac{p_{norm}(\mathbf{L})}{len(\mathbf{L}) \cdot p_{norm}(\mathbf{L})/u}) \cdot p_{norm}(\mathbf{L})$$

$$= \sum_{\mathbf{L} \in \mathcal{S}} len(\mathbf{L})^2 (1 - \frac{u}{len(\mathbf{L})}) \cdot p_{norm}(\mathbf{L})$$

$$= \sum_{\mathbf{L} \in \mathcal{S}} (len(\mathbf{L})^2 - u \cdot len(\mathbf{L})) \cdot p_{norm}(\mathbf{L})$$

$$= E[N_F^2] - u \cdot E[N_F] \quad (7)$$

where u is the normalization constant

$$u = \sum_{\mathbf{L} \in \mathcal{S}} len(\mathbf{L}) \cdot p_{norm}(\mathbf{L}) = E[N_F].$$

Substitution of u back into equation 7 makes the right-hand-side equal to $var(\mu)$, which implies that this particular (unrealizable) choice for $p_{skew}(\mathbf{L})$ yields an estimator with no variance! However, we can use this insight to construct $p_{skew}(\mathbf{L}) \approx len(\mathbf{L}) \cdot p_{norm}(\mathbf{L})/E[N_F]$.

From equation 7 we see that if constant of proportionality u is chosen with $u < E[N_F^2]/E[N_F]$ we should see a reduction in the sampling variance. The only constant of proportionality that *exactly* works is the unrealizable $u = E[N_F]$. In our approach we will construct p_{skew} dynamically, with each sampled link.

6. SKEWED SAMPLING STRATEGY

6.1 Method

We've seen that the strategy of trying to make $p_{skew}(\mathbf{L})$ proportional to $len(\mathbf{L}) \cdot p_{norm}(\mathbf{L})$ has the potential for variance reduction. We design a sampling strategy based on this observation. Earlier we saw that we can view an experiment under uniform sampling as a sequence of Bernoulli trials, where, at the jth trial, while we sample uniformly from among all un-sampled links we are implicitly choosing from set $F(\mathbf{L}_{j-1})$ with probability $|F(\mathbf{L}_{j-1})|/(N - j + 1)$, then choosing a specific link from that set with probability $p_f(\mathbf{L}_{j-1})$, thereby terminating the experiment. Under uniform sampling no specific knowledge of the membership in $F(\mathbf{L}_{j-1})$ or $\bar{F}(\mathbf{L}_{j-1})$ was required. Suppose though that the size of these sets *could* be determined explicitly. At the jth step, we could change the probability of selecting $F(\mathbf{L}_{j-1})$ to be any $\alpha_j \in [0, 1]$ we chose. We can then modify the expression for $p_{norm}(\mathbf{L})$ to create an expression for $p_{skew}(\mathbf{L})$:

$$p_{skew}(\mathbf{L}) = \alpha_{d(\mathbf{L})} \cdot p_f(\mathbf{L}_{d(\mathbf{L})-1}) \cdot \prod_{i=0}^{d(\mathbf{L})-2} (1 - \alpha_{i+1}) \cdot p_l(\mathbf{L}_i) \tag{8}$$

recalling that $p_f(\mathbf{L}_{d(\mathbf{L})-1}) = 1/|F(\mathbf{L}_{d(\mathbf{L})-1})|$ and $p_l(\mathbf{L}_i) = 1/|\bar{F}(\mathbf{L}_i)|$.

By careful selection of the α_j we can *try* to make $p_{skew}(\mathbf{L})$ proportional to $len(\mathbf{L}) \cdot p_{norm}(\mathbf{L})$ when $\mathbf{L} \in \mathcal{S}$. The choice of α_j will depend on the state of sampling prior to step j; what is needed is a procedure that, given $\mathbf{L}_{j-1}$, we compute α_j and then if possible, choose the next link from $F(\mathbf{L}_{j-1})$ with probability α_j.

The qualifications above on selecting and using α_j follow from the observation that, while in principle given a constant proportionality u and $\mathbf{L} \in \mathcal{S}$ one can ascribe probability $len(\mathbf{L}) \cdot p_{norm}(\mathbf{L})/u$ to $\mathbf{L}$, that does not necessarily imply that the method we've described to create a skewed distribution is always able to accomplish that objective. The point is subtle but important. As a consequence, as we construct the skewed distribution we need to ensure that it has non-zero probability on every sequence for which the uniform distribution has non-zero probability. For example, we will see in the equations used tα_i the possibility for the equation to give a value greater than or equal to 1. For a value which is supposedly a probability values in excess are obviously problematic; the case where the equation for $\alpha_i = 1$ and $\bar{F}(\mathbf{L}_{i-1}) \neq \emptyset$ is equally problematic, for it cuts off the possibility of sampling from $\bar{F}(\mathbf{L}_{i-1})$, which the uniform distribution can, and so must then the skewed distribution.

These issues not withstanding, we will do what we can to cause each $\mathbf{L}$ to have $p_{skew}(\mathbf{L}) \propto len(\mathbf{L}) \cdot p_{norm}(\mathbf{L})$, while

ensuring that the p_{skew} distribution has support everywhere that p_{norm} has support. Details will follow.

We must first start with a normalizing constant u, which we earlier saw might yield significant variance reduction if $u \approx E[N_F]$. We therefore estimate $E[N_F]$ analytically somehow, or do a few normal random trials to estimate $E[N_F]$.

Next we observe that if $F(\mathbf{L}_i)$ is empty, then $\alpha_{i+1} = 0$. As we sample then, the step where $F(\mathbf{L}_i)$ is first non-empty is important. Formally, given sequence $\mathbf{L}$, we define $b(\mathbf{L})$ to be the smallest index i for which $F(\mathbf{L}_i)$ is non-empty. We do not induce loss of service at any step $i \in [0, b(\mathbf{L})]$, so there obviously $p_{skew}(\mathbf{L}_i) = p_{norm}(\mathbf{L}_i)$. However, things change when $i = b(\mathbf{L}) + 1$. If it should happen that $F(\mathbf{L}_i)$ includes all links, then there is no skewing to be done; we'll sample a link, it will induce a loss of service, and the experiment will end. However if $\bar{F}(\mathbf{L}_i)$ is not empty we get to choose between the two lists, and $\alpha_{b(\mathbf{L})+1}$ will give the probability of sampling from $F(\mathbf{L}_{b(\mathbf{L})})$. We write

$$p_{skew}(\mathbf{L}_{b(\mathbf{L})+1}) = \beta_{b(\mathbf{L})+1} \cdot p_f(\mathbf{L}_{b(\mathbf{L})}) \cdot \prod_{i=0}^{b(\mathbf{L})-1} 1/(N - i)$$

which expresses the fact that when $F(\mathbf{L}_i)$ is empty we are sampling uniformly from all links. From this we express the property desired of $p_{skew}(\mathbf{L}_{b(\mathbf{L})+1})$:

$$\beta_{b(\mathbf{L})+1} \cdot p_f(\mathbf{L}_{b(\mathbf{L})}) \cdot \prod_{i=0}^{b(\mathbf{L})-1} 1/(N - i)$$
$$= \frac{(b(\mathbf{L}) + 1) \cdot p_{norm}(\mathbf{L}_{b(\mathbf{L})+1})}{u}.$$

with solution

$$\begin{aligned}
\beta_{b(\mathbf{L})+1} &= \frac{(b(\mathbf{L}) + 1) \cdot p_{norm}(\mathbf{L}_{b(\mathbf{L})+1})}{u \cdot p_f(\mathbf{L}_{b(\mathbf{L})}) \cdot \prod_{i=0}^{b(\mathbf{L})-1} 1/(N - i)} \\
&= \frac{(b(\mathbf{L}) + 1) \cdot \prod_{i=0}^{b(\mathbf{L})} 1/(N - i)}{u \cdot p_f(\mathbf{L}_{b(\mathbf{L})}) \cdot \prod_{i=0}^{b(\mathbf{L})-1} 1/(N - i)} \\
&= \frac{(b(\mathbf{L}) + 1) \cdot (1/(N - b(\mathbf{L})))}{u \cdot p_f(\mathbf{L}_{b(\mathbf{L})})} \\
&= \left(\frac{b(L) + 1}{u}\right) \cdot \left(\frac{|F(\mathbf{L}_{b(L)})|}{N - b(L)}\right). \tag{9}
\end{aligned}$$

There is no reason a priori why $\beta_{b(\mathbf{L})+1}$ so expressed necessarily satisfies $0 < \beta_{b(\mathbf{L})+1} < 1$. When this inequality is satisfied *and* $\bar{F}(\mathbf{L}_{b(L)}) \neq \emptyset$ we will assign $\alpha_{b(\mathbf{L})+1} = \beta_{b(\mathbf{L})+1}$. If it should happen that $\bar{F}(\mathbf{L}_{b(L)}) = \emptyset$ then obviously we must set $\alpha_{b(\mathbf{L})+1} = 1$. The final possibility is that $1 \leq \beta_{b(\mathbf{L})+1}$ and $\bar{F}(\mathbf{L}_{b(L)}) \neq \emptyset$. We have to allow for the possibility of sampling links from $\bar{F}(\mathbf{L}_{b(L)})$, and so choose the next link uniformly from among all links by assigning $\alpha_{b(\mathbf{L})+1} = |F(\mathbf{L}_{b(L)})|/(N - b(L))$. The choice of $\alpha_{b(\mathbf{L})+1}$ establishes the base for subsequent calculations of α_j for $j > b(\mathbf{L}) + 1$.

Continuing with the sampling, assuming no loss of service is induced up through step $j - 1$, we can assume that α_i has been appropriately defined for all earlier steps, and now seek to compute α_j. As with the first step we'll define a variable β_j whose value will define α_j in exactly the same circumstances as it did with $\alpha_{b(\mathbf{L})+1}$: $0 < \beta_j < 1$ and $\bar{F}(\mathbf{L}_{j-1}) \neq \emptyset$. From the requirement $p_{skew}(\mathbf{L}_j) = j \cdot p_{norm}(\mathbf{L}_j)/u$ we set up

$$\beta_j \cdot p_f(\mathbf{L}_{j-1}) \prod_{i=0}^{j-2}(1 - \alpha_{i+1}) \cdot p_l(\mathbf{L}_i) = \frac{j \cdot p_{norm}(\mathbf{L}_j)}{u}$$

which we rearrange to express β_j as a function of α_i with $i < j$:

$$
\begin{aligned}
\beta_j &= \frac{j \cdot p_{norm}(\mathbf{L}_j)}{u \cdot p_f(\mathbf{L}_{j-1}) \prod_{i=0}^{j-2}(1 - \alpha_{i+1}) \cdot p_l(\mathbf{L}_i)} \\
&= \frac{j \cdot \prod_{i=0}^{j-1} 1/(N - i)}{u \cdot p_f(\mathbf{L}_{j-1}) \left(\prod_{i=0}^{j-2}(1 - \alpha_{i+1}) \cdot p_l(\mathbf{L}_i) \right)} \quad (10) \\
&= \left(\frac{j}{u}\right) \cdot \left(\frac{|F(\mathbf{L}_{j-1})|}{N - j + 1}\right) \cdot \left(\prod_{i=0}^{j-2} \frac{|\bar{F}(\mathbf{L}_i)|}{(1 - \alpha_{i+1})(N - i)} \right)
\end{aligned}
$$

where the last step follows from simple algebra after using the definitions of $p_l(\mathbf{L}_i)$ and $p_f(\mathbf{L}_{j-1})$. As before, we cannot in the general case assert that β_j necessarily satisfies $0 < \beta_j < 1$. Therefore, just as with $\alpha_{b(\mathbf{L})+1}$, we assign α_j equal to β_j, 1, or $|F(\mathbf{L}_{j-1})|/(N - j + 1)$, depending on whether β_j is a probability that allows for sampling from non-empty $\bar{F}(\mathbf{L}_{j-1})$, must sample from $F(\mathbf{L}_{j-1})$ because $\bar{F}(\mathbf{L}_{j-1}) = \emptyset$, or is not a proper probability, respectively.

Note that for any given $\mathbf{L} \in \mathcal{S}$, the question of whether $p_{skew}(\mathbf{L}) = len(\mathbf{L}) \cdot p_{norm}(\mathbf{L})/u$ depends entirely on whether $\alpha_{len(\mathbf{L})} = \beta_{len(\mathbf{L})}$. If so, the proportionality exists regardless of the details of how α_i with $i < len(\mathbf{L})$ was defined. Equation 11 describes the requirements of proportionality, so that when the solution of that equation is used for $\alpha_{len(\mathbf{L})}$, we necessarily have $p_{skew}(\mathbf{L}) = len(\mathbf{L}) \cdot p_{norm}(\mathbf{L})/u$.

Upon selecting the kth link under the skewed sampling and discovering that its failure induces loss of service, we compute k times the likelihood ratio function and use that as the value representing the experiment. This is given by

$$
\begin{aligned}
&k \cdot \frac{p_{norm}(\mathbf{L}_k)}{p_{skew}(\mathbf{L}_k)} \\
&= k \cdot \frac{\left(\prod_{i=0}^{k-2} \frac{|\bar{F}(\mathbf{L}_i)|}{N - i} \cdot p_l(\mathbf{L}_i) \right) \cdot \left(\frac{|F(\mathbf{L}_{k-1})|}{N - k + 1} \cdot p_f(\mathbf{L}_{k-1}) \right)}{\left(\prod_{i=0}^{k-2}(1 - \alpha_{i+1}) \cdot p_l(\mathbf{L}_i) \right) \cdot \left(\alpha_k \cdot p_f(\mathbf{L}_{k-1}) \right)} \\
&= k \cdot \left(\prod_{i=0}^{k-2} \frac{|\bar{F}(\mathbf{L}_i)|}{(1 - \alpha_{i+1}) \cdot (N - i)} \right) \cdot \left(\frac{|F(\mathbf{L}_{k-1})|}{\alpha_k \cdot (N - k + 1)} \right)
\end{aligned}
$$

which is a form that suggests means of stable means of computation, provided that the α_i values used at each step are retained for use in this computation. That computation computes the ratio terms for each product index and multiplies the ratios. A naive computation would divide a very small number $p_{skew}(\mathbf{L}_k)$ into another very small number $p_{norm}(\mathbf{L}_k)$, which is a calculation rife with numerical issues.

The procedures described above will always create a skewed distribution that gives non-zero probability to any sequence that uniform sampling does. The degree to which that procedure yields reduction in variance depends on the structure of the network, configuration, and choice of u. We next consider those issues.

6.2 Variance Reduction

While the method we've described for constructing a skewed distribution strives to create values of $p_{skew}(\mathbf{L})$ that are proportional to $len(\mathbf{L}) \cdot p_{norm}(\mathbf{L})$, there will be $\mathbf{L} \in \mathcal{S}$ for which

this is not true. Let $\mathcal{S}_F$ be the set of $\mathbf{L} \in \mathcal{S}$ for which $\alpha_{len(\mathbf{L})} \neq \beta_{len(\mathbf{L})}$ from equation 11 or equation 9. For each $\mathbf{L} \in \mathcal{S}_F$ define $p_{prop}(\mathbf{L}) = len(\mathbf{L}) \cdot p_{norm}(\mathbf{L})/u$, i.e., the probability we would have liked to ascribe to $\mathbf{L}$ but could not because the rules for defining $\alpha_{len(\mathbf{L})}$ selected $\beta_{len(\mathbf{L})} = 1$ or $\beta_{len(\mathbf{L})} = |F(\mathbf{L}_{len(\mathbf{L})-1})|/(N - len(\mathbf{L}) + 1)$. Then for each $\mathbf{L} \in \mathcal{S}_F$ define $R_{prop}(\mathbf{L}) = p_{norm}(\mathbf{L})/p_{prop}(\mathbf{L})$, i.e., the likelihood ratio function value we'd ascribe to $\mathbf{L}$ if it had probability $p_{prop}(\mathbf{L})$. $R(\mathbf{L}) = p_{norm}(\mathbf{L})/p_{skew}(\mathbf{L})$ as before.

The equations for β_i never have a negative solution, so the only time that $\alpha_{len(\mathbf{L})}$ describes uniform sampling rather than $\beta_{len(\mathbf{L})}$ is when $1 \leq \beta_{len(\mathbf{L})}$. We can think of $\beta_{len(\mathbf{L})}$ as a factor by which we need to multiply another term in order to make $p_{skew}(\mathbf{L})$ proportional to $len(\mathbf{L}) \cdot p_{norm}(\mathbf{L})/u$. But since $\alpha_{len(\mathbf{L})} < \beta_{len(\mathbf{L})}$ we can assert the following.

LEMMA 1. *For every* $\mathbf{L} \in \mathcal{S}_F$, $p_{skew}(\mathbf{L}) < p_{prop}(\mathbf{L})$ *and so* $R(\mathbf{L}) > R_{prop}(\mathbf{L})$.

Note that for $\mathbf{L} \in \mathcal{S}/\mathcal{S}_F$, $R(\mathbf{L}) = R_{prop}(\mathbf{L})$. Define $\epsilon(\mathbf{L}) = R(\mathbf{L}) - R_{prop}(\mathbf{L})$, and observe that for all $\mathbf{L} \in \mathcal{S}_F$, $\epsilon(\mathbf{L}) > 0$. Recalling the derivation of the reduction of variance leading to equation 7, we express

$$
\begin{aligned}
var(\mu) &- var(\hat{\mu}) = \\
&\sum_{\mathbf{L} \in \mathcal{S}/\mathcal{S}_F} len(\mathbf{L})^2(1 - R(\mathbf{L})) \cdot p_{norm}(\mathbf{L}) \\
&+ \sum_{\mathbf{L} \in \mathcal{S}_F} len(\mathbf{L})^2(1 - R(\mathbf{L})) \cdot p_{norm}(\mathbf{L}) \\
&= \sum_{\mathbf{L} \in \mathcal{S}/\mathcal{S}_F} len(\mathbf{L})^2(1 - R(\mathbf{L})) \cdot p_{norm}(\mathbf{L}) \\
&+ \sum_{\mathbf{L} \in \mathcal{S}_F} len(\mathbf{L})^2(1 - (R_{prop}(\mathbf{L}) + \epsilon(\mathbf{L}))) \cdot p_{norm}(\mathbf{L}) \\
&= \sum_{\mathbf{L} \in \mathcal{S}} len(\mathbf{L})^2 \left(1 - \frac{u}{len(\mathbf{L})}\right) \cdot p_{norm}(\mathbf{L}) \\
&- \sum_{\mathbf{L} \in \mathcal{S}_F} len(\mathbf{L})^2 \epsilon(\mathbf{L}) \cdot p_{norm}(\mathbf{L}) \\
&= \left(E[N_F^2] - u \cdot E[N_F] \right) \\
&- \sum_{\mathbf{L} \in \mathcal{S}_F} len(\mathbf{L})^2 \cdot \epsilon(\mathbf{L}) \cdot p_{norm}(\mathbf{L}).
\end{aligned}
$$

This equation gives us insight into how variance reduction is impacted by choice of u. We recognize $E[N_F^2] - u \cdot E[N_F]$ from equation 7 and the insight that this term is $var(\mu)$ when $u = E[N_F]$. Unlike before though, the term summing weighted values of $\epsilon(\mathbf{L})$ reduces the amount of variance reduction. However if with u near $E[N_F]$ the nature of the network makes $|\mathcal{S}_F|$ very small relative to $1/p_{norm}(\mathbf{L}) = \prod_{i=0}^{len(\mathbf{L})-1}(N - i)$, then this summation will be very small showing that we can expect excellent variance reduction. Note further that as u increases the size of $\mathcal{S}_F$ decreases. For if $\mathcal{S}_{F,i}$ is defined by $u = u_i$ for $i = 1, 2$ and $u_1 > u_2$, then $\mathcal{S}_{F,1} \subseteq \mathcal{S}_{F,2}$. This says that if for u near $E[N_F]$ the number of terms in the sum is too large, the sum of *epsilon* terms can be made smaller by increasing u, but at the cost also of increasing the term $u \cdot E[N_F]$, which also reduces variance reduction.

7. EXPERIMENTS

We use a simple example to illustrate the potential for using importance sampling to reduce the number of samples

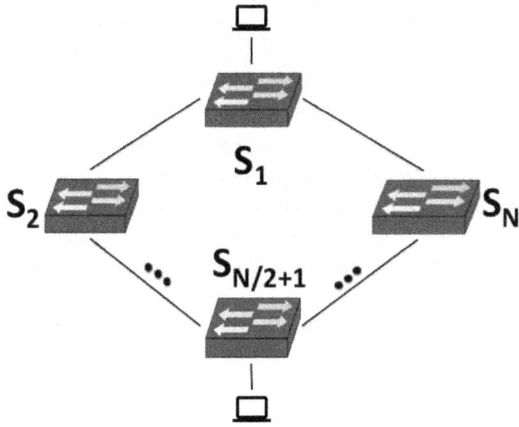

Figure 2: Ring architecture, with two hosts

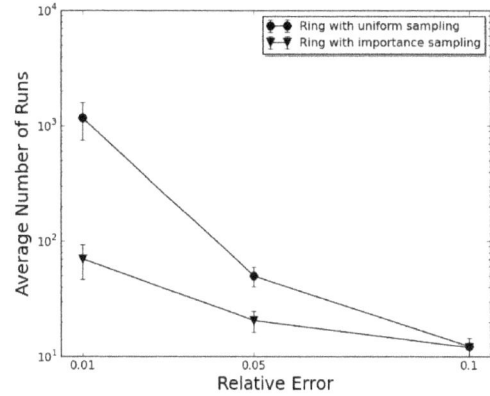

Figure 3: Replications required for given statistical accuracy

required to achieve high statistical accuracy. We consider a ring architecture, as illustrated in Figure 2, not only because of its simplicity but also because networks in the ICS domain of interest are in fact often rings. In this example all but two switches have just two ports; two switches have three ports, with an attached host. A flow is established between the hosts; rules are synthesized so that the backup link is the "other" inter-switch link at that switch.

The statistical accuracy asked of a Monte Carlo simulation is frequently given as "relative error", the ratio of the width of the confidence interval to the mean. So a relative error of 10% means that the confidence interval is one tenth the size in magnitude of the mean it surrounds. As we have seen earlier, to shrink the confidence interval by a factor of two normally requires a factor of four increase in the number of replications. This means that ordinary Monte Carlo simulation will tend to require significantly more replications to achieve a relative error of, say, 1% than a relative error of 10%.

Figure 3 gives the results of experiments we've done with **Flow Validator** on the ring topology with four switches. To understand the meaning of this data, think of each estimation task as a sample of the number of replications required to achieve a given statistical accuracy (in this graph, 1%, 5%, and 10%). Each such estimation task will have a variable number of replications; we plot the mean and standard deviation of 10 estimation tasks. We observe that there is very little difference between standard Monte Carlo and importance sampling for the relative error of 10%, but significant differences for more stringent accuracies. Note that the y-axis is logarithmic, and at a relative error of 1% importance sampling uses over an order of magnitude fewer replications to achieve that accuracy.

8. CONCLUSION

The application of software defined networking in an industrial control system context motivates the development of configurations that can tolerate link failures and minimize interaction with the controller. Assessment of these fail-over paths, along with many other properties is the objective of a tool under development called **Flow Validator**. This paper considers how we might use **Flow Validator** to assess overall resilience of an SDN to link failures, in the

sense of estimating the mean number of links that may randomly fail before any flow that formerly was routed can no longer be routed (necessitating involvement of the controller to attempt to repair the network.) The characteristics of **Flow Validator** make it possible for us to approach the problem via Monte Carlo sampling, and exploit deep knowledge about the network state to identify all as-yet un-failed links such that the immediate failure of any one of them will cause some loss of service. We show how to exploit this knowledge to design an importance sampling scheme for the Monte Carlo estimation of the mean of interest. We show in this paper conditions under which we can expect significantly less less variance in the sample statistic, with the potential for significant reduction in the computational effort needed to estimate resiliency with good accuracy. Preliminary experiments confirm this expectation.

Acknowledgements

This work was supported in part by Department of Energy contracts DE-OE0000679 and DE-OE0000780[1], and DHS contract 2015-ST-061-CIRC01[2].

9. REFERENCES

[1] H. Cancela, M. E. Khadiri, G. Rubino, and B. Tuffin. Balanced and approximate zero-variance recursive estimators for the network reliability problem. *ACM Trans. Model. Comput. Simul.*, 25(1):5:1–5:19, Nov. 2014.

[2] M. Casado, M. J. Freedman, J. Pettit, J. Luo, N. Gude, N. McKeown, and S. Shenker. Rethinking enterprise network control. *IEEE/ACM Transactions on Networking (TON)*, 17(4):1270–1283, 2009.

[3] O. N. Foundation. Openflow switch specification 1.3. "https://www.opennetworking.org/images/stories/downloads/sdn-resources/onf-specifications/openflow/openflow-spec-v1.3.0.pdf".

---

[1]The views and opinions of authors expressed herein do not necessarily state or reflect those of the United States Government or any agency thereof.

[2]The views and conclusions contained in this document are those of the authors and should not be interpreted as necessarily representing the official policies, either expressed or implied, of the U.S. Department of Homeland Security.

[4] P. W. Glynn and D. L. Iglehart. Importance sampling for stochastic simulations. *Manage. Sci.*, 35(11):1367–1392, Nov. 1989.

[5] P. Heidelberger. Fast simulation of rare events in queueing and reliability models. *ACM Trans. Model. Comput. Simul.*, 5(1):43–85, Jan. 1995.

[6] D. Jin and D. M. Nicol. Parallel simulation of software defined networks. In *Proceedings of the 2013 ACM SIGSIM conference on Principles of advanced discrete simulation*, pages 91–102. ACM, 2013.

[7] H. Kahn and A. W. Marshall. Methods of reducing sample size in monte carlo computations. *Journal Operations Research*, pages 263–278, 1953.

[8] P. Kazemian, M. Chan, H. Zeng, G. Varghese, N. McKeown, and S. Whyte. Real time network policy checking using header space analysis. In *NSDI*, pages 99–111, 2013.

[9] P. Kazemian, G. Varghese, and N. McKeown. Header space analysis: Static checking for networks. In *NSDI*, pages 113–126, 2012.

[10] A. Khurshid, W. Zhou, M. Caesar, and P. Godfrey. Veriflow: verifying network-wide invariants in real time. *ACM SIGCOMM Computer Communication Review*, 42(4):467–472, 2012.

[11] K. Kirkpatrick. Software-defined networking. *Commun. ACM*, 56(9):16–19, Sept. 2013.

[12] B. Lantz, B. Heller, and N. McKeown. A network in a laptop: rapid prototyping for software-defined networks. In *Proceedings of the 9th ACM SIGCOMM Workshop on Hot Topics in Networks*, page 19. ACM, 2010.

[13] P. J. Smith, M. Shafi, and H. Gao. Quick simulation: a review of importance sampling techniques in communications systems. *IEEE Journal on Selected Areas in Communications*, 15(4):597–613, May 1997.

Comparing a Scalable SDN Simulation Framework Built on ns-3 and DCE with Existing SDN Simulators and Emulators

Jared Ivey, Hemin Yang, Chuanji Zhang, George Riley
School of Electrical and Computer Engineering
Georgia Institute of Technology
Atlanta, GA, USA
{j.ivey, hyang350, Jenny_Zhang, riley}@gatech.edu

ABSTRACT

As software-defined networking (SDN) grows beyond its original aim to simply separate the control and data network planes, it becomes useful both financially and analytically to provide adequate mechanisms for simulating this new paradigm. A number of simulation/emulation tools for modeling SDN, such as Mininet, are already available. A new, novel framework for providing SDN simulation has been provided in this work using the network simulator ns-3. The ns-3 module Direct Code Execution (DCE) allows real-world network applications to be run within a simulated network topology. This work employs DCE for running the SDN controller library POX and its applications on nodes in a simulated network topology. In this way, real-world controller applications can be completely portable between simulation and actual deployment. This work also describes a user-defined ns-3 application mimicking an SDN switch supporting OpenFlow 1.0 that can interact with real-world controllers. To evaluate its performance, this ns-3 DCE SDN framework is compared against Mininet as well as some other readily available SDN simulation/emulation tools. Metrics such as realtime performance, memory usage, and reliability in terms of packet loss are analyzed across the multiple simulation/emulation tools to gauge how they compare.

Keywords

Network Emulation; Network Simulation; Software-defined Networking; Mininet; ns-3

1. INTRODUCTION

Software-defined networking (SDN) originated nominally as a means to separate the control and forwarding components of networks. Its initial focus stemmed from a need in campus networks to provide flexibility for research without interfering with regular network traffic. As SDN has grown in both academia and industry, its capabilities have expanded beyond these initial goals with more applications and use cases shedding light on what it can provide. With

Permission to make digital or hard copies of all or part of this work for personal or classroom use is granted without fee provided that copies are not made or distributed for profit or commercial advantage and that copies bear this notice and the full citation on the first page. Copyrights for components of this work owned by others than ACM must be honored. Abstracting with credit is permitted. To copy otherwise, or republish, to post on servers or to redistribute to lists, requires prior specific permission and/or a fee. Request permissions from permissions@acm.org.

SIGSIM-PADS '16, May 15-18, 2016, Banff, AB, Canada
© 2016 ACM. ISBN 978-1-4503-3742-7/16/05. . . $15.00
DOI: http://dx.doi.org/10.1145/2901378.2901391

newer and farther reaching applications being developed, it can prove beneficial both analytically and financially to employ modeling and simulation efforts toward initial developmental testing of these capabilities. In simulating SDN, an organization may examine topologies similar to those that it currently deploys to gather information about its network. This information may range from the feasibility of deploying initial SDN capabilities within its own network to troubleshooting and testing existing SDN deployments as a part of maintenance or enhancement of the overall system. In the former case of initial deployment, simulation of SDN can minimize initial costs of these kinds of exploratory efforts since network hardware is not immediately required. For existing networks, the degree of risk associated with introducing updates to an existing SDN network can be reduced as a number of issues can be identified and resolved within simulation prior to actual deployment.

This work introduces an SDN simulation framework within ns-3. It describes an ns-3 user-defined application, **SdnSwitch**, that supports OpenFlow 1.0. This application can be installed within ns-3 simulated topology nodes to provide a network of SDN-enabled switches. It also details how Direct Code Execution (DCE), a subproject of ns-3, can be used in conjunction with Python and the Python-based controller library POX, allowing real, deployable controller applications to be introduced into an ns-3 simulated topology. This work is not the first attempt to provide a framework for SDN simulation in ns-3. Efforts already underway within the ns-3 baseline have provided varying levels of SDN simulation capabilities. However, the framework provided by this work applies a novel approach toward achieving this goal. Providing a mechanism for using POX within DCE, controller applications written for this library can be developed and debugged in simulation and then immediately ported to a real-world deployment. Benefiting from the current capabilities provided by both ns-3 and DCE, this framework can achieve significant simulated node scales, providing the capacity necessary for adequately simulating enterprise and data center networks. Furthermore, the broad functionality of ns-3 enables opportunities in testing and simulating an immense variety of network configurations and topologies, offering wireless and LTE support, BRITE integration, real-world network connectivity and emulation, and many other useful tools.[1]

This work also examines a number of simulation/emula-

---

[1]Instructions for downloading and installing the SDN simulation framework may be found at https://github.com/jaredivey/dce-python-sdn.

tion libraries in addition to the previously described framework available for analyzing software-defined networks. The *de facto* standard for SDN emulation, Mininet, is compared against other available SDN simulation/emulation efforts. One such alternative is an extension to the flow-based simulator *fs* that allows real controller applications written in the Python-based controller library POX. Another option is actually a modification of Mininet that allows it to interface conveniently with the network simulator ns-3 to provide additional link capabilities not present in Mininet. Comparing realtime performance, memory usage, and reliability in terms of packet loss, the overall performance of each simulation/emulation tool can be compared against one another. Through this comparison, determinations can be made for when it is appropriate to use a specific tool.

The remainder of this paper is organized into the following sections. Section 2 provides a brief introduction of SDN, the OpenFlow protocol, and the SDN controller library POX. Section 3 describes currently available simulation/emulation tools for modeling SDNs. The SDN simulation framework using ns-3 and DCE is described in Section 4. The experimental setup and examined topologies are detailed in Section 5. Results are presented and discussed in Section 6. Section 7 identifies related work in the realm of SDN simulation/emulation, and the paper concludes with Section 8.

2. SOFTWARE-DEFINED NETWORKING

SDN is a paradigm that enables flexibility in communication networks by allowing them to be programmable. By most current conventions, this programmability is implemented by separating and logically centralizing the control of the network from its packet-level forwarding plane. In its early stages, SDN provided a means for virtualizing the network space such that networking research could occur and coincide seamlessly with regular traffic on physical campus networks[5]. Since that time, the concepts behind SDN have grown and evolved as more information elucidates this field.

Understanding SDN conceptually typically begins by examining currently implemented components that enable programmability of a network. Networks that strictly adhere to SDN internally will direct their packet traffic through very basic switches that examine the characteristics of incoming packets. These switches will perform actions on the packets (forward, drop, modify, etc.) through their switch ports based on installed rules. These rules are defined, installed, and managed by a logically centralized process referred to as the controller. The controller must communicate with its switches in a standardized manner, and the predominant method for normalizing this communication at the time of this writing is the OpenFlow protocol.

2.1 The OpenFlow Protocol

The OpenFlow communication protocol is a popular standard under which SDN may be deployed. The protocol itself arose from the need for an effective method for analyzing and testing new protocols realistically and scalably. Such tasks were previously cumbersome and difficult due in part to the rigidity of currently installed networks and a hesitance to interfere with them at the risk of compromising the base network functionality. The OpenFlow protocol was introduced as an attempt to address these issues. It is an open protocol that enables researchers to run experimental protocols on large scale networks while maintaining the integrity

of normal user traffic. With OpenFlow, the flow-tables contained in modern Ethernet switches and routers are simplified to accommodate a general set of functions and can be programmed according to these functions.

An OpenFlow switch integrates a flow table, a secure channel, and the OpenFlow protocol. The flow table consists of a set of flow entries. A flow is a match qualifier linked with a list of actions to take if the specific match is found. Each flow entry in a flow table is composed of a set of packet fields to match and actions to perform, such as sending the packet out through a certain port, modifying some field or fields in the packet before forwarding it, or simply dropping the packet. Based on the requirements of a particular switch, it may reasonably contain more than one flow table.

The secure channel of an OpenFlow switch connects it remotely to the controller process. Across this connection, the switch and controller can communicate commands and data. This communication is standardized by the OpenFlow protocol which provides a means to interface with the switch without directly programming it. Establishing a connection between the controller and a switch requires a specific set of steps similar to most network protocol handshakes. Establishing the connection involves a number of message exchanges, beginning with an OFPT_HELLO message followed by other messages for acquiring and/or designating various switch features and configuration settings.

When an OpenFlow switch receives a packet for which it has no matching flow entries, it may send this packet to the controller through an OFPT_PACKET_IN message. Upon receiving this packet, the controller will determine the appropriate action for the switch to take. This action may either be performed a single time by the switch, or the controller may direct the switch to install a flow entry with the appropriate action with an OFPT_FLOW_MOD message. This entry will hold certain characteristics of the received packet to compare against subsequent packets. Referred to as an `ofp_match`, this set of packet fields can prompt the switch to perform a given action when similarly matching packets are received in the future. The addition of flow entries is accompanied by the ability for the controller to remove flow entries from a switch flow table. This removal may occur through a direct action sent to the switch by the controller or through timeout values held in the flow entry [16, 17].

Requirements formally defining the OpenFlow protocol may be found in the *OpenFlow Switch Specification*. At the time of this work, versions extend from 1.0.0 to 1.5.0 [8]. This work focuses primarily on version 1.0.0.

2.2 POX

Multiple software libraries written in various programming languages are available for controlling network behavior in the context of SDN and OpenFlow. For this work, the POX controller library has been used. POX is the Python-based variant of NOX, the first controller library to support OpenFlow. POX provides a means for writing "Pythonic" controller applications compatible with OpenFlow. As a framework written in Python, its installation requirements are relatively low. Additionally, it possesses a low learning curve due to its design, and as such, has seen significant adoption in the academic realm as a mechanism to introduce SDN to the broader community. POX provides its own coordination library dubbed *recoco* that handles threading, timing, and other synchronization tasks. Accompanying the POX framework are numerous built-in controller applications that perform some basic forwarding functionality such as MAC address learning, link layer discovery, spanning tree, ARP requests, etc. At the time of this writing, POX supports OpenFlow 1.0 [1].

3. SDN SIMULATION/EMULATION TOOLS

This section examines the tools for SDN simulation and emulation that are the focus of this work. When modeling systems such as communication netowrks, both simulation and emulation aim to provide adequate representations of the behaviors of these systems. However, a notable difference between the two concepts is that simulation time is not intended to coincide with wallclock execution time. Indeed, it is preferred that simulations cover a greater simulated time span than the runtime execution time span. In contrast, emulation is intended to execute as closely as possible in lockstep with the wallclock time. Typically, emulated systems may need to interact with the real world in some way, and for this reason, the time that the emulation sees must coincide with the time in the real world. This difference between simulation and emulation is notable as it relates to the performance analyses in this work and has implications on the results that are examined in this study.

3.1 Mininet

Mininet is a network emulator that employs virtual Ethernet pairs and processes in network namespace in Linux to allow lightweight, rapid prototyping of SDNs. Through its Python-based API, scripts can be written to construct custom topologies of switches and hosts. Network traffic from the hosts may then be controlled and monitored through API commands to analyze the correctness and performance of the network. The hosts in Mininet are simple shell processes that are given their own network namespace. These hosts are given a virtual network interface and are children to the main Mininet process. Software switches supporting OpenFlow are given their own virtual interfaces as well and forward packets through the virtualized topology based on instructions from SDN controllers. The SDN controllers may exist internally or externally to the process space in which Mininet is run. As long as the system on which Mininet is run has network layer connectivity, the network interfaces of the virtualized switches can be configured to communicate with the controller process, regardless of its location. The links between all of these components (hosts, switches, controllers) are virtual Ethernet pairs, or *veth* pairs, that act as a wired connection [15].

Mininet provides a network testbed similarly to simply creating collections of virtual machines (VM) and connecting them in a specific topology. However, without the overhead of entire computer systems (OS, memory, etc.), Mininet is able to achieve similar results with significantly fewer resources. Even with the lightweight features that Mininet utilizes, it still presents some limitations related to performance and resource usage. All components in a topology created by Mininet require their own process space. At small scale (hundreds of nodes or fewer), performance impacts are not necessarily incurred since the memory usage of the system is not fully exploited. However, at scales of thousands of nodes and more, performance can significantly degrade as

more resources are required to fully realize the underlying components of each node in the topology. A workaround is available in the form of CPU limited hosts that only use a specified percentage of the total process space. With greater numbers of nodes though, this design choice can impede the realism of the virtualized hosts. Additionally, the use of CPU limited hosts only addresses memory usage for the hosts. Limitations are not imposed on the virtualized switches and internal or remote controllers so these components will use as much process space as they would typically need. The emulated default connections in Mininet also present a performance fidelity issue as the *veth* pairs will not provide specific bandwidth limits or quality of service. For cases where additional characteristics need to be added to the links, TCLinks that employ the Linux traffic control (tc) program may be used. Even so, the main Mininet process is still obligated to operate under the Linux scheduler of the system on which it is run. In this way, the emulated nature of Mininet will not guarantee identical results as simulation would.

3.2 Flow Simulator fs

The flow simulator *fs* is a flow-level discrete event network simulator written in Python [20], which can be easily used on any system on which Python can run. Instead of operating on packets, it operates on the higher-level notion of a *flowlet* as its network abstraction. A network flow is the complete stream of packets traversing a given route for a specific connection between a sender and its recipient. A flowlet is a portion of this network flow volume emitted along a path over a given time interval. By raising the level of abstraction, the number of events processed within an *fs* simulation can be reduced compared to packet-based simulation as fewer events are required to model groups of packets than each individual packet. With fewer total events to process, the simulation in *fs* is typically able to complete in less time – but with less precision as well – than a comparable packet-based simulation. The requirements of a specific user will determine if the trade off between speed and granularity is appropriate. To inject representative network traffic into an *fs* simulation, different simulated traffic conditions can be generated and configured via a directed specification in a JSON format or using Graphviz DOT language [9]. Configuration specifications define the network topology and its characteristics as well as the network traffic generation from specific nodes in the defined topology.

3.2.1 fs-sdn

SDN capabilities have been introduced into the *fs* platform in an extended framework referred to as *fs-sdn*. This framework is capable of directly incorporating the POX OpenFlow controller libraries and API without modification. To accommodate the real-world time and network handling required by POX, *fs-sdn* introduces runtime modifications that allow the POX controller methods to handle the simulated time and network of *fs*. New node capabilities are added to model an OpenFlow switch and OpenFlow controller and bridge the *fs-sdn* and OpenFlow worlds. The controller node simulates the arrival of OpenFlow control messages from a switch via the connection class. The switch node translates the data types between *fs-sdn* and POX and understands the notion of MAC addresses and ARP. Because the underlying *fs* system works at the flow level rather than the individual packet level, interfaces between *fs* and POX have been employed to deconstruct flowlets into individual packets and vice versa.

Even though the controller components developed for the POX platform can be used directly in *fs-sdn*, it is not completely transparent for executing all POX controller modules. According to its latest public version on [19], some kinds of packet headers have not been translated, e.g. MPLS shim headers, Ethernet frames. Furthermore, *fs* was originally designed to operate at the network layer (IP), so it is incomplete for handling lower layer protocols [10].

3.3 SDN Emulation with ns-3 and Mininet

The network simulator ns-3 provides simulation/emulation frameworks for developing network topologies and analyzing their network characteristics. It is developed in C++, and its libraries may be accessed in the same way or through Python bindings. Both formal and informal attempts have been made to provide varying levels of SDN capability in ns-3. An `OpenFlowSwitchNetDevice` class was added to the ns-3 baseline in ns-3.11. The implementation of this class suffers from two main drawbacks. The OpenFlow specification that it supports is 0.8.9, an early, experimental version that is not intended for commercial use. Additionally, the interface of the `OpenFlowSwitchNetDevice` is designed with a built-in controller as an embedded component of the implementation. This design prevents examination of controller applications written for real-world libraries. It also hinders proper link testing between controllers and switches in terms of topology checking and traffic verification [11]. This section describes efforts to overcome some of the limitations of both Mininet and ns-3 by combining their capabilities into a single, emulation framework.

3.3.1 Link Modeling in ns-3

In addition to its default simulator, the network simulator ns-3 provides an implementation that regulates the event processing of a simulation such that its execution coincides with wallclock execution time. In this "real-time" mode, ns-3 can operate as a network emulator. While the designs are vastly different, this concept provides a similar functionality to Mininet. Additionally, ns-3 provides mechanisms for allowing the simulated topology in the ns-3 process to interact with real-world network components. One of these mechanisms is the `TAPBridge`. Using the `TAPBridge`, packets sent from a simulated node in ns-3 may be sent out of the simulation to a real-world recipient, and conversely, packets may be tunneled in through the `TAPBridge` and received within the simulation.

With the `TAPBridge` capability in hand, the GitHub project "Link modeling in ns-3" aims to construct links between the components in a Mininet topology based on channels provided by ns-3 [13]. This project provides a foundation for utilizing a broader variety of network connections in a Mininet topology. The initial implementation provided link models based on the ns-3 `SimpleChannel` and `CSMAChannel` and anticipated its usage with the ns-3 wireless capabilities as well. This project has been developed using Python bindings within ns-3 for streamlined compatibility with Mininet, and as such, simulation scripts utilizing this project must be written in Python.

3.3.2 OpenNet

OpenNet extends the link modeling efforts described in section 3.3.1 to develop a simulator for software-defined wireless local area networks (SDWLAN)[6]. Besides utilizing the ns-3 link capabilities in that project, OpenNet provides enhancements for wireless ns-3 simulations that allow link layer handover of wireless hosts between access points (AP) that support OpenFlow and channel scanning for handovers between APs operating on different channels. Most importantly for this study however, OpenNet conveniently packaged the efforts of the link modeling project with its modifications, providing a simple installation process.

4. SDN SIMULATION WITH NS-3 AND DCE

This section outlines an SDN simulation framework that is implemented and executed entirely within ns-3. OpenNet presents a performance bottleneck in terms of scalability due to its TAP device interface between Mininet and ns-3. Mininet suffers from scalability issues as well due to its heavy use of network and process resources. The SDN capability in baseline ns-3 exhibits its own set of issues as previously described in section 3.3. For these reasons, an SDN switch application currently supporting OpenFlow 1.0 has been designed to interface with the DCE module of ns-3 to allow real, deployable controller applications to be executed on an ns-3 simulated topology.

4.1 SDN Switch Application in ns-3

The design of the classes specific to providing SDN simulation capabilities in ns-3 primarily center on implementing an OpenFlow-enabled switch as a user-defined application. This application is installed on nodes in the simulated topology, allowing them to receive packets, perform a given set of actions based on the nature of these received packets, and then forward them appropriately. Furthermore, the switch is designed such that it can communicate with external, real-world controller libraries.

The SDN switch application is comprised of the `SdnPort`, `SdnFlowTable`, and `SdnSwitch` classes. `SdnPort` provides the formal definition of a binding port for the switch to send and receive data. The `SdnFlowTable` provides the structure and control for a table of flow rules for the switch to use on incoming packets. The `SdnSwitch` provides the actual application to act as a switch.

4.1.1 SdnPort Class

The `SdnPort` class is used as an enclosing class for switch-to-switch and host-to-switch connections. Each `SdnSwitch` object has an `SdnPort` for every non-controller connection. When an `SdnSwitch` needs to send out a packet, it searches for the relevant `SdnPort` and sends through its associated connection.

4.1.2 SdnFlowTable Class

The `SdnFlowTable` is responsible for all the flows a switch controls at any time. The primary focus for an `SdnFlowTable` is handling packets that the `SdnSwitch` receives. This function places all headers from any given packet into an `ofp_match` for flow comparison. If a match is successful, all of the associated actions will be executed on the packet. The `SdnFlowTable` also allows for adding, modifying, and deleting flow entries based on messages received from the controller. `SdnFlowTable` maintains its own table statistics as well. These statistics include table-wide wildcards, the maximum number of allowed flow entries, the current active number of flows, the number of lookups computed in the table, and the number of matches found.

4.1.3 SdnSwitch Class

The `SdnSwitch` object is the main implementing class for an SDN-enabled switch. It functions as an ns-3 application upon any node on which it is installed. The `SdnSwitch` object maintains a number of components: the connection it established with the controller, an `SdnFlowTable` that maintains the current flow rules to apply toward incoming packets, and a map of `SdnPort` objects to their associated non-controller connections. When an `SdnSwitch` object is initialized, it examines the types of channels to which it is connected. Point-to-point channels are designated as controller connections since header information is not parsed for matching between switches and controllers. For all other connections found, the `SdnSwitch` will establish an `SdnPort` to the connection and create an entry in the port map. The `SdnSwitch` objects receive data via callbacks from each given connection. Controller data gets processed at the application level. Other connections get processed at layer 2 such that packets can be retrieved with all of their headers still prepended. In this way, the appropriate information can be handed to the `SdnFlowTable`. The `SdnSwitch` application also has a list of supported capabilities and actions with which the switch can operate.

The `SdnSwitch` applications can handle a variety of messages sent from a controller. It handles all messages necessary for the OpenFlow handshake. It also accepts OFPT_FLOW_MOD requests to change the flow table by adding, modifying, and deleting flows. OFPT_STAT_REQUEST messages require the switch to respond with information about itself. OFPT_PACKET_OUT messages require a switch to send a packet directly out a certain port and handle any customized actions the controller specified for the packet.

When an `SdnSwitch` handles data from a non-controller source, it sends the packet to the `SdnFlowTable`, allowing it to handle the packet and return the output port from which the packet must be sent. As the packet was received at layer 2, it must also be sent from layer 2. If a port of OFPP_NONE is returned from the table, the packet was not handled and must be sent to the controller via an OFPT_PACKET_IN message to request the appropriate action.

4.2 Direct Code Execution

DCE provides the capability to execute userspace and kernelspace network protocols and applications directly within an ns-3 simulation. It is an additional module that can interact with the ns-3 baseline to test real-world network applications. These real-world applications are installed on specified nodes within the simulated topology using DCE. The applications themselves typically require no modifications, but they must be rebuilt such that they can act as dynamic binaries rather than static executables. This procedure simply requires that some additional configuration flags be added to the compile and link instructions. Once installed on a node, the applications can interact with the rest of the simulated network through either the ns-3 simulated network stack or the Linux kernel stack. DCE interacts with the installed binary similarly to how an actual operat-

Listing 1: Source code for installing POX controller on a node in ns-3 using DCE.

```
DceManagerHelper dceManager;
dceManager.Install(controllerNode);

DceApplicationHelper dce;
ApplicationContainer apps;

dce.SetStackSize(1<<20);

// Python controllers
dce.SetBinary("python2-dce");
dce.ResetArguments();
dce.ResetEnvironment();
dce.AddEnvironment("PATH",
        "/:/python2.7:/pox");
dce.AddEnvironment("PYTHONHOME",
        "/:/python2.7:/pox");
dce.AddEnvironment("PYTHONPATH",
        "/:/python2.7:/pox");
dce.AddArgument("-S");

// POX arguments
dce.AddArgument("pox/pox.py");
dce.AddArgument("--unthreaded-sh");
dce.AddArgument("log");
dce.AddArgument("--no-default");
dce.AddArgument("openflow.discovery");
dce.AddArgument("openflow.spanning_tree");
dce.AddArgument("forwarding.l2_learning");

apps.Add(dce.Install(controllerNode);
apps.Start(Seconds(0.0));
```

ing system would. It handles process, memory, and environment management of the DCE-enabled nodes within the simulation. It also manages its own version of *glibc*, which is intended to handle certain system calls within simulation, such as those relating to sockets and threading. Calls that DCE does not need to manage internally, such as `string.h` or `math.h` functions, can be handed to the system *glibc*. During the simulation, DCE maintains specific file space for each node running DCE-configured applications, treating each of these applications as their own processes within the simulated userspace. The file space holds all output generated by the application and may also be used to hold any runtime file dependencies [12].

DCE is typically used for network protocols or applications written in either C or C++ that would reside in self-contained executable binaries. Applications such as *ping*, *iperf*, *iproute*, etc., are some of the simpler examples that have been employed. The main implementation of the high-level programming language Python, CPython, is itself an executable binary, and as such, becomes a potential candidate for DCE utilization. CPython acts as an interpreter of Python code, taking a Python script and executing C equivalents of its source lines. By building the CPython source code such that DCE can interact with it, the resulting binary can be used as a Python interpreter on a node in the ns-3 simulation. The build process for the CPython pack-

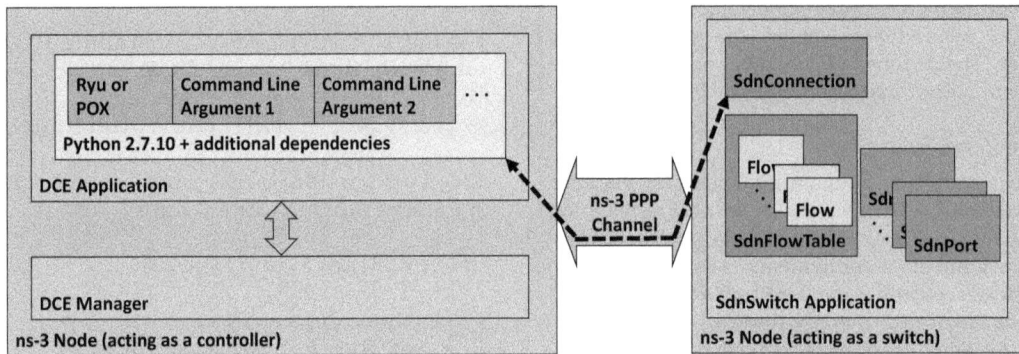

Figure 1: Structure and design of a DCE-enabled node acting as a controller and an SdnSwitch object. Communication occurs across the ns-3 point-to-point channel object. Packets are handled by the SdnSwitch through ns-3 simulated sockets maintained in the SdnConnection object. DCE handles packet coordination on the controller node.

age assembles most dependencies for Python scripts within either the Python executable or some of its shared libraries, making them readily accessible by DCE. Additional dependencies that are written as Python scripts themselves though are not readily accessible. This issue can be easily overcome by introducing the necessary files in the file space of the simulated node. With these considerations in place, it becomes possible to execute the POX controller and its applications within DCE.

4.3 Framework Integration

Using both ns-3 and DCE, the simulated switches would use the provided SdnSwitch class, and the simulated controllers would take DCE applications running POX. In this way, the controller applications examined would be directly portable to real network deployments. Setting up the entire framework utilizes the installation tool *bake* [4].

Figure 1 displays how a POX application on a DCE-enabled node would interact with the SdnSwitch object. The controller is managed by DCE. The DCE Manager maintains the simulated operating system space for the node and interacts within the node with the DCE Application. The installed application on this DCE Application is a locally built version of Python 2.7.10 with the appropriate library dependencies for POX. Python interprets the instructions of POX, executes the controller applications written for it, and communicates packets back and forth to the ns-3 point-to-point channel. Socket calls for packet transmission and reception by Python are translated to simulated socket calls for ns-3 by DCE. Listing 1 displays the code for configuring and installing POX on a DCE-enabled node. Python is set as the binary to execute, and environment variables are set to point the executed process to appropriate locations in the simulation filespace for Python scripts. The managing script for POX and specific applications then simply become arguments to be read by the Python binary. Notice that multiple arguments may be provided for interpretation by Python and POX.

5. EXPERIMENTS

Experiments have been performed on each of the emulation and simulation frameworks described in section 3.

These experiments and the topologies on which they have been executed are not identical across frameworks due to differences in design and supplied capabilities as well as various limitations that will be noted as necessary. Even so, the experiments have been designed in such a way to make them as similar in terms of topology, network configuration, and traffic generation as possible.

Traffic generation, although different nominally, has been configured to elicit similar host network traffic behavior across all frameworks. The intended behavior for each host is to send and receive 100 packets of 512 bytes each through a TCP connection. However, each framework has a different method for instantiating this behavior. For Mininet, and by extension OpenNet, traffic is generated with *iperf*. With *iperf*, hosts can act as either servers or clients based on the given configuration options. In the Mininet and OpenNet experiments, hosts are set to act as both through separate subprocess commands. As servers, the only additional configuration setting is the listening port. As clients, the subprocess command is set to send to a specific IP address and port a certain number (100) of packets of a given size (512B) through a TCP connection. For *fs-sdn*, hosts are assigned with an IP address, and packets can be transmitted between source and destination IP addresses/hosts. The Harpoon traffic generator is designed to generate application-independent IP-flow-level traffic that is statistically identical to traffic measured at a given point in the Internet. The total number of bytes for each flow, the total number of flows, and the packet size are defined by the Harpoon traffic generator. For the *ns-3-sdn* framework that can use the traffic generating applications of ns-3, the built-in OnOffApplication is used for traffic generation. This application can send to a specific IP address and port a maximum number of bytes (51200B) using a given packet length (512B). These packets can be configured to send through a TCP connection. By design, the OnOffApplication can be configured to generate traffic periodically rather than constantly. However, this capability is not used for these experiments. To confirm reception, the built-in PacketSink application can be configured to listen on the same port. Although each framework may use a different application for traffic generation, the intended behaviors of each application are similar enough that they can be configured to model nearly identical network traffic patterns. Traffic generators in Mininet and OpenNet are started sequentially in real time. Based on the design of *fs-sdn*, its traffic is started sequentially as well but only at a granularity of 1-second intervals within the simulated time. For the *ns-3-sdn* framework, traffic for each host is started with uniform randomness within a simulated time window similar to the time required for Mininet and OpenNet to start all of their applications.

5.1 Linear Network Topology

The linear network topology, as shown in figure 2, is designed as a linear network of switches. This single layer is comprised of a set of switches that connects to the hosts of the network. These access switches connect to each other as well as the controller. For this work, the number of host nodes connected to each switch is fixed at 16. The number of access switches is then varied as 10, 20, 30, 40, and 50. For traffic generation, each host will randomly select another access switch and then send its data to its corresponding host on that switch, i.e. host 2 on switch 0 might send to host 2 on switch 8.

A single POX controller is connected to each switch in the topology. This controller forwards traffic through layer 2 learning. In this way, the controller will direct switches individually to flood new traffic while recording the input port and source Ethernet address. If the switch later receives another packet destined for a previously recorded Ethernet address, it will forward the packet through the associated switch port.

Network connections are all wired links with the following characteristics:

- Host to Access Switch: 100Mbps, 1ms delay
- Access to Access Switch: 1Gbps, 1ms delay
- Controller to Access Switch: 1Gbps, 1ms delay

5.2 Campus Network Topology

The campus network topology examines a ring of simplified campus networks as shown in figure 3. Each campus network is simply a ring of switches that each connect to their own set of hosts. In this work, 8 switches in the ring are considered *access* switches, where each switch connects to a set of 4 hosts. An additional switch in the ring is considered a *gateway* switch that connects to a single *exchange* switch. The exchange switches then form a ring themselves to connect all of the campus networks. The number of campus networks is varied as 4, 8, 12, 16, and 20 rings, providing a simulation that examines a maximum of 861 total nodes in the topology (hosts, switches, and controllers). Each ring, including the exchange ring is controlled independently by a POX controller. These controllers execute link layer discovery to determine the part of the topology they control and a spanning tree application that prevents flooding loops from occurring. For forwarding traffic, the controllers employ layer 2 learning that will direct switches individually to flood new traffic and forward packets for destination MAC addresses for which the accompanying port has already been seen. For host traffic generation, each host will decide with equal probability whether to send data on its local ring or to a remote ring. Then, it will randomly select the switch and host to which it will send data.

Network connections are all wired links with the following characteristics:

- Host to Access Switch: 10Mbps, 1ms delay
- Access to Access Switch: 100Mbps, 1ms delay
- Access to Gateway Switch: 100Mbps, 1ms delay
- Access Switch to Controller: 1Gbps, 1ms delay
- Gateway to Exchange Switch: 1Gbps, 1ms delay
- Exchange to Exchange Switch: 1Gbps, 5ms delay
- Exchange Switch to Controller: 1Gbps, 5ms delay

Due to the design limitations of *fs-sdn*, a minor modification to the described topology has been conceded for its experiments. Since *fs-sdn* only operates at layer 3 and above, link layer discovery and spanning tree controller applications cannot adequately prevent flooding loops. To accommodate this limitation, one link from each ring in the network is deleted. In these simple ring topologies, this modification produces an effect similar to flooding loop prevention while maintaining roughly the same network behavior. The controller applications are all still allowed to execute as well to ensure as much network traffic is maintained as possible. For this specific topology, it is deemed adequate to administer this change for the experiments on *fs-sdn* while still comparing its results against the other emulators/simulators. However, it would not be appropriate for more complex topologies, such as any type of mesh network, as the network traffic would be more drastically modified by the topology change.

5.3 Data Center Network Topology

The data center network topology, as shown in figure 4, is designed as a simple *leaf-spine* architecture composed of two layers of switches. One layer, referred to as the access switches, forms the leaf switches and is conceived as a set of switches that connect to the hosts or servers of the data center. These access switches are also fully connected to the second layer, the spine of the network, which is composed of aggregate switches. As a simplification for the emulated/simulated systems, the aggregate switches connect to a single node, referred to as the "cloud" node. This "cloud" node models the gateway for the data center to either other data centers or the broader internet. For this work, the number of host/server nodes connected to each access layer switch is fixed at 8. The number of aggregate switches is set as 4, and the number of access switches is varied as 4, 8, 12, 16, and 20. For host traffic generation, each host will decide with equal probability whether to send data to the "cloud" or to a host on another switch. Then, if the host does not send to the "cloud" node, it will randomly select an access switch and send its data to its corresponding host on that switch similarly to the linear network experiments.

A single POX controller is connected to each switch in the topology. This controller executes link layer discovery to determine the topology and a spanning tree application that prevents flooding loops from occurring. For forwarding traffic, the controller employs layer 2 learning similar to the behavior described for the campus networks. However, switches are directed collectively such that new traffic will still be flooded but destination MAC addresses and their associated ports are learned by all switches. As described in the previous section, limitations in the design of *fs-sdn* prevent this simulator from adequately performing network

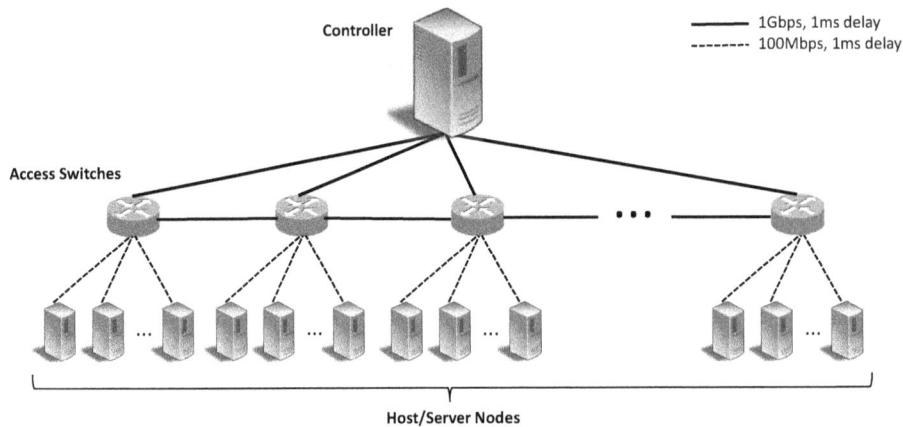

Figure 2: The linear network topology is a linear network of 10, 20, 30, 40, and 50 access layer switches. Connections between the switches have data rates of 1Gbps and 1ms delays. Each access layer switch is connected to 16 host nodes. Connections between the switches and the host nodes have a data rate of 100Mbps and a delay of 1ms. All switches connect to a single controller with 1Gbps channels with 1ms delays.

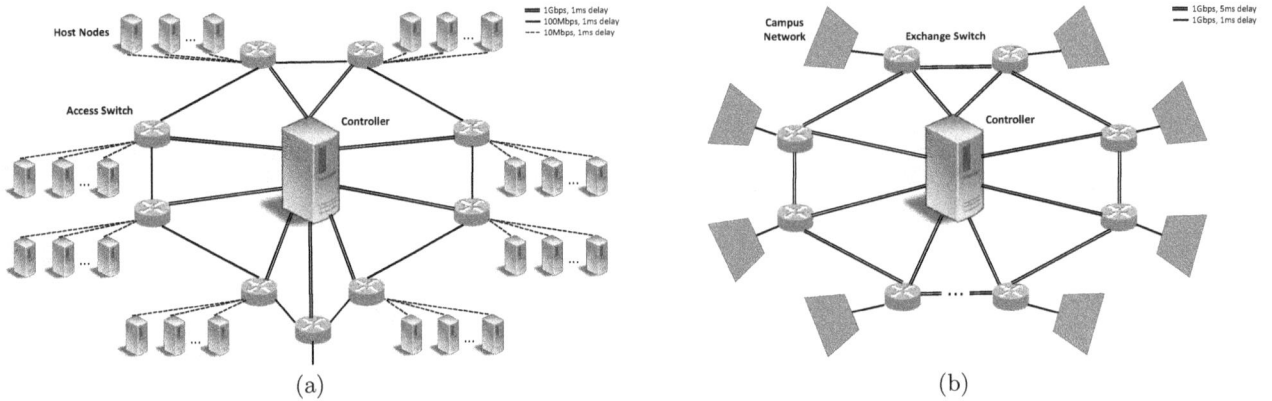

Figure 3: The campus network topology connects a ring of switches modeling a simplified campus network with identical rings, forming a ring of these smaller networks. Each campus network is composed of a ring of 8 access switches and a single gateway switch, where each access switch is connected to 4 hosts. Each gateway switch connects to an exchange switch which is connected to other exchange switches, forming a larger ring. Each set of switches connects to its own controller.

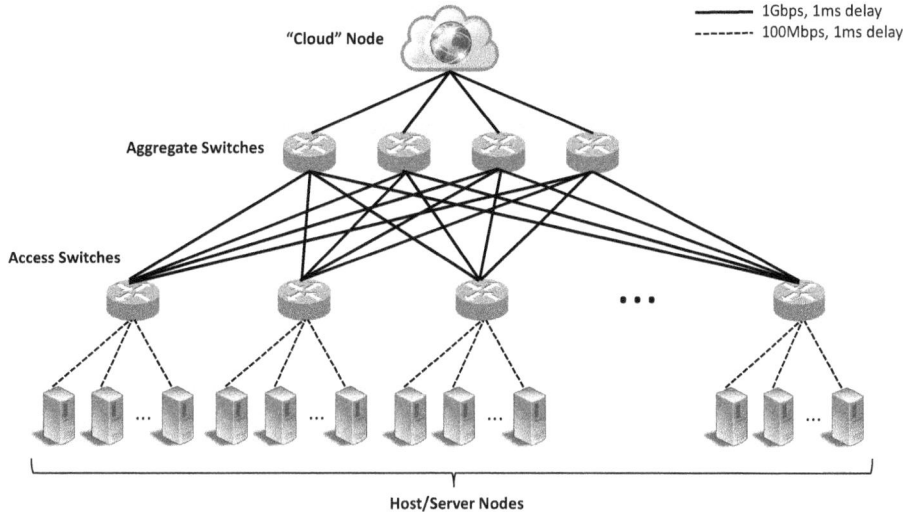

Figure 4: The data center network topology is a leaf-spine with 4 aggregate switches fully connected to 4, 8, 12, 16, or 20 access layer switches. Each access layer switch is then connected to 8 host/server nodes. The aggregate switches are each connected up to a single node, representing the "cloud." Connections between the cloud and the aggregate switches and the aggregate switches and the access layer switches have a data rate of 1Gbps and a delay of 1ms. Connections between the access layer switches and the host nodes have a data rate of 100Mbps and a delay of 1ms. Not shown: All switches connect to a single controller with 1Gbps channels with 1ms delays.

discovery and flooding loop prevention. Modifications to the actual topology would alter network traffic behaviors too significantly for a "fair" comparison, and as such, results are not gathered for the data center network topology using *fs-sdn*.

Network connections are all wired links with the following characteristics:

- Host/Server to Access Switch: 100Mbps, 1ms delay

- Access to Aggregate Switch: 1Gbps, 1ms delay

- Aggregate Switch to "Cloud": 1Gbps, 1ms delay

- Switches to Controller: 1Gbps, 1ms delay

6. RESULTS AND DISCUSSION

Experiments have been executed on an 8-core 3.6GHz Intel Xeon E5-1620 processor with 8GB of memory and running Ubuntu 14.04. Simulations are executed 10 times for each set of parameters to obtain the average total memory usage in MB and average wallclock execution time. Results for the linear, datacenter, and campus network topologies are shown in Figures 5, 6, and 7, respectively. As an additional consideration for the flow-based simulator *fs*, two definitions for the size of a flow are examined. For these experiments, a flow may model either 10 packets (denoted as "fs-sdn 10" in the figures) or 100 packets (denoted as "fs-sdn 100").

Gathering simulation/emulation completion times is a relatively simple task for gauging realtime performance. However, it is worth noting that these values across the simulation/emulation frameworks are divided further into times for topology and environment setup, traffic generation, and

cleanup. For the simulators *fs-sdn* and ns-3 with DCE, all stages of their simulations are accomplished intrinsically with most of the external resource overhead being handled when their processes are first instantiated. This situation significantly simplifies initialization and cleanup for these two simulators, reducing the time necessary for these tasks and leaving the majority of the process time to the pertinent part of the simulation, i.e. traffic generation and behavior modeling. For Mininet – and by extension, OpenNet – external resource overhead can be the main component of the network emulation at large enough scales. In this way, setup and cleanup for the topology requires much greater external allocation of resources and coordination between the operating system, the resources, and the main Mininet process itself. This inter- and intra-process coordination can impact the overall execution time for Mininet-based emulations.

Determining the resource utilization of each of the simulation/emulation tools varies based on the nature of the tool. Because *fs-sdn* and the ns-3 DCE framework are both simulators and handle all of their respective components internally, their memory usage can be considered the maximum usage achieved by the process under which they reside. For Mininet and OpenNet, it is not quite as simple. As emulators rather than simulators, these tools employ a number of components external to the process on which they reside. In this way, it becomes important to gather as many of these external components as possible. Each host, switch, and controller in Mininet requires its own user space, and their memory usages are best captured under the shell within which they reside. For each instantiation of traffic generation (*iperf*, *ping*, etc.), a process is spawned as well, and its information must be considered as part of the Mininet resource profile. Furthermore, for each controller required for a particular topology, its process data must be collected since it effectively participates in the emulation. For the largest campus network topology examined, 21 controller processes are examined as part of the Mininet and OpenNet emulations. Additionally, Mininet spawns *dhclient* processes to dynamically allocate IP addresses for all of the objects that it creates. However, OpenNet utilizes its ns-3 components for determining IP addresses so it does not require this extra process consideration.

For the simple linear switch topology, performance in terms of wallclock completion time does not differ too significantly for Mininet, *fs-sdn* with 10-packet flows, and the ns-3 DCE framework. However, the best performance is exhibited by *fs-sdn* with 100-packet flows. This result can be expected since the lower level of granularity at which *fs-sdn* is operating will cause fewer events to be created for processing. Furthermore, the flow granularity can be assumed to be at least part of the reason for the resource hierarchy between 100-packet flow *fs-sdn*, 10-packet flow *fs-sdn*, and the ns-3 DCE framework displayed in Figure 5(b).

For the campus network topology, shown in Figure 6, 100-packet flow *fs-sdn* again outperforms the other systems in terms of execution time and memory usage. However, 10-packet flow *fs-sdn* does not perform as well as Mininet or the ns-3 DCE framework. Resource usage in both Mininet and OpenNet demonstrate the overhead required by these two systems as they create greater numbers of *veth* pairs and occupy more process space with additional hosts. Again, at higher scales, the ns-3 DCE framework produces better performance times than Mininet and 10-packet flow *fs-sdn*, but scaling in terms of resource usage looks to become an increasing issue. However, the memory requirements for the ns-3 DCE framework remain significantly lower than those of Mininet and OpenNet, and at less than 1.5GB, remain in the comfortable realm of possibility for current computer systems.

The datacenter network topology indirectly displays the design limitations of *fs-sdn* while presenting a case where the ns-3 DCE framework can again outperform Mininet and OpenNet in terms of realtime performance and memory usage. The datacenter itself is a more complex topology than the previous two, but its scaling is not tested quite as heavily. The ns-3 DCE framework continues to outperform Mininet in terms of time and memory. Packet loss for OpenNet, while not achieving 100%, is still non-zero and increasing with the topology size. This particular result helps to illustrate how TAP bridge resource capacity is approached with greater topology sizes. For OpenNet, the resource usage for the datacenter topology actually begins to decrease for topologies with more than 12 access layer switches. This result suggests that as OpenNet nears the limits for TAP bridge allocation it uses less memory since fewer connections are successful. With fewer connections, the controller will not store as much network information and will not install as many flow rules, requiring less memory.

7. RELATED WORK

Besides the libraries studied in this work, two other network simulators have been identified that provide varying levels of SDN simulation capabilities. Efforts in the discrete event simulator OMNeT++ provided OpenFlow components based on OpenFlow version 1.0.0. These components were built using the INET framework. Successful implementation was demonstrated through an evaluation of

mean round trip time for the simulation of the OpenFlow-enabled Open Science, Scholarship, and Services Exchange (OS3E) infrastructure topology. However, the project designed its own controller rather than allowing for the use of external controller libraries such as POX[14]. This design would have made it difficult to compare with the frameworks examined in this work. The Estinet simulator/emulator, a commercial product based on the network simulator NC-TUns, provides one of the more well-rounded options for SDN simulation in that network traffic and topologies may be configured either textually or through a GUI. The Estinet design employs a mechanism for reentering the kernel. This process allows it to support the simulation of NOX, POX, and Floodlight controller applications with complete portability [21]. However, as proprietary software, it is difficult to accommodate for a complete performance analysis as the source code is not distributed with the product. This issue prevents a proper examination of the complete implementation of the Estinet design.

This work specifically analyzes simulation/emulation frameworks that can be executed on a single machine. However, other frameworks have been designed to allow simulations to be executed in a distributed environment to accommodate additional topology and traffic scale. Mininet CE allows Mininet networks on different machines to be run collectively as a single emulation [3]. The Distributed Open-Flow Testbed (DOT) emulates a network across multiple computer systems [18]. Differing from the clustered design of Mininet CE, DOT designates one computer system as a DOT Manager that controls the other involved systems, referred to as DOT Nodes. Otherwise, DOT implements its emulations similarly to Mininet with *veth* pairs. Furthermore, ns-3 provides distributed simulator capabilities based on MPI that can allow the discussed DCE framework to simulate topologies and network traffic at greater scales as well. This kind of effort would further demonstrate the capabilities of the framework while providing additional performance analysis.

In addition to the POX controller library, more software is available for designing applications for SDN controllers. Because of the emulated nature of Mininet and OpenNet, applications for other controllers written in any programming language can be readily examined with these tools. Further work within *fs* has provided a capability to debug controller applications for any controller library. This debugger specifically targets POX but can be extended to accommodate other controllers using a GDB wrapper [7]. Because the ns-3 DCE framework allows execution of Python scripts, such as POX, to be handled by DCE, other Python-based programs can be accommodated as well. The Ryu controller is one such Python-based controller library. It employs a different event-handling design from POX and supports OpenFlow versions from 1.0 up to 1.5[2]. It has been included for use in the ns-3 DCE framework in addition to POX. However, this study focused on POX, and as such, analysis of Ryu is saved for future work.

8. CONCLUSIONS AND FUTURE WORK

This work has introduced an SDN simulation framework based on ns-3 and DCE and compared it against other existing SDN simulation/emulation tools. For three different topologies, the presented framework provides comparable or better runtime performance than the Mininet testbed while

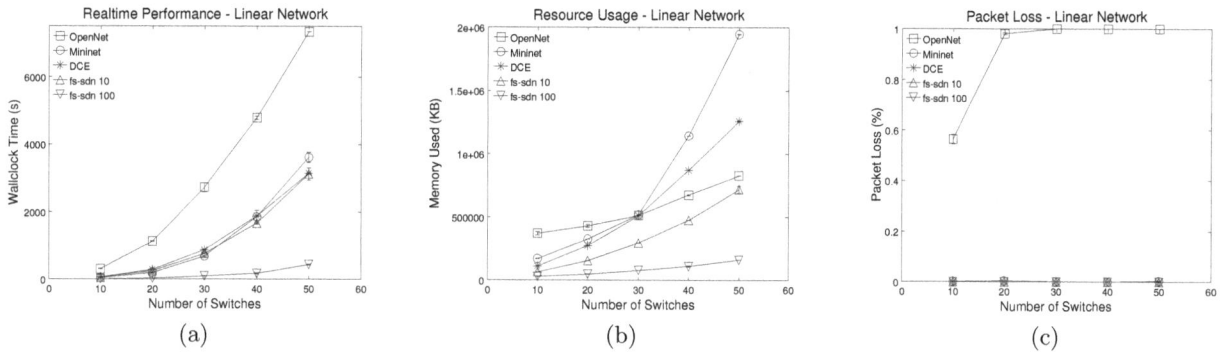

Figure 5: Linear network topology results for (a) realtime performance in seconds, (b) resource usage in MB, and (c) packet loss percentage. The topology is a linear set of switches that each connect to a set of 16 hosts per switch. A single controller manages and maintains layer 2 learning forwarding rules for the switches. Standard error bars are displayed for each data point and noted as negligible except for the Mininet points in (a).

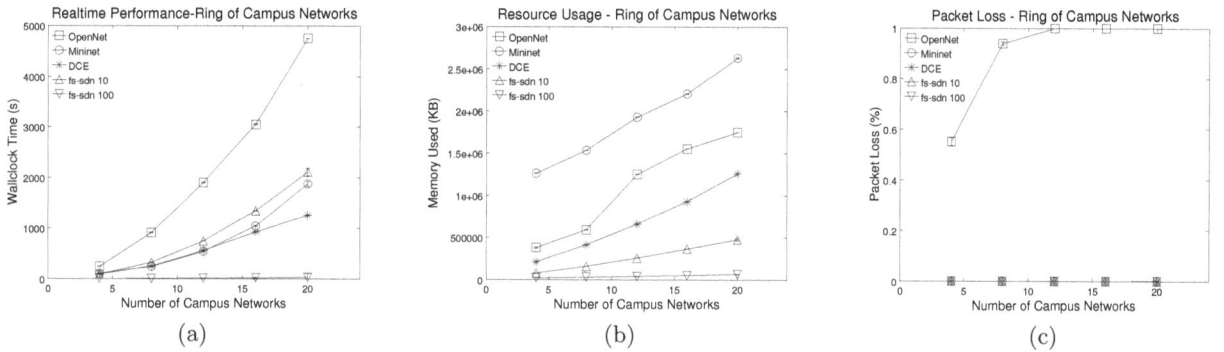

Figure 6: Campus network topology results for (a) realtime performance in seconds, (b) resource usage in MB, and (c) packet loss percentage. Each campus network is a ring with one switch connecting to the gateway ring of switches and 8 access switches that each connect to a set of 4 hosts per switch. Each campus network as well as the gateway ring has its own controller that manages layer 2 discovery and spanning tree of its own topology as well as layer 2 learning forwarding rules for its switches. Standard error bars are displayed for each data point and noted as negligible.

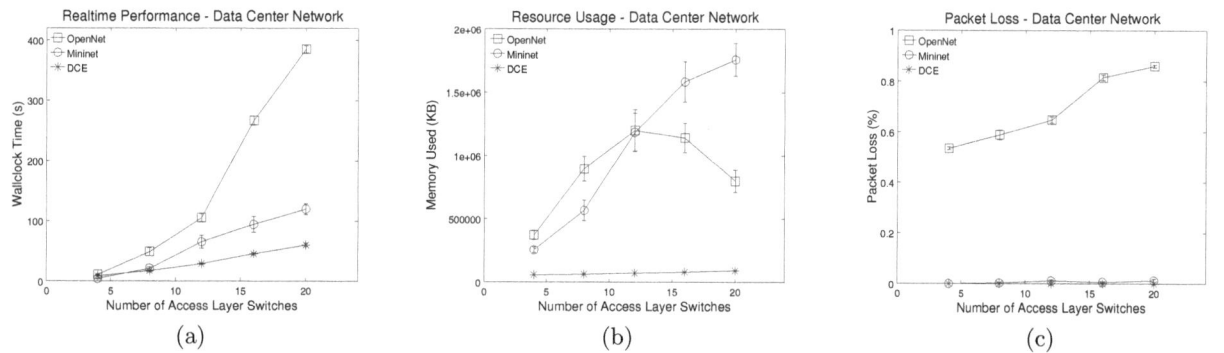

Figure 7: Datacenter network topology results for (a) realtime performance in seconds, (b) resource usage in MB, and (c) packet loss percentage. The datacenter is a leaf-spine architecture with 4 aggregate switches fully connected to the access layer. Each access layer switch connects to a set of 8 hosts per switch. A single controller manages layer 2 discovery and spanning tree of the topology as well as layer 2 learning forwarding rules for the switches. Standard error bars are displayed for each data point and noted as negligible except for Mininet points in (a) and OpenNet and Mininet points in (b).

163

exhibiting either lower or comparable memory requirements. The flow-based simulator *fs-sdn* has been shown to exhibit the best performance across all topologies that it can support. However, achieving this performance requires properly setting the number of packets that constitute a flow. Furthermore, the design of *fs-sdn* currently prevents it from supporting certain topology complexity that Mininet, OpenNet, and the ns-3 DCE framework are capable of supporting.

Further testing of the presented framework will involve examining it under the parallel simulator of ns-3 to expand its scalability and comparing it against other distributed SDN simulation/emulation options. Additionally, next steps for this initial framework include supporting OpenFlow 1.3 features for the `SdnSwitch` application in a more extensible manner than the baseline ns-3 `OpenFlowNetDevice`. With its use of Python as a binary within the DCE module, this work may also be considered a proof of concept and a foundation for studying the possibility of integrating the Java Runtime Environment with the described framework to examine Java-based SDN controllers, such as Floodlight and OpenDaylight.

9. REFERENCES

[1] About POX | noxrepo. Website, 2015. http://www.noxrepo.org/pox/about-pox/.

[2] Ryu resources. Website, 2015. http://osrg.github.io/ryu/resources.html\#documentation.

[3] V. Antonenko and R. Smelyanskiy. Global network modelling based on mininet approach. In *Proceedings of the Second ACM SIGCOMM Workshop on Hot Topics in Software Defined Networking*, HotSDN '13, pages 145–146, New York, NY, USA, 2013. ACM.

[4] D. Camara. Bake: Main page view. Website, 2015. http://planete.inria.fr/software/bake/index.html.

[5] M. Casado, M. J. Freedman, J. Pettit, J. Luo, N. McKeown, and S. Shenker. Ethane: Taking control of the enterprise. *SIGCOMM Comput. Commun. Rev.*, 37(4):1–12, Aug. 2007.

[6] M. Chan, C. Chen, J. Huang, T. Kuo, L. Yen, and C. Tseng. Opennet: A simulator for software-defined wireless local area network. In *Wireless Communications and Networking Conference (WCNC), 2014 IEEE*, pages 3332–3336, April 2014.

[7] R. Durairajan, J. Sommers, and P. Barford. Controller-agnostic SDN debugging. In *Proceedings of the 10th ACM International on Conference on Emerging Networking Experiments and Technologies*, CoNEXT '14, pages 227–234, New York, NY, USA, 2014. ACM.

[8] O. N. Foundation. Technical library - open networking foundation. Website, 2015. https://www.opennetworking.org/sdn-resources/technical-library.

[9] E. Gansner, E. Koutsofois, and S. North. Drawing graphs with dot. Website, 2006. http://www.graphviz.org/Documentation/dotguide.pdf.

[10] M. Gupta, J. Sommers, and P. Barford. Fast, accurate simulation for SDN prototyping. In *Proceedings of the Second ACM SIGCOMM Workshop on Hot Topics in Software Defined Networking*, HotSDN '13, pages 31–36, New York, NY, USA, 2013. ACM.

[11] B. Hurd. Openflow switch support – model library. Website, 2011. https://www.nsnam.org/docs/models/html/openflow-switch.html.

[12] Inria. Direct code execution (DCE) manual. Website, 2013. https://www.nsnam.org/docs/dce/release/1.5/manual/html/index.html.

[13] P. Jurkiewicz. Link modeling using ns-3. Website, 2013. https://github.com/mininet/mininet/wiki/Link-modeling-using-ns-3.

[14] D. Klein and M. Jarschel. An openflow extension for the OMNeT++ INET framework. In *Proceedings of the 6th International ICST Conference on Simulation Tools and Techniques*, SimuTools '13, pages 322–329, ICST, Brussels, Belgium, Belgium, 2013. ICST (Institute for Computer Sciences, Social-Informatics and Telecommunications Engineering).

[15] B. Lantz, B. Heller, and N. McKeown. A network in a laptop: Rapid prototyping for software-defined networks. In *Proceedings of the 9th ACM SIGCOMM Workshop on Hot Topics in Networks*, Hotnets-IX, pages 19:1–19:6, New York, NY, USA, 2010. ACM.

[16] N. McKeown, T. Anderson, H. Balakrishnan, G. Parulkar, L. Peterson, J. Rexford, S. Shenker, and J. Turner. Openflow: Enabling innovation in campus networks. *SIGCOMM Comput. Commun. Rev.*, 38(2):69–74, Mar. 2008.

[17] B. Pfaff, B. Heller, D. Talayco, D. Erickson, G. Gibb, G. Appenzeller, J. Tourrilhes, J. Pettit, K. Yap, M. Casado, M. Kobayashi, N. McKeown, P. Balland, R. Price, R. Sherwood, and Y. Yiakoumis. Openflow switch specification, version 1.0.0 (wire protocol 0x01). Website, 2009. https://www.opennetworking.org/images/stories/downloads/sdn-resources/onf-specifications/openflow/openflow-spec-v1.0.0.pdf.

[18] A. Roy, M. Bari, M. Zhani, R. Ahmed, and R. Boutaba. Design and management of dot: A distributed openflow testbed. In *Network Operations and Management Symposium (NOMS), 2014 IEEE*, pages 1–9, May 2014.

[19] J. Sommers. The fs flow record generator / network simulator. Website, 2014. https://github.com/jsommers/fs.

[20] J. Sommers, R. Bowden, B. Eriksson, P. Barford, M. Roughan, and N. Duffield. Efficient network-wide flow record generation. In *INFOCOM, 2011 Proceedings IEEE*, pages 2363–2371, April 2011.

[21] S. Wang, C. Chou, and C. Yang. Estinet openflow network simulator and emulator. *Communications Magazine, IEEE*, 51(9):110–117, September 2013.

Some Properties of Events Executed in Discrete-Event Simulation Models

Philip A. Wilsey
Dept of EECS, PO Box 210030
University of Cincinnati
Cincinnati, OH 45221–0030
wilseypa@gmail.com

ABSTRACT

The field of computer architecture uses quantitative methods to drive the computer system design process. By quantitatively profiling the run time characteristics of computer programs, the principal processing needs of commonly used programs became well understood and computer architects can focus their design solutions toward those needs. The DESMetrics project is established to follow this quantitative model by profiling the execution of Discrete Event Simulation (DES) models in order to focus optimization efforts within DES execution frameworks (and especially parallel DES engines). In particular, the DESMetrics project is designed to capture the run time characteristics of event execution in DES models. Because DES models tend to have fine grained computational processing requirements, the DESMetrics project focuses on the event dependencies and their exchange between the objects in the simulation. For now, we assume that optimization of the actual event processing is well served by conventional compiler and architecture solutions. Although, as will become clear later in Section 6, the possibility of identifying scheduling blocks of events that could potentially be schedule together can be achieved — at least within a single simulation object.

CCS Concepts

•Computing methodologies → Modeling and simulation; Discrete-event simulation; *Simulation tools;*

Keywords

Discrete event simulation; Profiling simulation models; Parallel discrete event simulation

1. INTRODUCTION

The field of computer architecture has been dramatically impacted by the use of quantitative methods to drive the computer system design process [12]. By quantitatively profiling the run time characteristics of computer programs, the principal processing needs of commonly used programs became well understood and

Permission to make digital or hard copies of all or part of this work for personal or classroom use is granted without fee provided that copies are not made or distributed for profit or commercial advantage and that copies bear this notice and the full citation on the first page. Copyrights for components of this work owned by others than ACM must be honored. Abstracting with credit is permitted. To copy otherwise, or republish, to post on servers or to redistribute to lists, requires prior specific permission and/or a fee. Request permissions from permissions@acm.org.

SIGSIM-PADS '16, May 15-18, 2016, Banff, AB, Canada

© 2016 ACM. ISBN 978-1-4503-3742-7/16/05. . . $15.00

DOI: http://dx.doi.org/10.1145/2901378.2901400

computer architects can focus their design solutions toward those needs. This has resulted in the widespread availability of high performance computing in the commodity processor and optimizing compiler markets.

This paper introduces a project to collect quantitative data from Discrete Event Simulation (DES) models in order to better understand their (primarily) computational needs. The primary motivation for this work is to better understand the properties of discrete event simulation models in order to pursue a more focused effort to build high-performance Time Warp [13, 11] synchronized parallel simulation engines. The project, called *DESMetrics*, follows the quantitative methods used by the architecture community. In particular, we instrument discrete event simulation engines to record (to a file) information on the events processed. This file is then analyzed to produce `csv` files that can be analyzed and displayed. Because DES models tend to have fine grained computational processing requirements, the DESMetrics project focuses on the event dependencies and their exchange between the objects in the simulation. For now, we assume that optimization of the actual event processing is well served by conventional compiler and architecture solutions.

In this paper, we present the processes and tools used in the DESMetrics project to collect and display this information. Furthermore, the event properties from several discrete event simulation models are captured and reported. In particular, two different discrete event simulation engines are instrumented and data collected. Two simulators are used in order to capture data from simulation models written by different authors and processed by different simulators. The purpose is not to compare the different simulators or to establish performance comparisons between the simulators. Instead the goal is to capture properties of various different simulation models in order to extract common properties from the simulation models that could serve to direct a focused optimization effort for some simulation engine. The chief contribution in this manuscript is to outline a general framework for data capture, analysis, and visualization and to demonstrate that different simulation models do in fact have common characteristics that can aid in optimization studies.

The DESMetrics project focuses strictly on the relations between events and the processes that process these events. By limiting the focus in this way, we have found it fairly easy to instrument a discrete event simulation engine to capture this data. Using this data, a variety of different analysis steps can be pursued. Of particular focus in this paper is: (i) the potential parallelism available, (ii) the number of LPs that each LP receives events from, (iii) the uniformity of events processed by the different objects of the simulation, and, (iv) the length of events in input queues that can be scheduled for execution from a fixed time point. This latter measure is called an *event chain* and will be described more formally in Section 6.3.

The remainder of this paper is organized as follows. Section 2 presents some background information. Section 3 reviews some previous work related to this paper. Section 4 gives a high level overview of the DESMetrics process and tools. Section 5 presents the simulation kernels and simulation models studied and reported herein. Section 6 presents the quantitative data captured from these simulation models. Readers are cautioned that several of the graphs in this section have significant data points and may take a minute or two to render, even on a higher performing desktop platform. While it is possible to reduce the resolution of these graphs for faster rendering, preserving the detail permits the interested reader to zoom in and observe the detailed results. As a result, we have preserved the detail. Finally, Section 7 contains some concluding remarks.

2. BACKGROUND & MOTIVATION

Capturing and understanding the properties of DES models can aid researchers in a variety of ways. The obvious aid is in providing guidance to areas to focus on performance improvement in simulation kernels (parallel and otherwise). To a certain extent, the focus of kernel optimization can be (and has been) by profiling the simulation kernel with tools like `valgrind`. However, that will only inform the developer of bottlenecks in an existing code base. Using results from the quantitative properties of the application domain directs the optimization focus on algorithm development for the key model specific properties and not (solely) toward improving the implementation of the algorithm.

A second area where a deeper understanding of the properties of DES models is in synthetic workload generation. A substantial amount of work has been directed at generating synthetic simulation models to exercise parallel simulation kernels [2, 7, 9, 18]. These synthetic models are commonly used by the research community to evaluate and report performance results. However, the utility of the specific configurations used to derive these synthetic workload generators is often not well established. Using profile data from actual models could dramatically improve confidence in the models generated for synthetic testing.

Related to algorithm optimization, simulation model profile data can sometimes be used to enable model setup and configuration for more optimal simulation. In fact, the trace data used from the WARPED2 simulation kernel [21] and used in this study is actually captured by translating information already captured by the kernel to perform LP partitioning [1].

Finally, the use of profile data could potentially be used to aid in the validation and verification of a simulation model (at a very coarse level). For example, simulation models with a scale-free network should have a specific communication profile between the objects of the simulation. Visualizations of the event connectivity between LPs could help confirm that the network does indeed follow the shape of communication expected.

3. RELATED WORK

Some of the earliest work analyzing the properties of discrete event simulation address, for example, the amount of parallelism available or the lookahead possible in simulation models. Early studies to perform *critical path analysis* [4, 14, 17, 15] are an at-

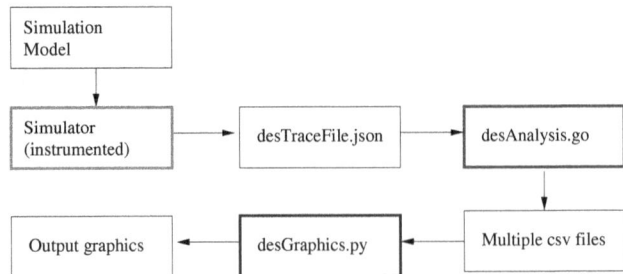

Figure 1: The DESMetrics Tool Flow

tempt to locate the shortest path through the collection of events in a discrete event simulation model. Two of these studies develop various algorithms that can be embedded in sequential simulators to locate the critical path [17, 15]. These studies can be used to show the fastest path to completion through the event pool of a simulation. Another common property of discrete event simulation analysis is to evaluate the lookahead available in simulation models [10]. Lookahead plays an important role in determining if a simulation model is suitable for parallelization using conservative synchronization techniques. This work extends those efforts by studying multiple properties of discrete event simulation models and working to understand how these properties could potentially be exploited to improve the performance of discrete event simulation engines — parallel and sequential.

4. THE DESMETRICS PROCESS

The approach in the DESMetrics project is to capture event information from existing simulation models by instrumenting DES simulators to capture said information. The captured information is then analyzed to produce summary data files that can then be visually displayed for inspection. This process is visualized in the graphic of Figure 1. Currently we have instrumented two different simulators (ROSS [5] and WARPED2 [21]) to capture the event information (only the sequential versions of both kernels can be used for this capture). These simulators are depicted by the red box in Figure 1. Analysis on the captured event data is performed by a `go` program named `desAnalysis.go` and depicted by the light blue box in Figure 1. This analysis produces a number of `csv` files containing the analysis results. Finally, a set of graphs are produced by a python/matplotlib program named `desGraphics.py` and depicted by the dark blue box in Figure 1. The next three subsections describe each of the main processing steps in the DESMetrics project.

4.1 Recording the Event Data

Event data is captured by instrumenting existing simulators to produce an event trace file. The capture process assumes that each simulator maintains a simulation time value and that the simulation is organized such that events are processed and exchanged by named simulation objects. The naming of the simulation objects is not critical and the names can be anonymously generated, however to facilitate analysis, the tools assume that events are exchanged by simulation objects and that the names are unique to the simulation objects in the simulation model. In the remainder of this paper we will use the term Logical Process or LP (from parallel simulation [8]) to denote a simulation object that processes and exchanges events.

```
1  {
2  "simulator_name" : "name of the simulator",
3
4  "model_name" : "name of the simulation model",
5
6  "capture_date" : "date/time that the profile data
       was captured",
7
8  // optional, but desirable; include if possible
9  "command_line_arguments" : "significant command
       line arguments",
10
11 // optional, include as needed
12 "configuration_information" : "anything
       significant",
13
14 "events" : [
15   ["source object",  send_time, "destination
        object", receive_time ],
16   //  "....forall events processed...."
17   ]
18 }
```

Figure 2: Format of JSON file holding simulation model trace data

The event information is captured in a `json` file format. Since even small simulation runs can easily produce gigabytes of event data, the `json` file format is somewhat more compact than might be expected. However, experience with more verbose formats resulted in file sizes that were quite difficult to process and therefore this compacted form is now used. The general format for captured data is (with non-json compliant comments added) shown in Figure 2. The fields of this format are defined as: the `send_time` is the simulation time when the event was generated and `receive_time` is the simulation time when the event is to be executed; the `source object` and `destination object` are the names of the LPs that, respectively, generate and process the event. Note that events sent by an object to itself are, if available, recorded as well as events exchanged between objects. Additional information on the event payload is not necessary and not captured.

4.2 The Analysis Phase

The analysis phase is performed by the `desAnalysis.go` program. This program takes considerable time (for example analyzing a 5GB file can take 10-15 hours on an 4-core/8-thread i7 x86 processor). It has been parallelized to optimize run time performance on multi-core processors. The analysis phase creates a collection of `csv` files that are then read by the tools in the visualization phase to produce plots (`pdf` or `eps`) for viewing.

The analyses performed in this phase are organized into the following classes:

Events Available for Execution: assuming unit time execution of each event, how many events are available at any given time for execution? This analysis attempts to compute a *conservative* estimate of how much potential parallelism exists among the events and as such, optimistic execution could easily uncover. The specific algorithm to compute events available is given in Section 6.1.

Events Executed by LP: how many events does each LP execute? Are the events self-generated (called *local* events) or remotely generated from some other LP (called *remote* events)?

Event Chains: are chains/blocks of events that could potentially be executed as a group from a fixed simulation time. That is, at a specific simulation time, how many events stored at that time would be available for immediate execution without the LP receiving any additional information? The algorithm computes the number of chains of various lengths. The details of this computation are given in Section 6.3.

Event Exchanges between LPs: for each LP, from how many different LPs does it receive events for execution? This analysis attempts to illustrate the degree of connectivity of events exchanged by the LPs in the simulation.

Lookahead data: for each LP, the analysis captures the delta of the send and receive timestamp of events exchanged between two LPs. The minimum, maximum, and average of this delta is captured. This data is captured separate for local and remote events as the lookahead information is critical only for event information exchanged between LPs on different compute nodes.

A detailed description of the analysis for above classes is described in the subsections of the results section (Section 6) below.

4.3 Visualizing the Analysis Results

The visualization phase is performed by the `desGraphics.py` program. This is a python program that uses `matplotlib` and `pylab` to produce `pdf` or `eps` files for visualization of the results.

5. SIMULATION MODELS STUDIED

The two simulators studied are ROSS [5] and WARPED2 [21]. A fork of the instrumented ROSS code base is available in the git repository https://github.com/wilseypa/ROSS. The WARPED2 code base (available at https://github.com/wilseypa/warped2) already captures the necessary event traces so only a short translation script is needed to convert the data into the desired format (available in the desMetrics code base). All of the tools for the DESMetrics project are release with open source licensing and available from the git repository https://github.com/wilseypa/desMetrics. The data files are available but their size (several GB each) prevent their online distribution.

In this paper, we report results from 4 simulation models, two from ROSS and two from WARPED2. All of the simulation models studied were taken from the standard code base of these tools. No modifications were made to the simulation models. The models used are:

traffic: a 2-d model of automobile traffic simulation model (ROSS).

pcs: wireless network model(s). The PCS model from ROSS is described in [6] and the PCS model from WARPED2 is based on the model described in [16]. The ROSS model uses a exponential distribution for event distribution; the WARPED2 model uses a Poisson distribution.

epidemic: an disease propagation model in WARPED2 derived from [3, 19].

167

In general the default configuration parameters for these models were used. However, in all cases, a shorter simulation time than the default (if one existed) was required. The command line used to capture these instrumented data for each simulation models is:

ROSS:
```
./pcs --synch=1 --end=10000
./Intersection --synch=1 --end=25
```

WARPED2:
```
./pcs_sim --statistics-type csv
  --statistics-file desMetrics.csv
  --max-sim-time 500
./epidemic_sim --statistics-type csv
  --statistics-file desMetrics.csv
  --max-sim-time 1000000
```

Algorithm 1: Compute the number of events available at each simulation cycle.

Input : LP[] array of all LPs, **where** LP[i].event_queue denotes the queue of events destined for LP[i]

Output: events_available[], counts of events available at each simulation cycle i

begin
  total_schedule_cycles ← 0
  forall the *i in 1:N* **do**
    events_available[i] ← 0
  end

  while *(at least one LP[i].event_queue.empty() != NULL)* **do**
    Set schedule_time to the lowest receive_time in the LP array.
    schedule_time ← minimum(LP[i].event_queue.front().receive_time)
    Count the number of LPs with events that were sent before schedule_time
    for *each i such that (LP[i].event_queue.front().send_time < schedule_time)* **do**
      events_available[schedule_time]++
      LP[i].event_queue.pop()
    end

    total_schedule_cycles++
  end

  for *i in range (1:schedule_time)* **do**
    plot i,events_available[i]
  end
end

---

6. RESULTS

The results are presented in five separate subsections. The first discusses results from the "*events available for execution*" portion of the analysis phase. This analysis orders the events by receiving LP and performs a simulated walk through an execution of the

events. The second subsection discusses the nature of *events executed by the LPs* in the running simulation. The primary objectives here are to show how many events are executed by the LPs and to classify events that are generated locally (by the executing LP) or remotely (by some other LP). Note that not all simulators will have locally generated events (*e.g.*, MiniSSF [20]), but in this study, both kernels do have local events. The third subsection studies *event chains*. Event chains are blocks of events in the pending event set that can potentially be scheduled as a block chain of events. Such chains are important to a parallel simulation engine on an SMP platform. More specifically if block chains of lengths greater than 1 are commonly present in simulation models, then a block scheduling of events can help reduce contention for the shared data structures maintaining the pending event set. The fourth subsection contains a review of our findings on the number of LPs that each LP receives remote events from. Finally, the fifth subsection contains a brief review of results regarding lookahead results.

6.1 Events Available for Execution

The computation of events available is developed to better understand the maximum potential parallelism in the simulation that guarantees safe execution of all events. The computation basically runs a simulated event execution engine to evaluate the number of events available at every simulation cycle (for simplicity, we assume that events available for execution are simulated instantaneously). While this sets an upper bound for parallelism in conservatively synchronized parallel simulation, it does not necessary find all of the parallelism that might be uncovered in an optimistically synchronized parallel simulation. The remainder of this section is subdivided into two parts. The first part presents the algorithm used to compute events available. The second part presents the principal findings with the simulation models studied.

Computing Events Available for Execution

The computation of events available performs a conservative estimate of what LPs have events that can be guaranteed to be safe for parallel execution. Essentially the computation orders the LP event queues by their `receive_time` and moves to the first event at each LP, called the *head event*. The head event with the lowest timestamp defines the *evaluation time*. The algorithm then counts as available every LP whose head event has a `send_time` before the evaluation time and a `receive_time` at or after the evaluation time. The head event for all counted LPs is advanced to the next event and the process is repeated until no more events exist in the set of LPs. For each LP report the number of local events executed and the total (local plus remote) number of events executed. The pseudo code of the algorithm used do perform this analysis is given in Algorithm 1.

The events available data computed by Algorithm 1 has several more steps and records several other data points of interest. At completion of this analysis phase, the results are dumped into several `csv` files that can then be processed for visualization or other analysis steps.

Results from Events Available Study

The plots in Figure 3 show the number of events available by simulation cycle. The label on the top of the graph shows the total number of LPs in the simulation, the bottom x-axis shows the number of simulated simulation cycles and their total. The left y-axis shows the raw number of events available at each simulation cycle

ROSS Traffic Model

ROSS PCS Model

WARPED2 Epidemic Model

WARPED2 PCS Model

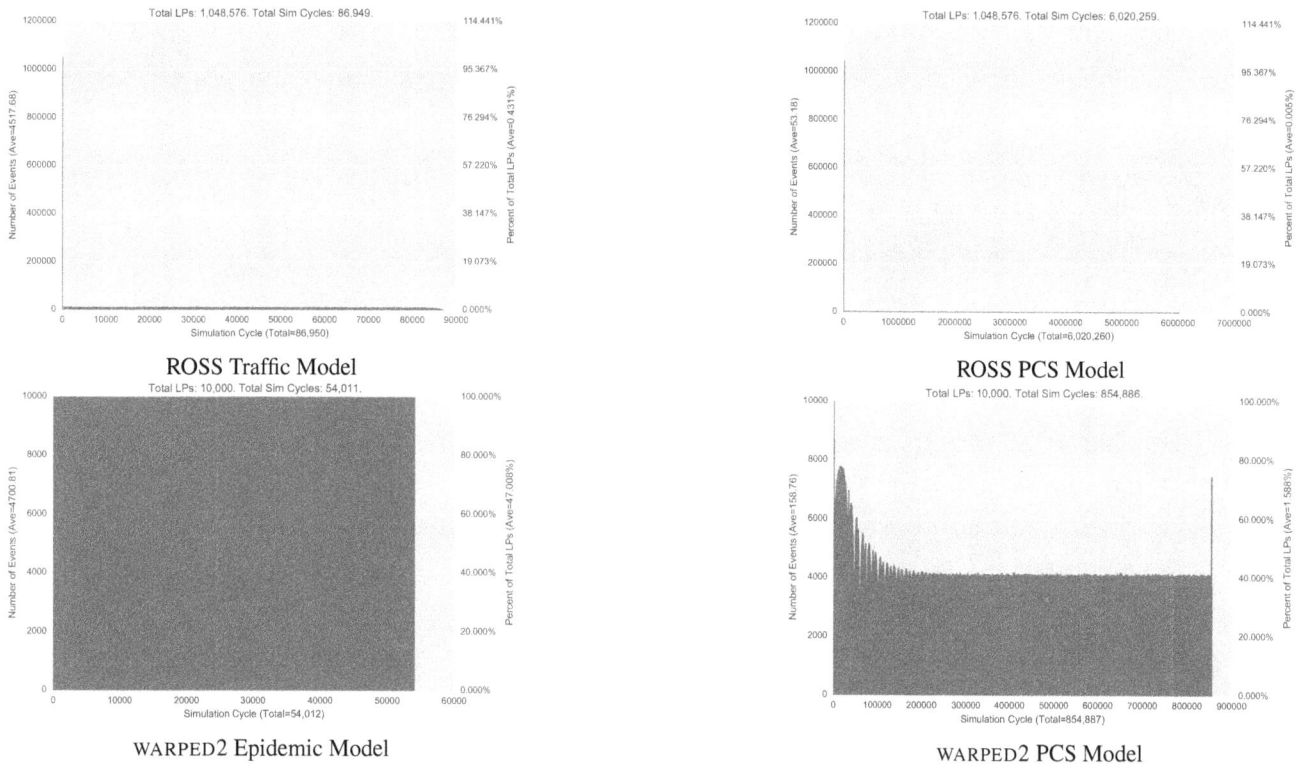

Figure 3: Events available for execution at each simulation cycle.

and the average over all of the cycles. The right axis is a scale of the events available as a percentage of the total LPs (and the average). That is, what percentage of LPs had an event available at that simulation cycle.

Unfortunately for the two ROSS models, there are an unusually large number of events available at simulation startup and teardown (not visible in the graphs); To a lesser extent, this also occurs in the WARPED2 PCS model. Since we are really trying to discover the "common case" of processing requirements, a more instructive visual might be to examine the data with outliers removed. Initially we developed plotting scripts that removed all data points that were greater than 2 standard deviations from the mean (Figure 4). This worked reasonably well, however, we found that trimming the first and last 1% of the evaluation cycles also achieved the desired effect. The advantage of this approach is that it attacks startup and teardown costs without discarding any wild variations that might exist during the main portions of the simulation. These results are shown in Figure 5.

Examining the results in Figure 5, we note that there is wide swings in the number of events available (*e.g.,* ROSS Traffic swings roughly between 2,000 and 8,000 events per simulation cycle). In terms of raw averages, we note that a only moderate percentage of LPs in the simulation have events available for concurrent execution (0.005%–47.0%). However, for any reasonably large simulation there are more than sufficient events available (52–4,700) for concurrent execution for a moderately sized parallel processing platform.

Figure 6 contains a histogram of the number of events available in the simulation. The x-axis is the number of events available, the left y-axis shows the number of simulation cycles, and the right axis shows the scale of percentage of the total simulation cycles. It

is interesting to note that both PCS models have a large number of simulation cycles with only a very few events available (indicating a relatively low degree of parallelism). In contrast, both Traffic and Epidemic have histogram maximums where the number of events available are in the thousands.

6.2 Profile of Events Executed by the LPs

During the events available analysis step, the DESMetrics tools also separates and records the events executed by each LP into two classes that we call *Local* and *Remote*. Local events are events that were generated and processed by the same LP. Remote events are generated by one LP and processed by another LP. As previously noted, not all simulation engines will send local events. However, both ROSS and WARPED2 do generate local events and the result of this analysis may be helpful for designing and optimizing pending event scheduling algorithms.

Figure 7 contains the results of events executed by LP. In this case, the LPs are sorted by the total number of events processed by it in the entire simulation (the blue line). The red line in these graphs shows the raw number of events that are locally generated. The green line shows the percentage of events that are locally generated. Except for ROSS Traffic, the percentage of events that are locally generated is quite high (averaging well over 50%). In the context of optimizing a parallel simulator, one could potentially create algorithms that short circuits the placement of a newly generated event into the input queue and, in some cases, simply directly executes it. This would bypass the locking overheads of accessing shared data structures of the pending event set and potentially have significant positive performance implications. This concept will be re-examined in the event chains discussion of the next section.

169

ROSS Traffic Model

ROSS PCS Model

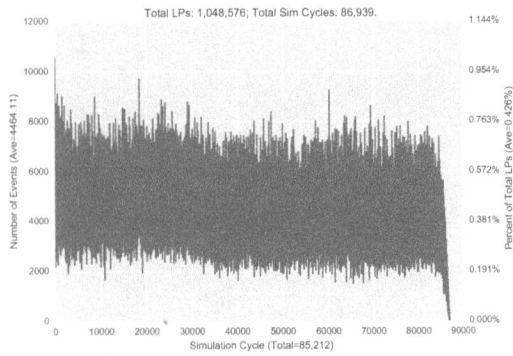

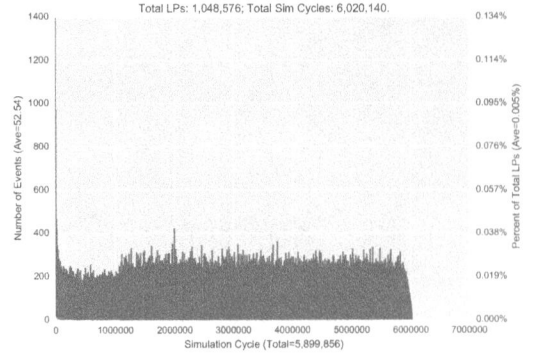

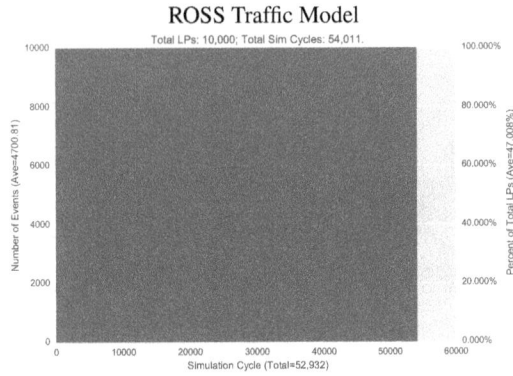

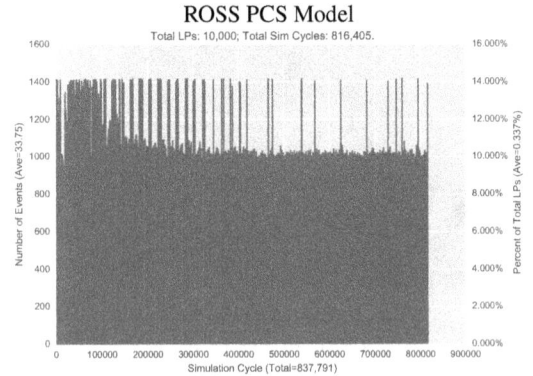

WARPED2 Epidemic Model

WARPED2 PCS Model

Figure 4: Events available for execution at each simulation cycle (outliers of $\sigma \geq 2$ removed).

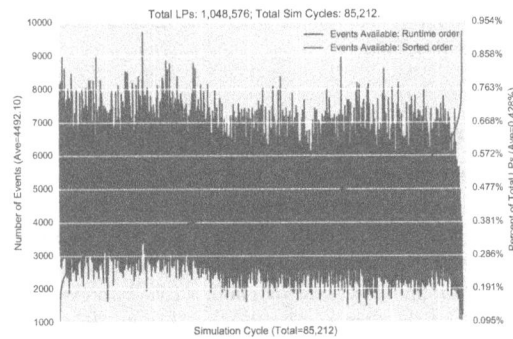

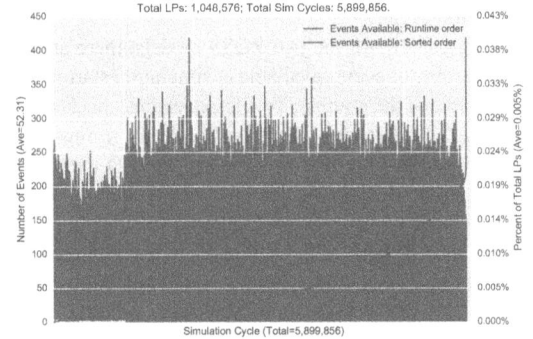

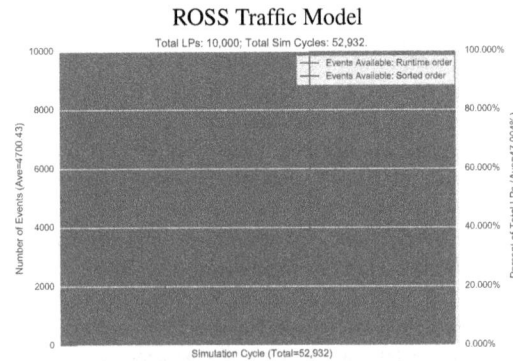

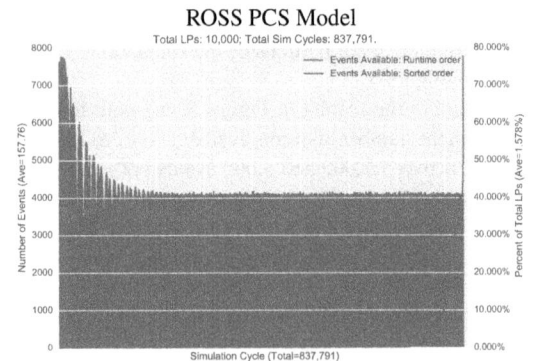

ROSS Traffic Model

ROSS PCS Model

WARPED2 Epidemic Model

WARPED2 PCS Model

Figure 5: Events available for execution at each simulation cycle (First and Last 1% of simulation cycles removed).

170

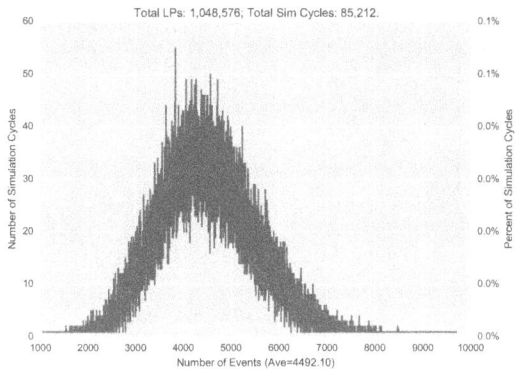

ROSS Traffic Model

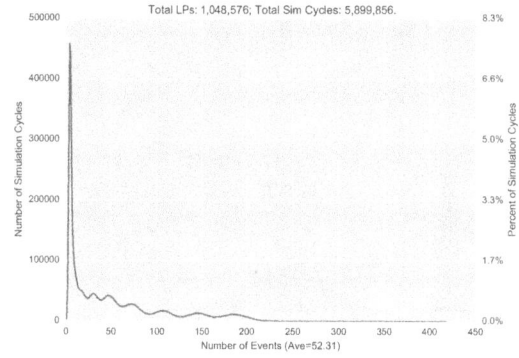

ROSS PCS Model

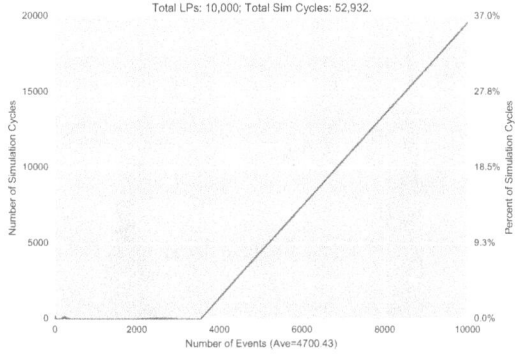

WARPED2 Epidemic Model

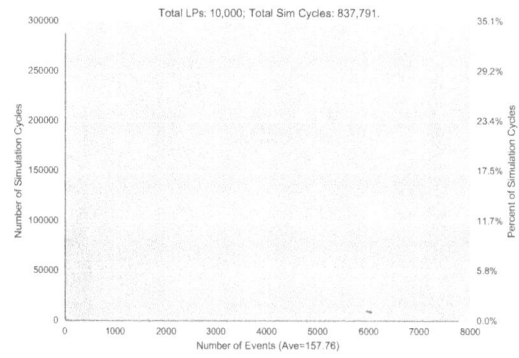

WARPED2 PCS Model

Figure 6: Histogram of events available for execution at each simulation cycle (First and Last 1% of simulation cycles removed).

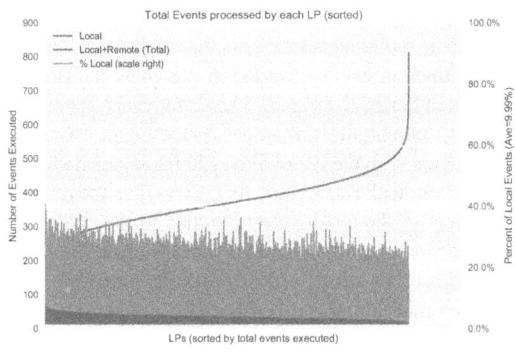

ROSS Traffic Model

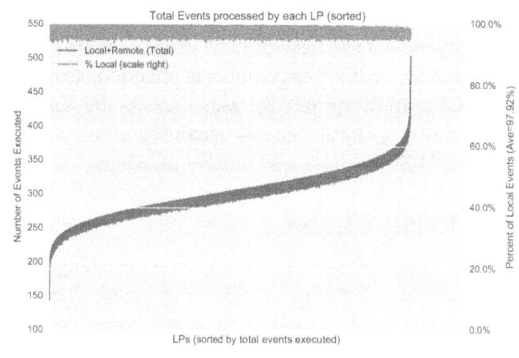

ROSS PCS Model

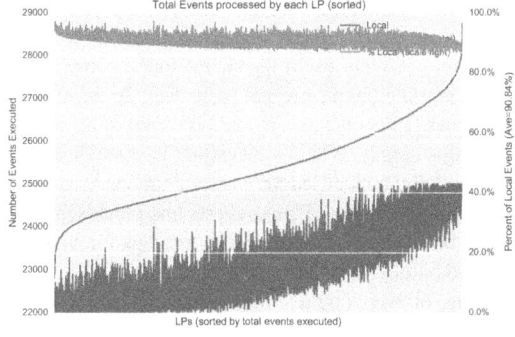

WARPED2 Epidemic Model

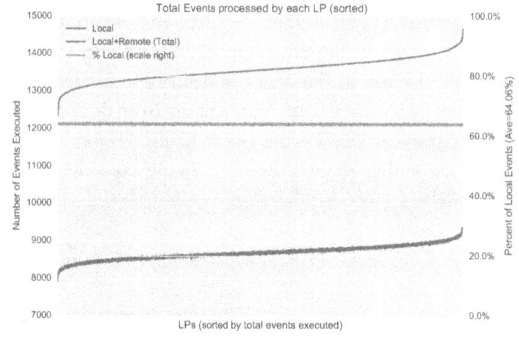

WARPED2 PCS Model

Figure 7: Total events executed by each LP (for all simulation cycles.

171

ROSS Traffic Model   ROSS PCS Model

WARPED2 Epidemic Model   WARPED2 PCS Model

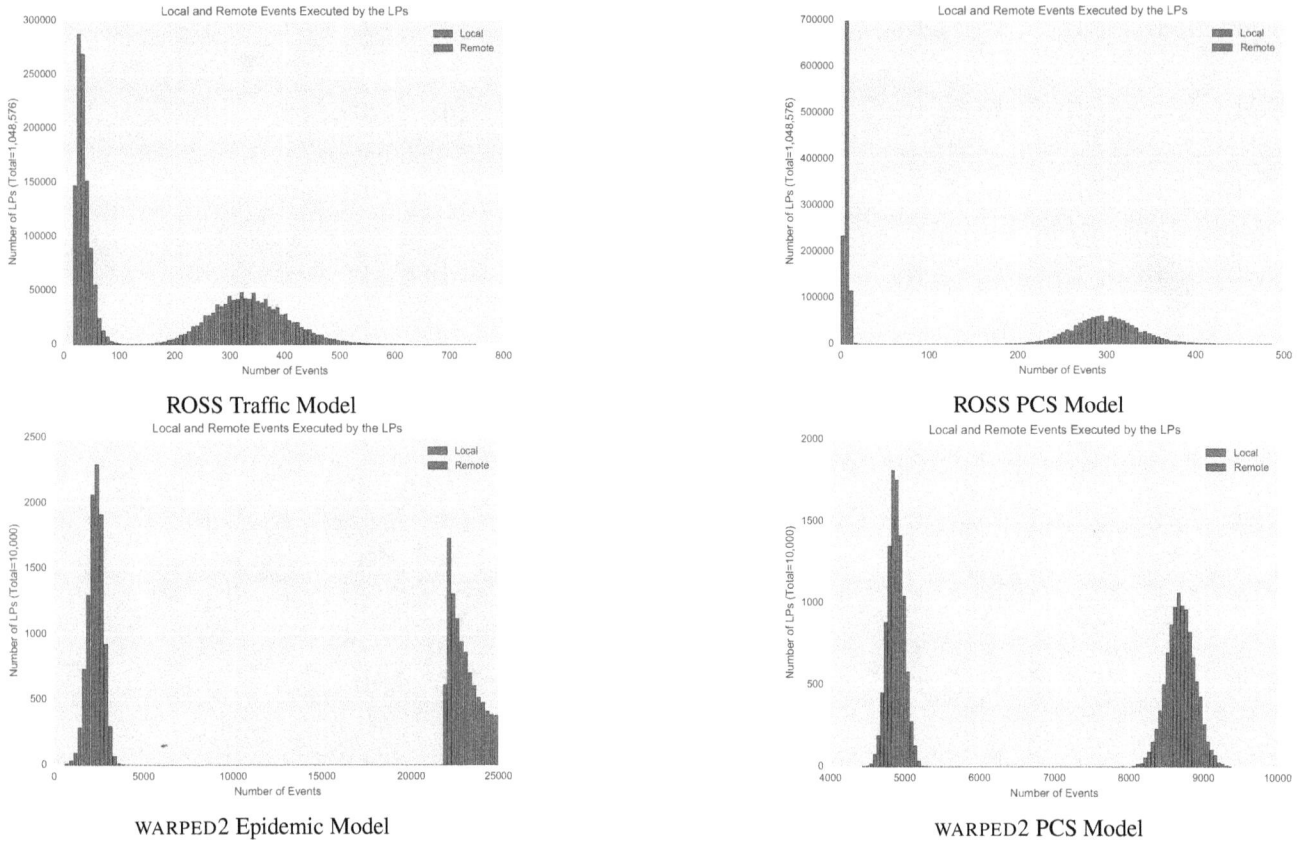

Figure 8: Histogram of events executed by each LP by event class (Local or Remote).

Figure 8 presents the data on local/remote events executed by LPs using the stacked histogram plotting capabilities of matplotlib. This graph summarizes the number of local/remote events executed by the LPs. In this graph, the x-axis shows the number of events executed (red — local, blue — remote) and the y-axis shows the number of LPs that have said number of events.

6.3 Event Chains

Event chains are blocks of events in the pending event set of an LP that could potentially be executed together. This computation is established independently of the events available execution loop shown in Algorithm 1. Instead, we examine the events processed by each LP independently. At each step, a chain is constructed and its maximum length counted. All of the events in the chain are treated as one and the algorithm then advances to the next event following the last in the chain to determine the length of the next chain. Formally, we define event chains from the `receive_time` timestamp of the head event in the chain. Thus, let e_0 denote the head event and e_i denote the event being considered for inclusion in the chain. Chain membership is established if

$$e_0.receive\_time > e_i.send\_time.$$

Event chains are further classified into three types, namely: *local*, *linked*, and *global*. To be members of local or linked chains, events must be locally generated events (generated by the executing LP). Membership in global chains places no constraint on which LP generates the event.

A *linked* chain is similar to the local chain except that the constraint on the `send_time` is relaxed so that any event with a `send_time` less than an event executed in the chain is also determined to be a member of the chain. Thus, any event generated by the chain is also potentially a member of the chain. That is, the linked chain begins with the list of events in the local chain and then includes any event with a send time that is less than the receive time of the last event in the chain. Events added to the chain can thus trigger the addition of yet more events into the chain.

In the DESMetrics implementation of event chain analysis, only chains up to a maximum length of 4. All chains longer than this limit are counted together and labeled ≥ 5.

Figure 9 shows the number of chains on the y-axis given their length shown on the x-axis. Note that the y-axis labels are in millions. Results for local (red), linked (blue), and global (green) are shown. Note that these counts are of the chains found corresponding to that length and the counts are not inclusive. To expand on this, Figure 10 shows the counts as a cumulative total of all chains at or greater than this length. What is interesting in these graphs is that sizable number of chains of length greater than one present in some of these simulation model. This suggests that block scheduling of events may be an effective optimization strategy for an Time Warp synchronized parallel simulation kernel.

Block scheduling of events by a simulator means that the event processing loop would dequeue and process multiple events from a single LP as a group. This could be especially beneficial for a kernel executing multiple event processing thread on an SMP machine. The key benefit to block scheduling is reduced time in the critical

ROSS Traffic Model

ROSS PCS Model

WARPED2 Epidemic Model

WARPED2 PCS Model

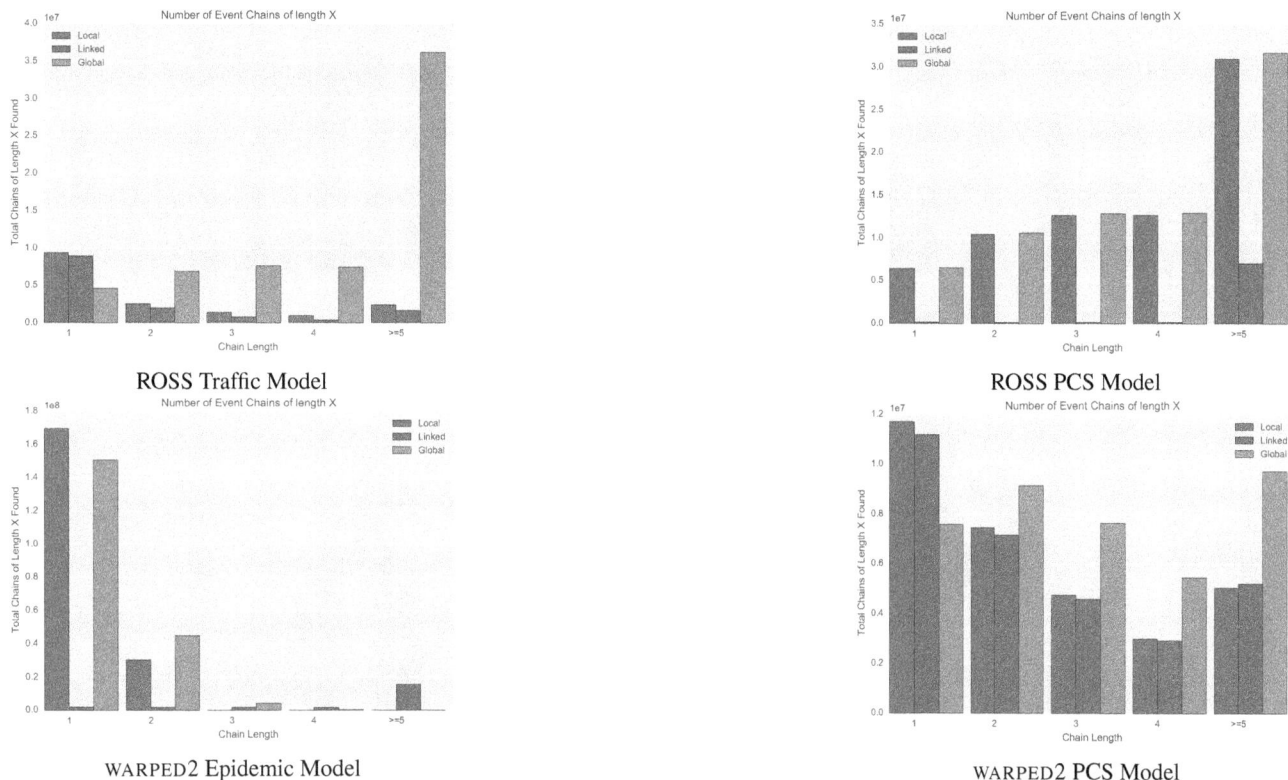

Figure 9: Number of event chains of length n.

region of the pending event set. Of course block scheduling might also lead to premature computation and thereby necessitate rollback. However, block scheduling of local event chains could potentially reduce the premature computation prospect. In any case, the data suggests it may be worth examining as a potential strategy for optimizing an SMP based platform simulation kernel.

6.4 Event Exchanges between LPs

In this analysis, we are attempting to discover how many LPs each LP sends events to. In order to better understand the connectivity of event exchanges among the LPs, this analysis counts the number of LPs that send an event to each LP. Basically this counts the number of LPs that send remote events to an LP. In addition to counting the total number of LPs that send a remote event, the analysis also computes how many events sends 95%, 90%, 80%, and 75% of the remote events. This allows us to better understand high connectivity and low connectivity of event exchanges among the LPs.

The results of this analysis are shown in Figure 11. In these graphs, the number of LPs that an LP receives remote events from is plotted on the y-axis. The data for each percentage shown is sorted (independently of the others) and then plotted on the same graph. For all of the simulation models, the number of sending LPs is a very small fraction (less than 1%) of the total LPs. While this does not show who is sending and therefore allows for the possibility that a small set of LPs communicate with all other LPs, our studies with partitioning of simulation models for parallel execution show that communication is distributed throughout the simulation model and that partitioning can largely localize communication between LPs [1]. As yet we have not discovered a better way to show this

result from the analysis performed here, we strongly believe that effective partitioning can significantly improve performance of a parallel simulator. In fact, the WARPED2 simulator has profile driven partitioning which shows significant performance implications for all of these simulation models.

6.5 Lookahead

In the final step of the analysis reported in this paper, we examine information related to lookahead. Specifically we plot results showing the minimum and average timestamp delta ($receive\_time - send\_time$) of remote events sent by each LP (Figure 12). The minimum timestamp is effectively the guaranteed safe lookahead on the channel of events sent between two LPs. The data shows that for the models studied, only the WARPED2 epidemic model has any significant lookahead.

7. CONCLUSIONS

This paper presented an approach for capturing simulation time properties of events exchanged and executed in a discrete event simulation model. The approach is to instrument a discrete event simulation engine to capture profile data. The profile data is then analyzed to produce various relations between the events and the LPs processing events in the simulation. The principal goal for this work is to help direct the algorithm development for investigations into solutions with parallel simulation. We believe that these results can directly impact the research directions of research in parallel simulation.

In summary, the data collected shows that ample parallelism exists in discrete event simulation models for parallelism to be successful. Furthermore, we find that simulation events are often lo-

ROSS Traffic Model

ROSS PCS Model

WARPED2 Epidemic Model

WARPED2 PCS Model

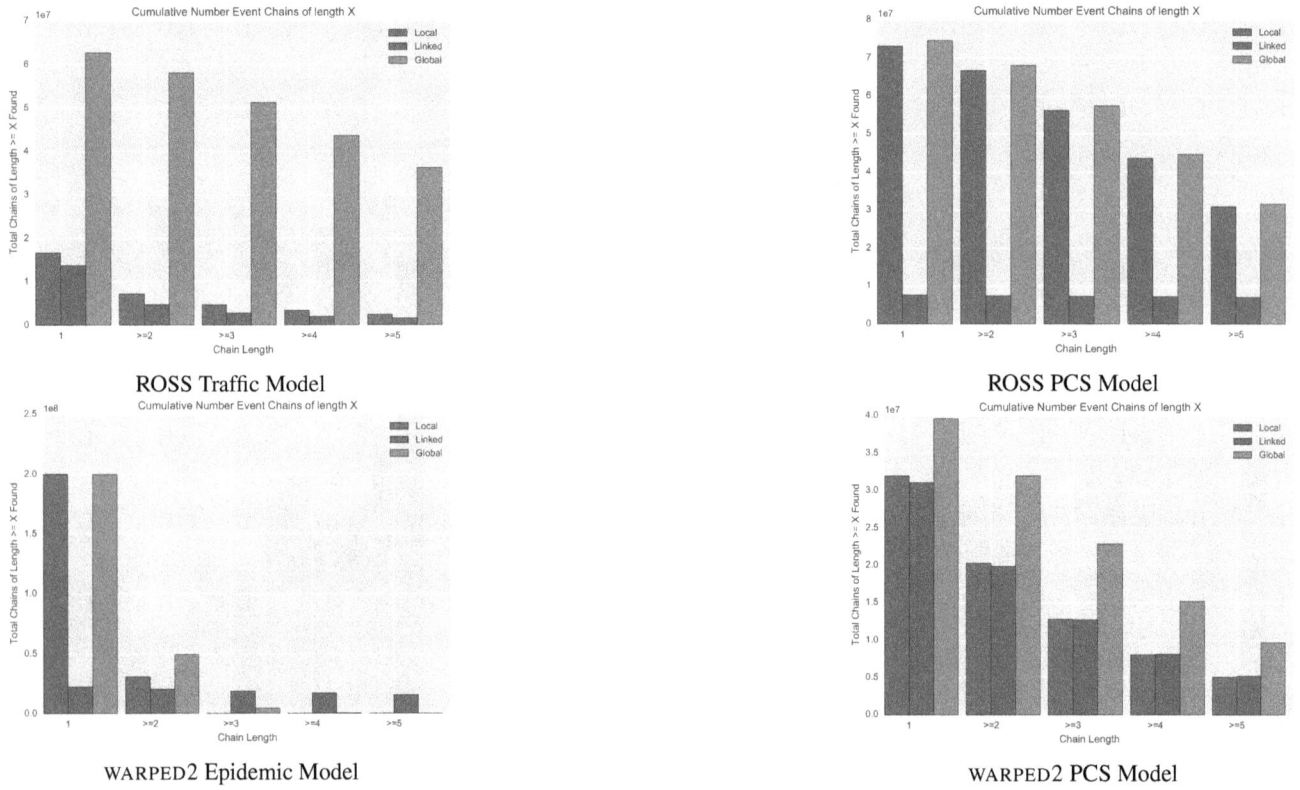

Figure 10: Cumulative number of event chains of with length $\geq$ n.

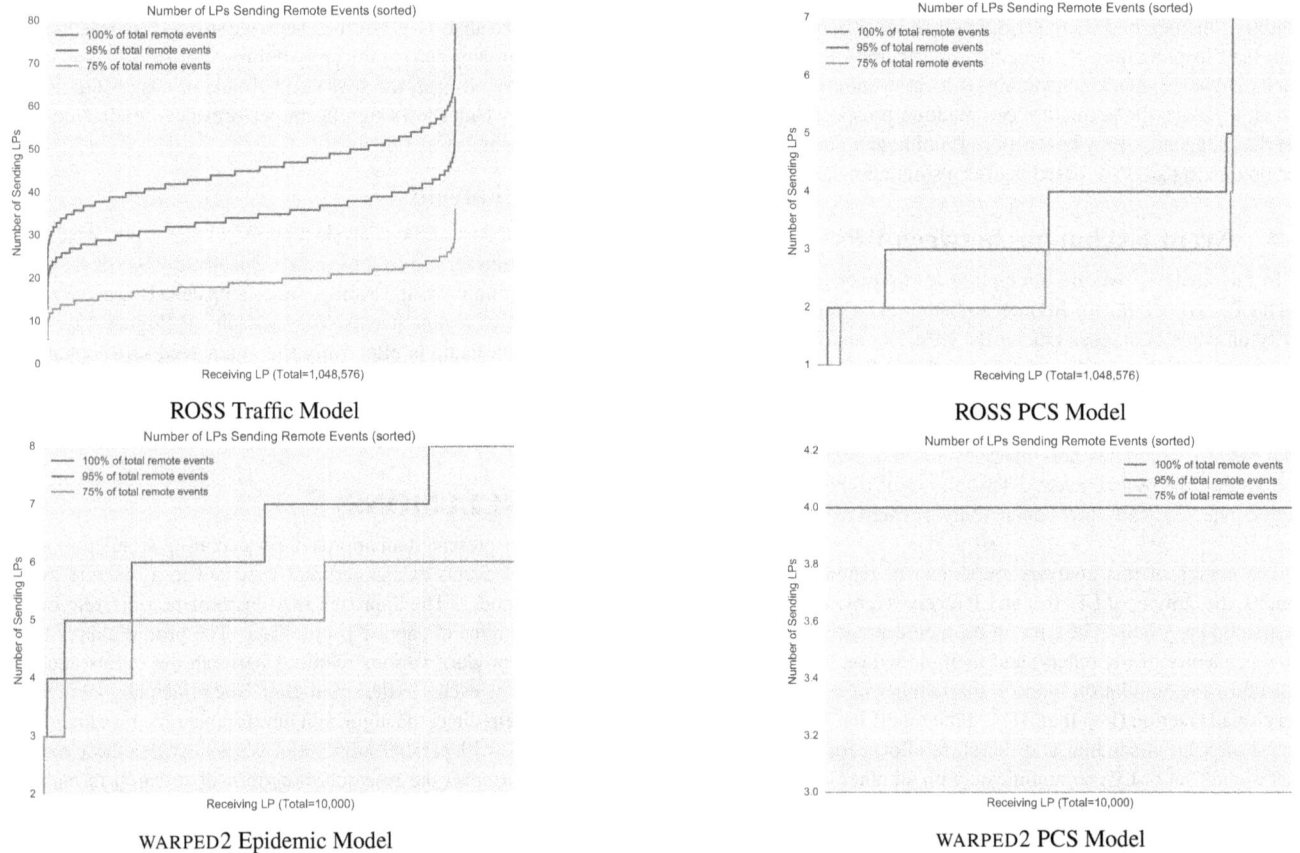

ROSS Traffic Model

ROSS PCS Model

WARPED2 Epidemic Model

WARPED2 PCS Model

Figure 11: Number of LPs sending various percentages of remote events

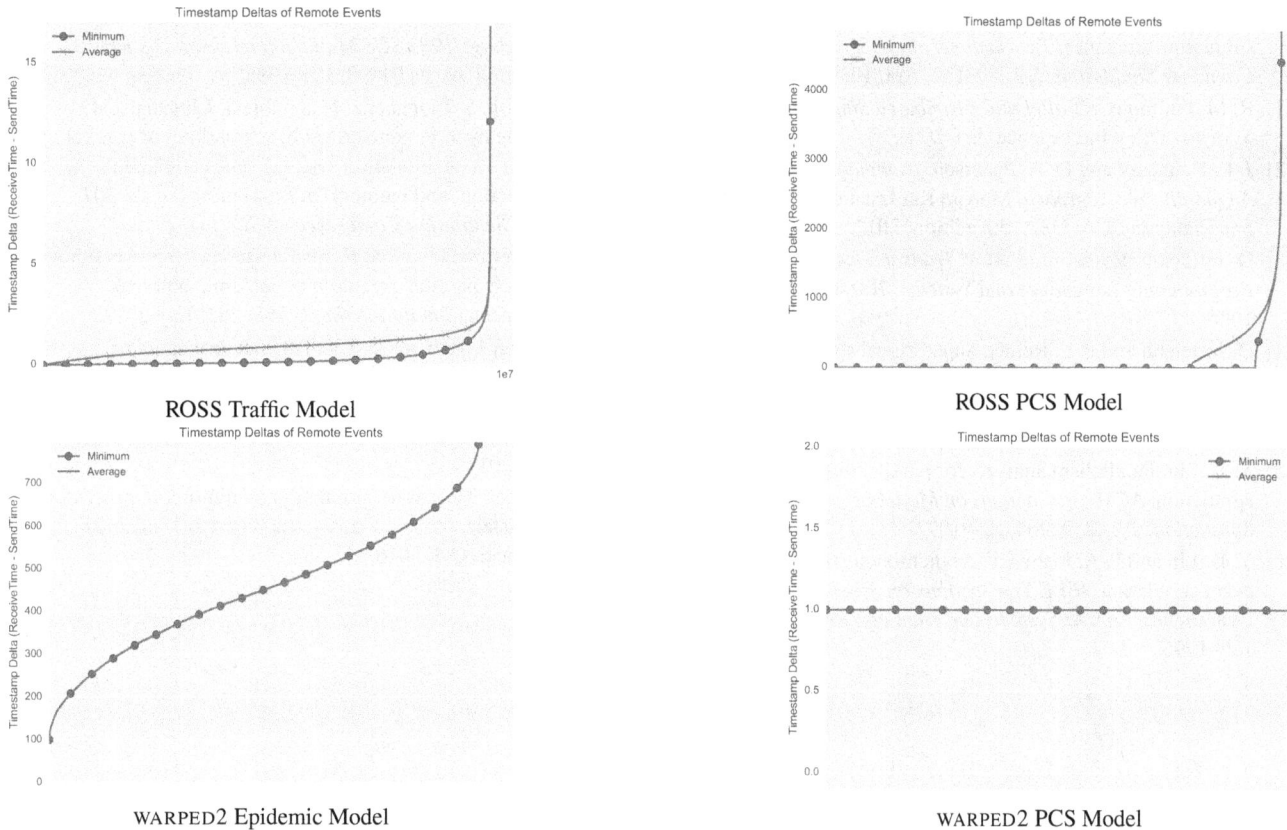

Figure 12: The Delta of the Send and Receive time of Remote Events (Lookahead).

cal within an LP and that "gang" scheduling of events in an LP should be a highly effective technique to dramatically improve performance on a shared memory platform. Finally, the impact of effective partitioning of the simulation model cannot be sufficiently emphasized. To fully unlock the potential of parallel simulation, the PDES field must embrace static analysis techniques to help organize the simulation model for high performance. With the proper application of static analysis techniques, we believe that parallel simulation can have significant performance impact on the execution efficiency of large simulation models.

8. ACKNOWLEDGMENTS

Support for this work was provided in part by the National Science Foundation under award CNS–0915337 and this material is based upon work supported by the AFOSR under award No FA9550–15–1–0384.

9. REFERENCES

[1] A. J. Alt and P. A. Wilsey. Profile driven partitioning of parallel simulation models. In *Proceedings of the 2014 Winter Simulation Conference*, Dec. 2014.

[2] V. Balakrishnan, R. Radhakrishnan, D. M. Rao, N. B. Abu-Ghazaleh, and P. A. Wilsey. A Performance and Scalability Analysis Framework for Parallel Discrete Event Simulators. *Simulation Practice and Theory*, 8:529–553, 2001.

[3] C. L. Barrett, K. R. Bisset, S. G. Eubank, X. Feng, , and M. V. Marathe. Episimdemics: an efficient algorithm for simulating the spread of infectious disease over large realistic social networks. In *Proceedings of the 2008 ACM/IEEE conference on Supercomputing*, SC '08, Piscataway, NJ, USA, 2008. IEEE Press.

[4] O. Berry and D. Jefferson. Critical path analysis of distributed simulation. In *Distributed Simulation*, pages 57–60. Society for Computer Simulation, 1985.

[5] C. D. Carothers, D. Bauer, and S. Pearce. ROSS: A high-performance, low memory, modular time warp system. In *Proceedings of the Fourteenth Workshop on Parallel and Distributed Simulation*, PADS '00, pages 53–60, Washington, DC, USA, 2000. IEEE Computer Society.

[6] C. D. Carothers, R. M. Fujimoto, Y.-B. Lin, and P. England. Distributed simulation of large-scale PCS networks. In *Proceedings of the Second International Workshop on Modeling, Analysis, and Simulation of Computer and Telecommunication Systems (MASCOTS '94)*, pages 2–6, Jan. 1994.

[7] A. Ferscha and J. Johnson. A testbed for parallel simulation performance predictions. In *1996 Winter Simulation Conference Proceedings*, December 1996.

[8] R. Fujimoto. Parallel discrete event simulation. *Communications of the ACM*, 33(10):30–53, Oct. 1990.

[9] R. Fujimoto. Performance of Time Warp under synthetic workloads. *Proceedings of the SCS Multiconference on Distributed Simulation*, 22(1):23–28, Jan. 1990.

[10] R. M. Fujimoto. Performance measurements of distributed simulation strategies. *Transactions of the Society for Computer Simulation*, 6(2):89–132, Apr. 1989.

[11] R. M. Fujimoto. *Parallel and Distributed Simulation Systems*. Wiley Interscience, Jan. 2000.

[12] J. L. Hennessy and D. A. Patterson. *Computer Architecture: A Quantitative Approach*. Morgan Kaufmann Publishers Inc., San Francisco, CA, USA, 5th edition, 2012.

[13] D. Jefferson. Virtual time. *ACM Transactions on Programming Languages and Systems*, 7(3):405–425, July 1985.

[14] D. Jefferson and P. L. Reiher. Supercritical speedup. In A. H. Rutan, editor, *Proceedings of the 24th Annual Simulation Symposium*, pages 159–168. IEEE Computer Society Press, Apr. 1991.

[15] Y.-B. Lin. Parallelism analyzer for parallel discrete event simulation. *ACM Transactions on Modeling and Computer Simulation*, 2(3):239–264, July 1992.

[16] Y.-B. Lin and P. A. Fishwick. Asynchronous parallel discrete event simulation. *IEEE Transactions on Systems, Man and Cybernetics, Part A: Systems and Humans*, 26(4):397–412, July 1996.

[17] M. Livny. A study of parallelism in distributed simulation. In *Proceedings 1985 SCS Multiconference on Distributed Simulation*, pages 94–98, Jan. 1985.

[18] E. J. Park, S. Eidenbenz, N. Santhi, G. Chapuis, and B. Settlemyer. Parameterized benchmarking of parallel discrete event simulation systems: Communication, computation, and memory. In *Proceedings of the 2015 Winter Simulation Conference (WSC '15)*, 2015.

[19] K. S. Perumalla and S. K. Seal. Discrete event modeling and massively parallel execution of epidemic outbreak phenomena. *Simulation*, 88(7):768–783, July 2012.

[20] R. Rong, J. Hao, and J. Liu. Performance study of a minimalistic simulator on XSEDE massively parallel systems. In *Proceedings of the 2014 Annual Conference on Extreme Science and Engineering Discovery Environment*. ACM, 2014.

[21] D. Weber. Time warp simulation on multi-core processors and clusters. Master's thesis, University of Cincinnati, Cincinnati, OH, 2016.

An Integrated Interconnection Network Model for Large-Scale Performance Prediction

Kishwar Ahmed
Mohammad Obaida
Jason Liu
Florida International University
{kahme006, mobai001, liux}@fiu.edu

Stephan Eidenbenz
Nandakishore Santhi
Guillaume Chapuis
Los Alamos National Laboratory
{eidenben, nsanthi, gchapuis}@lanl.gov

ABSTRACT

Interconnection network is a critical component of high-performance computing architecture and application co-design. For many scientific applications, the increasing communication complexity poses a serious concern as it may hinder the scaling properties of these applications on novel architectures. It is apparent that a scalable, efficient, and accurate interconnect model would be essential for performance evaluation studies. In this paper, we present an interconnect model for predicting the performance of large-scale applications on high-performance architectures. In particular, we present a sufficiently detailed interconnect model for Cray's Gemini 3-D torus network. The model has been integrated with an implementation of the Message-Passing Interface (MPI) that can mimic most of its functions with packet-level accuracy on the target platform. Extensive experiments show that our integrated model provides good accuracy for predicting the network behavior, while at the same time allowing for good parallel scaling performance.

CCS Concepts

•Networks → Network simulations; •Computing methodologies → Modeling and simulation;

Keywords

High-performance computing; interconnection network; performance prediction; hardware software co-design

1. INTRODUCTION

As we move towards exascale computing, the collapse of hardware scaling laws has led to the emergence of novel hardware architecture designs in high-performance computing (HPC) that include accelerator technologies (such as GPUs), high core-count compute nodes with shared memory, deep instruction pipelines, deep memory hierarchies with aggressive memory prefetching strategies, and sophisticated branch prediction for speculative execution. These

Permission to make digital or hard copies of all or part of this work for personal or classroom use is granted without fee provided that copies are not made or distributed for profit or commercial advantage and that copies bear this notice and the full citation on the first page. Copyrights for components of this work owned by others than ACM must be honored. Abstracting with credit is permitted. To copy otherwise, or republish, to post on servers or to redistribute to lists, requires prior specific permission and/or a fee. Request permissions from permissions@acm.org.

SIGSIM-PADS '16, May 15-18, 2016, Banff, AB, Canada

© 2016 ACM. ISBN 978-1-4503-3742-7/16/05. . . $15.00

DOI: http://dx.doi.org/10.1145/2901378.2901396

new architectural features enable massive *parallelism* and *latency hiding* that in principle allow software and codes to scale to next-generation HPC systems. For example, Intel's Knight's Corner node features 61 cores with shared main memory (albeit at a non-uniform access speed) that enables thread-level parallelism. In contrast, NVIDIA's Tesla GPU accelerators have up to $3,000$ CUDA Cores per CPU enabling vector parallelism. Different parallelization strategies were adopted in the these cases. CPU-based nodes use a significant fraction of their chip real estate to implement pipelining logic (to enable instruction-level parallelism) and memory prefetching logic at different cache levels (to enable latency hiding), whereas GPU designs tend to maximize core counts with arithmetic logic units (ALUs) for enabling vector parallelism.

These novel hardware technologies have turned out to be disruptive to existing software portfolios in many industries and government branches because simple re-compilation does not exploit these features very well. This in turn has led to massive code re-factoring in many sectors, including—and perhaps most pronounced—among users of high-performance computational physics code. Fast performance prediction of how well a new computational method or code will run on a novel architecture HPC platform is a key technique to achieve exascale computing because it allows the quick identification of algorithmic ideas that will or will not pair well with novel architecture platforms. Performance prediction on how fast and how energy-efficient a code will run on a platform is at the heart of computational co-design.

Performance prediction of large-scale parallel computers consisting thousands of node and more is a challenging task. In recent years we have witnessed the fast growth in supercomputer design that can perform operations at scale of quadrillions of calculations per second. The tremendous rise in the computational power is in part attributed to the government agencies that have been supporting (and encouraging) the growth of large-scale supercomputing infrastructures. For example, significant investment by the U.S. Department of Energy (DOE) on building state-of-the-art supercomputers through programs (such as FastForward [39], and recently FastForward 2 [38]) support the fact that exascale computing will continue to receive attention in years to come. Consequently, the community faces a significant challenge for complex large-scale scientific and engineering applications to keep up and take full advantage of the fast growth of supercomputing capabilities.

The Performance Prediction Toolkit (PPT) is a DOE co-design project that aims at developing a comprehensive prediction capability for computational physics code, algorithms and methods that perform on novel hardware architectures, thus enabling fast adoption of new code by quickly identifying and ruling out unsuccessful refactoring scheme. PPT models both hardware and software at levels of abstraction that are appropriate to the concrete question at hand, by applying a mix of discrete-event simulation, stochastic and analytical models at various layers on the software and hardware stack.

With changes in HPC system so frequent, it is imperative that performance prediction of future HPC system is properly realized. Of particular importance is the model for the interconnection networks as it is critical to the understanding of the communication cost and thus the performance limitations of large-scale applications on high-performance computing infrastructures. There has been significant research effort on performance prediction and modeling of extreme-scale interconnection network (e.g., [22,23,32,33]). However, few of these research efforts consider the effect of complex, dynamic application behaviors, such as the computational physics code, on the underlying large-scale interconnection network.

The contribution of this paper is three-fold. First, we present PPT's interconnection network model, which includes as an example a sufficiently detailed model of Cray's Gemini 3-D torus network. Second, our interconnection network model has been fully integrated with an implementation of the Message Passing Interface (MPI) model, which mimics all common MPI commands, including various send and receive functions, as well as collective operations. The MPI model can achieve packet-level accuracy at the target platforms. Third, we present extensive validation studies of our MPI and interconnect models, including a trace-based study using data obtained from executing real-life computational physics code on an existing high-performance computing platform.

PPT relies on the Simian [37], a parallel discrete-event simulation engine, and essentially consists of libraries of hardware models, application models, and middleware models. PPT, along with Simian, is designed to be lean, written in Python (or alternatively Lua) with minimal reliance on third-party libraries in an effort to keep the code simple, understandable, and yet offer high performance. In this paper, we report on scaling runs of our interconnect model, which confirm the scalability of the underlying simulation engine, albeit also point to some performance weaknesses in the Python version of Simian, which suggest directions of our further efforts.

The rest of this paper is organized as follows. Section 2 provides the background and related work. Section 3 provides an overview of our design. We provide the details of our model for the Gemini interconnection network in Section 4 and for the message-passing interface in Section 5. We conducted extensive experiments to validate our integrated interconnect model. The experiments are presented in Section 6. In Section 7 we present a trace-based simulation study to demonstrate the capability of our model for incorporating realistic applications. A preliminary study on the parallel performance of the interconnect model is presented in Section 8. Finally, we conclude the paper and outline our future work in Section 9.

2. BACKGROUND AND RELATED WORK

There exist a wide selection of HPC simulators. Some simulators, such as Gem5 [4], COTSon [3], and Simics [24], model the full-system architecture. Some simulators focus only on a specific component of the system, such as Cacti [41] for caches, M5 [5] for networks, and Graphite [25] for multicore design. These simulators are not appropriate for the performance prediction of large-scale HPC applications due to their limitations in scalability and scope.

An important aspect in HPC performance prediction is *scalability*. That is, how large the HPC system can one model? For example, BigSim is an early effort for performance prediction of large-scale parallel machines (in particular, Blue Gene/L machines), based on the actual execution of the real applications [35,43]. It is implemented using Charm++ and MPI, and applies parallel discrete-event simulation to scale up performance. BigSim adopts an optimistic approach using the inherent determinacy of the target parallel applications to reduce the overhead of the optimistic scheme. Experiments show that BigSim is capable of scaling up to 64K simulated processors. In the similar fashion, $\mu\pi$ is an MPI simulator based on an efficient conservatively-synchronized parallel simulator [32]. Experiments show that the simulator is capable of simulating hundreds of millions of MPI ranks on a Cray XTS with 216K cores. Compared to our integrated interconnect model, however, both BigSim and $\mu\pi$ provide a simpler network model [9,43].

The Extreme-scale Simulator (xSim) is a performance-prediction toolkit for future HPC architectures [6]. xSim applies parallel discrete-event simulation using lightweight threads to achieve scalability up to millions of application processes [15,16]. xSim also incorporates different network topologies, including star, ring, tree, mesh, and torus [17]. However, unlike our interconnect model, network congestion is omitted in xSim to gain scalability. As such, their simulator cannot accurately model the blocking behavior of the target interconnection network which may be of importance to the architecture/application co-design.

The Structural Simulation Toolkit (SST) [34] is a comprehensive simulation framework for modeling large-scale HPC systems, including processors, memory, network, and I/O systems. It attempts to achieve scalability using a conservative parallel simulation approach. SST can model hardware components with different granularity and accuracy. SST's network model in particular contains a variety of interconnect topologies: binary tree, fat-tree, hypercube, butterfly, mesh, and so on. The interconnect model, however, does not provide the necessary details for capturing important network behaviors for performance prediction. For example, it does not support network flow control and also the links are assumed to have infinite capacity. Our interconnect model, on the contrary, provides packet-level details that can support realistic network scenarios, such as the transient network congestion occurred during the execution of large complex applications.

Co-Design of Exascale Storage System (CODES) is a joint project between the Argonne National Laboratory and Rensselaer Polytechnic Institute [12]. The simulator is built upon the Rensselaer Optimistic Simulation System (ROSS), which is based on reverse computation [8]. Several detailed interconnect models have been implemented, which include torus [22], dragonfly [26], and fat-tree [23]. For example, in [27], the simulator predicts the performance of the torus

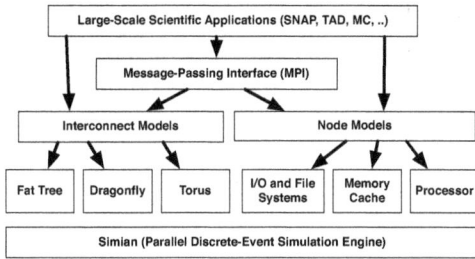

Figure 1: An architectural design of PPT.

network with high-fidelity using synthetic traffic patterns (such as diagonal pairing) on IBM's Blue Gene/P system. In [23], the simulator models large-scale fat-tree networks consisting of millions of compute nodes in a time-efficient manner. A recent paper has proposed a trace-driven simulator (TraceR) to replay large execution traces to predict and understand network performance and behavior [1]. TraceR is built upon ROSS-based CODES simulator and has been shown to be able to simulate a network consisting of half million nodes using traces produced by running BigSim applications.

The CODES project aims at enabling co-design of exascale storage systems. Although complementary to our approach in examining the communication cost of parallel applications (especially computation physics applications), CODES has a slightly different focus on storage systems. Our project aims at providing *fast evaluation* of computational physics algorithms and methods on novel large-scale parallel architectures. We have adopted a minimalistic design to facilitate easy integration of the interconnect model with the target applications (using interpreted languages, like Python and Lua) and provide scalability to accommodate large-scale parallel applications and high-performance architectures.

3. DESIGN OVERVIEW

To design an interconnect model for performance prediction, one need to take several important factors into account:

- *Scale*: The interconnect model must be able to accommodate high-performance computing platforms and applications at extreme scale.
- *Performance:* The interconnect model must run reasonably fast so that it can be used to explore design alternatives of system architectures, software, and parallel applications.
- *Accuracy:* The interconnect model must provide high fidelity sufficient to represent the effect of important design decisions, constraints and optimizations. Simple analytical models may not be sufficient for projecting the performance of dynamic, complex applications.
- *Integration:* The interconnect model must be easy to integrate with other models, including those for processors, memory, and file systems. It is also important that the model can be readily integrated with common software tools, such as MPI, so that various scientific applications can be easily incorporated in the performance study.

Fig. 1 presents an architectural design of our Performance Prediction Toolkit. The majority of target large-scale scientific applications use MPI. Consequently, we designed and implemented an MPI model, which makes it easy for us to incorporate various application models. An instance of the

MPI model can be instantiated at the simulated compute nodes, connected via the interconnect model. There are different interconnection network topologies, such as fat-tree, dragonfly, and torus. In this paper, we focus on the specific interconnect model for torus.

All our models are developed based on Simian, which is an open-source, process-oriented parallel discrete-event simulation (PDES) engine [37]. Simian has two independent implementations written in two interpreted languages, Python and Lua, respectively. Simian uses a conservative barrier-based synchronization algorithm [29] for parallel execution.

Simian has several distinct features. First, Simian adopts a minimalistic design. For example, the Python implementation of Simian consists of only around 500 lines of code. As a result, it requires low effort to understand the code and it is thus easy for model development and debugging. Second, Simian features a very simplistic application programming interface (API). To maximize portability, Simian requires minimal dependency on third-party libraries. Third, Simian takes advantage of just-in-time (JIT) compilation for interpreted languages. For certain models, Simian has demonstrated that it can even outperform the C/C++ based simulation engine.

To develop models on Simian, it is necessary to understand the Simian API, which contains only three main modules: the simulation engine, entities, and processes. A *simulation engine* is a logical process responsible for synchronizing with other logical processes. A simulation engine starts with the `run` method, which continuously pops events with the minimum timestamp from the event queue and invokes the corresponding event handler functions. The logical processes are synchronized using a simple window-based conservative synchronization mechanism. In particular, at the start of each window (beginning at simulation time zero), all logical processes find the timestamp of the event at the head of the event queue, add a system-wide minimum delay (lookahead), and then perform a min-reduction to determine the start time of the next synchronization window.

Entities are containers for state (such as a network switch or a compute node). Entities contain event handlers (called services in Simian) that may change the state. An entity can communicate with others by scheduling services at the other entities. Important methods for the entity include: `attachService`, `reqService`, `createProcess`, and `startProcess`. The `attachService` method attaches an event-handler function to the entity, while the `reqService` method schedules an event to be processed at a future simulation time. The methods `createProcess` and `startProcess` creates and starts a process, respectively.

Processes are independent threads of execution. Each process is associated with an entity. Simian uses lightweight threads to implement the processes—greenlets in Python and coroutines in Lua. The user can create a child process using the the `spawn` method and terminates one using the `kill` method. In addition, the user can put a process to sleep for a certain amount of simulation time (using the `sleep` method), suspend a process from execution (using the `hibernate` method), and later resume its execution to continue from the previous suspension (using the `wake` method).

In this paper, we focus on the torus interconnect model. In particular, we describe a model for the Cray's Gemini interconnect that has been commonly used by many supercomputing systems today. We also focus on an MPI model

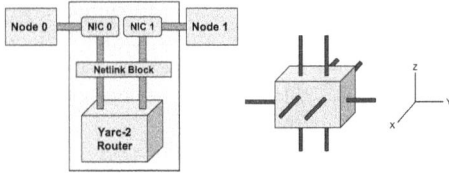

Figure 2: Cray Gemini ASIC block diagram.

that integrates with the Gemini interconnect model, allowing various scientific application models to be readily incorporated for performance evaluation and analysis.

4. GEMINI INTERCONNECT MODEL

We designed and implemented a relatively detailed model for the Gemini interconnection network. Gemini is a part of the Cray's XE6 architecture. Cray XE6 is a system currently used by many large-scale high-performance computing systems, including, for example, Hopper at National Energy Research Scientific Computing Center (NERSC), Cielo at Los Alamos National Laboratory (LANL), Blue Waters at the National Center for Supercomputing (NCSA), Titan at the Oak Ridge National Laboratory, and ISTeC at Colorado State University.

Each Cray XE6 compute node has two AMD Opteron processors, coupled with its own memory (either 32 GB or 64 GB) and communication interface. The Gemini network was first introduced in 2010 in Cray XE6 systems and was the most notable difference from the earlier Cray XT systems. In Gemini, the two AMD Opteron nodes are connected to the Gemini Application-Specific Integrated Circuit (ASIC) through two Network Interface Controllers (NICs). The NICs have their own HyperTransport (HT) 3 link to connect to the nodes, where the link offers up to 8 GB/s bandwidth per node and direction [31]. The NICs within an ASIC are connected through a Netlink block, enabling internal communication between the NICs. At the heart of Gemini is a 48-port YARC router (shown in Fig. 2), which is configured to construct a 3D torus topology. The router is connected to Netlink block through 8 links. Each router gives ten torus connection: two connections per direction in the "X" and "Z" dimension and one connection per direction in the "Y" direction.

Unlike some other interconnection networks, such as fat-tree, torus is a blocking network. It is possible that congestion may happen in the network where queuing delays may negatively affect the performance of parallel applications in a significant fashion. It is thus important to model the traffic behavior in the network imposed by high-level applications. To do that, we need to provide a detailed queuing model to capture the interactions of network transactions.

We implemented each compute node (which is also called a host) or interconnect switch as a Simian entity. Fig. 3 shows a diagram of the design. The hosts and switches are connected via network interfaces that simulate the queuing behavior. A network interface may consists of multiple ports to handle parallel connections between the switches (e.g., in the "X" and "Z" dimensions). Each port consists of an output port ("outport") and an input port ("inport") for sending and receiving messages. To send data from the output port, Simian schedules a service (i.e., an event handler), called

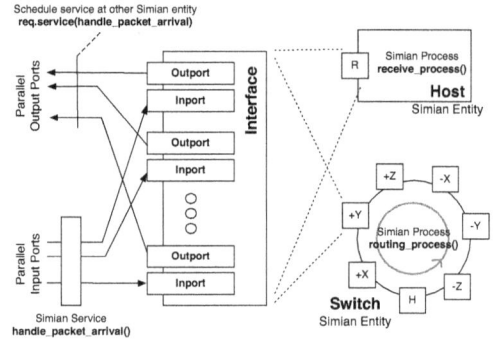

Figure 3: Interconnect model using Simian entities, processes, and services.

handle_packet_arrival, at the next node (which can be either a switch or a host), with a delay that is the sum of the current queuing delay at the output port, the packet transmission time, and the link propagation delay between the two nodes. Upon a packet's arrival at a switch, the handle_packet_arrival service inserts the packet into the buffer of the corresponding input port and informs the routing process. The routing process is a Simian process that takes packets from the input ports, calculates the next hop using the selected routing algorithm, and then forwards the packet to the corresponding output port. If a host receives the packet, the handle_packet_arrival service inserts the packet into the input buffer of the host interface and informs the receive process, which hands the packet to the corresponding MPI receiver accordingly.

Gemini supports multiple routing algorithms, such as deterministic, hashed, and adaptive [40]. Each routing algorithm follows dimension-order routing, where "X" dimension is always traversed first, then "Y" dimension, and finally "Z" dimension [30]. Different routing algorithms provide different level of flexibility in using links at dimensions. For example, the deterministic dimension-order routing provides least amount of flexibility, where links are predetermined in each dimension. The adaptive dimension-order routing provides most flexibility, allowing packets to be adaptively scheduled to lightly-loaded links. In our implementation, the user can explicitly select the routing algorithm when configuring the interconnect model.

5. THE MPI MODEL

The Message Passing Interface (MPI) is one of the most popular parallel programming tools on today's HPC platforms. A good MPI model is essential to studying the design and implementation of scientific applications.

The design of an MPI implementation is intricately influenced by the underlying interconnection network. For example, Cray's MPI implementation for the Gemini interconnect uses Fast Memory Access (FMA). It allows a maximum of 64 bytes of data transfer for each network transaction. A network transaction initiates a single request from the source to the destination, which triggers a response from the destination back to the source. A large message will get broken down into many individual 64-byte transactions. There are two types of transactions. A typical PUT transaction sends 64 bytes of data from a source to a destination. A PUT message consists of a 32-phit request packet (i.e., 96 bytes, where

```
from ppt import *

# config hopper (17x8x24 gemini interconnect)
model_cfg = { # a dictionary
  "intercon_type" : "gemini",
  "host_type" : "mpihost",
  "torus" : configs.hopper_intercon,
  "mpiopt" : configs.gemini_mpiopt,
}
model = HPCSim(model_cfg, ..)

# mpi main function, n is matrix dimension
def cannon(mpi_comm_world, n):
    ... # we describe this later

# start 16 mpi ranks, pass matrix dimension
model.start_mpi(range(16), cannon, 10000)

# simulation starts
model.run()
```

Figure 4: An example showing running 16 MPI processes on Hopper.

```
# cannon's algorithm on matrix multiplication
def cannon(mpi_comm_world, n):
  p = mpi_comm_size(mpi_comm_world)
  id = mpi_comm_rank(mpi_comm_world)
  # use p, id to calc i, j, and neighbor ranks

  # time for reading/initing submatrics
  sleep(sometime) # proportional to m^2

  # shift A(i,j) left by i columns
  mpi_sendrecv(left_i, None, m*m*8,
               right_i, mpi_comm_world)
  # shift B(i,j) up by j rows
  mpi_sendrecv(up_j, None, m*m*8,
               down_j, mpi_comm_world)

  for r in range(sqrt(p)-1):
    # time for multiplying A(i,j) and B(i,j)
    sleep(sometime) # proportional to m^3

    # shift A(i,j) to the left
    mpi_sendrecv(left, None, m*m*8,
                 right, mpi_comm_world)
    # shift B(i,j) upward
    mpi_sendrecv(up, None, m*m*8,
                 down, mpi_comm_world)

  mpi_finalize(mpi_comm_world)
```

Figure 5: Simulating Cannon's matrix multiplication.

each phit is 24 bits). Each PUT message is followed by a 3-phit response packet (9 bytes) from destination to source. A typical GET transaction consists of a 8-phit request packet (24 bytes), followed by a 27-phit response packet (81 bytes), including 64 bytes of data.

To design an MPI model for Gemini, we need to incorporated the FMA request and response scheme at the level of each network transaction. Cray's MPI implementation uses both PUT and GET protocols, the decision of which to use depends on the data size [30]. It was observed that, for data size up to 4K bytes and also beyond 256K bytes, Cray's MPI uses PUT. For data size between 4K and 256K bytes, MPI chooses GET. In our implementation, we only use PUT for simplicity. Since both PUT and GET transactions have a total of 105 bytes of traffic for each request and response pair between the source and the destination, we expect that the effect of selecting between PUT and GET, both in terms of network latency and bandwidth, would be rather insignificant.

In our model, upon receiving a send request of a large MPI message, the MPI sender needs to break down the message into individual PUT requests of at most 64 bytes each. Each message will be sent over the network with an extra 32-byte message overhead. Upon receiving the PUT request, the MPI receiver responses with a 9-byte ACK. We implemented a message retransmission mechanism to ensure reliable data delivery of the MPI messages.

To easily incorporate scientific applications that use MPI, we take advantage of Simian's process oriented design. As we mentioned earlier, each compute node (host) is by itself a Simian entity. Different compute nodes communicate by sending and receiving events (via scheduling services in Simian). We implemented each user MPI process as a Simian process on the compute node. This allows each user MPI process to run independently from other MPI ranks as well as other system-level simulation processes.

Fig. 4 provides an example showing how to start the MPI processes on a simulated HPC cluster. The program starts by calling **HPCSim** to instantiate the model for the entire cluster, including the interconnect model and the compute nodes. Model parameters are passed as an argument in the form of a python dictionary. Most common hardware configurations are preset in PPT for easy reuse and customization, including those parameters that are needed by the MPI implementation for specific interconnection networks.

The **start_mpi** function creates the MPI processes on the designated compute nodes. To allow maximum flexibility, we require the users to specify a mapping from the MPI ranks to the host IDs. The first argument to **start_mpi** is a list. In the example, the simulator creates 16 MPI processes and maps them to 16 compute nodes. On the other hand, if a compute node contains multiple cores (say, 4), one may want to allocate as many MPI ranks to the compute node. This can be easily achieved by specifying a list in python, like: **[i/4 for i in range(n)]**.

Each MPI process is simply a python function that takes at least one argument: **mpi_comm_world**. Like in a real MPI implementation, it is an opaque data structure that represents the set of MPI processes among which communication may take place. Our design, to a large extent, resembles the MPI API. To illustrate its use, we use a simple example of Cannon's matrix multiplication algorithm [7]. The algorithm applies a 2-D block decomposition of the matrices. Suppose the dimension of the matrices is $n \times n$, each processor would be in charge of calculating a sub-matrix of size $m \times m$, where $m = n/\sqrt{p}$, and p is the total number of MPI ranks (assuming it is a square number).

Fig. 5 shows a simulation of the Cannon's algorithm. As we see, the program captures the main execution skeleton of the algorithm. The timing calculation for loading and initializing the sub-matrices and for multiplying the sub-matrices depends on the processor, cache/memory, and file system models that we ignore here. The MPI calls are mapped to the real MPI functions. We implemented most common MPI functions. Table 1 summarizes the main func-

Table 1: Implemented MPI Functions

MPI_Send	blocking send (until message delivered to destination)
MPI_Recv	blocking receive
MPI_Sendrecv	send and receive messages at the same time
MPI_Isend	non-blocking send, return a request handle
MPI_Irecv	non-blocking receive, return a request handle
MPI_Wait	wait until given non-blocking operation has completed
MPI_Waitall	wait for a set of non-blocking operations
MPI_Reduce	reduce values from all processes, root has final result
MPI_Allreduce	reduce values from all, everyone has final result
MPI_Bcast	broadcast a message from root to all processes
MPI_Barrier	block until all processes have called this function
MPI_Gather	gather values form all processes at root
MPI_Allgather	gather values from all processes and give to everyone
MPI_Scatter	send individual messages from root to all processes
MPI_Alltoall	send individual messages from all to all processes
MPI_Alltoallv	same as above, but each can send different amount
MPI_Comm_split	create sub-communicators
MPI_Comm_dup	duplicate an existing communicator
MPI_Comm_free	deallocate a communicator
MPI_Comm_group	return group associated with communicator
MPI_Group_size	return group size
MPI_Group_rank	return process rank in group
MPI_Group_incl	create new group including all listed
MPI_Group_excl	create new group excluding all listed
MPI_Group_free	reclaim the group
MPI_Cart_create	add cartesian coordinates to communicator
MPI_Cart_coords	return cartesian coordinates of given rank
MPI_Cart_rank	return rank of given cartesian coordinates
MPI_Cart_shift	return shifted source and destination ranks

tions included in our MPI model, including blocking and non-blocking point-to-point communications, most collective operations, groups and sub-communicators.

6. VALIDATION EXPERIMENTS

In this section, we describe the experiments for validating our interconnect model. We measure the model-predicted MPI performance on Cray's Gemini network and compare that with published results in the literature to validate our interconnect model.

We consider a large-scale interconnect system in real deployment. Hopper was built by National Energy Research Scientific Computing Center/NERSC (a high-performance computing facility of the U.S. Department of Energy (DOE) [42]). It is a Cray XE6 system that consists of 6,384 compute nodes connected via the Gemini interconnect[1]. Each compute node contains two 12-core AMD Magny Cours processors running at 2.1 GHz, and DDR3 1.3 GHz RAM (32 GB for each of the 6,000 nodes and 64 GB for each of the rest 384 nodes). The entire system contains a total of 153,216 cores, 212 terabytes of memory, and 2 petabytes of disk. The peak floating point operations per node is 201.6 Gflops. The peak performance of the system has been demonstrated to reach 1.3 petaflops [20].

As mentioned earlier, Cray's Gemini interconnect is a 3-D torus interconnect of high performance [2]. Dimensions of Hopper's torus network are $17 \times 8 \times 24$. As outlined in the original design and considered in various literature [19], the peak link speed across the X and Z dimensions is 9.375 GB/sec and in the Y dimension is 4.68 GB/sec. Inter-node latency is measured about 1.27 μs between the

[1]Cray XE6 has been used by many of the largest supercomputing systems over the last decade [19].

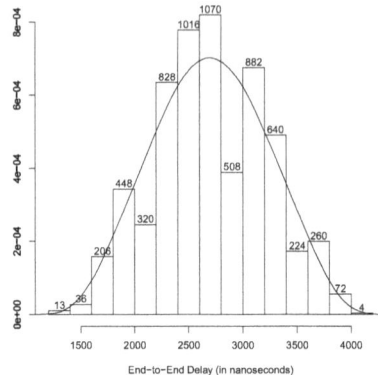

Figure 6: A histogram of end-to-end delay between compute nodes of the simulated HPC cluster.

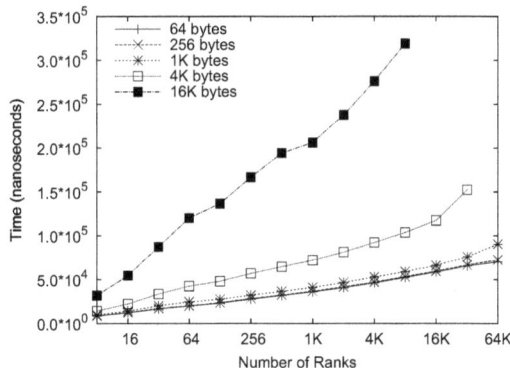

Figure 7: Duration of the MPI_Allreduce call for different number of ranks and data size on the simulated HPC cluster.

nearest nodes and 3.88 μs between the farthest nodes across the system. Although topologically it is a regular 3-D torus, Hopper's interconnect is wired specifically to optimize for the application performance, in which case the hosts are not necessarily named consecutively. To account for that in our model, we provide a mapping from the host IDs to the 3-D torus coordinates of the corresponding interconnect switches [28]. Using this one-to-one mapping, we design the hopper interconnect to closely represent the communication behavior of the applications running on the compute nodes.

The end-to-end latency between two end nodes is determined by the link (propagation) delay and the number of hops between the nodes. For Hopper, the inter-node latency has been reported to be 1.27 μs between the nearest nodes. Consequently, we configure the link delay between the compute nodes and the corresponding switch in our model to be half of that, which is 635 nanoseconds. The inter-node latency for the farthest nodes on Hopper is measured to be 3.88 μs. Since the network diameter for a $17 \times 8 \times 24$ torus is 24, we can subtract two node-switch link delays from the inter-node latency and divide the results by the network diameter. In this way, we obtain the link delay between the adjacent torus switches to be 108.75 nanoseconds. The result per-hop latency seems to be consistent with the empirical measurement reported in the original design paper [2].

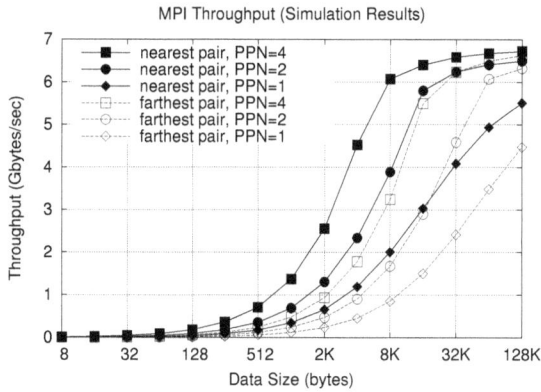

Figure 8: MPI throughput from simulation as a function of message size for 1, 2 and 4 MPI processes per node.

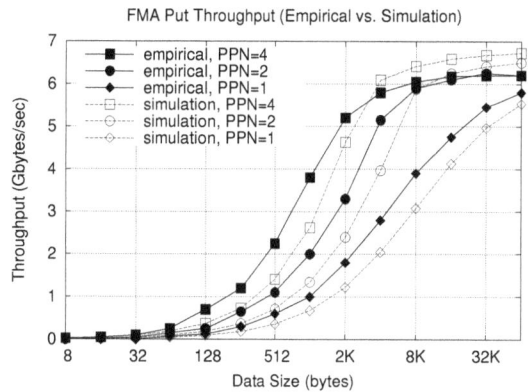

Figure 9: Gemini FMA put throughput (as reported in [2]) versus simulated throughput as a function of transfer size for 1, 2, and 4 processes per node.

We did a latency test by having an MPI process to send a 4-byte data to all other MPI processes mapped on different compute nodes and measure the end-to-end delay. Fig. 6 shows the histogram of the end-to-end delay. The delays are measured between 1.27 μs and 4.07 μs, which are considered within expectation. We also conducted a latency measurement for MPI collective operations. In particular, we measured the duration of a call to `MPI_Allreduce`, as we vary the number of MPI ranks and the data size. Fig. 7 shows the results. As expected, the collective operation has a logarithmic cost in the number of processes under the normal situation. When the number of processes increases along with the data size, part of the network becomes congested and the delay increase superlinearly.

To measure the MPI throughput, we select two compute nodes to run multiple MPI processes; we designate one compute node to run only the MPI senders and the other only the MPI receivers. We vary the number of the sender and receiver pairs (i.e., the number of processes per node, PPN) to be 1, 2 and 4. Each MPI sender sends a series of MPI messages of a given fixed size back-to-back, using `MPI_Send` call, to the designated MPI receiver on the other host. The MPI receiver simply loops and calls the `MPI_Recv`. We run different experiments varying the size of the MPI messages from 8 bytes to 128K bytes doubling each time between the experiments. To get reasonable bounds of the throughput, we select two extremes: one with the two compute nodes next to each other, and the other with the two nodes farthest apart over the interconnect network.

Fig. 8 shows the aggregate throughput of all MPI senders as a function of MPI message size. The performance levels off at 6.75 GB/s when the traffic becomes largely bandwidth constrained. As expected, multiplexing MPI sends at the source host achieves proportionally higher aggregate throughput for small data sizes when the total is less than the bandwidth cap. The throughput between the farthest nodes is lower than that between the nearest nodes due to the increased end-to-end latency.

In Gemini, Fast Memory Access (FMA) is a mechanism for user processes to generate network transactions. In our model, we implemented MPI only as FMA put, where the source can write up to 64 bytes at a time. In Fig. 9, we reproduce the Gemini FMA put throughput (solid lines) as a function of transfer size for 1, 2 and 4 processes per node (as

published in [2]). We noticed that the FMA put throughput is significantly higher than what we have achieved using MPI, especially at small transfer sizes, although both level off at above 6 MB/s for large transfer sizes. We speculated that this is due to the MPI overhead. On a quiet network, remote put has an end-to-end latency of less than 700 nanoseconds. But with MPI, the end-to-end latency increases to 3.88 μs between the farthest nodes. To verify that this is indeed the cause of the lowered throughput of our MPI performance, we artificially reconfigured the link delay so that the end-to-end delay for MPI becomes 700 nanoseconds. The results are shown in Fig. 9 (dashed lines), which clearly indicates a much closer match of the simulated results with the empirical measurements.

7. TRACE-DRIVEN MPI SIMULATION

In this section, we present a trace-based simulation study to demonstrate the capability of our interconnect model of incorporating realistic application behaviors, and further validate our model by comparing the communication cost predicted by our model against the actual performance of running the scientific applications on target HPC platforms.

In this study, we use real application communication traces provided by the National Energy Research Scientific Computing Center (NERSC). These traces are used for characterizing the demand of various DOE (US Department of Energy) mini-apps run at various large-scale computing facilities [13]. The traces contain single-node execution profiles of the mini-apps, which include the execution time, the execution speed (the number of instructions per second), the workload (the number of floating-point operations), as well as other cache/memory performance metrics, such as cache miss ratios at different levels. The traces also provide parallel speedup performance and MPI communication operations. The latter is of particular interest in our study.

The DOE mini-apps in the trace collection were run at DOE's three co-design centers, each covering two main applications. ExMatEx (Extreme Materials at Extreme Scale) [14] contains the traces of the Neutron Transport Evaluation and Test Suite (HILO) and the Livermore Unstructured Lagrangian Explicit Shock Hydrodynamics (LULESH). CESAR (Center for Exascale Simulation of Advanced Reactors) [10] contains the traces for the MOC emulator and

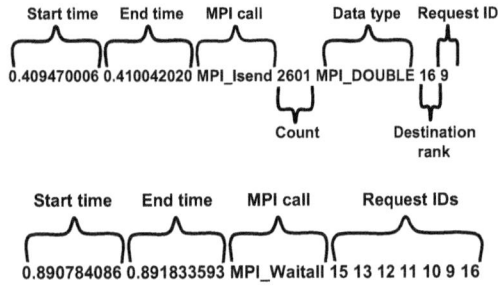

Figure 10: Format of MPI calls in the processed trace file (there is one trace file for each MPI rank).

Nekbone, which solves a poison equation using conjugate gradient iteration with no preconditioner on a block or linear geometry. ExaCT (Exascale Simulation of Combustion in Turbulence) [11] contains traces for a multigrid solver and CNS, a stencil-based algorithm for computing the Compressible Navier-Stokes equations.

The MPI traces was performed on Hopper (described earlier) using the open-source DUMPI toolkit [36] for different number of cores (e.g., 64, 256, and 1024 cores). For each run of the given application, there are a set of trace files, one for each MPI rank. The original trace files are in a binary format. We converted the binary files to text files, using the SST DUMPI toolkit [36] and then processed the files to assemble the necessary information of each MPI call in order, which includes the measured start and end time of the MPI call, and the specific parameters associated with the call, such as the source or destination rank, data size, etc. As an example, Fig. 10 shows two entries of a processed trace file, one for MPI_Isend and the other for MPI_Waitall. Note that, since the conversion from DUMPI traces to text format is done during pre-processing, this step does not contribute to the simulation runtime. An alternative solution is to parse the binary information directly. We did not choose this option as it depends on the knowledge of DUMPI's internal trace file format.

MPI_Isend is a non-blocking send; the function is expected to return immediately with a request handle, which the user can later use to query or wait for the completion of the corresponding non-blocking MPI operation. An entry associated with the MPI_Isend call includes the start time and the end time of the MPI call. The count indicates the number of data elements to be sent. Using the count and the data type, one can easily determine the true size of the MPI message. In the example, 2,601 elements of the MPI_DOUBLE type (8 bytes each) would give 20,808 bytes of data which is scheduled to be transferred for this MPI non-blocking call. The entry also provides the destination MPI rank and an ID to represent the request handle returned by the MPI call. MPI_Wallall waits for a list of MPI requests to complete. Accordingly the corresponding entry in the trace provides a list of the request IDs. The MPI function will not return until all corresponding non-blocking operations (which may include both MPI_Isend and MPI_Irecv calls) are completed.

To run the trace, we start the simulation with the same number of simulated MPI ranks. At each MPI rank, we read the corresponding processed trace file for the rank, one entry at a time. For each entry, we first advance the simulation

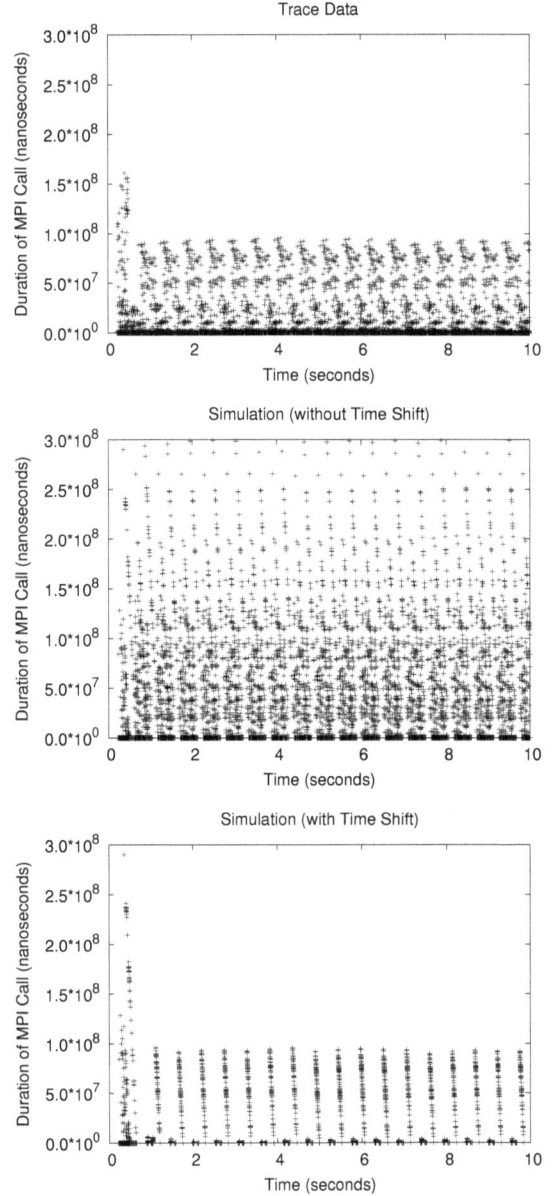

Figure 11: Comparing the duration of MPI calls between trace and simulation with and without time shift.

clock to the exact start time of the MPI call shown in the trace, by having the simulation process to sleep for the exact amount time equal to the difference between the MPI start time and current simulation clock. We then call the same MPI routine in our model and measure the time it takes to complete the MPI call in simulation. We record the time and later compare it against the end time of the MPI call in the trace.

Fig. 11 shows the results of our trace-driven simulation for LULESH from ExMatEx running on 64 MPI processes. Our method can be generally applied to all other traces. LULESH is a mini-app that approximates a typical hydrodynamics model and solves Sedov blast wave problem in 3-D [21]. It is a widely-studied proxy application, which can efficiently run on various platforms and has been ported to a number of programming models (including MPI, OpenMPI, Chapel, and Charm++) [18]. The particular trace runs for approximately 55 seconds. There are a total of 123,336 calls to `MPI_Isend` and the same number for `MPI_Irecv` and `MPI_Wait`. There are 12,864 calls to `MPI_Waitall`, 6,336 calls to `MPI_Allreduce`, 64 calls each to `MPI_Barrier` and `MPI_Reduce`.

The top plot of Fig. 11 shows the duration of MPI calls observed from the trace (by subtracting the start time from the end time). For easy exposition, we show only the first 10 seconds of the experiment (later time exhibits similar behavior). The middle plot Fig. 11 shows the trace-driven simulation result. At first glance, the simulation shows very similar pattern, yet the duration of the MPI calls spreads as much as three times of the empirical results. A closer inspection shows that the simulation clock sometimes may go beyond the start time of the MPI calls in trace. This is possible since the simulated process may take longer time to complete the previous MPI operation.

To eliminate this bias for comparing the duration of the MPI calls between the simulation and the empirical measurements, we introduce time shift for the trace. When the simulation process detects that its clock goes beyond the time of the trace, we shift the start time of all subsequent MPI calls in the trace by the difference so that the delay of the previous MPI calls in the simulation will not affect the subsequent calculations of the duration of the MPI calls.

The bottom plot of Fig. 11 shows the result of simulation with this time shift. We observe that the duration of the MPI calls becomes much lower. The outstanding spikes (up to around 100 milliseconds) are from `MPI_Waitall`. The staggering pattern seems to be related to the skew in the wall-clock time of the participating compute nodes in the original trace. This would explain the spread of the durations of the MPI calls observed in the original trace (in the top plot).

8. PARALLEL PERFORMANCE

To assess the parallel performance of our integrated model, we conducted a set of experiments on a 1,500-node compute cluster located at Los Alamos National Laboratory. Each compute node in the cluster is equipped with a 12-core Opteron 6176 12C 2.3GHz CPU. The compute nodes are connected by an Infiniband QDR interconnect.

To obtain strong-scaling results, we simulated 156,672 MPI processes running on the Hopper. That is, there is one MPI process running at each core of the target supercomputer platform. For the experiment, the MPI processes perform a collective operation, using `MPI_Allreduce`, with different data size (1K or 4K bytes).

Fig. 12 shows the performance results. We ran the model varying the number of compute nodes, from 1 (12 cores) to 256 nodes (that's 3,072 cores). For data size of 4KB, we ran the model with at least 48 cores to save compute time. The results demonstrate decent parallel performance of the simulator as we see the run time steadily decreases as we increase parallelism. However, the cost of using Simian's Python implementation is also obvious. The aggregate event rate is low, even for 3,072 cores. For this experiment, we did not use Python just-in-time (JIT) compilation, which is expected to significantly improve the performance. We are in the process of translating our model to Lua, for which Simian has demonstrated superior performance. Using JIT

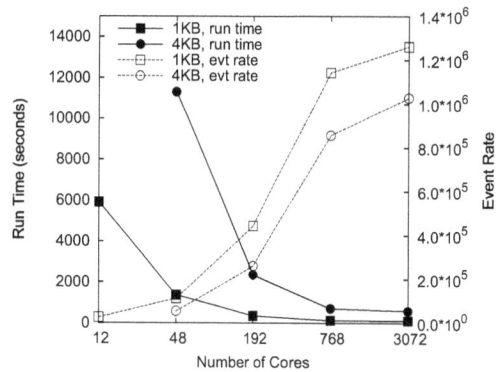

Figure 12: Observed run time and event rate for running Simian with an 156K-rank MPI model on a parallel compute cluster.

and with sufficient event granularity, Simian has been shown to achieve as much as three times the event rate of an optimized C++ parallel simulator [37].

9. CONCLUSIONS

In this paper, we presented an integrated HPC interconnect model for performance prediction. Performance prediction for large-scale scientific applications require an accurate representation of the communication cost between an extremely large number of compute nodes. Our interconnect model is fully integrated with an MPI implementation that includes all common point-to-point communication functions and collective operations with packet-level accuracy. We conducted extensive validation study of our integrated model, including a trace-driven simulation of real-life scientific application communication patterns. Results show that our model provides reasonably good accuracy.

For future work, we plan to include more interconnect topologies and integrate the interconnect model with detailed system models, including processors, cache, memory, and file systems. We plan to incorporate target scientific applications and perform scalability studies using large-scale application communication patterns (e.g., using those included on the DOE website [13]). We are currently in the process of translating our interconnect model to Simian Lua. By then, we will be able to study the parallel performance of our integrated models on large-scale HPC platforms.

Acknowledgments

We gratefully acknowledge the support of the U.S. Department of Energy through the LANL/LDRD Program for this work. We would also like to thank the anonymous reviewers for their constructive comments and suggestions.

10. REFERENCES

[1] B. Acun, N. Jain, A. Bhatele, M. Mubarak, C. D. Carothers, and L. V. Kale. Preliminary evaluation of a parallel trace replay tool for HPC network simulations. In *Euro-Par 2015: Parallel Processing Workshops*, pages 417–429. Springer, 2015.

[2] R. Alverson, D. Roweth, and L. Kaplan. The Gemini system interconnect. In *2010 18th IEEE Symposium on High Performance Interconnects*, pages 83–87. IEEE, 2010.

[3] E. Argollo, A. Falcón, P. Faraboschi, M. Monchiero, and D. Ortega. COTSon: infrastructure for full system simulation. *ACM SIGOPS Operating Systems Review*, 43(1):52–61, 2009.

[4] N. Binkert, B. Beckmann, G. Black, S. K. Reinhardt, A. Saidi, A. Basu, J. Hestness, D. R. Hower, T. Krishna, S. Sardashti, et al. The gem5 simulator. *ACM SIGARCH Computer Architecture News*, 39(2):1–7, 2011.

[5] N. L. Binkert, R. G. Dreslinski, L. R. Hsu, K. T. Lim, A. G. Saidi, and S. K. Reinhardt. The M5 simulator: Modeling networked systems. *IEEE Micro*, (4):52–60, 2006.

[6] S. Böhm and C. Engelmann. xSim: The extreme-scale simulator. In *High Performance Computing and Simulation (HPCS), 2011 International Conference on*, pages 280–286. IEEE, 2011.

[7] L. E. Cannon. *A Cellular Computer to Implement the Kalman Filter Algorithm*. PhD thesis, Montana State University, Bozeman, MT, 1969.

[8] C. D. Carothers, D. Bauer, and S. Pearce. ROSS: A high-performance, low-memory, modular Time Warp system. *Journal of Parallel and Distributed Computing*, 62(11):1648–1669, 2002.

[9] H. Casanova, A. Giersch, A. Legrand, M. Quinson, and F. Suter. Versatile, scalable, and accurate simulation of distributed applications and platforms. *Journal of Parallel and Distributed Computing*, 74(10):2899–2917, 2014.

[10] Center for Exascale Simulation of Advanced Reactors (CESAR). https://cesar.mcs.anl.gov/.

[11] Center for Exascale Simulation of Combustion in Turbulence (ExaCT). http://exactcodesign.org/.

[12] J. Cope, N. Liu, S. Lang, P. Carns, C. Carothers, and R. Ross. CODES: Enabling co-design of multilayer exascale storage architectures. In *Proceedings of the Workshop on Emerging Supercomputing Technologies*, pages 303–312, 2011.

[13] Department of Energy. Design forward characterization of DOE mini-apps. http://portal.nersc.gov/project/CAL/doe-miniapps.htm, Accessed December 1, 2015.

[14] DoE Exascale Co-Design Center for Materials in Extreme Environments (ExMatEx). ExMatEx: Extreme Materials at Extreme Scale. http://www.exmatex.org/.

[15] C. Engelmann. Scaling to a million cores and beyond: Using light-weight simulation to understand the challenges ahead on the road to exascale. *Future Generation Computer Systems*, 30:59–65, 2014.

[16] C. Engelmann and F. Lauer. Facilitating co-design for extreme-scale systems through lightweight simulation. In *Cluster Computing Workshops and Posters (CLUSTER WORKSHOPS), 2010 IEEE International Conference on*, pages 1–8. IEEE, 2010.

[17] I. S. Jones and C. Engelmann. Simulation of large-scale HPC architectures. In *Parallel Processing Workshops (ICPPW), 2011 40th International Conference on*, pages 447–456. IEEE, 2011.

[18] I. Karlin, A. Bhatele, J. Keasler, B. L. Chamberlain, J. Cohen, Z. DeVito, R. Haque, D. Laney, E. Luke, F. Wang, et al. Exploring traditional and emerging parallel programming models using a proxy application. In *Parallel & Distributed Processing (IPDPS), 2013 IEEE 27th International Symposium on*, pages 919–932. IEEE, 2013.

[19] D. J. Kerbyson, K. J. Barker, A. Vishnu, and A. Hoisie. A performance comparison of current HPC systems: Blue Gene/Q, Cray XE6 and InfiniBand systems. *Future Generation Computer Systems*, 30:291–304, 2014.

[20] V. Kindratenko and P. Trancoso. Trends in high-performance computing. *Computing in Science & Engineering*, 13(3):92–95, 2011.

[21] Lawrence Livermore National Laboratory. Livermore unstructured lagrangian explicit shock hydrodynamics (lulesh). https://codesign.llnl.gov/lulesh.php.

[22] N. Liu and C. D. Carothers. Modeling billion-node torus networks using massively parallel discrete-event simulation. In *Proceedings of the 2011 IEEE Workshop on Principles of Advanced and Distributed Simulation*, pages 1–8. IEEE Computer Society, 2011.

[23] N. Liu, A. Haider, X.-H. Sun, and D. Jin. FatTreeSim: Modeling large-scale fat-tree networks for HPC systems and data centers using parallel and discrete event simulation. In *Proceedings of the 3rd ACM Conference on SIGSIM-Principles of Advanced Discrete Simulation*, pages 199–210. ACM, 2015.

[24] P. S. Magnusson, M. Christensson, J. Eskilson, D. Forsgren, G. Hallberg, J. Hogberg, F. Larsson, A. Moestedt, and B. Werner. Simics: A full system simulation platform. *Computer*, 35(2):50–58, 2002.

[25] J. E. Miller, H. Kasture, G. Kurian, C. Gruenwald III, N. Beckmann, C. Celio, J. Eastep, and A. Agarwal. Graphite: A distributed parallel simulator for multicores. In *High Performance Computer Architecture (HPCA), 2010 IEEE 16th International Symposium on*, pages 1–12. IEEE, 2010.

[26] M. Mubarak, C. D. Carothers, R. Ross, and P. Carns. Modeling a million-node dragonfly network using massively parallel discrete-event simulation. In *High Performance Computing, Networking, Storage and Analysis (SCC), 2012 SC Companion:*, pages 366–376. IEEE, 2012.

[27] M. Mubarak, C. D. Carothers, R. B. Ross, and P. Carns. A case study in using massively parallel simulation for extreme-scale torus network codesign. In *Proceedings of the 2nd ACM SIGSIM/PADS conference on Principles of advanced discrete simulation*, pages 27–38. ACM, 2014.

[28] National Energy Research Scientific Computing Center (NERSC). Hopper system. http://www.nersc.gov/users/computational-systems/hopper/.

[29] D. M. Nicol. The cost of conservative synchronization in parallel discrete event simulations. *Journal of the ACM*, 40(2):304–333, April 1993.

[30] K. Pedretti, C. Vaughan, R. Barrett, K. Devine, and K. S. Hemmert. Using the Cray Gemini performance counters. *Proc Cray User Group (CUG)*, 2013.

[31] A. J. Peña, R. G. C. Carvalho, J. Dinan, P. Balaji, R. Thakur, and W. Gropp. Analysis of topology-dependent MPI performance on Gemini networks. In *Proceedings of the 20th European MPI Users' Group Meeting*, pages 61–66. ACM, 2013.

[32] K. S. Perumalla. $\mu\pi$: a scalable and transparent system for simulating MPI programs. In *Proceedings of the 3rd International ICST Conference on Simulation Tools and Techniques*, page 62. ICST (Institute for Computer Sciences, Social-Informatics and Telecommunications Engineering), 2010.

[33] K. S. Perumalla and A. J. Park. Simulating billion-task parallel programs. In *Performance Evaluation of Computer and Telecommunication Systems (SPECTS 2014), International Symposium on*, pages 585–592. IEEE, 2014.

[34] A. F. Rodrigues, K. S. Hemmert, B. W. Barrett, C. Kersey, R. Oldfield, M. Weston, R. Risen, J. Cook, P. Rosenfeld, E. CooperBalls, et al. The structural simulation toolkit. *ACM SIGMETRICS Performance Evaluation Review*, 38(4):37–42, 2011.

[35] N. Saboo, A. K. Singla, J. M. Unger, and L. V. Kalé. Emulating petaflops machines and Blue Gene. In *Proceedings of the 15th International Parallel &Amp; Distributed Processing Symposium*, IPDPS '01, pages 195–, Washington, DC, USA, 2001. IEEE Computer Society.

[36] Sandia National Laboratories. Dumpi: The mpi trace library. http://sst.sandia.gov/about/_dumpi.html.

[37] N. Santhi, S. Eidenzenz, and J. Liu. The Simian concept: parallel discrete event simulation with interpreted languages. In L. Yilmaz, W. K. V. Chan, I. Moon, T. M. K. Roeder, C. Macal, and M. D. Rossetti, editors, *Proceedings of the 2015 Winter Simulation Conference*, 2015.

[38] US Department of Energy. Department of Energy Awards $425 Million in Next Generation Supercomputing Technologies. http://energy.gov/articles/department-energy-awards-425-million-next-generation-supercomputing-technologies, 2014.

[39] B. Van Straalen and P. Collela. Resiliency and codesign. In *DOE Exascale Research Conference*, 2012.

[40] A. Vishnu, J. Daily, and B. Palmer. Designing scalable PGAS communication subsystems on Cray Gemini interconnect. In *High Performance Computing (HiPC), 2012 19th International Conference on*, pages 1–10. IEEE, 2012.

[41] S. J. Wilton and N. P. Jouppi. CACTI: An enhanced cache access and cycle time model. *Solid-State Circuits, IEEE Journal of*, 31(5):677–688, 1996.

[42] N. Wright, H. Shan, F. Blagojevic, H. Wasserman, T. Drummond, J. Shalf, K. Fuerlinger, K. Yelick, S. Ethier, M. Wagner, et al. The NERSC-Cray center of excellence: Performance optimization for the multicore era. *CUG Proceedings*, 2011.

[43] G. Zheng, G. Kakulapati, and L. V. Kalé. Bigsim: A parallel simulator for performance prediction of extremely large parallel machines. In *Parallel and Distributed Processing Symposium, 2004. Proceedings. 18th International*, page 78. IEEE, 2004.

Modeling a Million-Node Slim Fly Network Using Parallel Discrete-Event Simulation

Noah Wolfe, Christopher D. Carothers
Rensselaer Polytechnic Institute
110 8th St
Troy, NY
wolfen,chrisc@rpi.edu

Misbah Mubarak, Robert Ross,
Philip Carns
Argonne National Laboratory
9700 South Cass Avenue
Lemont, IL 60439
mmubarak,rross,carns@mcs.anl.gov

ABSTRACT

As supercomputers close in on exascale performance, the increased number of processors and processing power translates to an increased demand on the underlying network interconnect. The Slim Fly network topology, a new low-diameter and low-latency interconnection network, is gaining interest as one possible solution for next-generation supercomputing interconnect systems. In this paper, we present a high-fidelity Slim Fly flit-level model leveraging the Rensselaer Optimistic Simulation System (ROSS) and Co-Design of Exascale Storage (CODES) frameworks. We validate our Slim Fly model with the Kathareios et al. Slim Fly model results provided at moderately sized network scales. We further scale the model size up to n unprecedented 1 million compute nodes; and through visualization of network simulation metrics such as link bandwidth, packet latency, and port occupancy, we get an insight into the network behavior at the million-node scale. We also show linear strong scaling of the Slim Fly model on an Intel cluster achieving a peak event rate of 36 million events per second using 128 MPI tasks to process 7 billion events. Detailed analysis of the underlying discrete-event simulation performance shows how the million-node Slim Fly model simulation executes in 198 seconds on the Intel cluster.

CCS Concepts

•Computing methodologies → Discrete-event simulation; Model verification and validation; Parallel algorithms; •Networks → Network simulations;

Keywords

Slim Fly; Network topologies; Parallel discrete event simulation; Interconnection networks

Publication rights licensed to ACM. ACM acknowledges that this contribution was authored or co-authored by an employee, contractor or affiliate of the United States government. As such, the Government retains a nonexclusive, royalty-free right to publish or reproduce this article, or to allow others to do so, for Government purposes only.

SIGSIM-PADS '16, May 15 - 18, 2016, Banff, AB, Canada

© 2016 Copyright held by the owner/author(s). Publication rights licensed to ACM.

ACM ISBN 978-1-4503-3742-7/16/05. . . $15.00

DOI: http://dx.doi.org/10.1145/2901378.2901389

1. INTRODUCTION

Performance of interconnection networks is integral to large-scale computing systems. Current HPC systems have thousands of compute nodes; for example, the Mira Blue Gene/Q system at Argonne has 49,152 compute nodes [23]. Some of the future pre-exascale machines, such as Aurora to be deployed at Argonne National Laboratory, will have over 50,000 compute nodes [13]. The ability of the interconnection network to transfer data efficiently is essential to the successful implementation and deployment of such large-scale HPC systems. There is a trade-off of latency, cost, and diameter among the potential network topologies that currently exist. One topology that meets all three metrics is Slim Fly, as proposed by Besta and Hoefler [4]. High bandwidth, low latency, low cost, and a low network diameter are all properties of the Slim Fly network that make it a solid option as an interconnection network for large-scale computing systems.

In this paper, we present a highly efficient and detailed model of the Slim Fly network topology using massively parallel discrete-event simulation. Validating against the Slim Fly simulator by Besta and Hoefler [4], our Slim Fly model is capable of performing minimal, non-minimal, and adaptive routing under uniform random and worst-case traffic workloads. Our model is also capable of large-scale network modeling; and in this paper, we execute a million-node Slim Fly network on the RSA Intel cluster at Rensselaer Polytechnic Institute (RPI) Center for Computation Innovations. In addition, our model has been implemented to execute under optimistic event scheduling using reverse computation and achieves 36 million events per second while maintaining 99% efficiency. This level of performance establishes our Slim Fly model as a useful tool that will give network designers the capability to analyze different design options of Slim Fly networks.

The main contributions of this paper are as follows.

- A Rensselaer Optimistic Simulation System (ROSS) parallel discrete event Slim Fly network model that can simulate large-scale Slim Fly networks at a detailed fidelity and provide insight into network behavior by recording detailed metrics at this scale. The Slim Fly model is also shown to be in close agreement with the Kathareios et al. Slim Fly network simulator [14].

- We simulate and provide a detailed visual analysis of a Slim Fly network at a scale of 74,000 nodes, inspired by the Argonne Aurora supercomputer.

- This paper also models the largest discrete-event Slim Fly network to date at just over 1 million nodes and crossing the 7 billion committed events mark.

- In terms of the simulation performance itself, a strong-scaling study of our simulation demonstrates that our Slim Fly model is highly scalable and can achieve an event rate of 43 million events per second on 16 nodes, 128 processes of the Intel cluster at RPI [8]

The remainder of the paper is organized as follows. Section 2 provides the network simulation design in terms of the topology, routing algorithms and flow control. We also describe the details of the discrete event simulation implementation. Section 3 presents the validation experiments. Section 4 describes the network and discrete-event simulation performance results. Section 5 discusses related work, and Section 6 summarizes our conclusions and briefly discusses future work.

2. SLIM FLY NETWORK MODEL

In this section, we describe the simulation design of the Slim Fly topology as well as its implementation in the form of a discrete event simulation.

Table 1: Descriptions of symbols used

Topic	Symbol	Description
SF	p	Nodes connected to a router
	N_r	Total routers in network ($N_r = 2q^2$)
	N_n	Total nodes in network ($N_n = N_r * p$)
	k'	Router network radix
	k	Router radix ($k = k' + p$)
	q	Prime power
CODES/ ROSS	LP	Logical Process (simulated entity)
	PE	Processing element (MPI rank)

2.1 Slim Fly Topology

Introduced by Besta and Hoefler [4], the Slim Fly consists of groups of routers with direct connections to other routers in the network similar in nature to the dragonfly interconnect topology. Each router has a degree of local connectivity to other routers in its local group and a global degree of connectivity to routers in other groups. Unlike the dragonfly topology, however, the Slim Fly does not have fully connected router groups. Within each group, each router has only a subset of intragroup connections governed by one of two specific equations based on the router's subgraph membership. Furthermore, all router groups are split into two subgraphs. Each router possesses global intergroup connections only to routers within the opposite subgraph, forming a bipartite graph between the two subgraphs. These global connections are also constructed according to a third equation [4]. Figure 1. shows a simple example of the described structure and layout of the Slim Fly topology.

An important feature of the Slim Fly topology is that its graphs are constructed to guarantee a given maximum diameter. One example set of graphs, which we use in this paper, is the collection of diameter 2 graphs introduced by McKay et al. [16], called MMS graphs. MMS graphs guarantee a maximum of 2 hops when traversing the network layer and because they approach the Moore bound [18], these graphs

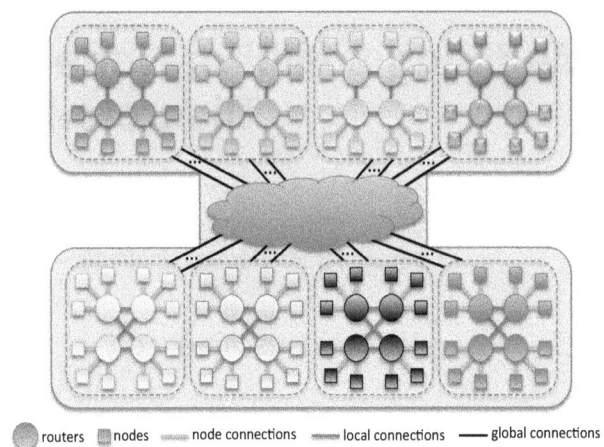

routers ● nodes ■ node connections ⋯⋯ local connections ═══ global connections ━━━

Figure 1: General structure and layout of MMS Slim Fly graphs. Global connections between subgraphs have been generalized for clarity. There are no intergroup connections within the same subgraph. Each router contains one global connection to one router in each of the q-many router groups in the opposing subgraph.

constitute some of the largest possible graphs that maintain full network bandwidth while maintaining a degree of 2. The 2-hop property holds true while scaling to larger node graphs because the router radix grows as well. For example, routers in a 3K node network require a 28 radix router, while a much larger 1M node network needs a 367 radix router.

2.1.1 Slim Fly MMS graph Construction

Following the methods derived in [12] and summarized and applied to the Slim Fly topology in [4], we developed a separate application to create the nontrivial MMS network topology graphs that govern the interconnection layout of nodes and routers in Slim Fly networks. The process requires (1) finding a prime power $q = 4w + \delta$ that yields a desired number of routers $N_r = 2q^2$; (2) constructing the Galois field and, more important, the primitive element ξ that generates the Galois field; (3) using ξ, computing generator sets X and X' [12] and using them in conjunction with equations 1–3 to construct the interconnection of routers; and (4) sequentially connecting compute nodes to routers.

$$\text{router}(0, x, y) \text{ is connected to } (0, x, y') \text{ iff } y - y' \in X; \quad (1)$$

$$\text{router}(1, m, c) \text{ is connected to } (1, m, c') \text{ iff } c - c' \in X'; \quad (2)$$

$$\text{router}(0, x, y) \text{ is connected to } (1, m, c) \text{ iff } y = mx + c; \quad (3)$$

An example MMS graph is provided in Figure 2. As shown, all routers have three coordinates (s, x, y) indicating the location of the router in the network. The $s \in \{0, 1\}$ coordinate indicates the subgraph, while the $x \in \{0, ..., q-1\}$ and $y \in \{0, ..., q-1\}$ coordinates indicate the router's group and position within the group, respectively. Following the coordinate system, Equation 1 is used to compute the intragroup connections for all groups of subgraph 0 shown in Figure 2. Equation 2 performs the same computation for all groups in subgraph 1, shown in red. Equation 3 determines the connections between the two subgraphs, shown in blue. For simplicity, Equation 3 connections are displayed only for router$(1, 0, 0)$.

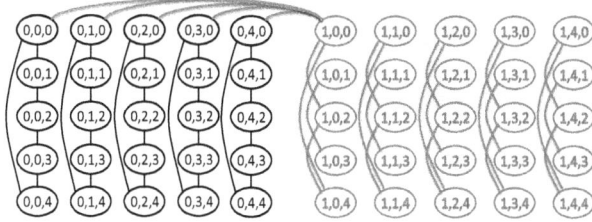

Figure 2: Example MMS graph with $q = 5$ illustrating the connection of routers within groups and between subgraphs.

2.2 Routing Algorithms

Our Slim Fly model currently supports three routing algorithms for studying network performance: minimal, non-minimal, and adaptive routing.

2.2.1 Minimal Routing

The minimal, or direct, routing algorithm routes all network packets from source to destination using a maximum of two hops between routers (property of MMS graphs guarantees router graph diameter of two regardless of the size of the graph). If the source router and destination router are directly connected, then the minimal path consists of only one hop between routers. If the source compute node is connected to the same router as the destination compute node, then there are zero hops between routers. In the third case, an intermediate router must exist that shares a connection to both source and destination router so the packet traverses a maximum of two hops.

2.2.2 Non-minimal Routing

Non-minimal routing for the Slim Fly topology follows the traditional Valiant randomized routing algorithm [25]. This approach selects a random intermediate router that is different from the source or destination router and routes minimally from source router to the randomly selected intermediate router. The packet is then routed minimally again from the intermediate router to the destination router. The number of hops traversed with valiant routing would be double that of minimal routing. In the optimal case when all three routers are directly connected, the path will be two hops. On the other end of the spectrum each minimal path to and from the intermediate router can have two hops, bringing the maximum number of possible hops to four.

2.2.3 Adaptive Routing

Adaptive routing mixes both minimal and non-minimal approaches by adaptively selecting between the minimal path and several valiant paths. To make direct comparisons for validating our model, we follow a slightly modified version of the Universal Globally-Adaptive Load-balanced (UGAL) algorithm [26] shown in [14]. First, the minimal path and several non-minimal paths (n_I) are generated and their corresponding path lengths L_M and L_I^i, $i \in 1, 2, ...n_I$ are computed. Next, we compute the penalty $c = L_I^i/L_M * c_{SF}$, where c_{SF} is a constant chosen to balance the ratio. Next,

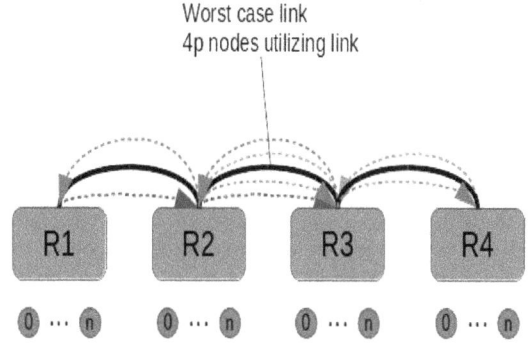

Figure 3: Worst-case traffic layout for the Slim Fly topology.

the final cost of each non-minimal route $C_I^i = c * q_I^i$ is computed, where q_I^i is the occupancy of the first router's output port corresponding to the path of route i. The cost of the minimal path is simply the occupancy of the first router's port along the path q_M. Then, the route with the lowest cost is selected, and the packet is routed accordingly. With this method, each packet has a chance of getting routed with anywhere from one to four hops.

2.3 Traffic Workloads

To accurately simulate and analyze the network communication using a Slim Fly interconnection topology, we implemented two traffic workloads. The first workload is the uniform random (UR) traffic pattern that selects a random destination compute node anywhere in the network that is different from the source and destination computes nodes. The second workload is a worst-case (WC) traffic pattern that simulates an application that is communicating in a manner that fully saturates links in the network and thus creates a bottleneck for minimal routing. In this workload, each compute node in a router, R1, will communicate to a node within a paired router that is the maximum two hops away. Another pair of routers that share the same middle link with the previous pair of routers will be established to fully saturate that center link. As shown in the example in Figure 3, all compute nodes connected to R1 communicate with nodes connected to R3 along the blue path. Also, the reverse communication is true, because all nodes connected to R3 communicate with nodes connected to R1 along the red path. The router pair R2 and R4 are set up in the same manner communicating along the gray and green paths, respectively. This setup of network communication puts a worst-case burden on the link between routers 2 and 3 as $4p$ nodes are creating $2p$ data flows. With all nodes paired in this configuration, congestion quickly builds up for all nodes in the system and limits maximum throughput to $1/2p$.

2.4 Congestion Control

Both virtual channel [10] and credit based flow control [11] are used in our Slim Fly model to prevent congestion. Following the approach in [4], we discretize our selection of virtual channels to the number of hops a message packet has taken. In other words, for every hop i that a message packet takes, when leaving a router, that packet uses the ith virtual channel. Packets that take a local route and have only one hop will always use $VC0$. Packets that take a global path (assuming minimal routing) will use $VC0$ for the first hop and then $VC1$ for the second hop. Clearly, the optimal number of VCs to use in minimal routing is two. In the case of non-minimal routing such as valiant and adaptive routing, the number of virtual channels used is four, because the maximum possible number of hops in a packet's route is four.

In terms of the implementation, an *output_vc* variable is added to the compute node message state structure and initialized to 0 when a message is created. Each time a router sends a message, it sends the message on the *output_vc* virtual channel and increments *output_vc* so that the next router on the path will use the next corresponding VC.

Each compute node and router also follows credit based flow control by utilizing a buffer space to store packets needing to be injected into the network. When a credit is received, indicating the requested link is available for transmission, a packet in the corresponding link buffer is transmitted.

2.5 Discrete-Event Simulation

Capturing performance measurements of extreme-scale networks having millions of nodes requires a simulation that can efficiently decompose the large problem domain. One such approach, used in this paper, is parallel discrete-event simulation (PDES). PDES decomposes the problem into distinct components called logical processes (LPs), each with its own self maintained state in the system. These LPs model the specific computing components in the simulation such as routers, nodes, and workload processes. LPs interact and capture the system dynamics by passing timestamped event messages to one another. These LPs are further mapped to physical MPI rank processing elements (PEs), which compute their corresponding LPs' events in timestamped order.

We have implemented our Slim Fly model using ROSS [6], a discrete event simulator with support for both conservative and optimistic parallel execution. Conservative execution uses the YAWNS protocol [21] to keep all LPs from computing events out of order. The optimistic event scheduler allows each LP to keep its own local time and therefore compute events out of order with respect to other LPs. Optimistic event scheduling is faster than conservative scheduling. However, this speedup comes at the cost of out-of-order event execution, which is handled by reverse computation [7]. When a temporal anomaly occurs and an event is processed out of timestamp order, all events must be incrementally rolled back to restore the state of the LP to just before the incorrect event occurred.

The rollback process uses a reverse event handler to undo the events. The reverse handlers for the model must be provided by the model programmers. The reverse event handler is a negation of the forward event handler performing inverse operations on all state changing actions. For example, in the Slim Fly model using non-minimal routing, when a message packet arrives at its first router from a node, that router LP performs forward operations in the router-receive forward event handler. The router LP (1) increments the number of received packets, (2) sends a credit event to the sending node LP, (3) computes the next destination by sampling a random number for the random intermediate destination, and (4) creates a new router-send event to relay the packet to the next hop router LP. The reverse event handler needs to undo these operations by (1) decrementing the received

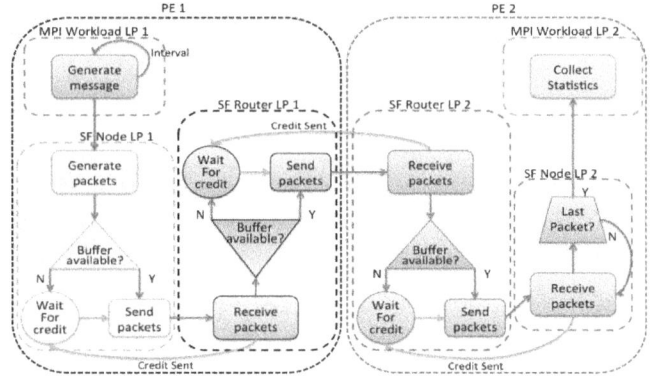

Figure 4: Diagram showing the general execution path of events in the Slim Fly specific ROSS parallel discrete-event simulation.

packets state variable, (2) sending an anti-message to the sending node to reverse the credit sent, (3) unrolling the random number generator by one, and (4) creating an antimessage (a message indicating an event was issued out of timestamp order and needs to be rolled back in optimistic execution) to cancel the router-send event.

We also implemented our Slim Fly model with CODES (Co-Design of Exascale Storage) [9]. This is a simulation tool kit built on top of ROSS that can be used to simulate storage [24] and HPC network systems. CODES helps facilitate the use of HPC network workloads and simulating network communication in the context of discrete event simulations. CODES also provides a range of network models including dragonfly [19], torus [20], and analytical LogGP [2]. Our Slim Fly network model is an addition to the CODES network models. Using the CODES simulation framework, dedicated MPI workload LPs (representing MPI processes attached to compute nodes) generate and receive messages. Messages generated by workload LPs are sent immediately to their corresponding attached compute node LPs with minimal delay in simulation time. Subsequent message generate events are created at a given interval to approximate the desired network injection rate, incorporating network latencies.

In our Slim Fly model, each LP represents one router, compute node, or simulated MPI workload process in the network. Also, each timestamped event represents a network packet transferring through the network. Figure 4 shows the general structure and event-driven procedure for the Slim Fly network simulation. In this figure, we are running the simulation on two physical cores with one MPI rank per core, resulting in two PEs. The LPs are distributed equally among the two PEs. Events/messages, represented by the arrows between LPs, are transferred between the LPs. For simplicity, only the LPs involved in the example are illustrated.

Upon receiving a message event, the compute node LP decomposes the message into packets and extracts the message destination. The compute node LP computes the next hop and corresponding output port for each packet using the selected routing algorithm. Prior to sending a packet, the sending node LP checks the occupancy of the selected port and virtual channel. If space exists, the packet is allocated, and a receive event is scheduled on the destination router with a time delay. This time delay incorporates the bandwidth and latency of the corresponding network link. If the buffer is full, the node LP follows credit-based flow control and must wait for a credit from the destination router to open up a space on the corresponding link.

In order to accurately analyze the Slim Fly network, various parameters and statistics are collected and stored in both the LPs and the event messages. These statistics include start and end times of packets on the network, average hops traversed by the packets, and the virtual channels being used.

Once a packet arrives at the router LP, a credit event is sent back to the sending LP to free up space in the sending LP's output buffer. The LP then extracts the destination node ID. The router LP determines the next hop and corresponding output port, once again using the routing algorithm specified. The router also follows the same credit-based flow control scheme as the compute node LP.

After the packet reaches its destination node LP, the node waits for all packets belonging to that message to arrive before issuing a message arrival event on the destination workload LP. At this point, we can collect the statistics stored in the messages, for example, packet latency and number of hops traversed.

3. SLIM FLY MODEL VALIDATION

In this section, we present a comparison with published Slim Fly network results by Kathareios et al. [14] to validate the implementation of our model. The specifics of the IBM-ETH-SF simulator are not provided, but the authors do mention that it is based on the Omnest simulator, which also employs parallel discrete-event simulation. This IBM-ETH collaborative work presents throughput results for a Slim Fly network with the configuration below. The configuration is of particular interest because it yields a total number of compute nodes that is similar to the number of nodes in the future Summit supercomputer [22].

- $q = 13$, $p = 9$, $N_n = 3042$, $N_r = 338$, $k = 28$.

Further network parameters include a 100 Gbps link bandwidth for all links with a latency of 50 ns. The routers utilize virtual channels, a buffer space of 100 KB per port (equally divided among the VCs), and a 100 ns traversal delay. Flow control is done with the use of credits and messages are 256 byte packets. Simulation time for the IBM-ETH-SF was 200 μs with a 20 μs warmup. In our simulation, we include the warmup time in the total execution and therefore run the simulation for 220 μs. The results include minimal, non-minimal, and adaptive routing for uniform random and worst-case traffic workloads. Our simulation results in comparison with the IBM-ETH-SF results are presented in Figures 5, 6, and 7. The metric comparison is throughput percentage and is computed according to Equation 4. Besta and Hoefler [4] approximate the upper bound for bisection bandwidth for the Slim Fly topology to be 71% link bandwidth per node when $p = \lfloor \frac{k'}{2} \rfloor$. Therefore, our simulated 100 Gbps link bandwidth translates to a maximum throughput of 71 Gbps per node. The *observed_throughput* is gained from our Slim Fly model by performing a sum reduction to get the total number of packets transferred by all compute nodes, multiplying by the 256 byte packet size and dividing by the total number of compute nodes.

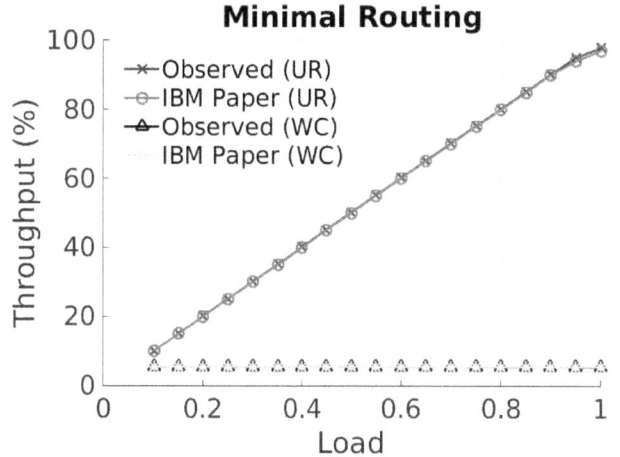

Figure 5: Throughput comparison of minimal routing for uniform random (UR) and worst-case (WC) traffic workloads.

$$throughput\_percent = \frac{observed\_throughput\_Gbps}{0.71 * 100Gbps} * 100$$

(4)

3.1 Minimal Routing Comparison

Figure 5 presents the throughput analysis for the minimal routing algorithm under input loads varying from 10% to 100% link bandwidth. Focusing on the uniform random workload case, our Slim Fly model closely matches that of the IBM-ETH-SF. As expected, the minimal routing algorithm excels under uniform random workloads. Both simulations show the Slim Fly network throughput matching the injection load from 10% load to about 95% load, at which point the throughput trails off to roughly 98% throughput at 100% load. In the worst-case workload results, the two results are again a close match. Both show a constant 5.5% throughput utilization from 10% to 100% load. Clearly, minimal routing is a poor choice for traffic that is not distributed throughout the network, because minimal routing has no means of selecting alternate routing paths to avoid congested links.

3.2 Non-minimal Routing Comparison

The results comparing throughput analysis for non-minimal routing are shown in Figure 6. In this case, all four sets of results are close together. Under both uniform random and worst-case traffic routing, the Slim Fly network achieves a throughput equal to the injection load until 50% load is reached. At this point, the network throughput reaches a bottleneck and maintains just under half-link bandwidth up to 100% injection load. Non-minimal routing underperforms compared with minimal routing for uniform random traffic because the maximum path length of all routes is twice as long at four hops compared with two hops in minimal routing. Therefore, non-minimal routing reaches congestion in UR traffic at roughly 50% load, roughly half the load of minimal routing. However, non-minimal routing outperforms minimal routing in worst-case traffic because of its ability to perform a uniform load balancing of traffic as it selects a random intermediate router along its path.

Non-minimal Routing

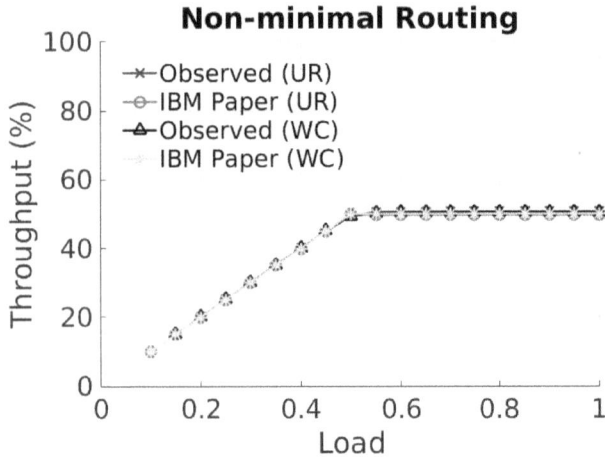

Figure 6: Throughput comparison of non-minimal routing for uniform random (UR) and worst-case (WC) traffic workloads.

Adaptive Routing

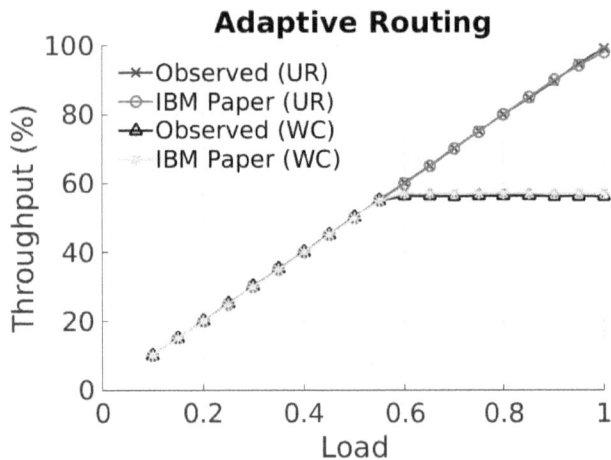

Figure 7: Throughput comparison of adaptive routing for Uniform Random (UR) and worst-case (WC) traffic workloads.

3.3 Adaptive Routing Comparison

The throughput comparison results for the adaptive routing algorithm are shown in Figure 7. In all cases, we set the number of indirect routes, $n_i = 3$, and $c_{SF} = 1$. Once again, the observed results for our Slim Fly model agree with those of the IBM-ETH-SF simulator. In both uniform random and worst-case traffic workloads, the network throughput matches the injection load until 55% load, at which point the worst-case traffic results reach congestion and are limited at 58%. The uniform random traffic results continue with optimal throughput and reach nearly full system throughput at 100% load. Adaptive routing is able to match the performance of minimal routing for uniform random traffic because it can continually select the minimal path for all packets. Adaptive routing outperforms both minimal and non-minimal routing for worst-case traffic because of its ability to dynamically select between the minimal and non-minimal routes.

3.4 Network Visualization

Continuing the analysis, we show visual representations of router occupancy and message sends and receives for both router LPs and compute node LPs during the above simulations. These visualizations provide insight into large, complex network simulations.

The router occupancy metric collects the number of packets sitting in queue waiting for space to open up on the necessary router output port. Since we use VCs for congestion control, the router occupancy metric can be further divided into virtual channels with 2 VCs per port per router used in the case of minimal routing and 4 VCs per port per router used in non-minimal routing. Since virtual channels help alleviate congestion, their occupancy can provide insight to help identify the source of congestion in the network.

Figure 8 presents a number of graphs visualizing the occupancy of all virtual channels for all ports on all routers in the simulation. All four Slim Fly test cases are from Figure 5, which run the 3K-node Slim Fly model using minimal routing for uniform random traffic. In this case, there are 338 routers with a network radix of 19 and 2 VCs per port. The result is a total of 6,422 ports, each with 2 virtual channels. Figures 8a–8d display the occupancy of VC0 with increasing load from 50% to 100%, and Figures 8e–8h display the same for VC1.

The 3K-node Slim Fly model experiences little congestion until about 90% injection load, where VC0 sees a uniform distribution of roughly 20% congestion in the network. At 100% injection load, the network begins to reach the buffer space limit as packets enter the network at an increased rate, further explaining why we see a slight dip in throughput performance for minimal routing under uniform random traffic in Figure 5. The VC0 buffer fills up first, indicating that the compute nodes are injecting packets into the network faster than the routers can relay them.

In addition to buffer occupancy, the number of message packets sent and received by all routers and compute nodes is visualized over the simulation time. The results are collected during the same simulation in Figures 8d and 8h and are displayed in Figure 9. The first noticeable feature is the large spike in the beginning of the compute node sends (Figure 9a). Occurring at the beginning of the simulation, this spike is a result of the initial packet burst into the system, which is followed by a balancing out as the network reaches a steady state. The same phenomenon is reflected as a slow start in router sends and receives plots in Figures 9c and 9d. These figures all resemble the uniform random traffic workload being simulated, except for the initial startup phase. We can also note that the steady-state section of the router sends graph has more of a yellow hue than does the router receives plot, indicating that the routers consistently receive message packets but have slightly more variance in the rate at which they are able to send packets, which can contribute to the slight drop in network throughput observed at 100% load.

The added capability of visual analysis of these important network metrics not only helps detect network congestion but also helps identify the time, location, and effect of congestion on the entire network simulation.

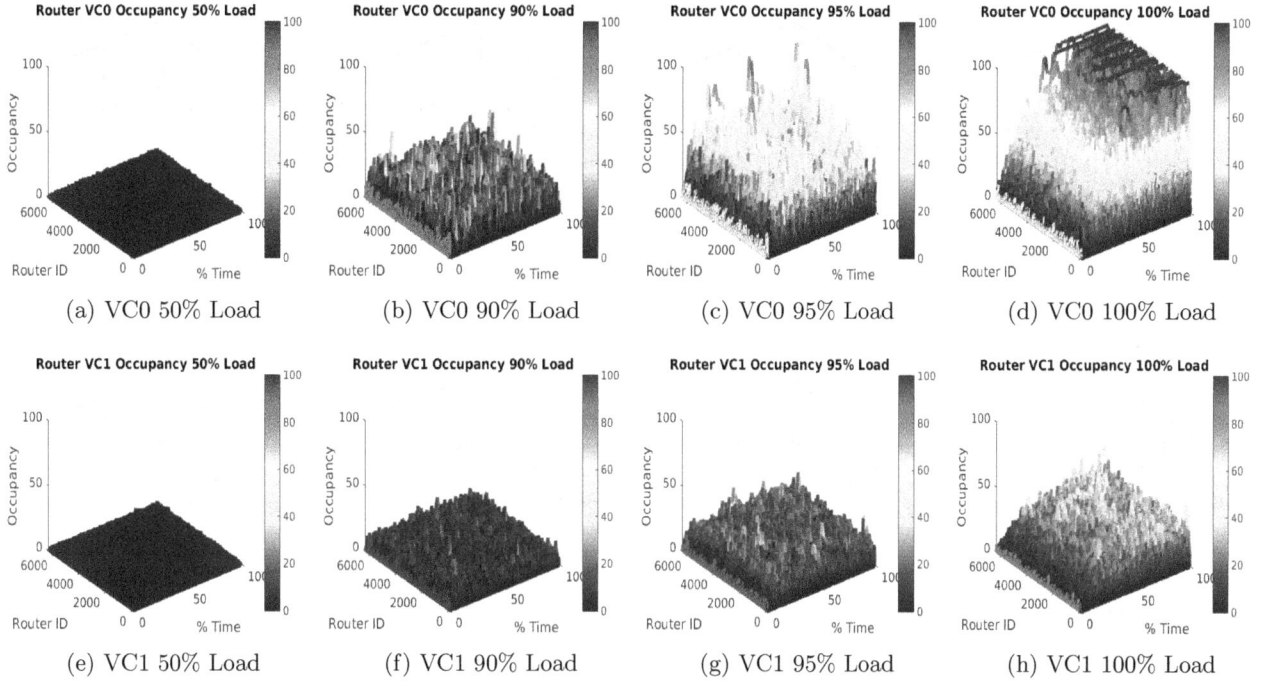

(a) VC0 50% Load (b) VC0 90% Load (c) VC0 95% Load (d) VC0 100% Load

(e) VC1 50% Load (f) VC1 90% Load (g) VC1 95% Load (h) VC1 100% Load

Figure 8: Router occupancy comparison for simulations using UR traffic and minimal routing with increasing injection load. Figures are best viewed in color.

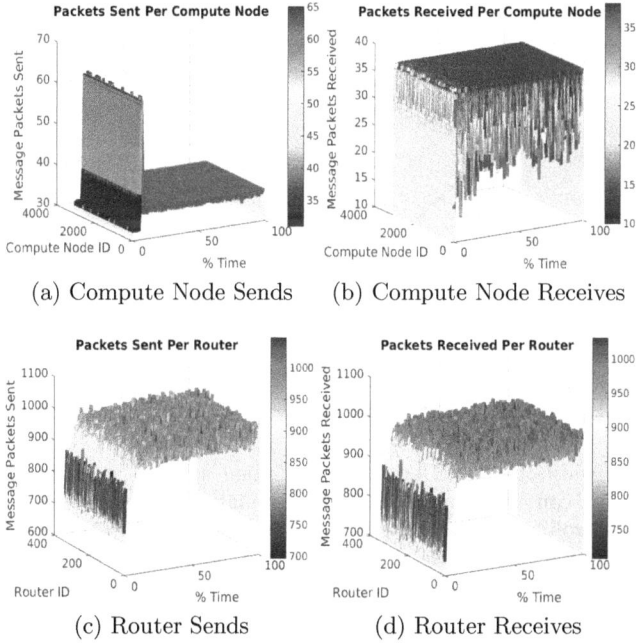

(a) Compute Node Sends (b) Compute Node Receives

(c) Router Sends (d) Router Receives

Figure 9: Messages sent and received over time for the simulation using UR traffic and minimal routing using 100% load. Figures 9a and 9b show the number of sends and receives sampled over the simulation run time for all the compute nodes. Figures 9c and 9d show the same for all routers in the simulation.

4. LARGE-SCALE PERFORMANCE

To show the full capabilities of the ROSS discrete event Slim Fly model simulator, we constructed and analyzed large-scale Slim Fly model configurations. The analysis includes discrete-event compute statistics and strong scaling on the Intel cluster at the Center for Computational Innovations at RPI to emphasize the efficiency of the new Slim Fly simulator. Following the same simulation parameters as in Section 3, we use 100 Gbps link bandwidth with a latency of 50 ns. Routers utilize virtual channels, a buffer space of 100 KB per port, and a 100 ns traversal delay. Each message consists of 256-byte packets. In all the adaptive routing cases, we set the number of indirect routes, $n_i = 3$, and $c_{SF} = 1$ μs. The increased model sizes result in much larger end-to-end runtimes (the time including the initial configuration of LPs in addition to the simulation processing time). However, we still maintain the simulated time of 220 μs, as in section 3.

4.1 74K-Node Slim Fly Model

In this section, we simulate the Slim Fly model at the scale of Aurora, the future supercomputer to be deployed at Argonne National Laboratory. Aurora is stated to have more than 50,000 nodes, which is significantly larger than Summit [13]. Assuming that the Knights Hill version of the Intel Xeon Phi, which will be the compute architecture for the system, is released with 3 TFLOPs, the future Aurora supercomputer will need to have 60,000 nodes in order to reach the quoted 180 PFlOPS of system performance. A network the size of the future Aurora supercomputing system results in a Slim Fly topology with the following configuration:

- $q = 37$, $p = 27$, $N_n = 73,926$, $N_r = 2738$, $k = 82$.

195

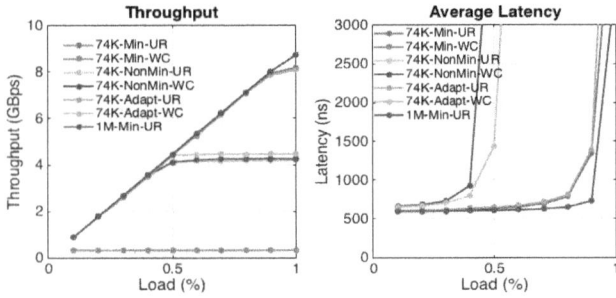

Figure 10: Million-node and 74K-node Slim Fly model performance analysis with uniform random traffic and minimal routing.

This 73,926-node model is the smallest configuration that can obtain at least 60,000 nodes without exceeding the $p = \lfloor \frac{k'}{2} \rfloor$ restriction for obtaining optimal system throughput.

We tested the model using all three routing algorithms—minimal, non-minimal, and adaptive—using both uniform random and worst-case traffic workloads. Both throughput utilization for the system and average packet latency are shown in Figure 10. The results follow the same general trend as was observed for the 3K-node Slim Fly validation model in Section 3. Minimal routing performs at nearly full bandwidth under uniform random traffic. Simulating worst-case traffic, minimal routing maintains roughly half the throughput achieved with 10% load of uniform random traffic. non-minimal routing hits congestion at 50% load under both uniform random and worst-case traffic. Again, this is the result of the non-minimal routing algorithm forcing path lengths to be twice as long as minimal routing. Adaptive routing achieves better throughput over minimal and non-minimal routing for worst-case traffic because it has the added benefit of selecting between the minimal or non-minimal route.

4.2 Million-Node Slim Fly Model

Further showcasing the scalability of the Slim Fly model, we scale the topology over 1 million nodes. To the best of our knowledge, this is the largest simulated Slim Fly network model. The million-node Slim Fly uses the following configuration:

- $q = 163$, $p = 19$, $N_n = 1,009,622$, $N_r = 53,138$, $k = 255$.

The feasibility of such a large Slim Fly topology must take into account the requirement of a router/switch containing at least 264 ports. Also, utilizing only 19 node connections per router leaves a significant amount of bandwidth on the network side of the router and provides the ability to scale the system up to 6.4 million nodes with up to p=122 nodes per router. This number of nodes reaches the desired $p = \lfloor \frac{k'}{2} \rfloor$ where we still achieve full link bandwidth throughout the system [4]. Unfortunately, this also raises the necessary router radix k' to 367.

Figure 9 presents the throughput and average packet latency results for the million-node simulation using minimal routing and uniform random traffic. Unlike the 74K-node Slim Fly performance, which trails off to a maximum throughput of 8.2 GBps, the million-node model achieves a

maximum of 8.7 GBps. As mentioned before, the million-node configuration has only 19 nodes per router, well below the suggested $p = \lfloor \frac{k'}{2} \rfloor$ nodes per router. Therefore, the million-node Slim Fly model will not experience any congestion under uniform random traffic with minimal routing because there is ample network bandwidth to satisfy the much smaller injection load bandwidth.

4.3 Scaling Analysis

In this section, we present the strong-scaling performance of the Slim Fly network model on the RSA Intel cluster at RPI. The system has 34 nodes, each node consisting of two 4-core Intel Xeon E5-2643 3.3 GHz processors and 256 GB of RAM. The million-node Slim Fly model is memory intensive and therefore limits the number of MPI ranks that can be executed per node to 4. The 74K-node Slim Fly model has a much smaller memory footprint, allowing 8 MPI ranks per node. All simulations are executed by using minimal routing, uniform random traffic, and an injection load of 10%.

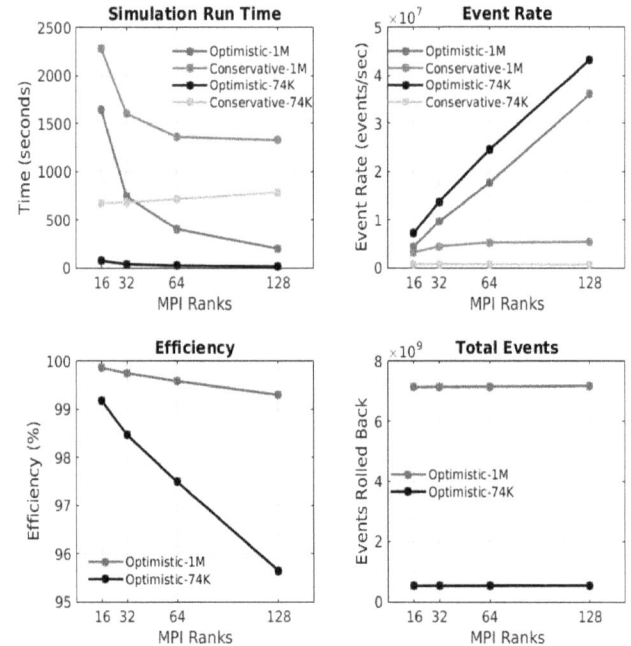

Figure 11: Million-node scaling analysis simulating 100 μs using minimal Routing, UR traffic, and 10% network load.

Additionally, ROSS uses simulation specific parameters that can be used to tune the simulation performance by controlling the frequency of global virtual time (GVT) calculation [6]. These parameters are the "batch" and "gvt-interval." The batch size is the number of events the ROSS event scheduler will process before checking for the arrival of remote events (events issued from other MPI ranks) and anti-messages (messages indicating an event was issued out of time stamp order and needs to be rolled back in optimistic execution). The GVT interval is the number of times through the main scheduler loop before a GVT computation will be started. The default values "batch=16" and "gvt-interval=16" are used in the optimistic event scheduling simulations and the default look ahead value of 1 is used in the conservative executions.

The scaling performance results are evaluated according to simulation run time (not including simulation configuration time), event rate, event efficiency, and total number of processed events. These measurements provide insight into how well the Slim Fly model performs as a ROSS discrete-event simulation. Event rate is a simple calculation of completed events per second, and event efficiency describes how much work is being performed in the positive direction. Instead of using traditional state saving techniques, ROSS uses reverse event handlers that undo untimely executed events. This technique saves state but requires extra compute to unroll the events. The simulation efficiency measures the amount of reverse computation using Equation 5 [3].

$$efficiency = 1 - \frac{rolled\_back\_events}{total\_events} \qquad (5)$$

As shown in Fig. 7, utilizing the ROSS optimistic event scheduler results in an ideal linear speedup of both the Slim Fly million-node model and the 74K-mode model. The largest event rate is achieved running the 74K-node Slim Fly model on 128 MPI ranks, executing just over 43 million events per second and processing 543 million events. Not far behind, the million-node model achieves a rate of 36 million events per second processing 7 billion events. Mapping the 7 billion events to 128 MPI processes translates to each process staying saturated with events and leads to an event efficiency above 99%. Running smaller Slim Fly configurations on as many processes leads to negative efficiency because of less available work. At 128 MPI processes, the smaller 74K-node Slim Fly model has a 3% lower efficiency than does the million-node model but manages to execute events at a 20% faster event rate. The smaller number of events per PE in the 74K-node model translates to less overhead reordering events to maintain timestamp order.

4.4 Discrete-Event Simulation Analysis

In order to understand the performance of the Slim Fly model within the context of the underlying discrete-event simulation engine, this section sheds light on which tasks the model spends the majority of its clock cycles. Figure 12 presents two area plots showing the distribution of time the 74K-node Slim Fly model simulation spends in each phase of the ROSS discrete-event computation. Each execution performs the same 220 μs simulation modeling minimal routing under uniform random traffic with an increasing number of MPI ranks (PEs). Also, each simulation uses a batch size of 16 and GVT interval of 16. The same general trends observed in these figures are consistent for all other combinations of non-minimal and adaptive routing with uniform and worst-case traffic.

Focusing first on optimistic execution in Figure 12a, we see the Slim Fly model spends the majority of the time making forward progress processing events. This trend is consistent regardless of the number of MPI ranks utilized. In addition, the distribution of time spent in each aspect of the simulation stays constant for optimistic scheduling as the number of MPI processes increases. This denotes an ideal distribution of events to LPs, and even further, an ideal distribution of LPs to PEs. It allows the simulation to scale linearly because there is an equal amount of work for each processor, preventing the case where some processors have less work. Less work causes the PE to advance its local time much

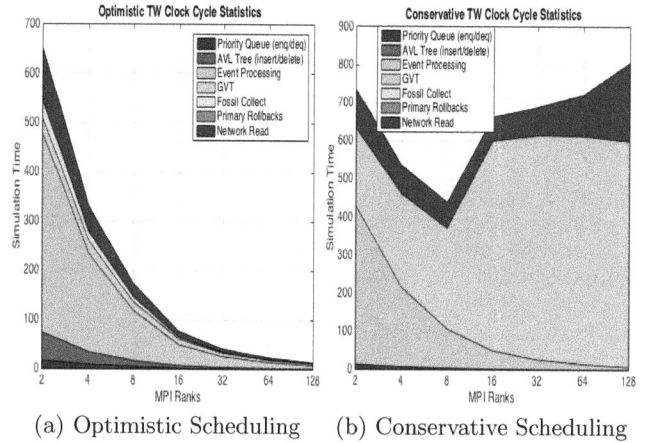

(a) Optimistic Scheduling (b) Conservative Scheduling

Figure 12: Distribution of simulation time for the 74K-node Slim Fly model with minimal routing, UR traffic, and 10% load.

further than the global virtual time and has a much higher chance of processing an event out of order and forcing a large number of primary and secondary rollbacks. All in all, the Slim Fly model excels under optimistic event scheduling.

In conservative event scheduling using a lookahead value of 1 and starting with 2 MPI ranks, we see a large portion of the Slim Fly model compute cycles spent in GVT. Unlike optimistic scheduling where each PE can maintain its own local time and process events accordingly, conservative execution forces all PEs to maintain the same virtual time, essentially executing in a semi-lockstep manner. This guarantees that no messages are processed out of order, but it requires more interaction from GVT, as shown in Figure 12b. Moving from 2 to 8 MPI ranks, the execution time decreases because of a linear decrease in processing time, while the GVT computation slightly rises. After 8 MPI ranks, the amount of work available for the number of processes decreases to the point that GVT must intervene more often to keep the processes in order, so we experience a large increase in GVT cycles. As the number of MPI processes increases, so does the number of number of PEs the event scheduler must keep locked at the same virtual time. This situation inevitably leads to PEs sitting idle waiting for GVT to advance the time window.

Overall, the ROSS-CODES Slim Fly network model is an efficient tool for modeling large-scale Slim Fly configurations. Using 128 processes on the Intel cluster, the 74K-node model gives the highest event rate of 43 million events per second, while the million-node case processes the most events at 7 billion committed events. Both Slim Fly models achieve strong linear scaling using optimistic event scheduling with the million-node model performing a 100 μs minimal routing simulation with 10% load under uniform random traffic in just 198 seconds.

5. RELATED WORK

Significant research has been done in simulating large-scale network interconnects and using visualization to gain further insight and understanding. Computing systems are increasingly emphasizing low-latency and low-cost networks.

Liu et al. [15] demonstrate the effectiveness of applying the fat tree interconnect to large data centers. The work focuses on the ability of fat tree networks to perform well under data-center applications at large scale. Unlike our work that currently focuses on HPC workloads, their work focuses on workloads approximating the Hadoop MapReduce model.

Mubarak et al. [19] [20] demonstrate the performance of both the torus and dragonfly network topologies using synthetic workloads at large scale. The simulations are also implemented on top of the CODES and ROSS discrete-event simulation frameworks and run on IBM Blue Gene/P and Blue Gene/Q systems. Our work, in contrast, studies the performance and scaling using an Intel cluster.

Bhatele [5] presents new methods that include visualization for identifying congestion in dragonfly networks and developing new task mappings to allow for efficient use of resources. Still a relatively new topology, the Slim Fly model does not have any real-world implementations. Therefore, it can benefit from the same methods of simulation and visual analysis to predict and limit congestion of possible future Slim Fly systems, especially when executing multiple concurrent tasks.

Acun et al. [1] present TraceR, a tool that replays the BigSim application traces on top of CODES network models. TraceR provides the ability to test CODES network models under real-world production application workloads. In contrast, our work simulates synthetic uniform random and worst-case traffic workloads. Since the TraceR tool has been interfaced with the CODES and ROSS frameworks, it can be experimented with on the Slim Fly model.

6. CONCLUSIONS AND FUTURE WORK

In this paper, we presented a Slim Fly network simulator developed using CODES and the parallel discrete-event simulation framework ROSS. Having implemented minimal, non-minimal, and adaptive routing algorithms specific to the Slim Fly model, we simulated the effectiveness of those routing methods under uniform random and worst-case synthetic traffic workloads. The results of the Slim Fly model have been verified by using published results from Besta and Hoefler [4].

Furthermore, the Slim Fly network model has been shown to scale in network size from a 3,042 and 73,926 node systems, inspired by the future Summit and Aurora supercomputers, to a million-node system topology. Additionally, the Slim Fly model scales linearly in execution up to 128 MPI ranks on the CCI RSA Intel cluster, achieving a peak event rate of 43 million events per second with 543 million total events processed for the 74K-node Slim Fly model. The million-node model achieves 36 million events per second processing 7 billion events.

Through visualization of network simulation metrics like buffer utilization and message packet transfers, we get an insight into the behavior of large-scale HPC networks. These methods provide the ability to view the entire network simulation and identify the cause and effect of congestion.

Further scaling of the million-node model can also be performed to make full use of the simulated $q = 163$ MMS configuration. A Slim Fly configuration can maintain maximum link bandwidth up to $p = \lfloor \frac{k'}{2} \rfloor$ total nodes per router. The million-node model we have simulated has a network radix of $k' = 255$ and $p = 19$ nodes per router. However, this $q = 163$ MMS configuration can use up to $p = 122$ nodes

per router to get a 6.4 million-node model capable of maintaining full network throughput. Adding additional realistic workloads that model real world applications is another future direction we plan to experiment with. We also plan to explore other applications for future large-scale Slim Fly network interconnects by possibly simulating a large-scale neuromorphic supercomputing system [17].

Acknowledgments

This work was supported by the Air Force Research Laboratory (AFRL), under award number FA8750-15-2-0078. This was also supported by the U.S. Department of Energy, Office of Science, Advanced Scientific Computing Research, under Contract DE-AC02-06CH11357.

7. REFERENCES

[1] B. Acun, N. Jain, A. Bhatele, M. Mubarak, C. Carothers, and L. Kale. Preliminary evaluation of a parallel trace replay tool for hpc network simulations. In S. Hunold, A. Costan, D. GimÃl'nez, A. Iosup, L. Ricci, M. E. GÃşmez Requena, V. Scarano, A. L. Varbanescu, S. L. Scott, S. Lankes, J. Weidendorfer, and M. Alexander, editors, *Euro-Par 2015: Parallel Processing Workshops*, volume 9523 of *Lecture Notes in Computer Science*, pages 417–429. Springer International Publishing, 2015.

[2] A. Alexandrov, M. F. Ionescu, K. E. Schauser, and C. Scheiman. Loggp: Incorporating long messages into the logp model—one step closer towards a realistic model for parallel computation. In *Proceedings of the Seventh Annual ACM Symposium on Parallel Algorithms and Architectures*, SPAA '95, pages 95–105, New York, NY, USA, 1995. ACM.

[3] P. D. Barnes, Jr., C. D. Carothers, D. R. Jefferson, and J. M. LaPre. Warp speed: Executing time warp on 1,966,080 cores. In *Proceedings of the 1st ACM SIGSIM Conference on Principles of Advanced Discrete Simulation*, SIGSIM PADS '13, pages 327–336, New York, NY, USA, 2013. ACM.

[4] M. Besta and T. Hoefler. Slim Fly: A Cost Effective Low-Diameter Network Topology. Nov. 2014. Proceedings of the International Conference on High Performance Computing, Networking, Storage and Analysis (SC14).

[5] A. Bhatele. Task mapping on complex computer network topologies for improved performance. Technical report, LDRD Final Report, Lawrence Livermore National Laboratory, Oct. 2015. LLNL-TR-678732.

[6] C. D. Carothers, D. Bauer, and S. Pearce. Ross: A high-performance, low memory, modular time warp system. In *Proceedings of the Fourteenth Workshop on Parallel and Distributed Simulation*, PADS '00, pages 53–60, Washington, DC, USA, 2000. IEEE Computer Society.

[7] C. D. Carothers, K. S. Perumalla, and R. M. Fujimoto. Efficient optimistic parallel simulations using reverse computation. *ACM Trans. Model. Comput. Simul.*, 9(3):224–253, July 1999.

[8] CCI. Rsa cluster, Nov. 2014.

[9] J. Cope, L. N., L. S., C. P., C. C. D., and R. R. Codes: Enabling co-design of multilayer exascale

storage architectures. In *Proceedings of the Workshop on Emerging Supercomputing Technologies (WEST)*, Tuscon, AZ, USA, 2011.

[10] W. Dally. Virtual-channel flow control. *Parallel and Distributed Systems, IEEE Transactions on*, 3(2):194–205, Mar 1992.

[11] W. Dally and B. Towles. *Principles and Practices of Interconnection Networks*. Morgan Kaufmann Publishers Inc., San Francisco, CA, USA, 2003.

[12] P. R. Hafner. Geometric realisation of the graphs of mckay-miller-siran. *Journal of Combinatorial Theory, Series B*, 90(2):223–232, 2004.

[13] Intel. Ushering in a new era: Argonne national laboratory's aurora system. Technical report, Intel Corporation, April 2015.

[14] G. Kathareios, C. Minkenberg, B. Prisacari, G. Rodriguez, and T. Hoefler. Cost-Effective Diameter-Two Topologies: Analysis and Evaluation. Nov. 2015. Accepted at IEEE/ACM International Conference on High Performance Computing, Networking, Storage and Analysis (SC15).

[15] N. Liu, A. Haider, X.-H. Sun, and D. Jin. Fattreesim: Modeling large-scale fat-tree networks for hpc systems and data centers using parallel and discrete event simulation. In *Proceedings of the 3rd ACM SIGSIM Conference on Principles of Advanced Discrete Simulation*, SIGSIM PADS '15, pages 199–210, New York, NY, USA, 2015. ACM.

[16] B. D. McKay, M. Miller, and J. Siran. A note on large graphs of diameter two and given maximum degree. *Journal of Combinatorial Theory, Series B*, 74(1):110 – 118, 1998.

[17] P. A. Merolla, J. V. Arthur, R. Alvarez-Icaza, A. S. Cassidy, J. Sawada, F. Akopyan, B. L. Jackson, N. Imam, C. Guo, Y. Nakamura, B. Brezzo, I. Vo, S. K. Esser, R. Appuswamy, B. Taba, A. Amir, M. D. Flickner, W. P. Risk, R. Manohar, and D. S. Modha. A million spiking-neuron integrated circuit with a scalable communication network and interface. *Science*, 345(6197):668–673, 2014.

[18] Miller, Mirka, Siran, and Jozef. Moore graphs and beyond: a survey of the degree/diameter problem. *The Electronic Journal of Combinatorics [electronic only]*, DS14:61 p., electronic only–61 p., electronic only, 2005.

[19] M. Mubarak, C. D. Carothers, R. Ross, and P. Carns. Modeling a million-node dragonfly network using massively parallel discrete-event simulation. In *Proceedings of the 2012 SC Companion: High Performance Computing, Networking Storage and Analysis*, SCC '12, pages 366–376, Washington, DC, USA, 2012. IEEE Computer Society.

[20] M. Mubarak, C. D. Carothers, R. B. Ross, and P. Carns. A case study in using massively parallel simulation for extreme-scale torus network codesign. In *Proceedings of the 2Nd ACM SIGSIM Conference on Principles of Advanced Discrete Simulation*, SIGSIM PADS '14, pages 27–38, New York, NY, USA, 2014. ACM.

[21] D. M. Nicol. The cost of conservative synchronization in parallel discrete event simulations. *J. ACM*, 40(2):304–333, Apr. 1993.

[22] NVIDIA. Summit and sierra supercomputers: An inside look at the u.s. department of energy's new pre-exascale systems. Technical report, NVIDIA, November 2014.

[23] M. Papka, P. Messina, R. Coffey, and C. Drugan. *Argonne Leadership Computing Facility 2014 annual report*. Mar 2015.

[24] S. Snyder, P. Carns, J. Jenkins, K. Harms, R. Ross, M. Mubarak, and C. Carothers. A case for epidemic fault detection and group membership in hpc storage systems. In S. A. Jarvis, S. A. Wright, and S. D. Hammond, editors, *High Performance Computing Systems. Performance Modeling, Benchmarking, and Simulation*, volume 8966 of *Lecture Notes in Computer Science*, pages 237–248. Springer International Publishing, 2015.

[25] L. G. Valiant. A scheme for fast parallel communication. *SIAM Journal on Computing*, 11(2):350–361, 1982.

[26] S.-J. Wang. Load-balancing in multistage interconnection networks under multiple-pass routing. *Journal of Parallel and Distributed Computing*, 36(2):189 – 194, 1996.

Profiling Energy Consumption in Distributed Simulations

Aradhya Biswas
School of Computational Science and
Engineering
Georgia Institute of Technology
Atlanta, Georgia USA 30332
aradhya.biswas@gatech.edu

Richard Fujimoto
School of Computational Science and
Engineering
Georgia Institute of Technology
Atlanta, Georgia USA 30332
fujimoto@cc.gatech.edu

ABSTRACT

An energy profile indicates the amount of energy consumed by different parts of a parallel or distributed simulation program. Creating energy profiles is not straightforward because high precision, low overhead energy measurement mechanisms may not be available, and it is not straightforward to determine the amount of energy consumed by different hardware components such as the CPU, memory system, or communication circuits that are operating concurrently throughout the execution of the distributed simulation. Techniques to create energy profiles of distributed simulation programs are described. A model is proposed that differentiates the energy consumed by the distributed simulation engine versus simulation application code, and energy consumed for computation versus that required for communication. A methodology and techniques are described to create energy profiles for these aspects of the distributed simulation. A study is described to illustrate this methodology to profile a distributed simulation synchronized by the Chandy/Misra/Bryant synchronization algorithm for a queuing network simulation. Empirical data are presented to validate the energy profile that is obtained.

Keywords

Distributed simulation; Energy profiling; Measurement; Performance; Design; Empirical studies; Discrete-event simulation

1. INTRODUCTION

Energy and power consumption of computations and communications are areas of increasing concern. Reductions in energy consumption for mobile computing applications will translate to increased battery life and/or reductions in the size and weight of batteries used to power the device. In high performance computing energy has become a major concern because power is a major cost in operating data centers. Another related area of increasing interest are micro-clusters [19, 23], i.e., energy-efficient high performance computing

Permission to make digital or hard copies of all or part of this work for personal or classroom use is granted without fee provided that copies are not made or distributed for profit or commercial advantage and that copies bear this notice and the full citation on the first page. Copyrights for components of this work owned by others than the author(s) must be honored. Abstracting with credit is permitted. To copy otherwise, or republish, to post on servers or to redistribute to lists, requires prior specific permission and/or a fee. Request permissions from permissions@acm.org.

SIGSIM-PADS '16, May 15 - 18, 2016, Banff, AB, Canada

ⓒ 2016 Copyright held by the owner/author(s). Publication rights licensed to ACM.
ISBN 978-1-4503-3742-7/16/05. . . $15.00

DOI: http://dx.doi.org/10.1145/2901378.2901395

platforms that utilize commercial processors that were originally developed for cellular phones or tablets. Micro-clusters offer the potential to realize computation intensive applications on energy-constrained platforms such as drones or space vehicles.

One class of applications where energy consumption is an increasing concern are dynamic data driven application systems (DDDAS) [10]. These are applications that interact closely with real-world systems typically with the goal of optimizing the system or to adapt the monitoring subsystem. DDDAS applications typically operate in a control loop that involves (1) collecting and processing data extracted from sensors and other devices, (2) executing algorithms or simulations utilizing these data to inform decision making processes, and (3) reconfiguring the system to optimize it along some dimension or to adapt the monitoring process. For example, in transportation system applications simulations may be used to predict future system states in order to guide mechanisms to manage congestion or adapt system monitoring. Because DDDAS applications interact directly with operational systems, it may be advantageous to embed computational devices within the system being managed, e.g., a sensor network. Here, our particular interest is in DDDAS systems where distributed simulations executing on mobile computing devices are used in the DDDAS control loop. For example, distributed simulations may be embedded within a mobile sensor network monitoring a forest fire or vehicular traffic in order to relocate sensors to track the evolving system or to concentrate monitoring activities in areas of particular interest.

There have been a myriad of studies and numerous methodologies have been proposed to measure and predict the energy consumption of specific smartphones applications, but most of these address the problem either within the context of a specific application program [4, 11] or address low level aspects concerning the hardware, compiler, or operating system [29, 20]. Energy consumption of distributed simulations have not been widely studied [15]. Very little is known concerning how energy is used in distributed simulations, or simulation applications in general. Clearly such knowledge is required before one can begin to develop approaches to effectively manage and reduce the energy consumed by distributed simulations or to understand tradeoffs among energy consumption, execution time, and model detail and accuracy.

This paper proposes a model that breaks down energy consumption of distributed simulations into a set of separate functional components. The intent of this model is to separate various aspects of the distributed simulation in order to quantify the energy consumed by each one, with the eventual goal to inform and guide the development of approaches to effectively manage and reduce energy consumption. We propose experimental methods to measure and separate the energy consumed by the functional components defined by the model and demonstrate their use in conducting an empirical study evaluating the energy consumed by a benchmark distributed simulation program.

The remainder of this paper is organized as follows. The next section presents related work. This is followed by a description of the model that is proposed for profiling energy consumption in distributed simulations. The section that follows discusses techniques for measuring and separating the energy consumed by various elements of the model. Results of an empirical study exercising these methods are then presented. Data supporting the validity of the experimental approach are presented followed by a discussion of future work.

2. RELATED WORK

The bulk of the work concerning energy profiling has focused on predictive modeling of energy and power [9, 30, 18, 20, 31] and embedded systems evaluations [17, 25, 26, 28]. Model based energy estimation tools are only as good as the training and accuracy of the model. This requirement along with the fact that these models generally depend on the hardware, usage [11] and/or platform restricts their applicability to a limited number of devices and/or platforms. A hybrid approach [11, 5] allows the models to be altered based on factors such as hardware and usage. Tools such as Trepn profiler [4], which rely on on-board power sensors, i.e. a fuel gauge, compute the energy consumed by the complete application but do not separate energy use among different portions of the program. Existing approaches to power or energy profiling do not allow the separation of energy required for all of the functional components of interest in optimizing energy use.

One way to profile the energy consumed by the different functional components is to compute the energy consumption of each machine instruction [24, 29]. This approach does not extend well to modeling components other than the CPU [5]. As will be observed later, the energy consumption of the non-CPU components, e.g., communications, can be large compared to the energy consumed by CPU in a distributed simulation. In addition the instruction-based approach suffers from the drawback of requiring hardware specific values that may not be readily available.

There have been only a small number of studies concerning the energy and power consumption of parallel and distributed simulations. In [27], the authors studied power consumption for disseminating state information in distributed virtual environments. This study highlighted dead-reckoning algorithms and tradeoffs between state consistency and power consumption. Studies described in [12, 14, 16, 13] focus on characterizing power consumption for scientific computing applications. [8] presents a preliminary study of energy consumption of Time-warp simulation on a shared memory multi-core processor with Dynamic Voltage and Frequency Scaling. The work described in [21] presents a study of power consumption of data distributed management (DDM) services defined in the High Level Architecture. One recent work examined the power and energy consumption of synchronization algorithms for parallel and distributed simulations [15]. To the best of our knowledge there has been no study that breaks down the energy consumption of a distributed simulation into its functional components, the primary focus of this work.

The approach proposed here does not assume or require any hardware or platform specific details and relies only on the availability of a coarse power measurement tool for the platform of interest that reports overall energy consumption for an entire application program. Numerous hardware and software platforms are currently available that have this energy measurement capability. Studies report that software tools such as the Trepn Profiler [4] used here indicate they can be as accurate as methods based on external hardware measurement devices such as the Monsoon power meter, but at a much lower cost [2].

3. A MODEL FOR ENERGY CONSUMPTION IN DISTRIBUTED SIMULATIONS

As discussed earlier, the purpose of the proposed energy model is to separate energy consumption for different aspects of distributed simulations programs. This model can be used to create profiles indicating the amount of energy consumed by different portions of the distributed simulator to pinpoint where improvements may have the greatest impact in reducing energy consumption. As is standard practice, we assume the distributed simulation application consists of a set of logical processes (LPs) that communicate by exchanging timestamped event messages.

We first differentiate between the *simulation engine* and the *simulation application*. We informally define the simulation engine as those portions of the distributed simulation that are fixed across all simulation applications. The simulation engine includes functions such as managing the execution of LPs, event lists, and synchronization. It also includes interprocessor message communications both for synchronization and exchanging application event messages. The simulation application includes all other software, and includes all software associated with the simulation model. Library functions such as random number generators are assumed to be part of the simulation application. While the distinction between the simulation engine and application is somewhat subjective for some simulators, distributed simulation systems typically define an applications program interface (API) that provides a clear separation between these two components. For example, in federated distributed simulation architectures, all software associated with the runtime infrastructure is considered part of the simulation engine, as well as much of the software within the federate such as that associated with event list management. We denote the energy consumed by the simulation engine by E_{SE} and that consumed by the application by E_{app}.

We can further divide software within the simulation engine into two major functional components: that implementing communication functions and that associated with simulation engine computation. Let E_{comm} denote the energy consumed by communication functions and E_{SEcomp} denote energy associated with computations performed within simulation engine, e.g., event list management and LP scheduling. We assume all interprocessor communication is performed by the simulation engine. These communications includes that required for sending and receiving event messages and other overhead communications, e.g., that required for synchronization. E_{comm} may be further broken down into the energy consumed for sending and receiving messages, denoted E_{send} and E_{rcv}, respectively, however, here we will be content to focus only on measuring E_{comm}. N_{event} indicates the total number of event messages received/sent by a node. Similarly, the number of messages transmitted for overhead functions, especially synchronization is defined as N_{sync}.

The total energy consumed by the distributed simulation (sequential simulations are viewed as a special case where E_{comm} and all its components are zero) is denoted E_{sim}. It is easy to see the relationships among the components making up our energy profile below.

$$E_{sim} = E_{SE} + E_{app} \qquad (1)$$
$$E_{SE} = E_{comm} + E_{SEcomp} \qquad (2)$$
$$E_{comm} = E_{rcv} + E_{send} \qquad (3)$$
$$N_{comm} = N_{event} + N_{sync} \qquad (4)$$
$$N_{event} = N_{eRcv} + N_{eSend} \qquad (5)$$
$$N_{sync} = N_{sRcv} + N_{sSend} \qquad (6)$$

4. CONSTRUCTING ENERGY PROFILES

An energy profile specifies the amount of energy consumed by each of the components defined in the model discussed in the previous section. The value of energy profiles is clear; just as time profiles are commonly used in optimizing the performance of software by revealing bottlenecks in a code, energy profiles may be used to guide optimization of energy use by revealing energy hogs. However, time profiles are easily constructed using a high-precision real-time clock or using sampling techniques. Constructing energy profiles is not so straightforward. One reason is because the hardware platform may not provide mechanisms to perform high precision, low overhead energy consumption measurements. Energy consumption may be measured by reading the instantaneous current used by the circuit and multiplying this value with the voltage used to obtain a power measurement, which in turn can be used to derive energy values. However reading the instantaneous current is often a system call that requires a significant amount of overhead when attempting to obtain high precision measurements. More seriously, even if high precision, low overhead current values can be obtained, the measured current includes that used by all hardware components including the CPU, memory system, and networking circuits that are all operating concurrently. There is no simple way to separate these. Models may be used to estimate the energy consumed by different hardware components, however this raises questions concerning the validity and applicability of the models, as was discussed earlier.

This section focuses on defining techniques to create energy profiles of distributed simulations with coarse energy measurement mechanisms. In the following section, we describe a methodology for measuring three major components of a distributed simulation, namely communication (*i.e.* E_{comm}), simulation engine computation (E_{SEcomp}) and application (E_{app}).

4.1 Measuring Energy for Communication

The main challenge in measuring the energy used for communication is to separate this energy from that used for computations not related to the communications. A technique is proposed that involves creating and measuring the energy consumed by a *pseudo distributed simulation*, or simply a pseudo simulation, that excludes all communication as discussed below. The total energy consumed by the distributed simulation less, that used by the pseudo simulation yields the amount of energy consumed for communications.

The *pseudo distributed simulation* must repeat the same computations performed by the distributed simulation execution but with all communications used by the distributed simulation removed. This is accomplished by first executing the complete distributed simulation in order to generate a log of all messages sent and received by the computation. The distributed simulation that includes all portions/aspects of the execution is called the *original simulation*. Coarse energy measurement tools can be used to measure the energy consumed by the original simulation. Then the distributed simulation on each processor is repeated without any interprocessor communication. No operation is performed when a message send is executed. Each time a message is received in the pseudo simulation the appropriate message is retrieved from the log rather than performing actual communications. The energy used by the pseudo simulation reflects the energy used by the computation part alone without energy expended for communication, and coarse energy measurement tools can be used to measure the overall energy consumption. Retrieving messages from the log consumes some energy, however as will be seen later, the amount is small and can be ignored.

Stated more succinctly, let the energy of the pseudo distributed simulation run be denoted E_{pseudo} and that of original simulation run be denoted by E_{orig}, then we can write the following

$$E_{sim} = E_{comm} + E_{pseudo} \qquad (7)$$
$$E_{sim} = E_{orig} \qquad (8)$$

From Eqn 7 and 8, we have

$$E_{comm} = E_{orig} - E_{pseudo} \qquad (9)$$

The message communication log is obtained from the original simulation run. It should be noted that the message communication log must be generated in a separate execution of the original simulation, as otherwise the energy consumed by the I/O operations required for the generation of the log would figure in E_{org}. The log must contain sufficient information to ensure each message is delivered at the correct point during the re-execution, i.e., in the execution of the pseudo simulation. It is sufficient to log (1) the contents of the message, (2) the simulation time stamp assigned to the event, and (3) a temporal value indicating the point during the execution when the message is delivered. In the experiments described later the simulation executive contains a loop that is concerned with processing events; the iteration number for this loop is used to specify this third value. By introducing necessary wait times, which might arise due to communication delays and non-uniform processing power of the nodes, this ensures that the run-time behavior of the pseudo simulation is similar to that of the original simulation. Note that the log includes both event messages as well as messages used for synchronization or other purposes. The message log is stored in secondary storage for use by the pseudo simulation.

When the pseudo simulation is executed the log of received messages is read and stored in memory during the initialization step of the pseudo simulation. This initialization step must be excluded from the measurements of energy consumption by the pseudo simulation. Loading the message log into memory during the initialization phase assumes there is sufficient memory to hold the entire log. If this is not the case one could load the message log into memory incrementally as needed during the execution of the pseudo simulation, however, one must be sure to exclude the energy consumed in reading the log into memory from the measurements of energy consumed by the pseudo simulation.

After the message log has been loaded, it is used to replace incoming messages received from other processors during the execution of the pseudo simulation run. This is achieved by incorporating (i.e. perform all the computations as if a real message was received) the ith message from the data in the *pseudo simulation run*, when the current simulation time of the pseudo simulation run is either greater than or equal to current_simulation_time of the original simulation associated with the ith message. This assures that the computations performed by the pseudo simulation are the same as that of the original execution.

This approach assumes the energy consumed to retrieve messages from the message log is negligible relative to other operations performed by the simulation. This is a reasonable assumption because the operations to retrieve messages from the log are simple and consume little time. This assumption was validated through experimentation, as discussed later.

Message send operations typically do not affect the computations performed by the application or simulation engine so they can be ignored in the pseudo simulation. In situations where the computation is affected by the message send, e.g., use of values returned by the send function, one would need to also log the results of these operations as well in order to ensure the pseudo simulation correctly reproduces the behavior of the program. Computations leading up to the sending of the message, e.g., buffer allocation and constructing the message itself are included in the computation portion of the energy consumption profile.

4.2 Measuring Energy Consumed by Simulation Engine Computations

Once the energy consumed for computations has been separated from that utilized for communication, the next step in the profiling process is to separate the energy consumed by the simulation application from that utilized by the distributed simulation engine. The main challenge is devising a way to separate energy consumed by application computations from that expended by engine computations.

One approach to separate application and engine computations is to start with the pseudo distributed simulation as described earlier and then delete all application code, leaving only the simulation engine code. Note the communications is also absent since we started with the pseudo simulation. The resulting code can be executed, and its energy consumption directly measured. With this approach interactions between the simulation engine and the applications,

e.g., function calls made by the application to the simulation engine must be logged, as well as the parameters used in those calls. The log is referenced when the engine is executed in isolation in order to ensure that the behavior of the simulation engine is correctly reproduced when it is executed without the simulation application.

A drawback of this approach is the energy consumed by the simulation engine executing in isolation may be different from that when it is executing with the application. While the simulation engine will execute the same machine instructions with or without the application being present, the timing and detailed operation of the CPU and memory system may not be the same. For example, if the application consumes a large amount of memory, the application may allocate cache memory and cause cache misses to occur within the simulation engine, an effect that is lost when the engine is executed in isolation without the application. One might argue that a similar error could arise when executing the pseudo simulation relative to the original distributed simulation because the communications part is missing, however we believe this impact will be less significant than an application consuming large amounts of memory.

In order to capture effects such as this, an alternative approach to measuring energy consumed by the computation portion of the simulation engine was developed. We start with the pseudo simulation that includes both the application and engine code. We add an additional copy of the engine code and associated data structures. Now, when the pseudo simulation is executed, we execute each engine operation *twice*, once as part of the normal execution of the pseudo simulation, and once in the replicated engine. We refer to this code as the *replicated engine code*. The replicated simulation engine code computes, or in other words decides its path of execution, based on the original state variables. This removes the requirement of replicating any computation which lies outside the simulation engine. It should be noted here that although the replicated simulation engine compute based on the original state variables, it only updates the replicated/dummy variables. The energy consumed by the replicated engine code is denoted $E_{SEcompX1}$. The subscript $SEcompX1$ indicates one additional execution of the simulation engine computations is included in the measurement. The amount of energy consumed by simulation engine computations is simply $E_{SEcompX1} - E_{psuedo}$ where E_{psuedo} is the energy consumed by the pseudo simulation including the application and one execution of the engine computations.

The introduction of a replicated copy of the simulation engine may have some impact on the execution of the original pseudo simulation because it too will utilize the memory system, introducing some error. We believe this impact will be small if the engine has a relatively large memory footprint, which is generally the case for real-world simulations. This would ensure that the misses remain relatively consistent even with replications. Empirical evidence supporting this claim is presented later.

It may be noted that this approach using a replicated engine avoids the need to generate a log of calls to the simulation engine. This simplifies the development of the instrumentation code.

In a well designed simulation engine the amount of computation used by the engine may be modest. To enable accurate energy measurements of the pseudo engine using coarse energy measurement tools one can simply execute k replications of the engine. Let $E_{SEcompXk}$ be the energy consumed by the pseudo simulation augmented with k replications of the engine. The energy used for simulation engine computations is easily computed as:

$$E_{SEcomp} = \frac{E_{SEcompXk} - E_{pseudo}}{k} \qquad (10)$$

4.3 Measuring Energy Consumed by the Application

The methodology presented in the previous section can be used to measure the portion of the energy consumption due to executing application computations. For example, one could take the original distributed simulation and create k additional replications of the application code. Let E_{AppXk} denote the energy consumed by this code, including message communications. If one subtracts the energy consumed by the original distributed simulation and divides the result by k the result is the power consumed by a single instance of the application code alone:

$$E_{App} = \frac{E_{AppXk} - E_{sim}}{k} \qquad (11)$$

Alternatively, once could use the pseudo simulation as the baseline. In this case the energy consumed by the application code is:

$$E_{App} = \frac{E_{AppXk} - E_{pseudo}}{k} \qquad (12)$$

It may be noted that E_{AppX1} (*i.e.* E_{AppXk} for k = 1) is not equal to E_{App}, because the former includes the energy of the baseline simulation (distributed simulation or *pseudo distributed simulation* depending on the implementation) in addition to one extra application part. Similar comments apply to $E_{SEcompX1}$ and E_{SEcomp}.

5. EMPIRICAL EVALUATION

A series of experiments were conducted to exercise the proposed methodology and validate the measurements. In this section we describe the setup used to empirically evaluate the energy model and methodology.

5.1 Distributed Simulation System

In this study, we use an implementation of a parallel discrete event simulation (PDES) program using the CMB (Chandy/Misra/Bryant) synchronization algorithm [6, 7]. LPs communicate directly with other LPs by sending messages to the appropriate nodes.

5.2 Experimental Configuration and Benchmark Application

The experimental configuration is intended to mimic an embedded simulation application where the distributed simulation executes within a set of mobile processors. Cellular phones are used for these experiments. The processor used in these phones is typical of what one might anticipate in future deployments of embedded distributed simulations. Specifically, a LG Nexus 5 cellular phone with a quadcore Qualcomm MSM8974 Snapdragon 800 processor,

2 GB memory, and 16 GB storage was used as the mobile computing platform. The phone runs the Android version 5.1 (Android Lollipop) operating system and was used in the experiments. Hardware-based techniques to reduce power consumption such as voltage or frequency scaling were not used in these experiments.

All inter-processor communications utilizes wireless links. The device's 802.11n WiFi network interface was used for communications between processors. A private wireless network was established among the devices to avoid interference resulting from Internet traffic. The cellular network capability of the phone is not used in these experiments.

Queuing networks provide an intuitive, efficient way to study systems that have waiting as a fundamental component. Hence it forms a building block of a very wide range of real-world discrete event simulation applications, e.g. network simulators such as NS3 [3] and DDDAS applications such as traffic simulators.

The benchmark program used in this study is a simulation of a closed queuing network with J jobs circulating among the nodes of the network. The queuing network is configured as a three-dimensional toroid topology. Each processor is assigned one two-dimensional plane of the toroid. Once a job receives service, which includes creating a temporary priority queue, pushing J jobs into it, and then popping them out and destroying the queue, it is routed to a randomly selected neighboring node. Each node of the network contains a single server with service time drawn from an exponential distribution. Jobs arriving at each network node are placed into a single queue, and are served in first-come-first-serve order. In these experiments the lookahead is enhanced by pre-sampling the random number generator to produce the service time of the next job to be processed by the server; if the pre-sampled value is P, then the time stamp of the next message generated by the LP must be at least P units of simulation time into the future [22]. The benchmark program is developed as a native android application.

5.3 Power Measurement Methodology

The energy and power consumption data are derived from direct measurement of the Android device. More specifically, Qualcomm's android app, Trepn profiler [4] was used for profiling. All the benchmark experimental results presented here are with *Deltas* enabled. When profiling with *Deltas* enabled the app profiles (collects power data) for the entire system for a baselining interval and then subtracts the average value of power, so obtained, from all subsequent raw values. All the experiments were conducted with a maximum possible baselining period of 30 second with wake lock for the entire period of profiling. The power profiles of the application were saved as csv files, which were then processed offline to compute the energy consumed.

5.4 Overall Energy Consumption

The energy consumed by the distributed queuing network simulation is computed by profiling a peer. The peer, denoted as the peer of interest, is simulated with 32*32 queues, each initialized with 10 jobs, for a simulation time of 200000 time units. Table 1 presents values measured from the original experimental run.

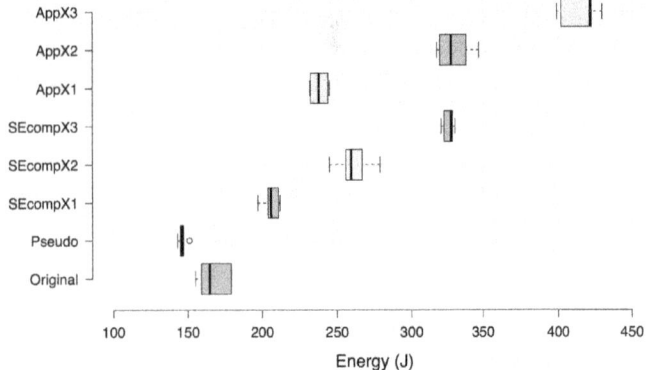

Figure 1: Ranges of experimental data

Events processed	99803
Sync messages received (N_{sRcv})	498
Sync messages sent (N_{sSend})	12515
Event messages received (N_{eRcv})	30341
Event messages sent (N_{eSend})	20104

Table 1: Measured values for peer of interest in original simulation

6. RESULTS

In this section, we start by presenting the energy consumed by each of the components of the distributed simulation (as described in Section 5.4 having the features listed in Table 1) as determined by the proposed methodologies discussed in section 4 and their corresponding implementations presented in section 5.

Multiple runs were conducted for each metric. Figure 1, generated using [1], presents the ranges of measured data that were observed for each metric. Table 2 presents the average values of the runs for each observable metric. We denote the values of components, which can be observed directly as a result of an experiment as *Observable metric* and those which have to derived using *Observable metrics* as the *Derived metrics*.

Metric	Avg. Value (J)
E_{sim}	166.83
E_{pseudo}	146.33
$E_{SEcompX1}$	206
$E_{SEcompX2}$	261
$E_{SEcompX3}$	325.4
E_{AppX1}	238.25
E_{AppX2}	325.6
E_{AppX3}	415.2

Table 2: Values of the observable metrics

There are three derived metrics of interest: the energy consumed by communication (E_{comm}), the energy consumed by the simulation engine (E_{SEcomp}), and the energy consumed by the simulation application (E_{app}). As indicated in eqn. 9, E_{comm} can be derived from the observable metrics E_{sim} and E_{pseudo} and is computed to 20.5 J.

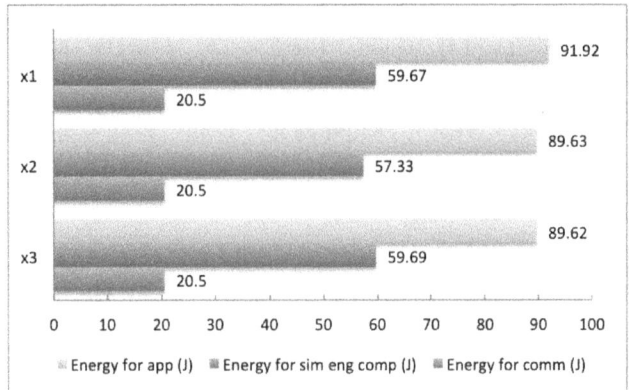

Figure 2: Aggregated results comparing energy profiles shows consistency in results of the proposed methodology for different values of k

The values of E_{Ecomp} and E_{app} can be computed using eqn. 10 and eqn. 12, respectively. Figure 2 shows the values of the derived metrics for different numbers of replications (k). It can be seen that varying k for these small values results in little variation, consistent with expectations.

7. EMPIRICAL VALIDATION

In this section we present two sets of validation experiments. Micro-validation experiments are used to validate the results obtained for individual parts of the proposed methodology. Macro-validation is used to validate the aggregated energy measurements made using the proposed approach.

7.1 Micro-Validations

7.1.1 Validating E_{comm}

For the purpose of validation the energy required for communication, we use micro-benchmarking. Another approach to determine E_{comm} is to view it as a sum of energy required for sending and receiving individual messages. A program was constructed that only performs message sends and receives. This approach ignores interference between the rest of the computation and the message sending and receiving code and uses a simplified model for the messages themselves, as discussed later. This limits the generality of this approach as a means of computing E_{comm} but is adequate for these experiments.

To determine the energy required for dispatch of an individual message (Here we assume the energy required for a synchronization message reception and dispatch is the same as that of an event message, but this methodology can be easily extended for asymmetric cases as well.), we compute the energy required, say E_{rcvXm}, for sending m messages and then divide it by m. That is,

$$E_{send} = \frac{E_{sendXm}}{m} \qquad (13)$$

Similarly the energy requirement of receiving a message can be computed as follows.

$$E_{rcv} = \frac{E_{rcvXm}}{m} \qquad (14)$$

Assuming E_{rcv} denotes the energy required for receiving a message and E_{send} as the energy required for sending a message, we have

$$E_{comm} = E_{rcv} \times (N_{eRcv} + N_{sRcv}) \\ + E_{send} \times (N_{eSend} + N_{sSend}) \qquad (15)$$

To implement the micro-benchmark the simulation code is modified to perform two functions. First, the simulation sends some fixed number of randomly generated messages using structures and sizes that are representative of the messages sent in the distributed simulation to other processors without actually simulating anything. Second, the microbenchmark simply receives messages and does not process them.

To determine the energy consumed in sending messages the microbenchmark simply sends the messages but does not receive any. The energy required for sending a message can be derived by using eqn. 13. Similarly, to determine the energy used to receive messages the processor only receives the m messages. The energy required to receive the messages can be determined using eqn. 14.

Using a value of m equal to 250,000, we find the average value of $E_{rcvX250k}$, over multiple runs, to be 28 J and that of $E_{sendX250k}$ to be 108.5 J. From eqn.14 and eqn.13, it follows that E_{rcv} is 1.12×10^{-4} J and E_{send} is 4.34×10^{-4} J.

Substituting these values into eqn.15 along with the values shown in table 1, we obtain E_{comm} is 17.61 J. This compares with a value of 20.5 J for E_{comm} obtained using the pseudo simulation. A somewhat higher value using the pseudo simulation is expected because it the communications executes in conjunction with the simulation engine and application codes.

7.1.2 Validating E_{SEcomp} and E_{app}

Energy measurements using the pseudo simulations for different values of k were presented in figure 2. It can be seen that the values of E_{SEcomp} varies by at most 4% for differnt values of k. This adds confidence that the methodology produces consistent measurements of application and simulation engine computations. Similarly, comparing the values of E_{app} for different values of k, we can see that they vary by at most by 2.5%.

7.2 Macro-Validation

To test the overall model for consistency we add the energy consumed by individual components, as determined by the proposed methods, and compare the result with the total amount of energy consumed by the distributed simulation that was measured, i.e., E_{sim}. Three major components of the E_{sim}, are energy for communication (E_{comm}), energy for computations of simulation engine (E_{SEcomp}), and the energy for the application (E_{app}). From the eqns.1 & 2, E_{sim} can be expressed as :

$$E_{sim} = E_{comm} + E_{SEcomp} + E_{app} \qquad (16)$$

Table 3 compares the observed value of E_{sim}, i.e., 166.83 J,

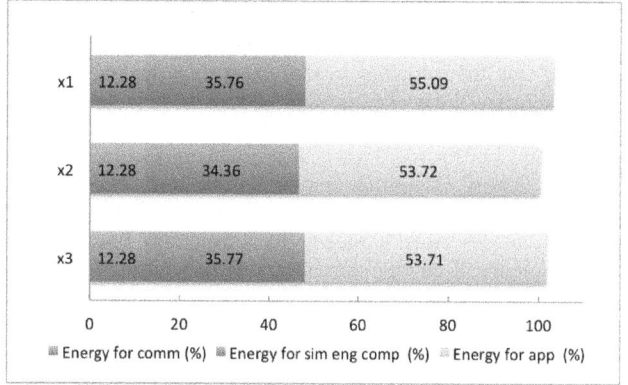

Figure 3: Energy measurements with respect to the observed value of E_{sim}, shows that energy computed for individual parts of the simulations adds up very close to total energy consumed by it

with the value of E_{sim} determined by eqn. 16. It can be seen that the error is small.

k	sum	error
1	172.08 J	3.15%
2	167.47 J	0.38%
3	169.81 J	1.78%

Table 3: Validating energy model by comparing computed values of E_{sim} with its observed value

Figure 3 shows graphically the energy profiles of the distributed simulation code for three values of k. These graphs illustrate the amount of energy consumed for communications, simulation engine computations, and application computations. This profile illustrates that for this benchmark all three components consume significant amounts of energy, however, that used for computation dominates that used for communication. Of course, these profiles will vary from one application to another depending on the intensity of communication required by the application.

8. CONCLUSIONS AND FUTURE WORK

We propose techniques to profile the energy consumed by major functional components of distributed simulation programs. Such profiles are needed to analyze and guide the development of energy optimization techniques. The methodology is followed by an empirical study, demonstrating use of the proposed methodologies and empirically validating the proposed energy model. Although this study focused on conservative synchronization algorithms, we believe the proposed methodology could be extended to apply to distributed simulation systems using optimistic synchronization algorithms. This is one area meriting further investigation.

One important observation from these measurements is that the energy overhead introduced by the distributed execution of the queueing network simulations examined here is significant. Specifically, the distributed simulation engine and communication functions consumed a significant portion of the total energy required to execute the simulations. These preliminary measurements suggest that techniques to optimize the energy costs associated with the distributed execution of simulations may yield significant benefits.

Using this methodology and tools a next logical step is to characterize the energy profiles of distributed simulations spanning a broad range of applications for different configurations and platforms. This can help inform future work to optimize energy use in distributed simulations. Another interesting area of research concerns continued development of the methods described here, e.g., to obtain more fine grained measurements of energy characterizing other functional aspects of the distributed simulation such as I/O operations.

9. ACKNOWLEDGMENT

This research was supported by National Science Foundation Grant 1462503.

10. REFERENCES

[1] Boxplotr. http://boxplot.tyerslab.com/. Accessed: 2016-01-22.

[2] How to measure power consumption using free software. http://mostly-tech.com/2015/05/28/how-to-measure-the-power-consumption-of-your-mobile-\ \app-using-free-software/. Accessed: 2016-01-22.

[3] Ns3. https://www.nsnam.org/. Accessed: 2016-03-22.

[4] Trepn profiler. https://developer.qualcomm.com/software/trepn-power-profiler. Accessed: 2016-01-22.

[5] J. Bornholt, T. Mytkowicz, and K. S. McKinley. The model is not enough: Understanding energy consumption in mobile devices. *Power (watts)*, 1(2):3, 2012.

[6] R. E. Bryant. Simulation of packet communication architecture computer systems. 1977.

[7] K. M. Chandy and J. Misra. Distributed simulation: A case study in design and verification of distributed programs. *Software Engineering, IEEE Transactions on*, (5):440–452, 1979.

[8] R. Child and P. A. Wilsey. Using dvfs to optimize time warp simulations. In *Proceedings of the Winter Simulation Conference*, page 288. Winter Simulation Conference, 2012.

[9] K. Czechowski and R. Vuduc. A theoretical framework for algorithm-architecture co-design. In *Parallel & Distributed Processing (IPDPS), 2013 IEEE 27th International Symposium on*, pages 791–802. IEEE, 2013.

[10] F. Darema. Dynamic data driven applications systems: A new paradigm for application simulations and measurements. In *Computational Science-ICCS 2004*, pages 662–669. Springer, 2004.

[11] M. Dong and L. Zhong. Self-constructive high-rate system energy modeling for battery-powered mobile systems. In *Proceedings of the 9th international conference on Mobile systems, applications, and services*, pages 335–348. ACM, 2011.

[12] J. Dongarra, H. Ltaief, P. Luszczek, and V. M. Weaver. Energy footprint of advanced dense numerical linear algebra using tile algorithms on multicore architectures. In *Cloud and Green Computing (CGC), 2012 Second International Conference on*, pages 274–281. IEEE, 2012.

[13] H. Esmaeilzadeh, T. Cao, X. Yang, S. M. Blackburn, and K. S. McKinley. Looking back and looking forward: power, performance, and upheaval. *Communications of the ACM*, 55(7):105–114, 2012.

[14] X. Feng, R. Ge, and K. W. Cameron. Power and energy profiling of scientific applications on distributed systems. In *Parallel and Distributed Processing Symposium, 2005. Proceedings. 19th IEEE International*, pages 34–34. IEEE, 2005.

[15] R. M. Fujimoto and A. Biswas. An empirical study of energy consumption in distributed simulations. In *Proceedings of the 2015 19th IEEE/ACM International Symposium on Distributed Simulation and Real-Time Applications*. IEEE Computer Society, 2015.

[16] R. Ge, X. Feng, S. Song, H.-C. Chang, D. Li, and K. W. Cameron. Powerpack: Energy profiling and analysis of high-performance systems and applications. *Parallel and Distributed Systems, IEEE Transactions on*, 21(5):658–671, 2010.

[17] I. Grasso, P. Radojkovic, N. Rajovic, I. Gelado, and A. Ramirez. Energy efficient hpc on embedded socs: Optimization techniques for mali gpu. In *Parallel and Distributed Processing Symposium, 2014 IEEE 28th International*, pages 123–132. IEEE, 2014.

[18] S. W. Keckler, W. J. Dally, B. Khailany, M. Garland, and D. Glasco. Gpus and the future of parallel computing. *IEEE Micro*, (5):7–17, 2011.

[19] K. L. Keville, R. Garg, D. J. Yates, K. Arya, and G. Cooperman. Towards fault-tolerant energy-efficient high performance computing in the cloud. In *Cluster Computing (CLUSTER), 2012 IEEE International Conference on*, pages 622–626. IEEE, 2012.

[20] R. Mittal, A. Kansal, and R. Chandra. Empowering developers to estimate app energy consumption. In *Proceedings of the 18th annual international conference on Mobile computing and networking*, pages 317–328. ACM, 2012.

[21] S. Neal, G. Kantikar, and R. Fujimoto. Power consumption of data distribution management for on-line simulations. In *Proceedings of the 2nd ACM SIGSIM/PADS conference on Principles of advanced discrete simulation*, pages 197–204. ACM, 2014.

[22] D. M. Nicol. *Parallel discrete-event simulation of FCFS stochastic queueing networks*, volume 23. ACM, 1988.

[23] Z. Ou, B. Pang, Y. Deng, J. K. Nurminen, A. Yla-Jaaski, and P. Hui. Energy-and cost-efficiency analysis of arm-based clusters. In *Cluster, Cloud and Grid Computing (CCGrid), 2012 12th IEEE/ACM International Symposium on*, pages 115–123. IEEE, 2012.

[24] A. Pathak, Y. C. Hu, M. Zhang, P. Bahl, and Y.-M. Wang. Fine-grained power modeling for smartphones using system call tracing. In *Proceedings of the sixth conference on Computer systems*, pages 153–168. ACM, 2011.

[25] N. Rajovic, P. M. Carpenter, I. Gelado, N. Puzovic, A. Ramirez, and M. Valero. Supercomputing with commodity cpus: are mobile socs ready for hpc? In *High Performance Computing, Networking, Storage and Analysis (SC), 2013 International Conference for*, pages 1–12. IEEE, 2013.

[26] N. Rajovic, A. Rico, J. Vipond, I. Gelado, N. Puzovic, and A. Ramirez. Experiences with mobile processors

for energy efficient hpc. In *Proceedings of the Conference on Design, Automation and Test in Europe*, pages 464–468. EDA Consortium, 2013.

[27] W. Shi, K. Perumalla, and R. Fujimoto. Power-aware state dissemination in mobile distributed virtual environments. In *Parallel and Distributed Simulation, 2003.(PADS 2003). Proceedings. Seventeenth Workshop on*, pages 181–188. IEEE, 2003.

[28] L. Stanisic, B. Videau, J. Cronsioe, A. Degomme, V. Marangozova-Martin, A. Legrand, and J.-F. Méhaut. Performance analysis of hpc applications on low-power embedded platforms. In *Proceedings of the Conference on Design, Automation and Test in Europe*, pages 475–480. EDA Consortium, 2013.

[29] V. Tiwari, S. Malik, A. Wolfe, and M. T.-C. Lee. Instruction level power analysis and optimization of software. In *Technologies for wireless computing*, pages 139–154. Springer, 1996.

[30] S. Williams, A. Waterman, and D. Patterson. Roofline: an insightful visual performance model for multicore architectures. *Communications of the ACM*, 52(4):65–76, 2009.

[31] L. Zhang, B. Tiwana, Z. Qian, Z. Wang, R. P. Dick, Z. M. Mao, and L. Yang. Accurate online power estimation and automatic battery behavior based power model generation for smartphones. In *Proceedings of the eighth IEEE/ACM/IFIP international conference on Hardware/software codesign and system synthesis*, pages 105–114. ACM, 2010.

A Case Study in Using Discrete-Event Simulation to Improve the Scalability of MG-RAST

Caitlin Ross,[‡] Misbah Mubarak,[†] John Jenkins,[†] Philip Carns,[†]
Christopher D. Carothers,[‡] Robert Ross,[†] Wei Tang,[*]
Wolfgang Gerlach,[†§] Folker Meyer[†]
[‡]Computer Science Department, Rensselaer Polytechnic Institute
[†]Mathematics and Computer Science Division, Argonne National Laboratory
[§]Computation Institute, University of Chicago
[*]Google, Inc. USA
rossc3@rpi.edu, mmubarak@anl.gov, jenkins@mcs.anl.gov, carns@mcs.anl.gov,
chrisc@cs.rpi.edu, rross@mcs.anl.gov, weitang@google.com,
wgerlach@mcs.anl.gov, folker@anl.gov

ABSTRACT

As the cost of DNA sequencing has decreased, computational biology data processing platforms are experiencing an increasingly large volume of data analysis requests. The metagenomics analysis server MG-RAST at Argonne National Laboratory, a computational biology data processing platform, is receiving several terabytes of data submissions per month. However, MG-RAST currently relies on a central object-based data store, Shock, for data access and storage that can become a bottleneck under high data transfer loads, adversely affecting the job response time for end users. In this work, we use a discrete-event simulation approach to explore the use of data proxies and an enhanced, proxy-aware scheduling methodology designed to reduce the movement of the intermediate data generated during workflow processing. In this approach, Shock is supplemented with proxy storage servers, employing solid state drives, to decentralize the management and hence reduce the movement of intermediate workflow results. Discrete-event simulation provides a way to evaluate the performance of MG-RAST with increased workloads without disrupting the production system. For our case study, we extrapolate scientific workflows obtained from MG-RAST to represent future usage trends. We demonstrate that the addition of proxies and the proxy-aware scheduling methodology significantly reduces the data movement overhead by distributing the data plane, leading to substantial improvement in end-user job response time.

---

[*]This work was performed while Wei Tang was a postdoctoral researcher at Argonne National Laboratory.

ACM acknowledges that this contribution was authored or co-authored by an employee, or contractor of the national government. As such, the Government retains a nonexclusive, royalty-free right to publish or reproduce this article, or to allow others to do so, for Government purposes only. Permission to make digital or hard copies for personal or classroom use is granted. Copies must bear this notice and the full citation on the first page. Copyrights for components of this work owned by others than ACM must be honored. To copy otherwise, distribute, republish, or post, requires prior specific permission and/or a fee. Request permissions from permissions@acm.org.

SIGSIM-PADS '16, May 15-18, 2016, Banff, AB, Canada

© 2016 ACM. ISBN 978-1-4503-3742-7/16/05...$15.00

DOI: http://dx.doi.org/10.1145/2901378.2901387

CCS Concepts

•**Computing methodologies** → **Discrete-event simulation;**

Keywords

discrete-event simulation, big data, clouds, MG-RAST

1. INTRODUCTION

Because of the decrease in DNA sequencing costs in recent years, the field of bioinformatics has seen an exponential increase in data submission, which poses significant challenges for data management and analysis. For example, MG-RAST [11], a metagenomics [20] analytic service provided by Argonne National Laboratory (ANL), processed 1 Tbp data (10^{12} base pairs) in the first five years, but since mid-2011 it has processed over 80 Tbp of sequence data with thousands of job submissions per month. It is currently receiving 8–16 TB of data per month, which we expect to double within 18 months. Therefore, it is critical to have scalable computing and storage resources that can efficiently handle the growth in data submission and subsequent analysis.

MG-RAST currently uses a centralized data management approach for data access and management [19]. While this approach simplifies security and long term data curation, it is a potential bottleneck when receiving a large number of data submission requests from clients, especially when the requests span multiple sites with compute resources connected by a wide area network (WAN). In addition, task scheduling in MG-RAST is currently first-come first-served (FCFS) and does not take advantage of data locality for multiple WAN sites. Since the tasks in the MG-RAST pipeline generate a large amount of intermediate data, significant WAN data movement can result, leading to increased job response times for end users. To mitigate the performance limitations of a centralized server and to minimize unnecessary data movement overhead between multiple WAN sites, we propose the addition of proxy storage servers to the MG-RAST infrastructure, along with a proxy-aware scheduling methodology that exploits data locality by placing storage proxies based on solid-state drives (SSDs) at each WAN site.

We chose to use storage proxies instead of a distributed

storage system for MG-RAST because the implementation of our proposed changes will require minimal changes to the existing MG-RAST infrastructure. Also, proxies help retain the useful properties of the central data store while providing the ability to load balance the data access requests and decrease the traffic to the central data server. The storage proxies used in this work are similar to web caches; however, web caches are used to store data that tends to be more frequently accessed, whereas in this situation, the proxies are being used as a local storage for the temporary intermediate data generated during job processing.

In this work, we use discrete-event simulation to evaluate the scalability of MG-RAST when using data proxies with and without a proxy-aware scheduling methodology. As opposed to modifying the production server, simulation is a valuable approach to quickly evaluate various configurations of data-analysis platforms in order to determine an efficient and cost-effective configuration. Our simulation work extends the MG-RAST workflow simulator developed by Tang et al. [18], which evaluated two data-aware scheduling policies running on the centralized MG-RAST design. The scheduling methodologies used in that work rely on the compute-to-data cost ratio of the tasks. Our work extends the simulation to explore a proxy-aware scheduling methodology that takes data locality into account by ensuring that all data related to a job is stored on a single proxy server local to a client. This approach helps reduce data transfers between the centralized data server and WAN sites and results in lower data movement overhead. The contributions of our work are as follows.

1. **Use of discrete-event simulation for evaluation of proxy-aware scheduling**: We use discrete-event based workflow simulation to evaluate the performance of the proposed proxy-aware scheduling methodology that exploits data locality to reduce the amount of data transfers over WAN sites. We can compare the performance of proxy-aware scheduling with FCFS and data-aware methodologies, both with and without the addition of proxy storage. We also perform simulations for two workload sizes, in order to show the behavior of proxy-aware scheduling as the MG-RAST servers become more congested.

2. **Improved performance of MG-RAST when using proxy-aware scheduling**: Our results show that the use of proxy-aware scheduling leads to decreased data movement overhead and improved job response time when compared with other scheduling methodologies that do not use storage proxies. When proxy-aware scheduling is used for a large workload, we get up to 286x speedup over FCFS scheduling and up to 150x speedup over other data-aware scheduling methods. The addition of the proxy servers necessary to implement the proxy-aware scheduling requires minimal changes to the current MG-RAST infrastructure. This fact, combined with the significant performance improvement, shows that our proposed setup is cost effective and highly efficient.

3. **Extrapolated traces to represent future workloads**: To represent the future data growth trend in MG-RAST, we have used representative extrapolated traces from the production service to evaluate the proposed proxy infrastructure for MG-RAST, as well as

compare the performance of proxy-aware scheduling against the previously proposed data-aware scheduling methodologies in [18]. The extrapolated trace is created through regression modeling of the relationships observed in the production trace data. Using the extrapolated traces in conjunction with discrete-event simulation enables the evaluation of MG-RAST under much larger workloads than would be possible using only the production traces.

The remainder of the paper is organized as follows. Section 2 discusses related work. Section 3 discusses the current and proposed infrastructures, while Section 4 describes the simulation design. In Section 5, we provide validation of the simulation as well as an evaluation of the proposed infrastructure. Section 6 summarizes our conclusions.

2. RELATED WORK

Tang et al. presented new approaches to workflow and data management systems, called AWE and Shock, respectively, that provided MG-RAST with scalable, portable, reusable, and reproducible data analysis capabilities [19]. Gerlach et al. presented an extension of the AWE and Shock ecosystem called Skyport [8]. Skyport uses Docker and Linux container virtualization technology to solve the problems involved in deploying software on multiple computing resources (e.g., dependencies on specific versions of software) while improving overall resource utilization compared with the previous virtual machine approach. Tang et al. additionally developed a discrete-event simulation framework, called AweSim, for evaluating MG-RAST deployments, focusing specifically on the effect of data-aware scheduling policies in deployments consisting of multiple sites connected by a wide-area network [18]. The WAN model of AweSim currently supports a latency and bandwidth network model that models contention at the endpoints, but not in the routing fabric. AweSim used production traces of MG-RAST workflows for evaluation, for which characterization work had previously been performed [17].

AweSim is based on the ROSS and CODES simulation frameworks. ROSS is the Rensselaer Optimistic Simulation System, a scalable discrete-event simulation framework providing sequential, synchronous parallel ("conservative") and speculative parallel ("optimistic") simulation capabilities [3]. The CODES simulation framework is built on top of ROSS and provides a comprehensive suite of HPC network, storage and workload models [6, 15, 12]. OMNeT++ [21] and ns-3 [13] are also discrete-event network simulation frameworks. Both frameworks provide various wired and wireless link layer protocol models; however, neither framework has HPC network models (e.g., dragonfly) readily available. We chose to use AweSim (and thus ROSS and CODES) in this work, because of the potential to extend AweSim in the future to use the HPC network models provided by CODES.

Event-driven simulation is also a commonly used approach to evaluate the performance of cloud systems. For example, CloudSim is a framework developed by Calheiros et al. that provides simulation of cloud infrastructures and services [2]. Network behavior can be modeled in CloudSim, however it uses a simple latency matrix that cannot capture network congestion. Chen and Deelman developed WorkflowSim, an extension of CloudSim, to allow for task dependency tracking and task clustering in workflow scheduling [4]. The system was subsequently used to model the Pegasus workflow management system [7].

The proxy approach has been employed in various situations. For example, Cirstea et al. provide a design for a prototype proxy cache for data located on a grid storage element [5]. Kungas and Dumas present a proxy cache implementation for SOAP traffic [10]. They show that the least recently used (LRU) replacement policy provides the best performance. Our work shows the addition of proxy servers in a different context: the proxy servers in our proposed infrastructure store the large volumes of intermediate data generated during job processing.

Finally, we discuss work being done in the area of job scheduling in scientific workflows at multiple WAN sites. Aside from Tang et al.'s exploration of scheduling in the context of MG-RAST [18], Jones et al. developed bandwidth-aware co-allocating meta-schedulers for mini-grids in order to improve the performance of simultaneously co-allocated jobs [9]. Specifically their methodology uses the intercluster network utilization to lower the impact of the network contention created by simultaneously co-allocated jobs. In contrast, our work explores a scheduling methodology that assigns a job to a single wide area site in order to reduce the movement of the intermediate job data generated. Szabo et al. [16] propose an evolutionary approach to task allocation on cloud resources that optimizes workflow runtime and the size of transferred data. Their approach uses a chromosome to encode the allocation of tasks to nodes and another chromosome to encode the execution order of tasks. Wang et al. [22] provide an improvement on work stealing methods. In their work, scheduling is distributed, and idle schedulers can steal the work of other schedulers, possibly incurring significant data movement overheads because of loss of data locality. Their solution is to organize work queues by data size and location in order to continue to provide load balancing while also taking data locality into account. The MG-RAST situation differs in that using proxy-aware scheduling allows for the exploitation of data locality to substantially reduce data movement overhead while also providing better load balancing of the tasks among clients at all WAN sites.

3. MG-RAST DESIGN

In this section, we first present the current design of MG-RAST, along with previously explored scheduling methodologies. We follow this with a discussion of our proposed proxy infrastructure, as well as our proxy-aware scheduling methodology.

3.1 Current Infrastructure

The system model of MG-RAST comprises the AWE [19] workflow management system and the Shock data management system [1].[1] The AWE workflow management system executes the biological analysis workflows on cloud resources. It is based on a client-server model where the AWE server schedules and assigns tasks of a job to the AWE clients, which then process the tasks locally. The AWE server receives job submissions, manages task dependencies, and performs scheduling.

The MG-RAST pipeline consists of various processing and

---

[1]AWE and Shock can be found at https://github.com/MG-RAST/AWE and https://github.com/MG-RAST/Shock.

analytical tasks. User submissions with one or more data sets are rendered into one job per data set at submission time. For each job, a number of potentially parallel tasks are generated by the AWE server using a workflow recipe. While there are data dependencies between the tasks of a given job, there are no data dependencies between tasks from different jobs. Each of the tasks is divided into one or more work units, each of which typically receives a small fraction of the input data due to the data-parallel nature of most steps.

The Shock object-based data management system is used to store biological sequences and the intermediate data generated during job execution on AWE clients. Shock is a centralized data server that handles all requests from the clients for transfer of data. It utilizes a REST API that makes it accessible from desktops, cloud, smartphones, or HPC systems.

With the increasing rate of data-processing requests being submitted to MG-RAST, workload execution is being outsourced to multiple cloud resources and user machines. A number of organizations already contribute to the compute-intensive steps of the pipeline (e.g., similarity searches) by providing their own virtual machine based instances to analyze data. Because MG-RAST uses the FCFS scheduling policy, it does not take advantage of data locality for workflow scheduling. This, combined with the use of a centralized data server with multiple WAN sites, contributes to significant data movement overhead, which can slow down the end user's job response time. Additionally, an enormous number of data access requests can transform the Shock server into a potential bottleneck.

Tang et al. [18] explored three scheduling policies: FCFS, best-fit, and greedy. Best-fit and greedy are data-aware methods in which the AWE server uses the compute-to-data cost ratio of work units for scheduling decisions, putting work units with high compute-to-data ratio on sites with lower effective bandwidth and work units with comparatively lower compute-to-data ratio on sites with higher effective bandwidth. This strategy is made possible through the ability to examine and make cost predictions of each type of task/work unit, as done in Tang et al.'s workload characterization research [17]. For best-fit scheduling, only the most computationally expensive tasks are scheduled at low-bandwidth sites. Greedy scheduling, on the other hand, allows less computationally intensive tasks to run on low-bandwidth sites if no more computationally intensive tasks are pending.

3.2 Proxies and Proxy-Aware Scheduling

We propose adding one storage proxy server to each wide-area site in MG-RAST which would distribute the load of the centralized Shock data server. We also introduce a proxy-aware scheduling policy that adjusts the distribution of jobs among multiple WAN sites in order to exploit data locality and thus reduce I/O time. Figure 1 shows an architectural diagram of the proposed proxy infrastructure and its interactions with the AWE clients/server and Shock. The Shock data server is shown as part of WAN Site 1 in the figure since it is hosted locally at ANL. This is because the clients and proxies at this site have a relatively higher bandwidth connection to Shock than any remote site that is communicating over a wide area link.

Steps 3 through 7 in the figure highlight the proposed

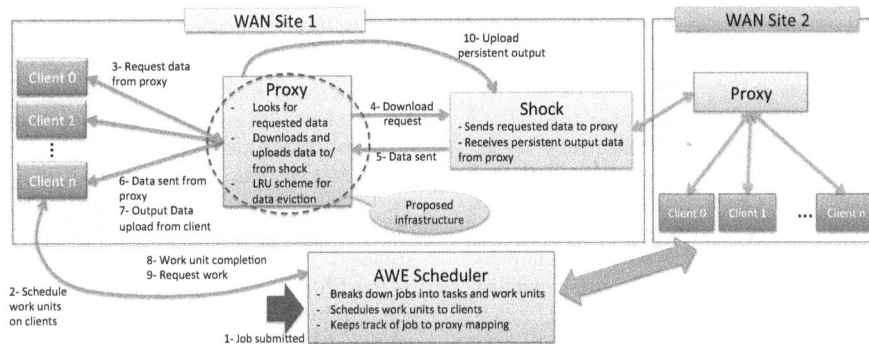

Figure 1: Proposed MG-RAST proxy infrastructure

changes to be made to the current MG-RAST infrastructure. As shown in the figure, the AWE server schedules the parallel tasks of a job so that all the data for a given job is stored on the same proxy. In proxy-aware scheduling, the AWE scheduler randomly chooses a proxy at either site when scheduling the first work unit in a job. For the given job, all work units will then be scheduled to a client at the same site as the chosen proxy. The AWE server keeps track of the job to proxy mapping so that the subsequent tasks and work units that comprise that job will be stored on that same proxy. Hence, all tasks of a job are computed at the same site, and the resulting data is stored in a single proxy, as opposed to sending tasks to different sites based on their compute-to-data cost ratio. This approach eliminates the need for proxies to transfer intermediate data between each other and the centralized Shock server, thus reducing the number of wide-area transfers. For MG-RAST, data dependencies are only between tasks within the same job. Therefore, intermediate data does not need to remain in proxy storage once its job is finished; it can simply be deleted from the proxy, instead of being sent back to Shock. Only the persistent and final output data from a job needs to be uploaded to Shock. As a proxy runs out of storage space, it will send final output data from completed jobs to Shock in order to free space for new job data.

As shown in Figure 1, clients send their data requests to a proxy server local to the clients, instead of directly to the centralized Shock server. When receiving a data access request from a client, a proxy checks whether it has the necessary data stored. If so, the proxy sends the data to the client. Otherwise the proxy requests the data from the Shock server before sending to the client. Since there is no one-to-one mapping from work units of a given task to work units of the next task in the pipeline, we design the proxies to store data at task-level granularity. Proxies also request data from Shock at task-level granularity, which reduces the number of accesses to Shock. In essence, when the proxies transfer data to and from Shock, all the data needed for the work units that compose that task is transferred. In contrast, transfers between proxies and clients is done at the work unit level, so the client receives only the data necessary for its assigned work unit. In the current MG-RAST infrastructure (i.e., without proxies), clients always request data from Shock at work unit granularity.

Figure 2 shows a representative example of best-fit scheduling and proxy-aware scheduling. In the figure, each horizontal line represents a different client at that site, with a limited bandwidth available between the two WAN sites. The figure shows Jobs A and B, with various work units being computed for each job. Each box represents a work unit, with work units from the same task being given the same coloring. Circles group work units that feed into the next task in the pipeline. For example, task 9 in the MG-RAST pipeline depends on both tasks 5 and 8, so work units for tasks 5 and 8 can be grouped together. The dotted lines pointing from one group of tasks to another show the dependencies of the tasks.

In the example, Job A initially has tasks 5 and 8 being computed concurrently because there are no dependencies between these two tasks. Task 9 is dependent on both tasks' output data. Job B shows tasks 2 and 3 being computed, where task 3 is dependent on task 2. The left side of the figure shows best-fit scheduling without using proxies. Task 5 is the most computationally expensive, as found in [17] (i.e., its relative cost of I/O is the lowest among all tasks), so its work units can be computed at either site. The right side of the figure shows the same situation using proxy-aware scheduling, where an entire job is computed by clients at a single site, because all intermediate data of a job is being stored on the same proxy.

In the best-fit scheduling example, task 5's work units at the remote site take longer to complete because of the need to retrieve the data from Shock and send the output back. The clients at WAN site 1 become idle waiting for the work units at WAN Site 2 to complete, so the AWE server starts scheduling another job's tasks to those clients. When Job A's task 5 is completed, those clients are now busy on another job, and have to wait longer to start Job A's task 9. In comparison, for proxy-aware scheduling the jobs can be split among sites, and the same jobs can be completed in less time.

4. SIMULATION DESIGN

To explore our proposed proxy architecture, we extended the AweSim simulator, introduced in Section 2. Although ROSS is capable of parallel execution, we use sequential execution in this work, because the scale of the simulations performed still experiences good performance with an event rate of up to 2.4 million events per second. We first provide a brief overview of AweSim before describing our extensions.

AweSim has five distinct simulation entities (known as logical processes, or LPs, in ROSS) to represent the MG-RAST analytic service: (1) an LP representing the Shock

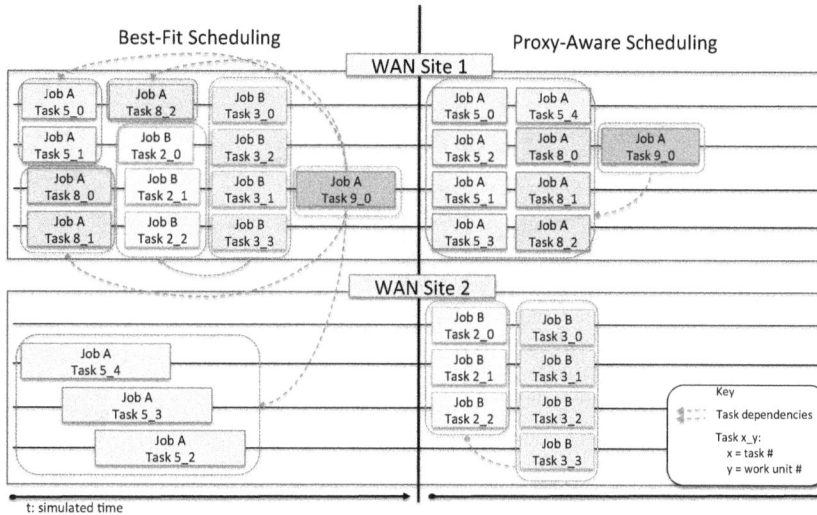

Figure 2: Representative examples of best-fit and proxy-aware scheduling

data server, (2) an LP representing the AWE scheduler, (3) an LP representing each AWE client, (4) a router LP representing the communication between the Shock server and AWE entities, and (5) an LP representing the WAN endpoints. All LP types have one instantiation, with the exception of the AWE client, which can have any number of instantiations, and the WAN endpoints, which have one instantiation per site. The AWE client LPs can be grouped into multiple sites, with different effective bandwidths to and from the Shock LP. The simulation proceeds through the issuance of time-stamped messages or events between LPs, representing data transfers, work unit executions, and control events, among others.

In this work, we have extended AweSim to include an LP representing the storage proxy discussed in Section 3.2. In the simulations, we place one proxy at each WAN site. The proxies have a configurable amount of storage and use a least recently used (LRU) protocol for evicting data. If the data evicted is intermediate job data that is no longer needed, it is simply deleted. Otherwise the data is sent back to the central Shock data server.

The event flow of the MG-RAST model is based on the the MG-RAST infrastructure diagram shown in Figure 1. The various event types used in AweSim are as follows:

- Work unit assignment: Upon scheduling a work unit to a client, the AWE scheduler issues an event to the client notifying them of the task type and which dataset to process.

- Data download request: This event is issued from client to proxy to request the data necessary for processing the assigned work unit. If the proxy does not already have the requested data, the proxy requests the data from the router, which forwards the request to the Shock server. In configurations that do not use the proxy LP, the client sends this event to the router instead, which then sends the download request event to Shock.

- Data download: After receiving a request for data download, Shock sends an event with the data to the

router, which forwards it to either the proxy or the client, depending on whether the configuration includes proxy LPs. The proxy also uses this event type to send the requested data to the client. The amount of time to transfer the data is based on the size of the dataset and the bandwidth configured between the endpoints.

- Data upload: After the client performs the necessary computation for its work unit, it sends an event to upload the output data to either a proxy or the router, dependent on the simulation configuration. If sent to the proxy, the proxy stores the data, evicting stored data by a LRU protocol if necessary. The proxy sends this upload event to the router for any evicted data that must be stored on Shock. Again, the time to transfer data is based on the size of the dataset and the configured bandwidth.

- Data upload acknowledgement: After the data is uploaded, Shock sends an acknowledgement event to the router, which sends the acknowledgement to either the proxy or client, dependent on the given configuration. In configurations where proxies are used, the proxy sends this acknowledgement to the client when it stores the data sent from the client.

- Work unit completion: Once a client has received an acknowledgement that its data has been uploaded, it sends the AWE scheduler an event to signify that the work unit has been completed.

- Work request: At the beginning of the simulation and anytime a client has received an acknowledgement from uploading a work unit's output data, it sends a message to the AWE scheduler to request work.

In the LP representing the AWE scheduler, we have implemented proxy-aware scheduling as previously described in Section 3.2. In our modified version, AweSim can also be configured to use proxies in conjunction with FCFS, best-fit, and greedy scheduling methodologies.

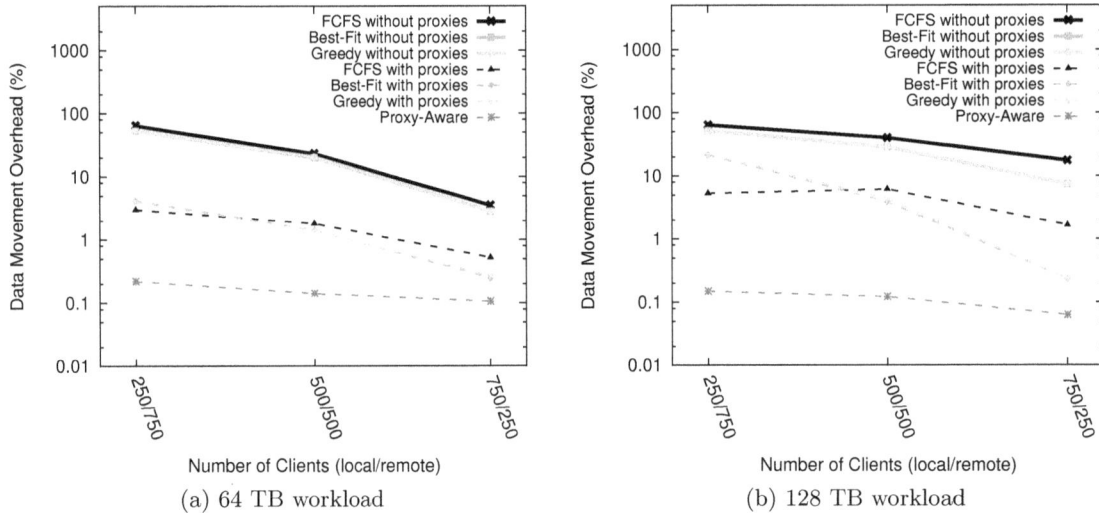

(a) 64 TB workload   (b) 128 TB workload

Figure 3: Average data movement overhead for proxy-aware, best-fit, greedy and FCFS scheduling algorithms with 1000 clients and an input of 64 TB (a) and 128 TB (b).

5. EVALUATION

In this section, we present an evaluation of the proposed proxy-aware scheduling methodology for MG-RAST using discrete-event simulation. First we describe the experimental setup. Then we provide validation of the simulation, followed by experimental results.

5.1 Experimental Setup

For the experiments, we perform two-site simulations. One site is configured as "local" with respect to Shock, with a comparatively faster connection to the centralized data store. The other site is configured as "remote," with a comparatively slower connection. Currently, MG-RAST runs with 50 to 150 clients [18]; however, with the anticipated increase in data submissions, more clients will be necessary. Therefore, we look at three configurations with a total of 1,000 clients: equal numbers of clients at each site (500 local, 500 remote), more clients at the local site (750 local, 250 remote), and more clients at the remote site (250 local, 750 remote). We configure each site to have one proxy with sufficient storage space to hold the intermediate output data. As stated previously, there are no dependencies between different jobs, so intermediate job data can be deleted from the proxy once it is no longer needed, freeing up storage space for new jobs to store their intermediate data. With our problem size, a 4 TB proxy storage size is sufficient.

We use the same Shock-to-site bandwidth as in the original AweSim work [18]: 500 MB/s download and 100 MB/s upload for the local site, and 10 times slower download and upload rates for the remote server. Between WAN sites, the bandwidth is 50 MB/s, which is the same as the download bandwidth between the remote site and Shock. The bandwidth between the clients and proxies at a given site is 750 MB/s, and the latency is 0.1 ms, which is based on the Samsung SSD PM863 specifications [23, 14].

The metrics we use for evaluation are job response time, client utilization, daily workload volume, and data movement overhead.

- **Job response time** is the elapsed time (in hours) from when a job is first submitted until the job is completed.

- **Client utilization** is measured as the percentage of time that clients spend processing a work unit, including the download and upload of inputs and results.

- **Data movement overhead** is the percentage of time to transfer data relative to the total compute and data transfer time for each client. We report the data movement overhead averaged over all clients.

- **Daily workload volume** is the total input data size in GiB divided by the simulated time to complete all jobs in days. This metric is constrained by the job arrival times in the workload trace being used for simulation, such that any given workload has a maximum daily workload volume regardless of the system configuration.

For the experiments, we use a production MG-RAST job trace that contains data for four months of job submissions. The trace contains 12,483 jobs, 124,830 tasks, and 190,205 work units. Since the number of data submission requests being submitted to MG-RAST is increasing tremendously, we extrapolate the production traces to create additional jobs on the fly during simulation. These extrapolated traces represent a future trend of the growth in data analysis requests. We used regression models to model the relationships in the trace data. The time it takes a client to execute a work unit is modeled with respect to the input size of the work unit coming from the trace. The output size of a work unit is also modeled with respect to its input size. The input size of a task is modeled with respect to the output size of the previous task that it is dependent on. This is necessary in cases where MG-RAST will output the data in multiple file formats for a task, but the next dependent task will use data from only one of the file formats. We also use a uniform random number generator to add randomness to the

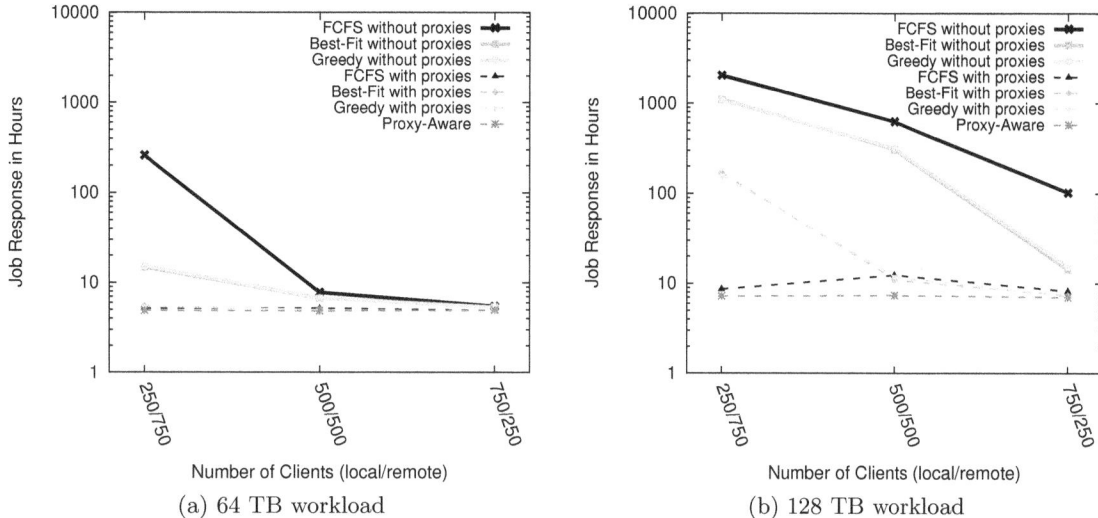

(a) 64 TB workload   (b) 128 TB workload

Figure 4: Average job response time for proxy-aware, best-fit, greedy and FCFS scheduling algorithms with 1000 clients and an input of 64 TB (a) and 128 TB (b).

trace values determined by the regression models. Job arrival times of the extrapolated trace are determined using a Poisson distribution.

We configure the simulations to model a time period of 100 days, and we perform the experiments with two workload sizes. The smaller workload uses a total job input size of 64 TB; the larger workload has a total job input size of 128 TB. The four-month production trace, which provides approximately 10.5 TB of input job data, is used with the extrapolated trace. Job arrival times of the four-month production trace were compressed to fit in this 100-day simulated time period. Using the extrapolated trace along with the production trace results in approximately 37,500 jobs, 375,000 tasks, and 806,000 work units for the 64 TB workload and 68,900 jobs, 689,000 tasks, and 1,560,000 work units for the 128 TB workload.

5.2 Validation

The behavior of the previous version of AweSim (i.e., without the proxy LP) was validated by Tang et al. [18] for one-site simulations by comparing simulation output with metrics computed by using production MG-RAST traces. To validate the behavior of AweSim with the addition of proxies, we compare the output of our extended version with the original simulator, in order to ensure that certain metrics stay the same. We are unable to perform further validation of the proxies with production MG-RAST data, as the proxies have not been implemented into MG-RAST. However, we perform both one and two site simulations and check that both versions perform the same amount of work and that the amount of data transferred is the same. For data transfer, we compare the amount of data uploaded and downloaded between clients and the central Shock server in the prior version (i.e., without proxies) with the amount transferred between clients and proxies in our extended version. We expect these values to be the same in each version because the proxies are now distributing the load of Shock and will, at some point, hold all job input and output data, as well

as intermediate job data. For the simulations with a 64 TB input workload, the amount of data uploaded by clients is approximately 354 TB and the amount downloaded is approximately 455 TB. For the 128 TB workload, the amount of data uploaded and downloaded by clients is approximately 725 TB and 929 TB, respectively.

5.3 Experimental Results

To explore the effectiveness of proxy-aware scheduling, we compare the FCFS, best-fit, and greedy scheduling policies with the proxy-aware scheduling. For FCFS and the data-aware methods, we perform simulations with and without proxy storage. Data movement overhead is shown in Figure 3 for both 64 TB and 128 TB workload simulations. In all three client configurations, FCFS, best-fit, and greedy scheduling without proxies have the highest data movement overheads. As the number of remote clients increase, so does the overhead for all three scheduling methodologies. In all configurations, using proxies in conjunction with these scheduling methodologies provides lower data movement overhead. When there are more local clients or equal numbers of clients at each site, best-fit, and greedy scheduling with proxies have a lower overhead than does FCFS with proxies. When there are more remote clients than local clients, this situation reverses, with the difference becoming more pronounced in the 128 TB workload. FCFS with proxies has a lower overhead in this client configuration, because best-fit and greedy are more restrictive in assigning work units to the remote site clients, making it is more difficult for scheduling at the remote site to exploit data locality to reduce data movement.

While adding proxies decreases the data movement overhead of all scheduling methodologies, proxy-aware scheduling is the only methodology to decrease to under 1% in all client configurations for both workloads. When the workload doubles, proxy-aware's overhead slightly decreases, because the time the clients spend computing increases at a faster rate than the time the clients spend waiting on data

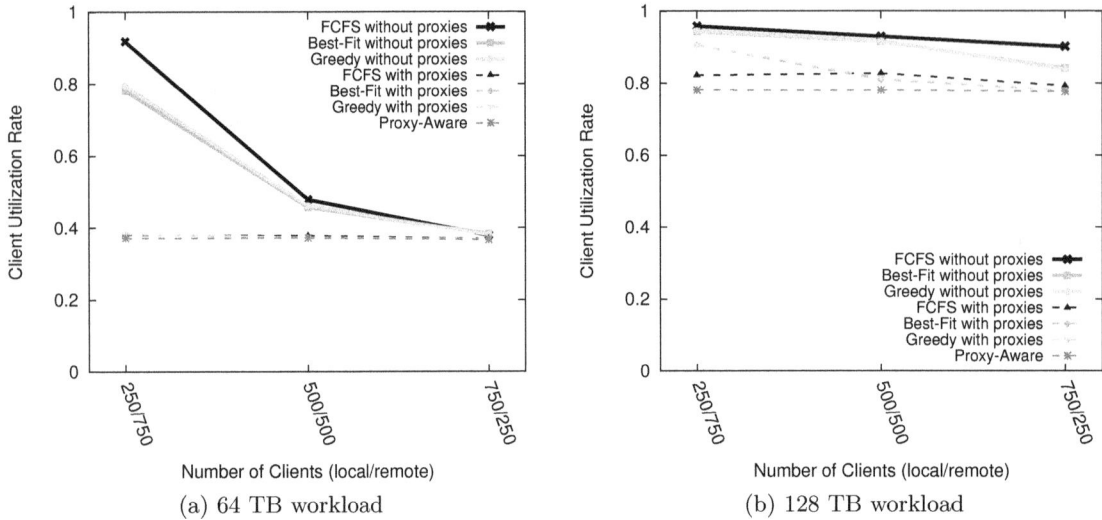

| (a) 64 TB workload | (b) 128 TB workload |

Figure 5: Average client utilization for proxy-aware, best-fit, greedy and FCFS scheduling algorithms with 1000 clients and an input of 64 TB (a) and 128 TB (b).

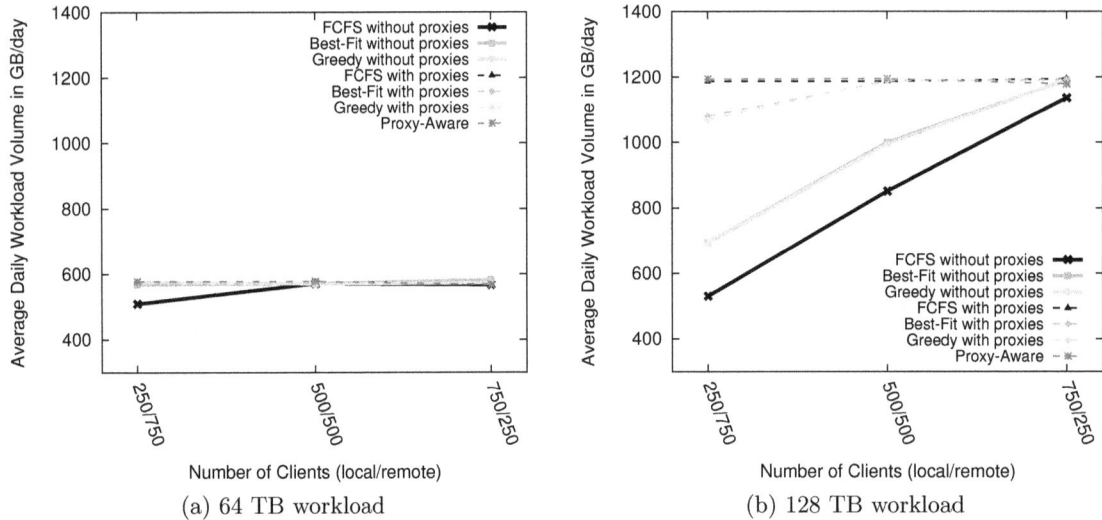

| (a) 64 TB workload | (b) 128 TB workload |

Figure 6: Average daily workload volume for proxy-aware, best-fit, greedy and FCFS scheduling algorithms with 1000 clients and an input of 64 TB (a) and 128 TB (b).

transfer. The reason proxy-aware scheduling provides low data movement overhead in all cases is that the data is almost always on the proxy when the clients request it, since the intermediate data generated by tasks are never transferred to the central data server. The data movement overhead metric is taking into account the movement of initial job data from Shock to the proxy and then on to a client; however, this transfer is negligible compared to the amount of time the clients spend actually computing work units. When using proxies (for any scheduling methodology), the transfer of a job's final output data from a proxy to Shock is not factored into the data movement overhead, as the clients do not have to wait on this transfer. The clients only need to wait for the acknowledgment that the proxy has re-

ceived the data before requesting more work from the AWE server. Whereas with the FCFS and the data-aware scheduling methods without proxies, the upload of final output data is accounted for in the calculation of data movement overhead, because the clients wait for an acknowledgment from the central Shock server before requesting more work.

The low data movement overheads observed in the proxy-aware scheduling also lead to a consistently small average job response time of approximately 5–7 hours, regardless of workload size, as shown in Figure 4. For the 64 TB workload, the addition of proxies improves the job response time, especially for the 250/750 client configuration, where the speedup is 3x over greedy and best-fit scheduling without proxies and the speedup is 52x over FCFS without proxies.

For the 128 TB workload, proxies still provide an improved job response time over not using proxies, but proxy-aware scheduling has the lowest job response time in all client configurations. In this larger workload, the largest improvements in job response time are seen in the case where there are more clients at the remote site. In this case, proxy-aware scheduling has a speedup of 286x over FCFS without proxies and 150x over greedy and best-fit without proxies. Proxy-aware scheduling has only a 1.1x speedup over FCFS with proxies, but a 22x speedup over best-fit and greedy with proxies. These large improvements in job response time with the addition of proxies are due to the fact that clients are spending much less time in downloading and uploading the data than with the previous scheduling methodologies.

Client utilization rate is shown in Figure 5. For the 64 TB workload, not using proxies results in a high client utilization rate in the case of more remote clients. The addition of proxies to any scheduling methodology keeps client utilization to approximately 37% in all client configurations. In the 128 TB case, client utilization is much higher for all scheduling methodologies in all client configurations. However, the addition of proxies results in a lower client utilization rate, with proxy-aware scheduling providing the lowest utilization in all configurations because clients are spending less time waiting on data transfer. Thus, with the addition of proxies, the clients can handle more work, even when there are a large number of clients at the remote site.

The results for average daily workload volume are shown in Figure 6. For the smaller workload, all scheduling methodologies, except FCFS without proxies, have a consistent average daily workload volume of approximately 575 GB/day in all client configurations. Since the workload volume is limited by the job arrival times in the workload trace, approximately 575 GB/day is the maximum daily volume for the 64 TB workload. Similarly for the 128 TB workload, approximately 1200 GB/day is the maximum. If the system is unable to keep up with the arrival rate of jobs for a given configuration, then the average daily workload volume for that configuration will be lower than the maximum. Proxy-aware scheduling and FCFS with proxies are the only methods that consistently meet the maximum average daily workload volume in all configurations, for both workloads tested. Greedy and best-fit scheduling with proxies perform the same except in the 250/750 client configurations, where the workload volume is reduced to approximately 1075 GB/day.

As discussed in Section 5.2, when proxies are not used, the amount of data downloaded from and uploaded to Shock in the 64 TB workload simulations is approximately 455 TB and 354 TB, respectively. In these simulations, Shock is accessed by the clients about 806,000 times. Adding proxy storage (to any scheduling policy) reduces the number of Shock accesses to approximately 37,000. The amount of data transferred to Shock is decreased as well, to approximately 64 TB downloaded and 39 TB uploaded. For the 128 TB simulations without proxies, the amount downloaded from Shock is 929 TB, the amount uploaded to Shock is 725 TB, and the number of accesses to Shock is approximately 1,560,000. Using proxies for any scheduling methodology reduces these amounts to 128 TB downloaded from Shock, 79 TB uploaded to Shock, and 69,000 Shock accesses.

6. CONCLUSION

MG-RAST, the metagenomics analytic service at Argonne National Laboratory, is seeing a tremendous growth in data processing requests. MG-RAST currently uses a central data store, Shock, for data management. While the central data store has the advantages of long-term data curation and added security, it can become a bottleneck for large volumes of data submissions. We propose the addition of proxy storage servers to the MG-RAST infrastructure, which store the intermediate data generated by jobs to help reduce the number of data access requests to Shock. We also propose a proxy-aware scheduling methodology, which takes data locality into account while scheduling jobs. Discrete-event simulation is used to evaluate our proposed changes to the MG-RAST infrastructure and the behavior of our proposed proxy-aware scheduling methodology. By extrapolating the production traces from MG-RAST, we are able to evaluate the various scheduling methodologies used for MG-RAST under increased workloads. We have demonstrated that the addition of proxy storage servers can substantially decrease the data movement overhead between multiple WAN sites and lead to a significant improvement in end-user job response time. Using proxies speeds the job response time for all scheduling methodologies evaluated, but using a proxy-aware scheduling methodology provides the most speedup over all client configurations in larger workloads.

Acknowledgments

This material was based upon work supported by the U.S. Department of Energy, Office of Science, Office of Advanced Scientific Computer Research (ASCR) under contract DE-AC02-06CH11357.

7. REFERENCES

[1] J. Bischof, A. Wilke, W. Gerlach, T. Harrison, T. Paczian, W. Tang, J. Wilkening, N. Desai, and F. Meyer. Shock: Active storage for multicloud streaming data analysis. In *2nd IEEE/ACM International Symposium on Big Data Computing*. IEEE, 2015.

[2] R. N. Calheiros, R. Ranjan, A. Beloglazov, C. A. De Rose, and R. Buyya. CloudSim: A toolkit for modeling and simulation of cloud computing environments and evaluation of resource provisioning algorithms. *Software: Practice and Experience*, 41(1):23–50, 2011.

[3] C. D. Carothers, D. Bauer, and S. Pearce. ROSS: A high-performance, low-memory, modular time warp system. *Journal of Parallel and Distributed Computing*, 62(11):1648–1669, 2002.

[4] W. Chen and E. Deelman. WorkflowSim: A toolkit for simulating scientific workflows in distributed environments. In *2012 IEEE 8th International Conference on E-Science*, pages 1–8. IEEE, 2012.

[5] T. C. Cirstea, J. J. Keijser, O. A. Koeroo, R. Starink, and J. A. Templon. A scalable proxy cache for grid data access. In *Journal of Physics: Conference Series*, volume 396. IOP Publishing, 2012.

[6] J. Cope, N. Liu, S. Lang, P. Carns, C. Carothers, and R. Ross. Codes: Enabling co-design of multi-layer exascale storage architectures. *Proceedings of the*

Workshop on Emerging Supercomputing Technologies, 2011.

[7] E. Deelman, K. Vahi, G. Juve, M. Rynge, S. Callaghan, P. J. Maechling, R. Mayani, W. Chen, R. Ferreira da Silva, M. Livny, and K. Wenger. Pegasus, a workflow management system for science automation. *Future Generation Computer Systems*, 2014.

[8] W. Gerlach, W. Tang, K. Keegan, T. Harrison, A. Wilke, J. Bischof, M. D'Souza, S. Devoid, D. Murphy-Olson, N. Desai, et al. Skyport: Container-based execution environment management for multi-cloud scientific workflows. In *Proceedings of the 5th International Workshop on Data-Intensive Computing in the Clouds*, pages 25–32. IEEE Press, 2014.

[9] W. M. Jones, L. W. Pang, W. B. Ligon, and D. Stanzione. Bandwidth-aware co-allocating meta-schedulers for mini-grid architectures. In *Cluster Computing, 2004 IEEE International Conference on*, pages 45–54. IEEE, 2004.

[10] P. Küngas and M. Dumas. Configurable SOAP proxy cache for data provisioning web services. In *Proceedings of the 2011 ACM Symposium on Applied Computing*, pages 1614–1621. ACM, 2011.

[11] F. Meyer, D. Paarmann, M. D'Souza, R. Olson, E. Glass, M. Kubal, T. Paczian, A. Rodriguez, R. Stevens, A. Wilke, J. Wilkening, and R. Edwards. The metagenomics RAST server - a public resource for the automatic phylogenetic and functional analysis of metagenomes. *BMC Bioinformatics*, 9(1):386, 2008.

[12] M. Mubarak, C. D. Carothers, R. B. Ross, and P. Carns. A case study in using massively parallel simulation for extreme-scale torus network codesign. In *Proceedings of the 2nd ACM SIGSIM/PADS conference on Principles of advanced discrete simulation*, pages 27–38. ACM, 2014.

[13] ns-3. https://www.nsnam.org/. Accessed Mar. 15, 2016.

[14] Samsung PM863 and SM863 for Data Centers. http://www.samsung.com/global/business/ semiconductor/minisite/SSD/downloads/document/ Samsung_SSD_PM863_and_SM863_Brochure_web.pdf. Accessed Jan. 21, 2016.

[15] S. Snyder, P. Carns, J. Jenkins, K. Harms, R. Ross, M. Mubarak, and C. Carothers. A case for epidemic fault detection and group membership in HPC storage systems. In *High Performance Computing Systems. Performance Modeling, Benchmarking, and Simulation*, pages 237–248. Springer, 2014.

[16] C. Szabo, Q. Z. Sheng, T. Kroeger, Y. Zhang, and J. Yu. Science in the cloud: allocation and execution of data-intensive scientific workflows. *Journal of Grid Computing*, 12(2):245–264, 2014.

[17] W. Tang, J. Bischof, N. Desai, K. Mahadik, W. Gerlach, T. Harrison, A. Wilke, and F. Meyer. Workload characterization for MG-RAST metagenomic data analytics service in the cloud. In *Big Data (Big Data), 2014 IEEE International Conference on*, pages 56–63. IEEE, 2014.

[18] W. Tang, J. Jenkins, F. Meyer, R. Ross, R. Kettimuthu, L. Winkler, X. Yang, T. Lehman, and N. Desai. Data-aware resource scheduling for multicloud workflows: A fine-grained simulation approach. In *Cloud Computing Technology and Science (CloudCom), 2014 IEEE 6th International Conference on*, pages 887–892. IEEE, 2014.

[19] W. Tang, J. Wilkening, N. Desai, W. Gerlach, A. Wilke, and F. Meyer. A scalable data analysis platform for metagenomics. In *Big Data, 2013 IEEE International Conference on*, pages 21–26. IEEE, 2013.

[20] T. Thomas, J. Gilbert, and F. Meyer. Metagenomics – a guide from sampling to data analysis. *Microb Inform Exp*, 2(3):1–12, 2012.

[21] A. Varga et al. The OMNeT++ discrete event simulation system. In *Proceedings of the European simulation multiconference (ESM 2001)*, volume 9, page 65, 2001.

[22] K. Wang, X. Zhou, T. Li, D. Zhao, M. Lang, and I. Raicu. Optimizing load balancing and data-locality with data-aware scheduling. *2014 IEEE International Conference on Big Data (Big Data)*, pages 119–128, 2014.

[23] Why SSDs are Awesome. http://www.samsung.com/ global/business/semiconductor/minisite/SSD/global/ html/whitepaper/whitepaper01.html. Accessed Jan. 21, 2016.

Automated Memoization for Parameter Studies Implemented in Impure Languages

Mirko Stoffers, Daniel Schemmel, Oscar Soria Dustmann, Klaus Wehrle
Communication and Distributed Systems, RWTH Aachen University
{stoffers; schemmel; soriadustmann; wehrle}@comsys.rwth-aachen.de

ABSTRACT

In computer simulations many processes are highly repetitive. These repetitions are amplified further when a parameter study is conducted where the same model is repeatedly executed with varying parameters, especially when performing multiple runs to increase statistical confidence. Inevitably, such repetitions result in the execution of identical computations, with identical code, identical input, and hence identical output. Performing computations redundantly wastes resources and the execution time of a parameter study could be reduced if the redundancies were avoided.

To this end, the idea of memoization was proposed decades ago. However, until today memoization is either performed manually or automated memoization approaches are used that can only handle pure functions. This means that only the function parameters and the return value may be input and output of the function whereas side effects are not allowed. In order to expand the scope of automated memoization to a larger class of programs, we propose an approach able to reliably detect the full input and output of a function, including reading and writing objects through arbitrarily indirect pointers with some preconditions. We show the feasibility of our approach and derive simple performance approximations enabling rough predictions of the expected benefit. By means of a simple case study performing an OFDM network simulation, we demonstrate the practical suitability of our approach, speeding up the execution of the whole parameter study by a factor of 75, while only doubling memory consumption.

CCS Concepts

•Computing methodologies → Massively parallel and high-performance simulations; •Software and its engineering → *Preprocessors*;

Keywords

Automatic Memoization; Accelerating Parameter Studies; Impure Languages

Permission to make digital or hard copies of all or part of this work for personal or classroom use is granted without fee provided that copies are not made or distributed for profit or commercial advantage and that copies bear this notice and the full citation on the first page. Copyrights for components of this work owned by others than the author(s) must be honored. Abstracting with credit is permitted. To copy otherwise, or republish, to post on servers or to redistribute to lists, requires prior specific permission and/or a fee. Request permissions from permissions@acm.org.

SIGSIM-PADS '16, May 15 - 18, 2016, Banff, AB, Canada

ⓒ 2016 Copyright held by the owner/author(s). Publication rights licensed to ACM.
ISBN 978-1-4503-3742-7/16/05. . . $15.00

DOI: http://dx.doi.org/10.1145/2901378.2901386

1. INTRODUCTION

Computer simulations are programs with highly repetitive computations. While a simulation is running, the same event handlers are executed repeatedly, often on the same input as before. In order to achieve sufficient statistical confidence, simulation experiments are repeated with the same parameters, but different random number streams. This inevitably results in performing a certain subset of computations again. Finally, to compare different configurations, certain parameters are varied while others are kept constant. This again causes a large set of computations to be repeatedly performed on the same input, necessarily resulting in the same output. From this observation we conclude that in a simulation parameter study a large fraction of the computations performed are in fact redundant. The opportunity to speed up the execution of computer software in general by avoiding such redundant computations has already been described by Michie in 1968 [16]. Michie developed the idea of so called memo functions (now known as *memoized functions*), which allow re-using previously computed results.

In order to apply this technique, two steps have to be performed: 1. The code blocks have to be identified, which are executed redundantly and comprise computations with a complexity greater than the memoization overhead. 2. Those code blocks have to be transformed into a variant that stores input and output of a computation and is able to directly reproduce the correct output if the same input re-occurs. In current practice, both steps are often applied manually.

While it would naturally be desirable to automate both steps, in this paper we focus on the second step. This is especially motivated by the observation that model developers are often domain experts in the simulated field, but not necessarily programming experts as well. We argue that the knowledge of the developed simulation model allows them to identify redundant computations. However, applying memoization manually requires to fully understand the underlying concepts. The developer has to carefully identify all side effects of a function and then create the code that detects whether the input has been seen before, applies the results, or computes and stores them. Once realized for a specific problem, this code can, however, not be reused for a different problem, requiring a repetition of much of this labor-intense and error-prone effort. Hence, we target an environment where the developer only needs to perform the first step and annotate the promising code blocks, saving the effort of manually applying the memoization.

We discuss previously developed techniques to tackle this second step (called *automated memoization*) in more detail in Sect. 5. We conclude that, unfortunately, all of them are designed for pure functions[1], whose availability is often supported by properties of the target programming language, especially prevalent amongst functional programming languages. However, most simulation models are not written in functional programming languages and computations heavily rely on the features that allow writing impure code. Hence, techniques restricted to pure functions can not be applied to a large set of simulation models.

We conclude that till today there is no approach to *automated memoization for impure functions*. We argue that such a technique could significantly improve performance of complex software with redundant operations, as common in simulation parameter studies, without requiring much effort or advanced programming skills from the developer. We propose an approach to automated memoization, which does not rely on the purity of the code to memoize. Our implementation operates on C++ [9], which is used to implement models for the popular open source simulation frameworks ns-3 [5] and OMNeT++ [22], and provides many features that pose challenges for memoization (such as pointers), hence we expect that our approach can be easily adapted to other languages with a less challenging feature set. We do not require that the computation to be memoized is pure, and in fact we allow using arbitrarily indirect pointers to read objects or cause side effects. However, it is another result of this work that it is necessary to pose certain restrictions on pointer usage, for example, to avoid undecidable problems like static aliasing analysis [12] (see Sect. 3.6).

To apply the automated memoization, we parse the provided C++ code using Clang[2], identify all input and output, and finally generate new C++ code with a memoized version of the original code. This can then be compiled by any C++14 compiler. On execution of our memoized code a lookup in a dictionary (the *Memoization Cache, MC*) is performed. On success the result is applied to the actual output, otherwise the result is computed as in the original code, intercepted, and stored in the MC. Hence, our approach works on pure *and* impure computations.

The remainder of this paper is structured as follows. We first analyze the problem and the resulting challenges more thoroughly (Sect. 2). After that, we introduce the design of our approach in detail and discuss its capabilities and limitations (Sect. 3). We demonstrate the practical feasibility by presenting evaluation results (Sect. 4). We then discuss related work (Sect. 5) before we conclude the paper (Sect. 6).

2. PROBLEM ANALYSIS

The major challenge of memoization is the correct identification of input and output. While this is an easy task for pure functions, impure functions can traverse the object graph arbitrarily and access any element. We need to determine which values are actually input or output of the computation and which are just used to find the finally relevant object in memory, but whose own value has no semantical meaning to the computation (e.g., a pointer that is being dereferenced to access another object).

[1] A *pure* function accesses no objects except compile-time constants, its parameters, and its local variables with automatic storage duration. Its parameters and return type are of value type and it never throws exceptions. It inspects no pointers and calls only pure functions.
[2] http://clang.llvm.org/

In this section, we first investigate adequate levels of granularity for automated memoization. We then discuss the language constructs which can conceivably be memoized, analyze the features of C++, and derive the implications on automated memoization for a representative subset.

2.1 Memoization Granularity

All existing approaches to automated memoization apply the optimization on a function level, i.e., a function is either memoized as a whole, or not at all. As these approaches rely on the input being solely the function parameters and the output being exactly the return value, a function level granularity is the only viable approach. However, as we allow side effects, we need to analyze the actual implementation anyway and the restriction to functions is no longer useful.

For this reason, we allow the memoization of (almost) arbitrary C++ *compound-statements*, better known as *blocks*. Blocks are the most general construct that has a concept of local variables with automatic storage duration and encapsulates them from the outer environment. Any statement that can be wrapped in curly braces to form a block without changing the semantics of the program can also be a memoization target. To this end, memoizing a function is performed by memoizing the block that constitutes its body. Similarly, a complete event handler could be memoized since an event handler is typically a function as well.

In general, the unit to be memoized should be a logical unit of the program's functionality. If two computations were memoized as a single unit, it is highly unlikely that the results can be reused as the input of both computations must have occurred before in that combination. On the other hand, if the memoization unit ends before a computation is complete, several intermediate results have to be retrieved rather than the final result. In simulations an event handler can be a good memoization target if it performs a single computation. However, a specific computation performed inside the event handler can as well be a more promising memoization target. The remainder of this analysis assumes that a C++ compound statement (block) shall be memoized, referred to as the *Memoization Unit (MU)*.

2.2 Variable Scope

Our first observation is that any object that is both created and destroyed inside the MU can obviously be neither input nor output. From this observation we deduce that it is helpful to distinguish variables by their scope and lifetime.

C++ allows a multitude of different scopes, from file-level variables, over class members to variables with block scope. However, for a variable which is not local to the MU or has a storage duration other than automatic (e.g., static) we observe: If it is read inside the MU without a prior write operation, its value is input of the computation. If it is written inside the MU, the effects are visible after completion of the MU, hence the variable must be considered output. Only if a variable v that is accessed inside the MU is also defined inside with automatic storage duration, the computation can neither depend on v nor can a result be stored in v.

We conclude: If a variable is local to the MU and has automatic storage duration, it is neither input nor output. In all other cases, read and write operations to that variable have to be analyzed and the variable has to be considered potential input and/or output. In the following, we use the terms *interior* for the first and *exterior* for the second case.

2.3 Pointers

For detecting input and output of a function, the most challenging feature of C++ concerns pointers as it is oftentimes impossible to statically predict which object a given pointer will point to at runtime. We identify the following important operations that can be performed on pointers:

- Pointers can be copied (e.g., p=... or ...=p).
- A pointer can be dereferenced to alter the object it points to (e.g., *p=...).
- A pointer can be dereferenced to read the object it points to (e.g., ...=*p).
- Instead of accessing the object the pointer points to, the address can also be used to access neighboring objects (e.g., *(p-4) or p[3]).
- Any object, including those of pointer type, can have its address taken (e.g., &p).
- Other notable operations on pointers are comparisons and conversions (e.g., !p or p!=nullptr).
- If the object a pointer points to is a pointer itself, the definition is recursive (e.g., *p[0]=****(***q+4)).

To evaluate a computation's actual input and output, we need to investigate the semantics of these operations. The most useful operations on pointers are those ending up dereferencing them to access another object. Consider *p=42. A simplistic approach would identify two memory accesses: First, the pointer object is read. Then 42 is stored to the target object. Hence, the pointer's value would be identified as input, inhibiting memoization in many common cases.

We can circumvent this problem by respecting the semantics of this operation, which is to modify the object located at the address p points to. Hence, the actual *value* of p (i.e., the address) is irrelevant. A smart approach to automated memoization has to store the *path* an object is accessed through and only the object itself should be considered input or output. For *p=42 it is hence necessary to store that the object pointed to by p is assigned 42.

We define such a path as an $(n + 1)$-tuple where n is the number of dereferenced pointers along that path. The first component of this tuple is the pointer name, followed by the difference between the current pointer value of the path component and the address of the object that is actually accessed. Hence, *p is simply represented by the tuple ("p",0). We represent expressions like a.b as ("a","b") which allows us to follow the C++ standard in representing a->b and (*a).b as the path ("a",0,"b") while easily retaining type information even in the case of unions.

This also allows representing arbitrarily complex pointer expressions like (p+4)[3]=q[8][-5][3]: The object at ("q",8,-5,3) is read and the object at ("p",4,3) is altered.

Similarly, we represent taking of addresses by adding the special value & to this notation to indicate the addressof operation. Hence, e.g., (&a)[3] is represented by ("a",&,3).

As these semantics imply that the actual value of a pointer is unimportant, we only allow conversions to bool (implicit, explicit, or by comparison to null pointer constant), which we represent by adding the special value bool to the path. For example, the expression p ? *p : 0 performs a read of ("p",bool) potentially followed by a read of ("p",0).

With respect to pointer comparisons two major cases have to be distinguished. Equality comparisons just test if the pointers point to the same object irrespective of the actual address. Ordered comparisons on the other hand are only

specified in C++ if both pointers point to subobjects within the same superobject, e.g., elements of the same array. This means that, again, the actual pointer value is unimportant, as in fact the offsets within the superobject are being compared. All comparisons are encoded in our path notation as the components of the path to the left hand pointer, followed by a special symbol representing the comparison type, and finally the components of the path to the right hand pointer, e.g., p<q would be encoded as ("p",<,"q").

Remark: We use this path notation not only as a theoretical concept but as well in the implementation of our approach. Hence, we need a value for the name of an object. For convenience, we simply use a string representing the name of the object throughout this paper. However, as 1. even when using fully qualified names this does not allow variables in sibling scopes or anonymous namespaces, and 2. string processing is inefficient, our transformation deterministically assigns each variable it encounters a unique, numerical ID. If, e.g., the symbol p is assigned the ID 42, the object p[3] is described as (42,3). We would like to stress the importance that this assignment be deterministic and independent of the surrounding context, to ensure that the One Definition Rule is not accidentally violated.

2.4 References, Arrays, and Containers

Similarly to pointers, reference types can be used in C++ to alias objects. However, references are not more expressive than pointers, i.e., everything that can be expressed by a reference could be expressed by a pointer as well. Hence, we can treat references as pointers with a different syntax.

Indexing C-style arrays needs no special handling, as a[1] is equivalent by definition to *(a+1). Hence, array-to-pointer conversion actually applies the indexing to a pointer.

Dealing with containers from the C++ standard library requires additional consideration. As the definition of a template such as std::array has to be available at compile time, it seems, at first glance, easy to consider class templates to be equivalent to user code. However, the C++ standard allows implementations significant leeway with respect to how these containers are actually implemented. One example of non-obvious optimizations is the use of SCARY iterators [20] to reduce the generated code size. Similarly, std::vector could conceivably be specialized for pointer-to-object types to always use the same non-generic implementation that is only available as a pre-compiled library with a C interface. We believe that in future efforts many of those operations can be serialized by making their semantics known during the memoization procedure. However, this is not important to demonstrate the general feasibility of automated memoization for impure functions.

2.5 Function Calls

If a function is called inside the MU, we need to differentiate two cases: If the function implementation is known to the compiler, it can be included into the analysis. However, this is not provided in general, e.g., for pre-compiled libraries. Such functions might or might not have side effects and might or might not depend on additional input. As this cannot be determined for functions whose implementation is unknown, we enable the user to annotate function signatures or calls as *transparent*. To this end, we define a transparent function as a function whose effects depend only on the parameters and are only of the following kinds: If a parameter of pointer or reference to a non-const object type is provided (e.g., ~~const~~ int *p), the value of the object may be changed during execution of the function (e.g., *p=42). The function may return an object or throw an exception. Other effects may occur if the user declares them negligible, e.g., logging or allocating temporary dynamic storage. As input we treat the parameter's values, or, for arguments of pointer or reference type, the object they point to.

For non-transparent functions whose implementation is known we need to differentiate whether the call is recursive. Non-recursive calls can just be handled like inline code. For recursive calls a fixpoint iteration is necessary to determine the full input and output. Since iterative programming is by far more commonly used in C++, we focus however on iterative functions and leave the fixpoint analysis of non-transparent, recursive function calls for future work.

Investigating the different methods to define and call functions in C++, we observe that all of them boil down to the simple base case. Member functions are just functions with an additional argument. For function pointers and virtual functions, either the pointer / call has to be annotated or the compiler needs to be able to statically determine which function is called and which code is executed. Lambda functions and function templates are just different ways to create functions. For implicit function calls (constructors, destructors, user defined conversions, and operators) the compiler can determine which function is executed and handle the implicit call just like an explicit call to that function. Hence, all kinds of functions can be treated as described above.

2.6 Unstructured Control Flow

C++ provides keywords that allow entering and leaving the MU not only at the beginning or end. Early exits (return, break, continue, throw, goto) have to be considered by the automated memoization as follows: Reads after the exit must not be considered input. While computing the results it has to be ensured that the output is stored in the MC prior to the early exit. When a result is retrieved from the MC, we need to ensure that the MU is left exactly the same way the original execution would leave the MU, including the correct argument to return or throw. This can be achieved by storing the kind of exit and potentially its argument as part of the output of the function.

Entering the MU at a point other than the beginning can only be achieved by jumping to a label in the MU. Though this can be allowed by extra care, we do not consider it in this paper as goto is not recommended anyway [1, 11] and memoizing a block that contains a label from a switch statement outside the MU is similarly discouraged.

As early *termination* (which, as opposed to early *exits* leaves not only the MU, but terminates the process) can occur in hard to predict ways (e.g., an exception falls through a noexcept function), we relax semantical correctness and allow that the output may not be fully actualized yet, which we deem an acceptable trade-off in the event of termination. Note, that memoization in this case is useless anyway, as the termination does not allow the same computation to reoccur during the execution of the program.

Finally, we deny the hardly used feature of non-local jumps (i.e., using setjmp and longjmp) inside the MU, since we introduce additional objects with non-trivial destructors, which would cause undefined behavior [9, 18.10§4] for many usages that would have been correct before memoization.

2.7 CV-Qualifiers

Our analysis of the cv-qualifiers const and volatile revealed: Pointer-to-const-parameters (see Sect. 2.5) allow us to deny their target to be output of a transparent function. Besides that, we do not rely on this qualifier as const-casts and the mutable keyword provide means to circumvent constness. The qualifier volatile guarantees that each implied memory access is actually performed in order. We argue that requesting to memoize a block containing volatile memory accesses is a fundamental contradiction.

2.8 Multi-Threading

Multi-threading is an optimization technique orthogonal to memoization. Our implementation assumes that only one thread is inside any MU at a time. Hence, we can demonstrate the feasibility on single-threaded programs. Future efforts clearly need to make the implementation thread-safe and investigate the impact on parallel programs.

3. AUTOMATED MEMOIZATION

In this section, we describe the design of our approach striving to provide automated memoization for pure or impure C++ code blocks using pointers in different ways, which can hence be used to avoid redundant computations in simulations. We specify the goals before we sketch the general approach and discuss the most important aspects in detail.

3.1 Design Goals

To maximize the benefit of our approach to automated memoization, we define the following three design goals:

Semantic Equivalence. Our approach converts an existing C++ code block into a memoized version of itself. It is the highest and most important goal that this transformation is sound, i.e., it does not change the results of the program. To this end, we define the transformed program to be *semantically equivalent* to the original if and only if it has the same semantics as defined by the C++ standard [9] except for: 1. a changed execution time and computational complexity, and 2. allocation and modification of additional memory (most notably the MC). Hence, we design our approach in a way that the perceivable effects and side effects of the original code and the memoized version are the same.

Maximize Memoizable Code. As discussed in Sect. 2, not every C++ statement can be memoized. For example, we cannot elude volatile reads without completely subverting the semantics of volatile qualification. Hence, we allow our approach to abort memoization if it would conflict with semantic equivalence, instead of issuing false results. However, we strive to maximize the number of supported C++ features. Our approach does support the basic C++ elements such as assignments, arithmetic operations, conditionals, loops, etc., as well as the challenging feature of input and output detection in the presence of pointer arithmetic. A detailed discussion of the actual capabilities and limitations follows in Sect. 3.6.

Optimize Efficiency. To maximize the benefit of the approach, its overhead should be as low as possible, such that its benefit can be reaped for computations of low computational complexity as well. To this end, the approach needs

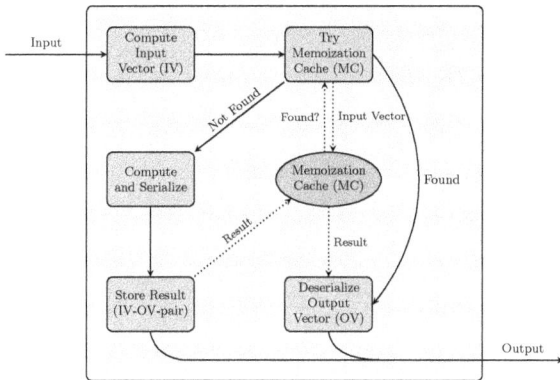

Figure 1: General memoization scheme.

```
1  void fib[[clang::transparent]](uint64_t* in) {
2      // the anchor is already hardcoded
3      // and does not need to be memoized
4      if(*in <= 1) return;
5      [[clang::memoize]] {
6          // we can dereference or index pointers:
7          auto in_minus_one = *in - 1;
8          auto in_minus_two = in[0] - 2;
9          fib(&in_minus_one);
10         fib(&in_minus_two);
11         *in = in_minus_one + in_minus_two;
12     }
13 }
```

Figure 2: Recursive Fibonacci computation with pointer usage to illustrate automated memoization. The transformed code is listed in Fig. 3.

to minimize the data it considers input or output, i.e., over-estimation should be avoided where possible. Additionally, the implementation can save overhead in three dimensions: 1. Each time a memoized code block is executed, the input has to be collected and the MC has to be queried for it. Minimizing this overhead improves performance of every execution of the memoized code. 2. When the result is found in the MC, it needs to be written to the corresponding output locations. Performing this as fast as possible maximizes the gain from using a cached result. 3. When the result is not found, it needs to be computed and stored in the cache. Not introducing too much overhead here is especially important for computations whose results can not be reused later on.

To demonstrate the feasibility of automated memoization we implemented it by code-to-code translation. A more efficient implementation could be realized by working at a lower level, though the implementation effort is much higher and we would not gain any additional scientific insights.

3.2 General Approach

Our approach to automated memoization works as follows. The developer annotates the MUs by adding the C++ attribute [[clang::memoize]]. This is the only manual action required; after handing the code to our tool, the memoization is performed automatically. A code-to-code translation rewrites each MU in a memoized way. Our proof-of-concept implementation utilizes a modified Clang to generate an abstract syntax tree as a basis for the memoization. This eases the implementation and allows debugging and verification of the generated, human-readable C++ code. For an efficient, product-level implementation we recommend integration into an actual optimizing compiler to further increase performance. However, this engineering effort is outside the scope of this paper. The transformed version performs the memoization as illustrated in Fig. 1. Fig. 2 lists the code of a recursive Fibonacci implementation using pointers to illustrate how memoization works with pointers. The transformed code is listed in Fig. 3, only slightly modified from the autogenerated code to fit in the paper: We renamed variables, applied indentation, changed line breaks, and removed parts not directly relevant to the memoization.

The automatic transformation identifies all read operations to exterior variables (cf. Sect. 2.2) and creates code that only reads these variables and serializes the input into the *Input Vector (IV)*. In the example, the only input is the object in points to, i.e., ("in",0). The IV is used as the key

to search the entry in the MC. If it is not found, we execute a version of the original code that is slightly modified, such that output is not only written to its location in memory, but also serialized to the *Output Vector (OV)*. In the example, the only output is ("in",0) as well. The IV-OV-pair is then stored in the MC. On later execution of the same MU with the same input, the IV will be found in the MC, and the corresponding OV returned. Our memoized version of the code then skips the (expensive) computation, and directly deserializes the OV to the corresponding memory locations.

To this end, the values in the IV and OV are simply bitwise copies of the original values, regardless of their semantics. Hence, our approach needs no special handling for floating point numbers, but just performs bitwise comparisons.

To improve the performance of our transformation we require that interior or exterior objects be only accessed via paths originating from variables of the same category. Additionally, our implementation does not perform the memoization when the same object is accessed via multiple different paths. In the following we describe the procedure and the rationale for these decisions in more detail.

3.3 Input Vector Computation

We need to extract all read operations on exterior objects from the original code and create code that does as little as possible besides reading those values and storing them in the IV. It is of special importance to ensure that no writes to exterior objects are performed at this stage, as they might interfere with later stages. The straightforward approach would be to search the code for all reads of exterior objects. However, if a conditional occurs inside the code, we would not only overestimate the input, but also potentially crash the transformed program by dereferencing a null pointer that was originally protected by an if-clause.

Our algorithm uses two basic ideas to tackle the IV computation. First, instead of synthesizing completely new code to compute the IV, we slice the original code in such a way as to compute the IV without causing any other side effects and then remove as much of the code as possible. Second, we intercept not only reads but also writes which we can then store in a Temporary Cache (TC) instead of writing to the exterior object. Of course this means that we need to test the TC for every read as well to prevent stale reads.

The transformation begins by adding interceptions for all accesses of exterior objects. While such reads and writes can

```cpp
#include <clang/memoize>
void fib[[]](::std::uint64_t *in) {
  // the anchor is already hardcoded and does not need to be memoized
  if (*in <= 1) return;
  /* transformed code begins here */ {
    try {
      auto __policy = ::std::clang::memoize::policy();
      static auto __dict = __policy.dict();
      auto __reader = __policy.reader();
      /* Read Key */ [&] {
        auto in_minus_one = __reader.read<1>(in, 0) - 1;
        auto in_minus_two = __reader.read<1>(in, 0) - 2;
      }();
      auto __iter = __dict.find(__reader.key);
      if (__iter != __dict.end()) {
        /* Check External Aliasing */
        for (auto const& __result : __iter->second.map) {
          switch (__result.first.baseid()) {
          case 1: __reader.alias(in, __result.first); break;
          }
        }
        /* Apply Result */
        for (auto const& __result : __iter->second.map) {
          switch (__result.first.baseid()) {
          case 1: __result.second.write_to(in, __result.first); break;
          }
        }
      } else {
        auto __results = __policy.results();
        auto __finalizer = ::std::clang::memoize::bits::at_scope_exit([&] {
          if(!__results.aliased()) __dict.emplace(::std::move(__reader.key), ::std::move(__results));
        });
        /* Compute Result */ {
          auto in_minus_one = *in - 1;
          auto in_minus_two = in[0] - 2;
          fib(&in_minus_one);
          fib(&in_minus_two);
          __results.write<1>(__reader, in, 0) = in_minus_one + in_minus_two;
        }
      }
    } catch (::std::clang::memoize::alias_exception const&) {
      auto in_minus_one = *in - 1;
      auto in_minus_two = in[0] - 2;
      fib(&in_minus_one);
      fib(&in_minus_two);
      *in = in_minus_one + in_minus_two;
    }
  } /* transformed code ends here */
}
```

Figure 3: Memoized version of the code in Fig. 2. This code has been automatically generated by our tool and then slightly edited for increased human readability and to fit in the paper format.

be caused in a multitude of ways (e.g., direct assignment, logical or arithmetic operation, passing arguments to functions), they can be reduced to the three basic cases of reads, writes, and reads followed by writes. For example, a += b performs a read on b, and both a read and a write on a.

To generate the IV, we simply store all reads on external objects that have not been read or written previously. Each value read is appended to the end of the IV to preserve the order. We can ignore repeated reads, as they cannot add any new information and we can ignore reads that follow writes to the same location, as the value that has been written is determined solely by reads that have been performed previously and thus been added to the IV already.

In the next section, we explain how our adapted dead code elimination allows the IV computation to be performed more efficiently while also explaining the need for a reliable alias

detection. To explain how the TC creates an overlay address space and perform alias detection at the same time, we then further discuss its design and implementation.

Adapted Dead Code Elimination.

It is essential to avoid complex operations during IV reading. To this end, we use a transformation derived from standard dead code elimination, which we extend for this purpose. As opposed to simpler analyses this allows us to deal efficiently with complex IV calculations. One interesting class of cases in which this is especially important is that of reading zero-terminated arrays, as the last part of the IV may be read only very close to the end of the computation.

To this end, we apply a very broad definition of *dead code* in the attempt to create a program slice that is narrowly defined by its purpose to generate the IV. The basic premise of the proposed technique is to consider everything expendable but reads from exterior objects that have not been read from or written to before. Most importantly, this also includes writes to external objects that are never read afterwards. By applying common dead code elimination techniques, operations which are no longer necessary are successively removed. For example, if a value x is stored in an exterior variable, which is never read afterwards, we remove the write and subsequently all the code that computes x up to (but excluding) the point were its input was read.

The effectiveness of this analysis depends on our ability to distinguish internal from external objects, which is problematic when considering not only scalar variables, but also pointers. Determining whether an object that is the result of a pointer expression is interior or exterior (as defined in Sect. 2.2) is not trivial. If the base pointer is interior, in most cases the final object will be interior as well. However, after creating a pointer locally, it might still be assigned the address of an exterior object. A similar problem occurs if an exterior pointer is assigned the address of an interior object.

In general, static code analysis does not allow to reliably deduce which object a pointer will point to in a given expression, as the decision whether it will point to an internal or an external object may depend on a runtime branch. A dynamic check could be performed, e.g., by determining whether the pointer points into the stack segment holding the local variables of the MU. However, the C++ standard does not guarantee the correctness of such an approach, instead it depends on the implementation of the compiler that later on translates the memoized version into executable code. Furthermore – and arguably more importantly – the runtime checks would introduce considerable overhead.

To be able to apply an efficient, standard-compliant solution, we restrict the usage of pointers inside an MU: An interior pointer must not store an address to an exterior object and vice versa. We discuss the impact of this decision in Sect. 3.6. Note that this property can easily be checked statically. This constraint allows us to determine whether an object reached by $(X, ...)$ references an interior or exterior object just by checking whether the symbol X itself is interior. Hence, we determine the input of an execution of the code block as a set $I = \{(X, ...) | X \text{ read} \land X \text{ not interior}\}$ and the output as $O = \{(X, ...) | X \text{ written} \land X \text{ not interior}\}$.

However, another requirement exists to ensure correctness: Since, in general, the same object may be reached via multiple different paths (as specified in Sect. 2.3), we had to assume that any write may change the result of any subsequent read, which would significantly inhibit the power of the dead code analysis. Instead, we perform the dead code elimination and read the IV as if aliasing would never happen. Although this tradeoff increases the potency of the dead code elimination, it also requires us to add another analysis that will ensure that no errors are introduced accidentally when attempting to memoize code that does indeed encounter aliased objects as discussed in the following.

In summary, our adapted dead code elimination leaves only the code to establish the IV as well as code that calculates what to include in the IV. It requires that objects are only ever accessed through a single path, a property that cannot be established at compile time. The TC discussed in the next section provides a way to detect aliasing and gracefully degrade to unmemoized execution in that case.

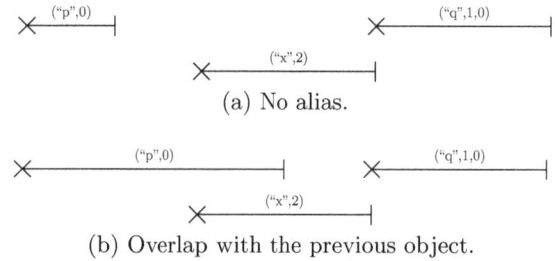

(a) No alias.

(b) Overlap with the previous object.

Figure 4: Alias detection: inserting ("x",2).

The Temporary Cache.

At the most basic level, the Temporary Cache (TC) is a dictionary that maps memory addresses[3] to paths, object values, and the length of objects. If a read or write causes a memory access that is not already in the TC, an entry is immediately inserted into the TC, which allows to satisfy all subsequent reads and writes. By using the TC to establish an overlay address space, all writes can be effectively prevented from being outwardly visible, while still being easily located when written objects are subsequently read again.

While, at first glance, the TC also seems to run into problems with aliasing, it is designed this way exactly to detect different paths leading to the same exterior object. Any possible alias falls into one of three categories: 1. The simplest case is that in which the alias is an exact match, as a simple lookup in the TC identifies the alias by comparing the stored path with the current one. 2. The current memory access begins in the range of a previously accessed object without matching exactly. To identify that case, it is only necessary to find the entry immediately preceding the target address, and check its end against the start of the current one. 3. The current memory access ends in the range of a previously accessed object without matching exactly. That is the case when the start address of the entry following the target address falls before the end address of the current memory access. A visualization of how the TC is used to detect aliases can be seen in Fig. 4, where the cross at the left hand of each element represents the base address and the line shows its size. Additionally, the TC contains a simple flag that tracks whether any alias has been found.

3.4 Performing Memoization

After computing the IV we need to determine whether the same input has occurred before. This operation is as trivial as searching for the IV in a hash map. On a hit, the MC returns the corresponding OV. Before actually applying the result, we need to finalize the aliasing check, which so far may miss locations that are only written (via two different paths). To this end we iterate over the OV and check the paths and locations found by tracing the path of each element to the actual memory location against the TC.

If the check shows that no aliases are encountered, the deserialization of the OV is performed by iterating over the OV again and storing the value in the object at that address. This effectively applies all side effects of the computation without having to execute the (complex) computation itself.

---

[3]We assume a flat memory model and that reinterpreting data pointers to ::std::uintptr_t values has the obvious implementation, which is valid for the x86_64 platform and all our target compilers.

Should the IV have not been found in the MC, the OV is computed, which will also perform the original computation. The next section explains how this computation will lead to the correct result in both presence and absence of aliases.

3.5 Output Vector Computation

Computing the OV is considerably simpler than computing the IV, as all that needs to be done is to keep track of all writes being performed. Writes are tracked by storing tuples of paths and object values, which can then later be deserialized by following the paths from their respective roots. Memory writes are not completely intercepted during computation of the OV, but rather stored in their originally intended locations as well. The advantage of using paths versus storing the address is, amongst others, that it also works with dynamic variables whose actual address changes depending on the depth of the current function stack.

Since the computation of the IV is designed to eschew as many writes as possible, its alias detection cannot be complete. All missing alias checks are performed during the OV computation, which must necessarily perform all writes. Therefore, the combined alias detection is complete. Should no alias be detected, the OV is stored in the MC to be retrieved during future computations. It is not necessary to immediately deserialize the OV, as the output will already have been stored as a side effect of the OV computation. For the same reason, no further action is necessary if an alias has been detected at this stage, instead the memoization degrades gracefully, i.e., no entry is created in the MC.

3.6 Discussion

While our approach is the first viable development in automated memoization for decades (see Sect. 5), it still has rather relevant limitations. The scope of our work is to answer the research question whether automated memoization can be applied in the presence of non-trivial pointer expressions[4], i.e., those going beyond what is correctly memoized by treating pointers as ordinary numbers. We focus on automating the memoization process, not automatically deciding where memoization is applied for the biggest benefit.

With our approach many cases of trivial and non-trivial pointer usages can in fact be used inside the MU, with the only exceptions being those listed below:

- The lifetime of objects is coupled to the scope of the MU, i.e., objects created outside must not be destroyed inside and objects created inside must not persist the scope of the MU[5]. In other words, the effects of creating or deleting objects cannot be stored in the OV, which only stores modifications of existing objects. The former can be added to our implementation, by allowing the OV to hold a representation of those effects and applying them – i.e., creating or deleting the corresponding objects – during OV deserialization.
- Addresses of exterior objects must not be stored in interior objects and addresses of interior objects must not be stored in exterior objects. We argue that the

former can easily be rewritten by not creating an interior copy of the pointer, but using the exterior variable, potentially with an interior index, instead. The latter form of pointer usage is never necessary as it does not provide any benefit if the pointer's lifetime is greater than the lifetime of the object it points to. Hence, an interior pointer could be used instead. A violation of either rule is easily discovered at compile time by also disallowing such assignments in unreachable code.

- As a result of this work, we found that aliasing is a severe problem to automated memoization. Assume two pointers p and q point to the same object o, and the object is modified via p before it is read via q. In this case the initial value of o is not read and hence not relevant to the computation. If, however, in the next execution of the MU, p and q point to different objects, the initial value of the object q points to is in fact read. Hence, the memoized code had to handle the two cases differently. Since aliasing cannot be generally checked at compile time [12], an implementation cannot be able to generate code for each possible case. To this end, we conclude that automated memoization with fully unrestricted pointer usage is infeasible as the runtime overhead associated with a dynamic approach would be overwhelming. We decided to perform a much simpler *dynamic* aliasing analysis (see Sect. 3.3), which detects aliases, but needs to abort the memoization in such a case. This enables applicability of memoization if no aliasing occurs, ensures correct results in either case by gracefully degrading to unmemoized execution, and can issue a warning to enable the developer to potentially resolve the aliasing by using only one pointer to access each object inside the MU.

Additionally, an obvious limitation is that we cannot analyze code that is not available to the memoizer (e.g., precompiled libraries). Hence, if function calls appear in the MU, the memoizer requires additional information. If the requirements for inlining the function call are fulfilled, the analysis can continue inside the function implementation. If, however, it cannot be statically determined which function is called (e.g., due to an untraceable function pointer), the implementation is not available to the memoizer (e.g., precompiled), or the number of function calls cannot be predicted (e.g., recursion), the user has to provide a transparency annotation or the transformation needs to be aborted with a warning. This poses an additional requirement to the user over the actual intent to only request for a single annotation to memoize a block. However, this cannot be avoided as unknown code cannot be analyzed. We argue that especially for libraries commonly used to perform expensive computations (e.g., mathematical functions), this could already be performed by the library maintainer. As an additional bonus, a manual annotation allows us to annotate functions as transparent that are not pure in the strictest sense[6].

Finally, certain features like multi-threading, which are not in the scope of answering the research question stated above, are not in scope of this work.

---

[4] And references, treated very similarly, see Sect. 2.4.

[5] Function-level static variables are not created during the first execution of the MU, but only initialized then. To ensure that this is performed correctly, they receive additional treatment – basically a simple flag – to ensure that they are initialized only once and the initialization expression only contributes to the IV once in the program execution.

[6] For example, we did encounter functions using variables with static storage duration as scratch space, instead of variables with automatic storage duration. Annotating that function as transparent is in line with our definition, as the changes to that scratch pad are irrelevant side effects – they are overwritten every time the function is called.

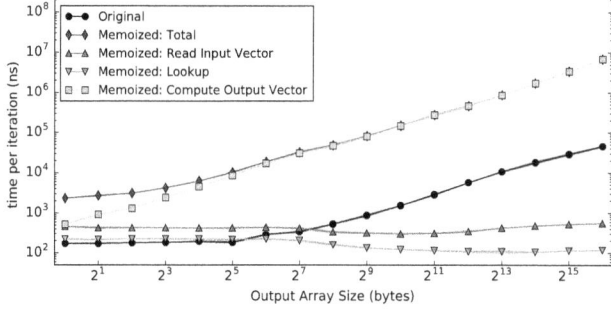

(a) $N_I = 1$ (varying OV size), 1. iteration of outer loop.

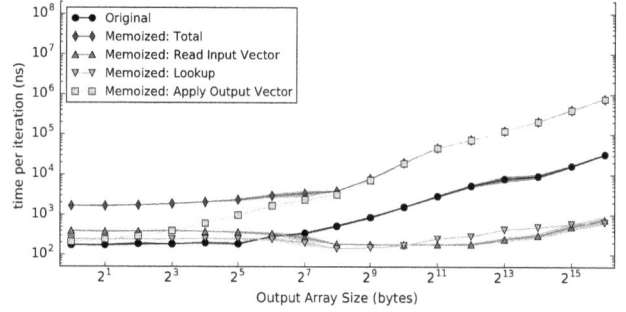

(b) $N_I = 1$ (varying OV size), 2. iteration of outer loop.

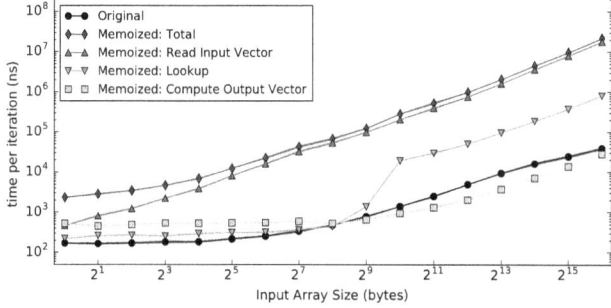

(c) $N_O = 1$ (varying IV size), 1. iteration of outer loop.

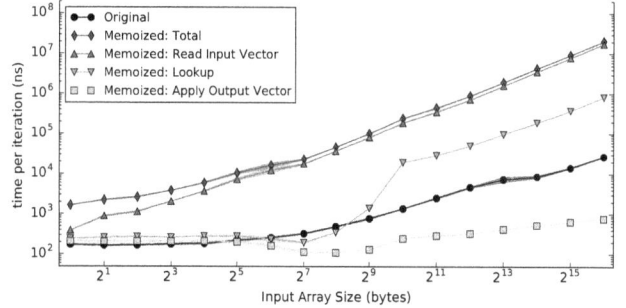

(d) $N_O = 1$ (varying IV size), 2. iteration of outer loop.

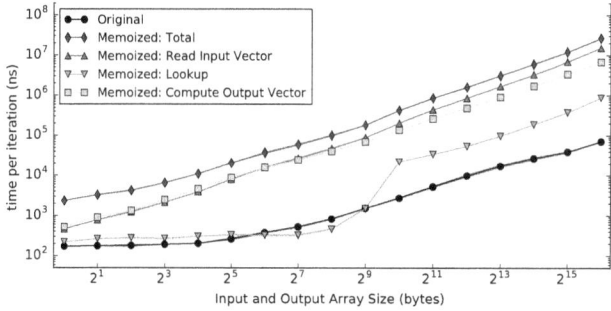

(e) $N_I = N_O$ (IV, OV varying), 1. iteration of outer loop.

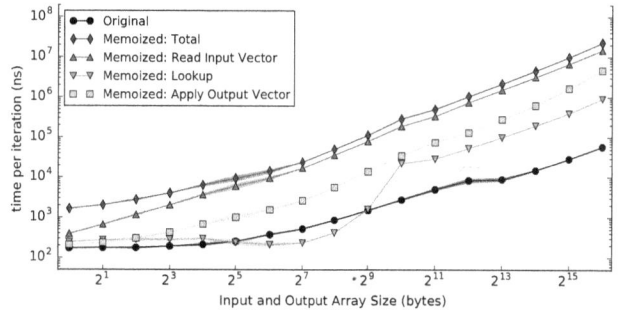

(f) $N_I = N_O$ (IV, OV varying), 2. iteration of outer loop.

Figure 5: Overhead evaluation: synthetic benchmark where memoization cannot gain benefit. Used to measure the overhead.

In summary, we found that pointers do not generally prevent automated memoization. If the above mentioned restrictions are met, a large and useful subset of pointer expressions can in fact be memoized in an automated fashion. We observed that especially complex computations whose memoization seems promising often use pointers to access (jagged multi-dimensional) arrays. Our approach of identifying objects via paths in fact allows this usage of pointers and enables us to determine the actual input and output of the MU. Hence, we conclude that we are able to apply automated memoization to programs using pointers in a multitude of ways, while certain restrictions have to be fulfilled to avoid undecidable problems.

4. EVALUATION

We evaluate our approach by first performing overhead measurements to derive simple formulae to give a basic esti-

mate when our approach is beneficial. These approximations can assist model developers in selecting appropriate regions for memoization and can as well be used in future research on automatic identification of such regions. Second, we implement the well-known Fibonacci-computation in a recursive implementation gratuitously using pointers to show the feasibility of our approach on recursive and pointer-based code. Finally, a case study performing a parameter study of an OFDM (orthogonal frequency-division multiplexing) network simulated by OMNeT++ [22] demonstrates the practical applicability of our approach in the simulation context.

All measurements are performed on a Xeon E5 compute server with 32 GB of RAM. Each experiment is repeated at least 5 times, all plots depict the means and 99 % confidence intervals. The latter are hard to perceive in many cases due to the low variance of the results.

As the optimization only makes sense if the quickly computed results are as well correct, we validated the output.

In each experiment we compared the computational results of the memoized version against the results of the original implementation. The results were identical in every case. Hence, we conclude that for every experiment performed in this chapter the transformation was performed correctly and maintained the semantics of the original program.

4.1 Overhead Evaluation

We measure the overhead by means of a simple synthetic benchmark: An array of N_I 8-bit numbers is read, the numbers are aggregated to a 64 bit variable, which is then xor-folded to yield an 8-bit result. An array of N_O 8-bit numbers is filled with numbers calculated by adding the array index of the respective element to the above mentioned result. Since the computational effort is almost negligible, the memoization cannot speed up the computation, instead allowing the memoization overhead to be observed. Varying N_I and N_O directly varies the size of the IV and OV, which are the primary influence factors for the memoization costs.

The surrounding evaluation program consists of two nested loops. The inner loop is repeated 250 times, each time with a different input. The outer loop is executed twice, such that the inner loop is executed again for each of the 250 inputs used in the first iteration. Hence, the memoized code adds 250 items to the MC in the first outer loop iteration while none of the lookups is successful. In the second iteration, each result is retrieved from the MC. In the original code, both iterations behave exactly identical.

We performed experiments while growing only N_I, only N_O, and growing both simultaneously. Fig. 5 depicts the average runtime per inner loop iteration for each of the two outer loop iterations. The runtime of the memoized version is decomposed into the components of the memoization (IV computation and MC lookup for both iterations, OV computation or application for the 1. or 2. iteration, respectively).

We observe that the MC lookup only contributes very little to the total runtime (note the logarithmic scale). For the first iteration we observe that for large output arrays the overall runtime is almost equivalent to the runtime of the OV computation whose cost primarily depends on N_O (at about $150\,\text{ns} \cdot N_O$). For smaller output arrays additionally the IV reading becomes relevant, which costs about $300\,\text{ns} \cdot N_I$. As a very rough approximation we conclude that the memoization overhead ranges about $T_F = 150\,\text{ns} \cdot N_O + 300\,\text{ns} \cdot N_I$ if the lookup is not successful. However, this simple approximation ignores, for example, the effect that increasing the input size as well influences the OV computation due to non-uniform memory access and growing data structures.

Similarly, we analyze the second iteration of the outer loop: The costs of computing the IV are the same as above, as the computation has to be performed in both cases, i.e., we observe overhead of about $300\,\text{ns} \cdot N_I$. For the application of the OV we observe about $15\,\text{ns} \cdot N_O$. We conclude that we can approximate the overhead for a successful lookup by $T_S = 15\,\text{ns} \cdot N_O + 300\,\text{ns} \cdot N_I$. Furthermore, we observed (without figure) memory overhead linear in both N_I and N_O.

From these approximations we derive that our approach to automated memoization pays off if sufficient memory is available to hold the MC and $p \cdot T_S + (1-p) \cdot (T_F + T_C) < T_C$ with the computational costs of the original MU of T_C and the fraction p of calls that can be served from the MC. Obviously, the bigger p and T_C the bigger the gain.

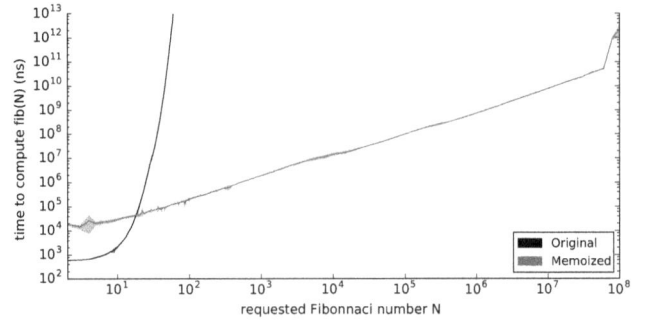

Figure 6: Performance of recursive Fibonacci computation using pointers.

4.2 Recursive Fibonacci with Pointers

To demonstrate the potential benefit of memoization and the versatility of our approach, we implemented a naïve recursive function (see Fig. 2) that gets an integer n and computes the nth Fibonacci Number ($F_n := F_{n-1} + F_{n-2}$, $F_0 := 0$ and $F_1 := 1$), or more precisely the bits of F_n that fit into an integer, i.e., $F_n \bmod 2^{64}$. To demonstrate the viability of our approach for impure code, the function takes a pointer to an integer that contains the actual input and stores the result in that same object. However, the function is transparent (see Sect. 2.5) and annotated accordingly to allow the memoization of this recursive function. It must be noted that, should the IV generation not be optimized well enough (cf. Sect. 3.3), this function would perform the whole computation before any memoization takes place.

Fig. 6 clearly shows the expected exponential runtime of the unmemoized algorithm (computing the nth Fibonacci Number recursively with this algorithm takes $\Theta(\varphi^n)$ time, with $\varphi \approx 1.618$ being the golden ratio), and that the memoized version also performs as expected by only requiring linear time up to $F_{6 \cdot 10^7}$. For $F_{8 \cdot 10^7}$ the compute server's memory doesn't suffice to store the MC and we observe a slowdown caused by swapping. The overhead of the memoization is also clearly visible for small n, where the unmemoized code is significantly faster. Since the axes are both scaled logarithmically, it is easy to overestimate the actual difference for small n – the memoized code runs in only a few microseconds. Starting at $n \approx 18$, the unmemoized code requires more time than the memoized code. This also means that a small table assist of 17 values would cause the memoized code to always outperform the unmemoized code.

4.3 Case Study: Network Simulation

To demonstrate the feasibility of our approach in a practical use case, we apply it to a parameter study of wireless network simulation. The simulation model is implemented for the open source simulation framework OMNeT++ [22] in C++. In the simulation model, a set of wireless nodes is placed on a 1 by 1 km area. A number of those nodes transmits frames in a fixed pattern. A channel model based on the Friis path loss model [3] and a complex OFDM fading model [23] calculates the received signal strength. In the parameter study the total number of wireless nodes is varied in 14 steps from 1 to 50, the fraction of transmitting nodes in 9 steps from 1 % to 100 %, and the time between two transmissions in 5 steps from 1 μs to 10 ms. Each experiment is

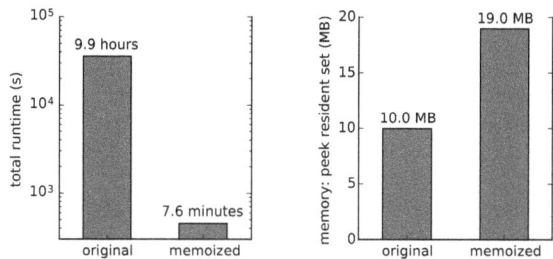

Figure 7: Case study: simulation parameter study.

repeated 10 times with different random number generator seeds, hence the total parameter study consists of 6300 runs.

We identified the fading computation as a good candidate for memoization as it is a complex operation, its input is small and repeated frequently. This fading computation heavily uses pointers to iterate over multi-dimensional arrays. Existing approaches to automated memoization would treat these pointers by their address, hence compute false results. However, as for the other experiments we compared the computational results to those of the original implementation and observed exactly the same results. As this fading computation seemed most promising, we only tagged this block for memoization. We executed the parameter study in the original as well as the memoized version, both with OMNeT++ 5.0b3 on the above described hardware.

The results of our experiments are depicted in Fig. 7. In the original implementation, each run took about 5-6 s, resulting in a total runtime of about 10 hours. In the memoized version, we observed a similar runtime for the first run, where no computations could be omitted. However, from the second run on, we observed significant speedups, certain runs were completed in as little as 5 ms. Completing the total parameter study then took less than 8 minutes, hence our automated memoization yielded a speedup of about 75×.

The MC, on the other hand, doubled the memory consumption of the program. We feel confident asserting that a penalty of less than 10 MB will be happily accepted by a user who now only has to wait minutes instead of hours.

5. RELATED WORK

Memoization was first introduced by Michie [15, 16] and implemented in a framework by Popplestone [19] in 1967. Though the framework provides an interface and assists the user, the challenging parts have to be realized completely manually. In particular, the user needs to implement a function deciding whether two inputs are equal, i. e., the user has to determine the input. Mostow and Cohen [17] provide an in-depth analysis of the memoization idea and the resulting challenges like side effects. They propose to display a list of side effects to the user and ask for permission to memoize, ignoring the side effects. This might be possible in certain cases, however, recognizing and applying side effects correctly makes our approach by far more generally applicable.

Several approaches realizing automated memoization have been implemented, for example those by Norvig [18], Hall et al. [4, 13, 14], and Hinze [6]. These approaches use Haskell and Lisp, but also C++ as the basis of their implementation. In the functional language Haskell every function is by definition pure, hence input and output is given by the function definition. Though Lisp supports imperative programming with functions modifying global state, i. e., inducing side effects, the approaches explicitly restrict themselves to pure functions. This also holds for the C++ implementation [14], which effectively adopts the Lisp approach from [13] to C++. Hence, input may only be provided in function parameters, only the return value may be output, and pointers are just handled like integers, i. e., pointers to the same address are treated equally even if the value at that address has changed, which inevitably introduces errors if the pointed to object is actually input. Similarly, in logic programming languages the concept of tabling is used to memoize results of previously evaluated (by definition pure) rules [24]. To the best of our knowledge no generic approach to automated memoization without restriction to pure functions has been proposed to date.

Tsumura et al. [10, 21] propose to integrate memoization functionality directly into the processor hardware. While this is probably the most promising approach to speed up any software independent of the programming language and paradigm, the proposed hardware is not available to most users, i. e., software implementations are essential for wide applicability. To this end, we provide an approach implemented in software and able to cope with impure code in impure languages to speed up simulations in practice.

To avoid unnecessary computations in simulation parameter studies simulation cloning [7, 8] and updateable simulations [2] should be mentioned. Both techniques share the motivation of our approach. However, simulation cloning clones any affected "virtual logical process" of the simulation as soon as the state of that process deviates. Hence, later occurring re-computations, which base only on parts of the state of that process, can not be avoided. Updateable simulations can avoid a large set of re-computations. However, the major limitation of that approach is the requirement to implement update functions realizing the necessary functionality to compute the differences between two runs. Like manual memoization this is a labor-intense, error-prone effort that needs to be carried out by the model developer.

6. CONCLUSION

In order to avoid redundant re-computations of intermediate results in simulation parameter studies by means of memoization, two major steps have to be approached. First, promising code blocks have to be identified whose effort can be saved using memoization. Second, the code blocks have to be rewritten in a way that the results are cached and can be retrieved from that cache instead of re-computation.

In this paper, we focus on automating the second step of this procedure and describe our approach for impure languages, realized in a proof-of-concept implementation for C++. While up to now every existing technique requires a function to be pure in order to be able to apply automated memoization, our approach detects the full input and output even if accessed via pointers, and hence eliminates this restriction. However, as discussed in Sect. 3.6, certain restrictions like absence of local aliasing are still required to be enforced as to avoid undecidable problems.

Once a developer has identified a suitable code block for memoization, the block can be annotated using a single attribute. Our tool then parses the code and generates a memoized version after detecting the full input and output. Hence, the approach is viable for both pure and impure computations even when using pointers in several ways.

Our evaluation shows the practical feasibility of the approach. In general, the approach is promising if the memoized computation is complex enough and executed several times on the same input. In Sect. 4.1 we derive simple approximations to estimate under which conditions the approach is promising. In a simulation parameter study we observed a 75× speedup while only increasing memory consumption by 9 MB. We conclude that automated memoization can significantly help reducing the time developers have to wait for their results with minimal manual effort.

Future efforts should address the automatic identification of promising computations, such that annotation by the user is no longer required. Additionally, instead of always adding an entry to the MC, selection strategies could be developed to reduce overhead and memory consumption if the result of a computation can be expected to not being reused later. Hence, the execution could switch between memoized and unmemoized versions of the code. Furthermore, our approach needs to cope with multi-threaded software, allowing multiple threads to concurrently and cooperatively utilize a common MC. This allows to combine the power of both PDES and memoization to benefit from both. Finally, the performance of the proof-of-concept implementation can be improved to reduce the overhead and make memoization promising for computations of less complexity. Nevertheless, our approach already demonstrates the feasibility of automated memoization for impure languages as used by many simulation tools and yields promising speedups.

Acknowledgments

The research leading to these results has received funding from the German Research Foundation (DFG) under Agreement n. 625799 (MemoSim) and from the European Research Council under the EU's Horizon2020 Framework Programme / ERC Grant Agreement n. 647295 (SYMBIOSYS).

7. REFERENCES

[1] E. W. Dijkstra. Go To Statement Considered Harmful. *Communications of the ACM*, 11(3):147–148, 1968.

[2] S. Ferenci, R. Fujimoto, M. Ammar, K. Perumalla, and G. Riley. Updateable Simulation of Communication Networks. In *Proc. of the 16th Workshop on Parallel and Distributed Simul.*, pages 107–114, 2002.

[3] H. T. Friis. A Note on a Simple Transmission Formula. *Proc. of the Institute of Radio Engineers*, 34(5):254–256, 1946.

[4] M. Hall and J. Mayfield. Improving the Performance of AI Software: Payoffs and Pitfalls in Using Automatic Memoization. In *Proc. of the 6th Intl. Symposium on Artificial Intelligence*, 1993.

[5] T. R. Henderson, S. Roy, S. Floyd, and G. F. Riley. ns-3 Project Goals. In *Proc. of the 1st Workshop on ns-2: the IP network simulator*, 2006.

[6] R. Hinze. Memo Functions, Polytypically! In *Proc. of the 2nd Workshop on Generic Programming*, pages 17–32, 2000.

[7] M. Hybinette and R. Fujimoto. Cloning: A Novel Method for Interactive Parallel Simulation. In *Proc. of the 29th Winter Simul. Conf.*, pages 444–451, 1997.

[8] M. Hybinette and R. M. Fujimoto. Cloning Parallel Simulations. *ACM Transaction on Modeling and Computer Simul.*, 11(4):378–407, 2001.

[9] ISO. *ISO/IEC 14882:2014 Information technology — Programming languages — C++*. International Organization for Standardization, Geneva, Switzerland, Dec. 2014.

[10] K. Kamimura, R. Oda, T. Yamada, T. Tsumura, H. Matsuo, and Y. Nakashima. A Speed-up Technique for an Auto-Memoization Processor by Reusing Partial Results of Instruction Regions. In *Proc. of the 3rd Intl. Conf. on Networking and Computing*, pages 49–57, 2012.

[11] D. E. Knuth. Structured Programming with go to Statements. *ACM Comp. Surveys*, 6(4):261–301, 1974.

[12] W. Landi. Undecidability of Static Analysis. *ACM Letters on Programming Languages and Systems*, 1(4):323–337, 1992.

[13] J. Mayfield, T. Finin, and M. Hall. Using Automatic Memoization as a Software Engineering Tool in Real-World AI Systems. In *Proc. of the 11th Conf. on Artificial Intelligence for Applications*, pages 87–93, 1995.

[14] P. McNamee and M. Hall. Developing a Tool for Memoizing Functions in C++. *ACM SIGPLAN Notices*, 33(8):17–22, 1998.

[15] D. Michie. Memo functions: a language feature with "rote-learning" properties. Technical report, Edinburgh University, Dept. of Machine Intelligence and Perception, 1967.

[16] D. Michie. Memo Functions and Machine Learning. *Nature*, 218(5136):19–22, 1968.

[17] J. Mostow and D. Cohen. Automating Program Speedup by Deciding What to Cache. In *Proc. of the 9th Intl. Joint Conf. on Artificial Intelligence*, pages 165–172, 1985.

[18] P. Norvig. Techniques for Automatic Memoization with Applications to Context-Free Parsing. *Computational Linguistics*, 17(1):91–98, 1991.

[19] R. Popplestone. Memo functions and the POP-2 language. Technical report, Edinburgh University, Dept. of Machine Intelligence and Perception, 1967.

[20] D. Tsafrir, R. Wisniewski, D. Bacon, and B. Stroustrup. Minimizing Dependencies within Generic Classes for Faster and Smaller Programs. *ACM SIGPLAN Notices*, 44(10):425–444, 2009.

[21] T. Tsumura, I. Suzuki, Y. Ikeuchi, H. Matsuo, H. Nakashima, and Y. Nakashima. Design and Evaluation of an Auto-Memoization Processor. In *Proc. of the 25th Intl. Multi-Conf. on Parallel and Distributed Computing and Networks*, pages 230–235, 2007.

[22] A. Varga. The OMNeT++ Discrete Event Simulation System. In *Proc. of the 15th European Simul. Multiconference*, 2001.

[23] C. Wang, M. Pätzold, and Q. Yao. Stochastic Modeling and Simulation of Frequency-Correlated Wideband Fading Channels. *IEEE Transaction on Vehicular Technology*, 56(3):1050–1063, 2007.

[24] N.-F. Zhou and T. Sato. Efficient Fixpoint Computation in Linear Tabling. In *Proc. of the 5th ACM SIGPLAN Intl. Conf. on Principles and Practice of Declarative Programming*, pages 275–283, 2003.

NeMo: A Massively Parallel Discrete-Event Simulation Model for Neuromorphic Architectures

Mark Plagge
plaggm@rpi.edu

Christopher D. Carothers
chrisc@cs.rpi.edu

Elsa Gonsiorowski
gonsie@rpi.edu

Department of Computer Science
Rensselaer Polytechnic Institute
110 8th Street
Troy, New York 12180-3590

ABSTRACT

Neuromorphic computing is a non-von Neumann architecture that mimics how the brain performs neural network types of computation in real hardware. It has been shown that this class of computing can execute data classification algorithms using only a tiny fraction of the power a conventional CPU would use to execute this algorithm. This raises the larger research question: *how might neuromorphic computing be used to improve the application performance, power consumption, and overall system reliability of future supercomputers?* To address this question, an open-source neuromorphic processor architecture simulator called *NeMo* is being developed. This effort will enable the design space exploration of potential hybrid CPU, GPU, and neuromorphic systems. The key focus of this paper is on the design, implementation and performance of *NeMo*. Demonstration of *NeMo*'s efficient execution on 1024 nodes of an IBM Blue Gene/Q system for a 65,536 neuromorphic processing core model is reported. The peak performance of *NeMo* is just over two billion events-per-second when operating at this scale.

Keywords

neuromorphic architecture; massive parallel; discrete-event; time warp; reverse computation; biocomputing; neural net architecture; non von Neumann architecture; neurosynaptic core

1. INTRODUCTION

In recent years, a new type of processor technology has emerged called *neuromorphic computing*. This new class of processor provides a brain-like computational model that enables complex neural network computations (e.g., data classification) to be done using significantly less power than von Neumann processors [23]. For example, IBM has created an instance of the *TrueNorth* architecture [1, 2, 10, 11] that has 5.4 billion transistors arranged into 4,096 neurosynaptic cores with a total of 1 million spiking neurons and 256 million

Permission to make digital or hard copies of all or part of this work for personal or classroom use is granted without fee provided that copies are not made or distributed for profit or commercial advantage and that copies bear this notice and the full citation on the first page. Copyrights for components of this work owned by others than the author(s) must be honored. Abstracting with credit is permitted. To copy otherwise, or republish, to post on servers or to redistribute to lists, requires prior specific permission and/or a fee. Request permissions from permissions@acm.org.

SIGSIM-PADS '16, May 15–18, 2016, Banff, Alberta, Canada.

© 2016 Copyright held by the owner/author(s). Publication rights licensed to ACM.
ISBN 978-1-4503-3742-7/16/05...$15.00

DOI: http://dx.doi.org/10.1145/2901378.2901392

reconfigurable synapses. This architecture consumes only 65 mW of power when executing a multi-object detection and classification program using real-time video input (30 fps) for 400×240 pixel images. TrueNorth could run for over one week on a single charge inside today's smartphones. For a list of TrueNorth-capable algorithms and applications, see Esser et al. [15].

This extremely low-power data analytics capability is particularly interesting as next generation High Performance Computing (HPC) systems are about to experience a radical shift in their design and implementation. The current configuration of leadership class supercomputers provides much greater off-node parallelism than on-node parallelism. For example, the 20 PFLOP "Sequoia" Blue Gene/Q supercomputer located at LLNL has over 98 thousand compute nodes with each compute node providing at most 64 threads of execution. In order to reach exascale compute capabilities, a next generation system must be 50 times more power efficient. This dominating demand for power efficiency is resulting in future designs that dramatically decrease the number of compute nodes while increasing the computational power and number of processing cores. Case in point, a recent NASA vision report [42] predicts that exascale class supercomputers in the 2030 time frame will have only 20,000 compute nodes and the number of parallel processing streams per node will rise to nearly 16,000.

To meet the computational demands of these future designs, it has become a widely held view that on-node *accelerator* processors, in close coordination with multi-core CPUs, will play an important role in compute-node designs [42]. These accelerators are currently used in two forms. The first are Graphical Processing Units (GPUs) that offer a single-instruction-multiple-data approach to parallelism, which matches the execution paradigm of graphics applications. GPUs offer a massive amount of numerical compute power at a very affordable price. The second form of compute node accelerators is a mesh processor architecture such as the Intel Phi [13]. Here, a collection of lower clock-rate x86 cores are interconnected over an on-chip mesh network.

Given the advent of neuromorphic computing, future research will need to address how might a neuromorphic processor be used as an accelerator to improve the application performance, power consumption, and overall system reliability of future exascale systems. This systems design question is driven by the recent DOE SEAB report on HPC [27]. This report highlights the neuromorphic architecture as a key technology (especially in the next generation of supercomputing systems) for large-scale data processing.

To address this larger research question, an open-source processor architecture simulation framework is being developed as part of the *Super-Neuro* research project (see: https://sites.google.com/site/superneuromorphic/). This effort will combine a number of modeling and simulation components to enable the design space exploration of potential hybrid CPU, GPU and neuromorphic supercomputer systems. The key focus of this paper is on the design, implementation and performance of the neuromorphic architecture modeling component called *NeMo*. In particular, the key contributions of this paper are:

- The design and implementation of an event-driven neuromorphic processor architecture model that is able to execute in parallel using optimistic event scheduling [28] and reverse computation [9].

- An initial validation of *NeMo*'s neuron model against the well known Izhikevich model [11, 24]. The Izhikevich model exhibits well-known features of biological spiking neurons. In particular, phasic spiking and tonic bursting models are validated.

- A demonstration of *NeMo*'s efficient execution on up to 1024 Blue Gene/Q nodes for a 65,536 core neuromorphic processor model performing an "identity matrix" type neuron computation that generates a significant amount of neuron firing traffic. The peak performance of *NeMo* is over two billion events per second when operating at this scale.

The design, implementation and integration of CPU, GPU and network modeling components as part of the *Super-Neuro* project will be presented in other papers and is beyond the scope of the research presented here. The remainder of this paper is organized as follows. Section 2 presents *NeMo*'s neuron model which is derived from the model used in the TrueNorth processor [11] followed by the discrete-event implementation in Section 3. The validation and performance results are then presented in Sections 4 and 5. Last, related work and conclusions are presented in Sections 6 and 7, respectively.

2. BACKGROUND

Parallel Discrete-Event Simulations (PDES) consist of *Logical Process* (LP) objects which communicate through messages or *events*. The LPs both encapsulate state and perform any computations within the simulation. However, in order for an LP to perform a computation or change its state, it must be triggered by an event. Thus, changes throughout the simulation system occur via events flowing from one LP to another. When preforming a parallel simulation, LP objects are placed on separate nodes connected across a network. While it is easy to ensure that events local to a node are in serial order, hiccups occur when events are arriving from the network.

PDES synchronization algorithms are used to keep simulation progress in sync across parallel nodes. Optimistic synchronization algorithms, such as Time Warp [28], do not keep each of the parallel nodes in lock step, but instead allow them to process events as they arrive. Nevertheless, there are still periods of global synchronization, called Global Virtual Time (GVT) calculation phases. The GVT calculations find the lowest timestamp on any unprocessed event. This allows the simulation system to reclaim memory from processed events.

Since there are no guarantees of global in-order execution of events, an LP may process a sequence of events out of serial order. To remedy this, the Time Warp algorithm keeps track of inter-event causality and requires LPs to have a "recovery mechanism" [30].

One method of LP recovery is called *reverse computation* [9]. This method uses a function to "un-process" a given event. This allows LPs to reverse the effects of a series of events and begin forward event processing with a more correct ordering.

When an LP detects out-of-order event, the event is said to cause the LP to *rollback*. This rollback may require that certain messages be canceled. This cancellation process is done through anti-messages. Within Time Warp systems there are two categories of rollbacks [18]:

- **Primary Rollback**
  A rollback triggered by receiving a late message. For an LP at time t, a primary rollback occurs when it receives an event at a time less than t. This may cause some anti-messages to be sent.

- **Secondary Rollback**
  A rollback triggered by an anti-message corresponding to a message which has already processed by an LP.

2.1 ROSS

Rensselaer's Optimistic Simulation System, ROSS, is a prominent PDES engine [4, 7, 9, 22]. This ANSI C engine includes a reversible random number generator and is designed for fast and efficient performance. ROSS performs optimistic simulation using the Time Warp algorithm with reverse computation. ROSS implements many other PDES scheduling algorithms, including the conservative YAWNS protocol [36, 37]. ROSS has been shown to be remarkable scalable [3].

2.2 Neuromorphic Computing Models

NeMo's neuromorphic processor architecture model is derived from the general neuron-synaspe-axion behavior used in the IBM TrueNorth processor [1, 10]. The TrueNorth Leaky Integrate and Fire (TNLIF) model is further derived from the Leaky Integrate and Fire (LIF) model [11]. We begin with an overview of hardware-based neuromorphic processor systems. We then present the LIF model, followed with details on the TNLIF model.

2.2.1 Neuromorphic Hardware

Neuromorphic computing refers to hardware implementations of cognitive computing techniques. More specifically, the goal of neuromorphic computation is the design and development of neuron inspired hardware in an energy efficient package [33].

Neuromorphic hardware development has significantly progressed, giving rise to new processor designs [1, 33, 34, 38]. These hardware designs are based on spiking neural networks. Spiking neural networks have input, internal connections, and output components. Input elements are referred to as *axons*, output elements are called *neurons*, and the connectors between axons and neurons are called *synapses*. Signals sent from a neuron are generally referred to as "spikes," as they are treated as binary signals. These terms stem from more general Artifical Neural Network (ANN) models, which in turn are borrowed from neuroscience [40]. Neuromorphic processors operate on a synchronized clock, allowing them to receive, process, and send new messages in between external clock cycles. For example, the TrueNorth hardware architecture has an external clock rate of 1 kHz, allowing each neuron to receive and send a spike 1,000 times per second [1].

The current generation of neuromorphic hardware implements a spiking neuron model with binary outputs. Signals

Integration:

$$V_j(t) = V_j(t-1) \sum_{i=0}^{n-1} [x_i(t)\, s_i] \qquad (1)$$

Leak:

$$V_j(t) = V_j(t) - \lambda_j \qquad (2)$$

Threshold Check and Spike:

$$\textbf{if} \quad V_j(t) \geq \alpha_j \qquad (3)$$
$$\text{Spike}$$
$$V_j(t) = R_j \qquad (4)$$
$$\textbf{end if} \qquad (5)$$

Figure 1: Leaky integrate and fire general neuron model

enter an axon, are passed to a synapse, then are processed by a neuron. The neurons in these models currently manage all of the computation—axons and synapses merely act as a signal transfer service to the neuron [21].

NeMo acts as a neuromorphic processor simulation model. It designed not as a complete, cycle-accurate, hardware simulation, but as a generic neuromorphic hardware simulator that implements the TNLIF neuron model described in [11].

The *NeMo* model can simulate neuromorphic processors of arbitrary dimensions, allowing for novel processor performance benchmarking. *NeMo* also has the ability to add message processing inside the axons and synapses, potentially simulating more powerful or energy efficient neuromorphic processors, as described in [21]. This is in contrast to the *COMPASS* simulator, presented in [39], which is designed for spike accurate TrueNorth hardware simulations.

2.2.2 The LIF Neuron Model

The LIF model is a simple neuron model that is able to emulate some biological neuron functions [25]. Because it is so straightforward (and does not rely on partial differential equations), the LIF model is used in most neuromorphic hardware.

Neurons that implement the LIF model follow a simple pattern of execution, shown in Figure 1 [43]. Execution consists of an integration period, leak calculations, threshold checking, firing, and then reset. In Figure 1, the general form of the neuron equations are presented. During integration, shown in Equation (1), the neuron updates its internal voltage based on each synapse i's synaptic weight, s_i. This is calculated based on the synapse's activity at time t, shown as $x_i(t)$ in Equation (1). Next, the LIF neuron calculates leak, by subtracting the set leak value, λ, from the current membrane potential, shown in Equation (2). Next, in Equation (3), the neuron checks the threshold value, α, against the current membrane potential. If the current membrane potential is greater than α, the neuron spikes. If the neuron spikes, Equation (4) executes, setting the neuron membrane potential to the reset voltage, R_j. This model forms the basis of the TNLIF neuron model, and thus the basis of the *NeMo* simulation model.

2.2.3 The TrueNorth Neuron Model

The TNLIF neuron model is a significantly enhanced version of the simple LIF model. *NeMo* fully implements this neuron model. In Figure 2, the full TrueNorth neuron model

is presented. Functions used in this model include signum:

$$sgn(x) = \begin{cases} -1, & x < 0 \\ 0, & x = 0 \\ 1, & x > 0 \end{cases}$$

a comparison function for stochastic operations:

$$F(s,p) = \begin{cases} 1, & |s| \geq p \\ 0, & |s| < p \end{cases}$$

and the Kroneker delta function: $\delta(x)$.

The TNLIF neuron model features a fully connected "neurosynaptic crossbar." This crossbar connects each input axon with all neurons. When an axon receives a spike, it sends signals to all connected synapses. The neuron integration equation is presented in Equation (6). At time t, if an axon ,i, is active, the synaptic activity, $A_i(t)$, is 1, otherwise it is 0. In the equation, $w_{i,j}$ represents connectivity between axons and neurons. If $w_{i,j}$ is 1, there is a connection between axon i and neuron j. If the value is 0, there is no connection.

Each neuron assigns a type, represented by G_i, to each axon. Weights are then assigned to each axon type. G_i is limited to four types, therefore each axon may be assigned one of four different weights by each neuron. Neuron weights are stored as signed integers, shown in the equation as $s_j^{G_i}$. $b_j^{G_i}$ sets deterministic or stochastic integration mode. If the value is 0, neurons update their membrane potential by taking the sum of each axon multiplied by each axon's weight: $\sum_{i=0}^{n-1} [s_j^{G_i}](A_i(t)w_{i,j})$

Neurons can be configured to use stochastic synaptic and leak integration. Setting $b_j^{G_i} = 1$ enables stochastic synaptic integration and setting $c_j^{\lambda} = 1$ enables stochastic leak integration. Stochastic integration functions similarly for both leak and synaptic weight. For each integration event (either a synaptic weight or a leak computation), a random number is drawn and stored as p_j. If the drawn random number is higher than the relevant weight (synaptic weight $s_j^{G_i}$ or leak weight λ_j), then the neuron adds $sgn(\lambda)$ or $sgn(s_j^{G_i})$ to its membrane potential. Synapse integration is shown in Equation (6), and leak integration is shown in Equations (7) and (8).

The TNLIF neuron model enhances the leak functionality of the LIF model by adding positive or negative leak values, and a "leak-reversal" ability. Normal leak operation calculates the sign of the leak value λ, stores this value as Ω, and then integrates this value into the neuron's membrane potential. Leak sign calculation is shown in Equation (7), and integration is shown in Equation (8). Leak-reversal mode changes the behavior of the leak function such that if the neuron has a positive membrane potential, λ is integrated directly, but if the neuron has a negative membrane potential, $-\lambda$ is integrated. In addition, if the membrane potential of a neuron is 0, then no leak is applied.

In addition to the deterministic threshold modes available, the TNLIF neuron model provides a stochastic threshold mode. Here, η_j is added to α_j and β_j. Then; η_j is calculated every cycle by first generating a random number value, p_j^T, then taking the bitwise AND of M_j and p_j^T, as seen in Equation (9). In Equations (10) and (12), η_j is added to the threshold values before they are checked against the neuron membrane potentials.

The TNLIF model also adds two new reset modes to the standard LIF model. TNLIF supports normal reset mode, a linear reset mode, and a non-reset mode. These values are

Integration:

$$V_j(t) = V_j(t-1) + \sum_{i=0}^{n-1} \left[A_i(t)\, w_{i,j} \left[(1 - b_j^{G_i})\, s_j^{G_i} + b_j^{G_i}\, F(s_j^{G_i}, p_{i,j})\, \mathrm{sgn}(s_j^{G_i}) \right] \right] \tag{6}$$

Leak Integration:

$$\Omega = (1 - \epsilon_j) + \epsilon_j\, \mathrm{sgn}(V_j(t)) \tag{7}$$

$$V_j(t) = V_j(t) + \Omega \left[(1 - c_j^\lambda)\, \lambda + c_j^\lambda\, F(\lambda_j, p_j^\lambda)\, \mathrm{sgn}(\lambda_j) \right] \tag{8}$$

Threshold, Fire, Reset:

$$eta_j = p_t^T \,\&\, M_j \tag{9}$$

if $\quad V_j(t) \geq \alpha + \eta_j$ $\hspace{6cm}$ (10)

$\quad$ Spike

$$V_j(t) = R_j + \delta(\gamma_j - 1)\,(V_j(t) - (\alpha + \eta_j)) + \delta(\gamma_j - 2)\, V_j(t) \tag{11}$$

else if $\quad V_j(t) < -[\beta_j \kappa_j + (\beta_j + \eta_j)(1 - \kappa_j)]$ $\hspace{3cm}$ (12)

$$V_j(t) = -\beta_j\, \kappa_j + [-\delta(\gamma_j)\, R_j + \delta(\gamma_j - 1)\,(V_j(t) + (\beta_j + \eta_j)) + \delta(\gamma_j - 2)\, V_j(t)]\,(1 - \kappa_j) \tag{13}$$

end if

Figure 2: **TrueNorth leaky integrate and fire neuron model (TNLIF)**

chosen through the variable γ_j, and used in Equations (11) and (12). Normal mode follows the standard LIF model. Linear reset mode subtracts the threshold value from the membrane potential. In non-reset mode, the membrane potential is not changed after a spike. These reset modes add additional functionality to the standard LIF neuron model.

TNLIF adds a negative threshold feature to the LIF. This negative threshold value is represented by β_j, an unsigned integer. This gives neurons the ability to have a membrane potential floor or a "bounce" feature. In the case of a floor setting, neurons with membrane potentials below $-\beta_j$ will set their values at $-\beta_j$. If the setting is set to a "bounce" value,, the neuron's membrane potential is reset to $-\beta_j$. The mode is set by changing the value of κ_j. Equation (12) shows the negative threshold check, and Equation (13) shows negative threshold reset and saturation.

The enhancements to the LIF model provided by TNLIF improves its flexibility and power. The additional stochastic integration and threshold features allow the TNLIF model to emulate continuous weight functions. Furthermore, the stochastic features allow neural networks trained with traditional backpropagation techniques to run directly on the hardware [16]. Cassidy et al. demonstrated the flexibility and power of this neuron model in [11] and Akopyan et al. implemented this model in hardware in [1].

The TNLIF model was originally developed through a software simulation tool called *Compass* [39]. *Compass* is a software tool provided by IBM to allow developers of neuromorphic software the ability to run code on a simulated TrueNorth processor. *Compass* is closed-source and proprietary, but there are some benchmarks available in [10,39]. Further discussion of *Compass* along with comparisons to *NeMo* can be found in Section 5.4.

3. NeMo DISCRETE-EVENT IMPLEMENTATION

Based on the TNLIF model presented in the previous section, the neuromorphic architecture model is realized as a discrete-event simulation using ROSS [3,4,8].

The TNLIF model has specific limitations due to its imple-

mentation in hardware. *NeMo*, however, is not designed as a simulation of the TrueNorth processor hardware, rather it is a more generic neuromorphic processor simulation model. With this set of design considerations, *NeMo* implements all of the features of the TrueNorth model. In addition, *NeMo* does not have the bit length constraints that are part of TrueNorth. *NeMo* may have a 64-bit signed integer value for weights, thresholds, and pseudo-random numbers. Furthermore, while *NeMo* operates with the same conceptual neurosynaptic crossbar that TrueNorth uses, the crossbar can be set to an arbitrary size, constrained only by memory. This allows *NeMo* to simulate neurosynaptic cores of any size. For the purposes of our benchmark runs, we set the number of neurons to 256, the same that TrueNorth hardware implements.

NeMo is also capable of simulating compute-on-synapse event models. This feature gives *NeMo* the ability to execute operations at the synapse or axon level, allowing for more complex neurosynaptic chip designs to be simulated.

NeMo partitions the model of a neuromorphic processor into individual components. Each axon, synapse, and neuron are modeled as a unique Logical Process (LP) type. By having individual elements of the neuromorphic chip running as individual LP types, *NeMo* is able to add processing features to the synapses and axons. Furthermore, advanced axon → synapse → neuron connections could possibly be modeled. A collection of axons, synapses, and neurons are contained within a logical container, referred to as a neurosynaptic core. *NeMo* can model thousands of neurosynaptic cores with each core containing hundreds of neurons and axons and tens of thousands of synapses.

The remainder of this section discusses the implementation of *NeMo*. This includes the forward and reverse event functions for ROSS as well as a discussion on techniques used to prevent excessive message generation using a fanout technique to maintain a stable message population.

3.1 Forward Event Computation

For the benchmarking and testing of *NeMo*, we implement a model with similar capabilities as the TNLIF model. Therefore, we do not add any computation to the axon and

236

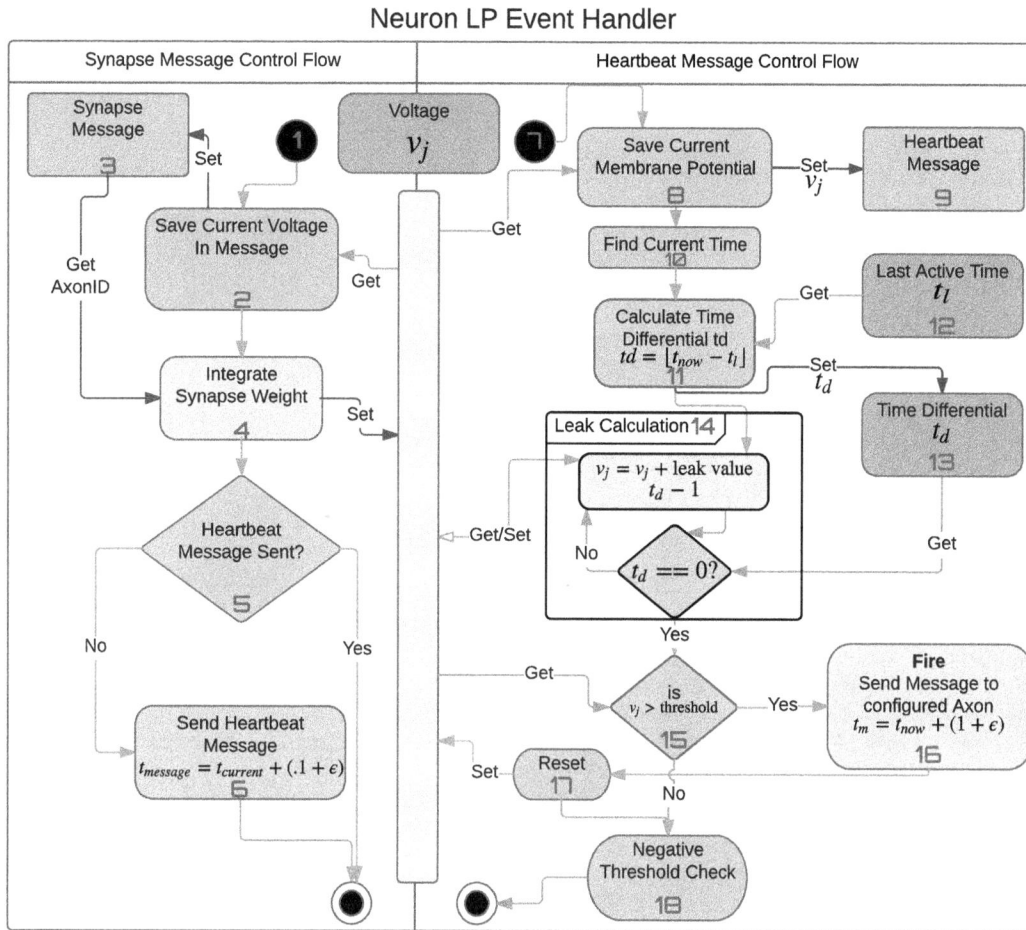

Figure 3: The *NeMo* neuron event flow. Details of each block, numbered 1 through 18, are discussed in Section 3.1.

synapse LPs. Section 3.1 shows the logical layout of neurons, axons, and synapses on a neurosynaptic core. When an axon receives a message it relays the message to each synapse in its row. In this model, the synapses simply relay any received message to the neuron in their column. Like the TNLIF model, there are no computations that occur when axons and synapses receive events; they simply relay thier messages to the next element in the model.

In Figure 3, Blocks 1–18, we show the *NeMo* neuron model control flow for the forward event handler. The flow starts at the current simulation time, t, where t is measured in microseconds. If $t > 1$, there has been at least one neurosynaptic tick since the simulation has started. There are two event types that neurons receive: synapse messages and heartbeat messages. Synapse messages are set at a nanosecond resolution, with events occurring at $t + 0.0001 + \varepsilon$. Heartbeat messages are sent at a larger time-slice, $t + 0.1 + \varepsilon$. In Figure 3, the synapse message processing is represented on the left column, and heartbeat messages are shown on the right. We use ε to represent a "jitter" factor, an extremely small random value used to ensure a deterministic ordering of events.

The synapse message process begins in Block 1, when the neuron receives a synapse message. The neuron first saves the current voltage value, Block 2, a double precision floating point value V_j, in the synapse message, Block 3. This is to

facilitate reverse computation, by saving V_j in the message, when rolling back messages neurons are able to revert changes made during forward computation.

The neuron then performs the integration function, shown in Figure 3 as Block 4. This updates V_j with a new value, computed by the integration function defined in Equation (6).

Neuron heartbeat messages are *NeMo*'s technique to synchronize neuron firing. In an LIF model, neurons integrate, leak, fire, and reset at specific intervals. To increase performance, a heartbeat message is sent only when a neuron activates. In Block 5, the neuron checks if it has already sent a heartbeat message. If it has not, it schedules a heartbeat message at $t + 0.1 + \varepsilon$, in Block 6. This action completes the neuron's integration function for a particular axon. By executing this flow every time an axon message is received, *NeMo* recreates the integration formula in Figure 2, Equation (6).

When a heartbeat message is received, as shown in Block 7, the neuron begins its leak, fire and reset function. The neuron also saves its current membrane potential in the received message Blocks 8 and 9.

The neuron then finds the current neurosynaptic time in Block 10. This is computed as $\lfloor t \rfloor$. In Block 11, the neuron calculates a time differential, t_d. This value represents how many neurosynaptic clock cycles have passed since this neuron has been active. By taking the last active time value, Block 12, and subtracting the current time, the neuron is able to determine how many times it needs to run the leak calculation, shown in Block 13. The neuron uses this time differential value to compute leak. By using a loop, the neuron is able to run the leak function, shown in Equations (7) and (8), t_d times, bringing its voltage to where it would have been if the neuron had been calculating the leak function in a synchronous fashion. This loop is shown in Block 14.

Once the neuron has computed the leak function, it proceeds to check the positive threshold Block 15, and either fire and reset, or just move on to the negative threshold check. If $v_j >$ threshold, the neuron will fire Block 16 and reset Block 17. A fire operation schedules a new message with ROSS at the next neurosynaptic clock time. Since the neurosynaptic clock operates at the integer scale, simply adding $1 + \varepsilon$ to the current time will schedule the fire event at the proper future time.

After the neuron completes the fire/reset functions, it then checks for negative threshold overflows Block 18. If the neuron's voltage is beyond the negative threshold, the neuron performs the negative threshold integration functions specified in Equation (13).

The neuron has now completed one neurosynaptic tick.

3.2 Reverse Computation

Reverse computation is handled through swapping states at key points in the neuron process and using bitfields to manage secondary state changes. The primary state change that occurs is V_j, the neuron's voltage. Neurons also contain a flag, marking when a neuron has sent itself a heartbeat message. When performing reverse computation, neurons must revert changes to both of these state elements.

Whenever a neuron receives a message from a synapse or receives a heartbeat message, before any changes are made to V_j, it saves the current current voltage in the incoming message. During reverse computation, neurons restore the saved voltage from the message. This reverts all integration, leak, and reset functions that changed V_j.

When a neuron receives a synapse message for the first time, it checks to see if it has sent a heartbeat message. If it has not, it changes an internal flag, and sends the message. The neuron also changes the flag when receiving a heartbeat message. Neurons record boolean flag changes in a bitfield in the incoming message. If there is a non-zero entry in the bitfield during reverse computation, the flag state is toggled.

3.3 Fanout

Since *NeMo* has individual LPs configured for each component, simulations have a large number of LPs running simultaneously. There are 2,164,260,864 LPs in our largest simulation experiment. If *NeMo* sent messages at every time stamp, it would send 66,048 messages per neurosynaptic core per tick. This large event population quickly becomes unmanageable due to memory constraints. To counter this,

Axons	Synapses			
0	0,0	0,1	...	0,n
1	1,0	1,1	...	1,n
$\vdots$	$\vdots$	$\vdots$	$\vdots$	$\vdots$
n	$n,1$	$n,2$	$n,3$	n,n
Neurons	0	1	...	n

Figure 4: A matrix representation of a neurosynaptic core.

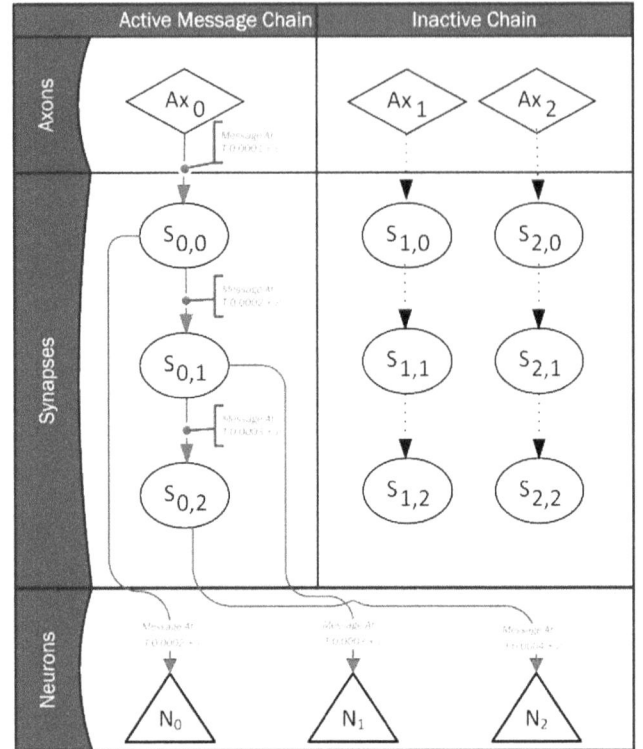

Figure 5: Example event chain in NeMo with 3 neurons per neurosynaptic core. In this diagram, an event is received at Axon 0 within a core at time t. At $t+0.0001+\varepsilon$ Axon 0 sends a message to Synapse 0,0. Synapse 0,0 then sends a message at $t + 0.0002 + \varepsilon$ to Neuron 0 and Synapse 0,1. Synapse 0,1 sends messages to Neuron 1 and Synapse 0,2 at $t + 0.0003 + \varepsilon$. Synapse 0,2 then sends a message to Neuron 2 at $t + 0.0004 + \varepsilon$. If no messages are received on Axon 1 and 2, no messages are sent. Neurons will send outgoing spike messages, if applicable, at $t + 1.0 + \varepsilon$.

NeMo implements a fanout technique for message transmission based on work done in [29].

In Figure 5, an example of the fanout message technique is shown. Here we see a neurosynaptic core with three axons, nine synapses, and three neurons. When a message is received by an axon, it sends an axon message to the first synapse in the neurosynaptic core at time $T + 0.0001 + \varepsilon$. The synapse then sends two messages: first to the neuron attached to it, second to the next synapse in the row, at $T + 0.0002 + \varepsilon$. The next synapse does the same, until the final synapse has been reached. This technique generates far fewer messages, preventing memory usage issues.

4. VALIDATION

Izhikevich implemented and reviewed 20 prominent features of biological neurons using a resonate-and-fire model [26]. The TNLIF model was used to recreate many of these behaviors, demonstrating the utility and validity of the TNLIF model [11]. *NeMo*, unlike Izhikevich's model and the *Compass* simulator used in [11], simulates TNLIF neurons using discrete events. Due to this difference, it is impossible to exactly replicate Izhikevich's models. Neurons only update internal state when an input message is received or if they are a self-firing neuron. However, we do recreate the neuron behavior observed by [11] in the TrueNorth neuron model.

To validate *NeMo*, we implemented two of the Izhikevich models Cassidey et al. implemented in [11]. Our goal was to match the behavior of these models, showing that *NeMo* correctly simulates the TNLIF model. To do this, we used similar parameters to the ones used in [11].Phasic spiking neurons were configured using the values shown in Table 1. A single axon was connected to this neuron that sent spikes out every 200 ticks. The results of this run are shown in Figure 6.

Table 1: Phasic Spiking Neuron Parameters.

Parameter	Neuron 0 Value
Synaptic Weights $\left(s_j^{G_i}\right)$	0,20,0,0
Leak Value (λ)	2
Positive Threshold (α)	2
Negative Threshold (β)	-10
Reset Voltage (R_j)	-15
Reset Mode	Normal Negative Saturation

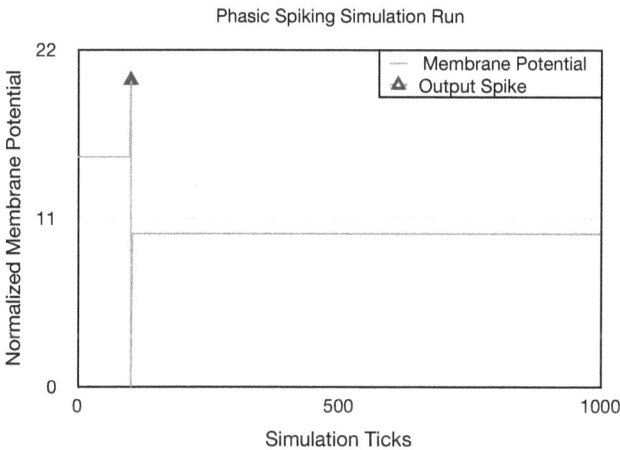

Figure 6: Izhikevich phasic spiking validation run.

We then implemented a tonic bursting neuron, again following the specifications set by [11]. In this configuration, we used two neurons and three axons. One axon was configured to send input spikes every 300 ticks. The neuron parameters used for this validation run are shown in Table 2, and the voltage results are shown in Figure 7.

The information shown in Figures 6 and 7 visually presents neuron behavior that is nearly identical to the behavior observed in [11]. Slight differences in the values are a result of neurons updating state only when events warrant. We also do not record the membrane potential of the input axons. Despite this, we do see qualitatively similar neruon behaviors. Thus, the *NeMo* simulation model is able to recreate the simulation results from [11].

5. EXPERIMENTAL PERFORMANCE

It is important to understand the performance of *NeMo* within massively parallel simulations. We first examine a weak scaling experiment, where we simulate up to 32,768

Table 2: Tonic Bursting Neuron Parameters.

Parameter	Neuron 0 Value	Neuron 1 Value
Synaptic Weights $\left(s_j^{G_i}\right)$	1, -100, 0, 0	1, 0, 0, 0
Leak Value (λ)	1	0
Positive Threshold (α)	18	6
Negative Threshold (β)	20	0
Reset Voltage (R_j)	1	0
Reset Mode	Normal Negative Saturation	Normal Negative Saturation

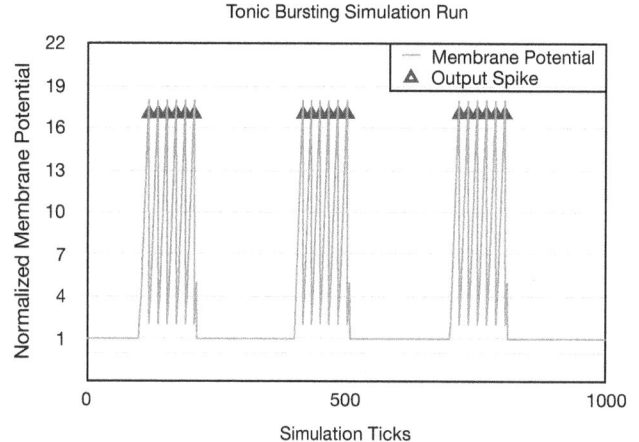

Figure 7: Izhikevich tonic bursting validation run.

neurosynaptic cores. Next we examine the strong scaling performance of a 8,192 neurosynaptic core simulation.

5.1 Experimental Setup

For each of the following experiments, we simulate TrueNorth-like neurosynaptic cores using the ROSS framework. Each neurosynaptic core connects 256 axon LPs, 65,536 synapse LPs, and 256 neuron LPs for a total of 66,048 LPs per core. We perform experiments with up to 32,768 neurosynaptic cores, giving a maximum number of 2,164,260,864 LPs in our largest simulation.

To fully test the performance of our model, we used a neurosynaptic core model which generates over 1,500 events per neurosynaptic core per tick. For this benchmark, each core consists of an "identity-matrix" of neurons. In this model, axon i will trigger synapse i, i, which triggers the neuron at i (see Section 3.1). The output destination of each neuron is set randomly with an 80% chance that it will output to a different neurosynaptic core. To start, each axon in the simulation fires. Overall, this creates an immense number of events, a larger workload than would be expected in a real-world application.

All simulations were performed on an IBM Blue Gene/Q machine. Each node of the Blue Gene/Q features eighteen 1.6 GHz processor cores, 16 of which are devoted to application use [20]. For the two remaining cores, one conducts operating system functionality while the other serves as a spare. All nodes are connected by an effective, high-speed communication network [12].

The 16 GB of DDR3 memory on each Blue Gene/Q node can be a limiting factor in memory intensive simulations. To allow for maximum utilization, each node is highly configurable in terms of parallelism. Each of the 16 processors can run up to 4 hardware threads (for a total of 64 MPI ranks per node) or the processor cores can be under-subscribed

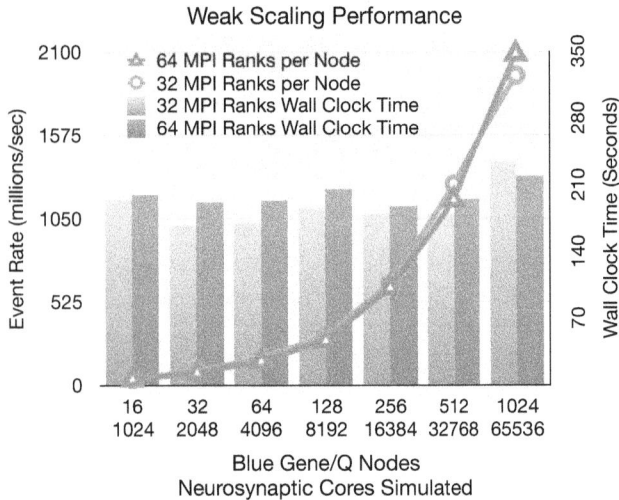

Figure 8: Weak scaling performance experiments.

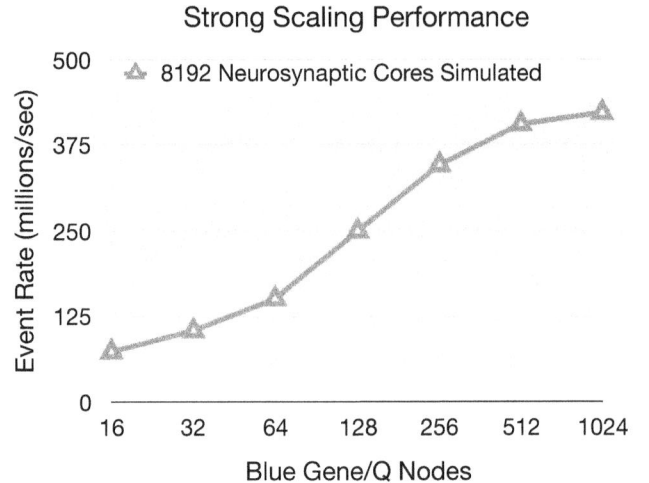

Figure 9: Strong scaling performance experiments.

Table 3: Breakdown of time spent during the simulation of 65,536 neurosynaptic cores on 1024 Blue Gene/Q nodes each with 64 MPI ranks.

Clock Cycle Category	Time Taken (seconds)	Percentage
Priority Queue (enq/deq)	1.8825	0.86%
AVL Tree (insert/delete)	0.0192	0.01%
Event Processing	38.2921	17.52%
Event Cancel	0.7486	0.34%
GVT	154.6155	70.75%
Fossil Collect	12.7742	5.85%
Primary Rollbacks	5.1278	2.35%
Network Read	5.0715	2.32%

(with a minimum of 1 MPI rank per node). Our experiments test several parallel configurations.

All experiments were performed using the time-warp based optimistic synchronization algorithm in ROSS.

5.2 Weak Scaling Experiment

Our first set of experiments tested two configurations: one and two neurosynaptic cores per MPI rank. These configurations ran on either 64 or 32 MPI ranks per Blue Gene/Q node, scaling from 16 to 1024 Blue Gene/Q nodes (see Figure 8). We achieved a peak performance of over 2 billion events per second when simulating 65,536 neurosynaptic cores on 1024 Blue Gene/nodes with 64 MPI ranks per node. These experiments simulated a total of 1,000 neurosynaptic core ticks.

Table 3 presents a breakdown of time spent during our peak performance simulation. These statistics are representative of all of our weak scaling experiments. The most noteworthy statistic is the time that the ROSS simulator spent performing GVT calculations. With less than 20% of simulation time being spent performing local event processing, we observe over 70% of the simulation time is spent performing GVT calculations. Since the GVT calculation is based around an `MPI_all_reduce` calculation, this indicates that there is a load imbalance within the simulation. That is, not all MPI ranks are reaching the blocking MPI reduction operation at the same time.

The slight load imbalance is to be expected. Every time a neuron fires, it has an 80% chance to send a signal to a neuron within a different synaptic core. Since the location of the receiver neuron is also chosen randomly, there is in an unpredictable, yet expected load imbalance across the simulation.

5.3 Strong Scaling Experiment

To understand the ways in which the *NeMo* model scales as parallelism increases, we ran a series of strong scaling experiments. Figure 9 shows performance results for a simulation of 8,192 neurosynaptic cores using 16 to 1,024 Blue Gene/Q nodes. These experiments were run for 1,000 ticks resulting in more than 13 billion net events. We achieved peak performance when we used 1,024 Blue Gene/Q nodes, where we observed over 421 million events per second. This benchmark was run with the same randomly generated neuron model as the weak scaling experements, with an 80% chance of neurons communicating to remote cores. One interesting thing to note is that *NeMo* does not place a neurosynaptic core across multiple MPI ranks. This is a limiting factor in the strong scaling results, as simulating 8,192 neurosynaptic cores gives a maximum of 8,192 MPI ranks. When running on 512 Blue Gene/Q nodes, there are 32,768 possible MPI ranks, and on 1,024 nodes there are 1,048,576 ranks available. We ran at these scales with 8,192 ranks, and the lack of increase in performance is attributable to this limitation in the *NeMo* system.

One interesting phenomena is observed when analyzing the running time and efficiency of the strong scaling experements, Figure 10. Here, we see that an unexpected correlation between overall simulation efficiency and the running time of the simulation: a *decrease* in efficiency corresponds to faster running times. This indicates a very low cost for performing an event rollback. Overall, the optimistic simulation is able to find more parallelism (and thus more speedup) despite incurring an increased number of rollback events.

Figure 11 shows a breakdown of the rollbacks observed during the strong scaling experiments. At first the number of rollbacks does increase as the parallelism increases however all experiments on 128 nodes or more each incur approximately 7.7 million rollbacks. This indicates that our simulations have a maximum amount of parallelism where increases in hardware do not correlate to increases in performance.

Efficiency Compared to Running Time for Strong Scaling Experiments

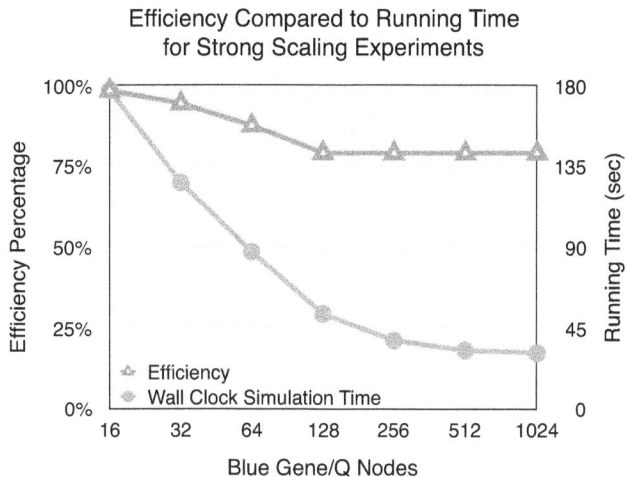

Figure 10: Comparison of the efficiency and the running time of the strong scaling experiments.

Rollbacks During Strong Scaling Experiments

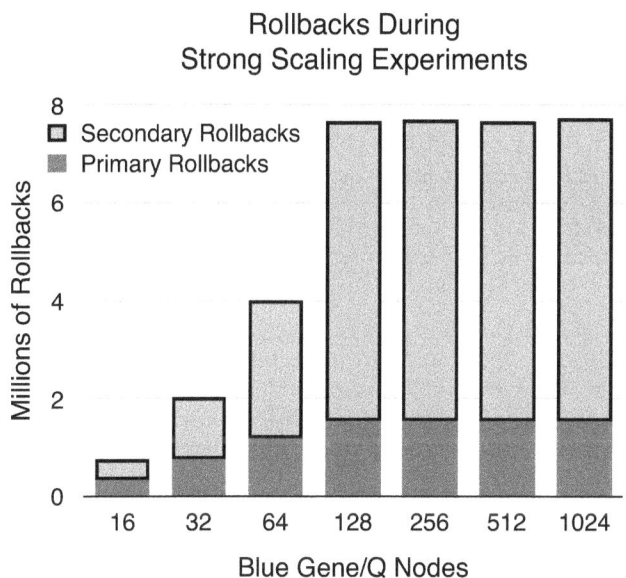

Figure 11: Breakdown of the primary and secondary rollbacks for the strong scaling simulation. Note that the net event population for these experiments is 13 billion events, but the maximum number of rollbacks observed is only 7.6 million.

Both Figure 10 and Figure 11 show that increasing the number of parallel nodes is only effective up to a point. At more than 128 Blue Gene/Q nodes, we see diminishing returns in performance scaling. In the 128 node experiment, each node simulates 64 neurosynaptic cores. We see that the overall workload is balanced (i.e., there is no decrease in performance which would indicate an over decomposition of the system). For the 128, 256, 512, and 1,024 node experiments, the communication overheads surpass the time spent doing local event processing. What is most intriguing about these experiments is that the number of rollbacks remains constant, despite an increase in parallelism.

5.4 Comparison with COMPASS

Comparing *NeMo* with IBM's own simulation software, *Compass*, poses some challenges. The intention of *NeMo* is to provide an open-source way to simulate various neuromorphic hardware designs. The *Compass* simulator is tuned for a similar purpose, but is tied into the TrueNorth architecture. Furthermore, *Compass* is proprietary software that we are unable to use on our benchmarking hardware. IBM Blue Gene/Q support for *Compass* was also eliminated in favor of focusing support on x86 architectures. These factors make a meaningful direct comparison impossible. However, in [39], benchmark runs of *Compass* are done using several models. Using these existing benchmarks, we can create a rough comparison between *NeMo* and *Compass*.

While both *NeMo* and *Compass* can exploit massively parallel supercomputer systems like the Blue Gene/Q, there are a number of key differences between the two. First, *Compass* employs a time-stepped algorithm which iterates over the set of neurons assigned to a particular thread (or MPI rank) and then iterates over each synaspe event that targets that neuron from the enclosing iteration loop. *NeMo* is implemented using a pure event-driven approach with all neuron, axon and synapse events being enqueued into a single priority queue. This approach avoids the cost of iterating over neurons which do not have any posted synaspe events.

In [39], *Compass* weak-scaling benchmarks are presented using the *CoCoMac* neuron model. We do not have access to the specific implementation details of the neuron model used in the paper, so we can not explicitly re-create the author's benchmarks in *NeMo*. CoCoMac is a message-sparse model, generating on average 1.3 spikes per simulated neurosynaptic core [39].

Given that we are not able to run the same model and we are not able to run *Compass* on our benchmark hardware, we have decided to compare the events per second produced by *Compass* with *NeMo*. To find this value for *Compass*, we took the number of spike events per simulated tick reported in [39] and made some reasonable assumptions about the underlying model. We took the values from the largest run of *Compass* that ran on 16 racks of IBM Blue Gene/Q that generated 22 million spikes per simulated tick. The paper does not specify if that value is for all spikes generated simulating the model, or if it was for remote-core spikes (spikes originating on a different node than the destination). To compare *NeMo*'s performance with *Compass*, we will assume the best-case scenario for *Compass*: that the 22 million spikes generated are only the remote spikes. The paper further specifies that the CoCoMac model simulated has some cores that generate a ratio of 80 remote spikes to 20 local spikes, and other cores that generate a 60/40 ratio. For the purposes of our comparison, we assume a best-case scenario for *Compass* and assume a 50/50 ratio of remote spikes versus local spikes. This assumption would mean that the 22 million spikes per simulated tick would be 50% of the total spikes generated by the simulation. For comparison, our benchmark model generated an average of 80% remote spikes per core.

The set of equations that approximate the performance of the *Compass* simulation are shown in Figure 12. To find the number of events per second, we assume that 1 axon and 256 synapse fan-out events, f are scheduled for each spike s event over the paper's reported 500 ticks t_{sim}, shown in Equation (14). We also multiply the total spikes reported, e_{total} by 2, per our assumption that 50% of the spikes are not remote. We then divide the calculated total number of events by the wall clock time taken by *Compass*, t_{wall} to get the spikes per second, e_{second}, shown in Equation (15). We then divide by the number of Blue Gene/Q racks used in

$$e_{\text{total}} = s_{\text{reported}} \times 2 \times f \qquad (14)$$

$$e_{\text{second}} = s_{\text{total}}/t \qquad (15)$$

$$e_{\text{second/rack}} = e_{\text{second}}/16 \qquad (16)$$

Figure 12: Calculating *Compass*'s events per second per Blue Gene/Q Rack

the simulation r, to get *Compass*'s events per second per rack, shown in Equation (16). The complete equation used is shown in Figure 12.

These values were chosen to help represent the number of events *NeMo* produces. For every neuron spike event in *NeMo*, there are 256 neuron events generated with one axon event. Our largest current *NeMo* simulation ran on one rack of Blue Gene/Q, thus comparing *Compass*'s event rate per rack p er second will provide a roughly accurate gauge of performance.

This gives $((22M \times 2 \times 257) \times 500\,\text{ticks})/194\,\text{secs}/16\,\text{racks} = 1,821M\,\text{events/second/rack}$. Our benchmark runs of *NeMo* showed an event rate of $2,082M\,\text{events/rack}$. The weak scaling experiments run on *NeMo* show $261M$ events per second more than *Compass*. While a direct comparison between *NeMo* and *Compass* is currently impossible, this result shows that *NeMo* is on par with the performance of *Compass*, and a viable option for simulation of neuromorphic hardware.

6. RELATED WORK

As indicated previously, the core neuron model of *NeMo* is based on the IBM TrueNorth chip which has a "spike" accurate simulator called *Compass* [10]. A detailed analysis of the differences between *Compass* and *NeMo* can be found in section 5.4.

A similar hardware specific neuromorphic system is the SpiNNaker Project [19]. SpiNNaker is a specialized machine that is designed to optimally transmit a very large number of very small packets to enable models of how the brain performs communication operations as part of an overall neuron/brain modeling capability. Here, 40 byte packets are efficiently transmitted across to 1 million processing cores. The machine is organized into "nodes" similar to a Blue Gene/Q except that the core processing engine of each node is 18 ARM968 processor cores. Each ARM core has 96 KB of local memory and 128 MB of shared memory across all the processors. SpiNNaker reports being able to model on a single core several hundred point neurons performing calculations on par with Izhikevich's model with about 1,000 input synapses to each neuron. This fan-out is about four times as big as currently supported in TrueNorth. However, the power consumed by SpiNNaker is much greater by several orders of magnitude. A 1,200 board system where each board support 48 nodes which can model on the order of 10 to 20 million neurons consumes 75,000 W of power whereas TrueNorth only consumes 65 mW (or 0.065 W) for 256 thousand neurons.

Future neuromorphic hardware predictions where recently made by Hasler and Marr [21]. Here, they present a road map for the construction of large-scale neuromorphic hardware systems. The metric used in this road map is called a MMAC which is a unit of neuromorphic computation in the "millions" of neural multiple and accumulate operations. Hasler and Marr argue that if computation were done not only in the neurons but in the dendrites which sit between the neuron

cell (e.g., soma) and synapses, then it is possible to perform one million MAC operations per picawatt of power. This scale of computational power in equivalent to performing an exa-MAC or 2^{60} MAC operations per watt of power which is on par with the computational power efficiency of the human brain.

In the computational neuroscience community, there are a number of spiking neuron simulators available that are using various modeling approaches to understand the biological function of neurons, dendrites, synapses, and axons. The most well known is NEURON [5] which is a simulation framework for creating and investigating empirically-based models of biological neurons and neural circuits. NEURON offers users the ability to select which numerical integration method to apply in solving the model equations. The default approach is an implicit Euler method. In [35], NEURON was extended to enable parallel neuron network simulations where each processor performs its own local equation integration over a subset of the neuron network. On the Blue Gene/P supercomputer it exhibited nearly linear speedup on 2,000 processing cores. Recently, Zhongwei et al. [31], constructed a multithread version of NEURON for reaction diffusion models that are implemented using a Time Warp with state-saving approach.

There has been work on simulating spiking neural networks using GPU acceleration as well. The "nemo" project, [17], uses GPU acceleration to simulate over 40,000 Izhkavitch neurons in a biologically plausible network. The "nemo" project is designed to accelerate simulation of biologically accurate neural networks, whereas our *NeMo* project is tuned to simulate neuromorphic hardware design. GPU acceleration for simulation of spiking neural networks is promising [6], and further work might be considered in simulating neuromorphic hardware using PDES techniques in tandem with GPU acceleration.

The Blue Brain Project[1] has attained world wide attention for its goals to construct high-fidelity, supercomputer-powered models of the human brain. This software is based on NEURON and uses the same numerical integration approaches. However, their brain models models can require very large data sets because each neuron and synapse is distinct [41] which results in the cellular model for a human brain requiring 100 PB of storage. This amount of data could be considered each and every time-step by the equation solvers in the Blue Brain simulator.

Finally, the only other optimistic neuron model with reverse computation is by Lobb et al. [32]. In this 2005 PADS *Best Paper* work, a Hodgkin-Huxley (HH) neuron model is implemented which demonstrates the performance viability of this approach. Speedups are demonstrated on an 8 node PIII cluster ranging from $1.5\times$ to $3.5\times$ for HH networks sizes of 25 to 400 neurons.

7. CONCLUSIONS & FUTURE WORK

We have presented *NeMo*, an open source[2] discrete event simulation model implemented using the ROSS simulation framework that allows for large scale, flexible, simulation of neuromorphic processors. This simulation model allows for the creation of arbitrarily sized neuromorphic processors based on the TNLIF neuron model. This simulation model will allow experimentation with new neuromorphic processor designs with new and novel problem domains.

The results of this work show that discrete event simulation is a viable option for simulation of massive neuromorphic

---

[1]Source: http://bluebrain.epfl.ch. Accessed on: Jan 4, 2016.
[2]Available At: https://github.com/markplagge/NeMo

systems. Near linear scaling was achieved running *NeMo* on a Blue Gene/Q system with weak scaling. Our largest run of *NeMo* simulated 32,768 neurosynaptic cores, each containing 256 neurons, 65,536 synapses, and 256 axons, for 1,000 neurosynaptic ticks. The largest run simulated 8,338,608 neurons and axons with 2,147,483,648 synapses with an event rate of just over 1 billion events per second. Larger simulations are possible, along with different neurosynaptic core designs.

NeMo is also capable of simulating new configurations of neuromorphic hardware. The number of neurons per neurosynaptic core can be set to any value within the limits of 64 bit computer hardware. Furthermore, experiments can be done simulating neuromorphic processors that process messages upon receipt, allowing for "what-if" hardware designs. Since *NeMo* is built with the ROSS discrete event simulation framework, integration between *NeMo* and supercomputer simulation systems is possible. Combining the *NeMo* simulation model with a supercomputer design simulator will allow for experimentation with hybrid neuromorphic supercomputer designs.

One of the goals of *NeMo* is the ability to simulate different neuron models and hardware configurations. With this future goal in mind, *NeMo* has been designed to allow for the addition of other neuron models. The first model implemented is the TNLIF neuron model [11]. However, *NeMo*'s neuron simulation is modular, allowing for new models to be "plugged-in" to the simulation. *NeMo* is capable of simulating any spiking neuron model, and is even capable of having multiple neuron types per neurosynaptic core. The next steps for *NeMo* include the addition of Izhikevich's simple spiking neuron models, as defined in [24].

Additionally, the design of *NeMo*'s message passing system does leave room for performance improvement. Significant simulation time is spent in GVT. Switching from ROSS's event based GVT to a real-time GVT algorithm potentially could improve execution speed. Further enhancements could be made to the way the neurosynaptic crossbar is implemented. Currently, *NeMo* forwards messages from synapses to neurons regardless if the neuron will act on the message. Adding connection information to the synapse would reduce message traffic, and potentially increase performance.

Finally, the other major goal of *NeMo* is to present it as a stand-alone simulation framework. Eventually *NeMo* should give users the ability to design and simulate custom neuromorphic hardware designs in an accessible way. We plan to add support for a high-level API, such as PyNN [14], or potentially a custom framework for describing neuromorphic hardware. We are also investigating including other neuron model support in *NeMo*, with the intention of creating a versatile neuromorphic hardware design simulation tool. Adding these features will be a major focus in the future work for this project.

8. ACKNOWLEDGMENTS

This work was supported by the Air Force Research Laboratory (AFRL), under award number FA8750-15-2-0078.

9. REFERENCES

[1] F. Akopyan, J. Sawada, et al. TrueNorth: Design and tool flow of a 65 mW 1 million neuron programmable neurosynaptic chip. *IEEE Transactions on Computer-Aided Design of Integrated Circuits and Systems*, 34(10):1537–1557, 2015.

[2] A. Amir, P. Datta, et al. Cognitive computing programming paradigm: A corelet language for composing networks of neurosynaptic cores. In *IJCNN '13*, pages 1–10, Aug 2013.

[3] P. D. Barnes, Jr., C. D. Carothers, D. R. Jefferson, and J. M. LaPre. Warp speed: Executing time warp on 1,966,080 cores. In *ACM SIGSIM PADS 2013*, pages 327–336, Montreal, Canada, May 2013.

[4] D. Bauer, C. Carothers, and A. Holder. Scalable time warp on blue gene supercomputers. In *ACM/IEEE/SCS PADS '09*, pages 35–44, Lake Placid, NY, USA, 22–25 June 2009.

[5] R. Brette, M. Rudolph, et al. Simulation of networks of spiking neurons: A review of tools and strategies. *Journal of Computational Neuroscience*, 23(3):349–398, December 2007.

[6] K. D. Carlson, M. Beyeler, N. Dutt, and J. L. Krichmar. GPGPU accelerated simulation and parameter tuning for neuromorphic applications. In *ASP DAC '14*, pages 570–577. IEEE, 2014.

[7] C. Carothers, D. Bauer, and S. Pearce. Ross: A high-performance, low memory, modular time warp system. In *ACM SIGSIM PADS '00*, pages 53–60, Bologna, Italy, 28–31 May 2000.

[8] C. Carothers, D. Bauer, and S. Pearce. Ross: a high-performance, low memory, modular time warp system. In *ACM SIGSIM PADS '14*, pages 53–60, 2000.

[9] C. Carothers, K. Perumalla, and R. Fujimoto. Efficient Optimistic Parallel Simulations Using Reverse Computation. In *ACM SIGSIM PADS '99*, pages 126–135, Atlanta, GA, USA, 5 1999.

[10] A. S. Cassidy, R. Alvarez-Icaza, et al. Real-time scalable cortical computing at 46 giga-synaptic ops/watt with 100x speedup in time-to-solution and 100,000x reduction in energy-to-solution. In *ACM SC '14*, pages 27–38, Piscataway, NJ, USA, 2014. IEEE Press.

[11] A. S. Cassidy, P. Merolla, et al. Cognitive computing building block: A versatile and efficient digital neuron model for neurosynaptic cores. In *IEEE IJCNN 2013*, 2013.

[12] D. Chen, N. Eisley, P. Heidelberger, R. Senger, Y. Sugawara, S. Kumar, V. Salapura, D. Satterfield, B. Steinmacher-Burow, and J. Parker. The IBM Blue Gene/Q Interconnection Network and Message Unit. In *ACM SC '11*, pages 1–10, Seattle, WA, USA, 12–18 Nov. 2011.

[13] G. Chrysos. Intel® Xeon Phi™ coprocessor-the architecture. *Intel Whitepaper*, 2014.

[14] A. P. Davison, D. Brüderle, J. Eppler, J. Kremkow, E. Muller, D. Pecevski, L. Perrinet, and P. Yger. Pynn: A common interface for neuronal network simulators. *Frontiers in Neuroinformatics*, 2(11):1–10, 27 Jan. 2009.

[15] S. Esser, A. Andreopoulos, et al. Cognitive computing systems: Algorithms and applications for networks of neurosynaptic cores. In *The 2013 Int. Joint Conference on Neural Networks*, pages 1–10, Aug 2013.

[16] S. K. Esser, R. Appuswamy, P. Merolla, J. V. Arthur, and D. S. Modha. Backpropagation for energy-efficient neuromorphic computing. In *Advances in Neural Information Processing Systems 28*, NIPS '15, pages 1117–1125. Curran Associates, Inc., 2015.

[17] A. K. Fidjeland, E. B. Roesch, M. P. Shanahan, and W. Luk. NeMo: A platform for neural modelling of spiking neurons using gpus. In *IEEE ASAP 09.*, pages 137–144, July 2009.

[18] R. M. Fujimoto. *Parallel and Distributed Simulation*

Systems. John Wiley & Sons, Inc., New York, NY, USA, 1st edition, 1999.

[19] S. Furber, F. Galluppi, S. Temple, and L. Plana. The spinnaker project. *Proceedings of the IEEE*, 102(5):652–665, May 2014.

[20] R. A. Haring, M. Ohmacht, T. W. Fox, M. K. Gschwind, D. L. Satterfield, K. Sugavanam, P. W. Coteus, P. Heidelberger, M. A. Blumrich, R. W. Wisniewski, et al. The ibm blue gene/q compute chip. *Micro, IEEE*, 32(2):48–60, 2012.

[21] J. Hasler and H. B. Marr. Finding a roadmap to achieve large neuromorphic hardware systems. *Frontiers in Neuroscience*, 7(118), 2013.

[22] A. O. Holder and C. D. Carothers. Analysis of Time Warp on a 32,768 Processor IBM Blue Gene/L Supercomputer. In *Proc. 20th Eur. Modeling and Simulation Symp.*, EMSS '08, pages 284–292, Amantea, Italy, 17–19 Sept. 2008.

[23] G. Indiveri, B. Linares-Barranco, et al. Neuromorphic silicon neuron circuits. *Frontiers in Neuroscience*, 5, 2011.

[24] E. Izhikevich. Simple model of spiking neurons. *Neural Networks, IEEE Transactions on*, 14(6):1569–1572, Nov 2003.

[25] E. Izhikevich. Which model to use for cortical spiking neurons? *Neural Networks, IEEE Transactions on*, 15(5):1063–1070, Sept 2004.

[26] E. M. Izhikevich. Resonate-and-fire neurons. *Neural Networks*, 14(6–7):883 – 894, 2001.

[27] S. A. Jackson, M. McQuade, R. Shenoy, R. G. S. Koonin, J. Hendler, P. Highnam, A. Jones, J. Kelly, C. Mundie, T. Ohki, D. Reed, K. Smith, and J. Tracy. Report of the task force on high performance computing of the secretary of energy advisory board. Technical report, DOE, August 2014.

[28] D. R. Jefferson. Virtual time. *ACM Trans. Program. Lang. Syst.*, 7(3):404–425, July 1985.

[29] J. M. LaPre, C. D. Carothers, K. D. Renard, and D. R. Shires. Ultra large-scale wireless network models using massively parallel discrete-event simulation. *Transactions of The Society for Modeling and Simulation Int.*, Oct. 2012.

[30] Y.-B. Lin and E. D. Lazowska. A study of time warp rollback mechanisms. *ACM Trans. Modeling and Comput. Simulation*, 1(1):51–72, Jan. 1991.

[31] Z. Lin, C. Tropper, M. N. Ishlam Patoary, R. A. McDougal, W. W. Lytton, and M. L. Hines. Ntw-mt: A multi-threaded simulator for reaction diffusion simulations in neuron. In *SIGSIM PADS '15*, pages 157–167, New York, NY, USA, 2015. ACM.

[32] C. J. Lobb, Z. Chao, R. M. Fujimoto, and S. M. Potter. Parallel event-driven neural network simulations using the hodgkin-huxley neuron model. In *Principles of Advanced and Distributed Simulation, 2005. PADS 2005. Workshop on*, pages 16–25, June 2005.

[33] P. Merolla, J. Arthur, F. Akopyan, N. Imam, R. Manohar, and D. S. Modha. A digital neurosynaptic core using embedded crossbar memory with 45pj per spike in 45nm. In *IEEE CICC '11 IEEE*, pages 1–4, Sept 2011.

[34] P. A. Merolla, J. V. Arthur, et al. A million spiking-neuron integrated circuit with a scalable communication network and interface. *Science*, 345(6197):668–673, 2014.

[35] M. Migliore, C. Cannia, W. W. Lytton, H. Markram, and M. L. Hines. Parallel network simulations with NEURON. *Journal of Computational Neuroscience*, 21(2):119–129, 2006.

[36] D. Nicol. The Cost of Conservative Synchronization in Parallel Discrete Event Simulations. *J. ACM*, 40(2):304–333, Apr. 1993.

[37] D. Nicol and P. Heidelberger. Parallel Execution for Serial Simulators. *ACM Trans. Modeling and Comput. Simulation*, 6(3):210–242, July 1996.

[38] E. Painkras, L. A. Plana, et al. SpiNNaker : A 1-W 18-Core System-on-Chip for Massively-Parallel Neural Network Simulation. *IEEE Journal of Solid-State Circuits*, 48(8):1943–1953, 2013.

[39] R. Preissl, T. M. Wong, P. Datta, M. Flickner, R. Singh, S. K. Esser, W. P. Risk, H. D. Simon, and D. S. Modha. Compass: A scalable simulator for an architecture for cognitive computing. In *ACM SC '12*, pages 1–11, Nov 2012.

[40] J. Schmidhuber. Deep Learning in Neural Networks: An Overview. *arXiv preprint arXiv: . . .*, abs/1404.7:66, 2014.

[41] F. Schürmann, F. Delalondre, et al. Rebasing i/o for scientific computing: Leveraging storage class memory in an ibm bluegene/q supercomputer. In *ICS 15' Conference Proceedings*, ISC 2014, pages 331–347, New York, NY, USA, 2014. Springer-Verlag New York, Inc.

[42] J. Slotnick, A. Khodadoust, J. Alonso, D. Darmofal, W. Gropp, E. Lurie, and D. Mavriplis. Cfd vision 2030 study: A path to revolutionary computational aerosciences. Technical Report NASA/CR-2014-21878, NASA, March 2014.

[43] R. Stein, A. S. French, and A. Holden. The frequency response, coherence, and information capacity of two neuronal models. *Biophysical journal*, 12(3):295–322, 1972.

Using DEv-PROMELA for Modelling and Verification of Software [*]

Aznam YACOUB
Aix-Marseille Université,
CNRS, ENSAM, Université de
Toulon, LSIS UMR 7296
13397, Marseille, France
aznam.yacoub@lsis.org

Maamar HAMRI
Aix-Marseille Université,
CNRS, ENSAM, Université de
Toulon, LSIS UMR 7296
13397, Marseille, France
amine.hamri@lsis.org

Claudia FRYDMAN
Aix-Marseille Université,
CNRS, ENSAM, Université de
Toulon, LSIS UMR 7296
13397, Marseille, France
claudia.frydman@lsis.org

ABSTRACT

Efficient modelling and verification of models need an accurate representation of systems. Especially, PROMELA cannot represent time as quantitative properties. That means some properties depending on time cannot be checked with SPIN model-checker. Discrete-Time approaches and dense representation of time were successfully introduced in SPIN as extensions but suffer of the expected statespace explosion problem. Another approach using discrete-event representation of time and simulation has been proposed to minimize this statespace explosion problem. In this paper, we show how this extension, DEv-PROMELA, can be used in order to model and verify software designs by combining simulation and formal verification.

CCS Concepts

•**Software and its engineering** → **Software verification and validation;** •**Computing methodologies** → *Model verification and validation;*

Keywords

Simulation; Formal Verification; Formal Methods; Model Checking; PROMELA; SPIN; Discrete-Event System; DEv-PROMELA

1. INTRODUCTION

Model-Checkers, and more generally formal verification tools, represent promising verification methods of models. Because they are able to potentially explore all the statespace, these methods appear as exhaustive and efficient methods. Accurate representation of temporal properties is another main key of the efficiency of these methods. However, time representation as quantitative properties leads, in the most of cases, to an explosion of the statespace, although many effort have been putting into the development of powerful algorithms and symbolic verification methods adapted to the verification of complex and big systems [7]. Consequently, formal verification tools must impose some restrictions about the model, and prefer a qualitative representation of timed properties. In this way, implicit-time representations seem to be a good compromise between accuracy and efficiency. This statement is well represented through Simple Promela INterpreter (SPIN) [12, 13] and its PRotocol MEta LAnguage (PROMELA). This well-known and wide-used model-checker, initially designed for the verification of asynchronous protocols, implements the main best algorithms of statespace reduction, but does not allow an explicit representation of the time. As a consequent, protocols which involved discrete-event properties cannot be neither represented or verified with accuracy. Discrete-Time and Dense-Time extensions [20, 5, 16] were introduced to allow the representation of timed systems. However, they suffer from a leak of precision and don't allow a precise representation of discrete-event systems.

In the area of Markovian systems, many works were done about Stochastic Model Checking. Probabilistic Model Checking is efficient for the analysis of systems which exhibit stochastic behaviour, and which can be modelled by Markov Chains. For instance, PRISM Model Checker [10, 14] supports the verification of both Discrete-Time Markov Chains (DTMC) and Continous-Time Markov Chains (CTMC). DTMC express probabilistic choices, in the sense that the designer expresses the probability of performing an action. In these models, time is modelled as discrete steps. CTMC model probabilistic choice and the continuous time, in the sense that designer can models the rate of performing a transition from one state to another. Then, stochastic model checking achieves the reachability analysis like traditional model checking, and computes likelihood of the occurrence of certain events during the execution of a system. But as stated in [18], *"this approach suffers the well known statespace explosion problem, i.e. it does not scale well when the system complexity grows"*. That is why Statistical Model Checking (SMC) [15] has been studied. Indeed, SMC uses discrete-event simulations in order to approximate the behaviour of a probabilistic system, and use hypothesis testing to infer whether the samples provide a statistical evidence for the satisfaction or violation of the specification. However, the main drawback is that SMC does not provide exact results.

---

[*]This work is part of the R&D project "MAGE", from French "Investing for the Future" national program.

Permission to make digital or hard copies of all or part of this work for personal or classroom use is granted without fee provided that copies are not made or distributed for profit or commercial advantage and that copies bear this notice and the full citation on the first page. Copyrights for components of this work owned by others than ACM must be honored. Abstracting with credit is permitted. To copy otherwise, or republish, to post on servers or to redistribute to lists, requires prior specific permission and/or a fee. Request permissions from permissions@acm.org.

SIGSIM-PADS '16, May 15-18, 2016, Banff, AB, Canada
© 2016 ACM. ISBN 978-1-4503-3742-7/16/05...$15.00
DOI: http://dx.doi.org/10.1145/2901378.2901388

As a transposition of this approach to non-probabilistic models, we proposed a new extension called Discrete-Event PROMELA (DEv-PROMELA) [22] which allows an accurate representation and verification of discrete-event systems. For that, DEv-PROMELA extends the syntax of PROMELA by allowing the modelling of the main concepts of discrete-event systems. Next, verification and validation of DEv-PROMELA models are based on a key notion which represents a promising fashion for the accurate verification of complex models: the combined use of formal verification and discrete-event simulation [21, 23]. Indeed, DEv-PROMELA is built so that a PROMELA equivalent model can be generated for the formal checking of non-timed and structural properties, whereas a Discrete-Event simulable model can be generated for the verification of timed and behavioural properties by simulation. As a result, time as a quantitative property can be taken into account in software designs, and the use of simulation earlier in the development process makes easier the discover of errors in specifications.

This paper is built as follow: section 2 and section 3 briefly introduce PROMELA and its timed extensions. Section 4 makes recall about DEv-PROMELA. Section 5 finally shows how DEv-PROMELA can be used to design and verify software through an exemple of video game.

2. OVERVIEW OF PROMELA

2.1 Concepts

PROMELA is specification language with an operational semantics and initially designed for the modelling and verification of concurrent protocols, involving synchronous or asynchronous communication between processes. Based on Djikstra's Guarded Command Language, its syntax is close to any imperative language, making their use very easy, compared with others formal methods. Because the language is very complete, we will focus there only on interesting concepts for the scope of this paper.

A PROMELA specification is thus a set of two separate parts: the system specification, on the one hand, which describes the behaviour of the model, and on the other hand, the properties to verify on the model.

2.1.1 System Specifications

A PROMELA system is a *finite* set of components: *instances* of *processes*. These ones can communicate each others thanks to different mechanisms as *buffered messages*, *shared global variables* or *rendez-vous handshakes*. Each instance of each process is modelled by a *finite* set of guarded or labeled command called *statements*. A statement is said non-blocked if the state of the system allows its execution, otherwise it is said blocked. Then, one execution of the specifications, at any time t_i, corresponds to the execution of one among all of non-blocked statements, without any assumption about duration of the statement execution.

Instructions are divided into two categories: statements that modify the system state and control-flow instructions. Statements relative to state changes are assignments and *message* exchange instructions. *Assignment* statements involve local and global variables, whereas communication statements involve buffered channels. It is important to note that, if assignements are always considered as *enabled* statements (i.e. they can be always executed), the instructions relative to channels can be *blocked* if the associated buffered

Program 1 A simple example of PROMELA program.

```
1: int z = 1;
2:
3: active proctype A {
4:     int x = 2, y = 2;
5:     if
6:     :: ( x == 2 ) → x = 3;
7:     :: ( y == 2 ) → y = 4;
8:     fi;
9: }
10:
11: active proctype B {
12:     int x = 2, y;
13:     do
14:     :: ( y == 2 ) → x = 2;
15:     :: ( x == 2 ) → y = 4;
16:     od;
17: }
18:
19: ltl {[](z == 1); }
```

channel is empty or full. *Control-flow* statements are classical conditionnal and loop instructions. These ones allow selection of the next statement among different branches regarding a guard. Because PROMELA processes are *non-deterministic*, if several guards are satisfied, a random one is selected. If none of them is satsfied, the control-flow structure is blocked. PROMELA also provides a *timeout* instruction (usable as a guard) which is enabled if all instructions are blocked in the whole system.

Datas in PROMELA are represented by local and shared variables. Local variables are those which are relative to only the process which they belong to, whereas global variables are shared by all processes. A variable is characterized by its value and its type, or any finite combination (structures) or finite arrays of these types. Each PROMELA type represent a finite set of values.

The immediate result is a PROMELA model can be represented by an underlying finite automaton.

2.1.2 Properties Specifications

SPIN supports the verification of Linear Temporal Logic (LTL) properties on the PROMELA models. LTL properties are converted into a *never-claim* process (comparable to any *normal* processes) which don't "participate" to the behaviour of the system. The goal of a never-claim process is only to guarantee the system satisfies the property which is encoded in it. In this sense, a never-claim process acts as a *monitor*. The study of LTL encoding is out-of-scope of this paper. Thus, we recommend the SPIN Reference Manual [11] to the interested readers for further informations.

Then, the formal verification of PROMELA specifications intuitively corresponds to the checking of all executable paths against a given property, without any assumptions of duration. It results that the next state of a PROMELA model does not depend on the time elapsed in a previous state. Because it is not possible to model this elapsed time, timed extensions were developed.

3. TIMED EXTENSIONS OF PROMELA

PROMELA does not allow the modelling of either real-time or timed processes with accuracy. However, correctness of a timed system strongly relies on the temporal coordination of its components. Being able to explicit time delays and time relations between components thus appears as needed to better model such a system, even the motivation of PROMELA is exactly the abstraction of time [11]. Three main extensions of PROMELA were thus developed in the litterature, permitting the explicitness of time as quantitative in PROMELA models. This section introduces these extensions. The algorithms for the verification of the resulting models are nevertheless not be treated in this paper.

3.1 Real-Time PROMELA

Real-Time PROMELA (RT-PROMELA) [20] was the first extension introduced to model real-time systems in PROMELA. The motivation was to introduce "*quantitative aspect of time*" into formal specifications, while "traditional formalisms dealt only with *qualitative aspect* of time, that is, the order of certain system events". Even this statement is not fully true from the point of view of discrete-event modelling as we will see in the next section, *quantitative* aspect of time is effectively important as said previously.

RT-PROMELA considers time as *dense*. Like Timed Automata (TA) [2], RT-PROMELA is not interested in the real order of events, but considers that a finite number of successive events can occur between two defined moments. More precisely, this means RT-PROMELA is only interested in intervals of time in which events can occur, not in the date and the full order of the events. Taking into account the semantics of PROMELA, RT-PROMELA introduces two new concepts: *clock* and *timed statements*.

As in TA theory, a clock measures the time which linearly elapses. By this, many clocks can be used and be compared in guards of timed statements. These latter are those which depends on time. Because statements represent transitions between states, a timed statement is thus an action which is fired when a certain quantity of time was elapsed. This can be interpreted as two manner:

1. either a system must stay in a state during at least or at most d units of time;

2. or an action is fired before of after d units of time;

If this is enough to explain relations between set of actions, RT-PROMELA does not explicitly enforce an order between *events*. Because the operator $==$ is defined, date of events can be precisely defined (on $\mathbb{N}$) with conjunction of process priority, but defining a precise order between events needs much effort, as presented in section 4.2.

3.2 Discrete-Time PROMELA

Discrete-Time PROMELA (DT-PROMELA) [5, 6] also relies on the notion of time bounds. Time is sliced into intervals of fixed size indexed by natural numbers (called *ticks*), and events are framed into each slices. By this way, events belonged to two different frames can be ordered with a good quantitative approximation of the time that elapses between them. But inside a same frame, events have only a qualitative relation (Figure 1). Like RT-PROMELA, DT-PROME
LA introduces *timers* which define the value of the current tick. In this sense, while RT-PROMELA uses a dense-time representation with a linear progression, DT-PROMELA assumes a discrete-time representation.

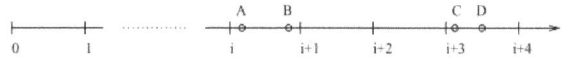

Figure 1: Time representation in DT-PROMELA [6].

Formally, a DT-PROMELA program is a PROMELA one, for which each action is guarded by an integer value that represents the time. This value is decreased (or increased) by a monitoring process, enabling then transitions which depend on it.

3.3 Timed PROMELA

A third extension called Timed PROMELA (T-PROMELA) [16] also relies on time bounds. Similary to RT-PROMELA, each statement is bounded by an upper or a lower value, but with the difference that T-PROMELA statements do not depend on clocks. An instruction can be simply delayed or executed at exactly after d units of time. By this way, a T-PROMELA can be seen as a RT-PROMELA with one clock. It results that the semantics of a T-PROMELA is likely the same than the semantics of TA (and that is why verification of T-PROMELA models is done through TA equivalents).

3.4 Extensions of PROMELA for Hybrid Systems

Finally, we shortly discuss about extensions of PROMELA for hybrid systems. "*A hybrid system is a system that evolves following a continuous dynamic, which may instantaneously change when certain internal or external events occur*" [8]. Hybrid automata [9] have been developed in order to model hybrid systems and some verification techniques have been studied for particular classes of hybrid systems. Mainly, Alur et al. [1] show that the reachability problem is undecidable for hybrid automata and propose techniques for verifying safety properties of piecewise-linear hybrid automata.

Bosnacki [4] propose an extension of PROMELA called HyPROMELA for modelling and verification of discrete-time rectangular automata. A discrete-time rectangular automaton is a rectangular automaton in which *implicit time transitions that represent the time flow and the evolution of the variables* is performed with a fixed duration of one time unit. In this way, an underlying discrete-time automaton of the rectangular automaton can be obtained and used for verifying properties.

In [8], the authors propose an non-intrusive methodology to extend SPIN and PROMELA for the verification and the analysis of some decidable classes of hybrid automata like linear hybrid automata, whose continuous variables evolve following constant differential equations, and rectangular hybrid automata. The verification is achieved by making a convex polyhedra abstraction of continuous behaviour of the system, as in Hybrid-PROMELA [19]. However, the proposed methodologies always face to the state space explosion due to the continuous components.

4. DISCRETE-EVENT PROMELA

4.1 Introduction to DEv-PROMELA

Even if timed extensions of PROMELA allow modelling of time, these formalisms suffer from two main problems:

they generate an explosion of the statespace and they imply restrictive constraints on time. For exemple, relations between clocks in RT-PROMELA are inevitably linear.

To overcome these constraints, we developed a new extension based on discrete-event simulation. DEv-PROMELA [22] is based on three key concepts:

1. Permitting the modelling of Discrete-Event Systems (DES) by keeping as much as possible the syntax and the structure of PROMELA. Thus, that allows modelling of any types of systems which can be modelled with PROMELA;

2. Verification of structural and non-timed properties on DEv-PROMELA models must be based on verification on PROMELA models;

3. DEv-PROMELA models must be simulable by any discrete-event simulation methods.

Some syntaxic elements were introduced in order to allow the modelling of DES concepts.

Firstly, a new data type called **real** was added. The purpose of **real** variables is to represent *infinite* and *unbounded* real values. Real variables can be local or global, and their declaration do not differ from any scalar variables:

```
real i,j,k;
```

Real variables can be combined in complex structures or used in arrays, without restriction. Real variables are mainly used in order to model the lifespan of instructions.

An implicit local clock is then associated to each process, whose the value can be accessed through the instruction **getCurrentDate**. In this way, like in Timed PROMELA, it is not necessary to introduce a specific type for clocks (because we ensure that each process has a clock). But, at the difference of others extensions, clocks can be used to define exactly the date of next events. In fact, the purpose of clocks is only to determine the next event by taking the minimum value of the dates of all next events.

Finally, we introduce the missing concepts of events, state lifespan and type of transitions. Each statement is expanded with a descriptor that describes the amount of time before its execution, and the type of event emitted when the statement is executed. This is done by following the grammar described in Backus-Naur Form, below:

```
<proctype_decl> ::= "[" priority "=" <int> "]"
                                      <proctype>
<event_stmnt> ::= "[" <timed_trans> "]" <stmnt>
                                      | <stmnt>
<timed_trans> ::= <clt_expr> | <evt_expr> |
                      <clt_expr> "|" <evt_expr>
<clt_expr> ::= "clt:" <real_expr> "->emit:"
                                      <evt_val>
<evt_expr> ::= "evt:" <evt_val> [ <op> <evt_expr> ]
<op> ::= "|"
<evt_val> ::= <mtype> | "silent"
<real_expr> ::= <real> | "infty" |
        /* Any C-function returning a real value */
```

For exemple, take a look at Program 2. The meaning of this model is that the condition in line 5 is checked *t1* unit of time after the execution of the last intruction. Before checking the condition, the **changex** event is emitted.

Program 2 Simple condition structure in DEv-PROMELA.

```
1: int x, y = 2;
2: real t1, t2;
3:
4: if
5: :: [clt : t1 → emit : changex] ( x == 2 ) → x = 3;
6: :: [clt : t2 → emit : changey] ( y == 2 ) → y = 4;
7: fi;
```

One of the advantage of a DEv-PROMELA model is that it is deterministic. It enforces modeller to specify more precisely the modelled system, which is crucial in software development. Indeed, as stated in [17], *"Application developers rely heavily on the fact that given the same input, a program will produce the same output."* The authors also states that *"such non-determinism is almost never required in the program's specification and comes directly as a consequence of parallelizing the program for improved performance on today's machines."* In another article, Bocchino et al. [3] argue that *"enforcing deterministic semantics simplifies composing, porting, reasoning about, debugging, and testing parallel software".*

We agree that non-determinism appears as an important feature in many formalisms, because it allows designers to think only about the system's behavior independently how the non-determinism is resolved, but this also leads unnecessarily to make heavier the verification. Indeed, non-determinism leads to verify paths which may have no sense and will never been executed in the real environment. Thus, enforcing determinism has two benefits: first, it enforces designers to fully define the behaviour of the system, and it mitigates the verification processes, by verifying only paths which have a sense.

In this sense, DEv-PROMELA ensures that the model will have the same behaviour for given inputs. Thus, it simplifies the reasoning about systems, makes easier the verification of timed properties, and increases the chance that the model meets the requirements. For properties in which time is less crucial or for non-timed properties, DEv-PROMELA capitalizes on the non-determinism feature of PROMELA.

4.2 Comparison between DEv-PROMELA and the Others Extensions

The advantages of DEv-PROMELA can be seen through a comparison with the others timed extensions.

Firstly, comparison between DEv-PROMELA and DT-PRO-MELA is easy. While in DEv-PROMELA time evolves along to events, DT-PROMELA provides a discrete representation of time, in which timed is "simulated" by increasing a tick. As a consequent, events cannot be fully ordered and systems modelled with DT-PROMELA are not event-based.

Timed PROMELA is based on the TA theory, with a dense-time representation. As we said previously, T-PROMELA is equivalent to RT-PROMELA, and suffers the same weakness as this latter.

Although RT-PROMELA provides a time support based on the same theory as TA, its semantics is very close to the DEv-PROMELA's one. The main problem is that clocks linearly evolve like in TA and can be compared only with integer values, restricting their possible valuation. Consequently, RT-PROMELA could generate also invalid paths in the sense of discrete-event systems (a non-deterministic

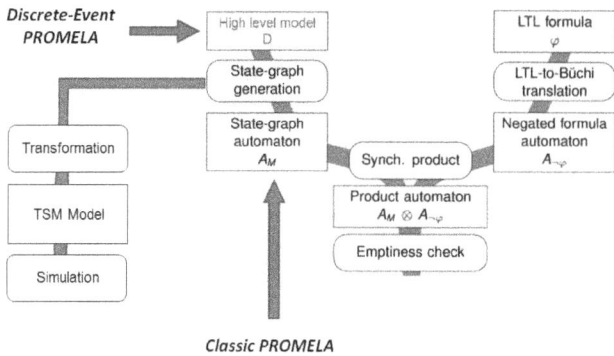

Figure 2: Combined V&V process of DE-PRO-MELA.

behaviour). Moreover, the operators $<=$ and $>=$ give a precision only about the time bounds. In opposite, DEv-PROMELA is not interested in bounds the clock valuation, and time can evolve following any polynomial or non-polynomial function (because the date of the next event is determined according to the lifetime function ta). Furthermore, the semantics of DEv-PROMELA is clear: a model will have the same behaviour for a given specific instance. This does not prevent that DES can be modelled with much effort with RT-PROMELA. If all clock constraints are encoded with the operator $==$, lifespan can be encoded in the same manner as in DEv-PROMELA (because the semantics of clock valuation is given by $s = (q, v)$ with v, the values of all clocks for the state q). Events are then encoded using channels, and priority using PROMELA priority concept, to resolve the problem of non-determinism. Obviously, RT-PROMELA cannot fully resolve the problem of linear evolution of the time, and ready will agree that the resulting specifications will be less clear.

5. APPLICATION

As seen in previous section, the verification of PROMELA model consists on checking all the executable paths without any assumption about time, because PROMELA model systems whose the state does not depend on the time elapsed in a previous state. This means, a PROMELA model is useful to check deadlock properties induced by the structure or to detect unreacheable states. But a PROMELA model suffers from the missing of computational aspects. On the other hand, a simulation model can be simulated to check the correctness of behavioural properties, but can't be formally verified.

One important thing in DEv-PROMELA is that it can be used to generate a PROMELA verification model and a DEVS simulation model, as shown in Figure 2. This property is really important because it implies that it is possible to combine verification and simulation from a unique model. It also allows designing software with a new approach: the specifications or a conceptual model can be translated into a DEv-PROMELA model which is checked, using formal verification, against structural and time-independent properties. Discrete-Event simulation is then used in order to predict the behaviour of the final software, and in order to validate the specifications.

We can illustrate this approach through the design of a video game.

5.1 Introduction to the Approach

Video games are software in which time is implicitly important. Indeed, video games specifications generally include continuous domains for data definitions, like velocity and acceleration which depend on time. However, as a game is a piece of software, it is by nature a finite automaton. Thus, the behaviour of the game is in fact discretized. For instance, the move of a character is seen as a finite suite of positions, in which each position corresponds to a snapshot of the game at a given time t_n. Moreover, the delay between two snapshots can change over the time. As a result, designers have to use methods of interpolation to approximate the values of datas from a snapshot to another. If we consider that a snapshot is done when an instruction is performed by the game, the immediate result is that the next state of the game depends on the time elapsed in the current state.

To illustrate that, we take the well-known Pacman as exemple. The specifications of Pacman are really simple: the game consists on moving a character that eats balls and avoids ghosts. Ghosts are controlled by the computer while Pacman is controlled by a player. If a ghost meets the Pacman, the game is over.

Figure 3: Example of Pacman.

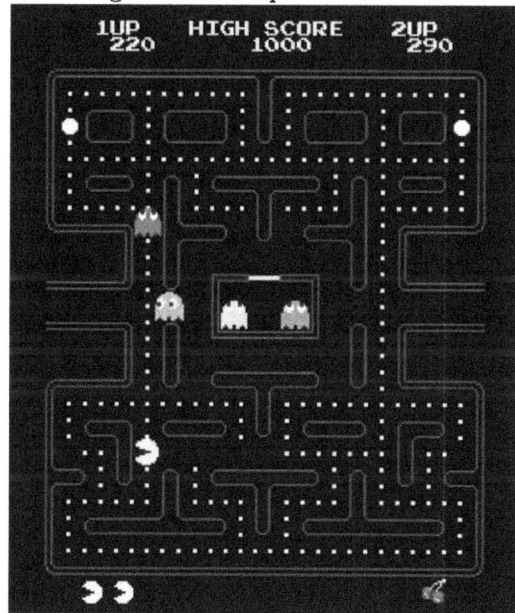

Behind these specifications, the notion of time and events are implicit: indeed, it is obvious that the position of the pacman at any time t depends on its speed. By extension, the speed depends on the time elapsed between two steps of graphical computations. Moreover, the pacman needs to respond to events generated by the player, and ghosts must respond to events generated by the system. Pacman and Ghosts can also be seen as asynchronous processes, and the game as an asynchronous protocol between pacman and ghosts.

Traditionnaly, developers model games using an object-oriented approach, and use model-checking to ensure correctness of some properties. Then, the game is validated by testing. But, we propose to model this game using DEv-PROMELA. Indeed, according to the previous reasonning, Pacman is a DEVS system and a protocol. We make a high level conceptual model of the game, by only translating the specifications. The model is then simulated and verified.

5.2 Modelling the Pacman

Algorithm 3 DEv-PROMELA model of Pacman Process.

```
 1: real pacman_x, pacman_y, opacman_x, opacman_y;
 2: bool end_game = false;
 3:
 4: [ priority = 1 ]
 5: active proctype PACMAN()
 6: {
 7:        real t = 1;
 8:        do
 9:        :: [clt:0.1→emit:silent] end_game == false →
10:                if
11:                :: [evt:PAC_LEFT] t = getElapsedTime;
12:                        if
13:                        :: atomic { (end_game == false
    && pacman_x < 5 && pacman_x > 0) →
14:                                opacman_x = pacman_x;
15:                                opacman_y = pacman_y;
16:                                pacman_x = pacman_x - t*1
17:                                }
18:                        :: else → skip;
19:                        fi;
20:                :: [evt:PAC_RIGHT] t = getElapsedTime;
21:                        if
22:                        :: atomic { (end_game == false
    && pacman_x < 5 && pacman_x > 0) →
23:                                opacman_x = pacman_x;
24:                                opacman_y = pacman_y;
25:                                pacman_x = pacman_x + t*1
26:                                }
27:                        :: else → skip;
28:                        fi;
29:                        // Stuff and other code ;
30:                fi;
31:                if
32:                :: atomic { (pacman_x == ghost_x) &&
    (pacman_y == ghost_y) →
33:                        end_game = true
34:                        };
35:                :: else → skip;
36:                fi;
37:        :: end_game == true → break;
38:        od;
39: }
```

Algoritm 3 shows the DEv-PROMELA model of the Pacman. Pacman is seen as a process. Each 0.1 unit of time (line 9), this process checks if the game is finished. If it is not the case, it waits an event from the player (the all PAC_* event), and updates its position according to the time elpased between the first check and the occurence of the given event. If the pacman and the ghost are in the same position, the game is over. Furthermore, the discrete-event nature of the game can be seen through two elements. Firstly, we can consider that each instruction is performed after a delay, which corresponds to the time needed by the processor

before performing the next instruction. In other words, this is the time before that the video game changes its state to another state by performing the next instruction. Thus, this delay corresponds to the lifespan of the current state. This is modelled by the constant 0.1 (line 9) for instance. The designer can change this constant by any value, or any variable or any function which can be evaluated as a real. When the lifespan of its current state expires, a process can emit an event to the others processes in order to notify them its change. This is done through the emit instruction.

Secondly, if a process can emit an event, it can also consume it. Thus, a process must react to an event which comes from another process or from the outside, for instance when the player press a button of its controller. An exemple of this type of external event is given in line 11. The assignment is done only if the event PAC_LEFT is received. Furthermore, DEv-PROMELA allows to combine a clt clause and with an evt clause. In this case, if the external event is received before the end of the delay, the internal transition is pre-empted by the external transition. DEv-PROMELA also allows mixing clauses in the selection constructs.

5.3 Modelling the Ghost

Ghost is just the symetrical of Pacman as shown in Algoritm 4. Each 0.1 unit of time (line 9), this process checks if the game is finished. If it is not the case, it waits an event from the computer (all the GHS_* events), and updates its position according to the time elpased between the first check and the occurence of the event. If the pacman and the ghost are in the same position, the game is over.

5.4 Methodology of Verification

Designers may want to verify some safety and liveness properties. For instance, one would like to check that:

1. Eventually the game finishes ?

2. Is it well impossible that the pacman leaves out the limit of the board ?

3. Is it well impossible that the pacman and the ghost intersect without the game ends ?

4. Can the life of the player be a negative number ?

5. Can any process always progress ?

6. Is there any unreachable state ?

7. Can the score be a negative number ?

Formal verification and simulation are used in this order. Formal verification can be used alone in two situations:

- when the property to check is a time-independant property. Indeed, this type of property can be true or false whatever the timed behaviour of the model;

- when the formal verification returns that a property is not verified. In this case, it is clear that the timed behaviour will not meet the requirement.

When formal verification returns that the checked property is verified by the model, then the simulation is performed to check timed behaviours against the same property. The main advantage is simulation is that we can inject some external events into the system (the PAC_* and GHS_*

Algorithm 4 DEv-PROMELA model of Ghost Process.

```
 1: real ghost_x, ghost_y, oghost_x, oghost_y;
 2:
 3: [ priority = 2 ]
 4: active proctype GHOST()
 5: {
 6:        real t = 1;
 7:        do
 8:        :: [clt:0.1→emit:silent] end_game == false →
 9:            if
10:                :: [evt:GHS_LEFT] t = getElapsedTime;
11:                    if
12:                        :: atomic { (end_game == false
   && ghost_x < 5 && ghost_x > 0) →
13:                                oghost_x = ghost_x;
14:                                oghost_y = ghost_y;
15:                                ghost_x = ghost_x - t*1
16:                            }
17:                        :: else → skip;
18:                    fi;
19:                :: [evt:GHS_RIGHT] t = getElapsedTime;
20:                    if
21:                        :: atomic { (end_game == false
   && ghost_x < 5 && ghost_x > 0) →
22:                                oghost_x = ghost_x;
23:                                oghost_y = ghost_y;
24:                                ghost_x = ghost_x + t*1
25:                            }
26:                        :: else → skip;
27:                    fi;
28:                    // Stuff and other code ;
29:            fi;
30:            if
31:                :: atomic { (pacman_x == ghost_x) &&
   (pacman_y == ghost_y) →
32:                        end_game = true
33:                    };
34:                :: else → skip;
35:            fi;
36:        :: end_game == true → break;
37:        od;
38: }
```

Table 1: Comparison between Results of Verification using Model Checking and Simulation.

	Formal Verification	Simulation
Property 1	At least one path	At least one scenario
Property 2	Impossible	Possible
Property 3	Impossible	Possible
Property 4	Always positive	Positive
Property 5	Always progress	Not in all cases
Property 6	No unreachable state	Unreachable states can exist
Property 7	Always positive	Positive

events). Because events are well-dated, simulation gives a full control over the execution path.

Table 1 gives a comparison between the results of verification using Model Checking and Simulation.

For instance, properties 1, 4 and 7 are verified using only formal verification, because they concern time-independent properties. Indeed, these types of properties can be true or false whatever the timed behaviour of the model. For exemple, property 1 is only about to know if the game can be over, i.e. if it exists at least one execution path that leads to the end. Property 4 is about to know if one path leads to a state in which the life of the player is a negative number.

What about properties 2 and 3 ? They concerns time-dependant properties. Indeed, moves depend on time, because the speed is computed from the time elapsed between two states of the system: the state before receiving a move event, and after the event, as described above. If we check these properties with formal verification, it would be like this time is equal to 1 step (because t would be equal to 1), meaning they are time-independent. This would mean that the Pacman and the ghost would evolve in a grid, and could only move from a case to an adjacent one, because the speed is one per unit of time according to l.25. And, obviously, if it is the case, these property are verified, and it is the result returned by the model checker. But the discrete-event simulation gives another interpretation. In the sense of the specifications, the timed behaviour represents the interpolation of the positions. In this model, Pacman and Ghost evolves in a continuous space as expected in the specifications. In this case, the moves depend on time as shown in l.25. Then, for exemple if the PAC_* event occurs with a delay of 0.1 unit of time, and the GHS_* event occurs with a delay of 0.2 unit of time, then the Pacman and the Ghost can cross themselves without the game is over, because line 31 are never true.

Readers can then ask how verification is done. In fact, GHS_* or PAC_* are external events. In other words, these inputs are injected into the simulation model at given dates. The distribution of these events can be randomly generated, but the semantics of DEv-PROMELA ensures that the behaviour of the model will be the same for a given set of input. Then, to check the behaviour, multiple simulations are performed with different scenarios identified as extreme situations by the designers. And this is one of the limitations of a simulation-based verification approach: the results of the verification depend on the experimental frame.

Concerning properties 5 and 6, the deadlock detected in simulation is caused by the absence of GHS_* or PAC_* events in certains played scenarii.

Because the model is done before the implementation, it allows designer to see that the specifications are incomplete. In this case, simulation helps designer to fix these errors. But note that if DEv-PROMELA makes easier the use of simulation earlier in the development process, it does not replace the validation phase.

5.5 Comparison with Others Timed Extensions

A legitime question is: could we model the Pacman game with others timed extensions of PROMELA ?

If RT-PROMELA provides mechanics to define timed constraints on statement, it does not provide any mechanisms to explicit states which depends on the past. Indeed, RT-PROMELA allows modelling of delays, in the sense that the next state will be chosen according to the time elapsed in the current state and a set of possible next states. In this interpretation, if the Pacman specifications used a grid for describing moves, the RT-PROMELA would be useful in order to explicit the fact that the entities would be sitting longer in a cell. In other words, the interpolation cannot be fully modelled with this extension. This statement is the same for DT-PROMELA and Timed PROMELA. Moreover, combining simulation with formal method in this manner limits the statespace explosion problem encoutered by timed verifiable models.

6. CONCLUSION AND FUTURE WORKS

We saw in this paper how to use the benefits of DEv-PRO-MELA to model and verify software models. DEv-PRO-MELA has the advantage to encompase formal verification and discrete event simulation through a mecanism based on morphisms of models. Comparing to other timed extensions, DEv-PROMELA has a stronger expressiveness, allowing accurate modelling of DES. Thanks to its structural preservation property, time-independent properties can always be checked with PROMELA and SPIN model-checker. Concerning the time-dependent properties, their verification and validation is done through discrete-event simulation. This simulation-based verification allows avoidance of checking of senseless executions. Because DEv-PROMELA is deterministic, the model is closer to the real system (because DEv-PROMELA enforces to fully define its behaviour). All these assets makes the using of DEv-PROMELA possible earlier in the development. Using this specification language, designers can check specifications before their real implementation. One of the outcomes mainly concerns the generation of scenarii for the simulation. The chosen scenarii, in other words the distribution of the incoming events, greatly impact the quality of the verification. Guidelines or methodology for helping designers to choose scenarii should be defined.

As future works, we can imagine that a fully workable code can be generated from the DEv-PROMELA model. This would help reducing the errors between the conceptual model and the real software. Indeed, because DEv-PRO-MELA is a syntactic language, automatic translation rules can be defined. And if an object-oriented architecture is defined, we can also imagine that a modular code can be generated to allow software working in two mode: in a simulation mode in which time follows a logical clock, and in a real execution mode corresponding to the final release of the application.

7. REFERENCES

[1] R. Alur, C. Courcoubetis, T. A. Henzinger, and P. H. Ho. *Hybrid Systems*, chapter Hybrid automata: An algorithmic approach to the specification and verification of hybrid systems, pages 209–229. Springer Berlin Heidelberg, Berlin, Heidelberg, 1993.

[2] R. Alur and D. L. Dill. A theory of timed automata. *Theoretical Computer Science*, 126:183–235, 1994.

[3] R. L. Bocchino, Jr., V. S. Adve, S. V. Adve, and M. Snir. Parallel programming must be deterministic by default. In *Proceedings of the First USENIX Conference on Hot Topics in Parallelism*, HotPar'09, pages 4–4, Berkeley, CA, USA, 2009. USENIX Association.

[4] D. Bosnacki. Toward modeling of hybrid systems in promela and spin. In *Proceedings of the 3rd International Workshop on Formal Methods for Industrial Critical Systems FMICS'98*, pages 75–96, 1998.

[5] D. Bosnacki and D. Dams. Discrete-time promela and spin. In A. Ravn and H. Rischel, editors, *Formal Techniques in Real-Time and Fault-Tolerant Systems*, volume 1486 of *Lecture Notes in Computer Science*, pages 307–310. Springer Berlin Heidelberg, 1998.

[6] D. Bosnacki and D. Dams. Integrating real time into spin: A prototype implementation. In S. Budkowski, A. Cavalli, and E. Najm, editors, *Formal Description Techniques and Protocol Specification, Testing and Verification*, volume 6 of *The International Federation for Information Processing*, pages 423–438. Springer US, 1998.

[7] E. Clarke. The birth of model checking. In O. Grumberg and H. Veith, editors, *25 Years of Model Checking*, volume 5000 of *Lecture Notes in Computer Science*, pages 1–26. Springer Berlin Heidelberg, 2008.

[8] M. d. M. Gallardo and L. Panizo. Extending model checkers for hybrid system verification: the case study of spin. *Software Testing, Verification and Reliability*, 24(6):438–471, 2014.

[9] T. A. Henzinger. The theory of hybrid automata. In *Logic in Computer Science, 1996. LICS '96. Proceedings., Eleventh Annual IEEE Symposium on*, pages 278–292, Jul 1996.

[10] A. Hinton, M. Kwiatkowska, G. Norman, and D. Parker. *Tools and Algorithms for the Construction and Analysis of Systems: 12th International Conference, TACAS 2006, Held as Part of the Joint European Conferences on Theory and Practice of Software, ETAPS 2006, Vienna, Austria, March 25 - April 2, 2006. Proceedings*, chapter PRISM: A Tool for Automatic Verification of Probabilistic Systems, pages 441–444. Springer Berlin Heidelberg, Berlin, Heidelberg, 2006.

[11] G. Holzmann. *Spin Model Checker, the: Primer and Reference Manual*. Addison-Wesley Professional, first edition, 2003.

[12] G. J. Holzmann. *Design and Validation of Computer Protocols*. Prentice-Hall, Inc., Upper Saddle River, NJ, USA, 1991.

[13] G. J. Holzmann. The model checker spin. *IEEE Trans. Softw. Eng.*, 23(5):279–295, May 1997.

[14] M. Kwiatkowska, G. Norman, and D. Parker. *Formal*

Methods for Performance Evaluation: 7th International School on Formal Methods for the Design of Computer, Communication, and Software Systems, SFM 2007, Bertinoro, Italy, May 28-June 2, 2007, Advanced Lectures, chapter Stochastic Model Checking, pages 220–270. Springer Berlin Heidelberg, Berlin, Heidelberg, 2007.

[15] A. Legay, B. Delahaye, and S. Bensalem. *Runtime Verification: First International Conference, RV 2010, St. Julians, Malta, November 1-4, 2010. Proceedings*, chapter Statistical Model Checking: An Overview, pages 122–135. Springer Berlin Heidelberg, Berlin, Heidelberg, 2010.

[16] W. Nabialek, A. Janowska, and P. Janowski. Translation of timed promela to timed automata with discrete data. *Fundam. Inf.*, 85(1-4):409–424, Jan. 2008.

[17] M. Olszewski, J. Ansel, and S. Amarasinghe. Kendo: Efficient deterministic multithreading in software. *SIGPLAN Not.*, 44(3):97–108, Mar. 2009.

[18] S. Sebastio and A. Vandin. Multivesta: Statistical model checking for discrete event simulators. In *Proceedings of the 7th International Conference on Performance Evaluation Methodologies and Tools*, ValueTools '13, pages 310–315, ICST, Brussels, Belgium, Belgium, 2013. ICST (Institute for Computer Sciences, Social-Informatics and Telecommunications Engineering).

[19] H. Song, K. J. Compton, and W. C. Rounds. Sphin: A model checker for reconfigurable hybrid systems based on {SPIN}. *Electronic Notes in Theoretical Computer Science*, 145:167 – 183, 2006. Proceedings of the 5th International Workshop on Automated Verification of Critical Systems (AVoCS 2005)Automated Verification of Critical Systems 2005.

[20] S. Tripakis and C. Courcoubetis. Extending promela and spin for real time. In *Proceedings of the Second International Workshop on Tools and Algorithms for Construction and Analysis of Systems*, TACAs '96, pages 329–348, London, UK, UK, 1996. Springer-Verlag.

[21] A. Yacoub, M. Hamri, and C. Frydman. A method for improving the verification and validation of systems by the combined use of simulation and formal methods. In *IEEE/ACM 18th International Symposium on Distributed Simulation and Real Time Applications, DS-RT 2014*, pages 155–162, Oct 2014.

[22] A. Yacoub, M. Hamri, C. Frydman, C. Seo, and B. Zeigler. Towards an extension of promela for the modeling, simulation and verification of discrete-event systems. In *Proceedings of the 27th European Modelling and Simulation Symposium (EMSS 2015)*, pages 340–348, September 2015.

[23] B. P. Zeigler and J. J. Nutaro. Combining devs and model-checking: Using systems morphisms for integrating simulation and analysis in model engineering. In *Proceedings of the 26th European Modeling and Simulation Symposium*, pages 350–356, 2014.

Extended Driving Simulator for Evaluation of Cooperative Intelligent Transport Systems

Maytheewat Aramrattana[*],
Tony Larsson
Halmstad University
Box 823, SE-301 18 Halmstad, Sweden
{maytheewat.aramrattana,
tony.larsson}@hh.se

Jonas Jansson, Arne Nåbo
The Swedish National Road and Transport
Research Institute (VTI)
SE-581 95
Linköping, Sweden
{jonas.jansson, arne.nabo}@vti.se

ABSTRACT

Vehicles in cooperative intelligent transport systems (C-ITS) often need to interact with each other in order to achieve their goals, safe and efficient transport services. Since human drivers are still expected to be involved in C-ITS, driving simulators are appropriate tools for evaluation of the C-ITS functions. However, driving simulators often simplify the interactions or influences from the ego vehicle on the traffic. Moreover, they normally do not support vehicle-to-vehicle and vehicle-to-infrastructure (V2X) communication, which is the main enabler for C-ITS. Therefore, to increase the C-ITS evaluation capability, a solution on how to extend a driving simulator with traffic and network simulators to handle cooperative systems is presented as a result of this paper. Evaluation of the result using two use cases is presented. And, the observed limitations and challenges of the solution are reported and discussed.

Keywords

Driving simulator; C-ITS; Traffic simulator; Network simulator

1. INTRODUCTION

Driving simulators have been used to study a variety of topics. For example, the area of human factors, vehicle dynamics, highway design, etc. Driving simulators can be used to evaluate the effect of C-ITS on the human drivers. Since the studies in driving simulators are focused on the human driver, the surrounding traffic is often simplified in a way that the behaviour of the human driver has almost no influence on the traffic. This is not the case in C-ITS, where vehicles are supposed to have interaction with each others. On the other hand, traffic simulators have the capability to

---

[*]Maytheewat is also with The Swedish National Road and Transport Research Institute (VTI).

Publication rights licensed to ACM. ACM acknowledges that this contribution was authored or co-authored by an employee, contractor or affiliate of a national government. As such, the Government retains a nonexclusive, royalty-free right to publish or reproduce this article, or to allow others to do so, for Government purposes only.

SIGSIM-PADS '16, May 15 – 18, 2016, Banff, AB, Canada

© 2016 Copyright held by the owner/author(s). Publication rights licensed to ACM.

ACM ISBN 978-1-4503-3742-7/16/05. . . $15.00

DOI: http://dx.doi.org/10.1145/2901378.2901397

model this type of influence between behaviours of vehicles with car-following models. A problem with traffic simulators is that the car-following models usually assume vehicles to follow most of safety criteria and traffic rules. Behaviours such as overtaking on two-lane rural roads or sudden lane changes are often not modelled in traffic simulators. Therefore, combining driving and traffic simulation environments together could produce more realistic ITS traffic models as presented in [11].

Driving and traffic simulators usually do not cover wireless communication, a key enabler to C-ITS, and a big research area by itself as summarized in [17][3][8]. Open source and widely used network simulators are *ns-2* [9], *ns-3* [5], and OMNeT++ [15]. However, these do not support modelling of the physical movements of objects, which is the case for vehicles in C-ITS. Therefore, researchers often need to generate trajectories of the vehicles before using them in the simulation. Otherwise, the network simulator has to be coupled with a traffic simulator as done in the Veins [14] framework, which integrates network and traffic simulators.

The three types of simulators mentioned above, i.e. driving, traffic, and network simulators, complement each other and cover most major components of C-ITS, as presented in Fig. 1. The black boxes indicate the components that are not covered in the study in this paper. To the authors'

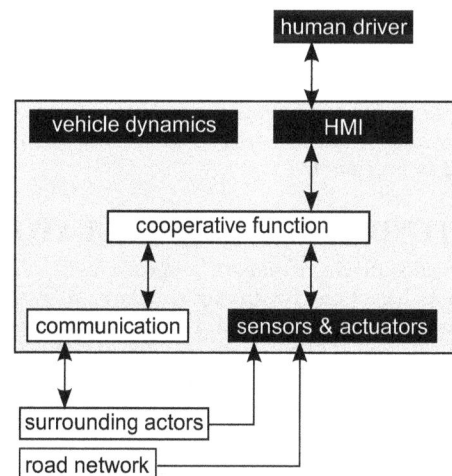

Figure 1: Major components in C-ITS from a vehicle perspective. In-vehicle components are inside the box.

knowledge, two similar attempts to extend the context of the driving simulator have been presented before. [11] presented the integration of driving and traffic simulation and related issues. Using AIMSUN [1] as the traffic simulation tool and Virtual Environment for Road Safety (VERA) as driving simulator. Aiming for connected vehicle applications design and evaluation, [18] claims that the integrated traffic-driving-network simulator in their work is technically feasible, with a number of challenges to be considered. Their solution used PARAMICS [4] as the traffic simulator, *ns-2* as the network simulator, and the University at Buffalo driving simulator.

Background regarding the traffic and network simulator used in this paper is presented in Section 2. An extended driving simulator is presented in Section 3. Section 4 elaborate on use cases of the simulator. Limitations, challenges, and perspectives are discussed in Section 5. Lastly, the paper is concluded in Section 6.

2. BACKGROUND

The traffic and network simulators to be used in the extended simulator presented in the following section is based on PLEXE [13], the platooning extension for Veins. It is chosen for two major reasons. First, it is already coupled with the traffic simulator, Simulation of Urban MObility (SUMO) [7]. Second, it is made for platooning applications, which in the authors' opinion, is a C-ITS application that represent a use case with high potential to be deployed in the near future. The author of PLEXE has implemented support for the platooning application in both Veins and SUMO, then released it as `plexe-sumo` and `plexe-veins`, denoted as SUMO and Veins in Fig. 2 respectively. The version in `plexe-dev` branch of Plexe on the Git repository [2] was used in this work. In the original `plexe-sumo`, there are car-following models implementing: cruise control (CC), adaptive cruise control (ACC), and two cooperative adaptive cruise control (CACC) controllers. The "actuation lag" modelled by a first order low-pass filter is added to the car-following model, to imitate the lag introduced by power-train. In `plexe-veins`, IEEE802.11p network interface is used by each vehicle. A basic message dissemination scheme and simple platooning application is also provided in `plexe-veins`.

Therefore, according to Fig. 1 from a driving simulator perspectives, `plexe-sumo` would cover simulation of surrounding actors and road network. Communication is simulated by `plexe-veins`. Lastly, cooperative function could be implemented in `plexe-veins` or driving simulator as elaborated in Section 4.

3. EXTENDED DRIVING SIMULATOR

The extended driving simulator proposed and evaluated in this paper is based on the driving simulator software from the Swedish National Road and Transport Research Institute (VTI) [6], i.e. VTI's driving simulator, in Fig. 2. This simulation software can run on both desktop environment and more advanced VTI's driving simulators. Fig. 3 illustrates a screenshot from the driving simulator.

Synchronization

SUMO simulation can be controlled using traffic control interface [16], where SUMO acts as server waiting for client

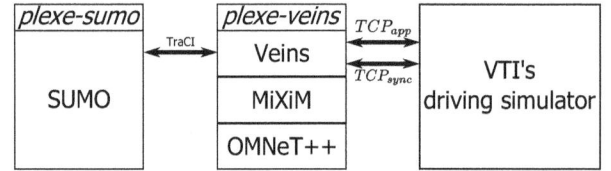

Figure 2: Overview of the extended simulator

Figure 3: A screenshot from VTI's driving simulator.

to be connected by setting up transmission control protocol (TCP) connection. When connected, the client, Veins in this case, has to trigger each simulation step in SUMO. Therefore, a similar approach was used to synchronize the driving simulator with Veins and SUMO. Before every simulation time step, the VTI's driving simulator sends a message to `plexe-veins` to trigger `plexe-sumo` to execute one time step as described above.

Modifications

A plug-in, attached to the VTI's driving simulator software was developed to exchange data with `plexe-veins`. The plug-in is executed before every simulation time step in the VTI's simulator. The VTI's driving simulator is running the plug-in at 100 Hz. Parameters of the vehicles in SUMO, which Veins subscribed to, are forwarded to the VTI's simulator. That then update position and speed of the vehicles according to the data. Moreover, a control logic can be implemented in the plug-in. The logic calculate speed to control a selected vehicle in SUMO. More details will be elaborate in Section 4.

No change were made on `plexe-sumo`. A number of changes have been made on `plexe-veins` to connect with the driving simulator. One TCP connection to the driving simulator was added (referred to as TCP_{sync} in Fig. 2). This connection was used to send vehicles' position and speed that `plexe-veins` received from `plexe-sumo` to the driving simulator. Synchronization between the driving simulator and `plexe-veins` is done through this connection. Moreover, another TCP connection was added to the application layer in `plexe-veins` to request and receive control data from the driving simulator (referred to as TCP_{app} in Fig. 2). Previously all vehicles in the simulation are controlled by car-following model in `plexe-sumo`. The modification allows driving simulator to control one of the vehicles by sending desired speed through the TCP_{app} connection. A detailed example is presented in the second use case of Section 4.

4. USE CASES

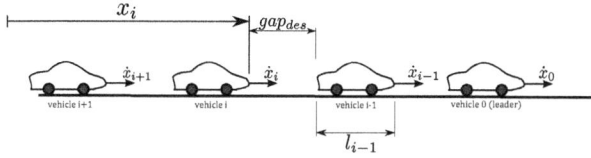

Figure 4: Platoon of vehicles with parameters

The proposed extended driving simulator is evaluated with two use cases related to a platooning application. A platoon consists of one leader and one, two, or more followers driving together with a desired gap between the vehicles. Fig. 4 illustrates a platoon of four vehicles together with their parameters, which will be mentioned in this section. The platoon leader is normally represented by index 0. Vehicle i normally refers to the ego vehicle and vehicle $i-1$ is its preceding vehicle. x_i represents the position of the vehicle i. gap_{des} is the desired gap between the vehicles.

Use Case 1

The first use case starts with a platoon of five vehicles running on a straight road. The VTI's driving simulator visualize the ego vehicle, which is the third vehicle in the platoon, from the driver's perspective. Two CACC controllers were compared in the simulation: a) CACC, which implements the CACC controller from [12, Chapter 7]; and b) Ploeg, the CACC controller presented in [10]. Default communication network parameters in plexe-veins were used. At 40 and 100 seconds, the speed of the platoon's leader was changed to 25 and 30 m/s respectively. And, after 60 seconds, a command to increase the gap is sent to all vehicles. The two controllers use different concepts of gap between vehicles. CACC implements fixed distance gap with the default value of 10 meters. On the other hand, the Ploeg controller uses the time head way concept, which means the gap is defined by the time that it will take the ego vehicle to reach the position of its preceding vehicle. The default time head way is 0.5 seconds. After receiving the "increase gap" command, the controllers then modify the parameter to 20 meters and 1 second respectively. Fig. 5 and Fig. 6 illustrates and distance between vehicles plotted from data collected in plexe-veins. This use case illustrates the capability of testing different control strategies with human drivers in the loop.

Use Case 2

The second use case perform similar scenario, with all vehicles controlled by CACC, except the third vehicle in the platoon. The driving simulator was used to control the third vehicle by executing the control logic shown in (1).

$$\dot{x}_i = \begin{cases} \dot{x}_{i-1} - 5km/h, & \text{if } gap_{des} < 12 meters \\ 120km/h, & \text{otherwise} \end{cases} \quad (1)$$

$\dot{x}_i$ represents desired speed of the ego vehicle and $\dot{x}_{i-1}$ is speed of its preceding vehicle. The desired speed was sent from the driving simulator to plexe-sumo via plexe-veins. The speed then go through the ACC model in plexe-sumo, which also implement the first order low-pass filter for power

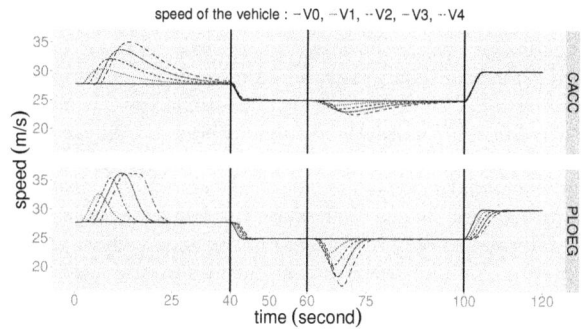

Figure 5: Speed profiles of the vehicles in the "increase gap" scenario.

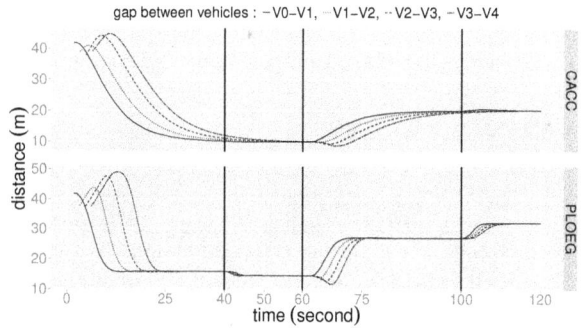

Figure 6: Distances between vehicles in the "increase gap" scenario.

train modelling as mentioned in Section 2. The result is compared with executing the same control logic in plexe-veins and presented in Fig. 7. The result shows that the simulation environment is synchronized and in phase. The controllers could be executed either by the driving simulator or plexe-veins. This use case elaborate on flexibility of the simulator, where different types of controllers are able to perform together in the same environment, not only limited to car-following models in plexe-sumo.

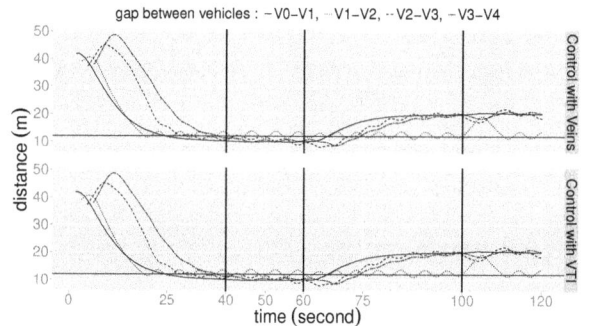

Figure 7: Plots of distances between vehicles with the ego vehicle of the platoon using the simple control logic in (1). The horizontal line is drawn at 12 meters.

5. LIMITATIONS AND PERSPECTIVES

One major limitation with the recent version of the proposed simulator is the lack of support for smooth lateral manoeuvres. This is since in traffic simulators like SUMO, the car-following models do not consider lateral acceleration. Consequently, lane changing manoeuvres are modelled as instantaneous, i.e. a vehicle can switch from one lane to another in one time step. Implementing more realistic lateral manoeuvres in the future would allow to perform more complex scenarios, requiring realistic lateral manoeuvres. For example, cooperative lane change, platoon merging, etc. Furthermore, currently the driving simulator does not have access to communication messages in vehicular network. Consequently, C-ITS functions that require data from the network are limited to be implemented only in plexe-veins. Development is needed to make the driving simulator aware of the messages sent in the simulated vehicular network. Lastly, involving a human driver in the scenarios is another evaluation goal of the simulator.

6. CONCLUSIONS

An extended driving simulator for C-ITS evaluation is presented. The VTI's driving simulator was extended with the plexe-sumo as the traffic simulator, and plexe-veins as network simulator. The thus extended simulator was then evaluated with the use case from a platooning application, implementing an extra ACC controller to elaborate flexibility of the extended simulator. Comparing two CACC controllers from human drivers perspectives is another use case used to illustrate benefits of the simulator. For instance, it may be clear from control theory point of view to only analyse the controllers numerically and with help of plots. But it is hard to judge the human drivers' preference. With the proposed simulation framework, users acceptance issues can also be studied. Moreover, the limitations of the simulator are presented as issues to be tackled in the future. Although realistic lateral manoeuvres are not available, the simulation framework will still be able to evaluate tactical decisions in C-ITS functions, e.g. decisions when to change lane, but not on the operational level, e.g. the manoeuvres. This work is still ongoing with the goal to answer the following research questions: *a)* how feasible is this approach with respect to evaluation of C-ITS? and *b)* what are the other limitations and challenges of this approach?

7. ACKNOWLEDGMENTS

The authors would like to thank Michele Segata from the Universities of Innsbruck (AT) and Trento (IT) for his valuable advices regarding modification and details of Plexe. Also, Jonas Andersson Hultgren from VTI for guidances on the VTI's driving simulator software.

8. REFERENCES

[1] Aimsun – http://www.aimsun.com/.

[2] Git repository of Plexe – https://github.com/michele-segata/{plexe-veins,plexe-sumo}.

[3] J. J. Blum, A. Eskandarian, and L. J. Hoffman. Challenges of intervehicle ad hoc networks. *Intelligent Transportation Systems, IEEE Transactions on*, 5(4):347–351, 2004.

[4] G. D. Cameron and G. I. Duncan. ParamicsÛparallel microscopic simulation of road traffic. *The Journal of Supercomputing*, 10(1):25–53, 1996.

[5] T. R. Henderson, S. Roy, S. Floyd, and G. F. Riley. ns-3 project goals. In *Proceeding from the 2006 workshop on ns-2: the IP network simulator*, page 13. ACM, 2006.

[6] J. Jansson, J. Sandin, B. Augusto, M. Fischer, B. Blissing, and L. Källgren. Design and performance of the VTI Sim IV. In *Driving Simulation Conference*, 2014.

[7] D. Krajzewicz, J. Erdmann, M. Behrisch, and L. Bieker. Recent development and applications of SUMO - Simulation of Urban MObility. *International Journal On Advances in Systems and Measurements*, 5(3&4):128–138, December 2012.

[8] J. Luo and J.-P. Hubaux. A survey of inter-vehicle communication. Technical report, 2004.

[9] S. McCanne, S. Floyd, K. Fall, K. Varadhan, et al. Network simulator ns-2, 1997.

[10] J. Ploeg, B. Scheepers, E. Van Nunen, N. Van de Wouw, and H. Nijmeijer. Design and experimental evaluation of cooperative adaptive cruise control. In *Intelligent Transportation Systems (ITSC), 2011 14th International IEEE Conference on*, pages 260–265. IEEE, 2011.

[11] V. Punzo and B. Ciuffo. Integration of driving and traffic simulation: issues and first solutions. *Intelligent Transportation Systems, IEEE Transactions on*, 12(2):354–363, 2011.

[12] R. Rajamani. *Vehicle dynamics and control*. Springer US, 2 edition, 2012.

[13] M. Segata, S. Joerer, B. Bloessl, C. Sommer, F. Dressler, and R. Lo Cigno. PLEXE: A Platooning Extension for Veins. In *6th IEEE Vehicular Networking Conference (VNC 2014)*, pages 53–60, Paderborn, Germany, December 2014. IEEE.

[14] C. Sommer, R. German, and F. Dressler. Bidirectionally Coupled Network and Road Traffic Simulation for Improved IVC Analysis. *IEEE Transactions on Mobile Computing*, 10(1):3–15, January 2011.

[15] A. Varga et al. The omnet++ discrete event simulation system. In *Proceedings of the European simulation multiconference (ESMŠ2001)*, volume 9, page 65. sn, 2001.

[16] A. Wegener, M. Piórkowski, M. Raya, H. Hellbrück, S. Fischer, and J.-P. Hubaux. Traci: an interface for coupling road traffic and network simulators. In *Proceedings of the 11th communications and networking simulation symposium*, pages 155–163. ACM, 2008.

[17] S. Yousefi, M. S. Mousavi, and M. Fathy. Vehicular ad hoc networks (vanets): challenges and perspectives. In *ITS Telecommunications Proceedings, 2006 6th International Conference on*, pages 761–766. IEEE, 2006.

[18] Y. Zhao, A. Wagh, Y. Hou, K. Hulme, C. Qiao, and A. W. Sadek. Integrated traffic-driving-networking simulator for the design of connected vehicle applications: eco-signal case study. *Journal of Intelligent Transportation Systems*, pages 1–13, 2014.

Toward Scalable Whole-Cell Modeling of Human Cells

Arthur P. Goldberg
Icahn School of Medicine at Mount Sinai
1 Gustave L. Levy Pl, NY, NY 10029
Arthur.Goldberg@mssm.edu

Yin Hoon Chew
Icahn School of Medicine at Mount Sinai
1 Gustave L. Levy Pl, NY, NY 10029
YinHoon.Chew@mssm.edu

Jonathan R. Karr
Icahn School of Medicine at Mount Sinai
1 Gustave L. Levy Pl, NY, NY 10029
Karr@mssm.edu

ABSTRACT

Whole-cell (WC) models comprehensively predict cellular phenotypes by simulating the biochemistry in individual cells. WC models have the potential to enable bioengineers and physicians to rationally design microorganisms and medical therapies. WC models are developed by combining multiple mathematically distinct pathway sub-models into a single multi-algorithm model. The only existing WC model represents a small bacterium. However, to enable medical therapy, new scalable methods are needed to model human cells that contain 100 times more molecular species and 10,000–100,000 times more molecules. We describe the design of a novel system for building and simulating WC models, including an expressive sequence- and rule-based modeling language and a multi-algorithm simulator that employs optimistic parallel discrete event simulation.

Keywords

Whole-cell modeling; Modeling human cells; Systems biology; Optimistic parallel discrete event simulation; Time Warp.

1. INTRODUCTION

A central goal of biology is to understand how genotype and environment influence phenotype. However, despite decades of research, a wealth of quantitative data, and extensive knowledge, we still do not understand these causal relationships [10].

Our long-term goal is to create whole-cell (WC) computational models that accurately predict how genotype influences phenotype by representing all of the biochemical processes inside cells. WC models have the potential to accelerate biological discovery by enabling unprecedented computational experiments. These models could transform microbial bioengineering and medicine. Microbial WC models could enable bioengineers to rationally design genomes to perform practical tasks, such as efficiently produce biofuels and drugs, or sequester carbon. Human WC models could enable physicians to personalize medical therapy for individual patients. For example, an analytical oncologist would use omics analyses of a patient's tumor to construct a personalized WC model, and then use the model to identify the patient's optimal drug treatment plan (Figure 1). WC models could also help scientists identify new drug targets.

Recently, we and our collaborators created the first WC model, which analyzes the bacterium *Mycoplasma genitalium* [5]. The model is composed of 28 mathematically distinct pathway sub-models. It describes the function of every biologically understood

Permission to make digital or hard copies of all or part of this work for personal or classroom use is granted without fee provided that copies are not made or distributed for profit or commercial advantage and that copies bear this notice and the full citation on the first page. Copyrights for components of this work owned by others than the author(s) must be honored. Abstracting with credit is permitted. To copy otherwise, or republish, to post on servers or to redistribute to lists, requires prior specific permission and/or a fee. Request permissions from Permissions@acm.org.
SIGSIM-PADS '16, May 15 - 18, 2016, Banff, AB, Canada
Copyright is held by the owner/author(s). Publication rights licensed to ACM.
ACM 978-1-4503-3742-7/16/05...$15.00
DOI: http://dx.doi.org/10.1145/2901378.2901402

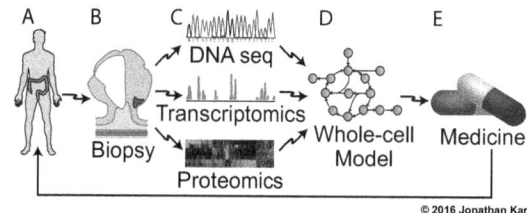

Figure 1. WC models could inform medicine. Patients (A) could be biopsied (B), tumors could be analyzed by omics techniques (C), this data could personalize WC models (D), and oncologists could use these models to design therapy (E).

gene and predicts the dynamics of every molecular species over the cell cycle of a single *M. genitalium*. The model was extensively validated against independent experimental data. We have used the model to discover novel biological insights, calculate the metabolic costs of synthetic circuits, and reposition antibiotics.

However, the model does not represent several cell functions or predict certain phenotypes, and the methods used to build the model were inefficient and not systematic. The model was developed over 4 years by manually curating hundreds of databases and scientific papers and by writing 3,000 pages of MATLAB.

WC modeling must be systemized in order to achieve models of human cells that have 40 times more genes and 10^4–10^5 times more molecules than *M. genitalium*.

To address the challenges above, we are developing a systematic and scalable six-step process for WC modeling: 1) comprehensively curate experimental data about the cell being modeled, and store the data in a database; 2) design and program the model; 3) simulate the model with high accuracy and speed; 4) estimate the model's parameters; 5) verify and validate the model; and 6) analyze model predictions to gain new biological insights, design genomes, or personalize medicine. This process will be iterated to improve the model.

This paper describes our designs for steps 2 and 3: a language for describing WC models and a multi-algorithmic, Time Warp parallel discrete event simulator for simulating WC models. In other work, we are developing new methods to accelerate steps 1 and 4-6. We motivate our designs with examples of the challenges presented by modeling human cells.

2. EXISTING MODELING METHODS AND THEIR LIMITATIONS

Multiple modeling formalisms have been developed to predict the dynamics of biochemical pathways. Here we discuss some of the most common approaches and their limitations.

Ordinary differential equations (ODEs) are frequently used to model biochemical systems. This method assumes that a cell is a well-mixed container of molecules. ODEs have been used to model several well-studied signaling pathways. However, ODEs cannot represent stochastic processes and cannot be used to model entire cells because they require more kinetic data than is available for some pathways.

The Stochastic Simulation Algorithm (SSA) is widely used to predict stochastic processes [2]. However, SSA also requires more kinetic data than is currently available for some pathways.

Flux Balance Analysis (FBA) [7] is commonly used to model cellular metabolism. Given a cell's metabolic biochemical reactions and the cell's chemical composition, FBA predicts the steady-state flux of each reaction. FBA does not require kinetic data. However, FBA cannot be used to model entire cells because it relies on assumptions which are only satisfied by metabolic pathways and it does not predict cellular dynamics.

Numerous other useful methods are also used to model various biochemical pathways in cells. These include rule-based modeling, partial differential equations, logical modeling, agent-based modeling, and Petri Nets.

2.1 Multi-algorithm WC modeling

No existing modeling formalism is suitable on its own for building fine-grained models of entire cells because the current fine-grained modeling methods require pathways to be modeled at the same level of granularity, and we do not have sufficient experimental data to finely describe every pathway.

Recently, we and others pioneered a *multi-algorithmic* approach to WC modeling [5]. This approach enables modelers to represent each pathway using the most appropriate mathematical representation driven by data availability. Separate sub-models are built for each pathway and combined into a single model. We used this approach to manually build a WC model of *M. genitalium* which is composed of 28 sub-models.

However, the WC modeling approach taken by this previous work is inadequate for efficiently developing WC models, especially of human cells. In particular, the biological properties of the *M. genitalium* model are difficult to understand because the model was described by a 3,000 page program, and the multi-algorithm simulation software was slow because it is single-threaded.

3. SCALING TO HUMAN WC MODELS

We aim to develop WC models of human cells which are orders of magnitude bigger and more complex than *M. genitalium* (Table 1). By comparison with *M. genitalium*, typical human cells contain 42 times more genes and approximately 100 times more protein types. In addition, their genomes are 6,000 times larger, and they contain qualitatively more biological compartments. Thus, human WC models will be far more complex and computationally expensive than any prior model.

Table 1. Relative sizes of *M. genitalium* and human cells.

	M. genitalium	*Homo sapiens*	Scale factor
Genes	525	21,983	42
Protein types	525	~50,000	~100
Volume	0.02 μm^3	500–5,000 μm^3	2.5 x 10^4 – 2.5 x 10^5

3.1 Computational complexity

Most human cells are 10^4–10^5 times more voluminous than *M. genitalium*. The computational cost of simulating larger cells increases linearly with cellular volume. This occurs because the SSA modeling formalism, which is used to model many well-

characterized pathways and is the most computationally costly formalism, has a cost that scales linearly with the number of reactions it models. The number of reactions modeled with SSA scales linearly with the number of molecules being modeled, which grows linearly with cellular volume because molecular size varies little between organisms. Thus, we expect the computing cost of simulating WC models to grow linearly with cell volume.

Based on the 1 core-day cost of simulating the *M. genitalium* model and the 10^4–10^5 times greater size of human cells, we estimate that it will take 10^4–10^5 core-days to simulate one cell-cycle of a human cell. Assuming a pragmatic maximum acceptable execution time of 10 days, human WC model simulations must therefore be parallelized on at least 10^3–10^4 cores.

4. SYSTEMIZING WC MODELING

To enable WC models of substantially larger and more complex cells, including models of human cells, we are developing new methods and software tools to formalize and accelerate every step of the WC modeling process.

WC models are primarily composed of chemical species and biochemical reactions which transform these species. In addition, WC models represent the cell wall and compartments inside the cell. These model components should be described concisely and comprehensibly so that WC models can be easily developed, understood, reused, and modified. To enable descriptions of WC models with these properties, we are developing a WC model description language.

To quickly and accurately simulate WC models, we are developing a new parallel multi-algorithm model simulator. The simulator will be a parallel discrete event simulation application (PDES) [4]. To enable highly parallel simulations, the species and reactions which compose WC models must be partitioned into large numbers of *modules* that interact infrequently with each other to provide adequate parallelism (Figure 2). The natural spatial locality of biological processes in cells and an analysis of the *M. genitalium* model (not shown) indicate that this clustering will be feasible because most pathways only interact with a small subset of all of the modeled species.

The simulation maintains the state of species in the cell. It stores the population of each species in each compartment. It also stores the configuration details of many individual macromolecules, such as DNA, RNA and proteins. To allow parallel access to the species state, it will be partitioned into *species modules* (Figure 2). Each species module will store the state of many species.

Simulation time will synchronize interactions between reaction modules and species modules.

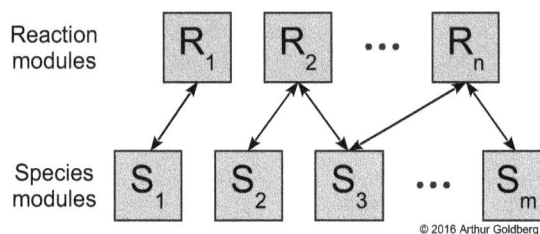

© 2016 Arthur Goldberg

Figure 2. WC model partitioning. To enable parallel simulation, WC models will be partitioned into species and reaction modules. Each module will run in a PDES logical process. Each reaction module will interact (arrows) with a small set of species modules.

5. DESCRIBING WHOLE-CELL MODELS

To provide maximum flexibility, the domain-specific WC model description language will be implemented as a software library. The language offers two novel features. First, the language will access a database of experimental data needed to build a WC model. This database is created by the curation in step 1 of the WC modeling process summarized in Section 1. These data contain extensive information about the cell, including its genome, metabolite concentrations, RNA and protein population counts, RNA and protein half-lives, biochemical reactions, protein-protein interactions, and kinetic reaction rates. Second, the language will support concise and powerful rules for using this data to describe species and reactions in a model. Thus, the language will enable WC modelers to seamlessly integrate genomics with large-scale dynamical modeling.

The modeling language will provide several critical innovations to allow scaling to human WC models: 1) The language will support multi-algorithmic modeling by enabling the modeler to specify the modeling algorithm of sets of reaction. 2) To describe the combinatorial complexity of biological systems, the language will support *data-based modeling*, or the definition of species and reaction patterns in terms of patterns based on biochemical, genomic, and other experimental data. Data-based modeling will generalize rule-based modeling and enable WC models to explicitly combine genomics with large-scale dynamical modeling. 3) The language will implement species as typed objects. This will enable the language to efficiently handle genomic and other specialized biological data.

5.1 Specifying species

Modelers will define species by instantiating objects with experimental data from the curated database. To help modelers efficiently develop models, the language will provide an extensive set of types of biological molecules, such as proteins and nucleic acids like DNA and RNA. The language will include many of the *species types* used in typical models. Each species type will incorporate attributes to represent the structural and functional properties of that biomolecule, such as the sequences and half-lives of RNA and proteins. Modelers will also be able to create new species types or extend existing ones.

Additionally, each species type will support an associated *species pattern* that will enable convenient retrieval of instances of the species that have attributes specified in the pattern.

The species types will be implemented as a hierarchy. For example, the messenger RNA (mRNA) and ribosomal RNA (rRNA) species types will be implemented as subtypes of the RNA species type. We will use object composition to support compound types such as complexes composed of RNA and protein subunits.

5.2 Specifying reactions as rules

The language will support the description of reactions as patterns that encode biological principles which generalize across many individual reactions. Because each biological principle can encompass numerous reactions, describing reactions as patterns can avoid a combinatorial explosion of reaction descriptions that would make models infeasible. For example, proteins that bind to DNA recognize specific DNA sequences known as *motifs*. The new language will enable modelers to store observed DNA binding motifs in the attributes of protein objects and then define a single reaction pattern that represents all of the reactions in which a protein binds to a chromosomal DNA region that has an observed sequence motif.

As discussed in Section 6 below, our new WC simulator will dynamically evaluate and expand these species and reaction patterns to determine the set of active reactions.

Figure 3 illustrates the instantiation of a reaction pattern that describes the binding of proteins to DNA. The modeling language will support analogous textual descriptions of reaction patterns.

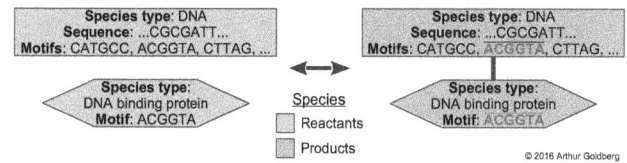

Figure 3. Instantiation of a reaction pattern. We visualize the instantiation of a specific reaction that matches a reaction pattern describing protein (lozenges) binding to DNA (rectangles). The reaction is bidirectional (arrow) with reactants on the left by convention and products on the right. The motif in the protein matches a motif in the DNA (red text in product) so they can bond (red line).

6. SIMULATING WHOLE-CELL MODELS

Most pathway simulation tools [3, 6, 8, 9] use only one modeling algorithm at a time. However, as discussed in Section 2.1, to represent all of the pathways in a cell, WC models must simultaneously employ multiple modeling algorithms. Furthermore, as discussed in Section 3, to scale up to WC models of human cells, WC models must be simulated in parallel. To achieve speedup using many cores and their memory we are developing a parallel WC simulator that will be implemented as a PDES application that runs on an optimistic PDES system, such as ROSS [1]. The simulation consists of both reaction modules and species modules. It will execute each reaction module and each species module inside a separate PDES logical process. The processes will communicate via PDES event messages (Figure 4).

Each *reaction module* will run in a PDES logical process, and use one biochemical modeling method. We will develop custom wrappers to interface continuous and static simulation algorithms such as ODEs and FBA with PDES. Multi-algorithm techniques for using continuous methods like ODEs in optimistic PDES processes are under study, but outside the scope of this paper.

Each reaction module will include the logic needed to retrieve the relevant species values from the species modules, run its modeling algorithm, and update the pertinent species values in the species modules.

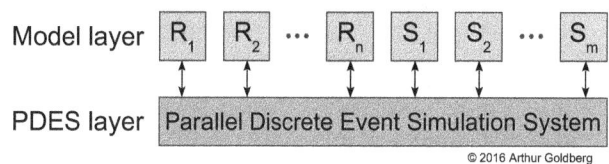

Figure 4. WC model as a PDES application. Each component of the model – reaction modules (blue) and species modules (green) – will be executed inside a PDES logical process. Reaction modules and species modules interact with each other via PDES event messages (arrows).

The simulator will support the most common biochemical modeling algorithms, including SSA, ODEs, and FBA. Wherever possible, we will reuse existing simulation libraries that support these modeling algorithms, such as libRoadrunner [9]. SSA will integrate naturally into a PDES application because SSA is a discrete event algorithm. In fact, PDES is well-suited for WC simulation because SSA is directly compatible with PDES and SSA is one of the most useful biochemical simulation algorithms.

6.1 Partitioning reactions into modules

As discussed in Section 3, to achieve practical simulation execution times and to effectively utilize PDES, we estimate that human WC models must be partitioned into at least 10^3–10^4 modules. Given this scale, the reactions in WC models must be partitioned algorithmically.

The partitioning algorithm's objective is to create a partition that minimizes simulation run-time. However, given the complexity of WC models, the run-time cannot be directly estimated. Instead, we use an alternative computable heuristic which minimizes the interactions between reaction modules.

This approach constructs a graph in which the nodes represent reaction patterns, edges connect reactions that share at least one common species, and edge weights represent the total frequency of the connected reactions. Reaction frequencies will be estimated from the reaction rate laws and rate parameters. Clustering algorithms will be used to partition the graph into loosely-connected reaction modules.

We anticipate that this clustering will improve simulation performance by reducing PDES network messages and Time Warp rollbacks [4].

6.2 Partitioning species into modules

We will use a similar approach to partition species into modules. The approach associates each species with the reaction module that most heavily uses the species (Figure 5). We will then co-locate these pairs of reaction and species modules to minimize network traffic and Time Warp rollbacks.

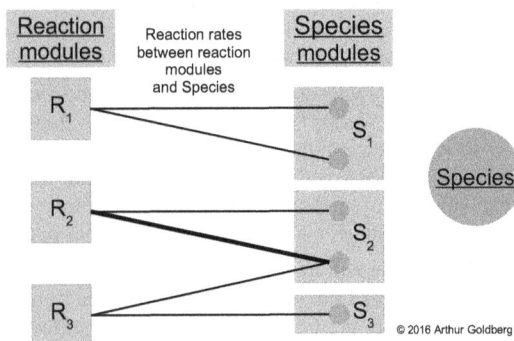

Figure 5. Heuristic for partitioning a WC model species state. First, reactions will be partitioned into modules (blue) as discussed in Section 6.1. Second, one species module (green) will be associated with each reaction module. Third, each species (salmon) is assigned to the species module associated with the reaction module that most heavily uses the species. The thickness of the black lines connecting reaction modules and species indicates the total rate at which modules use species.

7. SUMMARY

Our long-term objective is to use WC models of bacteria and human cells to advance biological science, bioengineering, and medicine. We envision using these models for a wide range of applications, including rationally designing microorganisms for a variety of industrial, agricultural and medical applications; predicting new drug targets; interpreting personal omics data; and identifying an optimal drug or drug combination for individual patients.

Significant research and engineering is needed to achieve these goals. We are beginning by developing algorithms and software for systematically building and simulating WC models. To ensure that the new tools meet all of the requirements for WC modeling and are practical, we plan to pilot the tools in conjunction with building the first human WC model. Thus, we anticipate that the tools will enable vastly more comprehensive and accurate WC models, including models of human cells.

We plan to publish the software tools open-source, along with extensive documentation, tutorials, and examples. In addition, we plan to integrate the software tools into a comprehensive, user-friendly platform for building, simulating, and analyzing WC models.

This platform will contain numerous innovations, including a WC modeling language that modelers can use to create compact and comprehensible multi-algorithm models, and an accurate, high-performance PDES whole-cell model simulator.

We anticipate that the methods and software outlined in this paper will dramatically advance WC modeling, thereby enabling routine use of whole-cell models in bioengineering and medicine.

8. ACKNOWLEDGMENTS

This work was supported by ERASynBio/NSF Grant 1548123 to JRK, by James S. McDonnell Foundation Postdoctoral Fellowship Award in Studying Complex Systems 220020377 to JRK, and by the Icahn Institute for Genomics & Multiscale Biology. We thank Amelia Goldberg for copy editing the manuscript.

9. REFERENCES

[1] Carothers, C.D. et al. 2000. ROSS: a high-performance, low memory, modular time warp system. *Proceedings Fourteenth Workshop on Parallel and Distributed Simulation.* 62, (2000), 53–60.

[2] Gillespie, D.T. 1977. Exact stochastic simulation of coupled chemical reactions. *The Journal of Physical Chemistry.* 81, 25 (1977), 2340–2361.

[3] Hoops, S. et al. 2006. COPASI—a COmplex PAthway SImulator. *Bioinformatics .* 22 , 24 (Dec. 2006), 3067–3074.

[4] Jefferson, D. et al. 1987. Time warp operating system. *ACM SIGOPS Operating Systems Review.* 21, 5 (1987), 77–93.

[5] Karr, J.R. et al. 2012. A Whole-Cell Computational Model Predicts Phenotype from Genotype. *Cell.* 150, 2 (2012), 389–401.

[6] Lopez, C.F. et al. 2013. Programming biological models in Python using PySB. *Molecular Systems Biology.* 9, 1 (2013), 646.

[7] Orth, J.D. et al. 2010. What is flux balance analysis? *Nat Biotech.* 28, 3 (Mar. 2010), 245–248.

[8] Sekar, J.A.P. and Faeder, J.R. 2012. Rule-Based Modeling of Signal Transduction: A Primer. *Computational Modeling of Signaling Networks SE - 9.* X. Liu and M.D. Betterton, eds. Humana Press. 139–218.

[9] Somogyi, E.T. et al. 2015. libRoadRunner: A High Performance SBML Simulation and Analysis Library. *Bioinformatics.* (Jun. 2015).

[10] Tomita, M. 2001. Whole-cell simulation: a grand challenge of the 21st century. *Trends in biotechnology.* 19, 6 (2001), 205–210.

Author Index

www.ingramcontent.com/pod-product-compliance
Lightning Source LLC
Chambersburg PA
CBHW061354210326
41598CB00035B/5983